A Cognitive Psychology of Mass Communication

A Cognitive Psychology of Mass Communication is the go-to text for any course that adopts a cognitive and psychological approach to the study of mass communication. In its sixth edition, it continues its examination of how our experiences with media affect the way we acquire knowledge about the world, and how this knowledge influences our attitudes and behavior. Using theories from psychology and communication along with reviews of the most up-to-date research, this text covers a diversity of media and media issues ranging from commonly discussed topics, such as politics, sex, and violence, to lesser-studied topics, such as sports, music, emotion, and prosocial media.

This sixth edition offers chapter outlines and recommended reading lists to further assist readability and accessibility of concepts, and a new companion website that includes recommended readings, even more real-world examples and activities, PowerPoint presentations, sample syllabi, and an instructor guide.

Richard Jackson Harris is Professor of Psychology at Kansas State University in Manhattan KS, where he has taught since 1974.

Fred W. Sanborn is Associate Professor of Psychology at North Carolina Wesleyan College, where he teaches a wide range of psychology courses. He is also the founding director of the NCWC's Teaching and Learning Center.

Routledge Communication Series
Jennings Bryant & Dolf Zillmann, Series Editors

Selected titles in the series include:

A Cognitive Psychology of Mass Communication

Sixth Edition

Richard Jackson Harris and
Fred W. Sanborn

Routledge
Taylor & Francis Group

NEW YORK AND LONDON

Sixth edition published 2014
by Routledge
711 Third Avenue, New York, NY 10017

Simultaneously published in the UK
by Routledge
2 Park Square, Milton Park, Abingdon, Oxon OX14 4RN

Routledge is an imprint of the Taylor & Francis Group, an informa business

First edition published by Lawrence Erlbaum Associates Inc 1989
Fifth edition published by Routledge 2009

Library of Congress Cataloging-in-Publication Data
Harris, Richard Jackson.
A cognitive psychology of mass communication / by Richard Jackson Harris,
Fred Sanborn. – Sixth edition.
     pages cm
Includes index.
1. Mass media–Psychological aspects. I. Sanborn, Fred W. II. Title.
P96.P75H37 2013
302.2301'9–dc23   2013001614

ISBN: 978-0-415-53704-9 (hbk)
ISBN: 978-0-415-53705-6 (pbk)
ISBN: 978-0-203-11090-4 (ebk)

Typeset in Goudy
by Cenveo Publisher Services

Printed and bound in the United States of America by Sheridan Books, Inc. (a Sheridan Group Company).

Richard

To my wife Caprice Becker, and children Clint (born 1989), Natalie (born 1991), and Grady (born 1991), who have taught me so much about what is really important in life. Watching them grow up in a world of rapidly changing media has provided much food for thought, which has affected the words on these pages in so many ways.

Fred

To my partner, Tony Hefner, who is also my favorite media consumption partner, and to my parents John and Lyna Sanborn, who taught me to be a savvy media consumer at an early age.

Contents

About the Authors

Richard Jackson Harris is Professor of Psychology at Kansas State University in Manhattan, KS, where he has taught since 1974. Growing up in suburban Pittsburgh, PA, he earned a B.A. at the College of Wooster in Wooster, OH and an M.A. and Ph.D. in Cognitive Psychology at the University of Illinois at Urbana-Champaign, IL. He is the author of over 100 published research articles on memory and comprehension of verbal material in media and elsewhere, as well as a textbook, *Learning and Cognition* (with Thomas Leahey), and some edited volumes of research papers.

Fred W. Sanborn is Associate Professor of Psychology at North Carolina Wesleyan College, where he teaches a wide range of psychology courses. He is also the founding Director of the NCWC's Teaching and Learning Center. Fred received his B.A. in Psychology and Psychological Services at Kansas Wesleyan University in 1996. He also earned an M.S. (2000), and a Ph.D. (2004) in Social and Developmental Psychology from Kansas State University.

Preface

Today's college-age students, born in the 1990s, have no memory of life before the Internet. In their minds it has always been possible to post videos online or edit an Internet encyclopedia. Photographs or videos have always been instantly downloadable to a computer. They can't remember arranging social gatherings without Facebook. E-mail is so last year, and calling on a phone tethered by a cord when you can't even text is almost unimaginable. They are as likely to watch a TV show on their computer, phone, or tablet as on a TV set. The world of media, and by extension entertainment and popular culture, has changed immensely in the last generation.

Yet, from a broader perspective, such a communications revolution is not entirely unprecedented. Still photography and telegraphy were transformative in the 1840s, telephones a few decades later, and cinema, starting around 1896, radically transformed the way people saw the world and communicated with each other. In the twentieth century, radio in the 1920s, television in the 1950s, video technology in the 1980s, and the Internet in the 1990s also transformed our lives within a mere decade in each case. In the new millennium, the explosion of social media and the opportunities for anyone to create and share media have been unprecedented.

A popular movie some years ago, *The Truman Show*, featured Jim Carrey as a man whose entire life had been a television show, filmed nonstop under a huge bubble that was his whole world. His eventual discovery of this situation is personally devastating, and Truman knows he can never be the same again. In a sense he is an exaggerated but apt metaphor for this entire book. Our lives, and all that we know, are far more heavily influenced by the media than most of us realize, even if our whole lives are not completely reducible to a reality TV show. Although by reading this book you will not, like Truman, find out that you have no identity except as an entertainment figure, you may discover that a surprising amount of what you know and how you behave is a direct product of your interaction with television, radio, print, and computer-mediated communications. In any event, you will probably never look at media the same way again! At least that is our hope.

Some real people are almost as much media creations as Carrey's Truman. In recent years there have been certain individuals who have received extensive media coverage more because they were celebrities than because of any artistic, athletic, or other accomplishments. Think of Paris Hilton, Lindsey Lohan, or the Kardashian sisters. People around the world cried over the deaths of Britain's Princess Diana in 1997, Michael Jackson in 2009, and Whitney Houston in 2012. These were not fake tears; the loss was real. The deaths were a true personal loss for millions of people who had only known them as friends through the media.

Sometimes the media and reality become intertwined in odd ways. A few years back the Westport Dry Cleaners in Manhattan, Kansas, was suddenly inundated with calls asking for "God" and delivering prayer requests. Why? The business happened to have the same phone number as the "God" character in the recently released movie *Bruce Almighty*. Didn't those callers know that it wasn't really God's telephone number? Maybe, but if they only meant to harass or play a joke, why not call any number and ask for God? Why this particular number? And why leave prayer requests?

This is the sixth edition of this text and much has necessarily changed since its inception. Seldom does the content of a textbook become obsolete so fast as when it deals with the media. Probably the major change overall in this edition has been the addition of much new material on computer-mediated communication, especially social media and the Internet. As recently as 2003, Facebook, YouTube, and cell phones with Internet capabilities did not even exist. Indeed, the whole media landscape has changed radically in the last ten years. We always shudder to think how much it will change in the next five and how obsolete and inadequate the words we have just written will be by the time you read this book.

Although we have updated examples and material throughout, we have also consciously tried to avoid the pitfall of creating an entirely ahistorical work. We firmly believe that we only understand the present and the future by understanding the past, so we have retained some particularly cogent and informative historical examples. If you don't understand some of these, ask your parents, grandparents, or professors for more information. They will remember and will be glad to tell you about them.

Beyond the obvious updating, we have reorganized some material within this edition. The same organization of twelve chapters that appeared in the fifth edition has been maintained here, with Richard having primary responsibility for the revisions of Chapters 2, 3, 6, 7, 8, and 12, and Fred for Chapters 1, 4, 5, 9, 10, and 11. We have reviewed each other's chapters and believe we have a very similar writing style, so we hope you don't notice much difference!

Some chapters have extensive new sections. The introductory chapter, on the general media landscape, has expanded material on the Internet and social media. Chapters 2 and 3 have expanded discussions of some important new psychological constructs involved in media. Chapter 4 has added material on gender, ethnic, and sexual minority portrayals. Chapter 5 has more material on the history of advertising as well as new, techno-savvy advertising techniques. Chapter 6 has expanded coverage of music. Chapter 7 has updated discussion of news, especially as communicated on new media. Chapter 8 has additional new material on the increasingly acrimonious political climate in the U.S. Chapter 9 has expanded material on violent video games and horror movies. Chapter 10 has additional historical background and updated statistics on media sex. Chapter 11 now has updated examples and research on prosocial media, including videogames. Chapter 12 has expanded and updated coverage of research and practice in media literacy.

Throughout the book, we have also introduced new boxes (now called "Close-Ups") with updated material and research that have appeared since the last edition. A large percentage of the references are from the 21st century, strong testimony to the impressive volume of quality research currently being done on media issues. In the process we have had to continually remind ourselves that we cannot read and include everything that has been written on the subject of media. If we have omitted some of your favorites, forgive us; the amount of research and scholarly literature on the media is staggering.

Although overall the book has a cognitive perspective, we think you will find it quite eclectic theoretically, as we believe it needs to be. Chapter 2 reviews the major theories that have been used to study mass communication, and these are all referred to throughout the text. We believe that each has something of value to offer, most of them being more useful in some areas than others. We would also argue that most theories of media effects have a strong cognitive component, which we have tried to highlight in these pages.

Our hope is that you enjoy reading this book as much as we have enjoyed writing it. We hope it will be a source of both great pleasure and much learning. It will amuse you in places and probably disturb you in others, but we hope it will always be interesting and relevant to your life. Students and teachers, please send us your comments. You can reach us by e-mail at rjharris@k-state.edu or fwsanborn@ncwc.edu. Your reactions are always helpful in improving the book in future editions. Also, please feel free to send us interesting examples to illustrate the principles discussed; maybe we can use them in the next edition.

Richard Jackson Harris
Fred W. Sanborn

A Note from Richard Jackson Harris

The first edition of this book appeared in 1989 and initially evolved from my development of the course "The Psychology of Mass Communication" at Kansas State University in the early 1980s. I am grateful to the students in this class over the years for their enthusiasm, inspiration, and challenge; their ideas and dialogue with the material have constructively affected each edition of the book. More and more I have became convinced that the area of mass communication is a wonderful area in which to apply theory and research methodology from experimental psychology. Media research deals with some of the major activities that occupy our time and addresses problems that people are vitally interested in, such as sex and violence, values in media, and images of different groups. Trained in the 1970s at the University of Illinois at Urbana-Champaign as a rigorous experimental psychologist with an emphasis in studying language, I became interested in applying what I knew about text processing to study the sort of language that people encounter every day. Some research I conducted on the cognition of deceptive advertising, starting in the late 1970s, first challenged me to start thinking seriously and more broadly about mass media consumption as information processing. Through this work the cognitive perspectives on the media came to influence my thinking.

When it became time to add a co-author, for this current edition, Fred Sanborn was a natural choice. Fred, an Associate Professor of Psychology at North Carolina Wesleyan College in Rocky Mount, NC, earned his Ph.D. in Social and Developmental Psychology from Kansas State University in 2004. During this time he assisted me with the Psychology of Mass Communication course, first as a TA and later teaching the class on his own, something he has continued to do at NCWC. From his first assignment as a TA for the course, Fred showed an amazing love, both for the material and for the process of teaching it effectively to students. He has gone on to have a distinguished career as a teacher and is founding Director of the Teaching and Learning Center at NCWC.

The support of the Psychology Department at Kansas State University and of the editors, first at Lawrence Erlbaum Associates and later at Taylor & Francis, during the writing of all six editions has been tremendous. I also greatly appreciate the Fulbright Visiting Lectureships I held in Belo Horizonte, Brazil in 1982 and Montevideo, Uruguay in 1994, and the Visiting Scholar position at Massey University in Palmerston North, New Zealand in 2005; these experiences gave me an internationalist perspective for which I am immensely grateful and which I have tried to bring to each edition of this book. Contemporary media are part of an international culture. Although this book disproportionately relies on U.S. media, since that is what we know best and that is what has been studied the most, the principles are equally applicable elsewhere, as we try to suggest with frequent examples from other nations' media.

Although countless present and former students have influenced the ideas on these pages, particular thanks are due to Steven Hoekstra, Jennifer Bonds-Raacke, Elizabeth Cady, John Raacke, Christy Scott, Jason Brandenburg, J. Andrew Karafa, Christopher Barlett, John Berger, Rebecca Schlegel, Lindsay Firebaugh, J. Bret Knappenberger, Sherry Wright, Christopher Rodeheffer, John Smyers, Jeff Hyder, Jorge Piocuda, Tuan Tran, Lindsay Cook, Natalie Barlett, Brynne Glynn, Kyle Bures, Michael Hinkin, Andrew Fiori, Abby Werth, and Chelsea Bartel for their helpful reactions and conversations over the years about this material.

Also, I would like to thank my parents, the late Dick and Helen Harris, for modeling incredibly effective media use in my home of origin, long before people were talking much about media literacy. For a long time I used to assume everyone grew up with the kind of positive media environment I knew. Our family media use was often quality family time. My own media literacy training started early, with my parents questioning what they saw on television and encouraging me to do the same. Many conversations around the television or the evening newspaper provided intellectual seeds that bear some fruit in this book. I remember them commenting on negative values, unfair stereotyping, and excessive violence from my earliest days of watching TV. Although TV was a part of our household, so were print media, whose use my parents faithfully modeled.

A Note from Fred W. Sanborn

I must admit that I didn't know much about the study of mass communication and psychology until I was assigned to be Richard Harris' teaching assistant, early in my graduate school career. I had signed on to graduate school at Kansas State University to study Social and Developmental Psychology, which I loved (and still love). However, when I learned that I could also study psychology in relation to media, which had fascinated, provoked, and entertained me my entire life, I was smitten. In common with many others, media have been a large part of my life since I was very young. As a child, television in particular was a window on the world for me, allowing for "encounters" beyond my own narrow set of experiences. Even now, when seeing something new, I sometimes catch myself thinking, "It's just like on TV!" Somewhere along the line in my experience with mass communication, I realized that media were indeed creating a reality for me and others. Understanding this "reality" is the focus of this book and the work that Richard Harris and I have done in writing it.

I moved on from being Richard's teaching assistant to eventually conducting research in the area of psychology and mass communication and teaching my own classes on the topic. When I received an appointment at North Carolina Wesleyan College in 2004, I found that the Psychology of Mass Communication blended beautifully with the Psychology Department's senior capstone course because it integrated many areas of psychology (cognitive, social, and developmental, among others) and had the added benefit of engaging students in a topic that affected their lives every day.

I thank especially Richard Harris who has nurtured my scholarship in so many ways. Through the years, he has provided me with an excellent model of a teacher, researcher, writer, colleague, and friend. I also am tremendously grateful to him for allowing me to contribute to his many years of work on this book in this latest edition. I have tried not to disappoint him or the readers. I also thank my parents, John and Lyna Sanborn, for being my first media teachers. Thanks go to my partner, Tony Hefner, for his support and encouragement as I worked on this book. Finally, I would like to thank all of the many students who have taken my Psychology of Mass Communication or Senior Seminar in Psychology/Media Psychology courses since 1999. You have contributed in countless ways to my passion for this topic and my desire to better understand it.

Chapter 1

Mass Communication in Our Wired Society

The Changing Media Landscape

Q: After a tornado hit the small city of Manhattan, Kansas, on June 11, 2008, how many amateur videos of the event were posted on YouTube?

A: 234 had been posted 36 hours after the hit. Most of these were poor quality home videos, though the selection also included coverage from local TV stations and at least one slide show of damage accompanied by a country music soundtrack, "Tornadoes" by the Drive-By Truckers.

Q: How much material is on the World Wide Web?

A: No one quite knows for sure. One 2011 estimate indicated that there were at least 17.9 billion indexed web pages, and that number is growing fast (The size, 2011). In fact, the growth of the web has been so rapid that the number of available web addresses dwindled from more than one billion in 2006 to 117 million in 2010, forcing a new internet protocol addressing system to be developed (Worthen & Tuna, 2011). Overall, the best estimate of the total number of web pages, as of 2011, is probably between 15 and 30 billion (The size of the World Wide Web, 2011).

Q: How have mobile phones revolutionized developing countries?

A: Developing countries with poor telephone infrastructure and long waiting lists for phone services have found mobile phones much more reliable and attractive than traditional, wired phones. In numerous countries, such as Botswana, Rwanda, Ivory Coast, Paraguay, and Venezuela, mobile phone users outnumbered conventional phone users by 2000 (Romero, 2000). Mobile "smart phones" in conjunction with social networking sites such as Twitter and Facebook have even been credited with helping dissidents organize revolutions in totalitarian countries such as Egypt and Tunisia (Preston, 2011).

In 2001, 13-year-old Jason Lind of Torrington, Connecticut, was hospitalized with second- and third-degree burns after he and a friend poured gasoline on his feet and legs and lit it in imitation of a stunt seen on MTV's popular show *Jackass*.

In 1969, a young news reporter from the British Broadcasting Corporation (BBC) was sent to cover the Vietnam War. Not being very experienced or knowledgeable about what he was observing, he led off his first televised report of an American attack on a Vietcong stronghold with, "My God! It's just like watching television" (Bogart, 1980, p. 209).

Two daughters of a White mother and indigenous Ecuadorian father were watching a Disney remake of *Little House on the Prairie*. Five minutes into the movie a character uttered, "I think we should kill all the Indians!" and seven-year-old Taquina burst into tears, crying "Turn it off. I'm too scared, Mommy!" (Carlsson-Paige, 2008, p. 115).

In different ways, these examples suggest the main theme of this book: that our experience with media is a major way that we acquire knowledge about the world. How we then act on this knowledge has consequences in terms of attitudes and behavior. We may call this a cognitive approach to mass communication because the emphasis is on the way that our minds create knowledge, a mental reality, about the world, constructed from our experience with the media. This mental reality then becomes the basis for developing our attitudes and motivating our behaviors, and thus has a great impact on our lives. Instead of the media being a more or less accurate reflection of some external reality, it has become the reality against which the real world is compared. The media view of the world has become, in many cases, more real than the real world itself!

Prevalence of Mass Communication

Mass communication in the form of print media has been with us almost since Gutenberg's invention of movable type and the printing press in 1456. However, the nature of mass communication, indeed of life in general, was radically changed in the 20th century by the advent of electronic media, starting with radio around 1920, followed by television around 1950, video and cable technology in the 1980s, the Internet in the 1990s, and social media since 2000. Television in particular has in the last 60 years transformed the day-to-day life of more people than perhaps any invention in human history. Radio and print media have been greatly changed, though by no means replaced, by TV as well. Computer-mediated communications may well be on their way to eclipsing television in terms of transforming society.

Americans spend more time watching television than doing anything else except working and sleeping, though Internet use is catching up fast, especially among youth (Kaiser Family Foundation, 2010). Every week residents of the United States spend about 15 to 20 of their average 39 hours of free time watching television, making it by far the most popular leisure activity. Only work and sleep take more of our time (Bureau of Labor Statistics, 2010; Kubey & Csikszentmihalyi, 1990; Numbers, 1997; Roberts, 2000). All other sources of leisure, such as spending time with friends, helping others, reading books, playing sports, and taking vacations, lag far behind. Besides changing the way we spend our time, media have also revolutionized the way we think and the way we view the world. The Internet and its various computer-mediated communication modes are currently revolutionizing our lives in the new millennium. The many effects of media on our perception and our cognition are particular emphases of this book. The media are not only the magic windows through which we view the world, but also the doors through which ideas enter our minds as we interact with them.

Media are far more than mere conduits of knowledge, although that role is not a trivial one. The act of transmitting that knowledge may itself become the event of note. We have come a long way from Gutenberg to the millions of newspapers, magazines, television channels, radio stations, and websites in the world today. To prepare to look at the effects of all of this, in this chapter we introduce the concept of mass communication and look at our use of the media from a cognitive psychological perspective.

Today, no place on earth is beyond the reach of mass media. For political reasons South Africa was for a long time the last large nation without TV, holding out until 1976 (Mutz, Roberts, & van Vuuren, 1993). The remote island states of the Cook Islands (1989), Fiji (1995), and St. Helena (1995) were among the last nations to welcome TV and the Internet (Wheeler, 2001), and the isolated, mountainous Himalayan kingdom of Bhutan may have been the very last, finally becoming wired to both in 1999.

In the 1970s, a unique study was carried out in Canada to assess the effects of the introduction of television. It involved three towns in interior eastern British Columbia which were very similar except for the fact that one ("Multitel") received several Canadian and U.S. TV channels, another ("Unitel") received only one channel, and the third, because of its particular isolated valley location, received no television signals ("Notel"). This study compared children and adults in the three towns before and after television was finally introduced to Notel. Children's creativity scores, for example, were higher before TV in Notel than in either (1) the other towns before TV or (2) any of the three towns after TV. See Macbeth (1996) for a summary of the findings and Williams (1986) for a collection of papers reporting the results of this research in more detail. For similar, more recent research for a smaller place, see Charlton, Gunter, and Hannan (2002), a study of the effects of the introduction of television to the remote South Atlantic island of St. Helena in 1995. These will probably be the last studies of their kind, because no such TV-less (or Internet-less) places now exist.

What Is Mass Communication?

What makes mass communication "mass"? First, the audience is large and anonymous, and often very heterogeneous (Wright, 1986). Groups of individuals can be targeted, but only with limited precision. Second, communication sources are institutional and organizational (Wright, 1986). Some, such as television networks, newspaper chains, wire services, or the conglomerates that own such businesses (and their accompanying websites), are among the largest and richest private corporations. Third, and perhaps most importantly, the basic economic function of most media in most nations is to attract and hold as large an audience as possible for the advertisers. In one way or another, advertising pays a very high percentage of the costs of newspapers, magazines, local TV and radio stations, television networks and cable channels, and the Internet. Even public television and government-subsidized networks like the Public Broadcasting Service (PBS), Canadian Broadcasting Corporation (CBC), or the British Broadcasting Corporation (BBC) are increasingly dependent on commercial revenues.

Despite some within the industry espousing high-sounding rhetoric about serving the public, the bottom line of commercial mass media is money, which comes from advertisers at rates directly determined by the audience size and composition. The size of the audience in turn determines the content. Thus, there is tremendous pressure for media to be as entertaining as possible to as many people as possible. This imperative to entertain also holds for non-entertainment content like news, sports, or advertising. All of this is not to say that editors and programmers are not concerned about responsibly meeting the needs of the public. In many cases they are, but such needs must necessarily be considered within the constraints of the economic realities of the media industry. If there is no audience, there is no money to support even the best programming. This is true at both the national and local levels, with local media outlets often as concerned, or more so, than national sources about ratings or circulation.

Often economic pressures, and sometimes political and ideological ones as well, influence the content of media. For example, magazines that accept tobacco advertisements print fewer stories about the health risks of smoking than those that have no cigarette ads (Lee & Solomon, 1991; Strasburger & Wilson, 2002). Similarly, the ABC television network, which is owned by Disney, has killed news stories reflecting negatively on Disney theme parks (Steyer, 2002). See Close-Up 1.1 for further discussion of both blatant and subtle censorship.

In addition to its mass nature, there is also "communication" in mass communication. In all communication there is a reciprocity that necessitates some kind of response from the audience. Even though the media user, especially the TV viewer, is often characterized as extremely passive, mindlessly absorbing the program content, such a picture is far from accurate. Although the meaning of a particular program certainly depends on the content of that program, it also depends on what is in the mind and experience of the viewer. A TV movie dealing with rape will have a very different effect on, indeed a different *meaning* for, a viewer who has herself been a rape victim than for someone else with no such personal experience. A violent pornographic

Close-Up 1.1: The Issue of Censorship

A major philosophical and legal issue with regard to media is censorship, which varies greatly across different societies. Although prior censorship (i.e., requiring approval of all content before broadcast or publication) occurs in some totalitarian societies, more subtle forms of censorship exist in all nations. Even in democracies, press freedom has never been absolute and always operates within certain constraints. For example, in most countries one may not print or broadcast material that is defamatory (i.e., libelous or slanderous), classified, obscene, or which incites people to violence or infringes copyright. In the United States, the Federal Communications Commission (FCC) assigns channels and issues licenses. Although it has the power to deny renewal of licenses, it has very seldom done so in its many decades of operation. The FCC also enforces application of the Equal Time rule to ensure that opposing points of view on controversial issues and political campaigns are aired. Pressures toward censorship exist, although it may not be called that, especially in the United States, where "censorship" is considered a very negative word. In rare instances, the FCC also levies fines against broadcasters whom it deems to have breached its mostly unwritten standards of decency; this was the case for the infamous 2004 "wardrobe malfunction" in which Janet Jackson's breast was briefly bared during a live broadcast of the Super Bowl halftime show (Fabrikant, 2004).

The National Association of Broadcasters (NAB), a professional organization of radio and television stations, has a fairly rigorous ethical code that it expects its members to adhere to, although court challenges and appeals, an atmosphere of deregulation, and changing social standards weakened adherence to the NAB code starting in the 1980s. Some content that may not be illegal per se may nevertheless not appear because broadcasters fear public outrage (e.g., graphic and explicit sex, violence, or surgery). Also, certain words (e.g., "shit," "fuck," many racial epithets, and any religious expletives stronger than "Oh, my God!") seldom occur on U.S. prime-time network television, although standards are becoming increasingly loose, even on basic cable TV. See Close-Up 10.1 for a more specific discussion of a decades-long censorship system known as the Hays Code that was once used by the U.S. movie industry.

Incidentally, standards change: 60 years ago we did not hear the words "damn," "hell," or even "pregnant," although we might have heard "nigger," "wetback," "jap," and other highly inflammatory ethnic slurs in the early days of radio or TV. Real or feared reaction from advertisers is another subtle source of self-censorship. Television networks and stations are loath to risk offending those who pay the bills for their livelihood. Advertisers occasionally threaten to withdraw their ads in protest. In 1979 General Electric was unhappy with ABC's Barbara Walters' plans to interview Jane Fonda about her antinuclear activism and pulled their ads in protest. However, ABC still aired the interview. Advertisers with many products to sell (and accompanying ad budgets) may hold influence that many of us don't realize. According to Gloria Steinem, co-founder of Ms. magazine, Procter and Gamble even issued an edict to publishers of women's magazines that "its products were not to be placed in any issue that included any material on gun control, abortion, the occult, cults, or the disparagement of religion" (Steinem, 1990, p. 26).

Concern over public reaction may be another source of self-censorship. All but one U.S. commercial network once refused to run an antismoking public service announcement (PSA) that showed a fetus smoking a cigarette in the womb. In 2005 all U.S. networks but the History Channel refused to run a PSA by the United Nations mine agency which showed suburban schoolgirls playing soccer when a landmine suddenly blows up, followed by screaming and a man carrying his daughter's lifeless body, and then a dark screen with the words, "If there were land mines here, would you stand for them anywhere?" (Huus, 2005).

website may incite one man to sexual violence because of the way his mind interprets and interacts with the content, whereas another man who sees the same content may be repulsed by it, showing no sexual arousal or antisocial behavioral response. See Close-Up 1.2 for a discussion of movie ratings related to sex and violence.

The nature of the media consumption experience must also be considered. Watching television or listening to the radio may be done alone or in small groups. Reading newspapers or magazines or using the Internet are typically, though not always, solo activities. The social situation of who else is watching, listening, or reading and how they react greatly affects the media consumption experience. Consider the difference between watching an exciting ball game alone, or with a group of friends, or with a group rooting for the other team. Your enjoyment and the level of fear you feel while watching a horror film can be affected by whether someone watching with you shrieks in fun, cries in severe distress, laughs, or shows no obvious reaction at all (Zillmann & Weaver, 1996). In one study looking at anticipated enjoyment of watching different types of movies with different viewers, college students found watching a sexual R-rated movie with their parents by far the most uncomfortable combination (Harris & Cook, 2011). Similarly, within families television may

Close-Up 1.2: The MPAA Ratings: Does Sex or Violence Carry More Weight?

Ever since their introduction in 1968, the Motion Picture Association of America's (MPAA's) ratings for movies have been controversial. The ratings have usually been made by 10 to 13 people whose identities are kept secret. The chair is the only publicly known member, and he or she hires all the others (Dick, 2006). Over time, there have been some adjustments to the ratings categories, most notably the addition of the PG-13 category in 1984 and the replacement of the pornography-tainted label of X by NC-17 (no one under 17 admitted) in 1990. The ratings are made based on violence, sex, nudity, language, and thematic content, although the specific rating criteria have never been made public and are not always applied consistently. By the turn of the millennium, over 60% of films submitted were rated R, almost none NC-17, and very few G. Sometimes a rating is negotiable; a studio will appeal an R rating or remove or edit an offending scene to obtain the PG-13 rating. The latter rating is often considered commercially the most desirable, since it neither excludes anyone nor has the "kiddie movie" stigma of G and even PG movies. There is widespread belief than many films that previously would have been R are now PG-13 and many PG films would have been PG-13 some years ago.

One specific continuing controversy concerns the relative weighting of the different factors, particularly sex and violence. Although the MPAA denies it, there is good reason to believe that sexual content and language carry greater weight than violence. Indeed, many PG and even G movies contain considerable amounts of violence, though a partial nudity scene may earn a film a PG-13 rating. Leone (2002) provided some empirical support for this, finding that scenes present in an NC-17 or unrated version of a film but removed from the commercially released R-rated version were more sexually explicit and graphic than they were violently explicit and graphic. Four times as many films are rated NC-17 for sex than for violence (Dick, 2006). In Europe, however, ratings are much more restrictive on violence and less so on sex.

In the final analysis, however, parents must use the movie ratings as part of their own parental mediation. It is important to look at not just the rating but what it is for (most DVD boxes and some film reviews give this information). There may be an occasional R-rated movie you would want your 12-year-old to see and some PG-13 movies you wouldn't want your older child to see. For additional discussion of MPAA ratings related to sex and violence, see Chapters 9 and 10, including the discussion of the era before these ratings in Close-Up 10.1.

either promote family harmony and interaction or be a divisive force, depending on how it is used (Bryant & Bryant, 2001).

The Media of Mass Communication

Now let us turn to how various forms of media have been used for the purposes of mass communication. Mass media have traditionally been divided into two basic types: print and electronic (or broadcast). Print media (i.e., newspapers and magazines), of course, disseminate information through the production and distribution of paper copies. In contrast to electronic media, print media tend to be more permanent, or at least they were before the advent of widespread video and audio recording. Print media also require literacy of the audience. There are no bandwidth limits in print media, whereas there has traditionally been a finite number of possible radio frequencies and television channels (though today, due to technological advances, these are rapidly increasing in number). There is no inherent limit to the number of newspapers or magazines that may be published. In general, print media lend themselves better to a more detailed treatment of most topics than do electronic media.

In contrast to print media, electronic media are technologically more recent, less permanent, and less dependent on formal literacy or accessibility of urban infrastructure. This last point becomes especially crucial in more isolated regions of the world. For example, one can use a portable radio without having any access to electricity, literacy, or urban life. Likewise, many developing countries rely on mobile phones for Internet access, although high-speed Internet remains elusive for many in rural areas, even within the U.S. Because of their limited channel capacity, radio and television are typically more tightly regulated by governments than are print media, for example in the assignment of television channels and radio frequencies. The more authoritarian the society, the easier it is for the government to control radio and (especially) television in times that are deemed to be threatening. Although television networks, both private and government owned, tend to be national in scope, they often have influence far beyond their country's borders.

This traditional print–broadcast distinction, while still useful, has become somewhat antiquated with the advent of computer-mediated communications (CMC). Although electronic in technology, CMC has permanence and effectively unlimited channel capacity, and in this way is more like print media. Computer technology offers opportunities for combining media in ways that never used to be possible. For example, YouTube archives video footage from anyone who cares to post something. Wikipedia offers an encyclopedia available for all to read and edit. Facebook and Twitter offer opportunities to post pictures, notes, or party invitations, and send messages to several hundred possible "friends." Anyone can start a blog and post for others to read. In addition, print media are increasingly crossing the line to become electronic media, in that many publications produce electronic versions of their printed content.

Given that we are studying the psychology of mass communication, let us now turn to look briefly at how we use the various media.

Media Use

Television

Although experimental sets appeared in the late 1930s, television was essentially unknown to the general public at the end of World War II, but whereas only 0.02% of U.S. homes had TV in 1946, that figure had risen to 9% by 1950 and 23.5% by 1951. By 1962, TV ownership had exploded, with 90% of U.S. homes having a set. By 1980, televisions were found in about 98% of U.S. homes, a figure that has remained constant since; today, there are an average of 2.9 TV sets in each American home (Andreasen, 1994; Nielsen Company, 2010a). Although most of the programming in the early years was by networks or local stations, the rapid growth of cable and satellite technology in the 1980s and 1990s greatly expanded the offerings, with a corresponding decline in the broadcast network market share. Associated with television sets are video cassette recorders (VCRs), which were in 98% of U.S. households of families with children by 1999 (Jordan, 2001). In the new millennium an increasingly popular technology, the digital video recorder (DVR), was present in 34% of households by 2010 (Nielsen Company, 2010a). By 2010 Americans were also increasingly "time shifting" their television viewing by accessing TV content online via the Internet (Nielsen Company, 2011). This has led some viewers to engage in "binge viewing," watching entire seasons of some shows in one sitting (Jurgensen, 2012).

Even though access to computers and mobile devices is high among young children, a 2011 study found that TV is still a dominant medium in that age group, with 65% of children under 8 watching television at least once a day, most for around two hours a day (Common Sense Media, 2011). By 2008, 60% of U.S. adolescents and 30% of preschoolers (26% of those under two) had television sets in their bedrooms, and 91% of American households paid for a television subscription through cable, satellite, or telephone companies (Carlsson-Paige, 2008; Kotler, Wright, & Huston, 2001; Nielsen Company, 2011). Figures for European children and families were slightly lower overall but varied greatly by country (d'Haenens, 2001).

The television phenomenon is almost as pervasive in developing countries as it is in the Western world. Even the worst urban slums in the Third World sprout a myriad of television antennas. The number of TV sets per 1,000 people worldwide doubled from 117 to 234 between 1981 and 1997 ("The Faustian bargain," 1997), although they are hardly distributed evenly across the globe. For example, in 1996 there were 906 TVs per 1,000 people in the Netherlands and 850 per 1,000 in the United States, but only 5 per 1,000 in Bangladesh and 9 in Kenya (Wresch, 1996). This worldwide television reach

Close-Up 1.3: Stages of Television Impact

Drawing on his studies of television use in several Brazilian communities with varying lengths of exposure to television, cultural anthropologist Conrad Kottak (1990) identified five stages of societal interaction with television. In Stage 1, the medium is new and strange and attracts people with glued gazes—no matter what the content is. "The medium rather than the message is the mesmerizer" (Kottak, 1990, p. 139).

Stage 2 usually occupies the next 10 to 15 years, with people beginning to interpret TV's messages and selectively accept or reject them. Due to its high status, television ownership displays conspicuous consumption and TV becomes a source of privileged information.

In Stage 3, the community is saturated with television and the length of exposure increases.

By Stage 4, adults have spent their whole lives in a culture permeated by television, and its lifelong impact on members of society is taken for granted.

Finally, Stage 5 occurs with the widespread appearance of cable TV and video capability. At this stage, there is much more individual control of TV, in terms of both time shifting and abundant selection of programming. Marketing is increasingly directed at homogeneous segments, not to the mass audience.

has led to a global audience for some events. For instance, as many as three billion people saw recent Olympic Games and World Cup soccer finals on TV. See Close-Up 1.3 for an anthropologist's views on the stages of a society's acceptance of TV.

The bulk of mass communications research has studied television, because we spend so much time watching it. A TV set is turned on in the average U.S. household between seven and eight hours each day, with the typical child, aged 8 to 18, watching over two and a half hours per day. Throughout childhood, the average U.S. child sees nearly 15,000 sexual references, innuendoes, and jokes per year, with only 1.1% of those dealing with abstinence, birth control, pregnancy, or sexually transmitted diseases (Kaiser Family Foundation, 2010; Strasburger & Donnerstein, 1999). By the time a child reaches the age of 18, he or she has seen an estimated 200,000 televised acts of violence (Huston, Wright, Rice, Kerkman & St. Peters, 1990).

Group Differences

The amount of television viewing changes through the lifespan. It rises sharply between ages 2 and 4, from about 15 minutes to 2.5 hours per day. It then levels off until about age 8, rising again to a peak of around 4 hours a day by age 12. It then starts to fall during the high school and college years and young adulthood, when people are busy with romance, studying, working, listening to music, and parenting young children. There is another rise, however, in the older adult years, after one's children are grown. In fact, elderly adults watch more television than most groups. Other groups who watch television more than average are women, poor people, and ethnic minorities (Roberts, 2000). It is interesting that many of the groups who watch the most television are the same groups that are the most underrepresented in TV programming, where characters are disproportionately middle class, White, male, professional, and affluent. We return to this issue in Chapter 4.

Time-of-Day Differences

Television viewing also changes sharply throughout the day. Typically the largest network TV audience is during "prime time"—8 to 11 p.m. Eastern and Pacific times in North America (7 to 10 p.m. Central and Mountain). These are the hours that earn the highest advertising charges and the greatest investment and innovation in programming. The most obvious pinnacle of such efforts may be seen in the prime-time "sweeps weeks" in February, May, July, and November, in which Nielsen audience size over a four-week span is used to calculate advertising charges for the next several months. These are the weeks when the networks outdo themselves presenting blockbuster movies, specials, and landmark episodes of top-rated series.

Video

Starting with Sony's slow introduction of $2,000-plus Betamax machines into the U.S. market in 1975 (five years later, less than 1% of U.S. homes owned a VCR), growth in VCR ownership took off in the early 1980s, until by 1995 it had reached 85% in U.S. homes (Hull, 1995). These days, the presence of VCRs has dropped to about 65% of households, most likely replaced with DVD players, DVRs, or Internet television and movie viewing (Nielsen Company, 2010a).

Although bitterly opposed to videotape at first, Hollywood studios later forged a very symbiotic and lucrative relationship between theater movies and home video. VHS and, more recently, DVD sales and rentals, have brought huge additional income and interest to the film industry. The widespread renting of movies has raised some new issues, however. Although the U.S. film rating system (G, PG, PG-13, R, NC-17) can have some effect in theaters, it has very little in rental stores, DVD rental kiosks, or online, where 13-year-olds generally have no trouble accessing an R-rated movie. More recently, increasing numbers of films have been produced solely for DVD distribution, or released in "unrated" or "director's cut" versions, bypassing both theaters and the need to have any rating at all. DVDs have been an additional boon to home movie viewing, since they are generally marketed with additional "special features," such as deleted scenes, interviews with stars and directors, and background information on filming. A growing trend is the tendency to view movies via cable on-demand and online streaming services. Indeed, this trend (combined with through-the-mail DVD services such as Netflix) has largely been responsible for the weakened presence or demise of brick-and-mortar video rental stores such as Blockbuster (Kehr, 2011).

One segment of television still distressed by video technology is advertising. Time shifting, which enables viewers to record TV shows and watch them later while fast-forwarding through the ads, has spurred new creativity in the ad industry, in an attempt to produce ads that viewers will be reluctant to fast-forward through. There are also increasing attempts to create ads with highlights that can be noticed while fast-forwarding. It is no accident that the ads have come to look more like the programming, using artsy montage and cinema verité techniques.

Some television markets have grown exponentially in recent years. China is now by far the largest TV market, with over 350 million homes having access (174 million having cable), reaching most of its 1.3 billion population. China moved from only 18 million people having access to TV in 1975 to one billion 20 years later, putting it first in the world in terms of the number of TV viewers. In contrast, the United States had only 98 million homes with TV, and third-place India 79 million (Madden, 2010; Thomas, 2003). The rapid growth of markets in developing countries will have far-reaching advertising implications in future decades.

An important emphasis in future media research, as indeed in all social science research, will be cross-cultural dimensions. Virtually every society in the world is becoming more multicultural, in part due to the increased ease of access to online information. We are all exposed to media from many different national and cultural sources, and it is necessary to understand how different cultures perceive the same message. Useful collections of papers on comparative and cross-cultural media research include: Kamalipour (1999), Korzenny and Ting-Toomey (1992), and Blumler, McLeod, and Rosengren (1992).

It is a common experience in much of the world to be able to watch a foreign language television program or film that has been dubbed or subtitled in the local language. For a discussion of how people process subtitles, see Close-Up 1.4.

Changing technology is accelerating fundamental structural changes in television. Broadcast network TV (e.g., ABC, CBS, Fox, and NBC in the U.S.), which accounted for over 90% of the audience as recently as 1978, has slowly but surely seen its audience decline as proliferating cable channels have vastly increased the number of offerings available. The psychological impact of all these choices is less clear; it is not obvious how receiving 500 or even 100 channels will change one's TV viewing. VCRs, DVRs, on-demand cable services, and the Internet have greatly increased audience control in program

Close-Up 1.4: Reading, Ignoring, or Not Having to Deal With Subtitles

In much of the world a considerable amount of television originates from places where a different language is spoken. Thus programs are either dubbed into or subtitled in the local language. Dubbing allows one to hear one's own language, though it may not match the movement of characters' lips on the screen. However, reading subtitles while simultaneously processing the visual content and ignoring the soundtrack in an unfamiliar language involves a set of cognitive skills that requires some practice (Perego, del Missier, Porta, & Mosconi, 2010). Belgian psychologist Gery d'Ydewalle and his colleagues (e.g., de Bruycker & d'Ydewalle, 2003; d'Ydewalle & de Bruycker, 2007; d'Ydewalle, Praet, Verfaillie, & Van Rensbergen, 1991) have measured eye movements as an indicator of people's relative attention to subtitles and visual content. They found that people look at subtitles in their own language and may find them distracting in cases in which they know both the languages involved (Lavaur & Bairstow, 2011). Belgians are very familiar with reading subtitles; most of their movies and much of their television is foreign and subtitled, sometimes bilingually, with two parallel subtitle lines in French and Dutch (the country's two languages).

Movies and TV shows with subtitles can even be used to learn a language (d'Ydewalle & Van de Poel, 1999; Koolstra & Beentjes, 1999). For example, the Italian newsmagazine *L'Espresso* promoted itself by giving away "MovieTalk" CD-ROMs of old *Beverly Hills 90210* and *Columbo* episodes to use for English lessons. In addition to the original voicing, users had the option of pressing another button to hear a slower, less slurred and more precise voiceover (Stanley, 2000).

The United States is unusual among nations in having virtually no subtitled television available. Presumably because so much domestic programming, almost all in English, is available, U.S. audiences have never had to become used to reading subtitles. Subtitled foreign films are shown, but with rare exceptions only as art films to highly specialized audiences. The conventional industry wisdom, accurate or not, is that American audiences will not watch foreign-language subtitled films or television. This largely untested assumption may exclude American viewers from seeing much high quality and potentially popular television.

selection and timing, as well as introducing the option of at least partially avoiding commercials. Although the days of the mass audience are not over (top-rated broadcast network TV shows like *American Idol* remain very widely shared experiences), movement in the direction of more precisely targeted audiences is probably unstoppable.

Other changes in television can be expected to grow. Pay-per-view television is beginning to catch on, especially for major events like boxing matches, although growth has been slower than its proponents had hoped. High-definition television (HDTV) was fully implemented in the United States in early 2009. TiVo and other DVRs can be programmed to record programs of interest to the viewer on whatever channel. Interactive TV projects allow viewers to, for example, press one button to see the original live feed and another to call up additional background information during newscasts or sports events. Yet another button can bring up a close-up shot of an athlete during a ball game, while another can provide an instant replay or start the game over. Opportunities for connecting one's computer, television, mobile phones, and music system together will change the face of mass communication, and further blur the boundary with personal media and entertainment.

Radio

The other traditional electronic medium, radio, rapidly permeated society in the 1920s, much as television would do 30 years later. The current network TV format of prime-time entertainment programming was borrowed from radio, which later, in the 1950s, reorganized into a primarily music-and-news format after TV had co-opted its programming agenda. More than television, radio is highly age- and interest-segmented (e.g., top 40, classical, country and western, Christian, oldies rock, easy listening, news and talk). Developmentally, radio is used infrequently by most children until preadolescence but becomes a central part of adolescent and young adult culture. Teenagers listen to music on radio, CD, or MP3 players three to four hours per day, more than the two to three hours per day they spend watching TV (Roberts & Christenson, 2001).

Worldwide, radio is the most available medium. It is crucially important in isolated societies because it depends on neither literacy nor electricity, nor on the purchase of a relatively expensive television set, computer, or mobile phone. Although there are premium satellite and Internet radio services available, most radio receivers are cheap and run well on batteries. Compared to television or print media, programming is very inexpensive to produce, especially talk and music formats. Talk radio, of course, can be anything from ennobling to dangerous. One of the most shocking abuses of radio was the Rwandan station that broadcast calls for genocide and fomented hysteria, culminating in the disastrous Hutu–Tutsi civil war and genocide of 1994 to 1995, chillingly recreated in the 2004 film *Hotel Rwanda*. However, more often radio serves as an important part of the social fabric, tying diverse constituencies together; even that infamous Rwandan radio station later broadcast a soap opera designed to encourage dialogue between Hutu and Tutsi (Phillips, Urbany, & Reynolds, 2008). See Close-Up 1.5 for an example of the role of radio in a country sorely lacking in modern infrastructure.

Close-Up 1.5: Radio in Namibia

Sparsely populated and largely undeveloped, the southern African nation of Namibia was plundered under German and then South African colonial rule, before its independence in 1990. Its only large city is its capital, Windhoek (population approximately 310,000). According to Wresch (1996), Namibian radio had a call-in talk show, *The Chat Show*, from 9 to 10 a.m., which listeners called with specific complaints about businesses, the government, or the police. The announcer played a humanistic therapist kind of role, listening to and summarizing the caller's concerns. After the show ended, station personnel would call the government agencies or businesses who received complaints. They recorded the officials' responses to the complaints and played those back, along with the original complaint, when the second installment of the show aired three hours later. However, in 2009 the state-run Namibian Broadcasting Corporation decided to pull the plug on *The Chat Show*, a move that was panned by several human rights groups.

In rural Namibia, radio serves an even broader communicative function. In areas with virtually no phones or mail service, one can relay messages through the local radio station, which will broadcast (free of charge) that a particular listener should, for example, call his grandmother or pick up the textbook for his correspondence course. Even if the intended recipient is not listening, someone who knows him or her usually is, and the message is delivered (Wresch, 1996).

Newspapers

The circulation of daily newspapers in the United States has been falling for many years, down from 62.3 million in 1990 to 46.2 million in 2010 (Pew Research Center, 2011b). Of even more concern is that most readers are older: in 2010, the percentage of adults who "read a paper yesterday" was 62% for those 65 and older but only 34% for those 35 to 44, and about 25% for those 18 to 34 (Pew Research Center, 2011b). Newspapers have also taken a hit in the past decade with decreased advertising revenue. This is especially true of the once-lucrative classified advertising market, which has largely moved online with free website services such as Craigslist (Pew Research Center, 2011b). However, by 2011, some newspapers were beginning to charge for access to online content, perhaps most notably *The New York Times* (Peters, 2011; Pew Research Center, 2011b).

More than television or magazines, newspapers have a local identity and are the preeminent source for local news, advertising, gossip, and sports. In fact, sports sections tend to be the most-read parts of newspapers. Even as the number of dailies continues to fall, the number of weekly newspapers keeps growing. Indeed, the largest decreases in circulation in the past few years have been seen primarily in big-city daily papers (Pew Research Center, 2011b), some of which (e.g., *Detroit Free Press*, *New Orleans Times-Picayune*) began curtailing their print editions. In the United States, newspapers are almost totally regional, with the important exceptions of *USA Today*, *The New York Times*, and the *Wall Street Journal*, though large national papers are the rule in many nations (e.g., *The Guardian* or *The Times* in the United Kingdom, *Le Monde* in France). In spite of their regional nature, newspapers are becoming increasingly similar, a trend attributable to a consolidation of media ownership and especially to an increasing reliance by most newspapers on a few international wire services like Associated Press (AP), Reuters, and Agence France-Presse (AFP) as news sources.

Demographically, groups who read more newspapers are generally those who watch the least TV: those who are older, Caucasian, better educated, and of a higher socioeconomic status. Newspaper readers like to keep up with the news. They are more likely than nonreaders to also view TV and Internet news. Those who consume news usually use multiple sources; alternatively, those who do not read newspapers usually do not watch TV news either (Pew Research Center, 2011b).

Magazines

Print magazines are the most narrowly targeted of the traditional media, having become increasingly so after an early period of popular general-interest magazines (e.g., *Life*, *Look*, *Collier's*, *Saturday Evening Post*) ended in the 1960s. An estimated 11,000 magazines were published in the United States in the mid-1990s (Wilson & Wilson, 1998), mostly devoted to special interests. However, traditional national weekly news magazines were suffering; by 2011 *U.S. News and World Report* had abandoned its print version, and *Newsweek* was sold by The Washington Post Company for $1 and the assumption of its debt (Pew Research Center, 2011b).

Magazines combine newspapers' permanence and opportunity for greater in-depth coverage with television's visual appeal. Reading magazines is primarily an adult activity, although there are children's magazines such as *Boys' Life*, *Sports Illustrated for Kids*, *Teen Vogue*, and *National Geographic Kids* that are useful in developing children's reading and print media habits. For girls, certain magazines, such as *Seventeen* and, later, *Glamour*, *Vogue*, and *Cosmopolitan*, are an important part of the female adolescent experience and are major contributors to the socialization of girls as women in Western society (see Chapter 4). The emphasis in these kinds of magazines tends to be on fashion, attractiveness, romance, and sex. There really are no comparable gender-role socializing magazines for boys, although many read *Sports Illustrated* and *Sports Illustrated for Kids*.

Computer-Mediated Communication (CMC)

It is increasingly difficult to draw clear boundaries to delineate what is included in mass communication. Many varieties of computer-mediated communication, such as the Internet, World Wide Web, instant messaging, e-mail, chat rooms, social networks, and blogs, have many characteristics of traditional print and broadcast media. The boundaries between mass and personal media are growing increasingly fuzzy. Personal messages or videos may be sent to mass audiences or posted on the Internet. Movies may be viewed on television and, increasingly, sent like a message to others. With the advent of online media, entertainment, most notably film, is looking like and is handled more like mass communication.

The capacity for very wide circulation of material on the Internet means it can share many characteristics with traditional print and electronic media. When large documents are released to the public, they are routinely posted first on the Internet. A major gaffe on camera by a politician or movie star is watched and rewatched on YouTube for the next several days. Whenever people want more information about anything, they go online and Google the topic or check Wikipedia.

Another capability which computers bring to mass communication is the ability to digitally alter photographs. With modern technology a photograph can be so totally changed as to be completely unrecognizable. The ethical boundaries are fuzzy here. Although few would have problems with digitally cropping a photo to remove irrelevant background, how about digitally composing a photo to put people together who were never in that particular place at the same time? No doubt a national leader would object to an altered photo that showed him shaking hands with a terrorist, but what about altering a student group shot for a university recruiting brochure to make it more ethnically diverse than the original? This actually arose as an issue at the University of Wisconsin-Madison, where an African American student was digitally pasted into a photo of a football crowd (Boese, 2006; Jacobson, 2001). Is this misrepresentation? The student was a UWM student and could have been at that football game, although in fact he wasn't (see Wheeler, 2002 for a careful discussion of this issue).

Do such alterations matter? Yes, they do. Experiment participants acting as newspaper editors reviewing a story about a hurricane saw either a picture of a village before the hurricane hit or the same village devastated after. Although there was no mention of personal injuries or death in the story, about a third of those who had seen the "after" picture falsely remembered the story as having mentioned injury or death, compared to only 9% of those seeing the "before" photo (Garry, Strange, Bernstein, & Kinzett, 2007). Doctored photos can also affect one's memory of public events widely covered in the news. Sacchi, Agnoli, and Loftus (2007) showed Italians either the original photo of a lone protester facing a line of tanks in the 1989 Tiananmen Square protest in Beijing, or a doctored photo of the same scene with masses of spectators watching. Participants in the study were also shown one of a comparable pair of photos of a 2003 Rome protest against the Iraq War. People who saw the doctored photos remembered the events as involving more people with more confrontation and damage to property.

As with print and broadcast media, the theories and research methodologies of mass communication (see Chapter 2) have been used to study computer-mediated communication (Mundorf & Laird, 2002). For example, Papacharissi and Rubin (2000) examined people's uses and gratifications for the Internet. Ferguson and Perse (2000) compared the uses and gratifications of watching television and using the Internet. Mastro, Eastin, and Tamborini (2002) looked at how use of the Internet arouses users and how they can also use that medium to arouse or calm themselves. Sometimes even technical aspects of the Internet can have measurable effects. Sundar and Wagner (2002), for example, found that the speed at which an Internet image is downloaded affects physiological arousal; slower-loading images produce higher arousal, as measured by skin conductance, although this is also affected by how inherently arousing the downloaded image is.

Walther, Gay, and Hancock (2005) discuss five qualities of the Internet that are particularly worthy of study and theory. The *multimedia* aspect of the Internet is not unique to CMC but is a central part of it. CMC stimuli may contain any or all of the following: written words, spoken words, pictures, sounds, video, and social interaction of the user with other users. Examining how these various channels are processed in parallel, or as task-switching, represents a major research challenge, made all the more daunting by the fact that users are often doing other, non-CMC activities at the same time!

Hypertextuality is perhaps the most unique characteristic of the Internet. The availability of multiple links to many other sites and stimulus sources makes the Internet perhaps the most profoundly nonlinear of the mass media. How people choose to navigate through the various links, how websites can be designed to facilitate navigation in the most efficient way, and how people mentally combine information from the various sources are all hugely important topics that need a great deal of further study. It is not clear how the nonlinear nature of most websites either facilitates or inhibits learning. Some research has suggested that print-format or linear web designs lead to better factual learning but nonlinear web formats contribute to a better understanding of connections among facts (Eveland, Cortese, Park, & Dunwoody, 2004; Eveland & Dunwoody, 2001, 2002).

Interactivity is not unique to the Internet but it is a major aspect of many of its uses. Whether it is talking to friends through instant messaging, posting on a Facebook wall, or shopping online, interaction is far more fundamental to CMC than to the traditional print or broadcast media. How do electronic conversations differ from face-to-face or written ones? How are experiences like shopping, information seeking, auctioning, or even visiting different, perhaps fundamentally so, on the Internet?

A fourth characteristic, *packet switching*, has received the least behavioral research attention, according to Walther and colleagues (2005). This is related to the fact that the Internet sends digital data, encoded with identity and routing information as well as content, over multiple paths, such that it can be retrieved in multiple ways through multiple links. This is useful, for example, in keeping access open in the face of hardware or infrastructure crashes, or in subverting authoritarian attempts to block Internet access. However, it poses challenges in other ways, for instance making it difficult to block child pornography, online predation, cyberbullying, and electronic piracy. Generally packet-switching technology is well ahead of the regulatory process and often far ahead of behavioral research in understanding how such processes work.

Finally, the characteristic of *synchronicity* is important. Four types of CMC synchronicity (Strasburger & Wilson, 2002) are a part of the world all children grow up with now, though only a short time ago none of them even existed. *One-to-one* asynchronous communication is traditional e-mail. Improving technology has allowed the sending of visual, voice, video, and all sorts of written material as attachments to e-mail. *Many-to-many* asynchronous communication involves electronic bulletin boards and distribution lists, in which a receiver signs up for a service or logs on to a program to access messages from a particular group, usually focused on some specific topic. If a user must seek out a site in order to asynchronously access information, it may involve one-to-one, *many-to-one*, or *one-to-many* source–receiver relationships. Also, synchronous communication includes texting, instant messaging, and the use of chat rooms. These are very popular forms of communication among preteens and teens but are also widely used by most segments of society. Chat rooms are organized around certain themes and allow users, for the first time in history, to find people like themselves without the issue of physical location being an issue. If someone suffers from an extremely rare disease, for example, there is probably a website, chat room, and a bulletin board to act as information sources and as a virtual support group for sufferers. Whether people are experiencing CMC in a synchronous or asynchronous manner can affect the way they process information and perform a cognitive problem-solving task (Münzer & Borg, 2008).

There are interesting age differences in the use of CMC. Although the stereotypes of the adolescent computer geek and the technologically clueless older adult still exist, increasing numbers of older adults are using the Internet effectively, though not necessarily in the same ways that their grandchildren do. Older adults are more likely to use the Internet for information seeking on topics of interest to them, as well as making frequent use of it for shopping and auctions (Hilt & Lipschultz, 2004).

Still, the young are especially frequent users of CMC, with 93% of teens saying that they use the Internet, the largest proportion indicating that they are online at least several times a day (Mastro, Eastin, & Tamborini, 2002; Pew Research Center, 2011a). The most common uses of the Internet are for e-mail, playing games, social networking, accessing databases, instant messaging, and talking in chat rooms and online discussion groups. By 2003, teens aged 13 to 14 already spent more time per week online (16.7 hours) than watching television (13.6 hours) (Weaver, 2003c). Often the Internet becomes the primary media source of information.

Teens and young adults also make huge use of social networking sites (e.g., Facebook and Twitter), which until recently were almost unknown, other than by name, to many adults. According to Facebook's own statistics, as of 2012 there were over 500 million daily users and 900 million monthly users of the website worldwide (Facebook, 2012). One 2008 study reported that 87% of college students had Facebook or MySpace accounts and spent 2.5 hours per day on their own and others' accounts (Raacke & Bonds-Raacke, 2008). The most common uses were to keep in touch with former and current friends. Another survey found that 47% of adult Americans reported using at least one social networking website (Pew Research Center, 2011a). In fact, according to at least one estimate, Americans spend more time on social networking sites than on any other online activity (Nielsen Company, 2010b). Interestingly, implicit rules have evolved for behavior on these sites (Walther & Bunz, 2005). There is a correlation between the amount of time adolescents spend on these sites and the likelihood that their social well-being will be affected by information received from the site (Valkenburg, Peter, & Schouten, 2006). On sites like Facebook, there are multiple cues (photos, wall postings, profile, and so on) that give information about a user, and we are only beginning to understand how people combine that information to form impressions of others in the absence of traditional, interpersonal, face-to-face cues (Anderson, Fagan, Woodnutt, & Chamorro-Premuzic, 2012; Lee, 2007; Walther, Van de Heide, Kim, Westerman, & Tong, 2008). The ways that personality affects one's level and quality of self-disclosure on social networking sites have also received some preliminary study (Schouten, Valkenburg, & Peter, 2007). Still, the psychological ramifications of social networking sites, including cyberbullying (Barlett & Gentile, 2012), are only beginning to be understood.

There is disagreement in the literature about whether Internet use is associated with social isolation or loneliness (Cole, 2000; Kraut et al., 1998; McKenna & Bargh, 1999; McKenna & Seidman, 2005; Sheldon, Abad, & Hinsch, 2011). Overall, Internet use is typically more social than television viewing or newspaper reading, in part due to social options like instant messaging and Facebook. At least one study found that young adults were happier following instant messaging communication than following comparable face-to-face interaction (Green, Hilken et al., 2005). There is also evidence that attempting to present oneself as extraverted on a blog, compared to writing private text documents, leads people to actually see themselves as more extra-verted (Gonzales & Hancock, 2008). Compared to face-to-face (FTF) interac-tions of two people, those who instant messaged each other drew interpersonal perceptions about the other person equally well, and even clearer social roles of dominant and submissive emerged in the CMC condition. These findings suggest that CMC is neither totally lacking in social cues, nor is it the "great equalizer" in terms of status (Boucher, Hancock, & Dunham, 2008). The strongest evidence for social isolation comes in the minority of the population who spend a very large number of hours online, perhaps due to a preference for online interaction fostering compulsive Internet use, which in turn results in negative social outcomes (Caplan, 2005). Effects of Internet use on social iso-lation are much weaker or nonexistent for moderate users. See Close-Up 1.6 for more about the issue of making friends online.

Close-Up 1.6: Making Personal Connections Online

Are relationships that are formed online, through e-mail, chat rooms, or social networking sites, inherently shallow and impersonal, even hostile and dangerous? Or, do they allow for liberation from the confines of physical locality and superficial aspects like physical appearance? In an early survey study of people in a variety of newsgroups and Usenet hierarchies, 60% of respondents reported making some sort of personal relationship online (Parks, 1996). Women were somewhat more likely than men to have such electronic friends, though age and marital status did not matter. Almost all had corresponded with their friend via e-mail and about a third had used phone, letter, or face-to-face contact as well. These relationships developed in many of the same ways that traditional relationships do. In the realm of romantic relationships, a 2006 survey revealed that 31% of adults in the U.S. indicated that they knew someone who had used an online dating website. About 15% reported that they knew someone who was in a long-term relationship that started on such a website (Pew Research Center, 2011a).

In a study comparing self-disclosure online and face-to-face, McKenna and Seidman (2005) found that people shared more of their true selves online than face-to-face and liked an Internet partner more than a face-to-face partner. Of course, individual differences are important. People prefer online relationships more strongly if they are socially anxious or lonely, or if their circumstances relating to current roles or relationships constrain face-to-face encounters. Thus, far from keeping people from interacting personally, computers may sometimes enhance the development of friendships, free of the usual constraints of first reactions to physical appearance and personal mannerisms.

The question of Internet "addiction" was examined by LaRose, Lin, and Eastin (2003). They argue that the sort of compulsive Internet use often popularly characterized with the addiction metaphor can better be conceptualized as deficient self-regulation. People who use the Internet excessively, at the expense of other activities and relationships, are poorer than most people at monitoring and regulating their own behavior, although their behavior is not usually as disturbed as those who fit the clinical definition of addiction.

Numerous questions about computer-mediated communication remain. Why do people e-mail, text, or use Facebook, and how do these new media complement or replace traditional communication means like the telephone and writing (Dimmick, 2003; Ramirez, Dimmick, Feaster, & Lin, 2008)? What is gained psychologically from instant messaging, texting, blogging, tweeting, and using Facebook? How do people search websites and evaluate the worth of the information they find? How do they make friends online?

Overview of the Book

This chapter has introduced mass communication from a psychological perspective. Chapter 2 explores, in some depth, the types of research methodologies that have been used to study media. It also looks at the various theoretical bases of research on mass communication, drawing on models from the different disciplines of communication, psychology, and other fields. The general, though not exclusive, emphasis is on a cognitive perspective. Chapter 3 then examines several psychological constructs important in understanding our interaction with media. The overarching theme of how we construct meaning from media and how that constructed meaning becomes our perceived reality is introduced.

Chapters 4 to 11 are topically organized, and explore several specific content areas. Chapter 4 explores the issue of group portrayals in the media. The emphasis here is on how media portray various groups of people and what the effects of such presentations are. We will see how media portrayals of groups may become a stereotyped reality in the minds of the public, especially in cases when the viewer has limited life experience with members of a particular group. Are men and women portrayed in stereotyped fashion? What about families? What are the effects of such portrayals on the socialization process for children? Also examined are African Americans, whose depictions have been more carefully studied than any other group in the history of TV. The portrayals of Latinos, Native Americans, Asian Americans, Arabs, older adults, sexual minorities, people with physical and psychological disabilities, and those in various professions are also examined. What are the effects of unrealistic or even nonexistent portrayals on the public's perception of these groups?

Chapter 5 examines the world as created by advertising. Advertising is a type of information to be processed—one very important way we learn about the world as well as its products. Techniques of persuasion are examined, focusing on various types of psychological appeals, especially as they involve persuasion through the creation of a new reality for the consumer (e.g., a reality full of danger in which one needs to buy locks and weapons, a reality in which most people are very thin and suntanned, a reality of status-conscious people that one has to continually impress with one's dress and possessions). We particularly examine the cognitive view of advertising, with a focus on the psychology of deceptive advertising. The issue of advertising to children is treated in some depth, identifying some surprising and disturbing trends and connections. Next, the issue of subliminal advertising is discussed to see if it is possible to persuade viewers at subconscious levels through subtle messages or embedded sexual figures in artwork. Finally, we look at the emergence of advertising in new places, such as in classrooms, product placements, the Internet, and prescription drug advertising.

Chapter 6 looks at three areas of media in which emotion is particularly central, namely sports, music, and religion. We examine how television not only transmits results and play-by-plays of athletic contests but also influences and changes the ways these sports are played. Rules and practices in sports have been changed by the demands of television coverage, and the nature of media coverage affects the public's interest and tastes in sports. Media coverage can encourage competition, cooperation, gender-role development, hero worship, and the enjoyment of sports violence. The second area—music—is a very important medium, especially for teens and young adults. The uses and gratifications of music consumption are examined, as well as specific issues like the nature of content in lyrics and how popular music has (and has not) changed over the years. The final emotion-laden topic, religion, is often curiously absent from the media, perhaps because it is so emotional that producers fear audience reaction. However, religion does creep into media in interesting ways, including through its presence in entertainment and its role in news. In fact, religious broadcasting and the electronic media revolution may have fundamentally changed religion itself.

Chapter 7 examines how the media's coverage of news affects our understanding of and attitudes to events in the world. News is perhaps the area in which people are most likely to believe that media merely reflect and report the reality that is out there. Drawing especially on agenda-setting theory, we make the argument that such is not the case, that in fact news reporting is by no means such a reality transmission, but is necessarily a constructed interpretation of reality, often based more on what is newsworthy than on what is really important. Even by choosing what to cover and what not to cover, media are setting an agenda. This necessarily involves only a partial presentation of reality, but this partial reality becomes the basis of our knowledge about the world, even affecting foreign policy.

Chapter 8 continues to examine news by looking at how politicians manipulate media coverage to convey their own intended reality. As practically all of our information about political candidates and officeholders comes through the media, the importance of mass communication in this area can hardly be overstated. Such issues as image building and the construction of an electronic personality are discussed. The impact of televised candidate debates is examined, followed by an in-depth look at the coverage of the extremely close 2000 U.S. Presidential election results and the subsequent vote-counting controversy. A final topic in politics and media concerns the appeals and effects of political advertising, including controversial negative or attack advertising. Types of appeals in political advertising and their effects on attitudes and voting behavior are examined.

In Chapter 9 we look at media violence, the most heavily researched issue in mass communication. Different effects of televised and filmed violence are examined, including induced fear, modeling, catharsis, desensitization, and the cultivation of fear. In addition, we explore what types of people are drawn to enjoy violent media and what different factors may interact with media violence to enhance or lessen its impact. Long-term effects of watching television violence and recent research on the effects of playing violent video games are also examined. The question of the effects on children of viewing violence turns out to be more complex than is often admitted by partisans on either side of this controversial issue, although the weight of the total body of research comes down strongly on the side of negative effects. These effects are substantial but usually in interaction with each other, suggesting a perspective of multiple risk and protective factors used to predict negative effects of watching violence.

Chapter 10 examines the history, character, and effects of sexual content in media, looking at both mainstream media and pornography. The creation and transmission of sexual values through media, as well as socialization in regard to sexuality and the behavioral effects of media sex, are addressed. Research on the effects of sexual violence, both in pornography and mainstream movies, is considered in some detail, pointing toward the conclusion that viewing sexual violence may be more damaging than viewing either sex or violence alone.

Turning in a more positive direction, Chapter 11 examines the media's prosocial uses, beginning with children's prosocial television. We start with a detailed look at *Sesame Street*, one of the longest-running and most evaluated TV shows in history. Other specifically prosocial TV shows are examined more briefly. The second part of the chapter deals with explicit attempts to use media to teach skills or persuade people to change their attitudes or behaviors in a more health- or safety-oriented direction. One section discusses principles of social, as opposed to product, marketing. The media's role in public health marketing campaigns to promote prosocial behaviors like stopping smoking, increasing exercise, or wearing seat belts is also considered. Public service announcements (PSAs) and other social marketing uses of media face greater obstacles, in many ways, than commercial advertising. A second part of this section looks at the use of mainstream entertainment media for explicitly prosocial ends (entertainment education), a format very common in developing countries and increasingly common, albeit it in more subtle ways, in Western countries.

Finally, Chapter 12 ties together themes from the entire book and explores how we, as consumers in the new millennium, can use the knowledge gained from this book to have a greater impact on the media, including their structure and programming. The issue of media literacy—how we can help children interact more productively with media—is examined in terms of both curricular development and what can be done in the home. Finally, some ways that we may influence the media and the ways in which media report social science research are presented.

Chapter 2

Research and Theory in Mass Communication

How Are Media Studied Scientifically?

Q: What is the gender breakdown of TV and movie characters that children see?

A: According to a 2008 study of almost 20,000 children's TV programs worldwide, only 32% of the main human characters were female, and only 13% of the nonhuman characters, like animals, monsters, and robots, were female. Of speaking characters in G-rated movies from 1990 to 2005, less than one-third were female (Fine, 2010).

Q: What percentage of felony defendants does the American public believe uses the insanity plea and how many actually do?

A: The public believes that 37% of defendants plead insanity, while in reality less than 1% do, most of whom are not successful ("Numbers," 1998).

Q: Why did several people receive hundreds of phone calls during the summer of 2003 from callers asking to speak with God?

A: In the movie *Bruce Almighty*, Bruce Nolan (played by Jim Carrey) was contacted by "God" on his cell phone. A particular phone number was shown, without area code. Hundreds of people around the United States called the number locally and asked to speak with God. The filmmaker had not followed the usual practice of using 555-prefix numbers (which are not real phone numbers), although this was added before the DVD release of the film. The poor fellow who had that 800 number received a phone bill for several thousand dollars!

In some sense everyone is a media critic. Few, however, have real answers to the questions and concerns that are so easy to raise. For example, it is easy to raise concerns about violence in the media but more difficult to precisely measure the effects of viewing that violence. It is easy to bemoan the lack of positive values on TV but more difficult to identify exactly what values television does communicate. The most reliable and useful answers come from scientific research. The results from such research are cited throughout this book, but in this chapter we look at what it means to do research on media and examine the theoretical frameworks that guide this research. In terms of the sheer amount of social science research on media, there is far more study of television than of radio, print, or computer-mediated communication. Many of the psychological questions discussed in this book apply equally to all media, although many have been examined primarily in regard to television. We begin by looking at some general approaches to studying media scientifically and examine the types of answers we can find. Then we move on to examine specific theories about media, drawn primarily from the disciplines of psychology and communication.

Media Research Frameworks

As well as being of great concern to the general public, the media are also of considerable interest to the worlds of commerce and science, both of which engage in research, studying media using various perspectives (see the chapters in Bryant & Oliver, 2009, for reviews). Much research has been done by or for TV networks, publishers, corporations, or ad agencies for commercial purposes; this is known as *administrative research*. For example, the Nielsen ratings of the television audience (see Close-Up 2.1) or marketing research studying the public's taste in colas is done for the purpose of increasing the profits of a corporation. Since most administrative research is not published in peer-reviewed journals, it is typically not even available to scientists or the public. The second general type of scientific study is usually performed by independent scientists, most often professors at colleges and universities, with the goal of understanding and explaining the effects of media and studying their role in society and in people's lives; this is called *critical research*. For example, studies of the effects of media violence or content analyses of sexist content in ads are generally done with no commercial motivation. It is this noncommercial critical research that is primarily cited in this book.

When we study media, we can examine the content itself, our exposure to this content, or the effects of that exposure. We begin by examining these three general ways of looking at media and then move on to specific theories.

Looking at Content

One very straightforward way to study media is to study its content. This is often an important precursor to research on exposure or effects. For instance, some studies count the number of characters of different racial, ethnic, or gender groups in TV shows. If we want to argue, for example, that television ads or shows are sexist, we must carefully define what we mean by "sexist" and then study the ads or shows to see if they fit those criteria. Studies of the effects of sex or violence make use of content-analysis studies to provide data on the prevalence of such themes and changing trends over time. In such research, *operational definitions* of important constructs are crucial. For example, if I am interested in studying how much violence there is on television, I must

Close-Up 2.1: Those All-Important Ratings

The Nielsen ratings are the all-important measures used to track audience size for television programming in the United States. It is on these ratings that programs, careers, and even broad social trends rise and fall. The A. C. Nielsen Company selects thousands of American homes as a sample. In many of these homes "people meter" machines are hooked up to their TVs, DVRs, cable boxes, or satellite dishes to measure when the set is on, who is watching, and what is being viewed. The Nielsen ratings provide two types of information. The rating itself is the percentage of the potential audience that is viewing a program (e.g., a rating of 30 means that 30% of the homes with TVs have that program on). The share compares that program's performance with the competition on at the same time. Network advertising charges are usually based primarily on the Nielsen ratings and shares measured during the four 4-week "sweeps" periods in February, May, July, and November. Advertising charges are based primarily on the number of homes reached by an ad, adjusted for demographics. For example, a higher proportion of 18- to 49-year-olds in the audience can translate into higher ad charges. The cost for a 30-second spot on the Super Bowl rose from $125,000 in 1975 to around $3 million by 2012. The even more lucrative 15-second spot typically sells for 55 to 60% of the 30-second price. Charges per minute are typically much lower for the non-prime-time slots and cable channels with smaller audiences.

carefully define what I mean by a "violent act." Without that, I do not know which acts to count. Without knowing other scientists' operational definitions, I am not able to interpret their research. That is why it is so important to include such definitions in published reports of research. We may not always agree with others' operational definitions, but knowing what they are allows us to interpret their results.

There are several important methodological issues involved in content analysis research, one of the major ones being interrater reliability and agreement (Lombard, Snyder-Duch, & Bracken, 2002; Tinsley & Weiss, 2000; for extensive discussions of content analysis as a methodology, see Neuendorf, 2002; Riffe & Freitag, 1997; Riffe, Lacy, & Fico, 1998).

Looking at Exposure

A second general way to study media is to study the amount of exposure people have to them. Who reads which newspapers or watches how much TV and when? How much do people use Facebook? Demographic information about different groups of people watching different shows comes from this type of study. This type of information does not always adequately assess real exposure, however. Just because the radio or television is on or someone is surfing the Internet is no assurance that he or she is devoting much attention to it, nor can we conclude that, merely because people are not paying full conscious attention to the source, they are unaffected by it. Often people are simultaneously doing something else besides listening to the radio or checking Facebook. Sometimes they leave the room altogether for some period of time, especially during TV commercials or while waiting for a friend to come online. To understand the cognitive processes involved in experiencing media, it is crucial to take seriously the amount and nature of attention devoted to the medium; we return to this issue in Chapter 3.

Looking at Effects

Probably the most common general perspective in studying media is to study the effects of exposure to mass communication. To the general public, most major concerns about the media probably center on their effects. The nature of these effects can take different forms. For example, these effects can be direct, conditional, or cumulative (Perse, 2001; Perse & Lambe, 2013).

With the *direct effects model*, effects appear quickly and are relatively similar across all audience members. The crudest version of a direct effects model is the theory of uniform effects. This model argues that most individuals in a mass society perceive messages from media in the same fashion and react to them strongly and very similarly. Media messages are thus "magic bullets" piercing the mind of the populace. Such a view had some influence in studies of propaganda popular in the so-called "hypodermic needle" model of the 1920s, whereby media were thought to "inject us with their venom." See Close-Up 2.2 for an interesting example from this period.

The assumption that media producers are evil thought controllers who manipulate everyone in a passive and helpless population in a uniform way has not been a serious theoretical position among communications researchers for many decades but is still implicitly assumed by some strident popular media-bashing critics, who blame the media for most social ills (e.g., Key, 1976, 1981, 1989; Winn, 2002). Indeed, a direct effects model is often implicitly held by members of the public critiquing media. An example of this is the belief of many regarding "subliminal" messages in advertising or music, which is discussed in Chapter 5.

With the *conditional effects model*, the media can still have substantial effects, but only under certain conditions or for certain audience members, often in less dramatic form than suggested by the most vocal critics. This is a model of selective effects based on individual differences (Oliver & Krakowiak, 2009). Different people perceive the same message differently and respond to it in different ways. For example, a violent TV program will probably not

Close-Up 2.2: *Reefer Madness*: A Hypodermic Needle?

An interesting study in the direct effects model is the 1936 film *Reefer Madness*. Originally released under the title *Tell Your Children*, the movie depicted frightening (if unrealistic) consequences of marijuana use. The story line has several clean-cut youths falling in with shady characters who persuade them to use marijuana. As the film progresses, characters resort to prostitution, rape, suicide, and murder as a result of their marijuana use. One character is even locked away in a mental asylum for the rest of his life, apparently the result of a mental break after using too much reefer.

Despite this over-the-top portrayal, *Reefer Madness* was not unique in its style. Similar films of the era included *Narcotic*, *Cocaine Fiends*, and *Sex Madness*. This movie genre has sometimes been labeled "cautionary film," the notion being that the producers' main goal was to warn viewers of the dangers of drugs, venereal disease, and the like. Such thinking reflects the direct effects/hypodermic model in the belief that audience members would be uniformly "immunized" by viewing the effects of others' sins. However, some see this view as naïve, calling movies like *Reefer Madness* "exploitation films," meaning that filmmakers intentionally played upon moviegoers' curiosity about lurid and taboo topics for profit. Summing up this notion, Feaster and Wood say: "Just as the exploiter's primary concern was not liberating his customers from the catacombs of ignorance, moviegoers also turned to exploitation for something beyond moral betterment. The explorations of vice promised vivid displays of human shame and debauchery, and it was for this dramatization that tickets were purchased" (1999, p. 18).

Reefer Madness has lived well beyond the 1930s. In the 70s, the movie became a cult favorite among many, with at least one pro-marijuana advocacy group screening it as a campy protest to governmental restrictions of the drug (Feaster & Wood, 1999). That cult popularity eventually led to a satirical *Reefer Madness* musical in the 1990s, and later a cable TV movie version of the musical. Whatever its original motivation, *Reefer Madness* has been fascinating audiences for decades.

incite all of its viewers to go out and commit mayhem, but it may reinforce the already existing violent tendencies of a small sample of the viewers and slightly dull the sensitivities of many others. Similarly, certain positive or negative aspects of media may affect exceptional children more than average children (Abelman, Atkin, & Lin, 2007; Grimes, Anderson, & Bergen, 2008; Sprafkin, Gadow, & Abelman, 1992).

A major effort of this type of research has been to discover other interactive variables that mediate or moderate the effects of consuming media. These may be demographic variables classifying the individual (e.g., gender, ethnicity, age), properties of the message (e.g., who commits the violence and whether it is reinforced), or the context of its reception (e.g., children watching television with their parents or alone). Taken together, these interactive variables may be considered *risk factors*; the effects will be stronger the greater the number of risk factors present in a particular person (Kirsh, 2006). The fact that the effects are not uniform does not reduce their importance. For example, even if a given effect occurs in only 0.01% of the viewers of a certain TV program, that still has an impact on 4,000 people out of an audience of 40 million!

The third model, *cumulative effects*, emphasizes the importance of repeated exposure to media stimuli and suggests that effects are due not so much to a single exposure as to the additive effects of many instances of exposure. For example, a single exposure to a *Seventeen* supermodel is unlikely to trigger an eating disorder, but repeated exposures to ultrathin, large-breasted women may cumulatively encourage a young woman to push her body in that direction, especially if she likes and identifies with the media models (Harrison, 1997). In looking for any effects of media, we must always keep in mind the importance of cumulative exposure. Most media messages or images are encountered dozens, if not hundreds or thousands, of times. Although such massive exposure is difficult to fully simulate in a laboratory setting and difficult to control in a field study, there are ways it can be studied. For a conceptual paper on defining what an "effect" of media is, see Potter (2011).

Behavioral Effects

There are four general classes of measurable effects of media. Probably the type most people think of first are behavioral effects, in which somebody performs some behavior after seeing a media model do it; for example, acting violently, buying a product, voting for a candidate, or laughing or crying. This is the particular emphasis among proponents of social cognitive theory (Bandura, 2009), which is discussed later in this chapter.

Although behavior may be conceptually the most obvious type of effect, it is often very difficult to measure and even harder to definitively attribute a causal role to the media. For example, we can know whether somebody sees a certain toothpaste commercial and we can check to see if that person buys that brand, but knowing for sure that he or she bought that product *because* of seeing the particular ad and not for other unrelated reasons is very difficult to demonstrate. Even in tragic cases like a school shooting by a teen who had recently seen a similar scene in a movie, it is very difficult, in either a legal or scientific sense, to demonstrate a cause-and-effect relationship between the teen seeing the movie and pulling the trigger himself.

Attitudinal Effects

Attitudinal effects make up a second general class of media effects. For example, an ad might make you think more highly of some product or candidate;
whether this attitude would be followed up in actual buying or voting behavior is another question. For example, U.S. and Japanese moviegoers viewing
the anti-General Motors documentary *Roger and Me* showed a more negative
attitude toward GM in particular and toward U.S. business in general
(Bateman, Sakano, & Fujita, 1992), but effects on car-buying behavior were
less clear.

Although attitudes consist of an intellectual (belief) component (e.g., reasons that you favor one political candidate's position over another's), much of
the psychological dynamic in attitudes is emotional (e.g., liking one candidate
more than another). Sometimes the intellectual and emotional components
may be inconsistent with each other, as when most U.S. voters in 1984 disa-
greed with President Ronald Reagan's positions on issues, but reelected him in
a landslide because they liked him and trusted him. Holding such inconsistent
attitudes simultaneously is labeled by social psychologists as *cognitive dissonance* (Festinger, 1957).

Positive feelings about products or candidates may be taught through the
process of classical conditioning, whereby a conditioned stimulus (a product)
is associated with an unconditioned stimulus that naturally elicits some positive response. For example, an attractive model paired with some product may
engender positive attitudes, especially positive feelings, through the association of the product with the sexy model, who naturally elicits that positive
response. The precise processes by which classical conditioning occurs in
advertising are discussed in more detail in Chapter 5.

Media may induce many sorts of attitudes on a given subject. For example,
a dramatic TV movie or documentary on human trafficking may sensitize
people to this problem and make them more sympathetic to its victims.
Stereotyped portrayals of social groups may contribute to prejudice in viewers.
Seeing horror movies in which women appear sexually aroused by being raped
or assaulted may teach viewers that women derive some secret pleasure out of
being victims of sexual violence. Attitudes are much easier to measure than
behaviors and are often of great importance, for they influence behaviors that
may follow and the way we cognitively process information in future.

Attitudes may have influence beyond one's opinion about a particular subject. Sets of attitudes may form a sort of mindset through which we view
the world. These attitudes color our selection of what we perceive in the
world and how we interpret it. The interaction of this knowledge gained from
media with our experience in the world can lead to what is called *cultivation*
(Gerbner, Gross, Morgan, Signorielli, & Shanahan, 2002; Morgan, Shanahan,
& Signorielli, 2009). For example, if we accept the cop-show image of large
cities being very dangerous places, that knowledge colors our attitudes about

cities, and can also affect cognitions and behaviors indirectly in ways that can be measured experimentally.

Cognitive Effects

The third class of media effects is cognitive effects, which alter what we know or think. When we are watching TV, using the Internet, or reading a magazine, we are continually processing, comprehending, and remembering the information we are exposed to (Harris, Cady, & Tran, 2006). The most straightforward type of example would be learning new information from media (e.g., facts about chimpanzees from a *National Geographic* article). There are also more subtle kinds of cognitive effects. Simply by choosing what news stories to cover, for example, media *set an agenda*. By covering American presidential primary campaigns much more thoroughly than complex but abstract economic issues like the world debt crisis or the shift from domestic to export agriculture, the media are telling us that the political details of all those primaries are very important, whereas the other issues are relatively less so.

Different media may stimulate different types of cognitive processing. In some early studies comparing cognitive effects of radio versus television in telling stories, children produced more original endings for incomplete stories heard on the radio than they did for stories seen and heard on television. This offers some research support for the intuitive claim that radio stimulates the imagination more than TV does. Children remembered verbal information better from radio but visual, action, and overall information better from television (Greenfield & Beagles-Roos, 1988; Greenfield, Farrar, & Beagles-Roos, 1986).

In some ways radio and newspapers may have more in common cognitively with each other than either does with TV. Both radio and print are largely verbal media, whereas television is disproportionately more pictorial. There is much similarity in the way that a story is comprehended from a book and from the radio, but less similarity between a story read and one seen on television (Pezdek & Hartman, 1983; Pezdek, Lehrer, & Simon, 1984; Pezdek & Stevens, 1984). This suggests that skills used for extracting information from television are different from those used to extract information from the words of radio or print.

Taking a field study approach to comparing information transmission through different media, Spencer, Seydlitz, Laska, and Triche (1992) compared the public's responses to newspaper and television reports of an actual natural hazard, in this case the saltwater intrusion from the Gulf of Mexico into the lower Mississippi River in 1988. Results indicated that newspapers were better at presenting complex and potentially ambiguous information about possible consequences of the hazard, whereas television was better at communicating material that was relatively simple and at making direct behavior-related appeals (e.g., buying bottled water). Similar effects of medium were shown in memory for news from the 2000 U.S. political campaign

(Eveland, Seo, & Marton, 2002). People gained more political knowledge when they accessed media information from various media modalities (e.g., print news combined with electronic news) than from one modality alone (Shen & Eveland, 2010).

Although cognitive effects are most often measured by testing the information acquired, other types of methods are also useful. For example, attention to TV may be studied by measuring the time the eyes are focused on the screen (Anderson & Kerkorian, 2006). The amount of cognitive effort required may be assessed indirectly by measuring the reaction time for remembering information and responding (Cameron & Frieske, 1994) or for doing some secondary task (Basil, 1994).

Physiological Effects

The fourth class of media effects involves the physical changes in our bodies resulting from exposure to the media. For example, increases in breathing and heart rate result from watching a scary movie or an exciting ball game. Sexual arousal from viewing pornography may be measured by sensors on the penis or vagina (Lohr, Adams, & Davis, 1997). Even such mundane material as television or radio commercials can induce changes in the heart rate and orienting reflex (Lang, 1990, 1994), electrodermal responses (Hopkins & Fletcher, 1994), facial electromyography (Bolls, Lang, & Potter, 2001; Hazlett & Hazlett, 1999), and changes in alpha waves given off by the brain (Reeves et al., 1985; Simons, Detenber, Cuthbert, Schwartz, & Reiss, 2003; M. E. Smith & Gevins, 2004). See Lang, Potter, and Bolls (2009) for a review of physiological measures of media effects and Ravaja (2004) for a review of research using the measures of heart rate, facial electromyography, and electrodermal activity to study attention and emotional responses to media.

One of the newest and most exciting physiological measures of media effects comes from functional magnetic resonance imaging (fMRI) scans of the brain. For example, Anderson, Fite, Petrovich, and Hirsch (2006) found complex patterns of activity in multiple brain areas were characteristically activated by watching video action sequences. When the action contains violence, other consistent areas are activated (Murray et al., 2006). Playing violent video games activates similar areas to those activated during actual violent behavior (Weber, Ritterfeld, & Mathiak, 2006) and may change, at least temporarily, the neural structure of the prefrontal cortex (Wang et al., 2009). As studies using fMRI techniques become more common, there will no doubt be additional findings regarding how media consumption affects the brain.

Caveat: The Third-Person Effect

One very general principle from social psychology, the *third-person effect*, is very important to consider when looking at media effects. As applied to media, this principle states that (1) people believe that other people are more vulnerable than themselves to persuasive messages and other media influences; and (2) such perceptions can influence behavior. This principle, soundly supported by research, suggests that people think other people are more influenced by ads, more distressed about their own bodies relative to supermodels, more corrupted by negative media values, or more likely to emulate violent media models than they themselves are. This effect has been shown for a wide variety of materials, including environmental news (Jensen & Hurley, 2005), political attack ads (Wei & Lo, 2007), Internet use (Li, 2008), video game playing and influence (Cruea & Park, 2012), perceived antisocial influences on young adults (Lambe & McLeod, 2005), responding to the "Y2K millennium bug" (Tewksbury, Moy, & Weis, 2004), tabloid newspapers and TV sitcoms (Reid & Hogg, 2005), and Internet pornography (Lee & Tamborini, 2005). There is even evidence that the third-person effect is particularly large when dealing with seriously antisocial behaviors, such as violence (Hoffner & Buchanan, 2002; Hoffner, Plotkin et al., 2001). A variety of explanations for this robust finding have been offered, as well as delineations of conditions affecting it (see Perloff, 2009, for a review; for meta-analyses see Paul, Salwen, & Dupagne, 2007; Sun, Pan, & Shen, 2008). Being one of several self-serving biases used to maintain a positive self-image (Tal-Or & Tsfati, 2007), the third-person effect leads people consistently to underestimate the media's influence on their own lives, even as they loudly decry its corrupting manipulation of others' lives.

A more general model derived from the third-person effect is the *influence of presumed influence* model (Gunther & Storey, 2003). This model postulates that people perceive that some particular media message will have an effect on others and that they then react to that perception. These perceived effects may be positive as well as negative. For example, Gunther and Storey (2003) evaluated the effect of a radio health campaign in Nepal targeted at health clinic workers. The broader population expected the campaign to affect health care workers, and this, in turn, raised their expectations about their own interactions with those workers, with the result that they held more positive attitudes toward those professionals and the quality of their interaction improved. Thus, the message directly affected the perceptions of people other than its target audience, and those perceptions in turn affected the behavior of the target persons.

The Strength of Effects

Although computing the precise strength of media effects is a very difficult task, there have been some attempts to do so, using statistical techniques like meta-analysis and computation of effect sizes (Perse, 2007; Perse & Lambe, 2013). For example, such strength measures have been developed for effects of media violence (Christensen & Wood, 2007), gender-role perceptions

(Herrett-Skjellum & Allen, 1996), ads targeted at children (Desmond & Carveth, 2007), and pornography (Allen, Emmers, Gebhardt, & Giery, 1995). Perhaps it will be surprising to you, but such studies generally show small to modest (though statistically significant) effect sizes. As would be expected, these effect sizes are almost always larger in laboratory studies than in field studies or surveys, due to the greater degree of experimental control reducing random error.

Why aren't the effects of media greater than they are? The major reason is that there are simply so many other influences, including some that most everyone would expect to be stronger. For example, parents' behavior and the level of community violence have greater effects on children's level of violent behavior than violent media do. Personal experience with a particular product has more effect on purchasing behavior than advertising does. Whether one's peers and parents smoke is a better predictor of whether a teen will start smoking than is exposure to cigarette advertising. None of this is surprising, however. Personal long-term influence has long been known to be highly influential on all sorts of behavior. A good way to look at this is through the idea of risk and protective factors (Kirsh, 2006). A child who will behave in extremely violent ways probably will not do so solely in response to watching a violent movie, being a product of parental neglect, living in a violent community, or getting involved with drugs or gangs, but the more of these risk factors he has, the greater the likelihood of violent behavior. In this sense exposure to violent media is one of numerous risk factors. Similarly, the more protective factors a child has (e.g., a safe community, supportive parents, good friends, a high level of empathy, a low level of sensation seeking), the less likely he or she will be to engage in violent behavior after watching violent media or playing first-person-shooter video games.

Just because media are not the strongest influence, however, does not mean their effects are trivial. In fact, there is good reason to believe that scientific studies may underestimate media effects, especially for very dramatic types of media. For example, studies of sex and violence, especially with children, do not show extremely graphic violence or pornography for ethical reasons. Would you give permission for your five-year-old to see *Pulp Fiction, Kill Bill,* or child pornography? Although we do not know for sure, it is quite possible that effects of highly graphic stimuli are greater than those already documented in the research with milder stimuli.

Also, effects may not always be linear though such linearity is often implicitly assumed by researchers and the public. It is probably not the case, for example, that advertising effects gradually increase the more times one sees a particular ad. There is evidence that this is true up to a point, but after that point people seem to grow tired of and even annoyed with the ad and its impact actually starts to decrease. Sometimes a particular media stimulus contains two different influences which have an opposite impact and thus cancel each other out. For example, watching violence may cause viewers to believe the world is a more violent place, but this belief may also cause them to stay inside more and thus avoid situations where they may be likely to behave violently.

Another issue is the direction of causal influence (Tal-Or, Cohen, Tsfati, & Gunther, 2010). For example, does watching pornography have a causative effect on one's attitude toward censorship, or are they merely correlated? Does seeing and remembering ads for a certain political candidate cause one to vote for that candidate? It is a challenging task for researchers to test and establish such causative relationships, especially in an environment in which many antecedents may have causal impact on a complex behavior.

Finally, because media affect different people so differently, it may be the case that a disproportionate amount of media effects occur with the relatively small number of audience members who experience a very large effect, while most others experience little effect. Thus group analyses may show overall small effects, but that may not be the whole story. For thorough discussions of these issues in more detail, see Perse (2001, 2007) and Perse and Lambe (2013).

Theories of Mass Communication

Now that we have looked at different media research frameworks and types of effects measured, let us turn to some specific theories that have guided mass communication research over the years. In their current versions, most contemporary theories are heavily cognitive in nature. By this we mean that they view perception and information processing of media messages as constructive; that is, people do not literally encode and retrieve information that they read or hear in the media (or anywhere else). Rather, as they perceive and comprehend media, they *interpret* in accordance with their prior knowledge and beliefs and the context in which the message is received. Comprehension of a TV program, for example, emerges through a continual interaction between the content of the program and the knowledge already in our minds. The mind is continually and actively thinking about what we see or hear and those thoughts become an important part of the constructive process of comprehension. See Bryant and Miron (2004) for a historical overview of uses of mass communication theory in research from 1956 to 2000.

Social Cognitive Theory (Social Learning, Observational Learning, Modeling)

The social cognitive approach originally grew out of stimulus-response (S-R or behaviorist) psychology as "social learning theory," first developed by social psychologist Albert Bandura and his associates in the 1960s (Bandura, 1977; Bandura, Ross, & Ross, 1961, 1963; Bandura & Walters, 1963). The basic premise of this theory is a simple one: We learn behaviors by observing others performing those behaviors and subsequently imitating them ourselves. The relevance to media occurs when a media actor becomes the source of observational learning. Over its years of development the social cognitive model has increasingly stressed cognitive processes and personal agency or choice.

There are four subfunctions of observational learning from media, according to Bandura (2001, 2002, 2009). The first is obvious. For modeling to occur, a person must be exposed to the media example and pay attention to it. Second, he or she must be capable of symbolically encoding and remembering the observed events, including both constructing the representation and cognitively rehearsing it when the media example is no longer present. Third, the person must be able to translate the symbolic conceptions into appropriate action. For example, a girl may see a character behaving violently in a movie when frustrated; when frustrated herself, the girl may mimic the violent behavior in her own life. Finally, motivations must somehow develop through internal or external reinforcement (reward) in order to energize the performance of the behavior. For instance, a movie character's violent behavior would be reinforced if that behavior elicited praise from others in the film or if the character enjoyed performing the behavior or received a monetary gain or beautiful companion as a result.

Social cognitive theory was initially applied to media in the context of studying the effects of violent media models on behavior (see Chapter 9). Although that is still the most-studied application, the model has many other applications as well, as in the modeling of sexual, prosocial, or purchasing behavior. For example, children randomly assigned to view high-risk behaviors on TV were more likely to later self-report their own tendency to engage in risk-taking behaviors (Potts, Doppler, & Hernandez, 1994). Such reported risk-taking was reduced by viewing a safety educational videotape showing high-risk behavior and its negative consequences (Potts & Swisher, 1998). The amount of social aggression (e.g., spreading rumors, social ostracism) that girls aged 5–10 watched predicted increased socially aggressive behavior at school (Martins & Wilson, 2012). Young women exposed to media portrayals of promiscuous sexual behavior (one-night stands) were more likely than those not seeing the media models to anticipate engaging in such behaviors themselves if they did not already have such life experience, regardless of whether the consequences were portrayed as positive or negative in the media depiction (Nabi & Clark, 2008). See Bandura (2009) for a recent and detailed formulation of the social cognitive model as applied to mass communication.

Cultivation Theory

This approach draws on a cumulative effects model to look at the way that extensive, repeated exposure to media over time gradually shapes our view of the world and our social reality. The more media we are exposed to, the more our views of the world will come to resemble the media worldview. According to this theory, media shape, nurture, indeed *cultivate* our worldview. Cultivation theory was initially developed by George Gerbner and his colleagues in the Cultural Indicators research project studying television at the University of Pennsylvania. See Gerbner, Gross, Morgan, Signorielli, and Shanahan (2002) and Morgan, Shanahan, and Signorielli (2009) for overviews of the theory, and Bilandzic (2006) for a recent integrated theoretical perspective.

One of the major constructs of cultivation theory is *mainstreaming*, the gradual homogenization of people's divergent perceptions of social reality into a convergent mainstream. This apparently happens through a process of construction, whereby viewers learn about the real world from observing the world of media. Memory traces from media experiences are stored relatively automatically (Shapiro, 1991). We then use this stored information to formulate beliefs about the real world (Hawkins & Pingree, 1990; Hawkins, Pingree, & Adler, 1987; Potter, 1989, 1991a, 1991b; Shrum & Bischak, 2001). When this constructed world and the real world of one's experience have a high degree of consistency, *resonance* occurs and the cultivation effect is even stronger. For example, a woman who has never been to New York City may hold a perception that it is a high-crime area due to portrayals in police dramas or news coverage (mainstreaming). If, upon visiting New York, she frequently sees police cars with lights flashing, her media-spawned idea of a crime-ridden city may be reinforced.

In terms of methodology, cultivation research usually compares frequent ("heavy") and infrequent ("light") viewers of television, researchers' usual medium of study, through correlational methods. A typical study finds that the worldview of heavy viewers is more like the world on television. For example, people who watch a lot of violent TV believe the world to be a more violent place than it really is, the so-called "mean world syndrome" (Signorielli, 1990). There is also a greater variance of views among light viewers, suggesting that one effect of watching a lot of TV is to inculcate a sort of middle-of-the-road view. For example, people who watch a lot of TV are less likely to be either extremely liberal or extremely conservative politically, whereas the political views of light viewers run the entire ideological spectrum. Mainstreaming pulls deviants from both directions back toward the middle.

The domains of social reality cultivated through mainstreaming take many forms, including gender roles (Morgan, 1982; Morgan & Shanahan, 1995; Preston, 1990); political attitudes (Gerbner, Gross, Morgan, & Signorielli, 1982, 1984; Morgan, 1989); estimations of crime risk (Shrum, 2001; Shrum & Bischak, 2001); views of science and scientists (Dudo, Brossard, Shanahan, Scheufele, Morgan, & Signorielli, 2011; Potts & Martinez, 1994); health beliefs and practices (Gerbner, Gross, Morgan, & Signorielli, 1981; Lee & Niederdeppe, 2011); degrees of materialism and life satisfaction (Schrum, Lee, Burroughs, & Rindfleisch, 2011); attitudes toward the environment (Shanahan & McComas, 1999; Shanahan, Morgan, & Stenbjerre, 1997); adolescent career choices (Morgan & Shanahan, 1995); effects of prolonged viewing of

---

Close-Up 2.3: Reality Shows as Feeding Delusion

Psychiatry professors and brothers Joel Gold and Ian Gold (2012) report several patients whose delusional beliefs took the form of believing they were characters in a reality television show, much like the 1998 movie *The Truman Show*, in which Jim Carrey plays a man whose whole life, unbeknownst to him, is a contrived reality show for the entertainment of others and where all his associates, even his wife, are hired actors playing parts. For example, one of Gold's patients began his first session with his psychiatrist by demanding to speak with the "director" of the reality show he was starring in. Another believed that his life was being continually taped for broadcast as part of a TV show. The Golds do not argue that reality TV has caused these delusions, but rather that existing illnesses such as schizophrenia, in which delusions are a common symptom, interact with major cultural events such as reality shows to give specific content to the delusions. They argue that cultural and media studies are an important component of understanding the cognitive aspects of delusions.

---

talk shows (Rossler & Brosius, 2001); and attitudes about the elderly (Hetsroni & Tukachinsky, 2006) and minorities (Gross, 1984; Volgy & Schwarz, 1980). Cultivation theory has also been applied cross-culturally (e.g., Appel, 2008; Morgan, 1990; Morgan & Shanahan, 1991, 1992, 1995). For an example of how reality shows may cultivate a belief that one is living in such a show, see Close-Up 2.3.

Meyrowitz (1985) and Postman (1982, 1985) argued that children are socialized into the role of adults far earlier since the onset of television than had been the case for the previous several hundred years. Television is the window through which children learn about the world of adults, which is no longer kept secret from them. The effect of television is thus a homogenization of developmental stages: children become more like adults, and adults become more like children. This has numerous social implications beyond the world of media. Children and adults dress more alike, talk more alike, and go to more of the same places than in the past. It is no longer the case that only children wear T-shirts or use slang and only adults wear designer clothes and swear. Similar blurring of the dichotomies of masculinity–femininity and politician–citizen are also posited and attributed to electronic media, increasing androgynous (gender-nonspecific) behavior and holding political candidates to personal standards. Whether such changes are positive or negative socially is probably a matter of personal opinion.

Although cultivation theory generally focuses on the cumulative effect of many repeated images, some images may be far more influential than others.

Greenberg's (1988) drench hypothesis says that a highly respected and popular TV character can have far more impact than a dozen other characters seen and identified with by far fewer viewers. Following this argument, Will and Jack, from the sitcom *Will and Grace*, or gay dads Mitchell and Cameron from *Modern Family*, may help improve people's attitudes toward gay men far more than numerous characters on less-often-seen shows (Bonds-Raacke, Cady, Schlegel, Harris, & Firebaugh, 2007).

In spite of being very influential, cultivation theory is not without its critics. Potter (1991b) argued that the cultivation effect really involves several components, some of which operate independently. Shapiro (1991) looked at the process of the formation of memory traces from television and their later effects on the construction of one's worldview. Several studies show that careful controls of certain other sociodemographic and personality variables tend to reduce or eliminate cultivation effects (Doob & Macdonald, 1979; Hawkins & Pingree, 1981; Potter, 1986; Wober, 1986). Cultivation studies have also been criticized on conceptual and methodological grounds, including concerns about response biases and problems with the measuring instruments (Hirsch, 1980; Perse, 1986; Potter, 1986, 1993; J. A. Schneider, 1987). There have also been criticisms of some of the assumptions underlying cultivation theory. For example, it seems to assume that the messages of TV are essentially uniform (Hawkins & Pingree, 1981) and that viewers accept what they see as perceived reality (D. Slater & Elliott, 1982). Tamborini and Choi (1990) pointed out the frequent failure of non-U.S. data to strongly support cultivation theory and suggested some reasons for this. See Rubin, Perse, and Taylor (1988) for a review of the methodological critiques of cultivation theory and Potter (1993) for a review of conceptual critiques.

Another adaptation of cultivation theory has been to add more cognitive variables, especially the encoding and storage of media messages in memory, in an attempt to increase its rigor and predictability (Shrum, 2002, 2009; Tapper, 1995). Some have reinterpreted cultivation theory in line with a uses and gratifications approach (see the next subsection), stressing the active mental engagement of the viewer while watching TV (Levy & Windahl, 1984; Weaver & Wakshlag, 1986). Cultivation then grows out of the viewer's active processing of information and construction of reality. Finally, taking into account cultural differences in media and societal factors and the degree of congruity between the two can help to predict why cultivation occurs in some areas but not in others (e.g., Morgan & Shanahan, 1995). See Close-Up 2.4 for an interesting effect of cultural differences in apologizing for sending someone e-mail spam.

Uses and Gratifications Theory

The uses and gratifications perspective places much emphasis on the active role of the audience in making choices and being goal-directed in its

Close-Up 2.4: Apologies in Spam: Do They Help Sell?

Apologies can be used for numerous reasons. Perhaps the major one is to acknowledge one's mistake and accept responsibility. Another is to establish empathy, a function that women express more often than men (Tannen, 1990, 2001). Apologies can also be used to elicit more positive feelings toward the sender ("saving face"), a device of potential use to the advertiser. One interesting area in which to examine the use of apology is via a particularly annoying and intrusive type of advertising, namely, spam (generally unwanted e-mail advertising). In a very clever cross-cultural content analysis study, Park, Lee, and Song (2005) found that far more (42%) of Korean e-mail spam contained apologies than was the case for American spam (3%). However, on a variety of effectiveness measures the spam messages with apologies were no more effective than those without apologies. Koreans did consider the spam with apologies more credible and "normal" than the spam messages without the apologies. They were also more likely than Americans to include an apology in their response to a spam containing an apology.

media-use behavior (Oliver & Bartsch, 2010; Palmgreen, 1984; Rosengren, Wenner, & Palmgreen, 1985; A. M. Rubin, 2009). The experience and effects of media depend, in part, on the uses one is putting those media to and the gratifications one is receiving from them. For example, the experience of watching a horror film will be very different for someone who is experiencing a good deal of empathy with the victim than for someone who is being only superficially entertained by the suspense of the plot. Watching CNN News or surfing Internet news sites may be a very different experience for someone trying to be entertained than for someone trying to be seriously informed on the details of a political candidate's positions.

Even the idea of entertainment is more complex than it first appears. Although much of the research and the public assumes that the wish to be entertained is hedonic, or pleasure-seeking, often it may be seen as nonhedonic, or eudaimonic, involving personal expressiveness, competence, autonomy, and self-development. In fact there is evidence that both hedonic and nonhedonic factors are important components of entertainment (Tamborini, et al., 2011). Thus, for example, we may enjoy playing a video game in part because of the sense of mastery or competence achieved, and we may be entertained by a sad film, which gives us some understanding of the human condition, though watching it may not exactly be a pleasurable experience (Oliver & Raney, 2011). What we find the most entertaining may also change over the life span. Bartsch (2012) found that young adults aged 18–25 were more interested than adults over 50 in emotionally intense entertainment, such as thrills from horror or adventure films and tear-jerking sadness from dramas. Older adults, on the other hand, preferred more contemplative entertainment experiences. This goes a long way to explaining why young people like horror and action films and their parents prefer quieter, more thoughtful dramas.

We may use media for many reasons besides basic entertainment or information-seeking. Perhaps it is to avoid studying or some other activity. Perhaps it is to escape into a fantasy world or be turned on by a particular sexy star. Maybe it is to find out what everybody's talking about in regard to some popular show or to be more like our friends. Sometimes we watch a program we strongly dislike simply to make ourselves feel less alone or to be emotionally stimulated. For many solo drivers, the radio or recorded music is a constant traveling companion. What draws different people to consume different types of media may be a critical issue; for example, it is very helpful to know the factors that cause some people to seek out and watch violent pornography. See A. M. Rubin (2002) and Conway and Rubin (1991) for discussions of psychological motives in uses and gratifications research.

A. M. Rubin (2009) identified several current research directions for uses and gratifications research. One is to develop taxonomies of communication motives. Others have compared motives across media, a particularly important area of research in regard to newer computer-mediated technologies, particularly social media (Quan-Haase & Young, 2010). A third approach has looked at different social and psychological circumstances of media use, including coviewers, personality, lifestyle, or religiosity (Harris & Cook, 2011). A fourth direction has looked at how motives for using media are satisfied or not satisfied. A fifth direction has examined the role of individual differences in experiences, motives, and exposure for the media experience. One interesting behavior genetics study comparing identical and fraternal twins concluded that up to one-third of the differences in media use habits and behaviors across people may be due to genetic influences (Kirzinger, Weber, & Johnson, 2012). Finally, some researchers have studied measurement issues like the reliability and validity of instruments measuring motivation.

One interesting problem to come out of the uses and gratifications perspective concerns the relationships we have with media figures we have never met in person, i.e., *parasocial relationships* or *interactions* (Klimmt, Hartmann, & Schramm, 2006; A. M. Rubin, Perse, & Powell, 1985; R. B. Rubin & McHugh, 1987; Tsay & Bodine, 2012). We may think of morning show hosts more as our breakfast companions than as news spokespersons. Evening news anchors are regular dinner guests, not merely people who read the news. This feeling of connectedness with public figures is occasionally dramatically illustrated, for example in the intense worldwide outpouring of grief following the sudden death of Britain's young Princess Diana in a car crash in 1997 (Brown, Basil, & Bocarnea, 2003). Her loss was a genuinely personal one to millions who knew her only through media. There were similar large-scale displays of public affection and mourning when Michael Jackson died in 2009.

Parasocial interactions and relationships are not limited to real people. For instance, actors who portray villains in ongoing television series have been known to receive hate mail from viewers. When decades-old soap operas have finally been canceled, faithful viewers feel a genuine sense of loss at the demise of beloved characters. One study that examined viewers' experiences with the last episode of *Friends* in 2004 found that there can be similarities between the distress of a "parasocial breakup" with a media "friend" when a long-running show ends and ending a relationship with a real person (Eyal & Cohen, 2006). Similar results were discovered in a study of Israeli television viewers and the potential loss of their favorite TV characters or personalities (Cohen, 2004). One can even develop parasocial relationships with video game characters (Coulson, Barnett, Ferguson, & Gould, 2012). Interestingly, however, there are no social conventions or social support for parasocial grieving, which in fact is often met by others with outright ridicule.

Parasocial interactions have many of the same characteristics as real inter-personal interactions (Perse & Rubin, 1989) and are strong predictors of television viewing motivation and behavior (Conway & Rubin, 1991; see Schiappa, Allen, & Gregg, 2007 for a meta-analysis of effects of parasocial interactions). People who form parasocial relationships tend to be higher in the Big 5 personality dimensions of agreeableness and neuroticism, though there is no relation to extraversion (Tsay & Bodine, 2012). These one-sided relationships can even lead to romantic feelings for celebrities whom fans have never met. McCutcheon, Ashe, Houran, and Maltby (2003) draw parallels between this kind of celebrity worship and erotomania, a psychological disorder in which a person has delusions of a romantic relationship with another. This level of parasocial interaction can be carried to extremes, for example when John Hinckley, Jr. attempted to assassinate President Ronald Reagan in 1981. Hinckley's delusional motivation was a belief that killing the President would win the heart of actress Jodie Foster, with whom he had become obsessed after watching her over and over again in the film *Taxi Driver*. In another instance, a teenager attempted suicide after a favorite musician became engaged to someone else (Haynes & Rich, 2002).

Nevertheless, parasocial media relationships may have a somewhat beneficial "social surrogacy" mental health effect. Derrick, Gabriel, and Hugenberg (2009) found that watching favorite TV shows provides a sense of belonging, particularly for those who are lonely. They even discovered that merely thinking about favorite TV shows while recalling a fight with a close other can help protect against drops in self-esteem. Interestingly, however, these sorts of effects only seemed to be present with *favored* TV shows, leading the authors to conclude that the effects were not due to mindless escapism through watching just any show. The intensity of a parasocial relationship can be affected by many factors. For example, attractive personalities engender more intense parasocial interactions, as do characters who directly address the audiences. Individuals higher in the individual difference factor of perspective-taking ability are more likely to develop more intense parasocial relationships. More intense parasocial interaction is also associated with greater enjoyment of the media experience (Hartmann & Goldhoorn, 2011).

As we have seen, whether positive or negative, parasocial media relationships can become intense. However, we have all probably felt some emotional connection to figures we know only through the TV, movie, or computer screen. See Giles (2002) for a literature review and proposed model for parasocial interaction. He argues for the importance of specifying the continuum of the relationship between social and parasocial and for identifying the stages in the development of parasocial relationships. Tsay and Bodine (2012) argue that we should consider parasocial interaction as a multidimensional construct.

Agenda Setting

This theory, which initially grew out of communications research on political socialization (Dearing & Rogers, 1996), defines agenda setting as the "creation of public awareness and concern of salient issues by the news media" (Heath & Bryant, 1992, p. 279). The idea here is that the media do not necessarily tell us *what to think*, but rather *what to think about*. For example, through heavy coverage of such issues in a political campaign, media may tell us that past marital infidelity of candidates is an important issue on which to base our vote. Other issues covered in less depth, such as their positions on taxation or foreign policy, are thus positioned as less important. See Chapters 7 and 8 for further discussion of agenda setting in regard to news, and McCombs and Reynolds (2002), Wanta (1997), Kosicki (1993), and Tai (2009) for theoretical conceptualizations.

Although it has been explored most fully in regard to news and politics, agenda setting is also relevant to other media issues. For example, in their basic ignoring of religion, mainstream entertainment media in the United States are sending a message that spiritual issues are not important factors in people's lives. Soap operas and movies that continually show characters engaging in seemingly unprotected casual sex with no apparent concern for consequences like HIV infection or pregnancy are subtly telling us that those concerns are not important. Characters' incessant preoccupation with body image tells viewers they should be concerned about that.

One way that an agenda can be set is through the use of *framing* (Borah, 2011; Entman, 1993; McCombs & Ghanem, 2001; Scheufele & Tewksbury, 2007; Tewksbury & Scheufele, 2009; Wicks, 2001). The way a problem is described selects or highlights certain aspects of its reality and neglects or downplays others. This framing will affect how people respond to it. For example, is some indiscretion described as a "caper," an "affair," or a "scandal"?

Jamieson and Waldman (2003) argued that press coverage of the U.S. Presidential election campaign of 2000 framed the candidates as the "lying panderer" (Al Gore) and the "ineffective bumbler" (George W. Bush) and that media and the public noticed details consistent with the frames and neglected details that were inconsistent (see Chapter 8 for further discussion of the framing of the candidates in the 2000 election). Framing effects can be quite persistent, particularly if the consumers have moderate, rather than high or low, levels of political knowledge about the issue (Lecheler & de Vreese, 2011).

There have been some attempts to integrate agenda setting with other theoretical approaches. For example, Wanta (1997) draws on the cognitive and uses and gratifications perspectives to develop a model of agenda setting that focuses more on the individual, rather than the issue, as the unit of measurement. Wanta tested this model and concluded that those most susceptible to agenda-setting effects are those who more actively process information from news media. McCombs, Shaw, and Weaver (1997) extended agenda setting to some new areas, including political advertising, economic news, and the comparative effectiveness of television and print media in agenda setting. Wanta and Ghanem (2007) offer a meta-analysis showing agenda-setting effects of news across a wide variety of studies.

Schema (Script) Theory

Part of what guides the perception and comprehension, and later memories of information from media are *schemas* (Brewer & Nakamura, 1984; Rumelhart, 1980). The schema construct refers to knowledge structures or frameworks that organize an individual's memory for people and events. A schema is a general mental construct or model about some knowledge domain. A person holds mental schemas based on past experiences; for example, our schemas about Latinos, schizophrenics, or the Arab Spring are connected to our memories and personal experiences. One consequence of holding these schemas for information processing is that the individual is likely to go beyond the information actually presented to draw inferences about people or events that are congruent with previously formed schemas (Harris, 1981; Rojahn & Pettigrew, 1992). For example, someone with a very negative schema about Mexican Americans might notice and remember all sorts of negative things about Latinos in response to watching a TV show set in Latino East Los Angeles, whereas someone with a more positive schema would notice and remember different, and more favorable, information from the same show. Typically, much of the content in schemas is culture specific. The schema that members of one culture may hold may cause them to interpret the same story very differently than members of a different culture (Harris, Schoen, & Hensley, 1992; Lasisi & Onyehalu, 1992). Cultural differences must be carefully considered by TV producers in international programming sales (see Close-Up 2.5).

Close-Up 2.5: The Internationalization of Popular Culture

Although the United States is a major exporter of television programming and movies, no country is able to totally dominate media today, if indeed this was ever possible (Chung, 2011; Straubhaar, 2007; Tunstall, 2007). What is actually happening is a globalization of all cultures (Legrain, 2003). McDonald's is becoming more popular worldwide, but so are Indian curry, Japanese sushi, and Greek or Arab hummus. Hollywood studios dominate world movie distribution, but film productions are multinational efforts. For example, many top "American" entertainment figures are not really American at all: Salma Hayek and Gael García are Mexican; Nicole Kidman, Hugh Jackman, Cate Blanchett, Simon Baker, Mel Gibson, and Russell Crowe are Australian; Hugh Grant, Kate Winslet, Ewan McGregor, and virtually the entire cast of the Harry Potter films are British; Sam Neill is from New Zealand; Michael J. Fox and Ryan Reynolds are Canadian; Antonio Banderas and Javier Bardem are Spanish; and Colin Farrell is Irish. Many top Hollywood directors are similarly from elsewhere than the United States: Peter Weir (Australia), Stanley Kubrick (Britain), Pedro Almodóvar (Spain), Alfonso Cuarón (Mexico), and Peter Jackson (New Zealand). In terms of music, despite the pressure to record in English, many of international music's biggest sellers are not Americans. A few of these are The Beatles and The Rolling Stones (UK), Shakira (Colombia), U2 (Ireland), Björk (Iceland), Justin Bieber, Arcade Fire, and Avril Lavigne (Canada), Abba (Sweden), and Julio and Enrique Iglesias (Spain).

The United States itself is a market as well as a producer. Many broadcast and cable markets now carry Univision and/or Telemundo, both Spanish-language channels headquartered in the U.S. Mexico's Televisa earns millions exporting its soap operas, with some of those sales going to the United States. The British BBC and Granada TV have exported programs to America's PBS for years. With the improvement in cable and satellite technology, there are now specialized American and/or international versions of some channels, such as BBC America, RT (Russia), and CCTV-4 (China). In addition, many American cable and satellite systems offer international channel packages with stations from around the world.

In mass media, activation of a schema in the mind of the audience member may be triggered by some particular information in the TV program, magazine article, or website. It may also be triggered by the content of certain formal features of the particular medium, such as flashbacks, montage, or instant replays in television or film. Young children do not understand these conventions and will interpret the input literally (e.g., thinking that a flashback or instant replay is continuing new action). Part of the socialization to the use of a medium like television is to learn about these formal features and how to interpret them (Bickham, Wright, & Huston, 2001; Calvert, 1988; Kraft, Cantor, & Gottdiener, 1991; Lang, Geiger, Strickwerda, & Sumner, 1993; Rice, Huston, & Wright, 1986; B. J. Wilson, 1991).

One place we learn schemas and scripts is from media (Luke, 1987). "Script" here does not mean "pages of dialogue," but rather refers to a schema about an activity. For example, when we watch a TV drama about a woman who discovers she has breast cancer, we may acquire a mental script for dealing with that particular situation. The viewer may learn specific activities like breast self-examination, how to tell her husband about her illness, how to seek out information about possible treatments, and how to cope with a mastectomy and chemotherapy in terms of her own self-image and sexuality. Through exposure to samples of activities following a particular script, that abstract script is inferred and gradually becomes a part of our permanent memory (Ahn, Brewer, & Mooney, 1992). This skeleton structure of an activity is then used to interpret future instances of that activity. For example, listeners of a British radio soap opera, *The Archers*, used knowledge of a general familiar script from that show to help them remember specific details from individual episodes (Reeve & Aggleton, 1998).

The potential consequences of learning scripts from media become especially clear when we consider a situation of which readers or viewers have little prior knowledge or scripts from their own life experience. For example, suppose a child's knowledge of dealing with muggers has resulted from watching TV adventure heroes trick and overpower the robber. If that child were to try that script on a real mugger by attempting the moves seen on TV, the consequences might be disastrous. As another example, consider a TV movie dealing with child abuse. A preteen in the story is being sexually molested by her uncle and is sufficiently troubled to mention this to a school counselor, a revelation that sets in motion a sequence of events that eventually, but inevitably, brings this event out in the open. Because child abuse was not discussed for so many years, many viewers, including some current or former victims, may have had no mental script for how to handle it. In this sense, such a movie, if done sensitively yet realistically, could help victims to come forward and seek help. It could provide information on how one may expect to feel about that experience and where to seek help, and, through the context of the drama, it could offer a scenario for what the effects of such a revelation might be.

In a more general sense, media fiction sometimes draws on very abstract scripts, such as "overcoming adversity." This implicit theme may be reflected in a story about a slave escaping from servitude in the antebellum South, a child learning to cope with alcoholic parents, or a burned-out police officer coming to terms with a vicious crime syndicate. Such a script is also used in many human-interest news stories.

There is a very general script for stories in Western culture (Kintsch, 1977). This narrative script is learned implicitly from the earliest days of childhood, when young children hear stories from their parents. Such stories are composed of episodes, each of which contains an exposition, complication, and resolution. That is, the characters and setting are introduced (exposition), some problem or obstacle develops (complication), and that problem or obstacle is somehow overcome (resolution). We grow up expecting stories to follow this general script. Children's stories such as fairy tales do so very explicitly ("Once upon a time there was a . . ."). Adult stories also follow the same script but often in a more complex fashion. For example, some of the complication may be introduced before all of the exposition is finished or there may be two subepisodes embedded in the resolution of a larger episode.

Entertainment media like television or film also draw on the narrative script to make their stories more readily understandable. Children's cartoons follow the script very explicitly. Most TV sitcoms and action-adventure shows also do so, although perhaps in a somewhat more complicated fashion; for example, there may be two interwoven episodes (subplots), each with its own narrative structure. The use of schemas enhances our information-processing capabilities. Meadowcroft and Reeves (1989) found that children had well-developed story schema skills by age 7, and such skills led to better memory for the central story content, a reduction in processing effort, and a greater flexibility of attention-allocation strategies. Soap operas traditionally hold an audience by concluding each day's story just before the resolution. Because we have this sense of our narrative script being incomplete, we are motivated to return the next day or the next week to complete it. This principle of the "cliffhanger" has been used in some prime-time season finales to ensure the interest and return of viewers for the first show of the next season.

Even many ads draw upon the narrative script. For example, a nice young fellow is ready to go out on a hot date (exposition); alas, he notices his teeth are yellowed (complication). But his mom and her amazing dental whitening strips come to the rescue to brighten his teeth just in time (resolution). Because of our familiarity with the narrative script, we are able to comprehend such a commercial very easily, which is of course to the advertiser's advantage. Also, because it fits the story structure of many programs, it seems more entertaining and is thus more likely than a traditional sales pitch to hold viewers' attention. The narrative script is a deeply ingrained knowledge structure; Esslin (1982) went so far as to argue that the 30-second story of an unhappy hemorrhoid sufferer has the same dramatic structure as a classic Greek tragedy!

Limited Capacity Model

Another heavily cognitive model is Lang's (2000) limited capacity model of media information processing. Drawing on basic cognitive psychology, Lang makes two basic assumptions: (1) people are information processors, and

(2) the ability to process information is limited. These information processes are sometimes automatic and sometimes controlled; that is, they involve conscious choice. The three major subprocesses are *encoding, storage,* and *retrieval.* These may be done partially in parallel, but the processing resources are limited, and heavy allocation to one may result in superficial allocation to another. One of the automatic selection mechanisms steering the encoding of information is the *orienting response.* When this occurs, as in our attention being captured by the television turning on, more cognitive resources are allocated to encoding the information from that source. Encoding of that information is enhanced, provided that the cognitive load is low. If, however, the cognitive load is high (e.g., a set of scenes that rapidly cuts from one location to another), the limited resources will be overwhelmed, and less encoding will occur. Increasing the cognitive load and resources required by speeding up the pace or having more arousing content decreases memory for the controlled processing of the verbal content, but not for the automatic processing of visual content (Lang, Potter, & Bolls, 1999).

Conclusion

The theoretical frameworks discussed here have all been influential in guiding the research on mass communication. Some have been particularly useful in certain content areas or with certain types of research designs. All are at least somewhat cognitive in nature, as they deal with the knowledge representation of information from the media and the processing of that knowledge through attention, perception, comprehension, and memory. The theories are not necessarily mutually exclusive, either. In fact, in many cases they are quite complementary, as they emphasize different aspects of our interaction with media. For example, social cognitive theory focuses on the modeling of behavior, while cultivation looks more at attitudinal effects, and schema theory and limited capacity say more about the information processing dimension.

Now we have some idea of what research in mass communication is all about and what sort of answers it seeks. There are different types of research and different theories to guide this research. In the next chapter we turn to look at various psychological constructs and topics which are important in understanding media.

Chapter 3

The Psychology of Media Use
Tapping into Our Deepest Selves

Q: What is the most uncomfortable combination of audience and movie type for college students?

A: Watching an explicit R-rated sexual movie with your parents is thought to be much more uncomfortable a situation than watching a sexual movie with anyone else watching a graphically violent movie with anyone, or anyone of several other combinations of audience and movie (Harris & Cook, 2011).

Q: When Disney's Animal Kingdom opened in Orlando, what was the major complaint about the live animals there from its first visitors?

A: That they were not "realistic" enough, that is, not like the active robotic animals elsewhere in Disney World (Turkle, 2011).

Q: When a television is turned on, how often is it for the purpose of watching a specific program?

A: About half the time people turn the TV on for a specific program, and about half the time they just turn it on and then find something. The best and easiest way to start controlling and limiting TV use in your home is to adhere to this rule: Never turn on the TV except to watch a specific program that you have in mind.

Q: During the 1980 U.S. Presidential election campaign, candidate Ronald Reagan liked to tell of a World War II pilot who stayed with an injured gunner rather than bail out after his plane was hit. When did this event occur?

A: Never, in real life. Reagan was remembering a scene from the 1944 war movie A *Wing and Prayer* (Schacter, 1996).

In the last chapter we looked at how scientists study media and what theories they use to guide them in that endeavor. We continue in this chapter by examining the psychology of using media. There are numerous psychological processes operating as we interact with media. We start out by looking at children in particular and some of the developmental issues related to media use. Then we look at several cognitive processes we use in understanding media, followed by various types of emotional processing. Finally, we conclude the chapter with a more in-depth look at the overall theme of this book, namely the perceived reality created by media.

Children's Distinctive Use of Media

Although young children regularly encounter fiction in both book and television format, because television looks more like "real life," children recognize at an earlier age when books, as opposed to television, are representing fiction rather than fact (Kelly, 1981). Thus, the world of television is more easily confused with reality than the printed equivalent.

Mental Effort and Social Interaction

The nature of a specific medium affects how a child can extract information from that medium and represent it in memory. In general, television involves less mental effort than print media, although this varies somewhat with age and type of program (Bordeaux & Lange, 1991). Historically, the invention of print several centuries ago permitted the widespread physical storage of information for the first time (Greenfield, 1984). People who had acquired the skill of literacy thus had access to vast amounts of information previously unavailable except through oral transmission. Literacy also had social implications, in that it was the first medium of communication that required solitude for its effective practice (Olson, 1994). Critics of television who fear that its advent has isolated children from social interaction are in fact concerned about a far earlier effect of print media; television only continued the requirement of physical isolation, it did not initiate it. In fact, research has shown no relationship between the amount of television watched and time spent in interpersonal activity.

Recent concerns have, of course, focused particularly on children's use of the Internet and social media. The fears expressed that web surfers are becoming socially isolated, perhaps even socially inept, sound amazingly like concerns expressed in the early days of print and later in the early days of television. In a very provocative book, Reeves and Nass (1996) argue that our interactions with computers, televisions, and other media are much more similar to the way we interact with other people than most of us realize. For example, at times we treat computers with politeness and emotion and perceive them as having personalities. See Turkle (2011) for a provocative look at how recent technology has changed (and not changed) social interactions.

Information Extraction and Memory

In some ways radio and newspapers may cognitively have more in common with each other than either medium does with TV. Whereas both radio and print are heavily verbal media, television more heavily involves the pictorial dimension, and the skills for extracting information from television are different from those used to extract information from the words of radio or print. Children derive more information from the visual component than from the verbal one (Hayes & Birnbaum, 1980), although a high degree of redundancy between the two generally aids comprehension. Overall, a story presented via television was better understood by second- and sixth-grade children than the same story presented via radio (Pezdek, Lehrer, & Simon, 1984), and was consistently remembered better, regardless of reading proficiency (Gunter, Furnham, & Griffiths, 2000). Material with previews and/or summaries or visual scene repetition, that is, some redundancies, were better remembered by 6–8-year-old children than the same material that was not repeated (Michel & Roebers, 2008). Presentations on television later led to fewer novel ideas from the child than did the same presentation on radio (Valkenburg & Beentjes, 1997). Thus, television is a very efficient way to transmit information to children, suggesting both greater potential and greater concern regarding this medium. Beagles-Roos and Gat (1983) had children retell a story which they had either heard on the radio or seen on television. The style of the retold stories differed in an interesting fashion. Retold stories from TV contained more vague references, such as the use of pronouns without identifying the referent, the use of definite articles ("the boy . . .") without first introducing the referent, and other forms presupposing more shared information with the hearer. Retold radio stories provided more information, much as a radio sports play-by-play provides more information than a televised play-by-play. Having children write a story from either TV or real life, Watkins (1988) found that the amount of television the child watched determined how elaborate and complex the TV story was. Greenfield (1984) suggested that one subtle effect of watching a lot of television might be the learning of a verbal style that is relatively vague in reference, much like talking face-to-face. In both cases, much shared knowledge may be assumed, and thus less need be explicitly explained. With radio and print, however, the language must be more explicit to compensate for the lack of a pictorial component.

Baggett (1979) found that adults recalled information from either a silent movie (*The Red Balloon*) or a constructed spoken version equally well, whereas young children remembered the silent film version better. Although this visual advantage in memory decreases somewhat with age, it is a natural characteristic of our cognitive processing system, not one that is produced by television exposure. The visual continues to have some advantage even with adults. In delayed testing a week later, Baggett found that adults also showed better memory for the visual than the verbal story.

The Medium and Imagination

Although media, especially television, have the potential to either stimulate or reduce children's creativity and imaginative play, overall there is much more evidence for some type of reduction effect (Valkenburg, 2001). Certainly creative play can be stimulated by watching certain TV shows, especially educational TV, but facilitated creativity does not appear to be a widespread effect. It has long been known that *Sesame Street* and especially the slower-paced shows like *Mister Rogers' Neighborhood* have been shown to stimulate imaginative play (Singer & Singer, 1976; Tower, Singer, & Singer, 1979), whereas action-adventure shows are associated with the lowest imaginative play scores (Singer & Singer, 1981).

Reductions in creativity or imaginative play could come for several reasons. First of all, there is some evidence that television watching displaces more creative play and interferes simply by replacing that activity. Other possible explanations remain possibilities but have as yet garnered less overall support (Valkenburg, 2001; Valkenburg & Peter, 2006). TV may induce passivity, which is inconsistent with imagination and creativity, and the rapid pacing of children's programs does not allow time for reflection and imagination. Finally, the highly visual nature of television may be so salient that it may distract from processing ideas creatively, a type of thinking that may be easier with print or radio presentation. Preschool children who watched more TV were less likely to have an imaginary playmate and showed lower scores on imaginative play (Singer & Singer, 1981). Does watching television interfere with the development of reading skills or fantasy play? It probably depends on what activity television is replacing.

Cognitive Components of the Media Experience

We now turn our attention to different cognitive processes involved in our experiencing media. By "cognitive," we mean the thought processes involved in attending, perceiving, comprehending, interpreting, and remembering the material that we encounter through media. The stimuli that we cognitively process may be in the form of language (written or spoken) or pictorial (filmed still or moving pictures), or some combination of the two. Often, as in the case with television and film, language and pictorial stimuli occur in parallel together, though sometimes they occur separately. There may also be multiple levels of pictorial stimuli; for example, the viewer may encounter cues about character movement and action but also background lighting, shadows, and other aspects of the visual stimulus, as well as nonlinguistic auditory stimuli like background music or sound effects. The way that the theatrical sets are laid out and the scenes filmed can affect the difficulty of the viewing process as well (Levin, 2010).

Now let us look at several different aspects of media cognition, starting with attention.

Attention

As a prerequisite to any comprehension of media, we must first select some information to attend to and process further; this necessarily entails neglecting other information. Although there are many ways, some very sophisticated, of measuring exposure to filmed media (Simons, Detenber, Cuthbert, Schwartz, & Reiss, 2003; Smith, Levin, & Cutting, 2012), it is naïve to assume either that viewers are fully processing everything that they encounter in media or that it is not affecting them at all unless they are paying full conscious attention. The issue is also relevant to other media. For example, how much do we process the typical newspaper or Internet ad as we read through the paper or scan a web page, paying little if any conscious attention to the ad?

Merely measuring when the television is on or how much time we allow a certain web page to remain before we click on another link does not give us complete information about how much is being understood or what influence it is having. A big question, particularly in the study of television, film, or the Internet, is how much attention viewers are paying to the screen while it is on. For example, the TV is often on when it is receiving less than the total undivided attention of viewers. Research studying people watching television has found that the typical adult or child over the age of 5 attends to the TV between 55 and 70% of the time it is on (Anderson & Burns, 1991; Anderson & Field, 1991; Anderson & Kerkorian, 2006; Schmitt, Woolf, & Anderson, 2003), varying depending on the time of day and the type of program being watched. For example, early morning news shows and commercials receive relatively less attention, and weekend shows such as sports and children's cartoons receive relatively more attention. Comedies receive a little more attention than dramas or news and much more attention than commercials (Hawkins et al., 2005). More attention is given to moving images than to static ones (Simons et al., 2003).

Children initially allocate considerable attention to difficult segments but quickly reduce that attention if the material is beyond their level of comprehension (Hawkins, Kim, & Pingree, 1991). Overall, children spend more time attending to "child content" than to "adult content" (Schmitt, Anderson, & Collins, 1999). The most common concurrent activities with TV viewing are socializing and playing (Schmitt et al., 2003).

Overall, both structure and content factors help determine the amount of attention allocated (Geiger & Reeves, 1993a, 1993b), and familiar content may partially compensate for structural confusion or lack of experience with film conventions (Schwan & Ildirar, 2010). Sometimes we may not be looking at the screen very much but may nonetheless be monitoring the sound for items of interest so we can redirect our vision toward it, if necessary. Even very young children are quite skilled at doing this (Rolandelli, Wright, Huston, & Eakins, 1991). Children are regular multitaskers well before adolescence, with greater multitasking for those high in sensation-seeking and those with televisions and computers in their own rooms (Jeong & Fishbein, 2007). Multitasking with respect to media may be particularly appealing because of our desire to meet multiple needs and achieve multiple gratifications (Wang & Tchernev, 2010). There are even a few people with exceptional multitasking ability, which goes beyond what most of us are capable of

(Watson & Strayer, 2010). At some point, however, our attention becomes overloaded. Despite the increasing popularity of multichannel information sources, such as *HLN*, which has multiple screens of different information and unrelated news crawls at the bottom of the screen, there is evidence that viewers are unable to grasp all of that information and actually acquire less information than they do from a less cluttered format (Bergen, Grimes, & Potter, 2005).

One fascinating aspect of attending to film is how much we do *not* see. The well-documented phenomenon of change blindness (Simons & Ambinder, 2005; Simons & Levin, 1997, 1998) refers to the fact we do not notice changes in a continuous visual scene as we watch it. In one famous experiment (Simons & Levin, 1998), the unwitting experimental participant was talking to someone else on campus when two workers carrying a door "rudely" walked between them. Unknown to the participant, one of those men switched places with the man who had been in the conversation. After the door passed, the conversation continued with the new speaker. Although the two men did not look particularly similar, about half the participants did not notice that their conversation partner had changed! Such effects are even more dramatic when watching a video, as in one famous example when people watch a group playing a basketball-like game but do not notice a gorilla walk across the visual field because they are occupied counting the number of ball tosses (Simons & Chabris, 1999).

In terms of filmed entertainment, change or inattentional blindness is a very good thing. Movie scenes are not filmed in the final order they appear on film. Multiple takes, often filmed at different times, are edited together much later to make what is hopefully a coherent story. Virtually every film ever released has multiple continuity errors, which, fortunately for our movie enjoyment, most of us never notice. For example, someone is eating a sandwich and later in the scene there is more sandwich on the plate than there was earlier, or early in the scene a woman is wearing a necklace and a minute later in the same scene she is not. Although we seldom see these discontinuities unless they are pointed out, descriptions (and sometimes clips) of many are readily available online (see, for example, http://www.moviemistakes.com).

Why don't we notice such "obvious" changes when we are attending to the screen? As we attend, our minds are constructing an interpretation of what we are seeing, with a focus on the action and characters. We do not notice changes in the background unless they are quite blatant. This constructive nature of film comprehension is a major reason that we can enjoy film and perceive it as continuous.

Although so far it has been studied primarily with regard to television, attention is also an important issue with newer computer-based technologies. With its numerous links that can be clicked, the Internet offers the chance to make many more choices than television does. One study found that allowing women to choose the type of ad they watched increased the attention subsequently devoted to that ad, although the effect was not obtained in men (Nettelhorst & Brannon, 2010).

One of the most controversial issues in attention in recent years has been the mobile phone, especially the possible distraction effects of using mobile phones while driving. In recent years many jurisdictions have passed laws forbidding talking or texting on handheld phones while driving. There is reason to be concerned, and not only for handheld devices. See Close-Up 3.1

Close-Up 3.1: Which Is Worse: Driving Drunk or While Talking On a Cell Phone? (The Answer May Surprise You)

Some of the most popular activities while driving in recent years seem to be talking or texting on a cell phone. Is this harmless fun or a dangerous distraction? University of Utah psychologist David Strayer and his colleagues (2005) used a high-fidelity driving simulator to answer this question and their findings are sobering. Compared to those in a control group devoting full attention to driving, those talking on a cell phone missed twice as many red lights, recognized fewer billboards they had driven by, took longer to hit the brake to stop while following another car, took longer to recover speed after passing the car, and had more accidents, in spite of leaving more distance between themselves and the next car.

Some additional conditions helped to better understand what was happening. Talking on a hands-free phone was just as bad as on a hand-held phone, so it is the cognitive distraction of the conversation, not the motor skill requirement of holding the phone, that is the major problem. Also, drivers who were listening to the radio or a recorded book or talking to a passenger in the car did not differ from the control group, so these conditions do not place strong demands on attention. One does not have to respond to the radio or talking book, and when the other conversant is in the car with you, he or she can also see the driving conditions and make adjustments in the conversation as conditions warrant, such as keeping quiet for a while. In one study, Strayer got his participants drunk to the minimum blood alcohol level for legal intoxication after they had driven in the control and cell phone conditions. In the car-following task, students who were legally drunk actually stopped and later regained speed faster than those talking on the cell phone, though they were slower in doing so than the controls. Thus, talking on a cell phone actually impaired driving more than being legally drunk!

This research used the experimental design of cognitive psychology to address a question of vital social importance. The results support recent legislation in many places banning cell phone use while driving, although limiting the ban to hand-held units may not completely do the job.

for some troubling results from some well-controlled experimental research on the effects of talking on the phone while driving.

Suspending Disbelief

Like movies or theater, television entertainment involves the social convention of the "willing suspension of disbelief," in which we, for a brief time, agree to accept the characters portrayed onscreen as real human beings so that we can identify with them and experience their joys and sorrows (Cohen, 2006; Esslin, 1982). We know that two actors are not really married to each other but we agree to suspend our disbelief and accept them as a married couple when we watch them in a weekly sitcom. Because of the continuing nature of a television series (often several years to a decade for a successful show), this suspension of disbelief for television is a far more enduring fantasy than it is for a two-hour movie or play. Producers in the early days of television may have doubted the ability of the public to suspend that much disbelief. Many of the earliest TV series featured real-life spouses playing TV partners (e.g., Lucille Ball and Desi Arnaz, George Burns and Gracie Allen, Jack Benny and Mary Livingston, Ozzie and Harriet Nelson). Apparently the public could handle this suspension of disbelief just fine, however, the phenomenon of married actors playing spouses on the screen has been rare since the 1950s.

Sometimes disbelief is suspended so long that the distinction between fantasy and reality becomes blurred. Although young children have difficulty understanding the difference between actors and the characters they portray (Fitch, Huston, & Wright, 1993), this problem is not limited to children. As any series actor knows, adult fans frequently ask an actor playing a doctor for medical advice or hurl epithets at an actress playing a villain in a soap opera. Such fantasies are covertly encouraged by spinoff series, where the same character moves from one series to another (e.g., Dr. Frasier Crane of *Frasier* was originally a supporting character on *Cheers*; actor Kelsey Grammer ended up playing the same character for nearly 20 years!). Children's cartoon or puppet characters like Mickey Mouse, Big Bird, Garfield, Dora the Explorer, SpongeBob SquarePants, or Barney the Dinosaur may reappear in commercials, toys, and kids' meals at restaurants, all of which support a belief in their reality apart from the show.

Sometimes television may provide a salient exemplar of an extremely unpleasant reality once the disbelief is suspended. Close-Up 3.2 explores the feared and actual effects of a much-hyped TV movie on nuclear war.

Transportation

Part of what happens when we willingly suspend disbelief is that we allow ourselves to be *transported* into a narrative world, that is, drawn into a story (Green & Brock, 2000, 2002; Green, Brock, & Kaufman, 2004). Any good

Close-Up 3.2: Nuclear War on TV

One of the most hyped television entertainment events of all time was the 1983 ABC TV movie *The Day After* (*TDA*), a drama depicting the aftermath of a nuclear attack on the American Midwest, aired at the height of the Cold War. Its anticipation became such a media event in itself that *60 Minutes* on the competing network CBS took the unprecedented step of covering *TDA* hype as one of its feature stories, an hour before the movie's airing. It also became a political event. Antinuclear groups encouraged people to watch it, whereas conservatives decried it as an unfair move in the battle to mold public opinion on arms control issues. Mental health professionals worried over its impact on impressionable young minds and warned people to watch it only in groups and not to allow young children to see it at all. All of this heavy media coverage, of course, ensured a large audience, which numbered over 100 million viewers, the largest audience to date for a TV movie.

Psychologists Scholfield and Pavelchak (1985) studied exactly what impact this controversial film's airing actually had. Contrary to some fears or hopes, the movie actually did little to change attitudes about arms control and related issues. Arguments such as the possible failure of a deterrence-through-strength policy had been widely discussed in the media and were not really new ideas to most viewers. Many viewers felt that, horrible as it was, *TDA*'s portrayal of the effects of a nuclear attack was actually milder than hype-weary viewers had expected and in fact was somewhat akin to many disaster and horror movies. The movie did have effects, however. Having seen the film, viewers were more likely to seek information about nuclear issues and become involved in disarmament activities, and they reported thinking about nuclear war twice as often as they had before seeing the film.

narrative medium transports us into the world of the story. This state of high engagement includes four dimensions: narrative understanding, attentional focus, emotional engagement, and narrative presence (Busselle & Bilandzic, 2009). Transportation involves both cognitive (e.g., attention, imagery) and emotional (e.g., empathy, suspense) activation. Someone who is more strongly transported into the world of the narrative enjoys the experience more (Krakowiak & Oliver, 2012) and is more likely to be persuaded by it (Appel & Richter, 2010). Although the content and emotion are often positive, they need not be. People also enjoy being transported into the scary world of a horror film or a war movie, for example. In the case of video games and some computer-mediated communication, we are also physically interacting with the medium, which cannot help but enhance the degree of narrative transportation (Barlett, Rodeheffer, Baldassaro, Hinkin, & Harris, 2008). Reading a book can enhance the degree of transportation later experienced upon seeing the movie based on the book (Green, Kass, Carrey, Herzig, Feeney, & Sabini, 2008).

Transportation as a construct is similar to and partially overlaps related constructs like narrative engagement, emotional involvement, cognitive involvement, immersion, and flow (Wirth, Hofer, & Schramm, 2012).

Identification

The amount of transportation that we experience while watching a filmed drama also depends on how much we identify with the character, that is, mentally compare ourselves to and imagine ourselves like that character (Cohen, 2001, 2006). It is easier to identify with characters with whom we have more experiences in common, although that is not a prerequisite for identification. Although both men and women identify more with same-sex characters who are successful and intelligent, women also identified with those who were attractive and admired, while men identified with media men who were violent (Hoffner & Buchanan, 2005). There is a certain universality in most good drama, however. The basic humanity of characters in very different historical circumstances may be portrayed so well that viewers can identify emotionally with them at some level without having experienced similar situations themselves. In fact, fictional portrayals often evoke stronger emotions and better memory than do documentaries on the same subject (Pouliot & Cowen, 2007).

The perceived reality of media is greater if our identification with the characters is such that they become significant persons in our own lives and we develop a parasocial relationship with them (Klimmt et al., 2006; see Chapter 2). We are more likely to imitate the behaviors or adopt the attitudes of characters we identify with. This has important social ramifications, and it is why, for example, there are greater antisocial effects of observing violent behavior by positive good guy characters than by criminal types (see Chapter 9). Perhaps the ultimate case of identification would be an actor's identification with the character he or she is portraying on screen. See Close-Up 3.3 for discussion of some cognitive research on how actors learn lines and construct a character.

Emotional Components of the Media Experience

Now that we have examined some cognitive components of the media consumption experience, we turn to another very important aspect of media experience: the emotional dimension.

**Close-Up 3.3: Using Cognitive Psychology to
Help Actors Learn Lines**

Cognitive psychologist Helga Noice and her actor and theater professor husband Tony Noice have collaborated for years on a fascinating research program studying how actors learn lines and develop characters in preparing a role for the stage. Surprisingly, most professional actors told the Noices they do not work hard to explicitly memorize lines but rather work hard to understand the character and be able to respond to the situation on stage as that character would. Many of the techniques they report using successfully are exactly those strategies suggested to students for learning material in an academic situation. For example, they elaborate the ideas, that is, think about what the character would be thinking as they speak those lines. Some directors even have their actors write a background biography of the character before they start rehearsal. Actors also report strongly taking the perspective of their character, trying to match their mood to the character, and trying to understand the motivation for every single line of dialogue and every blocking movement. In their research the Noices found that both professional actors and students using these techniques had better verbatim memory for lines than did those who tried explicitly to memorize the words. They coined the term *active experiencing* to refer to the process where an actor uses physical, mental, and emotional means to communicate to another. For example, a line of dialogue is intrinsically associated with the movement the actor makes while speaking it and the feeling he or she has at the time (Noice & Noice, 1997, 2006).

Empathy

Empathy, the ability to understand and feel what someone else is feeling, may be seen as emotional identification, and it is a very important factor in the enjoyment of media. Empathy is a trait, with some people naturally more empathic than others. However, everyone shows some empathy in some media situations, and that empathy enhances our enjoyment. We enjoy a comedy more if we can feel something of what the characters feel. We enjoy a ball game more if we have played baseball and can relate to the tense feelings of being at bat with two outs in the bottom of the ninth with our team down by one run. We enjoy a tragic movie more if we can easily empathize with the suffering of the characters (Mills, 1993). In fact, fMRI studies have shown that some "pain areas" of the brain, notably the anterior cingulate cortex and the anterior insula, respond similarly to physical pain and watching a movie character be embarrassed (Dahl, 2011).

In the case of media (Zillmann, 2006a), empathy is diminished somewhat by the relatively omniscient position we occupy relative to the characters. We generally know more of what is going on than they do, as when we know that the bad guy is just around the bend waiting to ambush our unsuspecting hero. If we know the final outcome, it is often difficult to become as emotionally involved as we could if we knew as little as the character did. Such enjoyment varies greatly depending on the genre, however. Audiences for reruns of sporting events are almost nonexistent, whereas audiences for reruns of comedies hold up quite well. Apparently, loyalty to the characters and show, and the empathy and degree of parasocial interaction with those characters, are crucial factors.

Empathy is composed of both cognitive and emotional components. Cognitive empathy involves the ability to readily take the perspective of another, whereas emotional empathy involves readily responding at a purely emotional level. Davis, Hull, Young, and Warren (1987) showed that the level of both of these types of empathy influenced emotional reactions to viewing the films Brian's Song (a sentimental fact-based drama about a football player dying of cancer) and Who's Afraid of Virginia Woolf? (a wrenching psychological drama about a vindictive and destructive marital relationship), but each type of empathy influenced reactions in different ways.

Empathy has also been conceptualized as a three-factor construct (Zillmann, 2006a), with dispositional, excitatory, and experiential components. One factor may override another that initially dominates. For example, a normal empathic response to an injured athlete may be overridden if one has a negative disposition toward that athlete (e.g., he's on the hated opposing team) and one may respond to the injury with booing. A natural empathic response may also be overridden by an abrupt change to material of a different mood, such as the shift from an intense TV drama to an upbeat commercial. Thus, what might otherwise elicit considerable empathy may not do so, in part due to the sound-bite nature of the medium of television. This could explain why it is much more difficult to become caught up emotionally in a movie broken up by multiple TV commercials than it is when seeing a film uninterrupted in a theater.

Another approach, not yet extensively examined in the research, is the extent to which media, especially television, teach empathy to children or could potentially do so, if more attention were given to such issues by writers, directors, and networks (Feshbach, 1988; Feshbach & Feshbach, 1997).

Suspense

Suspense is usually characterized as an experience of uncertainty whose properties can vary from noxious to pleasant (Vorderer & Knobloch, 2000). The suspense that we feel as we anticipate the outcome of an adventure show or drama is maximal if some negative outcome (e.g., the hero is about to die) appears highly likely but is not absolutely certain; everything points to disaster with just a slight hope of escape. If the negative outcome is either not very likely or absolutely certain, there is not much suspense. We experience a high level of suspense, for example, if our hero appears about to be blown up by a bomb, with just a slight chance of escape. Suspense is also heightened by the omniscient status of the viewer; we know something about the imminent danger that the character does not know, and that knowledge heightens the suspense we feel. The physiological excitation of suspense is relatively slow to decay and may be transferred to subsequent activities (Wang & Lang, 2012; Zillmann, 1996). Much of the positive experience of suspense is mediated by the presence of the pleasant relief that we feel after our hero has averted the imminent danger (Madrigal, Bee, Chen, & LaBarge, 2011).

Suspense may be studied either through an examination of the program script (text) or an analysis of the audience activities, expectations, emotions, and relationships with the characters (reception). See Vorderer, Wulff, & Friedrichsen (1996). The text-oriented approach examines such factors as outcome uncertainty, delay factors, and threats to the character. The reception approach studies the audience's identification with the character, their expectations and curiosity, their emotions, and their concurrent activities and social situation, which may enhance or detract from the experience of suspense. The fact that both text and audience aspects of suspense are important confirms how the experiencing of suspense emerges as the person interacts with the text of the medium.

Sometimes conventional wisdom about suspense does not hold up to hard scrutiny. See Close-Up 3.4 about how so-called "spoilers" do not necessarily spoil the suspense.

Humor

One very common emotional component of consuming media is the enjoyment that comes from experiencing something funny (D. Brown & Bryant, 1983; Zillmann, 2000; Zillmann & Bryant, 1991). But what makes something funny? Why is one line of comedy hilarious and a very similar one not at all funny, perhaps even offensive? Most comedy involves some sort of incongruity, inconsistency, or contradiction, which is then subsequently resolved, as in the punch line of a joke (Attardo, 1997; Perlmutter, 2000; Vaid, 1999; Wyer & Collins, 1992). For example, Attardo (1997) offers a three-stage model of humor, beginning with the setup, followed by some incongruity, and finally a resolution of that incongruity. Neither the incongruity nor the resolution by itself is necessarily very funny, however. Although the joke, "Two elephants got off the bus and left their luggage by the tree" is highly incongruous, it is not particularly funny because there is no resolution. "Two soldiers got off the bus and left their trunks by the tree" has a resolution, but it is not very funny either, because there is no incongruity. Only "Two elephants got off the bus

Close-Up 3.4: Do Spoilers Really Spoil?

Does knowing the end of a story remove the enjoyment from reading or watching it? Many people apparently believe so, as evidenced by the irate responses to movie reviewers who reveal the ending of the film or friends who tell their friends how a story ends before the friends see it. Jonathan Leavitt and Nicholas Christenfeld (2011) decided to test this popular idea to see if it was in fact true. In three experiments they asked college students to read three short stories each, some literary, some mystery, and many with an ironic twist at the end. After reading them, students rated how much they had enjoyed the story. Some had an opening paragraph with a "spoiler" telling how the story ended, and some did not. Surprisingly, readers actually *preferred* the stories that included the spoiler. Why would readers actually prefer to know the surprise ending at the beginning? The authors suggest that this knowledge allowed them to organize the information in the story somewhat differently as they read it. This more omniscient perspective, although very different from that of the character in the story, may actually heighten pleasure, perhaps by allowing the reader to anticipate events and think more deeply about them.

Apparently NBC was confident enough of the lack of a spoiler reaction when broadcasting the 2012 Summer Olympics. Although previous Olympics had held off broadcasting events until the edited evening presentations, in 2012 NBC showed live coverage on its various cable channels hours ahead of the edited evening summary broadcasts. Evening audience figures did not suffer.

and left their trunks by the tree" has both incongruity and resolution (and perhaps humor!).

The best jokes offer some intellectual challenge, but not so much that we cannot "get it." Some of the most satisfying jokes are very esoteric, as in jokes involving knowledge from a particular group, such as a profession. What presents an adequate challenge for one person may not do so for another. For example, many children find certain very predictable, even dumb, jokes funny, whereas adults do not. They are simply not novel or challenging enough for adults. Sometimes the relevant in-group may be the viewers of a show themselves; some jokes on *The Big Bang Theory* may be funny only to regular viewers of the show, especially as they experience solidarity with others as they watch the show together.

Another important concept in understanding media humor is the psycho-dynamic notion of catharsis, the emotional release of tension we feel from expressing some repressed feelings. For example, if you are very worried about some problem but talk to a friend and feel better just for having "gotten it off your chest," what you are experiencing is catharsis. Humor is often seen as a healthy and socially acceptable outlet for dealing with some of our darker feelings. For example, we may be able to deal with some of our own hidden sexual or hostile impulses by listening to a caustic stand-up comedian insult people. Although we might never say such things ourselves, though we might secretly want to, hearing someone else do it partially fulfills our need to do so. Catharsis is often invoked to explain why people appreciate racist, ethnic, sexist, or sexual jokes (Scheele & DuBois, 2006). It is also frequently proposed as a socially beneficial outcome of consuming sexual or violent media, although research has failed to confirm such a conclusion (see Chapters 9 and 10).

Social factors can make a lot of difference in the experience of humor (Apter, 1982; Vaid, 1999). Sometimes the presence of others watching with us enhances our enjoyment, particularly for broader, more raucous humor. The presence of others may genuinely enhance our enjoyment, or we may only outwardly pretend to enjoy it, due to peer pressure to conform to our co-viewers. If we are in a room full of people laughing uproariously at a movie, it is hard to avoid at least a few smiles, even if we are not particularly amused. This is the principle behind the inclusion of a laugh track on some sitcoms. The person who tells the joke is also an important factor. A joke making fun of Mexican-Americans may be very funny if told by a Latino but highly offensive if told by an Anglo or an African American.

There are individual and cultural differences in appreciation of humor. Some people prefer puns, others prefer physical humor or practical jokes; still others prefer sexual or ethnic jokes. Also, societal standards change over time. In the very early days of television, in the early 1950s, *Amos 'n' Andy* could make fun of African-Americans as dim-witted (see Close-Up 4.5); a few years later Ralph Kramden could playfully threaten his wife with physical violence on *The Honeymooners* ("One of these days, Alice, pow! Right in the kisser!") and the audience roared with laughter. We have the chance to laugh at more sexual innuendo on TV now than we could then, but Andy and Ralph's actions do not seem quite so funny.

All of these factors affect the dispositional consequences of moral assessment, as theorized by Zillmann (2000; Zillmann & Bryant, 1991). According to this view, the recipient of the humor is a "moral monitor" who either applauds or condemns the intentions of the other character(s). A lot depends on whether that response is positive or negative. For example, a sitcom character who responds to a witty putdown from another character with a retort in kind is implicitly offering approval, and the viewers experience humor and liking for both characters. On the other hand, if the recipient character is offended and lashes back at the first character, it sets the stage for an antagonistic relationship, where viewers' emotional support goes to the "good guy" (usually the unfairly wounded party) and roots for the discomfort of the "bad guy." Both types of responses are common in comedy, but the dynamics are different and the experience of viewing is different.

Different ages find different things humorous. For example, in an analysis of humor in Dutch television commercials, Buijzen and Valkenburg (2004) found that slapstick, clownish humor, and misunderstanding were common in commercials aimed at young children, while ads aimed at adolescents tended to use satire, parody, and surprise. Ads aimed at a broad audience often used slapstick, irony, surprise, and occasionally sexual or hostile humor. Ads targeted at men and boys used relatively more irony, satire, and slapstick, while those aimed at girls and women used more clownish humor. Sometimes a TV show or movie has multiple aspects of humor in order to appeal to a broader audience. For example, young children's TV shows like *Sesame Street* or *SpongeBob SquarePants* contain numerous witty retorts and popular culture allusions designed to appeal to teens and adults. Many animated movies like the *Shrek* and *Toy Story* series, *Finding Nemo*, *Wall-E*, or *Ratatouille* are filled with double entendres, pop culture references, and parodies, to appeal to older audiences without making it inappropriate or uninteresting for the youngest viewers.

Different cultures find different themes and approaches funny. In North American society, for example, certain topics are off limits or very touchy, at least for prime-time humor (late-night TV and some cable programs are more permissive). Jokes on U.S. TV about racism, feminism, violence against women, or mainstream religion are risky; such humor does exist, but people are likely to take offense and thus producers and comedians are very cautious. On the other hand, a Brazilian TV commercial for a department store chain during one Christmas season showed the Three Wise Men walking to Bethlehem. Suddenly, to a rock beat, they throw open their robes and start dancing in their pastel underwear, featured on sale at the store. It seems unlikely that such an ad would be aired in the United States. See Close-Up 3.5 for some examples of humor that ran up against powers who were not amused.

One function of media humor is a sort of leavening in the context of a more serious offering. A little so-called "comic relief" in the midst of a serious drama can be much appreciated, although if done badly it runs the risk of being perceived to be in poor taste and offending people. If done well, it can increase motivation and interest and make the characters seem more human. If the humor is too funny, of course, it may distract from the major content.

Effects of humor in serious drama are complex and depend on many other factors, including viewer gender, character status (hero vs. villain), and context (King, 2000). This is particularly a concern with commercials. Some of the funniest and more creatively successful TV commercials have not been very effective at selling because the humor overshadowed the commercial message. People remember the gag but forget the product—not a situation that advertisers want!

Close-Up 3.5: Humor in Unfriendly Political Contexts

Sometimes political realities conspire against humor. When the producers of *Sesame Street* tried to launch an Israeli version designed to promote harmony between Israelis and Palestinians, they ran into difficulty. Palestinians did not want their Muppets living on the same street as the Israeli Muppets. A later proposal to have the show set in a neutral park foundered on the problem of which side owned the park. In another example, a former president of Zimbabwe, Canaan Banana, banned all jokes about himself after he tired of banana jokes. Perhaps the most extreme case is North Korea, where all satire is banned because "everything is perfect in the people's paradise." There are those who resist even draconian restrictions, as in the case of one enterprising Chinese wit in the 1990s who created a computer virus that destroyed the hard drive of anyone who answered "no" to the question, "Do you think that Prime Minister Li Peng is an idiot?" ("What's so funny?" 1997).

Mood Management

Another emotional function of media use, especially entertainment media, is to maintain good moods and alleviate bad ones. People in good moods will often seek the least engaging stimulation in order to perpetuate their current state, while people in negative moods may seek stimulation to alter that bad mood (Knobloch-Westerwick, 2006; Knobloch-Westerwick & Alter, 2006; Potts & Sanchez, 1994). This could help explain why happy people frequently turn on some mindless sitcom rerun, or unhappy people watch an outrageous comedy that could distract them from their negative mood. Mood repair can occur through satisfaction of psychological needs (Reinecke, Tamborini, Grizzard, Lewis, Eden, & Bowman, 2012). High sensation seekers, who are more easily bored than others, may seek highly arousing fare in order to achieve and maintain a high arousal level (Zuckerman, 1994, 2006). Severely depressed people may not take full advantage of this mood-altering function of media and might helpfully learn to do so (Dillman Carpentier et al., 2008). Media may also helpfully direct attention away from ourselves and our failure to meet our ideal standards (Mosalenko & Heine, 2003).

Media as Perceived Reality

Now that we have examined some of the psychological constructs involved in our enjoyment of media, let us return for a more careful look at the theme briefly introduced in Chapter 1: the reality created by the media.

The Reflection Myth

A common popular view of the media is that they merely "reflect" the world around them. News stories report what happened in the world that day. Sitcoms reflect the values, lifestyles, and habits of society. TV dramas and magazine fiction reflect the concerns and issues that viewers are struggling with. The presence of violence, pornography, Internet predators, and offensive stereotypes merely reflects the ugly reality of an imperfect world. Advertising reflects the needs and wants that we really have. Media, in this view, are a sort of window on reality. This view is used in authoritarian societies which attempt to control media and thus control people's view of reality; see Close-Up 3.6 for what may be the most extreme modern example of such control.

Close-Up 3.6: North Korean Cinema as Manipulator of Reality

Perhaps the most rigidly controlled authoritarian society in the modern world is the North Korean police state ruled, until his death in 2011, by Kim Jong-Il, and before him, from shortly after World War II, by his father Kim Il-Sung. As well as being a ruthless dictator, Kim Jong-Il was also a film fanatic, particularly enjoying American and Hong Kong action and horror films, which he saw at private screenings, although they were not available to his countrymen. He was thought to particularly enjoy the *Friday the Thirteenth* films and gangster movies like *Scarface* and *The Godfather*. All North Korean films are made in accordance with Kim's 1973 book, *The Art of Cinema*, and are overtly for propaganda purposes. They show only a positive image of their country, which is in fact one of the most desperately poor and backward in the world. The soldiers are usually the heroes who come to rescue the people. For example, in one film, soldiers carried buckets of water for miles and joined hands to form a human dam to hold back a flood. Help comes from the army and from working harder, never from foreign nations, the UN, or nongovernmental organizations. Kim also had a film made to model another favorite film, *Titanic*. This film told of the sinking of a North Korean ship in 1945, and even had a love story modeled on the Rose and Jack romance in the 1997 film. Perhaps Kim's most outrageous act was to kidnap the admired South Korean film director Shin Sang-Ok. He was captured and put to work making North Korean films, among them *Pulgasari*, an imitation of the Japanese *Godzilla*, transformed into an iron-eating lizard who fights with the peasants against their feudal overlords ("North Korean movies' propaganda role," 2003).

Would anybody believe such heavy-handed messages so far removed from reality? Probably so. North Koreans are not allowed to leave their country or have any exposure to foreigners or foreign media, and they have heard this heavy propaganda all their lives. Even the autocratic ruler Kim Jong-Il hardly ever left his country; he may very well have believed that his beloved American horror and gangster movies actually portrayed typical American life. It remains to be seen if his son and successor, Kim Jong-Un, who actually studied in Europe, might allow any small cultural or political opening up.

The reflection view is not the only way to view mass communication, however. It may be that we think certain events and issues are important *because* the news tells us they are. Sitcoms may portray certain values, lifestyles, and habits which are then adopted by society. Dramas deal with certain issues that are then considered by the viewers. Media stereotypes implicitly teach young viewers what different groups of people are like, and the presence of media violence teaches that the world is a violent place. Advertising convinces us that we have certain needs and wants that we did not know we had before. In this view, media are not merely reflecting what is out there in the world. Rather, they are constructing a world that then *becomes* reality for the consumer. This world may be accepted by heavy media users, who are often unaware that such a process is happening, as they believe they are only being entertained. Soon the world as constructed by media may become so embedded in our minds that we cannot distinguish it from reality.

Do the media reflect the world as it is or create a new reality? Certainly media do in many ways reflect what is out there in the world. However, they also choose what to tell us about what is out there in the world (agenda setting), and we accept that interpretation, which then becomes part of our memory and our experience. In this book, we examine how media create a world which then becomes our reality. This cognitive perspective focuses on the mental construction of reality that we form as a result of our contact with media. An individual's constructed reality often differs substantially from objective reality in ways not always open to our conscious awareness. The plan of this book is to examine various content areas from a cognitive psychological perspective, structured around this theme of how media create a reality.

The Study of Perceived Reality

Each of the theoretical approaches discussed in Chapter 2 has something to say about studying the perceived reality that we cognitively construct through interaction with media. For example, agenda setting (McCombs &

Reynolds, 2009) tells us what is important to think about. Social cognitive theory (Bandura, 2009) examines how we learn the behavioral component of this reality. Cultivation theory (Morgan, et al., 2009) focuses on the construction of a worldview. Uses and gratifications theory (Rubin, 2009) looks at the uses we make of media and the gratifications they give us, increasingly connecting this research to an examination of the effects of media. Schema/script theory and the limited capacity model (Lang, 2000) both look at the knowledge structures that we create from exposure to the media.

When we speak of the reality constructed from the media, this is actually a more complex idea than it may first appear. At least two different components are involved (Fitch et al., 1993; Potter, 1988). The first component in perceived reality is *factuality*, or *magic window*. This is the belief in the literal reality of media messages. This reality can be conveyed at the level of either style or content. The style of news reporting, for example, may convey a message of factual correctness more strongly than would the style of an entertainment program. The content of action-adventure shows, presenting a world that is very dangerous, may cultivate a view that the real world is also like that (Morgan, et al., 2009; Signorielli, 1990).

The understanding of factuality develops gradually (Chandler, 1997; Davies, 1997; Wright, Huston, Reitz, & Piemyat, 1994). Two-year-olds do not understand the representational nature of filmed images at all and will try to answer a TV personality who talks to them. By around age 10, children's factuality judgments are essentially equivalent to those of adults. During the transition period, as they learn to "read" TV programs, their emotional experience may be affected by the complexity of the plot and also by how realistic they perceive the program to be. For example, Weiss and Wilson (1998) found that, the higher the degree of realism attributed to a sitcom episode, the more concerned elementary school children were about similar negative emotional events in their own lives. Even relatively mundane factors can affect perceived reality. For example, a larger screen size can lead to greater arousal and involvement of the viewer (Detenber & Reeves, 1996; Grabe, Lombard, Reich, Bracken, & Ditton, 1999; Lombard, Reich, Grabe, Bracken, & Ditton, 2000).

One does not have to believe in the literal reality of media to have it become real, however. The second component of perceived reality is *social realism*, which refers to the perceived similarity or usefulness of the media representation to one's own life, even while recognizing its fictional nature. For example, a viewer with a strong belief that soap operas present real-life situations would expect more application to her own life than another viewer who feels that soap operas present wildly unrealistic and purely escapist content (Rubin & Perse, 1988). Stories where events happen as we would predict them are seen as more realistic (Shapiro, Barriga, & Beren, 2010), as are those which adhere more strongly to familiar narrative structures such as following the familiar narrative script of exposition, complication, and resolution discussed in Chapter 2 (Igartua & Barrios, 2012; Kintsch, 1977). Viewers rely heavily on typicality to judge the social reality of television; the more typical a situation seems, the more real it is judged to be (Shapiro & Chock, 2003). Because of their shorter life experience, young children often see greater social realism in television content than adults do, in that they have less experience with which to compare the media representation to assess its reality. In general, media have greater effects on people who attribute a higher degree of social realism to them. This has important consequences whether we are talking about violence, sex, advertising, news, or prosocial media.

When we make assessments of the degree of social realism, those judgments may differ depending on whether the particular relevance is at the personal or social level (Chock, 2011). For example, a high degree of identification with a character may lead us to judge that show as relatively more realistic for ourselves, while identification would be less important in judging the perceived realism for others. Also, different shows, or even commercials, contain cues to the degree of realism (Shapiro & Kim, 2012). With the increase in reality TV shows, we may also have the odd situation of objective factuality without much social realism. Even though the people on *Jersey Shore* or *American Idol* are acting as themselves and unscripted, the application to a viewer's reality may be quite limited (Skeggs & Wood, 2012).

Social realism can be enhanced by the degree to which viewers believe that a character is important in their own lives. In extreme cases there is a tremendous outpouring of grief for these parasocial media friends we have never met, for example, the worldwide mourning that occurred following the death of Princess Diana in 1997 or Michael Jackson in 2009. The character need not even be real. When Colonel Henry Blake of M*A*S*H was shot down and killed on his way home from the Korean War, the network was deluged with letters from grief-stricken and irate fans who did not appreciate the intrusion of wartime reality into their sitcom (see Chapter 2 for further discussion of these kinds of parasocial grief reactions).

The explicit use of media to build character is a largely untapped domain that may have considerable potential. For example, Niemiec and Wedding (2008) use Peterson and Seligman's (2004) list of character strengths and virtues from positive psychology to identify and discuss movies that can be used to build character and virtues. They use six different virtues—wisdom and knowledge, courage, humanity, justice, temperance, and transcendence—with several character strengths within each virtue. In their book they discuss different movies which encourage the building of particular character strengths and offer discussion questions and specific applications.

As human information processors, we are always monitoring the sources of what we know and judging whether those sources are reliable or not (Johnson, 2007). However, much of this *reality monitoring* process fails to accurately remember the source and thus may assign far too much credibility to some memories. On a more social or cultural level, we expect media sources to exercise reasonable reality monitoring. Failures to do so have significant consequences, for example, when a news writer is caught fabricating a story. The proliferation of unreliable news sources such as tabloid journalism and unchecked Internet sources may tend to lower these expectations overall, contributing to a greater mistrust of media in general.

Conclusion

The rest of this book will take a fairly eclectic cognitive approach, drawing on various theoretical perspectives, as appropriate, to approach the study of how media construct reality. The different theories are not necessarily mutually exclusive in all ways and may in fact be quite complementary. The meaning of something in the media, at either a cognitive or an emotional level, depends on how that information is processed during our experience of interacting with the medium. Elements of the different theories and psychological processes are brought in as appropriate in discussion of the topics in the rest of the book.

The media create a reality for us in many different areas, drawing on different psychological processes as they do so. Next, let us turn to the first set of those perceived realities created by media, namely our knowledge of what different groups of people are like.

Chapter 4

Media Portrayals of Groups
Distorted Social Mirrors

Q: What percentage of teenage girls from Fiji suffered from eating disorders in 1995, before the advent of television in the island nation, and how many after?

A: Three percent in 1995. Three years later, 15%, with another 29% "at risk" of eating disorders. Seventy-four percent of the teens said they felt "too big and fat" (Becker, 2004; Goodman, 1999; "Numbers," 1999).

Q: How do today's advertising models compare in weight to real women?

A: The models weigh 23% less than the average woman, compared to only 8% less in the 1970s. They are also taller and generally of a very unusual body type (tall, thin, small hipped). If they have large breasts, they are probably implants, since women of that body type seldom have large breasts (Kilbourne, 1995, 2010). All this is happening at the same time as the average woman's size has increased from 8 to 14 since 1985! (Kher, 2003).

Q: How well does *Sports Illustrated* represent women?

A: Not very, at least according to one study that found, during a three-year time span, only 10% of the photos in the magazine were of women. Further, 55% of these photos were classified by the authors of the study as showing a "non-sport setting" (Fink & Kensiciki, 2002).

What do you know about Mexican Americans? Arabs? Jews? Farmers? People with schizophrenia? Older adults? One of the major perceived realities that media help create for us involves information about groups of people. Through media we are exposed to a much broader range of people than most of us would ever encounter in our own lives. Not only are media our introduction to many different kinds of people, but sometimes media are practically the *only* source of our information about them. Sometimes almost everything that we know about some groups of people comes from media.

Some rural White North Americans have never met any Arabs or Jews in person. Many urban dwellers have never met a real farmer. Most people in the world have never met someone from the United States. In such cases, the media portrayal of Arabs, Jews, farmers, or Americans is reality for them. In one of the earliest studies of this issue, children several decades ago reported that most of their information about people from different nationalities came from their parents and television, with TV becoming increasingly important as the child grew older (Lambert & Klineberg, 1967). In this chapter we examine the media image of different groups of people and look at the consequences of such portrayals. The concerns regarding some groups (e.g., women, African Americans) are widely known and investigated, while portrayals of other groups have received relatively little research attention. Although the issue is relevant to all media, television and movies are of particular concern, especially with regard to programming and advertising. For example, if the world of TV is presented in a positive multicultural fashion, that could have enormous socializing effects on children (Asamen & Berry, 2003). Although the focus of research has been on media, especially television, in the United States, the same principles (if not all the specifics) hold true for any nation's media. Of course, with the advent of the Internet, international boundaries for media are weaker than ever, and popular culture is increasingly international.

Most American producers of television and films tend to be rather affluent, and they tend mostly to live in New York City or Southern California. The media grossly overrepresent the world of those who produce the programming, which therefore tacitly presents their world as far more typical of life in general than is really the case. Most American shows and films are set in Los Angeles or New York, few in Tennessee or South Dakota. Some research suggests that exported programs showing glitz and glamour may be cultivating negative images of Americans for viewers elsewhere (Harris & Karafa, 1999; Kamalipour, 1999). Popular TV and films about the rich are by no means a uniquely North American phenomenon; many developing countries' domestic shows also present such affluent lifestyles. The telenovelas of Mexico and Brazil present characters with income levels and lifestyles wildly beyond the reach of most of their viewers.

Although concerns about stereotyped group portrayals in media have been widely discussed and some good content analyses have been performed, rigorous scientific research addressing the effects of group portrayals has been much less common. It is difficult to isolate media effects from other influences to establish firm causal relationships. All the theoretical perspectives discussed in Chapter 2 have made their contributions in this area, and the prevailing portrayals of some groups will increasingly come to be the reality perceived by those who partake heavily of the media.

Portrayals of the Sexes

To begin with, let us examine gender portrayals. What do media say about what it means to be a man or woman? Although this question will be addressed here, for reviews and meta-analyses of research on gender portrayals see Durkin (1985a, 1985b), Gerbner (1997), Gunter (1986), Herrett-Skjellum and Allen (1996), Oppliger (2007), and Signorielli (2001).

The View of Women

We have heard a lot in recent years about stereotyping of women by the media, but what exactly does content analysis research tell us about the way women are portrayed? Some of these concerns may be very familiar, whereas others are more subtle.

Numbers

Perhaps the most basic gender asymmetry is that there are far fewer females than males throughout media. According to the 2010 U.S. Census, the nation's overall population consisted of 49.2% males and 50.8% females (Howden & Meyer, 2011). These roughly 50–50 proportions have been the case for at least the past century.

However, content analyses of characters in television shows in the 1970s through the 2000s showed about twice as many males as females in prime-time dramas and up to three or four times as many in children's shows (Gerbner, 1997; Signorielli, 1993; Smith & Cook, 2008; Thompson & Zerbinos, 1995). On a wide variety of ensemble shows, including C.S.I., The Office, Saturday Night Live, The Daily Show with Jon Stewart, Seinfeld, Cheers, Futurama, South Park, and Sesame Street, a large majority of the characters have been and continue to be male. The percentage of female characters on U.S. TV only increased from 28 to 36% between 1975 and 1995, and only 20% of characters aged 45 to 64 were women (Gerbner, 1997). Until the advent of such mid-1980s shows as Cagney and Lacey, The Golden Girls, Designing Women, and Kate and Allie, shows with all-female lead characters were largely nonexistent in the United States, with very infrequent exceptions like One Day at a Time and the arguably sexist Charlie's Angels and Police Woman of the 1970s. However, virtually all-male shows have been common through much of the history of television, including most Westerns and police shows, and many kids' shows like Teenage Mutant Ninja Turtles, Power Rangers, or even Mickey Mouse, Bugs Bunny, and Roadrunner cartoons. In fact, children's cartoon characters are male two to three times as often as they are female (Dobrow & Gidney, 1998; Thompson & Zerbinos, 1995; Smith & Cook, 2008), and are especially likely to be male in cartoons that focus on adventure or comedy (Leaper, Breed, Hoffman, & Perlman, 2002).

The same general patterns have emerged in the realm of film. For example, one study found that female characters only accounted for 33% of all characters among the top 100 U.S. domestic grossing films in 2011 (Center for the Study of Women in Television and Film, 2012). In another study, a content analysis was conducted that examined male and female characters in all G, PG, and PG-13 rated films released in the U.S. between 2006 and 2009 (Smith & Choueiti, 2010). Results revealed that 71% of speaking characters in these "family films" were male, with only 29% being female. Further, female characters were more likely than male characters to be portrayed in "sexy, tight, or alluring attire" (p. 3). Another study examining top-rated G-rated films found that only 28% of speaking characters were female (Smith & Cook, 2008).

Although 46% of characters in television commercials were female by1998 (Ganahl, Prinsen, & Netzley, 2003), the voice-over announcer was male 71% to 90% of the time (Bartsch, Burnett, Diller, & Rankin-Williams, 2000; Bretl & Cantor, 1988; Ferrante, Haynes, & Kingsley, 1988; Lovdahl, 1989; Paek, Nelson, & Vilela, 2011), a figure virtually unchanged from the early 1970s (Dominick & Rauch, 1972). Music videos show at least twice as many males as females and tend to reinforce traditional gender stereotypes (Sommers-Flanagan, Sommers-Flanagan, & Davis, 1993; Toney & Weaver, 1994; Took & Weiss, 1994; Vincent, Davis, & Boruszkowski, 1987). Print media is no exception to this pattern of underrepresenting females. Photos of men outnumber photos of women everywhere in the newspapers except the lifestyle section (Luebke, 1989).

A substantial minority of TV news anchors and weathercasters are now women, although very few sportscasters are. In a content analysis of guests interviewed on ABC's *Nightline* from 1985 to 1988, Croteau and Hoynes (1992) found that only 10% were women. Not surprisingly, when children were asked to name their favorite characters on informational TV programs, both boys and girls were more likely to think of male than female characters and remembered more traditionally masculine than feminine behaviors (Calvert, Kotler, Zehnder, & Shockey, 2003).

Physical Appearance

A second concern is that women are too often portrayed as youthful beauties whose duty it is to stay young and attractive in order to please their men. Once a woman is no longer so young and is therefore considered less attractive, she becomes an object of ridicule. Support for this criticism comes especially from the messages that say a woman must not allow herself to age. This anti-aging theme appears especially, although not exclusively, in advertising, the media area with the most stereotyped gender portrayals. Women in media became slimmer during the 20th century (Percy & Lautman, 1994), but the weight gap between models and real women widened. By the mid-1990s, models weighed 23% less than the average woman, a figure up from 8% less in 1975 (Kilbourne, 1995). *Seventeen,* among the most widely read magazines for teen girls, devotes two-thirds of its editorial content to fashion and beauty topics, with most of the remaining articles being about relational topics like finding boyfriends and being popular (Phillips, 1993).

Wrinkles, gray hair, or a "mature" figure are to be avoided at all costs. At least until recently, women obviously over 30, and especially those over 50, have been grossly underrepresented on television and in movies, and in all sorts of advertising. When present, they were often seen as stereotyped "old ladies" whom no one would want to grow up and be like. Women in TV ads tend to be younger than men (55–70% vs. 40% under 35, respectively), with ratios essentially unchanged since the early 1970s (Dominick & Rauch, 1972; Ferrante et al., 1988; Stern & Mastro, 2004).

The obsession with youth is so strong in advertising that sometimes grown women are depicted as eroticized young girls. One example of this is an ad campaign by Calvin Klein in the 1990s that intentionally mimicked child pornography with photos of scantily clad and very young-looking models. At the same time there also seems to be a tendency among some marketers to sexualize young girls by equating them with sexually mature women. One example of this is the Bratz doll line marketed to young girls. Typically, these popular dolls feature short, tight-fitting clothing and heavy makeup, which most adults would find inappropriate on a child. There is also an interactive website in which girls can have their dolls shop for clothing, shoes, pet accessories, salon services, and even furniture. Not to be outdone, Mattel introduced a Bratz-like My Scene Barbie collection (with accompanying website) and even Lingerie Barbies, some of which had see-through underwear and bustiers (Levin & Kilbourne, 2009). This trend even extends to clothes designed to be worn on girls' own bodies. In a content analysis of popular clothing websites, it was discovered that about 30% of clothes marketed to girls had sexualizing characteristics (Goodin, Van Denburg, Murnen, & Smolak, 2011).

The idealized portrayal of feminine beauty, especially in advertising, involves a highly unusual body type, namely very tall, very thin, and small-hipped. These characteristics co-occur in less than 5% of the adult female population, but models are usually of this type. The other common supermodel characteristic, large breasts, is an attribute so infrequent for this body type that at least one leading scholar in the area concludes that, if present, they almost surely must be implants (Kilbourne, 1995). Computerized image construction of models and the use of body doubles, even for very attractive stars, are common. For example, in a prominent movie poster for *Pretty Woman*, what appeared to be actress Julia Roberts was, in fact, composite body parts selected from the best of several models, plus computer graphic enhancement. Some of her sex scenes in the film used body doubles with even more beautiful bodies or body parts (Kilbourne, 1995). Interestingly, one analysis even concluded that thin, small-waisted, large-chested female characters were more common in animated than in live-action movies (Smith & Cook, 2008). See Close-Up 4.1 for a more detailed discussion of how body image is related to the complex interaction of food, sex, and weight loss.

Although the stress on women's physical beauty is important in many cultures, there are some differences. For example, many African cultures see

Close-Up 4.1: Food, Sex, and Weight Loss in the Ideal Woman

The next time you're in a supermarket checkout line, pay attention to the cover headlines of magazines geared toward females. According to Kilbourne (1995, 2010), two major themes of magazine articles and advertising aimed at women are food and weight loss. Food is often presented as a way to deal with emotional needs (e.g., break up with a guy and indulge in some ice cream) and is sometimes even presented as a substitute for sex, as when a woman comes close to having an orgasm from eating fine chocolate or when Oreos are described in ads as "the most seductive cookie ever." Metaphors of addiction and loss of control are commonplace ("I can't control myself with this candy"), sometimes even modeling binge eating (e.g., downing a whole quart of ice cream). At the same time, however, women (but not men) are made to feel ashamed or guilty for eating, with supermodel thinness presented as the moral equivalent of virginity, both resulting from keeping one's appetites under control. Never mind the fact that no amount of dieting could possibly turn most women's bodies into supermodel shapes. This fear of losing control and losing one's figure is a powerful appeal in the advertising of everything from diet programs to cigarettes. Do such appeals work? With half of teens and adult women on diets, most of which fail, and 75% of normal-weight women thinking they are fat, it would appear that they do.

plump women as healthy and attractive and very thin women as emaciated and unattractive. In some parts of Nigeria, young women are sent to "fattening farms" to be fed and massaged to gain weight to be more attractive for their future husbands. In parts of Niger, in a desperate attempt to gain weight, some women risk their health by taking steroids or food or vitamins designed for animals. A woman who is too thin is seen as not being well provided for by her husband (Onishi, 2001). Facial piercing has long been popular among South Asian women, and large body tattoos and corpulent physique are popular among some Polynesians of both genders. One content analysis of fashion ads in the United States, Singapore, and Taiwan concluded that a pretty face was the central beauty focus in the two East Asian cultures, while a shapely body was more central in the American ads (Frith, Shaw, & Cheng, 2005).

Pregnancy and Breast-Feeding

Women's pregnant bodies may evoke either a positive response of love or a more ambivalent response of discomfort. Goldenberg, Goplen, Cox, and Arndt (2007) have suggested that the discomfort may stem from a feeling of mortal vulnerability made more salient by seeing a pregnant woman. They tested this idea by having young adults read an essay, either one describing the similarity of humans to other animals or one describing human uniqueness. After reading the essay, they saw a photo of either a popular movie star (Demi Moore or Gwyneth Paltrow) who was very obviously pregnant or the same film star not pregnant. Those reading about humans' similarity to other animals rated the Demi Moore photo as more offensive and Gwyneth Paltrow as less competent and intelligent, compared to those who read the uniqueness essay or saw the nonpregnant photo.

In terms of entertainment media, women's breasts are often presented in media as sexual organs, even in the context of their intended biological use. Consider the case of breast-feeding, now recommended by virtually the entire medical community as the preferred method of providing infant nutrition. Ads, and even photos in feature magazine stories on breast-feeding, sometimes show women breast-feeding in very revealing poses so that it appears as though the entire breast must be bared in order to nurse, when in fact an infant may be nursed in public quite discreetly. Advocates of breast-feeding worry that such media images discourage mothers from offering the best nutrition for their infants (Dettwyler, 1995). Inexperienced mothers who see such revealing images may be turned away from nursing, thinking they do not want to disrobe to that extent in public. Their husbands may fear that their wives' nursing requires an inappropriate sexual seductiveness. Employers who see such images may be less inclined to allow breast-feeding in the workplace, mistakenly believing that considerable undressing or sexually revealing poses are necessary in order for a woman to nurse.

Concerns of Women

Women in the media are still disproportionately seen as homemakers and mothers, with their business, professional, and community roles downplayed or not represented at all. This has been especially true of advertising through the years (a slogan from one 1970s print ad for dinnerware: "A chip on your dinnerware is like a spot on your dress!") (Knill, Pesch, Pursey, Gilpin, & Perloff, 1981; Stern & Mastro, 2004). However, the range of occupational roles for women in ads has increased (Ferrante et al., 1988), and the stereotyping of women in advertisements is not limited to the United States but occurs in many societies, including Australia, Mexico (Gilly, 1988), and South Africa (Luyt, 2011). Women are often seen as dependent on men and needing their protection. Even relatively egalitarian TV families generally show the wife deferring to the husband more often than the reverse, although the behaviors showing this are much more subtle than those of 40 years ago. Women are not seen making important decisions or engaging in important activities as often as men. Advertising often portrays women as terribly perplexed, even obsessive, about such matters as dirty laundry or spotted glassware. Women squeezing toilet paper or berating others about soiled clothing or wasted cell phone minutes also make this point. Early sitcoms such as *I Love Lucy* showing women playing bridge or gossiping with neighbors all day also illustrate this concern. Although we have come a long way from the *Father Knows Best* dad telling his daughter in 1959, "Be dependent, a little helpless now and then. The worst thing you can try to do is beat a man at his own game" (Douglas, 1997, p. 24), some of the most gender-stereotyped TV shows are those aimed at children. Often the females in children's shows have been rather frilly and wimpy supporting characters like Baby Bop of *Barney and Friends* and April O'Neill of *Teenage Mutant Ninja Turtles*, both of whom, even into the 1990s, seemed mainly to nurture and support their male colleagues (Douglas, 1994). Some shows beginning in the late 1990s and 2000s, particularly on cable networks like Nickelodeon and Disney, offered more complex and positive role models for girls (e.g., *Hannah Montana, Dora the Explorer, That's So Raven, iCarly*), and there is some evidence that gender roles on recent children's and teen shows are somewhat less stereotypical than in earlier decades (Aubrey & Harrison, 2004; Kaveney, 2006).

Sometimes the power that women do exercise is used in very underhanded and conniving ways, often directly or indirectly involving sexuality. The ruthless businesswoman character who sleeps her way to the top is a classic example. There are subtle messages that it is not ladylike to confront men (or even other women) directly, but it is perfectly acceptable to behave deviously in order to trick them. Portraying sexuality as a weapon of power subtly deemphasizes and even degrades its tender and relational aspects. Even strong female characters like those in *Sex and the City* or *Desperate Housewives* are very interested in sex and do not hesitate to use it to further their interests. Less sexual wielding of female power also occurs; for example, Lucy in the cartoon *Peanuts* dominates the boys through intimidation. Even relatively powerless victims of possible sexual harassment are often presented as conniving, devious, and manipulative. For example, some news media portrayals in the 1990s of various women allegedly involved with President Bill Clinton (e.g., Monica Lewinsky, Paula Jones, Gennifer Flowers) often received this treatment.

Some current gender differences in media may be more subtle than those in the past. For example, a content analysis by Zhao and Gantz (2003) found that male fictional TV characters initiated more disruptive conversational interruptions, while females initiated more cooperative interruptions, but only if the interrupter was of higher status than the interruptee and if the conversation was about work. This suggests that gender asymmetry in portrayals of the workplace might be more unbalanced than in friendship conversations (see Tannen, 1994 for an excellent discussion of language, power, and gender issues in the workplace). These kinds of media models of gender-appropriate communication may even translate into behavior. For example, Ben-Zeev and colleagues (2012) found that when exposed to a "hypermasculine" communication style in a movie (a film clip of a heterosexual male character who refuses to discuss emotions with a female partner), male college students indicated they would be less likely to facilitate an emotion-laden discussion themselves than male college students who had seen a control clip.

The Superwoman

The unrealistic superwoman who can effortlessly "have it all" has increasingly appeared as media attempt to represent modern women more accurately and fairly. Although women characters in TV series are often employed outside the home, this only occurs about half as often on TV as in real life (e.g., 34% on TV vs. 67% in reality, in 1998). Those who are depicted as employed are most often in professional or managerial positions, and many are also mothers. Although some of these characters are truly positive role models of professional women, they appear to handle the demands of career, marriage, and parenting with amazingly little stress and difficulty (Heintz-Knowles, 2001). Real women in two-career families need such positive role models, but they also need some acknowledgment that the great difficulties they experience balancing all of those responsibilities are not abnormal. The supermoms make it all look too easy.

The superwoman myth is also reinforced by advertising. For example, one notorious perfume commercial that began airing during the Women's Movement of the 1970s (and was probably designed to reflect the times) could be considered damaging. Specifically, the ad said that a woman can "bring home the bacon, fry it up in a pan, but never let him forget he's a man." In other words, a woman can (or at least should) work outside the home all day, come home and cook dinner for her husband, and still have enough energy left to be sexy for him that evening! Another notable ad slogan from that era was, "You've come a long way, baby," used by Phillip Morris to advertise Virginia Slims, cigarettes marketed specifically to women. This message also played on feminist themes and seemed to suggest that, unlike their grandmothers, modern women should have it all, including their own brand of smokes! Are these realistic messages to send to young girls about what it means to be a woman in today's society? Are these helpful expectations to transmit to young boys about what they can expect from the women they may eventually marry? Do advertisers place similar, multi-role expectations on males?

Women and Violence

A final concern is that women are subtly linked with violence, especially as victims of sexual violence. Some advertising or entertainment playing on the seductiveness of women (especially women of color) also suggests that they are animals to be tamed, something wild to be brought into line by men (Kilbourne, 2010). A high-fashion ad selling negligees by showing a scantily clad woman being playfully attacked by several fully dressed men, or an auto magazine ad showing a woman in a bikini chained inside a giant shock absorber (perhaps not-so subtly) link sexuality and violence. Perfume ads may stress the wildness, the toughness, and the challenge that women provide for men. "Blame it on [the perfume]" seems to justify an attack from a man in response to some irresistible fragrance on the woman.

Although we may not find Ralph Kramden's (from the 1950s TV show *The Honeymooners*) mock threat of violence to his wife ("One of these days, Alice, pow! Right in the kisser!") as amusing as we did in 1955, far more graphic instances of violence toward women are common, especially in the so-called "slasher" films popular since the 1970s (e.g., the *The Texas Chainsaw Massacre, Friday the 13th, Nightmare on Elm Street,* and *Halloween* series) aimed at teenagers, and in violent pornography sold to adults. The association of women with violence is a lesser concern in relation to network television series, although it does occur. When Luke and Laura on *General Hospital* fell in love and married after he raped her, a message was sent to men that, when a woman says "no," she may really mean "yes." In fact, this image of a woman resisting but secretly wanting a man to force himself on her has a long cinematic tradition, including such classics as *Gone with the Wind* and numerous John Wayne Westerns. Possible desensitization effects of such portrayals are examined in Chapter 10.

Although we have so far focused on women, there are also some serious concerns about the media portrayals of men. Although these have received less general attention and scientific research than portrayals of women, unrealistic stereotyping is also a problem here.

The View of Men

The predominant image of men in our media is as calm, cool, self-confident, decisive … and totally lacking in emotion. Although this may be positive in some ways, it sends the message to young boys that this is what men are supposed to be like, and if a man cannot deny his feelings or at least keep them all inside, he is not a real man.

Emotionless Beings

The Marlboro Man is the quintessential media man, but many classic TV fathers and detectives come in a close second. Who could imagine Ward Cleaver (*Leave It to Beaver*) or your classic TV cop (like *Dragnet's* Joe Friday) shedding a tear? This picture has changed somewhat; modern TV dads like Homer (*The Simpsons*) or the heterosexual male characters on *Friends, How I Met Your Mother,* and *Modern Family* are allowed to cry occasionally, although even they are generally somewhat embarrassed and ashamed to do so. Most men and boys in advertising are looking blankly at no one with a vacant stare (often shielded by sunglasses), whereas women and girls in ads appear to be looking at someone and are often smiling or giving some other hint of what they are feeling.

Physical Appearance

Like women, men are portrayed as young and attractive, but the rules are a little different. Well-developed upper-body muscles are an important part of the male beauty ideal. A study of images of men and women in heterosexual erotic magazines found that photos of women were more sexualized and idealized than photos of men (Thomas, 1986). Also, it is not quite as bad for a man to age as it is for a woman. A little gray hair may make a man look "distinguished" or possibly even sexy, whereas it just makes a woman look old. It is not unusual to see a man with some gray hair reporting the news, sports, or weather, but seeing a woman with gray hair in these roles is far less common.

In spite of this, the message to stay young is still a strong one for men. For example, although many men begin losing hair in their 20s or 30s, few sympathetic leading male characters in TV series, movies, or advertising ever have even the slightest receding hairline. A bald character, when he appears at all, is usually at least an object of subtle ridicule (e.g., the stupid husband who needs his wife to find him the right laxative), or at best a character (like the eccentric guy who doesn't believe oatmeal really could have all that fiber). Even sympathetic middle-aged or elderly male characters usually have full heads of hair. The occasional man who openly wears a hairpiece is almost always the butt of tired old toupee jokes. The few positive exceptions, like Picard of *Star Trek: The Next Generation*, are middle-aged or older, although bald (apparently shaved) heads are increasingly common among some actors and characters.

There is alarming evidence that men are becoming increasingly obsessed with their bodies and feeling increasingly inadequate in comparison to the heavily muscled media models (Pope, Phillips, & Olivardia, 2000). Some (see Labre, 2005) have attributed this, at least in part, to the advent of magazines such as *Men's Health* and *Men's Fitness*, which became increasingly prevalent starting in the late 1980s. Just as so many women see an unrealistically thin body as normal, so many young men see a heavily muscled upper body as normal and readily attainable. In one study cited by Pope and colleagues (2000), over half of a sample of boys ages 11 to 17 chose as an ideal body build a type completely unattainable without steroids.

Male models of the 21st century have far more defined "six-packs" and chests than models of 20 or 30 years earlier. This trend has even been transferred to toys. Star Wars, Batman, and G. I. Joe action figures since 2000 have been far broader in the shoulders, beefier in the chest, and smaller in the hips than their 1970s counterparts. For example, proportionally, the 1998 G. I. Joe Extreme had a 55-inch chest and 27-inch biceps, compared to the 44-inch chest and 12-inch biceps of the 1973 model (Pope, Olivardia, Gruber, & Borowiecki, 1999). This look would be all but unattainable by real men and certainly not without the use of dangerous anabolic steroids.

Besides the need for bulging "pecs" and "delts," many young men are concerned with other shortcomings of their bodies, including hair (must have
plenty of it on your head but not on your back or chest), height (must be taller
than your woman), genital size (need enough bulge under your pants), and
even breast size (can't be too large and thus look feminine). When these concerns become strong enough to be seriously maladaptive in one's life, one may
suffer from body dysmorphic disorder (BDD), a body-image condition therapists report seeing increasingly often in males.

Friendships

Although media images of friendship are common for both men and women,
the nature of those friendships is often different (Spangler, 1989, 1992).
Women characters tend to show a greater degree of emotional intimacy
in their friendships than men do. TV images of male bonding go back to
the Westerns of the 1950s, in which a cowboy and his sidekick went everywhere together. Sitcom friends like Ralph and Ed on *The Honeymooners*,
Hawkeye and B.J. on M*A*S*H, or the Chandler-Joey-Ross triad on *Friends*
were clearly close emotionally, although that was seldom explicitly discussed,
unlike the more overtly emotional women's friendships of Lucy and Ethel on
I Love Lucy, Mary and Rhoda on *The Mary Tyler Moore Show*, or the women
on *Sex and the City*. This gender difference may fairly accurately reflect real life
in terms of the different communication styles of the sexes (Tannen, 1990),
though most scholars agree that the feminine model is the healthier one (see
Close-Up 4.2 for a closer look at the masculine socialization messages in beer
commercials and Close-Up 11.5 for a discussion of teen cross-sex friendships
in movies).

Domestic Roles

Although men are generally portrayed as competent professionally, they are
often seen as ignorant and bungling with regard to housework and child care.
TV fathers of year-old infants often do not know how to change a diaper; this
is unlikely to be true in even the most traditional real families. Men in commercials often seem to know nothing about housekeeping, cooking, or household appliances, and have to be bailed out by their wives, who, in the domestic
sphere, are portrayed as the knowledgeable experts. Even TV psychologist Dr.
Phil was shown ineptly shopping, cleaning, and baking during a "role reversal"
episode of his show (Henson & Parameswaran, 2008). Over the last 30 years
there have been periodic TV shows and movies portraying the ineptness of
men dealing with children (*Full House*, *Mr. Mom*, *Home Improvement*, *Two and
a Half Men*, *Everybody Loves Raymond*). Although the characters typically
learned and grew as persons from the experience, these men's initial inepti-
tude would seem to suggest that childcare is not a part of the normal male role.

Close-Up 4.2: Messages of Masculinity in Beer Commercials

In a content analysis of TV beer commercials, Strate (1992) argued that there is strong socialization occurring about what it means to be a man. Specifically, he claimed that five questions are addressed by such ads:

What kinds of things do men do? First of all, they drink. This almost always occurs in the company of others in the context of good times. Beer is seen as a reward for a job well done (particularly after physical activity) and is a common marker for the end of a work day, such as stopping for a drink with friends after work.

What kinds of settings do men prefer? Beer is identified with nature and the outdoors, through images like a cowboy, horses, or a clear mountain stream. The second popular setting is the bar, which is always clean, smokeless, and full of polite and non-intoxicated, upper middle-class people. Also, no one ever seems to pay for a drink, either in cash or consequences.

How do boys become men? Beer serves as a reward for a challenge or an initiation or rite of passage. "To earn acceptance, the younger man must demonstrate that he can do things that men do: take risks, meet challenges, face danger courageously, and dominate his environment" (Strate, 1992, p. 85). Apparently, he does this mainly through drinking beer.

How do men relate to each other? Men relate to each other primarily in groups (interestingly enough, a contrast to the frequent loner image of masculinity). Beer drinking is the shared activity that brings the group together and is never seen as being harmful.

How do men relate to women? Although women are largely absent in beer commercials, they are occasionally there as rather passive and peripheral accessories. The male group is clearly more important.

Anybody watching sports events or other programming with many beer commercials receives a heavy dose of such messages. Many of these viewers are children. What are boys learning from beer commercials about the use of alcohol and what it means to be a man?

In a similar vein, men in the media are often portrayed as insensitive and interpersonally unskilled. For example, they are usually very awkward in not knowing how to talk to their children about sensitive personal issues. Seeing a father struggle to avoid talking to his daughter about menstruation sends the message that men do not do that and should not want to; how much better it would be to show him talking effectively to her, perhaps providing dads in the audience with a cognitive script about how to have that conversation. In another example, a nice young man in a pharmaceutical ad talks about how he suffered from acid reflux for years and finally *his mother* sent him to the doctor's office, where he received a prescription for this miracle drug. Why was this grown man too dim-witted to manage his own health, and need to be bailed out by his mother?

Class Issues

There are sometimes interesting interactions of gender and social class in the media. For example, in a study of African American Upward Bound high school students' reactions to episodes of *Good Times* and *The Cosby Show*, Berry (1992) found that a majority of the youth found the lower-class and more authoritarian James Evans of *Good Times* a more positive role model than Dr. Cliff Huxtable of *The Cosby Show*, contrary to what the producers had probably intended. Perhaps James better fit what the youth thought a real man should be like.

To help balance the bias of scientific study on middle- and upper-class people, New Zealand psychologist Darrin Hodgetts and his colleagues (Hodgetts & Chamberlain, 2002; Hodgetts & Rua, 2010) have studied the media image of what they call the "bloke culture"; that is, working-class men who earn their living by manual labor. Hodgetts argues that there are many similarities between the Pakeha (European New Zealander) and Maori (indigenous Polynesian New Zealander) men in the way that they interact with the media images to construct their own sense of self. Contrary to the "Marlboro Man" lone-wolf image, much of this sense of self is defined relationally, in terms of the men's roles as partner, parent, and friend.

Effects of Gender Stereotyping

Although it is relatively easy to critique gender role portrayals in media, empirically demonstrating their effects is a far more difficult research problem. Nevertheless, Oppliger (2007) concludes in a meta-analysis that increasing exposure to gender stereotyping in media is followed by increasing sex-typed behavior and stereotypical gender-role attitudes. Negative or narrow gender images become a serious concern if they are seen as representative of real life. Although no single exposure to a sexist commercial is likely to irreparably harm anyone, the huge number of commercials we see (100,000 or more ads by the time we graduate from high school, see Chapter 5) is likely to have an effect, given what we have learned from cultivation and modeling research. In general, effects of repetition are often underestimated; if the same themes about how men and women are supposed to look, behave, and think keep recurring on show after show and in ad after ad, that "reality" is more likely to be perceived as accurate. For example, women may expect men to dominate them and to be relatively insensitive, or men may expect women to be submissive to them and to be preoccupied with their appearance.

Not only may we take the media portrayals of the other sex as reality, we may take the portrayals of our own gender as cues to the ways we should look and behave. When we fail to meet these standards, that failure sets us up to experience low self-esteem. For example, women who watch more entertainment TV have lower sexual self-concepts than women who watch less of this kind of media (Aubrey, 2007). A woman who feels frazzled meeting the demands of career, family, and homemaking may well feel very inadequate comparing herself to the media superwoman who does it all so well. Similarly, a man losing his hair or a woman losing her youthful figure may feel inadequate when using TV bodies as the standard (Myers & Biocca, 1992).

There is even empirical evidence of greater objectification of women compared to men. In one study, college students looked at upright or inverted photos of men and women in swimsuits or underwear. They later recognized the upright and inverted photos of the women equally well but found the inverted images of the men much harder. This was interpreted as reflecting the brain's perception of the men as uniquely human, whereas women were perceived objectively, without the usual human advantage of the upright orientation (Bernard, Gervais, Allen, Campomizzi, & Klein, 2012).

Such concerns are especially important when considering effects on children. Children tend to prefer to watch entertainment characters of their own gender and ethnicity (Knobloch, Callison, Chen, Fritzsche, & Zillmann, 2005). Further, children who are heavy viewers of TV also hold more traditional sex-role attitudes than children who don't watch much TV (O'Bryant & Corder-Bolz, 1978; Saito, 2007). This relationship is particularly strong when considering sitcoms and soap operas with traditional gender-role orientations (Ex, Janssens, & Korzilius, 2002). Using a cultivation argument, Kimball (1986) found that children's sex-role attitudes were less sex-typed than average in a town with no access to television but became more stereotypical after the introduction of television.

On the other hand, exposure to media models can sometimes have beneficial social effects. For example, repeated TV appearances of women in traditionally male occupations can lead to more open attitudes in preteen girls toward considering those occupations (Wroblewski & Huston, 1987). Similarly, exposure to advertising that portrays women in egalitarian fashion is followed by more accepting attitudes in young viewers (Geis, Brown, Jennings, & Porter, 1984; Jennings, Geis, & Brown, 1980).

More often the effects are not so positive, however. Botta (1999) found that media variables played a big part in adolescent girls' drive for thinness, feelings of body dissatisfaction, bulimic behaviors, and thin ideal endorsement, accounting for 15 to 33% of the variance in measures of these variables. Women exposed to TV ads portraying women as sex objects judged their own current body size as larger and men judged their current body size thinner, compared to control groups (Lavine, Sweeney, & Wagner, 1999). A similar study found that adolescent girls exposed to TV with conspicuously overweight female characters were more likely to exhibit symptoms of eating disorders (Harrison, 2000; Harrison & Cantor, 1997). College women and preadolescent girls (though not boys) watching more entertainment TV later showed more disordered eating (Bissell & Zhou, 2004; Moriarty & Harrison, 2008). However, adolescent girls given instructions supporting the use of larger-size female models in ads rated their own attractiveness and self-esteem as higher than a control group supporting supermodels (Loken & Peck, 2005).

These effects don't end with adolescence. In another study, women seeing slides of slender models with diet- and exercise-related story lines later ate less in front of female peers, while men seeing slides of muscular men ate more in front of male peers, compared to control groups seeing other images (Harrison, Taylor, & Marske, 2006). Unrealistic body portrayals may even affect our problem-solving ability. Men handling highly muscular action figures as part of a research study responded more slowly to positive emotion words on a lexical decision task than those playing with action figures that had more "normal" physiques (Barlett, Smith, & Harris, 2006).

Obviously we cannot expect any given type of portrayal of the sexes to have a uniform effect on the public. For example, McIntyre, Hosch, Harris, and Norvell (1986) found that men and women with less traditional gender-role attitudes were more sensitive to and more critical of stereotypic portrayals of women in TV commercials than were people with more traditional gender-role attitudes. Further, women with a relatively greater difference between their ideal and actual body self-perception may be affected more negatively by ads of thin women than are women with less discrepancy (Bessenoff, 2006). Likewise, dieting women may react differently to thin media images than non-dieting women (Mills, Polivy, Herman, & Tiggemann, 2002). Sometimes behaviors related in people's minds (e.g., reading women's magazines and anorexia risk behaviors) in fact have different roots (Thomsen, McCoy, Gustafson, & Williams, 2002). Parental discussion and mediation can lessen the negative effects of media body-image stereotyping (Nathanson, Wilson, McGee, & Sebastian, 2002). The perceived reality differs across individuals.

Families

Now that we have looked at the images of women and men, let us examine the images of families in media. For reviews of research on media and families, see Gunter and Svennevig (1987), Pitta (1999), and the papers in Bryant and Bryant (2001).

Family Composition and Portrayals

A content analysis of 630 U.S. network TV shows featuring families over 45 years from 1950 to 1995 showed that overall about 55% of the children were boys, and that families were almost exclusively White until the 1970s, with African Americans the only sizable ethnic minority since then. The proportion of traditional nuclear families fell from 38% to 25% of the total families from the 1950s to 1960s but has remained constant since. The numbers of extended family configurations have increased (18% to 26%), and the number of childless families has declined (24% to 12%). Interestingly, single-father families have always outnumbered single-mother families on TV, but the reverse is true in real life (Robinson & Skill, 2001). Divorced major characters did not appear on U.S. TV until the debut in 1975 of *One Day at a Time*, featuring a divorced mother and her two teenage daughters, although divorced adults have been fairly common on TV since that time (see Close-Up 4.3 for a discussion of an early "reality TV" depiction of divorce).

Close-Up 4.3: TV's First "Reality" Family

An interesting portrayal of American family life that reflected its times was the 1973 documentary series *An American Family*. Airing in 12 one-hour episodes, the PBS show tracked the upper-middle-class Loud family of Santa Barbara, CA.

The series was groundbreaking in many ways, most notably because the Louds allowed a film crew to record nearly every aspect of their lives for seven months, years before reality shows like *Cops*, *The Real World*, and *Survivor* first started to become popular. At the time, even noted cultural anthropologist Margaret Mead wrote that the docu-series was, "as new and significant as the invention of drama or the novel—a new way in which people can learn to look at life, by seeing the real life of others interpreted on camera" (Mead, 1973, p. 21).

Drawing relatively good ratings for the fledgling PBS network, *An American Family* also dispelled many wholesome myths of family life common in sunny sitcoms of the day like *The Brady Bunch* and *The Partridge Family*. For example, viewers watched gay adult son Lance openly discuss his life with his parents, even taking his mother Pat to a New York drag show in one episode. Perhaps the most compelling aspect of the show, however, was when Pat asked her husband Bill to move out of the house after having had enough of his alleged adultery. In later episodes, viewers saw Bill move into an apartment and the family try to make sense of separation and divorce. Fans of the show said it was an unblinkingly accurate depiction of what many families were experiencing, particularly in those turbulent times. Some critics argued that it was sensationalistic and exploitative. Interestingly, after the series aired, the Louds (like some of their later reality show counterparts) said that the show had been edited primarily to highlight the negative aspects of their lives (Ruoff, 2002).

How are families portrayed on television? Family interaction patterns tend to show more harmonious conflict-resolution behaviors in traditional (i.e., mother-father-children) than in nontraditional families (Skill, Wallace, & Cassata, 1990). Working-class families are far rarer on TV than upper-middle-class families, and they show more distressed and less happy relationships than the middle and upper classes do (Douglas, 2001). Sibling relationships are positive overall, though less deep and meaningful than in real life (Larson, 2001a). On a positive note, one study indicated that the psychological health of TV families in the 1990s was rated quite high in the categories of cohesion, adaptation, and communication skills, suggesting some positive role modeling (Bryant, Aust, Bryant, & Venugopalan, 2001).

In recent decades, most often both parents in TV families have had careers outside of the home, or one parent brings his or her career into the home. However, a major departure from reality is the way that modern TV families appear to manage career and family demands so successfully and effortlessly; indeed, the difficulties inherent in managing two-career families are glossed over, if not totally ignored (Heintz-Knowles, 2001). There are few appearances of child-care providers or day care on television, and more often than not one of the employed parents works at home and is completely available to the children. The spheres of home and career on TV are presented as separate domains which seldom intersect, providing a "misrepresentation of the lives of most American adults [that] can send a powerful message to viewers struggling with these collisions, and to their employers and colleagues" (Heintz-Knowles, 2001, p. 197).

These kinds of content analyses show that TV family portrayals present a fairly positive picture overall. Family members are most likely to be of traditional gender-role orientation, and children tend to be very precocious. Interactions among family members are most often cooperative and helpful. Where conflict exists, most often between siblings, it is generally handled positively and resolved by the end of the half-hour episode. The use of power in families is usually reasonable, with mutual concern and respect as predominant values. Family happiness is not related to financial status, with family unity being stronger for middle-class than for wealthy families (Comstock & Strzyzewski, 1990; M. S. Larson, 1989, 2001a; J. D. Robinson & Skill, 2001; Skill, Robinson, & Wallace, 1987). Even in the context of traditional families, some of the patterns of interaction have greatly changed from the more authoritarian days of the 1950s. Parents and children on TV these days are much more likely to talk out differences, often complete with yelling and immature behavior on both sides.

Perhaps the most pervasive family image in media is that of family solidarity (loyalty, support, and love for one's family). This is most clearly seen in the family sitcom. The basic message here, as true for *The Simpsons, Modern Family*, or *Family Guy* in the 21st century as it was for *Leave It to Beaver* decades earlier, is that one's family is more important than money, power, greed, status, or career advancement. Even the most irreverent family shows teach a family cohesiveness that tends in the final analysis to strongly affirm traditional values; for example, when Homer Simpson lost his job, the whole family pitched in to help save money (see A. S. Brown & Logan, 2005, for an interesting set of readings on the psychology in *The Simpsons*).

One may ask if such family solidarity is a realistic reflection of our society. It clearly is for many families and just as clearly is not for many others, whose troubled family dynamics would more typically be characterized by vicious backstabbing, betrayal, and generally putting oneself above other family members. Still, even those families might agree that the family solidarity characterization is a worthy ideal to hold up as a model, even if it is not totally realistic. Maybe this is a socially helpful model to portray and can help offer some useful new cognitive scripts to viewers in dysfunctional families. It may be particularly helpful in showing positive relations with extended families and nontraditional families, such as the positive interaction of a gay couple and their children with traditional extended family on *Modern Family*.

Such solidarity may occur in groups other than biological families. Television shows which feature a group of friends (e.g., *Cheers*, *Friends*, *Seinfeld*, *How I Met Your Mother*, *Sex in the City*) basically uphold the friend group as the de facto family unit. Typically, the loyalty to this social family is even stronger than to one's biological family, which the featured group has apparently replaced. Another common setting for both sitcoms and dramatic shows is the workplace, which essentially becomes a surrogate family (e.g., *The Mary Tyler Moore Show*, *Grey's Anatomy*, *The Office*, *30 Rock*, *Scrubs*, *Parks and Recreation*). The strong message in these shows is always love your coworkers (even if you really don't) and put their needs above your own. This, far more than traditional family solidarity, is more tenuously tied to reality.

One aspect of workplace solidarity is probably a direct consequence of the TV series format. This is the way that characters are so intimately involved in the personal lives of fellow workers, employers, and employees. Although real-life coworkers may sometimes be close friends, such intimacy is not typical, and it is almost unheard of in the real world for all of the workers in a unit to be close personal friends. Yet this is typical in television land. For example, when one character delivers her baby, the entire crew from the office may be on hand for the delivery. In real life this would not only be unlikely, but probably obtrusively inappropriate and unappreciated, even if for some reason it did occur.

Perhaps even more of a deviation from reality is the way that this workplace solidarity is extended to the clients of a professional. For example, one of the doctors on *ER* or *Grey's Anatomy* might spend her day off finding a lost family member of a patient or smoothing out a domestic quarrel that she believed was interfering with the recovery of the patient. In real life, physicians seldom do this sort of thing and might be considered derelict in their duty at the hospital if they did. Still, such an image of a professional is appealing because that is what we want to think our doctor would be like.

Even if I have never been a patient in a hospital, it comforts me to feel that a doctor I might have would be as caring as the doctors on *Grey's Anatomy*.

One important genre of apparent exceptions to this pro-family theme is soap operas, and similar movies and miniseries. The mean-spirited and self-serving backstabbing between dysfunctional family members would seem to be as opposite as can be from family solidarity; see Pingree and Thompson (1990) for a discussion of the nature of the family in daytime soaps and Liebes and Livingstone (1992) for a comparison of British and U.S. soap operas.

The Influence of Media on Family Life

Do media enhance or detract from the quality of family life? The conventional wisdom is that media have a negative influence, but that conclusion is by no means certain or simple. In some instances, family TV viewing can be a positive time of family discussion and interaction, including commenting on the programs or laughing and crying together. In other instances, it can be very negative; for example, if it induces conflict among family members over what program to watch or whether to turn off the set. Particular quarrels can occur around certain events like meals, bedtimes, or children's disagreement with parental prohibitions of certain programs.

A uses and gratifications approach to studying family TV use looks at motivations for watching, which may vary greatly depending on the program or the individuals' moods. For example, Kubey (1986) found that divorced and separated people watch TV more when they feel down and alone than married or other single people do, perhaps due to their use of TV for solace and comfort to replace a lost relationship. Men and women may view television watching differently. For example, men and boys are more likely to control the remote and channel surf; this behavior is often the source of TV-based marital conflict (Gantz, 2001; Walker & Bellamy, 2001). The gender difference is stronger with older than younger couples, although younger people do more channel surfing in general. In terms of uses and gratifications, women see TV viewing as more of a social activity and are also more likely to be doing other activities (e.g., housework) concurrently, whereas men are more likely to devote full attention to the program. Men see TV-watching as "earned recreation," whereas women see it as a "guilty pleasure," a distraction from homemaking duties (Morley, 1988).

Now that we have looked at media's view of the sexes and families, let us turn to ethnic minorities, starting with a developmental model of the portrayals of minorities in media.

The Four Stages of Minority Portrayals

A useful model presented many years ago by Clark (1969) identified four chronological stages of the portrayals of minorities on television, although the model can easily be extended to all media. The first stage is *non-recognition*, in which the minority group is simply excluded. It is not ridiculed; it is not caricatured; it is simply not present. Someone from an alien culture watching the media would never know that such people even existed in that society. For example, many early films and TV shows had no African American characters at all, even when it might have been logical for them to be present (one wonders, for instance, why there were no Blacks in the Southern town of Mayberry on the *Andy Griffith Show*). Until fairly recently, non-recognition was also largely the position of gay and lesbian people in U.S. media.

The second stage of minority portrayals is *ridicule*. Here the dominant group bolsters its own self-image by putting down and stereotyping the minority, presenting its members as incompetent, unintelligent buffoons. Very early television programs like *Amos 'n' Andy* and movie characters like Stepin Fetchit or Jack Benny's TV valet Rochester reflect this stage in terms of portrayals of African Americans. In current media, Arabs are a good example of a group at the stage of ridicule; we seldom see positive or likable Arab or Arab-American characters in U.S. TV or film.

A third stage is *regulation*, in which minority group members appear as protectors of the existing order (e.g., police officers, detectives, spies). Such roles were typical of the first positive roles open to African Americans in the 1960s; one often sees Latino/as in the same types of roles today.

The final stage is *respect*. Here, the minority group appears in the same full range of roles, both good and bad, that the majority does. This is not to say that there is never a stereotyped character or that all the characters are sympathetic, but just that there is a wide variety: good and intelligent characters as well as evil and stupid ones.

Now let's turn to looking specifically at the media's portrayal of several particular ethnic minorities, starting with African Americans, the minority receiving the most public attention and scientific study for the longest time.

African Americans

Probably the most-studied ethnic group portrayal anywhere has been the U.S. media image of African Americans. Although they comprised about 12–13% of the U.S. population in the 2010 census, until the 1960s there were very few African Americans in mainstream U.S. advertising (Colfax & Steinberg, 1972; Kassarjian, 1969; see also Close-Up 4.4).

How Are African Americans Portrayed?

The percentage of African Americans among people in ads (across all media) rose from .57% in 1949 to 16% in TV advertising by 1986 (Zinkhan, Qualls, & Biswas, 1990). The only African Americans on prime-time TV programming in the early days were limited to a few stereotyped and demeaning roles, such as the reliable maid *Beulah* and the affable but dim-witted African

Close-Up 4.4: Historical View of African Americans in Advertising

African Americans have been a part of advertising in America as far back as ads for the sale of slaves or return of runaways (Kern-Foxworth, 1994). In the late 19th and early 20th centuries, Blacks became common in advertising targeted at European Americans, which in this era included all advertising except that in specifically Black publications. Often the portrayals were pictorially demeaning (huge lips, bulging eyes, cannibals, mammy figures like Aunt Jemima) and verbally insulting (with brand names like Nigger Head canned vegetables and stove polish). Many of these figures thankfully disappeared quietly, but some of these symbols evolved in interesting ways. For example, Aunt Jemima was first developed in 1889 by Charles Rutt, with his introduction of the first ready-mixed pancake flour. In the early years, Aunt Jemima in ads (and in her personal appearances, as played by various actresses) was right off the antebellum plantation, with her characteristic headdress, uneducated speech style, and subservient behavior. Aunt Jemima gradually became less slavelike over the next 80 years, though the greatest change came in 1968, when she wore more of a headband than a slave bandanna and also appeared younger and more intelligent. Only in 1989, in her 100th year, did Aunt Jemima lose the headgear altogether (Kern-Foxworth, 1994). There has been a similar (although less pronounced) evolution of the African American Uncle Ben (Rice) and Rastus (Cream of Wheat) characters.

American friends on *Amos 'n' Andy* (see Close-Up 4.5 for a discussion of the *Amos 'n' Andy* show).

In the United States, media reflected this prejudiced viewpoint before radio or television ever appeared. One of the earliest movies was *Uncle Tom's Cabin* in 1903. Based on a well-known book, it featured highly stereotyped African American characters. The groundbreaking but intensely controversial 1915 Civil War epic film *Birth of a Nation* presented the Ku Klux Klan as heroic saviors of the Reconstruction Era. Such treatment persisted in films for many years (Bogle, 1973). In 1942 the NAACP convinced the Hollywood studio bosses to abandon the characteristic negative roles for African Americans and to try to integrate them into a variety of roles; this agreement did not produce overnight results, but change did come eventually.

The civil rights movement of the 1960s ushered in significant changes in media (Berry, 1980). African American models began to be used in advertising, with none of the feared offense taken by Whites (Block, 1972; Soley, 1983). African Americans also appeared for the first time in leading

Close-Up 4.5: The *Amos 'n' Andy* Phenomenon

The history of the show *Amos 'n' Andy* in many ways parallels the history of White social attitudes toward African Americans in the early to mid-20th century, being "partly a tale of White obtuseness" (Ely, 2001, p. xiv). Starting off as a radio show in the 1920s, *Amos 'n' Andy* employed two White actors using their interpretations of Black English to portray the title characters. The show became wildly popular on the radio, with reports of listeners speeding to get home and refusing to go to movies until after the program had ended. There was even one account of prisoners rioting when a warden refused to let them listen to the show (Shankman, 1978). As further evidence of this popularity, there were also Amos 'n' Andy candy bars, greeting cards, toys, and records (Ely, 2001).

Movie producers tried to translate the radio success of *Amos 'n' Andy* to film in 1930 with the movie *Check and Double Check*, using the White radio actors as Amos and Andy in blackface (Shankman, 1978). With the advent of television, CBS decided to create an *Amos 'n' Andy* TV show in 1951. This time, however, Black actors were cast in the roles.

As might be expected, *Amos 'n' Andy* was controversial in the African American community. Although many Black listeners of the early radio show were happy to hear *some* portrayal of African Americans, it was disheartening to many. One editor of a Black newspaper lamented that "the men playing the characters are White. The company employing *Amos 'n' Andy* is White. The people reaping the financial gain from the characterizations are all White" (Shankman, 1978, p. 239). The TV show was also disappointing to many, with the NAACP pressuring sponsors to withdraw support. Although it received fairly high ratings (and even an Emmy nomination in 1952), the show was canceled by CBS after two seasons, due (at least partially) to the controversy (Ely, 2001). Although some tried to forget that a show such as *Amos 'n' Andy* ever existed, the story behind it provides an interesting cultural history of early portrayals of African Americans in electronic media. See Ely (2001) for a very thoughtful and thorough examination of the show.

roles in prime-time TV during this era, most notably in *I Spy* with Bill Cosby, and *Julia*, the first African American family sitcom. In addition, there were African Americans as part of the starring ensemble on 1960s drama programs like *Mission Impossible*, *Peyton Place*, and *Mod Squad*. Although these were generally positive portrayals, many such shows have been criticized as having been out of touch with the civil rights struggles of those times. It is interesting to note, for example, that the title character in *Julia* was a widowed, single mother who worked for a White employer, had predominately White neighbors, and seemed to have only White friends (Miller & Pearlstein, 2004).

In the 1970s and 1980s, there were usually some African American characters on TV, although they tended to be heavily concentrated in sitcoms and were largely absent from daytime soap operas and children's programming. Some of these characters were more well-rounded than early TV African Americans but still retained some stereotypical characteristics, such as the buffoonery and posturing of J. J. on *Good Times*, George Jefferson on *The Jeffersons*, and Fred Sanford on *Sanford and Son*. In the 1970s, about 8% of prime-time TV characters were African American (Gerbner & Signorielli, 1979; Seggar, Hafen, & Hannonen-Gladden, 1981; Weigel, Loomis, & Soja, 1980), with less than 3% in daytime soaps (Greenberg, Neuendorf, Buerkel-Rothfuss, & Henderson, 1982).

A landmark event occurred with the phenomenal commercial success of the 1977 TV miniseries *Roots*, based on Alex Haley's multigenerational saga of his ancestors' forced journey from West Africa into American slavery and their later emancipation. Although widely praised for both its artistic and entertainment value, *Roots* was also controversial. Some called it biased for presenting few sympathetic European American characters, whereas others took it to task for transforming the horrors of slavery into an epic triumph of the American dream (Riggs, 1992). Nevertheless, *Roots* is considered by many to be monumental, in that it was one of the first times that age-old race issues were confronted in an approachable yet powerful prime-time TV dramatization (Miller & Pearlstein, 2004).

The current media situation is vastly improved from the *Amos 'n' Andy* days, though some argue that there are still subtle indicators of racism on television (Greenberg, Mastro, & Brand, 2002; Taylor, Lee, & Stern, 1995). African Americans are still underrepresented in most TV genres except sitcoms and are largely absent in high-level creative and network administrative positions (Miller & Pearlstein, 2004). Although the phenomenal success of *The Cosby Show* (1984–1992) presumably laid to rest any commercial concerns about Whites not watching "Black" shows, that show's relevance to the experience of the large majority of less affluent African Americans was hotly debated. Cliff Huxtable and his family were clearly positive role models, but they also enjoyed a lifestyle that was beyond the reach of most African American families (and, for that matter, most of the rest of the population as well). By 2011, TV shows with predominately African American casts were largely absent from U.S. broadcast networks, although such shows were increasingly common on cable networks such as BET (with shows like *The Game*) and TBS (*House of Payne*) (Armstrong, 2011).

American advertising's portrayals of African Americans has a long history. Although we seldom, if ever, see the racist ads or programming from the pre-civil rights era, some blatantly racist cartoons from as far back as the 1940s are still available in video anthologies; some villains have dark skin, big lips, and even exhibit cannibalistic behaviors. Barcus (1983) found cartoons to be the most ethnically stereotyped of all television genres. More recently, video game villains have tended to be darker skinned than the heroes (Carlsson-Paige, 2008).

There are still some biases in news coverage related to Blacks (Entman, 1990, 1992, 1994a, 1994b; Heider, 2000). For example, Romer, Jamieson, and DeCoteau (1998) examined 14 weeks of local TV news on three stations in Philadelphia in 1994. They found that people of color (most often African Americans) were disproportionately represented in stories about crime and were more likely to be presented as perpetrators than as victims, relative to the actual demographics from local crime statistics. This finding was generally replicated in a study of Los Angeles and Orange County, California local news by Dixon and Linz (2000) and in a study of *Columbus*, Ohio's newspapers (Lundman, Douglass, & Hanson, 2004).

Black Viewers

African Americans of all ages watch more television than Whites, even when controlling for socioeconomic status (Graves, 1996; Kern-Foxworth, 1994). They especially watch more sports, action-adventure shows, and news. African Americans also tend to watch shows with Black characters and Black-oriented networks like BET in relatively greater numbers than White Americans (Goldberg, 2002). However, there is no evidence that other groups avoid such shows because of the African American characters (Comstock, Chaffee, Katzman, McCombs, & Roberts, 1978; Graves, 1980), even though children of all races tend to identify more with characters of their own race (Eastman & Liss, 1980; Greenberg & Atkin, 1982). Overall, African American children prefer sitcoms, whereas White American children prefer action-adventure shows. Compared to light TV viewers, heavy viewers believe that African Americans and European Americans are more similar overall, African Americans are more middle class, and racial integration is more widespread (Matabane, 1988). This may be interpreted in terms of cultivation theory to suggest that television mainstreams viewers into the optimistic view that African Americans have "made it" and that segregation and racism are no more.

Effects of African American Portrayals

One focus of research has been on the comparative effects of African American TV portrayals on both White and Black Americans (for reviews, see Graves, 1980; Greenberg, Mastro, & Brand, 2002). Like everyone else, African Americans are more likely to identify with and emulate characters who exhibit personal warmth, high status, and power. Often these models have been White, yet African Americans will readily identify with media Blacks as role models, especially with the more positive ones (Ball & Bogatz, 1970, 1973; Jhally & Lewis, 1992). This can boost children's self-esteem, especially with regular viewing and when accompanied by appropriate parental communication and explanation (Atkin, Greenberg, & McDermott, 1983; McDermott & Greenberg, 1985). Sympathetic characters like the Huxtable children on *The Cosby Show* or the African American teens on *Sister Sister* and *That's So Raven* thus become potentially very important models for young African Americans. Studies of White children have shown that prolonged exposure to television comedies or *Sesame Street* with regular African American and Latino/a cast members influences the attitudes of White kids in a more accepting, less racist direction (Bogatz & Ball, 1971; Gorn, Goldberg, & Kanungo, 1976).

Although everyone identifies more with characters who are perceived to be like themselves on whatever relevant dimensions (*identification theory*), being a member of a minority group makes certain attributes more salient (*distinctiveness theory*). Thus, one's race is a larger part of one's identity for a person of color in a largely White society than it is for the majority. Similarly, being left-handed, gay, red-headed, or six-foot-six is more salient than being right-handed, heterosexual, brown-haired, or five-foot-nine. In one study, Black viewers recalled Black characters better than White characters, while White viewers showed no difference in their recall of White and Black characters (Appiah, 2002).

Even a very positive portrayal developed with the best intentions may contribute to misconceptions, however. For example, some White viewers of *The Cosby Show* cited the Huxtable family as examples of why affirmative action was no longer necessary (Jhally & Lewis, 1992). If the affluent Huxtables have attained their share of the American dream and they are assumed to be representative of African Americans, then those who haven't made it must not be trying very hard. Consistent with cultivation theory, White heavy viewers of entertainment TV believed that African Americans were relatively well off socioeconomically, although those who were heavy viewers of TV news believed African Americans to be relatively worse off economically (Armstrong, Neuendorf, & Brentar, 1992), suggesting different images of African Americans in news and entertainment television.

Several studies have confirmed a link between Whites watching stereotyped images of African Americans, especially as associated with crime, and later showing more negative attitudes toward affirmative action and welfare programs (Fujioka, 1999, 2005b; Tan, Fujioka, & Tan, 2000; Valentino, 1999). Exposure to a particular African American stereotype like a "mammy" or a "jezebel" primed later implicit prejudice responses toward an African American woman (Givens & Monahan, 2005).

Sometimes TV can unexpectedly reinforce preexisting stereotypes. For example, more traditional White viewers tended to identify with the bigoted Archie Bunker of the 1970s sitcom *All in the Family* and accept his racist views, although less prejudiced people decried these views and found Archie's attitudes offensive or laughable (Tate & Surlin, 1976; Vidmar & Rokeach, 1974). The same inconsistent reactions were found with viewers of the Indian TV feminist drama *Hum Log* (W. J. Brown & Cody, 1991).

In contrast to this picture of considerable progress in the portrayal of African Americans, the media image of another American minority of similar size is far less hopeful.

Latino/as

Although Hispanics, or Latino/as, are growing very rapidly in numbers in the United States (15–17% of the population in the U.S. by 2010, collectively surpassing African Americans in number), they comprise only 5% of characters on prime-time TV (Mastro & Behm-Morawitz, 2005; Mastro & Greenberg, 2000; Monk-Turner, Heiserman, Johnson, Cotton, & Jackson, 2010; see Table 4.1). Hispanics are, in fact, several very diverse groups of Americans with ethnic origins in Cuba, Puerto Rico, Dominican Republic, Mexico, Central America, South America, or Spain. Latino/as are racially and culturally diverse. Although many Cubans, Puerto Ricans, and Dominicans have some African ancestry, most Mexican Americans are mestizos (mixed White and Indian/Native American) and seldom have African ancestry. Many Hispanic New Mexicans are of purely Spanish descent, whereas some recent Guatemalan refugees are pure indigenous peoples who speak Spanish as a second language, if at all.

The North American histories of various Latino/a groups are also very different. Although Spaniards have lived in New Mexico since before the Puritans settled in Massachusetts, some Mexicans and Central Americans are very recent immigrants. They are economically diverse, ranging from wealthy Cuban Americans in South Florida or Spanish New Mexicans in Albuquerque and Santa Fe, to the poor immigrant underclass of southern California and Texas. Latino/as are also politically diverse, from the staunchly Republican and conservative Cuban Americans in Florida to the politically liberal Mexican Americans flexing their voting muscles in Texas and California. Since 2000, the greatest relative increases in Latino/a numbers in the United

Table 4.1 Ethnic Group Members in U.S. Population and on Prime-Time TV in 2009–2010 (Humes, Jones, & Ramirez, 2011; Monk-Turner et al., 2010)

Racial/Ethnic Group	% U.S. Population 2010	% Prime-time TV Characters 2009
African American	12.6	16.0
Asian	4.8	<2.0
Caucasian	63.7	74.0
Latino	16.3	5.0

States have come in places which have historically been home to few of them, such as Rhode Island, Iowa, and North Carolina.

In spite of their growing importance in the United States, there are several pervasive stereotypes of Latino/as in the media (Greenberg et al., 2002; Ramirez Berg, 1990, 2002; Rivadeneyra, Ward, & Gordon, 2007). Portrayals and characters tend to be disproportionately lower class, criminal, inarticulate, and poor. The greasy, dirty Mexican bandit stereotype of the Westerns of the early to mid-20th century has been updated as the drug runner of more recent movies. Variations of the bandit appeared in advertising, with the heavily accented Frito bandito of the 1970s or the Taco Bell chihuahua of the 1990s. Other stereotypes include the harlot, the loose woman interested only in sex, and the buffoon or clown, such as Ricky Ricardo of *I Love Lucy* or Rosario of *Will and Grace*. Another stereotype is the sensual and musical but slightly laughable Latin lover of early films (1920–1945). On American television, characters who were criminals were one and a half times more likely to be Hispanic than European American. There have also been few Latino/a characters appearing on Saturday morning kids' television (Subervi-Velez & Colsant, 1993). Latino/as were overrepresented in the criminal justice system on TV, as both police officers and criminals (Dixon & Linz, 2000; Mastro & Greenberg, 2000; Mastro & Behm-Morawitz, 2005).

As early as the 1980s, there were a few signs that movie studios and the TV networks were beginning to discover the largely untapped Latino/a market (Ramirez Berg, 2002). Spanish cable channels offered popular options to Spanish-speaking populations. In the mid-1980s, the unexpected commercial success of films like *La Bamba* and *Born in East L.A.* inside and outside of Latino/a communities allowed several new Hispanic films to be released shortly thereafter, but this trend did not continue. Even the modest success of the *Spy Kids* trilogy of the early 2000s, a series of sort of James Bond movies for kids in which the hero family just happens to be Latino/a, failed to give much boost to Latino/a movie fortunes.

U.S. television has been an even more dismal story. Following the commercial failure of several very short-lived Latino/a-oriented sitcoms in the 1970s and 1980s, the networks appeared to be wary about more such shows. Some shows have achieved limited success (e.g., *George Lopez*), but a Latino/a *Cosby Show* has remained elusive. There are some signs of hope, as in the Nickelodeon bilingual preschool show *Dora the Explorer* (and a spin-off, *Go, Diego, Go!*), which has become very popular and profitable. There have also been several Latino/a breakout TV stars such as Mario Lopez (*Saved by the Bell*), Wilmer Valderrama (*That '70s Show*), America Ferrera (*Ugly Betty*), and Sofia Vergara (*Modern Family*).

Still, overall, Latino/as in media are at a point somewhat similar to that of African Americans of 50 or 60 years ago—largely invisible or in negative or regulatory roles when they do occur. There are also documented negative effects of the stereotyped portrayals (Mastro, Behm-Morawitz, &

Kopacz, 2008). Heavy TV viewers see Latino/as as more criminal-like and less intelligent and hardworking than do light TV viewers (Mastro, Behm-Morawitz, & Ortiz, 2007). Heavy TV-viewing Latino/a adolescents show lower self-esteem than their light viewing peers (Rivadeneyra et al., 2007), thus supporting a cultivation effect. Greenberg and Brand (1994) attributed this at least in part to the low level of minority employment in the broadcast industry, due not necessarily to overt discrimination but more often to the low entry-level salaries that are not attractive enough to the relatively few qualified Latino/as, who may have multiple job opportunities. Because decision makers and those at management level are mostly Anglo, it is their world that tends to appear on television.

Native Americans

Arguably the most mistreated group in the history of North America, Native Americans were the object of extermination campaigns in the 18th and 19th centuries. Today their surviving descendants collectively comprise less than 1% of the U.S. population, with a large proportion living below the official poverty line. Stereotyped negative images have been pervasive in both news and entertainment media throughout U.S. history (Bird, 1996, 1999; Merskin, 1998; Weston, 1996).

By far the best-known image is the bloodthirsty and savage Indian of old movies and early television. Westerns were one of the most popular genres of television and movies through the early 1960s. Indians were usually depicted as vicious killers or, at their very best, as lovable but dim-witted sidekicks to White men, such as *The Lone Ranger*'s Tonto (Morris, 1982). Some of the stereotypical behaviors may actually have come from other groups; for example, some argue that historically "scalping" was performed by European Americans on Native Americans before Native Americans ever began the practice. Later, slightly more serious portrayals of Indian men were most often the "doomed warrior" or "wise elder" characters (Bird, 1999). For the most part, when Westerns declined in popularity, Native Americans disappeared from the screen altogether. When Mastro and Greenberg (2000) did their content analysis of the 1996–1997 prime-time TV season, they found no examples of Native-American characters at all! At best, there have been only very occasional supporting characters, such as those in shows like *Northern Exposure* and *Dr. Quinn, Medicine Woman*.

Although there are over 500 officially recognized Native American tribes today, those who have appeared in the media (usually in Westerns) have almost always been Plains Indians, and behaviors like living in teepees and hunting bison came to be identified with all Native Americans, although they were no more characteristic of the northeastern Iroquois, southwestern Navahos, or northwestern Tlingits than they were of the English or Africans. The overemphasis on Plains Indian peoples was still seen in a few 1990s films like *Dances with Wolves* (1990), *Thunderheart* (1992), and *Geronimo* (1993). Women seldom appeared, and when they did, they tended to be passive and rather dull background figures. The powerful women in matriarchal societies like the Navaho and Mohawk have never been seen on TV or film. Most media Indians are seen in the historical setting of Westerns; the few modern characters are usually presented as militant activists, alcoholics, or casino owners. There is hardly any Native American news and what does appear is usually about land claims litigation or controversies over Indian-run casinos. Without a large national constituency, substantial change may come only from Native American film and television production (Geiogamah & Pavel, 1993), which is largely nonexistent.

To add to the misrepresentation, one of the few places that Native American ethnic identity appears in mainstream culture is in the names of school and professional sports teams that have nothing to do with their heritage. A very controversial issue in many places is the use of Native American names and themes for U.S. sports teams (e.g., Atlanta Braves, Kansas City Chiefs, Washington Redskins, Cleveland Indians). Although the most visible examples are names of professional teams, the same issue exists at a local level, where many high schools and colleges use Indian names and mascots.

Mostly named many years ago, before much consciousness of ethnic stereotyping existed, such labels probably arose to suggest the strong, fighting, even savage nature associated with the Indian image from Westerns. Now it is time, many argue, to replace these names with others that do not demean any ethnic or racial group or co-opt and cheapen its cultural symbols (Pewewardy, 1999; Springwood & King, 2001a, 2001b). The issue first received widespread attention during the 1991 baseball World Series, when fans of the Atlanta Braves had a hand motion called the "tomahawk chop" to support their team. Critics argued that the use of comparable symbols or names from any other minority group would not be tolerated; could one seriously imagine teams called the Chicago Jews, Seattle Caucasians, or the Dallas Orientals? (Although, interestingly enough, we do have teams named the Notre Dame Fighting Irish and the Minnesota Vikings.) Similarly, Native American ethnic names alone among social groups are widely used for names of products (e.g., Sioux Bee Honey, Red Man tobacco, Crazy Horse Malt Liquor, Jeep Cherokee, Winnebago motor homes).

In 2001, the U.S Commission on Civil Rights declared that Native American nicknames and mascots were "inappropriate and disrespectful" and the NCAA in 2005 asked the remaining 31 colleges and universities using such names or mascots to file a report about their use (Wills, 2005). By the early 21st century, many high school and college teams (though almost no professional teams) had changed their names or mascots, but old traditions die hard, especially among alumni. Many argue that such names and traditions are not demeaning but respectful of the native culture. Sometimes circumstances prevail to make change especially difficult. For example, when controversy arose over the University of North Dakota's "Fighting Sioux" mascot in 2000, the university's president convened a commission to study the issue and make recommendations to him. Before its work was complete, however, the school's major alumnus donor, Las Vegas casino mogul Ralph Engelstad, wrote a letter threatening to withdraw his latest $100 million gift for a luxurious hockey arena already under construction if the school dropped the Sioux mascot. Shortly after, the state Board of Higher Education issued a unanimous preemptive strike to keep the name, and the money (Brownstein, 2001). This issue was not finally settled until 2012, when, under NCAA threats of sanctions, a state referendum struck down a state law keeping the Fighting Sioux name. Traditions die very hard.

In other places, media outlets were taking stands. For example, the Portland *Oregonian* (1992), the state's largest daily, the Lincoln (Nebraska) *Journal Star* (2003), and several papers near the University of North Dakota announced they would no longer publish names or nicknames of sports teams that used racial or ethnic stereotypes. The teams would hereafter be referred to only by their city or school. Some radio stations or broadcasters in different places have similar policies. Predictably, many called the whole flap much ado about nothing, but Native Americans were almost uniformly pleased. This controversy is not going away any time soon.

The history of oppression of the native peoples is by no means unique to North America. They have been similarly marginalized in Australia, New Zealand, and European-oriented Latin American countries like Argentina, Chile, Brazil, Uruguay, and Costa Rica. An interesting exception to this pattern is Mexico, which, unlike its neighbors to the north, has always had a very large indigenous population. At the time of the Spanish conquest in 1521, the Aztec capital Tenochtitlán was one of the world's most populous cities. In spite of early, severe oppression by the Spanish conquerors, the Indian identity came to be fused with the Spanish into a unique culture that is the essence of modern Mexico. The last Aztec ruler, Cuauhtémoc, not the conquering Spaniard Cortez, is the Mexican national hero.

Asian Americans

Among the fastest growing minorities in the United States, Canada, Australia, and New Zealand in recent decades are Asians (Wu, 2002), although in the United States their immigration history goes back to the large numbers of Chinese brought over to build the railroads in the American West in the 1800s. Many Japanese emigrated to the United States, as well as to Brazil and elsewhere, in large numbers in the early 20th century. Asian emigration in large numbers to Australia and New Zealand has only occurred since around 1970. Koreans and Filipinos came to America, often as spouses of U.S. military personnel formerly stationed abroad. Vietnamese and other Southeast Asians came in large numbers as refugees following the end of the Vietnam

War in 1975. There is also a substantial number of South Asian Americans, from India, Pakistan, Bangladesh, Sri Lanka, and Afghanistan, as well as large numbers of Iranian refugees who came to the West following the 1979 Islamic revolution.

As with Native Americans, there is a long history of media stereotyping of Asians in movies, such as the Fu Manchu and Charlie Chan characters, often played, incidentally, by White actors (Iiyama & Kitano, 1982). On television there have been few Asian Americans. The 1970s *Kung Fu* series had the Asian lead played by White David Carradine. Interestingly, Chinese American actor Bruce Lee was turned down for the same role (Miller & Pearlstein, 2004). The 1970s and 1980s saw some improvement, with the addition of some minor Asian American characters in shows like *Hawaii Five-O* and M*A*S*H, although they were often villains or in stereotyped occupations like Chinese running a laundry or restaurant (Mok, 1998).

Often the villains of choice on entertainment TV follow news events. After the 1989 Tiananmen Square massacre, Chinese officials from the People's Republic of China (PRC) were frequent villains on action-adventure shows. During waves of U.S. concern about Japanese commercial power and ascendancy in the 1980s, Japanese businessmen were portrayed as buying up America in a sort of "yellow scare." Newspaper stories about Asian immigration featured headlines like "Asian Invasion" or "Containing Japan" (Funabiki, 1992). Parallels were drawn between Japanese economic power and the nation's earlier World War II militarism. As with African Americans, some very nasty old stereotypes live on in children's cartoons in video anthologies. For example, only in 1995 did MGM-UA Home Video pull a 1944 World War II–era Bugs Bunny cartoon in which Bugs hands out bombs concealed in ice cream cones to a crowd of Japanese people as he says, "Here you go Bowlegs, here you go Monkey-Face, here you go, Slant Eyes, everybody gets one." Prior to the withdrawal, about 800 copies had been sold in the 1990s ("What's Up, Doc?" 1995)!

Nevertheless, overall, Asian Americans are probably portrayed more positively than most other minorities in U.S. media. In fact, there is one positive stereotype that is increasingly troubling to some Asian Americans: the model minority image of the group that succeeds academically, commercially, and socially (S. J. Lee, 1996). Taylor and Stern (1997) found Asian Americans to actually be overrepresented in TV commercials relative to their proportion in the population, but they were usually in business settings, rather than home or social relationships. Sometimes this perceived success image is used to ignore problems that the group has or as an excuse to criticize other minorities for doing less well and thus seeming lazy.

Sometimes prejudice against different groups can interact in complex ways. For example, reading news stories about Asian Indians tended to increase hostility toward African Americans (Ramasubramanian & Oliver, 2007) or Mexican Americans (Ho, Sanbonmatsu, & Akimoto, 2002), perhaps due to valuing one group and subtly denigrating another for not being able to "make it." Intergroup feelings can sometimes be strained. For example, in the 1992 Los Angeles race riots, some of the major targets of angry African American looters and arsonists were Korean-American businesses. The high academic success of Asian Americans for a while led the University of California system to set an Asian quota, a limit on the number of Asian American students that could be admitted; critics argued unfairness, as no other group had such a quota.

Arabs and Arab Americans

A much smaller American minority offers a look at a stereotype that is currently among the most unsympathetic and derogatory portrayals on U.S. media. As of 2007, there were an estimated 3 million Arab Americans. Stereotyping of this group, as well as Arabs in the Middle East and elsewhere, is widely seen in both news coverage (Suleiman, 1988) and entertainment (Shaheen, 1984, 2001, 2008). There seems to be an implicit identification of Arabs with the Islamic religion, although Muslim Arabs worldwide represent only 20% of all the world's Muslims, who collectively represent about one-fifth of the planet's population (Shaheen, 2008). As for Arab Americans, a vast majority of them are Christian. In addition, Islam as a religion is often portrayed as cruel and vicious, in total contrast to the Judeo-Christian faith and civilization. Because most North Americans know very little about Islam except media reports of its extremist fringe, this may easily become their perceived reality about one of the world's major religions. Although many Americans have sufficient knowledge to recognize a Christian cult extremist on TV as very atypical of Christians, they may not have the necessary knowledge to similarly critically evaluate a media presentation of an Islamic suicide bomber, who is thus taken to be a typical Muslim.

According to Shaheen (2008), there have been over 1,150 films that denigrate or stereotype Arabs and only 29 (all post-2001) which present any positive image. Over the years, there have been several stereotypic ways that Arab men are portrayed, all very negative. One is as the terrorist. Although only a minuscule fraction of real Arabs are terrorists, there are many of these on television, especially since September 2001. A second stereotype of Arab men is the wealthy oil sheik, who is often greedy and morally dissolute. His wealth, often suggested as being undeserved, is spent on frivolities like marble palaces, fleets of Rolls Royce cars, and garishly kitschy homes in Beverly Hills. A third stereotype is that of a sexual pervert, often portrayed as selling Europeans or Americans into slavery. This is an older stereotype, perhaps originally arising from medieval Christian Europe's enmity against the Muslim "infidels," who were, incidentally, primarily non-Arab Turks. Although probably less prevalent than the terrorist or oil sheik portrayal today, this image does appear occasionally. A fourth stereotype is the Bedouin desert rat, the unkempt ascetic wanderer far overrepresented on TV and in advertising, in relation to the approximately 5% of Arabs who are Bedouins. Visual images and jokes about camels, sand, and tents are frequent in connection with U.S.-media Arabs.

Arab men are generally seen as villains, a stereotype especially rampant in children's cartoons (e.g., Daffy Duck being chased by a crazed, sword-wielding Arab sheik or Heckle and Jeckle pulling the rug from under "Ali Boo-Boo, the Desert Rat"). More significantly, portrayals of these barbaric and uncultured villains are not usually balanced by those of Arab heroes or good guys. One of the very few positive media models was probably Lebanese American Corporal Max Klinger on M*A*S*H. He was a sympathetic and rounded character, yet (especially in early episodes) he dressed in drag and made comments about his relatives having unnatural relations with camels. A more recent cable reality series, The Shahs of Sunset, profiled wealthy Iranian Americans living in Southern California. Some reviews said the show presented the castmates as likeable, but being a reality series it also portrayed them at times as vain and shallow.

How about Arab women? They are seen far less often than Arab men on U.S. TV and in U.S. movies, but, when they are seen at all, it is usually as oppressed victims or in highly stereotyped roles such as that of a belly dancer or a member of a harem. The reality, as Shaheen points out, is that harems were never common and today are nonexistent in Arab countries. The public veiling of women is presented as the Arab norm, rather than as a characteristic of some, but not all, Islamic traditions.

Arab children are practically nonexistent on U.S. television, even though the negative adult Arab stereotypes are perhaps more prevalent in children's cartoons than on any other type of programming. Even as we routinely see African American, Latino/a, and Asian faces on programs like Sesame Street, few if any Arabs appear.

Historically, Arabs may simply be the latest villains in a long list of groups who have been maligned by the U.S. media. The vicious Arabs of contemporary entertainment were preceded by the wealthy but cruel Jews of the 1920s, the sinister Asian villains of the 1930s, and the Italian gangsters of the 1950s. Each of these stereotypes has been tempered and balanced following protests by the offended groups. Such media portrayals provide unwitting social support for racist and discriminatory policies and legislation, such as the network of Jim Crow laws and racist practices against African Americans in the century following the American Civil War.

Recent historical events have, at times, encouraged unflattering media portrayals of Arabs: the OPEC oil embargoes of the 1970s, various hostage-taking incidents, the Lebanese civil war, the Iran–Iraq War of 1980 to 1988, the Persian Gulf War of 1991, the Iraq War beginning in 2003, continuing Israeli–Palestinian conflicts, and, most dramatically, the Al-Qaeda terrorist attacks of September 11, 2001, and the ensuing "War on Terrorism." The actual and potential backlash against Arabs and Arab Americans since the 9/11 attacks stresses the urgency of better understanding this group. The concern is not that there are some negative portrayals of Arabs and Arab Americans. Rather, it is that such portrayals are not balanced by positive portrayals to feed into the perceived mental reality constructed by viewers. There is very little programming on Arab culture or society. The Arab world was more intellectually and technically advanced than Europe in the Middle Ages and gave us many of the basics of modern science, mathematics, and music, but how many Americans know that? The close family values and other positive features of the Islamic faith and Arab culture also do not receive much play in U.S. media. Sometimes we do not even realize how mainstream a strongly negative portrayal has become. For example, a 2011 TV reality show profiling real Arab-American families was forced off the air when a major sponsor pulled its advertising in response to criticism that this realistic portrayal was unfair pro-Muslim propaganda!

Immediately after the Oklahoma City bombing in April 1995, investigating authorities and the general public immediately suspected Arab terrorists, although there was no evidence of such a link. When a pair of White Americans was arrested and later convicted of the crime, there were a lot of embarrassed faces. However, the stereotypes persist on entertainment TV and in movies, and still there are almost no positive models. This is not without its consequences. For example, Arab nations argue rather convincingly that Western coverage of the Israeli–Palestinian dispute over the West Bank is severely biased toward Israel due to anti-Arab prejudice.

The concern about stereotypical portrayals of groups is not limited to gender, race, and ethnicity. Let us look at the media portrayal of a formerly invisible minority.

Sexual Minorities

Although there were some early film intimations of homosexuality, such as the effeminate "sissy" characters of some 1930s movies or the gender-ambiguous characters like those played by Marlene Dietrich (*Celluloid Closet*, 1995), the Production Code of 1930 (see Close-Up 10.1 for a further discussion) formalized the voluntary exclusion of all gay and lesbian portrayals from Hollywood films (V. Russo, 1981). Still, some negative stereotypes occurred, with just enough sexual ambiguity to elude the censors. These included lesbians as villains or prisoners and gay men as suicidal. *Victim* in Britain and *The Children's Hour* in the United States in the early 1960s were the first films with explicitly gay or lesbian heroes. *The Boys in the Band* (1970), a movie about a group of gay men, was a ground-breaker, followed two years later by the much more widely seen *Cabaret*. Several more films with gay characters followed, although the first with a major theme of a gay love affair was *Making Love* in 1982.

When television entered the picture, the code of silence regarding sexual minority characters (gay, lesbian, bisexual, and transgender individuals) was maintained, not to be broken until very occasional openings started in the 1950s and 60s (Capsuto, 2000). A televised version of the play *Lady in the Dark* on NBC in 1954 depicted the first clearly gay (and somewhat sympathetic) character on American TV (Paley Center for Media, 2010). A CBS documentary titled *The Homosexuals* aired in 1967, with many of the film's subjects in disguise. Norman Lear's *All in the Family*, debuting on television in 1970, occasionally dealt with some gay and lesbian themes. A sympathetic dramatic TV movie, *That Certain Summer* aired in 1972, followed by a gay character in the sitcom *Soap* in the late 1970s. Still, depictions of sexual minority characters were rare on TV throughout the 70s. However, during that time there also may have been an interesting case of the viewing public not seeing what was in front of them. Specifically, two popular TV stars of the era (Paul Lynde of *Hollywood Squares*, Charles Nelson Reilly of *Match Game*) tended to be very flamboyant on game show celebrity panels. Although both Lynde and Nelson Reilly were both later revealed to be gay, sexual orientation was never mentioned on the shows.

The advent of AIDS in the early 1980s greatly altered the media perception of sexual minorities, particularly gay men. Although neglected and marginalized at first as a problem of the gay and drug subcultures, the death from AIDS of romantic leading man Rock Hudson in 1985 helped bring AIDS coverage "out of the closet," although the media tended to redefine coverage of sexual minorities as "epidemic" coverage, with gay people cast in the role of villains carrying the dread disease or as victims of it, or both. There were some sympathetic portrayals of gay AIDS victims, though they were almost always male and upper-middle class, as in the groundbreaking 1985 TV movie *An Early Frost*.

By the 1990s, greater numbers of gay men (and less often lesbian) characters began to appear in positive TV and film roles, some of them saintly, and most of them appearing rather mainstream and being well accepted by their straight friends. Physical contact was rare; a lesbian kiss on the sitcom *Roseanne* was almost vetoed by ABC in 1994, but Roseanne Barr insisted on it. The most publicized gay character in the history of TV was featured in the on-screen coming out of *Ellen*'s lead character Ellen Morgan in April 1997, which coincided with the off-screen coming out of the actress Ellen DeGeneres. Although the coming-out episode set ratings records and was itself the subject of many news stories at the time, the formerly high-rated sitcom was canceled at the end of the following season (Dow, 2001). Despite this setback, DeGeneres eventually found success and mainstream acceptance as a talk show host. Although the *Ellen* sitcom was canceled, another network comedy (*Will and Grace*), about a gay man living with a straight woman, became a mainstream hit (Battles & Hilton-Morrow, 2002) in the 1990s and 2000s. *Queer as Folk*, a British series adapted for premium cable in the U.S., featured predominately gay characters in the early 2000s and was followed by *The L Word*, about a group of lesbian friends. There was even a gay-themed basic cable channel (Logo) launched in 2005. Interestingly enough, however, some of the most daring programming with gay themes came on animated shows, such as *The Simpsons* and *South Park*. Music videos, the occasional soap opera, and other sitcoms (e.g., *The Office*, *My Name is Earl*) also began to feature some prominent gay themes or characters.

By 2009, two highly successful television shows, *Glee* and *Modern Family*, both featured main characters and story lines involving sexual minorities. In *Glee*, high school students Kurt and Santana dealt with romance, coming out to their families, and bullying by other students. *Modern Family* featured committed couple Cameron and Mitchell raising a young daughter together. In 2011, for probably the first time, a transgendered person, Chaz Bono (formerly Chastity, child of Sonny Bono and Cher), was featured on the highly rated reality series *Dancing with the Stars*. For a detailed history of gay men and lesbians on TV (and radio), see Capsuto (2000).

Although numerous films and even TV shows with gay and lesbian characters appeared in the 1990s, the topic continued to generate some controversy. The 2005 "gay cowboy" film *Brokeback Mountain*, about two Wyoming cowboys falling in love in the 1960s, poignantly dramatized the tragedy of such a union in a time and place that did not accept such love. The fact that it won several Oscar nominations brought unprecedented attention to the issue of gay media portrayals.

A few studies suggest that positive media portrayals such as Will Truman in *Will and Grace* or Kurt Hummel in *Glee* can be instrumental in improving tolerance and acceptance of gays and lesbians in the broader society. Riggle, Ellis, and Crawford (1996) found that viewing a documentary film about a gay politician led to significantly more positive attitudes toward homosexuals. Bonds-Raacke et al. (2007) found that just thinking for a few minutes about a positive gay or lesbian media character of one's choice led to improved attitudes toward gay men. These results suggest a potentially important role for media entertainment in reducing prejudice in this area.

As recently as 1991, sponsors successfully pressured ABC not to rerun an episode of the drama series *thirtysomething* that had one brief peripheral scene of two minor, non-regular gay male characters sitting in bed with each other (and only talking). An image of two same-sex people touching romantically in an ad was thought to turn off many heterosexual viewers, with obvious marketing implications (Bhat, Leigh, & Wardlow, 1998). Controversy was not limited to electronic media. When the comic strip *For Better or For Worse* had Lawrence, a friend of teenager Michael, come out in 1993, some papers refused to run the strip, although most did (see Close-Up 4.6). By 2012, however, gay kissing and other affectionate touch had quietly appeared on prime-time TV such as *Modern Family* and *Glee*.

How gay rights and gay pride events and issues are communicated via news media is also an important consideration. Gays and lesbians are treated qualitatively differently from ethnic, religious, or other social minorities.

Close-Up 4.6: When Lawrence Came Out in the Comics

For one month in the spring of 1993, Lynn Johnston's popular family comic strip *For Better or For Worse* dealt with the theme of a gay teen, as occasional character Lawrence, a friend of principal family teen Michael, came out to his friends and family on the comic pages of about 1,500 North American dailies. Canadian cartoonist Lynn Johnston drew on the experience of her gay brother-in-law and others as she wrote the story over several weeks (Lawlor, Sparkes, & Wood, 1994).

Lawrence initially came out to his parents, who had a very difficult time with the news, and later to Michael. Lawrence's father first threw him out of the house but later relented and offered a grudging acceptance, though not total understanding. There was some predictably negative reaction from the Canadian and U.S. markets. About 40 papers refused to run the strips on this theme, and 16 canceled permanently in protest at the content. However, the controversy seemed to generate new interest, and the strip experienced unprecedented growth in subscriptions over the succeeding months. In Lawlor and colleagues' analysis of almost 2,200 letters received by Johnston, the newspapers, and the distributing syndicate, 70% were positive, many offering poignant personal stories of readers' own experiences (Lawlor, Sparkes, & Wood, 1994). There were, of course, some angry responses, though fewer than had been feared. In any event, it seemed clear that the funnies weren't just for laughing any more.

For example, Moritz (1995) points out that the Ku Klux Klan and neo-Nazis are not sought out for minority opinions for "journalistic balance" in coverage of issues concerning African Americans or Jews. However, spokespersons from the political right who would ban and suppress all expression, even all discussion, of homosexuality are routinely sought out to present the "other side" in coverage of sexual minority issues. This is one group that it is still socially, politically, and, for many, morally acceptable to publicly despise.

Once limited to coverage of gay pride parades or protests, in the new millennium news coverage of gay issues has increased, along with public discussion of issues such as the U.S. military's "don't ask, don't tell" policy and same-sex marriage. One study (Moscowitz, 2010) found that such television news coverage of gay marriage tended to be dominated by a "straight perspective" that emphasized the traditional, heterosexual viewpoint. In fact, the study revealed that in many news stories, "gay and lesbian citizens were also given a shorter sound bite, speaking less than most other sources speaking on their behalf such as straight allies and gay rights activists" (Moscowitz, 2010, p. 36).

Older Adults

One of the most underrepresented demographic groups in U.S. media, especially television, has been the older adult (Dall, 1988; Davis & Davis, 1985). Although the percentage of the U.S. population over 65 has climbed from 4% in 1900 to about 13% in 2010 and is projected to be near 20% by 2100, only about 3% of characters on television are over 65 (Cassata & Irwin, 1997; Hajjar, 1997; Roy & Harwood, 1997). Even the relatively few older people who appear on TV are not particularly representative of the population. For example, 62% to 70% of the TV elderly in commercials were men, as compared with about 40% in the over-65 population (Hajjar, 1997; Roy & Harwood, 1997). A disproportionate number of the TV elderly appear in sitcoms, with very few in action-adventure or children's shows. Studies of print media also show underrepresentation and stereotyping in portrayals of aging (Buchholz & Bynum, 1982; Nussbaum & Robinson, 1986; J. D. Robinson, 1989). If that were not bad enough, content analyses show this age group has the largest portion of television characters treated with disrespect (70% of men, 80% of women) (Gerbner, 1997). Often, the older adult is portrayed as more of a stereotype than a fully rounded character. These stereotypes take several forms.

Overall, older people on TV are often seen as quite healthy, perhaps even unrealistically so (Cassata, Anderson, & Skill, 1980; R. H. Davis, 1983; Kubey, 1980). Those who are sick, however, are ailing very badly, often seen as infirm, feeble, and sometimes senile. Although in terms of numbers of stories, newspapers do the best job of any medium in covering the elderly, a high percentage of such stories are obituaries (Buchholz & Bynum, 1982; J. D. Robinson, 1989)! Moreover, the elderly are usually portrayed as sexless. The major exception to this is the other extreme, the so-called dirty old man (or female "cougar"), who is preoccupied with sex and usually a highly ludicrous character. The very active and healthy senior citizen may be an object of ridicule, such as the grandmother who rides a motorcycle or cruises bars to meet men. Narrow-minded older persons often complain, criticize, and generally make a pain of themselves. As with the physically weak stereotype, the crotchety complainer is usually at best a laughable buffoon and at worst an object of scorn and derision. Older people tend to be seen doing relatively trivial things like playing bingo and sitting in rockers on the front porch. Such identifying symbols of aging are especially common in advertising. For example, a woman in a magazine ad for cookies is placed in a rocker to make sure we recognize that she is a grandmother.

In marked contrast to the unusually attractive young adults on TV, television's elderly are often stoop-shouldered, mousy-haired, badly wrinkled, and wearing out-of-style dowdy clothing. Such markers may be given to them so that we do not mistake them for younger people. Whether intentional or not, this also contributes to their being perceived negatively. Seefeldt (1977) found that elementary school children viewed physical signs of aging as horrifying and saw the elderly as infirm and incapable of doing much.

An interesting class of exceptions to these generalizations can be seen in TV commercials. Although the elderly are as underrepresented there as in the programs, the characterization is a bit different. The elderly in ads often appear as the "young-old," with few of the stereotypic signs of aging except the gray hair, which is almost always there. Although they suffer more health problems than young people in ads, they retain their vigor. It is as if the producers give the character gray hair so we all realize that he or she is supposed to be older, but allow that person to show very few other signs of age that our society finds so distasteful. Baldness, wrinkles, and otherwise general dowdiness are unseemly. One content analysis of TV commercials in 1994 found the portrayals of older people to be largely positive (Roy & Harwood, 1997). Still, older adults are neglected. Ad agency Grey Worldwide found that less than 10% of U.S. television commercials are aimed at those over 50, in spite of the fact that this group has over half of all the disposable income in the country (Lippert, 2003). Since the onset of prescription drug advertising in the U.S. in 1997, the largest number of older models have appeared in pharmaceutical ads, which are very prevalent on TV shows aimed at an older demographic.

Even in cases when the elderly are portrayed very positively, they tend to be shown in rather a restricted and stereotyped range of roles. They are almost always in roles in relation to family, very often as grandparents, but sometimes as the antagonist in a relationship with their adult child. We seldom see an older executive or professional. The older detectives of *Murder She Wrote*, *Matlock*, and *Diagnosis Murder* offer a couple of exceptions.

When NBC's sitcom *The Golden Girls* (1985–1992) featured four single women (three widowed, one divorced), aged about 50 to 80, sharing a house in Florida, what was new was the age of the stars. Never before had a sitcom, or perhaps any U.S. TV show, had its regular cast consist entirely of older adults. There were no precocious children, no smart-mouthed teenagers, no hunks or supermodels, and no angst-ridden yuppie couples, yet the show had consistently high ratings. The characters were also not the stereotyped TV old ladies. Three of the four were working professionals, and all showed depth of character beyond the typical TV grandma. However, they were criticized for being excessively interested in sex, although that criticism may primarily reflect the critics' discomfort with sexual interest in the mature adult. Also, the humor of the show sometimes perpetuated stereotypes of aging by poking fun at counter-stereotypical portrayals (Harwood & Giles, 1992). In spite of the success of *The Golden Girls*, it was not followed by other ensemble shows of older characters. However, as the U.S. population ages sharply over the next few decades, a greater variety of portrayals of older adults is practically assured.

In spite of inadequacies in their portrayal on TV, older people are heavy users of television. Robinson (1989) offered a uses and gratifications interpretation of this. A reduction in the number of friends and family seen regularly, perhaps in part due to decreased mobility as a result of health limitations, leads to a proportionately greater reliance on media, especially television, with its high level of redundancy in the visual and auditory modalities. If one sense is impaired, the other may partially compensate. In the case of the sound track, the volume may be turned up, so some elderly TV viewers may actually hear more of what is spoken on TV than what is spoken by people around them.

Persons with Physical or Psychological Disabilities and Disorders

People with disabilities, either physical or mental, are very concerned about their media image (Balter, 1999; Cumberbatch & Negrine, 1991). Unfortunately, in many ways, media portrayals of these groups have also not been kind.

Physical Disabilities

Disabilities appear in less than 1% of series characters on TV; by comparison, 10 to 20% of the population have some sort of physical disability (Balter, 1999). However, people with disabilities have occasionally appeared, often in the form of the "bitter crip" or "supercrip" stereotypes. In the former, the person with a disability is depressed and bitter due to the disability and other people's failure to accept him or her as a full person. Often such story lines revolve around someone (typically someone who is not disabled) challenging the character to accept him- or herself. Often the character with the disability finds that this self-acceptance miraculously leads to a physical cure, perhaps subtly suggesting that happiness does in fact come only from being physically whole.

The supercrip image, on the other hand, is seen in characters like the superhuman and selfless paraplegic who wheels hundreds of miles to raise money for cancer research or the blind girl who solves the baffling crime by remembering a crucial sound or smell that sighted people had missed. Sometimes the two even coexist in the same person, as in *The Miracle Worker*'s Helen Keller, at first bitter and inept, almost animalistic, until she is "tamed" by the saintly teacher Annie Sullivan, after which she goes on to be almost superhuman. A covert message of both of these portrayals is that individual adjustment is the key to disabled people's lives; if they only have the right attitude, things will be just fine. Factors like prejudice and social and physical barriers in broader society are underplayed (Longmore, 1985).

Positive images do count. The old TV show *Ironsides* featured a lead detective who worked from a wheelchair. Dr. Carey on *ER* used a crutch, but it did not define her character. Heather Whitestone, who is deaf, was chosen Miss America in the 1990s. *Glee*'s Artie, who is in a wheelchair, generally goes about the business of being a teenager, as does Down syndrome character Becky (played by Down syndrome actress Lauren Potter). It is not uncommon to see an advertising model in a wheelchair. A teacher in the comic strip *For Better or For Worse* is a positive example of a character who just happens to have a disability requiring her to use a wheelchair. Such portrayals can have substantial impact. When a popular Brazilian soap opera introduced a character who was ruggedly handsome and very sexy but also deaf, interest in learning sign language soared nationwide.

Psychological Disorders

The media image of psychological disorders (mental illness) is also an issue. A content analysis of week-long program samples from 1969 to 1985 showed that 72% of the prime-time adult characters who were portrayed as mentally ill actually injured or killed others, and 75% were victims of violence (Signorielli, 1989), whereas in reality about 11% of persons with psychological disorders are prone to violence, the same ratio as in the overall population (Teplin, 1985). A comparable bias exists in print media coverage of mentally ill persons (Day & Page, 1986; Matas, Guebaly, Harper, Green, & Peterkin, 1986; Shain & Phillips, 1991). One of the few truly violent disorders, antisocial personality disorder (those affected are sometimes labeled "psychopaths" or "sociopaths"), is greatly overrepresented among the media mentally ill (W. Wilson, 1999). The media image is one reason for the stigmatization of mental illness, which becomes a major barrier to improving health care delivery (Hinshaw, 2007).

Besides the violent mentally ill person, another stereotype is the person with disorders as object of humor or ridicule (Wahl, 1995). Although mental illness is seldom ridiculed directly, there is frequent use of metaphors that many find demeaning and insulting. For example, in advertising, an ad portrays a straitjacket as appropriate for someone crazy enough to buy the competitor's product; a lawn mower is described as "schizophrenic"; a line of peanuts called Certifiably Nuts is sold by picturing cans of the product wearing straitjackets. Ads describe sunglasses as "psycho," and vicious criminals are labeled "psychotic killers" as if the two words were synonymous. These stereotypes even creep into political discourse. In the 1992 U.S. Presidential election campaign, third-party candidate Ross Perot happily told his followers, "We're all crazy again now! We got buses lined up outside to take you back to the insane asylum" (Willwerth, 1993).

A popular movie *Me, Myself, and Irene* poked fun at a character labeled as schizophrenic but having the symptoms of dissociative identity (formerly multiple personality) disorder, two completely different disorders frequently confused in the public mind. People who have dealt with the tragedies of schizophrenia, depression, or other illnesses find such language and images very hurtful.

A third stereotype is that people with disorders are "a breed apart," that is, totally different from the rest of us (Wahl, 1995). They may be presented as being obviously different, unmistakably symbolized by wild hair, disheveled clothing, bizarre behavior, and odd facial expressions. This encourages two inaccurate beliefs: (1) mental illness is immediately identifiable by one's appearance, and (2) people with an unusual appearance are obviously mentally ill and thus objects of suspicion and perhaps fear. Such attitudes support the stigmatization of mental illness that discourages people from disclosing their own disorders and perhaps even dissuades them from seeking much-needed treatment. Media discussion of this stigma is perhaps most clearly seen in coverage of its role as political poison (Rich, 1997). Traditionally, seekers of high political office admit their own use of counseling or psychiatric resources only at their peril. One of the most celebrated political casualties of such prejudice is probably U.S. Senator Thomas Eagleton, the original Democratic Party vice presidential nominee in 1972. He was replaced on the ticket after "admitting" he had been hospitalized for depression some years before. Presidential candidate Michael Dukakis lost ground in 1988 after a rumor that he had sought therapy to deal with grief over his brother's suicide some years before. How sad when the desirable behavior of seeking help for problems is considered a moral failing or character flaw! Would someone make a better politician if he or she ignored a problem and did not seek help?

Occasionally there are reassuringly helpful images. One of the most influential was the 2001 Oscar-winning film *A Beautiful Mind*, the true story of Nobel Prize-winning mathematician John Nash's descent into schizophrenia and largely successful treatment for it. In spite of some cinematic license (visual hallucinations instead of auditory ones, more successful treatment than is often the case), the illness and its treatment were presented realistically and sensitively. Important issues were dealt with, such as the gradual detachment from reality, the necessity of maintaining medication therapy, and the devastating impact on one's family. Someone watching this film will learn a lot about schizophrenia (though nothing about multiple personalities!), as well as being greatly entertained for two hours. See Wedding, Boyd, and Niemiec (2005) and Dine Young (2102) for excellent discussions of portrayals of mental illness in movies, and Close-Up 4.7 for further discussion of stereotyping of mental illness in movies.

Occupations

Finally in this look at portrayals of groups, our attention focuses briefly on another large area of group stereotyping on television, namely that of various occupational groups. Wroblewski and Huston (1987) found that fifth and sixth graders saw television as a major source of information about occupations. However, such TV portrayals are often inaccurate.

Close-Up 4.7: Mental Illness in the Movies

According to Hyler, Gabbard, and Schneider (1991; see also Dine Young, 2012), there are several common movie stereotypes of persons with mental illness: These include: the rebellious free spirit (e.g., Randle McMurphy in *One Flew Over the Cuckoo's Nest*, Joon Pearl in *Benny and Joon*); next is the homicidal maniac (e.g., Michael Myers in *Halloween*, Norman Bates in *Psycho*); third is the seductive woman (e.g., Alex Forrest in *Fatal Attraction*, Catherine Tramell in *Basic Instinct*); fourth is the narcissistic parasite who sponges off society and gives nothing in return (e.g., several characters in *Annie Hall*). Other characterizations include the zoo specimen—the curiosity whom others like to look at and feel glad they are not like themselves—and the enlightened member of society, whose greatness is unrecognized and whose creativity is mistakenly and cruelly labeled mental illness.

Hyler (1988) suggested three common themes in movies that tend to establish and support these stereotypes. First of all, there is the "presumption of traumatic etiology," which seems to assume all mental illness has its origins in some traumatic event in childhood. Related to that is the "blame the parent" theme, which assumes that the mental illness not only has its origin in childhood trauma but in one caused by a parent, perhaps through abuse, neglect, or even treating the child unfairly. Finally, and perhaps most perniciously, is the frequent theme that harmless eccentricity is labeled as mental illness and tragically treated as such, often with extreme measures like frontal lobotomies or mind-numbing drugs or shock treatments. Have you seen these themes in movies you remember?

Nevertheless, the presence of positive media models in certain occupations can greatly increase the numbers of those entering that profession. For example, the number of medical school applicants surged sharply from 1962 to 1963, apparently due to the debuts of the popular medical TV dramas *Dr. Kildare* and *Ben Casey* (Goldberg, 1988). The number of journalism students mushroomed after the Watergate scandal of the early 1970s, when investigative reporters became heroes, especially with movie portrayals such as *All the President's Men* starring Robert Redford and Dustin Hoffman. More recently, the number of college students wanting to go into forensic science has skyrocketed with the advent of TV shows like the *CSI* series (see Close-Up 4.8). Although the number of such jobs is minuscule, students often do not realize that. The effects of media portrayals of occupational groups are not always so dramatic, however. Here we examine a few especially interesting groups and look at how the media present these professions.

Close-Up 4.8: The *CSI* Effect? Have TV Forensic Science Shows Affected Juror Verdicts?

One particularly interesting way that media may be becoming reality concerns the area of forensic science in criminal investigations. Since 2000, several prime-time TV shows (at one point eight out the top 20 shows) have been police forensic science dramas, most notably the *CSI* series. Many prosecutors and judges are growing concerned that jurors are failing to convict defendants with strong evidence against them because of a lack of DNA evidence of the sort that exists in the TV shows but is often absent in real life. Has there been such a change in verdicts, or is this impression purely anecdotal? In spite of the widespread concern, controlled scientific studies have so far largely failed to confirm such an effect on juror verdicts (Houck, 2006; Tyler, 2006), although work is continuing.

Even if the *CSI* shows are not directly affecting verdicts, they are clearly having huge effects in other ways. For one thing, police are gathering much more physical evidence than they used to, often hundreds of items, placing large burdens on the overworked, minimal staff whose job it is to analyze and store all this material. For example, the entire state of Massachusetts in 2006 had 11 DNA analysts. Also, the shows have higher-tech equipment than the real world does, and jurors may not always understand this. One forensic scientist estimated that 40% of the forensic science shown on *CSI* does not exist in real life (Houck, 2006). Finally, enrollment in forensic science programs in universities has exploded since 2000. The program at West Virginia University had four graduates in 2000 but six years later was the third largest major on campus, with over 500 students! Criminal forensic science is an area most people have had little or no life experience in; these TV shows have stepped in to become the reality.

Lawyers and Courtroom Trials

Some controversy has arisen around realistic courtroom TV shows like *Divorce Court* and *The People's Court*, as well as the truTV (formerly Court TV) cable channel. All of these present legal proceedings, either dramatizations of real cases (*Divorce Court*) or actual court proceedings (*The People's Court, Judge Judy*). In shows like *The People's Court*, an actual judge presides over small claims court cases in which both parties agree to have their case settled on the show in lieu of a more traditional setting. The cases are real, as are all parties in those cases. On the one hand, such shows have been praised for making the court system more available to the public, who now can better understand how this phase of our judicial system functions. In fact, the number of small claims cases rose considerably after the advent of *The People's Court* in the 1980s, although not necessarily because of that show. Speaking to this point, however, critics argue that many such cases are frivolous and that these shows trivialize the legal system by making impatient judges (and sometimes pseudo-judges) TV stars. Chief among these is Judith Sheindlin of the highly rated *Judge Judy*, who seems to delight in sassy one-liners such as, "You spent $72 getting your hair done? You wasted your money!" (IMDB, 2012). Some court personnel report that litigants in many courtrooms have become more contentious, dramatic, and emotional in court, apparently following the model of the parties on shows like *The People's Court*. Is the public well served by such shows? Do we have a more accurate perception of how courts function or is our reality colored by some "Hollywoodization" of the courtroom by the producers of these real-life judicial programs?

What is the effect of such shows on people's knowledge and beliefs about lawyers? Cultivation theory would predict that such knowledge in heavy TV viewers would come to approximate the image of occupations presented on TV. Using this framework, Pfau, Mullen, Deidrich, and Garrow (1995) examined prime-time portrayals of lawyers and the public perception of attorneys. They found that public perceptions were affected in the direction of the TV portrayal, which in this case, interestingly enough, was more positive than expected. Others (e.g., Thaler, 1994) argue that television cameras in the courtroom are turning trials into entertainment, something they have never tried to be before.

Psychologists and Psychiatrists

Other highly stereotyped careers in entertainment media are the helping professions, including psychiatry, clinical psychology, marriage and family therapy, and counseling, which are generally not distinguished from each other in entertainment. In the 1990s, 17% of Hollywood movies contained at least one helping professional (Young, Boester, Whitt, & Stevens, 2008). Sometimes the therapist is a source of humor (*Frasier, What About Bob?, The Bob Newhart Show*, various movies by director Woody Allen). Very often professional boundaries are violated, most blatantly by the character having sexual relations with his or her patients (*Prince of Tides, Basic Instinct, Eyes Wide Shut*). Other boundary violations include physically assaulting a patient (*Good Will Hunting*), violating confidentiality and making fun of a patient (*Frasier, What About Bob?*), being a socially repressive force (*One Flew Over the Cuckoo's Nest*), and being severely disturbed oneself (*Silence of the Lambs, Anger Management, Web Therapy*) (Bischoff & Reiter, 1999; Dine Young, 2012; Gabbard & Gabbard, 1999; Young et al., 2008). Is it any wonder that many people who need help are reluctant to seek it, if this is their image of those who provide it?

However, there are also some positive and realistic images scattered out there. The therapists portrayed in *The Sixth Sense* and *The Sopranos* have won high marks, and perhaps the all-time best cinematic portrayal was Judd Hirsch's Dr. Berger in the 1980 Oscar-winning film *Ordinary People*. Of even more concern than fictional portrayals, though, are media therapists like Dr. Phil (McGraw) and Dr. Laura (Schlesinger) who actually do some semblance of psychotherapy on the air. Although sometimes the therapist is qualified (Dr. Phil has a Ph.D. in psychology from the University of North Texas, although Dr. Laura's Ph.D. is not in psychology or counseling) and the therapy is well-motivated (Dr. Phil has off-air follow-up therapy for his clients), television is at heart an entertainment medium with all the attendant pressures of ratings. Thus the "therapy" by these real "Frasier Cranes" must first and foremost be entertaining to the audience. This goal is utterly inconsistent with competent psychotherapy, which requires thoughtful reflection, privacy, and freedom from an audience. Amusing one-line zingers, dramatic on-air confrontations, and pat answers do not treat mental illness. If the public learns that this is what therapy is, that may be just as harmful as the distorted fictional portrayals.

Farmers and Rural Life

As a rule, farmers and rural life in general are not highly visible in media, although the few rural TV shows have been among the most extremely stereotyped and unrealistic in the history of the airwaves. In earlier days, it was *The Beverly Hillbillies* and *Green Acres*, then *Hee Haw* and *The Dukes of Hazzard*. All of these shows portrayed rural people as uneducated, stupid rubes totally lacking in worldly experience and common sense. True, there was also *The Waltons*, perhaps the most popular rural show of all time, but its historical setting detracted from its use as a model of modern rural life. Many, if not most, of the farm shows have been set in rural Appalachia, one of the poorest and most atypical of rural regions nationwide. There is an occasional depiction of the other extreme: the rural refuge of the very wealthy. However, the *Dallas* and *Falcon Crest* of the 1980s were as unrepresentative of rural America as *Hee Haw* was, although for entirely different reasons.

This stereotype is not limited to television. Use of Grant Wood's American Gothic-type figures in advertising reflects an archaic stereotype. The popular comic strip *Garfield* occasionally features Jon Arbuckle's farming parents who come to visit him in the city wearing overalls and not knowing how to use indoor plumbing and other modern conveniences. Much humor is based on the fact that there is nothing to do on the farm except count the bricks in the silo. The relatively few films set in rural America often have people speaking in southern drawls, even if the setting is Montana or Michigan. Sometimes one sees rather silly rural symbols, such as a tractor driving down Main Street, used to remind us that we are not in a city.

Problems facing the profession of agriculture have typically been underreported in the news, probably because complex issues like the farm debt crisis of the 1980s or the worldwide food shortages of the 2000s are difficult to encapsulate into a brief TV or newspaper story. Also, the people involved with producing media are virtually 100% urban, usually from New York or Los Angeles or other large cities, with no roots or connections to any rural community.

College Students

Finally, let us consider the occupation of most of the readers of this book. According to movies, television shows, and advertising, how do college students spend their time? Perhaps the foremost portrayal involves drinking lots of beer and partying into the wee hours. Sometimes wildly excessive and destructive behaviors are presented as normal and amusing, as in the movies *Animal House*, *Revenge of the Nerds*, and *Road Trip*. Advertising provides other examples. For instance, a phone company ad targeted at college students showed a fellow passed out on his bathroom floor after celebrating his 21st birthday by binge drinking. By presenting this sort of behavior as normal, such marketing could encourage binge drinking and all its serious consequences. Second, one would think from ads in university newspapers that almost everybody takes a spring break trip to some beach community where there is lots of fun, sex, and alcohol. Where is the studying or struggle to earn enough money for next month's rent? Where is the volunteer work? Where is the search for a job after graduation?

Does it matter? People in some communities have limited personal interaction with college students, and therefore this media image becomes reality. One student reported that she had trouble finding a summer job back in her hometown because no one wanted to hire college students, thinking they would be constantly partying and would not be responsible workers. See Conklin (2008) for a thorough examination of the image of college students in American movies from 1915 to 2006.

Conclusion: So What If They're Stereotyped?

The concern about group portrayals may extend to any sort of group; the ones we have discussed are only some of the most maligned and most studied. Many other groups still struggle to gain a balanced and realistic treatment from television and other media. We have talked a lot in this chapter about rather narrow and negative media portrayals. But what is the impact? Many variables may moderate the effects of stereotyped portrayals. For example, it might be that comedy neutralizes some of the negative aspect of portrayals that would otherwise be considerably more offensive (Park, Gabbadon, & Chernin, 2006).

Although we have already discussed some effects research on gender and ethnic images, we close here with a couple of controlled experiments (Murphy, 1998; Slater, 1990). Murphy (1998) exposed people to either a gender-stereotypical or counter-stereotypical fictional or factual portrayal of a person. Subsequent (apparently unrelated) judgments about different people were affected by exposure to the previous portrayal. Particularly for men, exposure to the stereotypical portrayals led to less credibility given to different women in sexual harassment and acquaintance rape cases. It did not matter much whether the stereotype was a factual or fictitious person. Counter-stereotypical portrayals had the opposite effect, though it was not as strong. Slater (1990) presented people with information about some social group. The information was attributed to fiction (from a novel) or nonfiction (from a news magazine) and was about a group that was either familiar or unfamiliar to the participants. If the group was unfamiliar, the fictional portrayal was actually *more* influential in forming beliefs than was the nonfictional portrayal, whereas the reverse was true for the familiar group. This suggests the great power of fictional portrayals on knowledge and attitude formation, especially when life experience with the group in question is lacking.

For the groups described in this chapter, media are major, perhaps the predominant, sources of information for most of us. However, they are usually not the only source; there is often at least some reality to temper the media image. Thus, the perceived reality that our minds construct will not be totally taken from media, although it may be very heavily influenced by it. Occasionally, however, media may be the *only* source of information. Consider the example of prostitutes. Practically all adults know what prostitutes are and could give some basic facts about them (what they do, what they look like, why they are doing it). Few readers of this book, however, have probably ever known a real prostitute. Where does our perceived reality about prostitutes come from? In most cases it comes not mostly, or partly, but *entirely* from television and movies. The garishly dressed TV hooker standing on the street corner in the short, short skirt, high heels, and too much makeup is the reality of prostitutes, as far as most of us know. We might describe someone we see dressed this way as "looking like a hooker." But is this what hookers really look like, or is it just the way media portray them? Even as the authors of this book, we honestly do not know the answer. All we know is what we see in movies. If we were to meet a woman tomorrow who was identified as a prostitute, the media stereotype (schema) would come to mind to guide the processing of information about this woman. It would not matter if that image was accurate or not. It would be the *perceived reality*. This is what is happening with children growing up learning from television about groups of people. Many children have had no more personal contact with Arabs, Jews, African Americans, Latino/as, farmers, lesbians, or college students than their exposure in the media. This is why stereotypes matter.

Chapter 5

Advertising
Baiting, Catching, and Reeling Us In

Q: When did the first TV commercial air?
A: During a 1940 baseball game on WBNT-TV in New York. The ad was for Bulova watches (Silvulka, 1998).

Q: How many TV commercials do children see every year?
A: About 30,000–40,000, a large majority of them for unhealthy food like candy and sugary cereals (Fonda, 2004; Kaiser Family Foundation, 2007a).

Q: How much does advertising cost?
A: Corporate advertisers paid around $3.5 million for a 30-second spot during the 2012 Super Bowl. In terms of a regular series, the highest-priced ad was $2 million for a 30-second spot in the final episode of the sitcom *Friends* in 2004. The finales of *Everybody Loves Raymond* in 2005 and *The Oprah Winfrey Show* in 2011 charged around $1 million per commercial.

Q: Did Elliott's use of Reese's Pieces candies to lure E.T. in the 1982 movie have any effect on candy sales?
A: Sales of Reese's Pieces rose 65% after their appearance in the movie (Rimmer, 2002).

Q: How many 7th to 12th grade smokers preferred Camel cigarettes before and after the Old Joe smooth character ad campaign began in 1988?
A: Less than half of 1% chose Camels before Old Joe. Two years later, 33% did (DiFranza et al., 1991).

The bottom line of media is advertising. With the exception of public television and radio and premium cable networks such as HBO, most television channels in the U.S. are almost 100% dependent on ad revenues for financial support. Newspapers have traditionally derived around 70% of their revenue from advertising, although, as discussed in Chapter 1, this revenue source is declining. Magazines sometimes sell subscriptions below cost simply to raise the readership rate to allow them to charge higher advertising rates. The Internet is increasingly dependent on advertising revenue for support. Everything in media except advertising costs money, whereas advertising brings in all the money. This simple fact explains much of the content of the media. Ultimately it is the advertiser, not the audience, who must be pleased.

In spite of the tremendous costs of producing ads and buying time (or space) to broadcast (or print) them, advertising is still a remarkably efficient and inexpensive way to reach the buying public. Because of the huge size of the audience for highly rated TV shows, for example, the cost per viewer is often in the neighborhood of a quarter to a half a cent per ad. These costs, of course, only include the purchase of air time; production costs are extra. On a smaller scale, local newspaper and radio ads are far more reasonable in cost but still reach the target area of interest to the advertiser quite effectively. Perhaps the cheapest of all to produce and distribute are Internet ads and spam e-mails, which can yield a minuscule response rate and still be profitable.

Advertising makes very heavy use of psychology, and the study of the psychology of advertising could easily fill an entire book. This chapter examines certain aspects of the perceived reality created by advertising but is by no means a comprehensive examination of its effects. After some initial introductory and historical material, we consider some psychological appeals in advertising, followed by a more specifically cognitive examination of ads, especially the issue of deceptive advertising, in which the perceived reality is at particular odds with objective reality. Next we examine how sexual appeals are used to build a reality of positive feelings and associations about a product. In this section we also consider the issue of subliminal advertising, which is claimed to affect us without our awareness. Next, we look specifically at advertising directed to children and adolescents, one of the fastest-growing demographic markets in terms of amount of disposable income. Finally, we examine the many new places where advertising is appearing, infiltrating all corners of our lives. It has become increasingly difficult to separate advertising from the more general category of marketing, because, while advertising has traditionally been restricted to mass media, it is increasingly appearing in new places which are not quite media, but are definitely marketing (Stewart, Pavlou, & Ward, 2002).

One surprisingly difficult aspect of studying advertising is how to definitively answer the most important question about it, namely, does it work? Because there are so many other influences besides advertising that affect a purchase decision, it is very difficult to design a critical experiment to test if an ad has the desired effect or not. Thus, surprisingly, actual purchase behavior is measured infrequently. Rather, more indirect measures such as purchase intention, attitude toward the product or the ad, and belief about performance of the product are typically used. See Dillard, Weber, and Vail (2007) for a meta-analysis and discussion of the effectiveness of persuasive messages.

Historical Background

The earliest known written advertisement, from around 1000 BC in Thebes, Greece, offered a "whole gold coin" for the return of a runaway slave. Advertisements in mass communication did not really exist before Gutenberg's invention of movable type in the mid-15th century, however. Newspapers started carrying ads regularly in the mid-1600s. The rapid commercial growth associated with the Industrial Revolution in the 19th century gave great impetus to advertising, as did the rise of magazines during the same period, when transportation infrastructure, especially railroads, allowed the distribution of national publications for the first time, especially across a large country like the United States (see Close-Up 5.1 for a brief account of the history of marketing an everyday "necessity"—personal hygiene products). The rise of radio after 1920, television after 1945, cable TV in the 1970s and 80s, the Internet in the 1990s, and social media in the 2000s provided new outlets for advertising dollars and creativity.

Close-Up 5.1: Personal Hygiene Products: A Basic Necessity or a Marketing Creation?

The history of personal hygiene products and how they have been marketed, particularly in the U.S., is an interesting study in advertising and persuasion. Of course, if one goes back far enough in history, even the most basic hygiene product—soap—was nonexistent. However, eventually the utility of cleaning agents became apparent, and homegrown recipes for soap developed. When soap first began to be sold in stores, it was usually broken off a large cake and sold by the pound. In the early days, there was no distinction between hand, laundry, dish, or body soaps (Sivulka, 2001). That all changed, however, when it was discovered that a market could be created for brand-name soaps. "Along with patent medicine manufacturers, early soapmakers pioneered the merchandising and packaging of brand-name goods... Manufacturers also recognized that they could charge a higher price for goods with memorable brand names and attractive packaging" (Sivulka, 2001, p. 72). This led to soap being among the first nationally marketed products around 1900, with companies like Procter & Gamble and Palmolive devoting large advertising budgets to convince consumers, mostly women, to buy their products. Early ads ran in magazines that targeted women, such as *Good Housekeeping* and *Ladies Home Journal* (Sivulka, 2001). At the time, advertisers considered women easy targets whose "minds were vats of frothy pink irrationality" (Parkin, 2006, p. 15).

Over the years, advertising strategies for soap changed, from appeals to beauty and sex beginning in the 1910s, to patriotism around the time of World War I, to playing on health concerns and fear of germs in the 1920s to 1940s (Sivulka, 2001). Deodorant was first marketed to women in the 1920s as a way to protect against men perceiving them as smelly and unattractive. By 1935, advertisers realized that they could also market deodorant to men, playing on Great Depression-era insecurities like fears of losing a job due to perspiration odors (Everts, 2012). Personal hygiene products were even marketed as an important marker of social status, with those who bought and used the products portrayed as being of a higher class. For example, a 1927 ad stated: "The Safe Solution of Women's Greatest Hygienic Problem, over 80 percent of the better class of women in America today employ Kotex" (Sivulka, 1998, p. 163).

Beginning in the 1920s, advertisers also focused consumers on making a good first impression by protecting against "halitosis" (bad breath) and "b.o." (body odor). Both of these serious-sounding afflictions were invented by manufacturers and advertisers (halitosis by Listerine and b.o. by Lifebuoy Soap) to help instill a sense of need for the products. It worked. Most Americans today would not dream of going on a first date, a job interview, or even leaving the house with conditions such as b.o. or halitosis. According to Sivulka, "Nationally advertised, brand-name soap, toiletries, and even bathrooms made their way from seldom-used luxuries to necessities of American life in a remarkably short period of time—less than 65 years spanning the period between 1875 and 1940" (2001, p. 291). Today, the deodorant industry is worth approximately $18 billion (Everts, 2012).

Of course, the first electronic ads appeared on radio. Although there were early experiments with radio by Marconi in Italy in the 1890s and De Forest in the United States in 1906, the first radio station was set up in 1919 in a Pittsburgh garage by some Westinghouse engineers. Station KDKA broadcast the 1920 Presidential election results. There were 30 stations on the air by the end of 1920 and 400 by 1922. Ensuing concerns and debate about how to finance this new medium culminated in the Radio Act of 1927 for licensing and control of radio stations. This legislation established the free enterprise model to pay for radio; that is, total revenue would come from the sale of advertising time with no government subsidy. At about the same time, Great Britain made a very different decision in establishing the BBC, which was funded by license fees paid by consumers. Both of these economic models were carried over from radio to television in the late 1940s and still frame much broadcasting in their respective societies, although the United States now has some public broadcasting and Britain has had commercial television since the 1960s. One or the other of these two economic models of broadcasting has since been adopted by most of the countries of the world.

Types of Ads

Advertising is the one type of communication most clearly designed to persuade (i.e., have some effect on the viewer or hearer). This effect may be behavioral (buy the product), attitudinal (like the product), or cognitive (learn something about the product). Ads may be for particular categories of products (e.g., milk, coffee, beef, cotton) or brands of products (e.g., Coca-Cola, Nike, Toyota), or for services or businesses (e.g., banks, plumbers, dentists).

Frequently, the most direct purpose of an ad is not selling as such but rather image building or good will. For example, when a multinational corporation spends 30 seconds on TV telling us how it provides fellowships for foreign study, it is trying to encourage viewers to think of it as a fine, upstanding corporate citizen. This is done by associating the company with very positive images. Image-building advertising is especially prevalent after a corporation or industry has received a public relations black eye, such as the 1989 Exxon Valdez oil tanker spill in Alaska or the 2010 BP oil spill in the Gulf of Mexico. It also is common when a corporation tries to become involved in consciousness-raising on some issue of importance and public interest, such as when a distillery runs an ad encouraging people not to drive drunk. They believe that the goodwill they achieve by being perceived as taking a responsible public position will more than offset any decline in sales arising from people buying less of their product due to concern about driving under the influence.

A different kind of persuasive media message is the Public Service Announcement (PSA), usually sponsored by some government agency or nonprofit organization, or coordinated by the non-profit Ad Council. Historically, the U.S. Federal Communications Commission (FCC) has mandated that radio and TV stations must offer free time for PSAs but does not usually specify when that time should be; thus PSAs frequently air heavily at off-peak hours, late at night or during weekdays. With the deregulation and weakening of U.S. regulatory agencies starting in the 1980s, the placement and frequency of PSAs suffered even more.

A final kind of advertising is political advertising, usually designed to persuade viewers to support some candidate, party, or issue. In many ways political advertising is very similar to commercial advertising, although there are some important differences. Political advertising is considered in Chapter 8 and thus is not discussed further in this chapter.

All types of ads try to affect the reality perceived by the consumer (i.e., give us a new image of a product, candidate, or company or make us feel we have a need or desire for some product). Such processes involve attempts to change our attitudes.

Our attitudes about products (or anything else, really) consist of three components. The belief or cognition is the informational content of the attitude. For example, Kyle prefers Toyota cars because of certain features they have. The affective (emotional) content of the attitude is the feeling toward that product. Kyle prefers Toyotas because he trusts them, likes them, and feels safe with them. Finally, the action is the attitude's translation into behavior. In the case of ads, the advertiser typically hopes the final step in the chain will be a purchase; in our example, Toyota hopes that its advertising has created the right beliefs and emotions in Kyle that will translate into him actually buying a Toyota himself. However, some ads are designed primarily to influence our beliefs, and others are designed to influence our emotions.

Psychological Appeals in Advertising

Any type of advertising uses a variety of psychological appeals to reach the viewer. In one way or another, ads attempt to tie the product or service to our deep and basic psychological needs. Implicitly, then, the message is that buying the product will do more than give us something useful or pleasant: it can help us be better people as well.

Informational Appeals

Although not the most common appeal, some ads primarily provide information in an attempt to influence the belief component of our attitudes. A good example of this would be an ad for a new product; such an ad may explain in some detail what that product does, what its features are, and how those features differ from those of existing products. As a medium, newspapers are particularly well suited to conveying this sort of information in ads (Abernethy, 1992).

Some of the most common belief appeals are exhortations to save money or receive a superior product or service. The feeling that we are getting a good bargain is a powerful motivator in deciding to purchase something. It is so powerful that often the official list prices are set artificially high so that products may be advertised as costing considerably less, when in fact they may have never been intended to sell at the full list price. Framing (Entman, 1993) is also very important. For example, advertising a discount or offering a coupon for some amount off the price is more appealing than saying the price goes up after some time, even if the cost the consumer actually pays is the same. For example, most people prefer to receive a discount of $3 off the regular price of $30 for paying early than to pay a penalty of $3 on top of a regular price of $27 for being late, even though in both cases they are paying $27 on time or $30 if late (Kahneman, 2011).

How to word advertising slogans and other information in the ad is an important consideration. In a strongly informational appeal, the advertiser wants to convey as much information as possible in a very short time but not overload or confuse the consumer. However, research suggests the most appealing wording may not always be simple. Although simpler syntactic structures (such as active voice or simple clauses) are generally recognized better than complex structures (such as passive voice or subordinate clauses), there are some cases in which moderate syntactic complexity might be more effective than either very simple or complex structures (Bradley & Meeds, 2002).

Emotional Appeals

Very often ads appeal to the affective (emotional) component of our attitudes. Influencing emotions is often the best first step to influencing beliefs and, ultimately, behavior. For example, there are many ads that appeal to our love of friends, family, and good times, and the good feelings that they bring us. We are asked to buy diamonds, flowers, and greeting cards to show how much we care, and drink certain products with friends as part of sharing a good time. Such classic slogans as "Reach out and touch someone" or "Friends are worth Smirnoff" illustrate such appeals. The message is conveyed that products are an integral part of showing our love and caring for others. This message has been especially targeted at women, who can presumably show love for their families by buying food products (e.g., "Put a little love in lunch with Skippy"; Parkin, 2006). The more closely the advertiser can link the product with the natural and positive emotions of love and connection, the more successful the ad. A baby food company once advertised that it helped babies learn to chew. Such an appeal links the product with a very basic developmental event in the baby's life, thus giving it a much more central role in the child's growth than any mere product, even an excellent product, would have. A car advertises itself as "part of the family"—not merely offering something to the family but actually being a member of it.

Closely related to family and love appeals is the linking of the product with fun. This is especially clear in ads for soft drinks and beer and almost anything marketed directly to children. Photography and copy that link images of a product with people having a good time at the beach or the ski lodge, or just relaxing at home with friends, encourage people to think about that product whenever they have or anticipate having such times. For example, Corona has had an advertising campaign for years associating their beer with the beach, Adirondack chairs, and relaxing on vacation. The product becomes an integral part of that activity, and, more importantly, of the positive feelings associated with that activity. Watching a sports event on TV with friends may naturally cause us to seek that advertised product (such as beer), which has become part of the event.

Certain cultural symbols have come to evoke warm feelings in viewers, which advertisers hope will transfer to warm feelings about the product. A boy and his dog, grandma baking an apple pie, the national flag, or a family homecoming are examples. For example, Folgers coffee has often run a commercial during the Christmas season depicting a college student returning home for the holidays and waking his family with the fresh smell of brewing coffee. Such symbols appear frequently in advertising of all sorts. Connecting a product with the positive feelings that people have for such symbols can associate a lot of positive emotion with that product. Even the name of the product can evoke certain feelings, perhaps connected with a particular culture or country (see Close-Up 5.2).

Close-Up 5.2: Challenges and Pitfalls of Choosing Foreign Product Names and Slogans

If you want to choose a foreign name for your product, how do you do that? The reality is more complicated than simply finding a real foreign word in some appropriate language (e.g., French for a perfume, Spanish for a tortilla, Norwegian for skis). It has to be a word that, for example, *looks* French to people who don't know any French. The American clothing brand Le Tigré, for instance, added the accent to the real French word for tiger ("tigre," with no accent). In doing so, they in fact made the word less French, but made it look more French to English speakers, who know that French uses accents and English doesn't. In another example, Häagen-Dazs ice cream has always been American but chose its unusual name "to convey an aura of old-world tradition and craftsmanship," according to the company's website. In reality, the words in the name don't mean anything in any language.

Reactions to foreign product names vary a lot depending on the product and the country (Chang, 2004; Harris, Garner-Earl, Sprick, & Carroll, 1994; Hong & Wyer, 1989, 1990). Perhaps the area of greatest danger is that a brand name means something quite different in the language of a target market. When marketing its 1970s Pinto subcompact in Brazil, Ford discovered belatedly that *pinto* is a vulgar term for "small penis" in Brazilian Portuguese. Only after their introduction in Germany was it learned that the facial tissue brand name "Puffs" is slang for whorehouse. For a short time, the Japanese were puzzled why their popular soft drink Calpis (pronounced "cow-piss") did not sell well in a U.S. test market, where it was a vulgar expression for cattle urine. Similarly, brand-name changes for the American market might be in order for the Iranian detergent Barf (American slang for vomit), the Mexican bread Bimbo (American slang for an attractive but dim-witted and/or promiscuous woman), the Uruguayan real estate company Yucky, or another Japanese drink, Sweat.

English advertising slogans are also sometimes lost in translation. For example, Perdue chicken's tagline, "It takes a tough man to make a tender chicken" ended up on Mexican billboards in Spanish as, "It takes a hard man to make a chicken aroused." For a time, Coors used the slogan, "Turn it loose." In Spanish, it came out as, "Suffer from diarrhea." In Chinese, Kentucky Fried Chicken's famous slogan "finger lickin' good" came out as "eat your fingers off" (Sivulka, 1998).

Sometimes product names can be changed in the short term in response to political whims. For example, during the anti-German frenzy of World War I, Americans took to calling sauerkraut "liberty cabbage," frankfurters and wieners "hot dogs," and hamburgers "liberty sandwiches." Such silliness is not purely a historical relic. In 2003, after France refused to support President George W. Bush's invasion of Iraq, the U.S. House of Representatives cafeteria began serving "freedom fries" instead of French fries (Rawson, 2003).

Perhaps the most effective selling pitch focuses on how the product will affect one's individual psychological well-being and deep-seated personal needs. For example, a camera ad once said, "Look how good you can be" using the camera, not simply "Look at the good pictures you can take." The product goes beyond merely providing you with something worthwhile to purchase; the product actually makes you a better person! Nike's well-known "Just do it" and Home Depot's "You can do it, we can help" slogans also appeal to this kind of sentiment. When the U.S. Army recruited with the slogan "Be all you can be," it suggested the psychological appeal of self-actualization, whereby somebody is motivated to develop his or her fullest potential. Who knows what psychologist Abraham Maslow would make of advertisers appealing to this self-actualization top rung in his classic hierarchy of needs, a level he believed was achieved by only the most psychologically well-adjusted and enlightened.

Sometimes the emotion elicited may change over time. For example, State Farm Insurance a few years ago considered retiring its longstanding "like a good neighbor" campaign, first introduced in 1971. Although the company had an amazing 98% brand name recognition and nearly 70% of Americans could fill in the blank in "Like a good neighbor, ____ is there," younger and more urban consumers increasingly saw a "good neighbor" in different terms. Apparently, to many contemporary young adults, a good neighbor is one who stays on his or her side of the fence and leaves you alone, not one who gets involved in your life and helps you, as State Farm was trying to suggest (Elliott, 2002a).

Often an emotional appeal is centered on the uniqueness of the product or consumer. Interestingly enough, this type of appeal is especially common from the largest corporations, trying to fight an image of large, impersonal, and uncaring corporate institutions. For example, Burger King's "Have it your way" and Wendy's ads against "assembly-line burgers" illustrate this approach, as does General Motors' "Can we build one for you?" and Microsoft's "Where do you want to go today?" campaigns. This theme was also apparent in advertising for the now-defunct Saturn automobile, which stressed the importance of the individual consumer and, in fact, never even mentioned that Saturn was a General Motors product! Walmart has used such appeals very effectively, with its mini-bios of happy families shopping at Walmart and contented employee-models who love working there. Such marketing not only makes it look like a fun place to shop but also counteracts its image as a megastore that pays low wages and forces small, local businesses into bankruptcy. Personal attention to the individual is almost always appealing.

Different emotional appeals can work to varying degrees in different cultures. For example, in a content analysis of print ads in news and women's magazines in collectivist Korea and the individualist United States, Han and Shavitt (1994) found that American ads more often stressed individual benefits and pleasures, such as standing out from the crowd and being personally happy, while Korean ads more often pitched collective benefits, such as drawing closer to others or making an office work better together. Sometimes a marketing appeal developed in one culture does not translate well to another. For example, when Nissan developed magazine ads to introduce its luxury Infiniti auto line to the U.S. market with several pages of scenes of nature with the name of the car only at the end of the sequence, the approach did not work. In more holistic, collectivist Japan, where people and nature have an inherent connectedness not appreciated in the West, this appeal had been successful (Nisbett, 2003). Even different subcultures sometimes call for different marketing appeals (see Close-Up 5.3).

Patriotic Appeals

Appeals to consumers' national pride are common in ads. They are particularly abundant during the quadrennial Olympic and World Cup events, as well as during events like the U.S. Bicentennial (1976), the French Bicentennial (1989), or Queen Elizabeth II's Diamond Jubilee (2012). The nationality of the manufacturer is of minor importance. Toyota is just as likely as General Motors to use an American patriotic appeal to sell cars in the United States. Volkswagen in New York salutes U.S. Olympic victories; McDonald's in Dublin helps raise money for the Irish Olympic team. In terms of advertising themes, patriotism is where the market is, not where the home office is located.

How do people respond to patriotic messages? Generally, very positively; for example, in a post-9/11 study, Seiter and Gass (2005) had restaurant

Close-Up 5.3: Advertising to Latino/as

The largest ethnic minority group in the United States is Latino/as, with over 50 million by 2010, about 16% of the population (Humes, Jones, & Ramirez, 2011). The billions they spend annually on goods and services has recently started to attract major advertising attention, helping to integrate Hispanic tastes and culture into the national mainstream. In 2002, NBC bought the second-largest Spanish-language network, Telemundo, for $2.7 billion. Many magazines publish Spanish-language versions (e.g., *People en Español*) and Spanish-language TV is widely available in many U.S. markets. However, the Latino/a audience also watches much English-language programming and a large percentage are bilingual and bicultural.

Procter & Gamble aired a Crest Toothpaste commercial in Spanish during a recent Grammy Awards Ceremony. Many companies, including Pepsi and Nike, have used some Spanish in their mainstream TV ads. Kraft Foods now sells a milk-based Jell-O (O Gelatina Para Leche), a Kool-Aid flavor "Aguas Frescas," and a lime-flavored mayonnaise. Pepsi and Nestlé sell fruit drinks with flavors like mango and tamarind, and Nabisco began selling three Latin American cookie brands in the United States in 2003 (Weaver, 2003a). Many mainstream supermarkets have also expanded their offerings to include large Latino sections.

servers write various messages on the bottom of their customer checks. Customers who received "United We Stand" left significantly higher tips than those receiving "Have a Nice Day" or no message.

Sometimes nationalism crosses the line into tasteless jingoism, as when a small-town U.S. restaurant published an "Iranian coupon—good for nothing," or when some advertisers took heavy-handed Japan-bashing approaches during times of intense feelings over Japanese trade practices. Public outcry against excessively mean-spirited patriotic appeals backfires on the advertiser in ways that tend to discourage such campaigns, at least in their most blatant forms. After the terrorist attacks of September 2001, advertisers were extremely cautious about doing anything that might appear to be capitalizing on those events, but Americans still saw an increase in patriotic public symbols in advertising, whether it was the Statue of Liberty, the American flag, or "new" heroes like firefighters and emergency personnel.

Fear Appeals

Advertising fear appeals involve some kind of threat of what may happen if one does not buy the product, such as a scenario of children trying unsuccessfully to phone parents when in danger because their mobile phone is unreliable. Selling home computers by asking parents, "You don't want your child to be left behind in math because you wouldn't buy him a computer, do you?" is a subtle but powerful emotional appeal to guilt and fear. Somewhat less subtle appeals involving the safety of one's children also occur, such as when one car manufacturer showed an apparent sonogram of a fetus in utero as the most important reason to buy its car. There may be a similar notion behind the well-known Michelin slogan "because so much is riding on your tires."

Psychological research on persuasion shows that fear appeals have varying effects. The conventional wisdom in both social psychology and advertising for many years has been that there is an optimal level of fear at which persuasion is the strongest. A weaker appeal will be less effective, but if the fear induced becomes too strong, the ad may turn people off and make them defensive, in which case they tune out the message. As Rotfeld (1988) pointed out in a careful review paper on fear appeals and persuasion, however, the research lacks consistency (see also King & Reid, 1990, regarding fear appeals in PSAs). It is hard to draw firm conclusions because what each researcher has defined as a strong, moderate, and low fear appeals has varied widely, and there has typically been little assurance that the participants in the studies have viewed the appeals similarly to the researchers. Indeed, sometimes ads are viewed much differently by various segments of the audience, some of whom may be highly offended; see Close-Up 5.4 for a particularly controversial example. Fear appeals in ads can be effective, but exactly which ones are most effective is not yet entirely clear.

Achievement, Success, and Power Appeals

Another popular theme in ads is striving to win, whether the prize is money, status, power, or simply having something before the neighbors do. A candy ad may blatantly say "Winning is everything," picturing a chocolate Olympic-style medal, or it may more subtly suggest that only the people who use the particular product have really arrived. The idea that using some product enables us to be winners is a powerful appeal, whatever the prize. Even an appeal to pure altruism in a PSA can use an appeal to win, by calling on us to achieve a "moral victory" by helping to fund leukemia research.

Advertising appealing to success sometimes crosses a line into appealing to snobbery. This is sometimes the case in ads for expensive liquor, jewelry, clothing, and cars. The message seems to be that only the finest products will do. Occasionally, the snob appeal also becomes humorous. For example, in a classic Grey Poupon mustard commercial, two high-class gentlemen in Rolls Royce sedans share their high quality mustard through their car windows. In another commercial, a rube at a fancy dinner party asks for "jelly" rather than "Polaner All Fruit," a faux pas causing one society woman at the table to faint in horror.

Close-Up 5.4: Bad Taste or Brilliant Marketing?

A Nike ad that ran during the 2000 Summer Olympics became very controversial. The ad showed a horrified 1500-meter Olympian Suzy Hamilton running from a masked pursuer wielding a chainsaw. She escapes him due to her superior running shoes and her own athletic ability. Nike defended the ad as one that empowered women and celebrated their strength. Critics assailed it as an insensitive "glorified rape fantasy" making light of violence toward women. NBC dropped the ad in response to complaints (Fussell, 2000).

Some other ads that have been pulled after consumer complaints include a pair of bungee jumpers in which one survives because he is wearing Reeboks, a Just for Feet ad in which a barefoot African runner is tackled by White westerners who put shoes on his feet, and various Calvin Klein ads with apparent preadolescents in sexually suggestive positions that appeared to many to be uncomfortably close to child pornography.

What do you think? Are these creative artistic endeavors or tasteless, insensitive marketing? One thing that is not in dispute is that all these ads were noticed.

Humorous Appeals

Humor is often used as an effective selling tool in ads; funny ads are often among the most popular and best remembered. The audiovisual capabilities of television offer a particularly rich set of possibilities for humor, although there is much humor in print and radio advertising as well. Indeed, some humorous ad campaigns have become classics of popular culture (e.g., Alka-Seltzer's "I can't believe I ate the whole thing" campaign of the 1960s, the Wendy's "Where's the beef?" of the 1980s, the Budweiser frogs of the 1990s, the quacking AFLAC ducks of the 2000s, or the Geico gecko of the 2010s). Radio's "see it on the radio" campaign drew on people's ability to use visual imagery to imagine a humorous situation described only through sound (Bolls & Lang, 2003).

One caution regarding the use of humor concerns its distractibility potential. Up to a point, humor clearly attracts attention and increases motivation and general positive feeling about the product or service. Sometimes humor in ads may lead to improved memory for the content (Furnham, Gunter, & Walsh, 1998). However, sometimes a very funny spot may be so entertaining that it detracts from the advertiser's message. Viewers may remember the gimmick but forget what product it was selling (Gelb & Zinkhan, 1985).

A related concern in regard to humorous ads is their longevity. Any ad campaign depends on repeated presentations to reinforce its message. However, if an ad appears too often in too short a time, its effect may wear out and even become counterproductive by turning people off due to overexposure. Although all ad campaigns eventually wear out, humorous ads have a particularly short lifespan. They become older, more tired, and much more annoying faster than other ads (Pechmann & Stewart, 1988).

Testimonials (Product Endorsements)

In the testimonial ad, some identified person, often a well-known entertainer or athlete, offers a personal pitch for some product or service. This person may clearly be an expert in the particular field or be no more informed than the average person (e.g., what does Michael Jordan know about underwear that you don't?). Social psychological research on persuasion indicates that we are more likely to be persuaded by a prestigious and respected figure, even if that person has no particular expertise in relation to the product being sold (Heath, Mothersbaugh, & McCarthy, 1993; Kahle & Homer, 1985). We tend to trust that person more due to our parasocial relationship (see Chapter 2) with him or her (Alperstein, 1991; Giles, 2002; Klimmt et al., 2006), and the positive associations and feelings we have about the person may be transferred in part to the product, thus transforming its image (Walker, Langemeyer, & Langemeyer, 1992). When 1996 Presidential candidate Bob Dole later became a pitchman for Viagra, the hope was that the trust viewers felt for Dole and his long years of public service in the U.S. Senate would transfer to the medication.

Although typical spokespersons in testimonial ads are famous athletes, entertainers, or politicians, they can also be animated (Garfield the cat plugging Embassy Suites, Bart Simpson eating Butterfinger candy bars). Another variation on testimonials involves the "person-in-the-street" endorsement of a product. Here, of course, the hope is that the viewers will identify with the everyday person and want to use the product like he or she does.

One of the oddest types of testimonials is the posthumous plug. For example, Mahatma Gandhi has sold Visa cards and Apple Computers, Albert Einstein has sold Fuji film and Chrysler cars, and John Wayne has sold Coors beer. Although the companies don't have to worry about their deceased pitchman getting caught in some scandal that renders him worthless in testimonials (think O. J. Simpson or Tiger Woods), they still have to pay royalties to the departed's estate. In 2004, decades after their deaths, Marilyn Monroe earned an estimated $7 million and Einstein $1 million from advertising, while Elvis Presley earned most of all, at $40 million (Taylor, 2005)!

One advantage of testimonials is that they often allow fairly precise age targeting. Betty White and Justin Bieber clearly reach different age demographics. Sometimes a product can be identified so strongly with a particular age group that others might be less interested. For example, Chrysler originally tried to market its 1930s-retro look PT Cruiser to young adults. Although this appeal was not particularly successful, their baby-boomer parents bought the car in droves and it later became identified with that generation. Similarly, the small, economical Toyota Echo appealed not to young buyers but to their parents. The same was true for the Saturn Vue SUV and the boxy Honda Element. In spite of these cars being pitched to them, the young adults instead preferred sportier cars like the Dodge Stratus, Mitsubishi Lancer, and Hyundai Tiburon (Fonda, 2003). An age-connected image can be hard to crack. High median ages of buyers for Buick (63) and Cadillac (55) make a strong youth appeal in marketing difficult. General Motors once tried to market against this image by advertising a certain model was "not your father's Oldsmobile" and even eliminating the Oldsmobile nameplate from some models. Young consumers didn't buy it; to them it *was* their father's Oldsmobile. GM stopped manufacturing Oldsmobiles altogether shortly afterward.

Can Appeals Be Unethical?

Just because an ad appeals to genuine human emotions does not mean that it is necessarily appropriate in a broader ethical sense. One of the most controversial international media campaigns in history centered on the selling of infant formula as an alternative to breast milk in poor countries. Although it was sold as being healthier than mother's milk, the fact that it was often mixed with unsafe water or in dirty containers actually led to a far greater danger of disease than using breast milk, to say nothing of the added expense for already desperately poor families. Concern over the alleged social irresponsibility of such media campaigns led to a worldwide boycott of Nestlé products (Fore, 1987).

The ubiquitous presence of television around the world has led to numerous advertising campaigns whose appeals have come under fire on grounds of social responsibility. Poor children often spend what little money they have on expensive junk food and soft drinks rather than on wholesome school lunches, thanks in part to the influence of advertising. For instance, even though 40% of Mexico's population has no access to milk, poor people are increasingly starting the day with a soft drink in part due to massive TV ad campaigns for Coca-Cola and Pepsi. Faced with flat or declining sales in North America, tobacco companies have increasingly turned to developing countries as markets, finding less knowledge of health risks, fewer limits on smoking, and less draconian advertising regulation. The percentage of smokers in China, for example, has skyrocketed in recent decades. How the commercial demands of television and other media confront the real world of desperate poverty leads to many questions about media transmission of values. Is it the media's responsibility to promulgate a more culturally sensitive set of values?

A Theoretical Model

Although advertising may be studied from a variety of theoretical perspectives (see Chapter 2), one of the most useful in recent years has been the *elaboration likelihood model* (or *ELM*; see Petty, Priester, & Briñoll, 2002; Petty, Briñol, & Priester, 2009). The ELM was initially developed to account for situations when full attention to processing was lacking but some influence might still be occurring; that is, exactly the situation with the typical exposure to advertising.

The central distinction in ELM is the postulation of two distinct routes to persuasion: the central and the peripheral. The *central route* involves effortful cognitive processing, in which we bring to bear our conscious thought processing and relevant information retrieved from long-term memory. Arguments of the persuader are thoughtfully evaluated to determine their merits, and a conclusion is rationally arrived at. The informational appeals discussed earlier in this chapter typically make use of the central route.

In contrast to the central route is the *peripheral route*, which does not have to involve conscious, effortful processing. In fact, in the real world of responding to ads, it is neither possible nor desirable to bring the cognitive resources to perform central processing on every TV commercial or billboard. Peripheral processing tends to make an initial, often emotional, response to one salient aspect of the message. For example, we like a commercial because of the familiar rock music sound track or the cute animated tiger, or we dislike one because it features our most hated comedian. When the likelihood of active cognitive elaboration is high, the central route predominates; when it is low, the peripheral route does. When our psychological involvement with a product is low, the peripheral route tends to dominate. Emotional, patriotic, fear, power, and humorous advertising appeals (among others) make use of the peripheral route, and peripheral route ads predominate relative to those that appeal to the central route.

Thus far we have primarily focused on the general psychological appeals in ads. In any real ad, of course, there may be multiple appeals. Sometimes it is not entirely clear what appeal is being used (see Close-Up 5.5). We now turn to look more closely at the cognitive aspects of advertising.

Cognition and Advertising: Ads as Information to Be Processed

The cognitive approach to advertising views an ad as information to be processed (Thorson, 1990). An ad is a complex stimulus, involving language (presented orally or in writing) and often pictorial stimuli as well. Television is a particularly complex medium, because it contains both the visual and auditory modalities. Typically, there is a close relationship between the audio and video portion of a TV commercial, but this is not always the case, such as

Close-Up 5.5: Ad as Social Statement: Case of United Colors of Benetton

One of the most controversial international ad campaigns of recent decades has been the United Colors of Benetton campaign by the trendy Italian clothing company. Instead of picturing their product, Benetton ads present powerful visual images of social issues. Some of these, such as the Hasidic Jew and the Palestinian embracing, or world leaders (including President Obama) kissing, suggest uplifting possibilities. Others, such as a burning car or a guerrilla fighter holding a human leg bone, are more troubling. Still others, such as a Black woman nursing a White baby, Black and White hands shackled together, or a rack of vials of blood with names of world leaders on them, are very striking but vaguely disquieting.

Why such a campaign? In part, it seems to be a personal statement of company President Luciano Benetton and creative photographer Oliviero Toscani. Benetton has long been politically active and was a member of the Italian Senate. Toscani has been a fierce critic of advertising and its promotion of consumerist values. United Colors is clearly a product of its leaders' social beliefs. Still, the ads have greatly increased the attention given to the company's products, there has been increased discussion of their ads, and this has probably helped lead to large increases in sales during this period. Critics, however, are troubled by the apparent exploitation of social problems to sell trendy clothing. The framing of social issues as products seems to demean or commodify them. Various United Colors ads were banned, or proposed for banning, in different North American and European countries (Tinic, 1997).

when a disclaimer is presented only in writing across the bottom of the screen (Kolbe & Muehling, 1992). The question of how the consumer processes and integrates information from the verbal and visual components of TV commercials is a complex and important issue in itself (Cook, 1992; Gardner & Houston, 1986; Percy & Rossiter, 1983; Shanteau, 1988). What part of an ad a person looks at and for how long depends both on the content of the ad and the reason the viewer is looking at the ad (Rayner, Miller, & Rotello, 2008).

Stages of Processing

When we perceive and comprehend an ad, there are eight stages of processing involved in understanding and acting upon it (Shimp & Gresham, 1983). First of all, of course, we must be exposed to the ad (e.g., seeing an ad in a magazine or online, hearing a commercial on the radio). Second, we choose to attend to it, perhaps selectively perceiving some parts more than others. Peripheral cues such as humor or sex appeal that catch our attention may cause us to attend to some ads more than others. Third, we comprehend the message. This is usually a fairly straightforward process, but can be more difficult with strange or obtuse ads. Fourth, we evaluate the message in some way (e.g., agree or disagree with it based on our own thoughts, feelings, and experiences). Fifth, we try to encode the information into our long-term memory for future use (e.g., remembering the name of an intriguing new product for the next time we're at the store). Sixth, some time later, we try to retrieve that information (perhaps when we're ready to buy the product). Seventh, we try to decide among available options, such as which brand or model to purchase. Finally, we take action based on that decision (e.g., actually buying the product or not). If any one or more of the stages is disrupted in some way, the overall comprehension or impact of the ad may suffer.

These eight stages are involved in our processing of every aspect of the ad. Even something as simple as the choice of a name or slogan for a product can have important ramifications for processing, depending on the nature of that name or slogan. For example, the memorability of a name may vary depending on various characteristics. A name that lends itself to an interactive logo or mental image may be remembered due to its amenability to organizational working memory strategies called chunking, which leads to a greater number of possible avenues of retrieval from long-term memory (Alesandrini, 1983). For example, a basement waterproofing sealant named Water Seal once used a logo of a seal (animal) splashing in water in the middle of a seal (emblem). This choice of a name allowed information about the product name (Water Seal), its use (sealing), and its sound (/sil/) to be unified into one visual image that is easy to remember. Characteristics of an ad may affect how many attentional resources are allocated to processing it. A major challenge to advertisers, especially in the age of multitasking, channel-surfing, and pop-up Internet ads, is to grab the attention of viewers. For example, Bolls and Lang (2003) found that highly "imageable" radio ads draw more attention than less imageable ones, perhaps because of the extra cognitive effort expended in comprehending them. Bradley and Meeds (2004) found that adding explanatory language to print ads for electronics facilitated comprehension but also improved attitude toward the product and heightened intention to purchase.

The context in which an ad appears will also affect how well it is processed and remembered. For example, Furnham, Bergland, and Gunter (2002) tested students' memory for a beer commercial embedded in the popular prime-time British drama series *Coronation Street*. The target ad was remembered better if it appeared as the first ad in the commercial cluster than if it was shown later. They also found that similar program content (characters drinking in a pub) which appeared just after the break led to improved recall of the beer ad compared to a control group, but that the same content before the ad led to poorer recall of the ad. This may have been due to cognitive interference of the program content with the ad, although recall was also good when the program had characters drinking both before and after the commercial break.

One of the most common types of entertainment programming on television involves high levels of violence (see Chapter 9). Violence also finds its way into advertising. It may surprise you, however, that violent TV programming actually reduces memory for the commercials in those shows and reduces the chance that people will intend to buy those products (Bushman, 1998, 2005). In attempting to explain this finding, Bushman suggests one reason may be that watching violence raises one's physiological arousal by making people angry and putting them in a bad mood. An angry mood can prime aggressive thoughts, which in turn may interfere with retrieval of the ad content. Negative moods are known to interfere with the brain's encoding of information. Also, the effort taken to try to repair the bad mood may distract from attending to and processing the ad. Thus, it may be that advertisers are not getting as much "bang for their buck" with violent content as with nonviolent content. This also suggests that other material being processed during violent entertainment might not be retained as well. In addition, the use of such a context runs greater risks of substantial portions of the audience being offended by the material. Thus, in terms of memory, perhaps students shouldn't study while they watch violent entertainment (see Bushman & Phillips, 2001, for a meta-analysis on this topic).

Whether or not the commercial itself contains violence may also make a difference to how well it is remembered. Gunter, Furnham, and Pappa (2005) found that a violent version of a commercial appearing in a violent film sequence was remembered much better than a nonviolent version of the same commercial in the same program. However, the nonviolent ad was remembered better in the context of a nonviolent program. Thus the congruence of the ad and program was important.

Sometimes the stimulus may be altered in ways that do not substantially affect its processing. One interesting phenomenon called *time compression* involves compressing a 36-second ad into 30 seconds by playing the ad at 120% of normal speed, an acceleration rate small enough that it is not readily detected and does not produce higher pitched sounds or other noticeable distortion (Hausknecht & Moore, 1986; Moore, Hausknecht, & Thamodaran, 1986).

A Constructionist Framework for Understanding Advertising

The cognitive principle known as *construction* argues that people do not literally store and retrieve information they read or hear, but rather modify it in accordance with their beliefs and the environment in which it is perceived.

The encoding and later retrieval of information about the product is guided by knowledge structures called schemas (see also Chapter 2). A *schema* is a knowledge structure or framework that organizes an individual's memory of information about people and events. It accepts all forms of information, irrespective of the mode—visual or auditory, linguistic or nonlinguistic. The individual is likely to go beyond the information available to draw inferences about people or events that are congruent with previously formed schemas (Harris, 1981; Harris, Sturm, Klassen, & Bechtold, 1986; Stayman & Kardes, 1992).

For example, imagine a commercial for "Lucky Soda" with a group of happy young adults running on a beach and opening a cooler filled with cola. In bold letters at the bottom of the screen are the words "Get Lucky." The slogan and picture elicit a "beach party" schema from memory, which helps the viewer draw inferences about the scene, going beyond what is specified directly in the ad. The viewer uses the schema to infer information not specifically stated in the ad, such as (1) the people have been swimming; (2) the weather is hot; (3) the people are thirsty, and, most importantly; (4) drinking Lucky makes the people happy and playful.

Deceptive Advertising

One issue of great concern to the general public is the issue of deceptive, or misleading, advertising. This relates directly to the theme of perceived reality and is at heart a cognitive question. The comprehension of an ad may be tested to determine whether the consumer constructs a meaning at variance with the facts; that is, whether the consumer is deceived (Harris, Dubitsky, & Bruno, 1983; Richards, 1990). From a cognitive perspective, the question is more complex than merely determining the literal truth or falseness of the ad itself (I. L. Preston & Richards, 1986; I. L. Preston, 1994). Advertising that directly states information which is not true is clearly both illegal and bad business, and thus fairly unusual, with the possible exception of ads for weight-loss and muscle-building products. An FTC study of weight-loss advertising (Sommerfeld, 2002) found that nearly 40% of the ads contained claims that were almost surely false, such as "You will lose 30 pounds of fat the first week." Although there is no scientific evidence supporting sustained weight loss as an effect of over-the-counter supplements, Americans spend billions of dollars each year on these products and services. People are so eager for a quick fix for losing weight that does not require them to decrease calorie intake or increase exercise that such outrageous claims continue to sell products.

Sometimes an ad may state a claim that is literally false, but we comprehend it in some nonliteral way that is consistent with reality, and thus we are not deceived. For example, claims like "Our cookies are made by elves in a tree"; "A green giant packs every can of our vegetables"; or "At this price these cars will fly out the door" are unlikely to be understood literally; thus consumers are not deceived. Sometimes photographic conventions raise interesting issues as to whether a picture is deceptive (see Close-Up 5.6).

Assuming that an ad does contain factual, rather than purely evaluative, information, determining whether or not an ad is deceptive is not the same as assessing its literal truth value. Truth may be considered a legal or linguistic question, which may be resolved by examining external reality. Deception, however, is a function of the understanding of the consumer and is thus a cognitive psychological question. It is covert and unobservable and must be inferred from an assessment of one's understanding of an ad. One may be deceived by an ad that is either true or false in some objective sense.

Close-Up 5.6: The Creative Work of Food Stylists

Food stylists prepare food for photography and try to make it look as good as possible. Sometimes the realities of the studio conventions call for surrogate munchies, and what you see in the ad may not be the real thing. For instance, ice cream is likely mashed potatoes covered with chocolate sauce, because ice cream melts too fast under hot studio lights. The head on beer is often shampoo or soap suds, because real beer bubbles do not last long enough for photography. White glue is added to milk to make it look whiter and creamier, and roasted chickens are spray-painted golden brown to look like they've been in the oven for hours—but aren't wrinkled (Wilson & Wilson, 1998). Pancakes are sprayed with Scotchgard to keep the syrup from soaking in so you can see it run appetizingly down the sides of the pancake. Pieces of cereal may be glued into white cardboard in a bowl so they won't ever get soggy. These conventions have been justified on the grounds that the falseness actually presents the product less deceptively and more honestly than literal truth (e.g., real ice cream would look like creamed soup, not ice cream, whereas mashed potatoes look like ice cream). Some cases, however, have been more questionable and sometimes have been disallowed by the Federal Trade Commission or the courts. For example, how many marbles should be allowed in the bottom of a soup bowl to buoy up the solid ingredients before it is deceptively suggesting more solid ingredients than are really there? How about the shaving cream commercial in which the sandpaper being shaved was actually loose sand grains on clear plastic? The razor would in fact shave sandpaper, but only fine grade sandpaper, not coarse. Because fine sandpaper looked like regular paper on TV, the advertiser used the sand grains on plastic. This particular case was argued in the courts for years (I. L. Preston, 1975).

True-but-Deceptive Ads

The type of advertising claim that is potentially the most damaging is the statement that is literally true but deceives consumers by inducing them to construct a meaning that is inconsistent with reality. Psychologists have long recognized the inferential nature of information processing, and studies on inference strongly suggest that, in order to derive the meaning of a statement, people typically interpret beyond what is explicitly stated. When applied to advertising, the consumer may be led to believe things about a product that were never explicitly stated (e.g., an ad states that a mouthwash *fights* germs and the reader infers that it *destroys* or *eliminates* germs).

There are several different types of linguistic constructions that may deceive the consumer without actually lying. All such claims invite the consumer to infer beyond the information stated and thus construct a stronger interpretation. This inference-drawing tendency plays on our knowledge, in the form of mental schemas, as discussed earlier, and is a natural component of our information-processing system.

One common class of claims that are true but potentially deceptive are *hedge words* or expressions (e.g., "may," "helps," "could help"), which considerably weaken the force of a claim without totally denying it; for example, "Scrubble Shampoo *helps* get rid of dandruff *symptoms*"; "Rainbow Toothpaste *fights* plaque"; or "Although *I can't promise to make you a millionaire by tomorrow*, order my kit, and you too *may* become rich."

Another common type of linguistic construction that may imply false information is the *elliptical comparative*; for example, "The Neptune Hatchback gives you *more*"; "Fibermunchies have *more* vitamin C"; or "PowderPower laundry detergent cleans *better*." Comparative adjectives or adverbs necessarily involve some sort of standard to which something is being compared. When a product merely says it gives "more," the statement is largely empty without a basis for comparison (more than what?). As long as anything true could be used to complete the comparative, the statement cannot clearly be considered false. However, our brains tend to construct the most plausible basis of comparison, not necessarily the most accurate.

Often a causal relationship may be implied when no more than a correlational one in fact exists. Making further inferences beyond what is stated directly increases the active cognitive processing by the consumer, which in turn typically improves memory. One particular technique is the *juxtaposition of two imperatives*, as in, "Help your child excel in school. Buy an Apricot home computer," or "Shed those extra pounds. Buy the Blubber-Buster massage belt." In neither of these cases does the ad state that buying the product will have the stated effect, but the causal inference is very easy to draw.

Such a cause-and-effect relationship may also be implied in a more general sense. For example, consider a commercial for diet cola in which a young woman talks about using and liking the product. Then, at the end of the ad, an attractive man says, "And I like the way it looks on her, too." Listeners may infer that drinking that product will cause female listeners to be more attractive to men, although the ad never states that directly.

Sometimes something unfavorable may be implied about a competitor's products or services without stating that directly; this is sometimes known as an *implied slur*. For example, consumers may infer from statements like "We don't skimp on the quality of our ingredients," or "If we do your taxes and you are audited by the IRS, we will accompany you to the audit" that competing companies do not provide the same service or quality, whereas most in fact do so. The claim is true but not distinctive to that product.

Reporting of scientific evidence in incomplete fashion may also imply considerably more than what is stated. In reporting results of surveys, "Three out of four doctors recommended Zayer Aspirin" would not be false if only four people were questioned. Claiming that "2,000 dentists recommended brushing with Laser Fluoride," without reporting the dentist sample size or "In a survey of 10,000 car owners, most preferred the Venus Zip" without reporting the number responding is seriously incomplete and potentially misleading, and can be labeled *pseudoscience*. Our minds tend to fill in the missing information in ways favorable to the advertiser.

Comparative advertising may employ very selective attribute comparisons to imply a much more global impression. For example the *piecemeal comparison*, "The Egret Pistol has more front-seat leg room than a Honda Accord, more rear-seat headroom than a Nissan Altima, and a larger trunk than a Toyota Camry" may imply that the car has a more spacious interior on most or all dimensions than any of the competitors, which is not necessarily a warranted inference from the given statements.

Studying Deception Scientifically

In experimental studies, people do in fact make the inferences as suggested and remember the inferred information as having been stated in the ad (e.g., remembering that a toothpaste prevents cavities when the ad only said it fights cavities). This is a very strong and stable finding that occurs with a variety of dependent measures (Burke, DeSarbo, Oliver, & Robertson, 1988; Gardner & Leonard, 1990; Harris, Pounds, Maiorelle, & Mermis, 1993; Harris, Trusty, Bechtold, & Wasinger, 1989; Richards, 1990; Russo, Metcalf, & Stephens, 1981).

Training people *not* to make such inferences is actually very difficult, because the tendency to infer beyond the given information is so strong. In a series of studies, a training session did have a significant effect in teaching people to put a brake on this natural inference-drawing activity; however, accomplishing this involved a multi-step process in which participants had to individually analyze ads, identify unwarranted inferences that could be drawn, and rewrite the ads to imply something more or less strongly (Bruno & Harris,

1980; Harris, Dubitsky, & Bruno, 1983). Such research has direct application to the preparation of consumer education materials, including some media literacy programs (see Chapter 12).

Sometimes changing the wording of an ad (i.e., framing it in a different way) may induce very different interpretations; for example, consider a meat advertised as "75% lean" versus one that is "25% fat." Consumers tend to evaluate the first example more favorably than the semantically identical second example (Levin & Gaeth, 1988). The "positive frame" leads us to construct a more positive image of the product. One type of currently popular advertising where one must carefully watch the wording is ads appealing to environmental or nutritional consciousness (see Close-Up 5.7).

Close-Up 5.7: Green Advertising

One of the most currently popular kinds of social responsibility appeals in advertising relate to the environment. Being able to advertise one's product as being biodegradable, organic, reducing carbon footprint, or otherwise conserving the earth's resources is a popular concern and would seem initially to be a socially responsible position. In fact, the emphasis in green advertising is much more on the means of production and on the consumption process (Iyer & Banerjee, 1993), presumably because that is where the environmental impact is at issue. However, this may not be the best way to reach the consumer.

Green advertising has suffered from a problem of low credibility; consumers apparently do not believe its claims. Sometimes the scientific reality is more complex than what is presented in the ad (T. M. Smith, 1998). For example, one popular kind of trash bag advertised that it was made of biodegradable plastic. Although this sounds good, once a sealed bag of contaminants is in a landfill, it may actually be better for the environment if it is not biodegradable, rather than slowly decomposing over several years, gradually releasing toxic content into the groundwater system. Some such products rely on the sun to initiate the decomposition process, and it is questionable how much sun the typical bag buried deep in a landfill would receive.

Sometimes some guidelines can be helpful to consumers. For example, in October 2002, the U.S. Department of Agriculture implemented legal definitions of "organic" foods. If a label says "100% Organic," the ingredients must contain no synthetic pesticides, herbicides, chemical fertilizers, antibiotics, hormones, or artificial preservatives. "Organic" means that at least 90% of the ingredients meet or exceed the USDA specifications, while "Made with Organic Ingredients" requires only 70% (Bjerklie, 2002).

Now we turn to some noncognitive aspects of advertising, focusing on the use of sex to sell and more generally on the question of whether we can be persuaded by messages we are not even aware of—so-called subliminal advertising.

Sex and Subliminal Advertising

One of the most common types of appeals in advertising is sex. Although some products such as perfume and cologne are sold almost exclusively through sex appeals, practically any product can be marketed through associating it with a beautiful, sexy, or scantily clad person. The sexual association and allure, and, even more, the overall good feelings engendered, then become a part of the perceived reality of that product for many consumers.

Classical Conditioning

A psychological process called classical conditioning sheds some light on how sex in advertising can affect us. Classical conditioning is the process discovered by the Russian physiologist Ivan Pavlov, who studied the physiology of hunger in dogs in the early years of the 20th century. In his studies he noticed a curious fact: his dogs would often start to salivate merely at the sight of an empty food dish. Given that there is no natural connection between dishes and drooling, why did they do this? Pavlov eventually decided that they had been classically conditioned. This process became one of the cornerstones of experimental (especially behaviorist) psychology and is as important for consumers of ads as it was for Pavlov's dogs.

An *unconditioned stimulus (UCS)* naturally, without learning, elicits an *unconditioned response (UCR)*. For example, meat (UCS) naturally produces salivation (UCR) in a dog. Similarly, the sight of a gorgeous woman (UCS) naturally elicits mild sexual arousal or at least some positive feelings (UCR) in most heterosexual males. At this point in the process, there is no conditioning. The conditioning occurs when the UCS is paired (associated) with the *conditioned stimulus (CS)*, which does not normally elicit the UCR. For example, Pavlov's dog dish (CS) was associated with meat (UCS), just as the attractive model (UCS) is associated with a product (CS) in a commercial. There may be some natural and obvious connection between the model and the product, such as a perfume ad that suggests a woman will attract sexy men if she wears that fragrance, or there may be no intrinsic connection at all, such as the beautiful woman who merely appears repeatedly next to the steel-belted radial tires.

After sufficient pairing of the UCS and the CS, the CS by itself comes to elicit the *conditioned response (CR)*, which in most cases is very similar to the UCR. Just as Pavlov's dogs eventually began to salivate (CR) with the empty food dish (CS), so may we continue to have positive feelings (CR) about the product (CS) when we see it without the gorgeous model. This basic classical conditioning paradigm is the psychological process being employed by most ads using sexual stimuli, for example, associating a nonsexual product such as beer with a sexy model in a beer commercial. Ironically, sometimes advertisers themselves may be loath to be associated with certain stimuli that they feel evoke strong negative responses in a large segment of the population. For example, at one point condom manufacturers were wary of becoming too closely associated with the gay community for fear of alienating potential heterosexual customers.

Subliminal Advertising

Although we could view classical conditioning as a subliminal effect in the broadest sense, people are more likely to worry about subliminal persuasion, especially as applied to advertising. In the late 1950s several popular press articles reported a study by advertising expert James Vicary wherein he reported increasing the sales of Coke and popcorn in a New Jersey movie theater by flashing the messages "Eat popcorn" and "Drink Coke" for a few milliseconds every 5 seconds during a film. Although the research was never published and in fact was admitted by Vicary in 1962 to have been a complete fabrication, intended only to increase his advertising agency's business (Pratkanis, 1992), the public became very alarmed, and the FCC and the National Association of Broadcasters (NAB) outlawed the practice. Excited about its prospects, however, a few radio stations threatened by the competition of television started broadcasting sub-audible messages like "Isn't TV dull?" and "TV's a bore" (Haberstroh, 1994).

Even today, large numbers of people continue to uncritically accept the existence of subliminal persuasion, in spite of there being no credible scientific evidence for its existence or effectiveness. "Subliminal" means below the threshold of conscious perception; by definition, if something is subliminal, we are not aware of it. Such stimuli may be a subaudible sound message in a store ("Don't shoplift"), a very brief visual message in a movie or TV show ("Buy popcorn"), or a visual sexual stimulus airbrushed into an ad photograph (S-E-X spelled in the lines on crackers or sex organs drawn inside ice cubes). What are the alleged effects of such stimuli? Do they in fact work to sell products?

A helpful distinction to bear in mind in considering this question is the difference between establishing the *existence* of some subliminal stimulus and demonstrating that such a stimulus has some *effect*. Books like Wilson Bryan Key's *Media Sexploitation* (1976), *The Clam-Plate Orgy* (1981), and *The Age of Manipulation* (1989) focus on demonstrating the existence of subliminal messages and sexual implants, but they give few arguments that demonstrate any effects of such stimuli. Such authors often implicitly assume that showing the existence of subliminal media stimuli necessarily entails that it has some effect. This assumption is completely unwarranted, however. Although there is some reputed evidence of an effect (Cuperfain & Clarke, 1985; Kilbourne, Painton, & Ridley, 1985), much of the so-called evidence is anecdotal or open to other interpretations. Many examples, such as allegedly obscene images or messages in Disney animations like *The Lion King, Aladdin,* and *The Little Mermaid,* are mostly the result of big imaginations, rumors, free time, and pause and rewind buttons (Bannon, 1995). In fact, there is little evidence that subliminal messages affect people very much (for reviews see Merikle & Cheesman, 1987; T. E. Moore, 1988; Pratkanis, 1992; Pratkanis & Greenwald, 1988).

Moore (1982) identified three types of stimuli: subliminal visual perception, subaudible speech, and embedded sexual stimuli, and carefully examined research evidence on possible effects in each. The conclusion was that there is some evidence (although it is far from compelling and not directly related to advertising anyway) that subliminal stimuli may in some cases have a weak positive effect of a general affective nature (i.e., they make us feel a little better about the product, probably due to classical conditioning). However, there is no evidence for any effects of subliminal stimuli on *behavior.* Saegert (1987) looked at the very few studies that seem to suggest effects from subliminal stimuli and argued that other interpretations are possible. The conclusion at this point seems to be that subliminal stimuli may exist on occasion but that their effects are minimal, fleeting, and/or nonexistent. Subliminal advertising seems to be a perceived reality in the mind of much of the public, but not an actual reality that stands up to scientific scrutiny. The same is true for subaudible recordings which, for example, purport to decrease smoking behavior (Greenwald, Spangenberg, Pratkanis, & Eskenazi, 1991; Merikle, 1988; Merikle & Skanes, 1992).

Similar issues are involved in heated controversies over subliminal messages in rock music. In 1990, the family of two teenage suicide victims in Nevada brought suit against the group Judas Priest and CBS Records, on the grounds that subliminal and backmasked (recorded backwards) messages on the album *Stained Class* had directed the boys to take their own lives; the judge ruled against the family (Wilson & Wilson, 1998). Another concern has been allegedly satanic messages recorded backwards into certain rock music recordings. See Close-Up 5.8 for details of a carefully designed research program to test for effects of such stimuli.

Now let us turn to advertising aimed at the youngest segments of our population.

Advertising to Children

Children are an enormous and growing market for advertising. There are actually three distinct markets for children: the primary market, the influence market, and the future market (Valkenburg, 2004). The *primary market,* in which children spend their own money, has exploded in recent years, as

Close-Up 5.8: Satanic Messages in Rock Music?

Periodically one hears the claim that some rock music contains embedded messages recorded backward. Although no one claims that these messages can be consciously easily perceived when the record is played forward, concern has been expressed that, unbeknownst to the listener, there may be some unconscious effect. Furthermore, some have even been concerned that such messages may be satanic, and they caused legislation to be introduced in several states in the 1980s that called for warning labels about such messages to appear on album jackets.

Psychologists John Vokey and Don Read (1985) of the University of Lethbridge in Alberta conducted a careful series of studies designed to test the effects of such messages—assuming for the moment that they exist (an assumption that is not at all established, but we will leave that for now). When verbal messages on tape were played backwards, research participants showed no understanding of the meaning; identifying the sex or voice of the speaker was about all that they could perceive. Next, they tested for unconscious effects by giving a spelling test in which some of the words were homophones (e.g., read, reed). A biasing context sentence ("A saxophone is a reed instrument") was played backward, but listeners were no more likely than a control group to write "reed" instead of "read." When backward messages were played and subjects were merely asked to assign the statement to the category Christian, satanic, pornographic, or advertising, based on its content, they could not do so at greater than chance level. The only time that people ever perceived and reported anything at greater than chance level was in one study in which the experimenter picked out phrases in advance and asked the participants to listen for them. Only under conditions of such strong suggestibility could people comprehend anything from the backward messages.

Vokey and Read's studies clearly demonstrate that, even if backward messages do exist in music, it is highly unlikely that they could be having any effect on the hearers. This conclusion is all the more striking considering that in their studies there was no competing forward message as there is with real music CDs. In at least a couple of cases, proposed record-labeling legislation was withdrawn based on results of this research. If you want to hear some backward speech and music with alleged messages, see jeffmilner.com/backmasking.

parents are having fewer children later in life with more money to spend on them. Children in the United States spent $27 billion of their own money in 2003, and advertisers spent $15 billion to influence that spending, up from only $100 million in 1983 (Carlsson-Paige, 2008). Although most of these ad dollars were spent on television, substantial amounts also went to Internet and point-of-purchase advertising, and product placements in children's programming. A meta-analysis (Desmond & Carveth, 2007) found that advertising exposure results in more positive associations with advertised brands and more likelihood of selecting those brands, although the effect sizes were small. Children at different ages are affected by different sorts of persuasive techniques because of their particular stage of cognitive development and level of media literacy (Livingstone & Helsper, 2006). For example, very young children are more persuaded by a lively visual appeal and older children by a social norms appeal.

The second child advertising market is the *influence market*, whereby children influence their parents' buying decisions either through direct request or demands or more indirectly by parents taking children's wishes into account when they make their purchases. Preschool children can readily identify corporate logos and characters they have seen in advertising (Fischer, Schwartz, Richards, Goldstein, & Rojas, 1991; Valkenburg & Buijzen, 2005). In addition, children by age 2 already request specific products when shopping with parents in stores, and this specific pressure increases to a peak around age 7, after which it starts to decline, being gradually replaced by more mature discussions and influence on purchasing (Buijzen & Valkenburg, 2008). It has been estimated that the overall influence of children on family purchasing is around 28 to 30%, varying for different products from a high of 70 to 80% for toys and video games to a low of 10% for the family car (McNeal, 1999; Valkenburg, 2004). As children grow older, they exert more influence on family purchases, although that influence becomes increasingly indirect. The influence of children on parental spending is growing rapidly and tends to have a negative effect on the quality of parent–child relationships.

The third child advertising market is the *future market*, in which children are developing brand preferences that often carry over into adulthood. Children as young as 3 have good recognition for specific product names and logos, with McDonald's golden arches being the highest. Children ages 3 to 6 already consistently ask for specific product or restaurant names. Some of these will become lifetime favorites and advertisers work hard to establish brand loyalty early.

One of the most important media concerns in regard to children is television commercials aimed specifically at kids, such as those aired on Saturday morning and after-school shows, and child-oriented cable channels like Nickelodeon and Disney. Keep in mind, however, that children's programming constitutes only a minority of the hours of TV that children watch, although the percentage of that time filled with commercials has increased in the United States since the 1980s. This "kidvid" programming represents only about one-quarter of the total TV time for 6-year-olds and a mere 5% for 11-year-olds. The rest of the many thousands of commercials that a child sees every year are those appearing on general programming (i.e., prime-time and daytime offerings such as game shows, soap operas, dramas, reality shows, and syndicated sitcom reruns).

Turning now to kidvid ads specifically, about 80% of them advertise products in only four or five categories: toys, cereal, candy and snacks, sodas/soft drinks, and fast-food restaurants (Kunkel & Gantz, 1992; Kaiser Family Foundation, 2007a; Kunkel & McIlrath, 2003). These figures are unchanged since the 1980s. Almost half of these ads are for food products, mostly high-calorie, low-nutrition foods (Stitt & Kunkel, 2008). In fact, only 3% of the ads are for healthy foods. Almost half of the food ads (43%) are for breakfast cereals, and 20% are for fast food restaurants (Bower, 2002). The toy ads are many but highly seasonal, being primarily concentrated during the pre-Christmas season, with numbers much lower during the rest of the year. According to economist Juliet Schor, U.S. kids receive 45% of the toys manufactured worldwide, averaging 70 new toys a year per child (Carlsson-Paige, 2008)!

Children's ads are technical marvels, full of color, movement, and animation, with most of them emphasizing how much fun children can have with the product. Special visual and sound effects are common and captivating. The pace is fast. Even less hard information is presented than in adult ads, and there is even more of a global association of the product with fun times. There is lots of alliteration (e.g., Frosted Flakes, Cap'n Crunch, Kit Kat) and word play (e.g., "fruitiful," or a character yodeling "Cheerio-ios"). Many use animated spokespersons, which increase the young child's level of attention, recognition, and positive attitude toward the product (Neeley & Schumann, 2004). The most common theme is fun (27%), followed by taste and flavor (19%) and product performance (18%). In contrast to adult ads, appeals based on price, quality, nutrition, or safety accounted for less than 1% of kids' ads each (Kunkel & Gantz, 1992).

Valkenburg and Cantor (2001) identified four stages that a child goes through in understanding advertising. During the first two years of life, the child primarily notices bright and colorful television images (many of the best of which happen to be in commercials) and starts asking for products seen on TV as early as 18 months to 2 years of age. In the preschool years (2–5), children understand TV literally and are very vulnerable to its appeals. By the third stage (ages 5–8), they have somewhat more cognitive sophistication and begin to develop strategies for negotiating with parents over purchases. In the last stage (ages 9–12) the child makes the transition to more adult styles of consuming.

Within this sequence of development, there are several particular issues of concern.

Differentiating Ads and Programs

One major concern about children and commercials is that very young children do not discriminate between commercial and program content and do not understand the persuasive intent of ads or the economics of television.

Although children can identify commercials at a very early age, this identification seems to be based on superficial audio and video aspects rather than on an understanding of the difference between programs and commercials (Raju & Lonial, 1990; S. L. Smith & Atkin, 2003). Children younger than 4 or 5 have little understanding that commercials are meant to actually sell products. Depending on how such understanding is tested, elementary school children show various stages of development in understanding the purpose of ads (Bever, Smith, Bengen, & Johnson, 1975; Martin, 1997; Sheikh, Prasad, & Rao, 1974; Smith & Atkin, 2003; Stephens & Stutts, 1982; Ward, Wackman, & Wartella, 1977). The insertion of video and audio separators ("bumpers") to mark the transition between program and commercials has not made this discrimination easier (Hoy, Young, & Mowen, 1986; Stutts, Vance, & Hudelson, 1981). Perhaps the separators are just too brief to be noticed, or perhaps they look much like the adjacent programming. Discriminating between ads and programs is especially difficult if a primary character in the show is also the spokesperson in the ad, a situation called host-selling (Hoy et al., 1986; Kunkel, 1988; Neeley & Schumann, 2004).

As they grow older, children show increasing understanding of the selling purpose of ads (see Martin, 1997, for a meta-analysis). Only about a third of 5- to 7-year-olds understand this purpose, but almost all do by age 11 (Blatt, Spencer, & Ward, 1972; Ward et al., 1977; Wilson & Weiss, 1992). Typical explanations of middle elementary children center around the truth (or lack thereof) of the material; however, not until late elementary school is the distrust based on perceived intent and an understanding of the advertiser's motivation to sell the product.

Disclaimers

Another important issue in children's advertising is the question of disclaimers, those little qualifying statements like "some assembly required," "batteries not included," "some pieces sold separately," or "part of a nutritious breakfast." For obvious reasons these are seldom the central focus of the commercial. In fact, the disclaimers often occur in vocabulary far beyond the age of the targeted child and typically occur only in small script superimposed at the bottom of the screen or hurriedly read by an announcer. Of course, this is completely lost on a pre-reading child and probably on an older one as well, because the colorful activity in the background is so much more enticing and interesting. In a content analysis, Kunkel and Gantz (1992) found that over half of the commercials aimed at children had some sort of disclaimer, with 9% having two or more. These usually appeared as an adult voiceover, often in rapid hushed tones (Muehling & Kolbe, 1999). Unlike the rest of the ad, most of the disclaimers used adult terminology. Most preschoolers do not understand such language (Stutts & Hunnicutt, 1987), although some disclaimers were less difficult to understand than others.

Incidentally, disclaimers and other fine print information flashed at the bottom of the TV screen are not limited to children's ads. A content analysis of prime-time TV ads overall found two thirds of them contained some sort of disclaiming "footnote" (Kolbe & Muehling, 1992). Such disclaimers are especially noticeable in the possible side effects mentioned during prescription drug ads on TV (for a more complete discussion of prescription drug ads, see the section dedicated to these products later in this chapter).

Television, Toymakers, and the Military

In 1983 Mattel's popular He-Man toy made the move to television (*He-Man and the Masters of the Universe*) and within a year became the second-best-selling toy in the country. This successful marketing approach has been massively copied since then and has raised a new issue in regard to children's TV ads, namely the commercial-as-show phenomenon. In succeeding years, dozens of television shows were linked to toys in some way, including *The Transformers*, *She-Ra: Princess of Power*, *Teenage Mutant Ninja Turtles*, *Power Rangers*, and *The Care Bear Family*. Toy companies, TV networks, video game makers, processed food companies, and even restaurants routinely promote the toys and their tie-ins together (Pecora, 1997). One of the most successful was the Pokémon craze of the late 1990s. Although beginning as 150 cartoon characters in a Japanese Nintendo game, Pokémon was simultaneously launched worldwide in 1998 as a TV cartoon, collector card series, video game, and toy merchandise. This was shortly followed by a Warner Brothers movie, Burger King kids' meal toys, children's clothes, and other merchandise (Strasburger & Wilson, 2002). Thus television and the toy industry have been wedded almost as significantly and profoundly as sports and TV (see Chapter 6).

A relatively new partner is the movie industry. Although toys tied to films have been around for some time (see the *Star Wars* franchise), movies based on toys began in the 2000s with big budget films like *Transformers*. In 2012, there was even a movie, *Battleship*, based on the old Milton Bradley board game. The movie in turn inspired the sale of additional toys and action figures.

This marriage of the film, TV, toy, video game, and food industries raises several concerns. Critics have argued that children's programming is driven too much by the marketability of associated toys rather than by the quality of the shows (Carlsson-Paige, 2008; Carlsson-Paige & Levin, 1990; Kline, 1992). Toy and broadcasting executives defend the policy by arguing that creative animated shows are preferable to tired syndicated sitcom reruns. Still, producers of non-toy-related children's programming report difficulty funding and selling their products. Programming is routinely initiated around an existing (or soon to be marketed) toy. Although merchandising toys from successful TV shows has long been practiced (*Mickey Mouse Club*, *Sesame Street*), until the 1980s the show came first, not the toy. In large part, that is no longer the case. There is also some evidence that the combination of toys and TV shows that feature the toys have an inhibiting effect on imaginative play, especially for older children able to play more creatively than the toy's use in the show's context would suggest (Greenfield et al., 1993). While the toy–show connection may help the youngest children see play possibilities, in older children it restricts their play options to what is suggested by the show.

The toy–television alliance has also helped to produce increasing marketing segmentation by gender (Carlsson-Paige, 2008). The violent shows and accompanying toy weapons and action figures (never called "dolls" if marketed to boys) are sold to boys, whereas girls are offered the soft, cuddly shows and toys like My Little Pony, Rainbow Brite and Barbie dolls. Successful "boy" toys have been repackaged and sold to girls, as in pink Barbie Jeeps and computers or the "Adorable Transformables" that change from a dog into lipstick, instead of from a car into a robot. Although food ads are likely to portray boys and girls together, ads for toys are usually gender-segmented, most often selling action figures or video games to boys and Barbie dolls and beauty products to girls. Also, the types of interaction are different; ads to girls have been found to show cooperation 80% of the time, while only 30% of the ads to boys did so (Larson, 2001b).

The huge success of boy-oriented action figures, as well as violent video games, has led to another odd but troubling alliance. Toymakers such as Hasbro regularly work with the military in developing new battle toys (W. L. Hamilton, 2003). The new offerings closely follow world events. Firefighter and police action figures sold well after September 2001. After the invasion of Iraq in 2003, action figures like "Delta Force Sniper" and "Marine Force Recon" sold well, as did "Josh Simon," a "Desert Nuclear, Biological, Chemical Trooper," and Army National Guard "Homeland Security Amy."

The U.S. Army has developed a video game "America's Army," in which players work as a team to conduct missions and raids. As well as being entertaining, it just might be useful as a subtle recruiting tool (Carlson, 2003). Perhaps more surprising is that this military–toymaker alliance is not one way. The Pentagon looks to toymakers for inspiration in developing new weapons, which new military recruits who have grown up with these toys and video games can use very naturally. Pentagon spokesperson Glenn Flood says that the M-16 rifle was based on a Mattel toy, quick-loading assault weapons were inspired by super-soaker water guns, a Marine Corps remote-controlled truck called the Dragon Runner is guided by a keypad modeled after a Sony PlayStation, and unmanned robotic vehicles use gaming control panels from electronic games (W. L. Hamilton, 2003). The Institute for Creative Technologies, founded by the U.S. Army in 1999, brings together computer scientists, video game manufacturers, the entertainment industry, and the army to cooperatively develop "immersive" (i.e., highly realistic) training simulations. This high degree of realism is important both in military training and in video games, an issue we return to in Chapter 9.

Many of the toy-related TV shows and games, especially those targeted at boys, are highly violent in nature. This in itself is not new; children's cartoons have always been the most violent shows on TV, in terms of numbers of violent incidents (see Chapter 9). A particular concern with the newer shows, however, is that the availability of toys makes it easier to act out the violence modeled by the cartoon characters. Whereas children have always played war games of sorts, in the past they have usually had to employ their imagination to make a stick into a sword or a cardboard cutout into a gun. In so doing, they also developed their creative capacities (Carlsson-Paige, 2008). A plastic Uzi or AK-47, however, can only be used to play killing people and thus requires no particular imagination. The more highly defined the violent purpose of the toy, the more it directs the child's play in a violent direction, even in a child who might not otherwise be inclined toward violent play. It also encourages the child to look on the real thing as just a toy. There are many serious consequences of the failure to distinguish toy weapons from the real thing: children using toy guns have been killed by police officers who thought they were about to be fired upon with real weapons. For this reason, some jurisdictions have banned such realistic-looking toy guns, though, curiously, the real guns are still legal.

Sometimes the marrying of toys, violence, and advertising goes to amazing lengths. For example, a popular toy for Christmas 2002 was a bombed-out dollhouse with bullet holes and smashed furniture. An Easter 2003 promotion in which Easter baskets included military action figures and weapons was withdrawn from Walmart and Kmart after public complaints. Even a neo-Nazi group has joined the fun, with a game called Ethnic Cleansing, in which players run through a rotted city killing African Americans, Latino/as, and Jews (Carlson, 2003).

Tobacco Advertising and Role Modeling

A final area of particular concern in relation to marketing to children and teens is tobacco advertising, especially advertising that is allegedly aimed at nonsmoking youth. Historically, tobacco has been the most heavily advertised product in the United States—in spite of a ban on broadcast advertising since 1971! Almost all smokers start in their teens or pre-teens, most often at ages 11 to 13, and almost never after age 20. Magazines are the major media outlet for tobacco advertising, and those publications that accept it have less coverage of health-related issues than those which do not accept such ads. Tobacco companies have become more creative in marketing, however. Sponsorship of sporting events, logos on shopping carts and baskets, and designer clothing and tote bags advertising the brand names are common and (as of the time of writing, at least) perfectly legal in the United States.

Movies are a particular concern. In spite of a huge drop in smoking among U.S. adults between 1960 and 1990 (down from over half to about 25%) and in smoking by TV series characters (down to 2% by the early 1980s), the rate of smoking in movies remained relatively high throughout the 1990s and was about three times the rate of smoking in the population. This may in part be due to product placements, which the tobacco industry claims to have discontinued; for example, Philip Morris (now known as Altria) reportedly paid over $350,000 to have Lark cigarettes smoked in the 1989 James Bond movie *License to Kill* (Strasburger & Wilson, 2002). Various studies showed tobacco use in 85 to 90% of the most popular movies in the 1990s, cutting across all genres of film (Roberts, Henriksen, & Christenson, 1999). Even over half of the animated G-rated movies issued from 1937 to 1997 featured smoking, and many of these old films are still classics viewed by millions of modern children (Strasburger & Wilson, 2002). The good news is that, as a result of public awareness and the work of some advocacy groups, smoking in U.S. movies appears to be on the decline. According to a report released by the Centers for Disease Control and Prevention, between 1991 and 2010, instances of smoking in movies seemed to peak around 2005, when 67% of top-grossing films contained smoking. By 2010, that percentage had dropped to 45% (Glantz et al., 2011).

However, there is increasing evidence that smoking by characters in movies, especially if they are admired characters and actors, can lead young people to start smoking (Dal Cin, Gibson, Zanna, Shumate, & Fong, 2007; Dalton et al., 2002; Distefan, Gilpin, Sargent, & Pierce, 1999; Sargent et al., 2001; Tickle, Sargent, Dalton, Beach, & Heatherton, 2001). Many teens perceive smoking in films as common and an accurate reflection of reality, seeing it as a model for dealing with stress and developing one's self-image, and as a marker of passage into adulthood (McCool, Cameron, & Petrie, 2001). As long as the "hot stars" like Gwyneth Paltrow, Reese Witherspoon, Brad Pitt, and Ben Affleck smoke on screen, this behavior is likely to be modeled by their adoring fans.

There is evidence of a causal relationship between advertising and tobacco consumption (Tye, Warner, & Glantz, 1987) and huge profits from sales of tobacco to minors and to those who became addicted to tobacco as minors (DiFranza & Tye, 1990). Tremendous criticism was leveled at the Joe Camel character used to sell Camel cigarettes in the 1980s. At one time he was recognized by 98% of adolescents, though by only 72% of adults. This occurred at the same time that sales of Camels to minors were skyrocketing from less than half of 1% to a third of the youth cigarette market (DiFranza et al., 1991)! Selling the image of smoking as cool and the "in thing" to do pays off. Children who believe that smoking will enhance their popularity or attractiveness are 4.7 times more likely to smoke than children who do not believe that (DiFranza et al., 1991).

Advertising to children has always been regulated more than advertising to adults, but the extent of the oversight has varied considerably depending on the political whims of the time, and questions have been raised as to the ethics of advertising aimed at children (see Close-Up 5.9). Whatever the government or industry regulation, there is still a tremendous need for media literacy in the home and elsewhere.

Advertising in New Places

In recent years advertisers have had to scramble, trying harder and harder to attract and keep our attention. Although ads seem to be everywhere, we also

---

Close-Up 5.9: Advertising Regulation, the FCC, and the FTC

In the United States, the consumer watchdog agency overseeing advertising is the Federal Trade Commission (FTC). The FTC was established in the early 20th century during the trust-busting era of increasing concern over abusive monopolistic practices of large corporations. Its sister organization, the Federal Communications Commission (FCC), oversees radio and television and was set up primarily to deal with issues such as assigning frequencies and channels and ensuring access and fair practices, although at times the FCC has gotten involved in matters of perceived decency (see Close-Up 1.1).

There have usually been stricter regulations and laws regarding children's advertising than for ads aimed at adults. For example, drug advertising aimed at children has usually been prohibited. In the late 1970s the FTC was probably at its most aggressive as a proconsumerist organization, in relation to issues such as deceptive advertising and children's ads. One interesting incident that apparently helped prompt this approach involved children's television host Soupy Sales in 1965. During an early morning show, Sales prompted his child viewers to go find their sleeping fathers' wallets and look for "some of those funny green pieces of paper with all those nice pictures of George Washington, Abraham Lincoln, and Alexander Hamilton, and send them along to your old pal, Soupy, care of WNEW, New York" (Sivulka, 1998, p. 323). Apparently, many did!

The FTC's protective stance changed in the early 1980s, with increasing deregulation and the Reagan administration's pro-business philosophy. For example, in 1983 the FCC abolished its children's TV guidelines and in 1984 it lifted the limits on allowed commercial time per hour. In the 1980s the FTC became far less aggressive in pursuing claims of misleading advertising based on the implication of a false claim. In the 1990s the pendulum started to swing the other way, as can be seen in the Children's Television Act (1990), which required broadcasters to air some educational programming ratings for television shows.

The FCC later interpreted the 1990 act to require at least three hours of "educational and informational" programming per week (Steyer, 2002).

Some places have stricter regulation. For example, Norway, Sweden, and Quebec province have all banned TV commercials targeting children. Italy permits no ads during children's cartoons, and Greece permits no ads for toys between 7 a.m. and 11 p.m., and no ads for war toys at all (Carlsson-Paige, 2008). If characters eat on kids' TV shows airing in the U.K., the BBC requires them to consume healthy foods on camera (Fonda, 2004). Even in the United States, *Sesame Street*'s classic Cookie Monster has started eating vegetables. Do you think advertising aimed at children is ethical?

have more technology to delete or subdue them (e.g., muting or fast-forwarding videos, pop-up blockers, delete keys, spam filters). In response, the advertisers have become increasingly clever in placing ads in places we can't ignore, sometimes even in places where we do not even realize there are ads. This section of the chapter looks at several of these.

High-Tech Billboards

Digital technology has allowed all sorts of more involving variations on the traditional outdoor advertising of the billboard (Tsiantar, 2006). Clear Channel LED billboards change image every 8 seconds along Interstate 90 in northeast Ohio, and vary their products by the time of day. A digital Absolut vodka ad featuring Lenny Kravitz invites viewers to send a text message to enable their smart phones to download a free four-minute MP3 track. Other billboards send digital coupons to one's cell phone, to be used in nearby stores. Digital LED screens on London's famous double-decker buses and on escalators in its famed Underground change their ads frequently.

In-Store Advertising

Point-of-purchase advertising in stores has long been used, from standing boards advertising products, to shopping baskets with product logos, to display ads in the aisles to call attention to a particular product shelved there. However, stores are becoming ever more creative at injecting advertising into the shopping experience itself. For example, Premier Retail Networks (PRN) produces mini-television networks for stores like Walmart, Best Buy, and Sears, customizing the entertainment and especially the ads, at 12 minutes per hour, for that store. For example, Walmart has used in-store TV since 1997, and a 2005 study found that customers watched an average of 7 minutes per shopping trip. More importantly, they showed 65% brand recall, compared with 23% for commercials from regular television. Advertisers pay up to $300,000 for four weeks of ads in Walmart, but they have the huge advantage that the weekly audience of 138 million is already in the store ready to buy (C. B. Thomas, 2005)!

Product Placements

When your favorite actor in a TV show or movie drinks a Pepsi, smokes a Marlboro, or talks on an iPhone, is the choice of a brand coincidental? Hardly. The manufacturer has probably paid thousands of dollars through a placement agent or somehow contributed to the film or TV show as part of a deal to have those products used. For example, Nokia paid to have Jennifer Aniston use one of its cell phones in *Friends*, and producers of *The Saint* actually shot more footage after the film wrapped, in order to include several scenes featuring Volvo's latest model, in response to Volvo's offer of an ad campaign to promote the car and the film together (Gornstein, 1997). Ramses Condoms paid over $10,000 to feature its product in *Lethal Weapon II*, while Safetex paid around $15,000 to have Julia Roberts pull a Gold Circle condom out of her boot while sitting on Richard Gere's desk in *Pretty Woman* (Wilson & Wilson, 1998). James Bond films feature some of the most blatant and ubiquitous product placements, for products including Visa card, Avis car rental, Smirnoff vodka, Ericsson cell phones, British Airways, Omega watches, Heineken beer, L'Oreal makeup, and Mercedes automobiles (Rimmer, 2002). Reality-based TV shows like *Survivor* and *The Amazing Race* have taken product placement to new heights, including many scenes of the "cast" using the products. And don't think it's an accident when judges on *American Idol* sip Coke, the host recommends texting your vote on an AT&T phone, and contestants drive Fords! According to one analysis, *American Idol* had the most product placement occurrences among primetime shows in 2011, with 577 during 39 episodes; it was also the highest-rated show of the 2010–2011 season ("Primetime Shows," 2012). TV and movies are not the only modalities for product placement, however. Even video games routinely make these sorts of agreements with manufacturers (Nelson, 2002).

Often the payment for such positioning is more subtle than a flat fee for the appearance of the product. For example, Plantronics placed its headsets in *Minority Report* and *Die Another Day* in 2002 by paying "marketing dollars" for costs toward promotion of the film (Rimmer, 2002). This way, film advertising, trailers, and merchandising can promote both the product and the film at the same time.

There are three different levels of product placement, according to the *landscape model* (Yang & Roskos-Ewoldson, 2007). The shallowest level is *background*, in which a product is shown onscreen but not used by a major character. The second level, *use*, is when the product is actually used by the character. Finally, at the *story connection* level, the product actually is an active "enabler" in the plot to help the character solve some problem; for example when Elliott used Reese's Pieces candies to attract the alien in *E.T.*, or a Junior Mint candy is accidentally dropped into a patient during surgery on *Seinfeld*.

Do product placements work? As noted in the opening pages of this chapter, after Elliott used Reese's Pieces to lure the alien from his hiding place in the family's backyard in *E.T.* in 1982, sales of the candy increased by 65%. Mars had initially declined an offer to use M&Ms in this role (Rimmer, 2002). Although there has not yet been a lot of research on the behavioral effects of product placements, one study on product placement and attitudes showed research participants a 20-minute clip from the movie *Die Hard*, in which the lead character either smoked or did not smoke; those who saw him smoking found him more appealing than those who saw the nonsmoking clip (Gibson & Maurer, 2000). Generally products are recalled better, especially in explicit memory measures, if they have deeper involvement in the plot (Yang & Roskos-Ewoldson, 2007).

Variations on product placement are becoming more numerous and more creative. In 2002, cosmetics giant Revlon cut a deal with ABC to have a part on three months of the soap opera *All My Children*, when the story line had a protagonist spying on a rival firm (Eisenberg, 2002). There are even product placements within other ads (Elliott, 2002b). For example, a Toyota ad featured a Sony Vaio laptop computer to highlight the feature of a 110-volt outlet inside a car, burnishing the prestige of both products at the same time. Sometimes the juxtaposition can be more humorous, for the purpose of attracting attention. For example a Chevrolet TV commercial featured the two "lonely Maytag repairmen" cruising around in a Chevrolet. Guest appearances on talk shows may even involve product placements of a sort. For example, drug companies sometimes pay celebrities like Lauren Bacall, Kathleen Turner, or Rob Lowe for pushing their products on talk shows (Eisenberg, 2002). These guest appearances are often not noted as paid appearances. Advances in technology are also creating new opportunities for product placement. For example, in 2011 when a rerun of a 2006 episode of *How I Met Your Mother* aired, a movie poster for the 2011 movie *Bad Teacher* was digitally pasted into a scene (Stransky, 2011)!

Although product placement may seem like a savvy new marketing phenomenon, it has been going on for years. For example, in *I Love Lucy*, Ricky and Lucy very conspicuously smoked Philip Morris cigarettes (a product line which actors Lucille Ball and Desi Arnaz also endorsed in commercials). Other radio and early TV shows even had product names in their titles, for example, *General Electric Theater*, *The Dinah Shore Chevy Show*, and *The Colgate Comedy Hour*.

Is there an artistic or ethical problem with product placements? If the script, the blocking, and the editing are driven by motivation to show a product rather than artistic and script-driven concerns, there may be a compromise of artistic quality. Particularly troubling is the case of modeling the use of unhealthy or dangerous products, such as tobacco or alcohol. For example, although instances of smoking on U.S. TV are very low (far lower than the 20–25% of the population who smoke), smoking is far more common in movies. Much of this difference has been attributed to product placement of tobacco in movies.

Classrooms and Schools

As school districts and universities become increasingly financially strapped, they are turning to private industry for additional funds. One type of arrangement is a sales contract whereby a school agrees to exclusively sell one brand of soft drink, for example, on its campus for some period of time in return for a substantial sum. One university concluded a contract with Pepsico to sell only Pepsi drinks on campus in return for $5 million for the university library. At a time when journal subscriptions and library hours were being cut, $5 million was a big help.

Public schools have long had corporate tie-ins, like the Pizza Hut Book-It campaign, in which an elementary school child receives a coupon for a free Personal Pan pizza from Pizza Hut if he or she completes an agreed-upon number of pages of reading per month. Sometimes if everyone in the class meets the requirements the whole class gets an in-school pizza party at the end of the semester. Children are encouraged to read, and Pizza Hut socializes a new generation of customers for its restaurants.

Sometimes there are required sales quotas to actually receive the money. For example, a Colorado Springs, Colorado school district was somewhat behind on its agreement with Coke to sell 1.68 million units of Coke products. Not wanting to risk losing the $8 million, 10-year contract, the district administrator moved vending machines to more accessible areas, encouraged principals to allow drinking Cokes in class, and generally exhorted staff and students to drink more Coke products as a way to support their school (Labi, 1999).

Advertising has become a major presence in schools. School buses and athletic scoreboards sell advertising space, and students watch the commercials on daily news summaries on CNN or Channel One, which is required viewing for an estimated 40% of American secondary students (Carlsson-Paige, 2008). Fast food chains like Taco Bell and Pizza Hut sell their products in many food court-like school cafeterias, and soft drinks machines are everywhere (Wartella & Jennings, 2001). Corporate-sponsored curriculum kits are also increasingly common, and one study suggested a strong bias in 80% of these, as when an Exxon curriculum emphasized the earth's resilience to recovering from oil spills (Carlsson-Paige, 2008).

Sometimes ad money can go to other good uses. The bottled water company Evian refurbished a rundown public swimming pool in the southwest

London suburb of Brixton and tiled the bottom with its brand name. Although this was not readily seen by swimmers, it just happened to be highly visible to passengers in planes that were taking off and landing at Heathrow Airport (Eisenberg, 2002).

Advertisers are forever finding new places to put ads; see Close-Up 5.10 for some of the newest and most creative locations.

Close-Up 5.10: Captive Marketing

The advertising industry is forever finding new places to hawk its wares. Some of the newest agencies, with names like Flush Media, Cunning Stunts, and Captivate Network, take advantage of places where people find themselves necessarily looking at a flat surface for whatever reason. Public restrooms are one of the most potentially profitable of these new "captive marketing" sites. Print ads or even video screens are appearing above sinks, urinals, and inside toilet stall doors in restrooms. The user is captive for a minute or so, a building owner can make some profit off the otherwise non-income-producing restroom, and very precise gender-targeted marketing can occur. Another popular new advertising site is the elevator, a non-revenue-producing space where both the advertiser and building owner can now make a profit. Increasingly we are also seeing video ads in theaters, airplanes, buses, taxis, and even golf carts (Orecklin, 2003). In 2011, Budget Rent a Car started a marketing campaign in which they sold large advertising "wraps" that could be placed on their cars. These wraps, similar to those on some city buses, advertise products such as energy drinks. Car rental customers who agree to drive a wrapped car receive a discount on their rental rate (Haines, 2011).

Sometimes we meet marketing where we least expect it. Big Fat Promotions of New York has hired people to pose as bar customers and talk up certain drinks to the clientele, mothers to talk up a laundry detergent at their children's ball games, and commuters to play with a certain PDA on the train home from work (Eisenberg, 2002). A British agency even rents college students' foreheads to display corporate logos, in semipermeable color transfers made from vegetable dye. These last about a week, and students receive $6.80 an hour for the 3 to 4 hours a day they are visible to other students. Cunning Stunts spokesperson Nikki Horton reports reaction from financially struggling students was "overwhelming" (Payne, 2003). Movie theaters now routinely show a few commercials before their movie trailers, and British and Irish theaters have begun to present 3-minute live commercials before their nightly shows begin.

Advertising on the Internet

One of the fastest-growing areas of advertising is the Internet. In 2010, web advertising revenue surpassed newspaper advertising for the first time, totaling $26 billion in the U.S. (Worden, 2011). However, Internet advertising has also provided marketers with some distinct challenges (Schumann & Thorson, 1999). The pop-up, pop-under, and banner ads familiar to us on most websites tend to be as annoying as they are ubiquitous; and the more salient they are, the more annoying they are. The ads that pop up and are hard to get rid of risk alienating the potential market, yet the advertiser has to get people's attention. The most explosive growth in ads on the Internet in recent years has come in the form of spam, or e-mail advertising, which grew almost 1900% in the United States between 2002 and 2003 alone, to 4.9 trillion pieces of mail (C. Taylor, 2003). Many of these are for cheap loans, weight-loss products, Viagra and other drugs, computer accessories, and, more distressingly, breast- and penis-enlargement products, pornography, and solicitation of sexual encounters. How to screen out the spam has been a major challenge for e-mail providers and programs in recent years. Some are even asking whether the huge volume of spam will soon begin to make e-mail not worth the trouble (B. Sullivan, 2003).

One of the most attractive but also challenging new fields for ads has been social media, especially Facebook. The number of ads on Facebook has been increasing, but so have the complaints about them. When Facebook went public with its initial IPO in 2012, its price fell far below what was expected. This was attributed in part to Facebook's inability to come up with a convincing business model for advertising income. The audience was huge but volatile, and Facebook feared losing numbers if it went too far with more obtrusive advertising.

How effective are Internet ads and how do people respond to them? Social psychologist Brad Sagarin and his colleagues have conducted some research to begin to answer that question (Sagarin, Britt, Heider, Wood & Lynch, 2005). First of all, they found an extreme version of the third-person effect (Perloff, 2002); practically everyone thought that they themselves paid no attention and were not affected at all by Internet ads. In fact, although they found the ads annoying, most people seemed willing to go along with the "exchange" of putting up with the ads in return for free Internet use and website access. However, Sagarin and colleagues found some subtle ways that people were affected by Internet ads, unbeknownst to them. For example, the ads did sometimes distract users doing a problem-solving task, even though they did not remember paying attention to them.

Sometimes children using the Internet may not even be aware they are being targeted by advertisers. For example, fun online games are available on companies' websites. Nabiscoworld.com has a game in which players dunk Oreo cookies, go to a Chips Ahoy party, or race in a Triscuit 4×4

(Fonda, 2004). Young players are unlikely to see this as any different from playing a video game.

Other electronic media are gathering marketing data without our awareness. For example, e-readers like Nook and Kindle routinely gather data about what a consumer chooses to read and how he or she reads it (e.g., straight through, or in fits and starts) (Alter, 2012). This may allow individual niche marketing of future books of interest but it also creates a record of what someone is reading, including reading of books on topics that one might not care to have made public.

Perhaps the most troubling aspect of computer-mediated advertising is the advertising of pornographic materials and solicitations through website advertising and through e-mail. Offers to sell products to augment penis or breast size, improve sexual potency, view sexually explicit photos, and meet sexual partners, come frequently and routinely by mass mailing to e-mail accounts. Many children have such accounts, especially through free providers like Hotmail, Yahoo, or Gmail, and regularly receive such e-mails. Spam filters help somewhat but do not screen out everything. Although the specter of porn on the Internet is often magnified to an irrational frenzy, the threat is real, and the legal system and social norms have not caught up with technology in figuring out how to deal with it. Child pornography in particular has become much easier to circulate via the Internet and e-mail, in spite of being illegal almost everywhere.

Prescription Drug Advertising

Although not a new place for advertising, one of the fastest growing areas of advertising, in terms of type of product, is the pharmaceutical industry. Emerging from being almost nonexistent at the start of the 1990s, to spending an estimated $1.7 billion on TV advertising alone in 2000, to over $4 billion spent on print and electronic ads by 2008, the selling of prescription drugs directly to consumers (DTC) is a major growth industry (Belkin, 2001; Howard, 2009). By 2000, 14% of prime-time shows in the United States advertised prescription drugs, while half of adult prime-time programming and 43% of popular teen shows have ads for over-the-counter drugs (Christenson, Henriksen, & Roberts, 2000). A 1997 loosening of requirements which had formerly required including all consumer warnings in every ad greatly facilitated this trend. One positive effect of this change is some increased empowering of the public to learn about these drugs and request them from their physicians. Although this probably has brought needed treatment to some who would otherwise remain undiagnosed, it has also quite likely resulted in unneeded treatment of some looking for a quick fix to all of life's problems or those seeking treatment for ailments they probably do not actually have. Although a physician's prescription is usually still necessary, this is sometimes obtained without a consultation, particularly with drugs purchased over the Internet.

The 2007 Drug Administration Amendments Act sought to greatly increase funding and legal power for the FDA to enhance enforcement, curb abuses, and generally better inform the public. Although it will be a few years before all the changes are fully implemented, some expected changes to advertising include presenting side effects warnings in a "clear, conspicuous, and neutral manner" and including hotline numbers in print ads to report adverse side effects.

DTC prescription drug advertising is unusual in several ways. Unlike most product advertising, it pitches to consumers who cannot directly purchase the product. However, they can and do request the drugs from their physicians. They also are subtly encouraged to think even more than they did previously in terms of chemical solutions to a wide variety of problems, many of which have not been traditionally thought of in this way, such as psychological disorders. Consumers tend to hold DTC prescription drug advertising in higher esteem than most advertising because they see it as providing useful information (Deshpande, Menon, Perri, & Zinkhan, 2004). However, this evaluation may be becoming more negative over time. They also see such ads as increasing their confidence in talking to their doctors and their motivation to comply with treatment (Murray, Lo, Pollack, Donelan, & Lee, 2003). Physicians, however, are somewhat more skeptical, being concerned that consumers may be confused by the ads and may put undue demand on physicians for inappropriate drugs, although they do recognize that DTC ads have helped motivate some patients to seek care (Murray et al., 2003; A. R. Robinson, Hohmann, Rifkin, Topp, Gilroy, & Pickard, 2004; Wilkes, Bell, & Kravitz, 2000). In terms of the perceived effect of such ads on others, those consumers very familiar with DTC ads thought their influence to be greater than did those consumers less familiar with such ads, while physicians estimated their influence to be less than did consumers (Huh & Langteau, 2007).

Conclusion

This chapter is in no way a comprehensive review of all the psychological effects of advertising or even of all the issues relevant to the perceived reality of advertising. Rather, the emphasis has been on looking at a few areas in which advertising attempts to create a reality within our minds that is conducive to purchasing a product. We are taught positive emotional associations about the product through classical conditioning or association of the product with positive experiences in our past. Natural information-processing tendencies like drawing inferences and invoking knowledge schemas are used by advertisers to encourage us to make particular interpretations of ads. Knowledge of the way that the mind processes information allows the advertiser to produce ads designed to encourage us to construct a meaning favorable to the advertiser's ends. On the other hand, knowledge of such processes also allows consumers to take steps to reduce the extent to which they are manipulated. Advertising is not going to go away, and in fact new places in which it can be embedded will continue to be found.

Chapter 6

Sports, Music, and Religion
Emotion to the Forefront

Q: What event captures the largest TV audience in the world?

A: Some part of the 16-day 2004 Athens Summer Olympics was seen by an estimated 3.9 billion viewers worldwide, 61% of the entire world's population at the time! World Cup Soccer competition draws up to 3 billion viewers watching some part of the multigame series, with 620 million worldwide watching the 2010 World Cup final (Ghosh, 2012).

Q: What percentage of popular songs mentioning alcohol portray its use as having no consequences to the user?

A: Ninety-one percent. Only 9% mentioned any negative consequences (Roberts, Henriksen, & Christenson, 1999).

Q: What movie was film critic Roger Ebert describing when he said the following: "The movie is 126 minutes long, and I would guess that at least 100 of those minutes, maybe more, are concerned specifically and graphically with the details of . . . torture and death . . . . This is the most violent film I have ever seen."

A: Ebert was reviewing *The Passion of the Christ*, about the crucifixion of Jesus, one of the most popular films of 2004 in the U.S. (Kirk, 2011, p. 23).

Although emotion is a major component of many, if not most, types of media use, there are some domains in which both what we feel in response to consuming the media and how we express those feelings are particularly central to the experience. This chapter looks at three of those content areas: sports, music, and religion. These would seem to be hugely diverse areas of media but all centrally involve emotion, though in very different ways. To get started, let's look a little at the psychology of emotion.

The Emotional (Affective) Side of Experiencing Media

What Is Emotion?

Something that makes the study of emotion difficult is that we cannot directly observe emotion, sometimes called "affect" (with an *a*) by psychologists. We do not see anger or hear happiness. We see violent behavior and feel angry; we hear laughter and feel happy. Emotions themselves are internal states and must be inferred from behavior. This can be tricky because sometimes the obvious inference is not the correct one. We may see someone crying over a TV movie and infer that she feels sad, when in fact she might be crying for joy or in anger, or for that matter she might have an allergic condition and her crying does not reflect emotion at all. The behavior we observe is not the emotion felt inside by the person behaving, and it is not always even a good clue to that emotion.

Emotions are an integral part of the appreciation of media, especially radio, television, and film. Perhaps no kind of programming hooks into emotions more strongly than music and sports, but many other genres of shows do so as well, including action-adventure shows, soap operas, game shows, reality shows, and comedies. What we feel while watching or listening is a central part of the whole psychological experience. If the emotional aspect is absent, we miss an important dimension of the experience. Consider the unsatisfying experience of watching a ball game between two teams when you have little knowledge of the teams and no interest in who wins. It's not very exciting, is it?

There are two components of emotion: the physiological and the cognitive. When we are aroused, certain changes occur in our bodies such as increased heart rate, respiration, sweating, and changes in electrodermal (skin) measures. We also *think* about our feelings and attribute causes and interpretations to them. For example, at some moment your body may be very hyped up, but you would have a different interpretation of that state of bodily arousal depending on whether you had just consumed ten cups of coffee or escaped from the clutches of a crazed killer. The emotions we feel are a product of both our aroused bodily state and our cognitive appraisal of that state (Schachter & Singer, 1962; Zillmann, 2006b).

Media as Vicarious Emotional Experience

Watching a crime show on TV allows us to experience some of the emotion felt by the characters without ourselves being in any physical danger. Thus we can become aroused safely through this *vicarious* experience; that is, we experience the emotion through someone else's experience. This indirectness allows us to focus on the excitement of a police show or enjoy the humor of a sitcom. If we actually experienced those situations in real life, the danger or embarrassment might overpower the positive aspects and they would not be nearly as much fun as they are on TV. Many emotions are more enjoyable to experience vicariously. Many comedies show people in embarrassing situations that are more humorous when happening to someone else. TV characters may do things we would like to do but have moral or ethical proscriptions against. We can, however, with a clear conscience watch others have extramarital affairs, verbally insult their bosses, drive recklessly, or drop bags of groceries all over the floor.

Game and reality shows are representative of programming genres in which participants are particularly encouraged to be highly emotionally expressive. In fact, a major screening characteristic for participants is high emotional expressiveness. The producers want bubbly, emotive, expressive people who yell, scream, cry, and hug. Such "reality" shows involve a far from representative sample of real people; in fact, the participants have been highly selected to be very emotionally expressive.

Occasionally a particular live media event is so emotionally compelling as to make a lasting impact, for example the collapse of the twin towers of the World Trade Center after the September 2001 terrorist attacks. When the U.S. space shuttle *Challenger* exploded in January 1986, this event was seen live at the time on TV or later that day by 95% of the population of the country (Wright, Kunkel, Pinon, & Huston, 1989). In a study of the reactions of schoolchildren to the event, Wright and colleagues found evidence of strong emotion evoked by the tragedy, especially among girls, though that may reflect in part the gender stereotyping of girls being willing to admit to feeling more emotion.

Emotional Expression and Media

Mainstream North American and Northern European societies often discourage direct expression of intense emotions. Media popular culture, however, sets some new, more flexible rules. It is more acceptable to yell and shake your fist at a referee in a ball game on TV than to do the same at your boss. In some societies sports is one of the very few arenas where heterosexual adult men may show physical affection toward other men without intimations of homosexuality, and some of the same license is transferred to viewing sports on television. Thus, two men may playfully slap each other or even embrace after watching a spectacular play in a televised ball game. To some extent listening to music also allows masculine expression of emotion. Such behavior from the same men would he highly unlikely watching a movie, however.

The social situation of watching TV also makes a difference in our experienced emotion. Watching a ball game or scary movie might be very different if one is alone, as opposed to at a party with friends. There is often more overt expression of emotion when in a group. A cheesy horror movie might be scary to watch alone but funny with a group. Even though the stimulus is the same in both cases, the experience, especially the emotional experience, may be quite different. The social experience of teenagers going to a horror film together is often very different from what one might predict purely from considering the content of the film; for example, they may laugh at graphic horror (Zillmann & Weaver, 1996; Zillmann, Weaver, Mundorf, & Aust, 1986).

Children may learn from media, helpfully or otherwise, how to deal with and express emotions they feel in various situations. Some years ago, young children learning to play tennis cursed and threw their racquets in imitation of tennis great John McEnroe, whose angry antics on the court became a model for dealing with frustration in sports. In a more serious case, if media regularly portray men who feel frustrated with women as expressing such feelings through violence (battering or rape), children may learn that these anti-social ways of dealing with such feelings are acceptable. When dramas and comedies regularly show smoking and alcohol consumption as common ways of dealing with stress, children and teens will learn that as a coping strategy. There is also ample evidence of *emotional contagion*, whereby we unconsciously mimic and synchronize our language and behavior with those around us (Hatfield, Cacioppo, & Rapson, 1992, 1993). This mimicking and synchronicity then lead to an emotional convergence with the person being mimicked. Such persons may be from the media as well as in real life. Sometimes TV and radio take advantage of this process by intentionally eliciting and manipulating negative emotions for their own ends, to entertain and promote a particular agenda. See Close-Up 6.1 for some particularly egregious and outrageous examples of this emotional manipulation.

Close-Up 6.1: Talk Shows that Elicit and Manipulate Negative Emotions for Entertainment

Popular radio talk-show host Rush Limbaugh calls feminists "feminazis who look like rhinoceroses" and called a Georgetown University law student a "slut," after she testified before Congress in 2012 about the need for health care to cover birth control.

The Jerry Springer Show allegedly encourages yelling, screaming, crying, and even hitting among its guests. Nikki and her new husband Chico once appeared on the show without being told what the producers really had in mind. During the taping it was revealed that Chico was still seeing his old girlfriend Mindy and also had a male lover, Rick. Both of them were on the show with the couple, and Mindy even assaulted Nikki. The audience was encouraged to show contempt for them. "It's white trailer trash! I love it!" said an 81-year-old farmer from Oregon (Collins, 1998). The show offers to pay for counseling for guests afterward, but few accept the offer.

In one of the most notorious cases of reality talk shows gone wild, the *Jenny Jones* show guest Jonathan Schmitz was told he would soon meet his secret admirer who had a crush on him. The mystery person turned out to be another man, Scott Amedure, who spoke of fantasies of tying Schmitz in a hammock and spraying him with whipped cream and champagne. Schmitz was very distraught and three days later was arrested for killing Amedure. He told the police that the embarrassment from the program had eaten away at him (Gamson, 1995).

Are such programs freak shows that exploit guests and bring out the worst in the audience, or are they legitimate forums for people's stories that otherwise we would not (but perhaps should) hear? By the way, in case you ever wondered where these shows find these people, there is a National Talk Show Guest Registry, a database of thousands of people who tell stories or have problems they are willing to vent about on the air.

Although emotion is present in, and evoked by, most types of media, in this chapter we examine in more detail two domains of media where the emotional response is absolutely central, namely sports and music, and a third area, religion, which plugs into some of our most central and deeply held feelings.

Sports

Media sports are a part of most everyone's consciousness today, even those who have no great interest in sports. Events like the Super Bowl, World Cup, and Olympics have become cultural phenomena that touch the lives of many people, and not only regular sports fans. Over one-third of all network programming on broadcast television involves sporting events (Bryant & Raney, 2000). The media, particularly television, are the way many of us learn about sports. Our perceived reality about particular sports is largely a media creation. In the case of sports not played locally, media may be the *only* source of information. The marriage of sports and television is so accepted and taken for granted today that it is easy to overlook the enormous influence that television and other media have had on the games themselves. See Close-Up 6.2 for a look at sports and media in the days before TV.

We begin with a brief look at the influence of media, especially television, on the games themselves. Then we examine several psychological issues related to sports and see how media have become formative influences in our perceived reality of those sports.

Close-Up 6.2: Sports and Media before Television

In spite of the profound recent effect of television on sports, the marriage of athletics and the media is not a new relationship. The first sports story in an American newspaper appeared in 1733, when the *Boston Gazette* reprinted a story about a boxing match in England. The first British sports publication appeared in 1801, followed in the U.S. in 1819 by the oddly titled *The American Farmer*, which included results of hunting, fishing, shooting, and bicycling events, plus essays on the philosophy of sport. U.S. newspapers began regular reporting of sports in the 1850s (Rader, 1984). By 1890, most major daily newspapers had established sports departments, and sports pages continue to be the most widely read section of newspapers.

Magazines were a late entry to sports media but quickly became important players. *Sports Illustrated* has been a top-circulation magazine since its 1954 inception. Many newer and more specialized magazines reflect interest in particular sports, including some sports that receive relatively little coverage from newspapers or television (*Dirt Bike, Runner's World, Cycle News, National Dragster*). Overall, sports magazine readers are disproportionately male, middle class, and well educated, although this varies some according to the sport.

Baseball games were broadcast almost from the inception of radio in 1920. In July 1921, the Dempsey–Carpentier fight was broadcast from Jersey City. One month later, pioneer Pittsburgh radio station KDKA broadcast a Pirates–Phillies game live. The first regular play-by-play season programming of baseball and football was in place by 1925, although for some years it was primarily the World Series that was carried play-by-play. A famous early sportscaster was future U.S. President Ronald Reagan, who recreated the Chicago Cubs' games for Des Moines station WHO. The first televised sporting event was the Berlin Olympics of 1936, which was broadcast only to the area immediately around Berlin. The first American TV sportscast was the 1939 live broadcast to the 200 TV sets in greater New York of a Columbia–Princeton baseball game and the Lou Nova–Max Baer boxing match (Guttman, 1986). Widespread TV ownership had to wait, however, until after World War II (1939–1945).

How Television has Changed Sports

Audiences for major sporting events are among the largest for any programming, and television has become an integral part of the financing of most professional sports, including nominally amateur sports such as the Olympics and NCAA college football. Initially broadcast on weekend afternoons in the late 1950s, sports offered TV a chance to greatly increase the audience at traditionally low-viewing times. However, the great popularity of sports soon led to prime-time broadcasting of games as well, for example ABC's *Monday Night Football*, evening baseball games, and the Olympics. The advent of popular all-sports cable channels like ESPN and Fox Sports has greatly increased the amount of TV sports available. Over the years, the television audience has become considerably more important than spectators in the stadium, and sports have changed to adapt to the needs and desires of TV and its viewers much more than to those of the fans in the stadium. For economic reasons, the perceived reality of the TV audience has come to be more important than the reality of the fans in the stadium.

Social Changes and the Growth of Sports and Media

Although television greatly affected sports in its early years, there were other profound social changes occurring during that time that played into sports-media growth. After the end of World War II in 1945, unparalleled economic prosperity fueled a building boom and a massive migration from the central cities to the burgeoning suburban areas (Coontz, 1992). The suburbs were far more dependent on the automobile than the cities had been, signaling the shift from primary use of public transportation to private cars. Soon this led to the construction of better highways and the subsequent decline or loss of public transportation. With all of these changes came a privatization of leisure. More people owned their own homes, with more space inside and lovely yards outside, so recreation and leisure time increasingly centered on the home or, at most, the neighborhood. See Close-Up 6.3 for a closer look at the alleged "golden age" of the 1950s. One major activity of this home-based leisure was watching television. No longer did one have to go to the theater or to a distant stadium; sports were available for free and far more conveniently from television. The financial bonanza from selling television rights gradually came to be fully appreciated (Bryant & Holt, 2006).

The New Look of Games

Television has changed sports in a myriad of ways (Sullivan, 2006). There is much more color in sports than there used to be. Before TV, tennis balls and players' outfits were always white. For centuries a sport of the elite, tennis was brought to the masses by television coverage of major tournaments. Before TV, football stadiums had less colorful end zones. Uniforms also became more colorful, with players' names written on the backs for TV audiences to read. Increasing numbers of domed stadiums have lessened the number of boring rain delays that play havoc with TV schedules. Computer graphics technology has allowed for lively and colorful scoreboards and video screens, which offer

Close-Up 6.3: The Real Story of the Golden Age of the 1950s

Critics of modern media and society in the United States often lament that we have lost the solid family values of the 1950s, the last decade before all the social upheavals of the 1960s. Historian of the family Stephanie Coontz (1992, 1997) looks more carefully at this alleged golden age and finds that all was not in fact as golden as we collectively remember it.

Coontz argues that the 1950s was a decade unlike any before or since. First, it was an era of unparalleled economic expansion; there was more growth in real wages in any year of the 1950s than in the entire period 1980 to 1995. Birth rates skyrocketed, approaching those of India. Even under the Republican Eisenhower administration there was greater federal assistance to families than there has ever been before or since. With the GI Bill paying college tuition, large amounts of money available for first home purchases and education costs, and numerous jobs available building interstate highways, expanding infrastructure, and in heavy industry, the 1950s were one of the very few eras in U.S. history when a large number of families could thrive on a single income. The divorce rate was lower than in the years that followed but also lower than those of the preceding years: one third of pre-World War II marriages had ended in divorce or abandonment. There was also a massive shift in family structure. People were moving to the suburbs and farther away from extended families, thus putting all of their energy into the nuclear family, a model reinforced by the cheery sitcoms of the time. Not everyone was prospering, however. Most minorities were largely excluded from the American dream. Rates of domestic violence, crime, incest, and child abuse were high but ignored, since their principal victims were racial, ethnic, and gender minorities; a large percentage of children were living in poverty. Coontz argues that the 1950s are a time we could never return to if we wanted to, and she questions whether we should even want to.

considerable entertainment in themselves as well as putting the game on the screen, a sort of television for fans in the stadium.

Continuing technical advances in broadcasting have affected sports. One of the most dramatic is the instant replay, first seen in 1963. The same play can be seen over and over at different speeds, from different camera angles. Technical advances allow the editing and delayed broadcast of lengthy events with interpretation added and uninteresting sections deleted. Increased sports coverage has given some exposure to sports long considered too minor and unprofitable to broadcast. ESPN Classic (formerly The Classic Sports

Network) showed there was an audience for watching classic ball games (anyone interested in watching the 1960 World Series or the 1990 Super Bowl again?). CBS Sports Network (previously College Sports Television) devotes many hours a day to college sports, particularly the so-called minor sports not already captured by the major networks. Thus, for the first time a broader audience can see football or basketball from largely unknown conferences, as well as many collegiate sports previously absent altogether from television, including baseball, lacrosse, track, soccer, volleyball, and others (Gregory, 2003a).

Sometimes the major sports price themselves out of a major network TV market and newer sports can take their place. For example, after NBC lost $300 million on the last two years of its contract with the NBA, it replaced it with the much more affordable Arena Football League (AFL) in 2003. This gave a much-needed boost to the indoor football league, which had been around since 1987 but had languished without much TV exposure (Gregory, 2003b).

The Telegenic Factor

Some sports are more naturally suited to the format of commercial television than others. Baseball, with its many half-inning divisions, is a natural for commercial breaks. Football and basketball have fewer structured breaks, but do have frequent time-outs. The continuous action and low scoring of hockey and soccer make them relatively poor TV sports. Some have suggested this to be why professional soccer, by far the most popular spectator sport worldwide, has never caught on to a large degree in the United States. However, this lack of TV friendliness is not an entirely satisfactory explanation, since soccer (usually called "football" outside North America) draws huge TV audiences in many countries. The quadrennial World Cup series is the most-watched professional sporting event worldwide, with an estimated viewership of over 3 billion.

In spite of what one might think, some of the most popular sports in terms of fan attendance are not particularly popular on television. Two of the top American sports in gate receipts are NASCAR auto racing and horse racing, yet, until quite recently, only the very top contests—like the Indianapolis 500 or the Triple Crown of thoroughbred racing (the Kentucky Derby, Preakness Stakes, and Belmont Stakes) have been seen by large TV audiences. There are also considerable regional differences in sports interest (see Close-Up 6.4).

Institutional Changes

There have been some dramatic structural changes in the institutions of sport due to television. For example, the 59 baseball minor leagues in the late 1940s were down to about 15 leagues 30 years later. The chance to see major league baseball on television from all over the country largely eroded the appeal and

Close-Up 6.4: Geographical Differences in Sport

There are huge international differences in which sports are popular, both in terms of participation and TV watching. The two most popular TV sports in the United States do not command much worldwide interest. Baseball is very popular in some of East Asia (especially Japan and Taiwan), the Caribbean, and northern Latin America as far south as Venezuela, but remains largely unknown in Europe, Africa, and most of Asia and South America. Football is big in the United States and somewhat in Canada but practically nowhere else, with the name "football" often used for soccer. Rugby is the most popular sport in Australia, New Zealand, and some Pacific Island nations, and one of the most popular in the UK, Ireland, and France, but it is not much more than an athletic footnote elsewhere. In Britain and some Commonwealth countries such as India, Pakistan, some Caribbean and east African nations, and South Africa (but few other places), cricket is popular. Bullfighting is popular on the Iberian peninsula and in northern Latin America but nonexistent elsewhere.

Even within the United States and Canada there are considerable regional differences in sports preferences. Throughout Canada and the extreme northern United States, ice hockey is the major sport. U.S. hockey teams depend heavily on Canadian talent. Even at the college level, hockey far eclipses football and basketball in quality and popularity at far-northern schools like the University of Maine and the University of North Dakota, which regularly send their graduates to the NHL. Although college football is popular all over the United States, it is particularly so in the Midwest and South; in Canada and elsewhere outside the United States, big-time collegiate sports are nonexistent. Basketball is most popular in the U.S. Mid-Atlantic states and especially in the state of Indiana, which, uniquely, begins interscholastic competition in elementary school and regularly draws college recruiters from all over the country.

---

financial viability of the minor leagues. However, there may be a limit to growth of the TV audience. The formation of the United States Football League in the early 1980s and the XFL 20 years later were colossal failures. There are also signs of tedium and lower than expected ratings as division playoffs and tournaments extend the seasons of different sports longer and longer. People often tire of baseball by late October, or NBA basketball and Stanley Cup hockey playoffs in June.

The large-scale reshuffling of NCAA athletic conferences in the early 21st century is largely due to desire for television revenue. The postseason college football bowl games sold TV rights for multimillion-dollar deals as early as the 1960s, and the larger conferences depend on bowl appearances to recruit strong talent and bowl receipts to finance their programs. The proliferation of postseason bowl games and their corporate sponsorship (e.g., Tostitos Fiesta Bowl, GoDaddy.com Bowl) has opened new advertising and revenue opportunities. By the early 21st century, interest and attendance at some bowl games had declined, amid growing controversy about bowl team selection processes. Although TV has brought big-time college football into the lives of many who would never have attended a game, it has been at the cost of heavily commercializing the football programs of the major schools and depleting the audience for small college football, whose supporters often prefer to watch top-rated teams on TV instead of attending a local game in person (Sperber, 2001).

Although college football had been popular since the 19th century, pro football was more of an athletic footnote on the U.S. sports scene before the age of television. Pro football learned how to deal with television more adeptly and in a more unified fashion than did baseball. Television close-ups and cogent interpretation by the sportscaster made a previously opaque and uninteresting game fascinating to large numbers of new fans, who now were able to follow what was happening.

One of the most brilliantly marketed events in media history has been the Super Bowl, which began in January 1967. By the early 1970s, the Super Bowl had overtaken the baseball World Series and the Kentucky Derby in TV audience size in the United States. Unlike other major sporting events, the Super Bowl was a creation of television, not a preexisting institution adapted to the medium. Super Bowl Sunday practically became an annual holiday, complete with ebullient media hoopla starting weeks in advance. The games themselves were frequently watched in over half of U.S. households. The broadcast in itself became the event; what happened in the game was almost irrelevant. By the 1980s, major advertisers, paying top dollar for ad time, launched new ad campaigns with commercials presented for the first time during the game; this annual advertising debut became a significant spin-off media event. A whole series of satellite events sprang up, such as numerous televised parties and pre- and postgame specials. This large audience is sometimes even used for other purposes, such as collecting "Souper Bowl" food donations for food banks and consciousness-raising about the problem of wife-battering, that takes place during and after the Super Bowl (Gantz, Wang, & Bradley, 2006).

The Olympics

Some immensely important sporting events, in terms of their TV impact, are the quadrennial Summer and Winter Olympics. Although in modern times they have been held since 1896, interest has soared exponentially since television, and they have become totally financially dependent on television. NBC paid $1.8 billion dollars for all broadcast and Internet rights to the 2012

Summer Games in London. Due to the traditionally amateur status of the Olympics, the TV coverage has popularized sports that have not otherwise been sources of large revenues. Most notable among these have been women's sports, which have received a tremendous boost from Olympic coverage. By 2012 a majority of the medal winners of the most successful countries, like the U.S., China, Russia, and the UK, were female. Certain sports that have little audience elsewhere (e.g., gymnastics and figure skating) are very popular in the Olympics. For such sports, television serves an important educational function: people learn about new sports from watching the Olympics, which sometimes translates into their own participation in these activities.

Sometimes the commercial pressure to pay back the enormous cost of the broadcasting rights may lead to low-quality television, with a high total ad time and poor timing of ads, for example, when hockey goals are scored or figure skating results are announced. Organizing committees plan schedules to include three weekends of prime sports broadcasting time and make sure top-rated teams do not play each other until the finals.

As with sport in general, emotional aspects of the athletes are often highlighted, leading to some criticisms that broadcasting the sport itself has taken a back seat to the tearjerker side-stories. This trend may reflect attempts to increase the numbers of female viewers. Competition is underlined, even if somewhat artificially, as with the heavily hyped rivalry between American swimmers Michael Phelps and Ryan Lochte at the 2012 Summer Games. Probably the most dramatic such competition was the Nancy Kerrigan–Tonya Harding feud ("Dueling Figure Skaters") of the 1994 Winter Games. Harding and her boyfriend were implicated in a knee-bashing sabotage attempt against Kerrigan. This nasty side-issue almost eclipsed the actual skating competition, although ironically it delivered a record boost to the figure skating audience.

A more common melodramatic theme is that of the triumph of the human spirit over adversity. Whether it be an athlete's cancer-stricken father watching his daughter earn her final gold medal or the first runner to compete in the Olympics with two prosthetic legs, the emotional drama is framed as prominently as the athletic competition. When the expected heroism does not actually occur, there is shame and derision, as at the 2012 Summer Games when several badminton players were disqualified for throwing matches in the round-robin tournament, to try to obtain an easier route through the competition.

Occasionally, more light-hearted treatments can raise some eyebrows. At the 2012 Games, American gymnast Gabby Douglas was hailed for winning medals but also criticized for her unkempt hairdo, a journalistic detail many found inappropriate. During the baseball games at the 2000 Summer Olympics in Sydney, every foul ball (even a grounder) was accompanied by a sound effect of breaking glass. Beach volleyball had its own comic host, "Lifeguard Dave," who worked the crowd like a stand-up comedian. Roy Slaven and H. G. Nelson, Australian late-night comedians, ran Greco-Roman

Olympic wrestling coverage to a sound track of Barry White love songs and commentary pondering why large men would try to grope and mount each other. Their show's mascot "Fatso the Fat-Arsed Wombat" became so popular that Olympic athletes all wanted to pose with it, until the International Olympics Committee (IOC) requested that they stop doing so (Luscombe, 2000). Do you think such coverage enhances or detracts from the Olympics?

Olympic coverage may be used to further the host country's political or economic goals. China used the 2008 Beijing Summer Games to showcase its economic progress. This spotlight is not without some risk for the host, however. China also received unwanted attention from groups that protested against its occupation of Tibet and had to institute draconian vehicle restrictions during the Olympics to keep the highly polluted Beijing air breathable for the athletes. Britons' complaints about elevated prices and separate highway lanes for Olympians in 2012 were a mild embarrassment to London, though the city largely benefited from its newly spruced-up East End. Viewers learned during the 1992 Summer Games that host city Barcelona spoke Catalan, not Spanish, and felt primary identity with the autonomous region of Catalonia, rather than with the nation of Spain. In 1996, every single independent country in the world, 197 in all, for the first time had some presence at the Summer Games (Wulf, 1996). By 2012, every nation had sent at least some women athletes as well as men; the last holdouts had been Qatar, Brunei, and Saudi Arabia, all of whom sent women to London in 2012. As recently as 1996, 26 nations had sent only men.

So far we have looked at how the media have changed the sports themselves and the reality about them that we perceive. Next we examine several psychological factors that are directly affected by the perceived reality of media sports.

Psychological Issues in Sports and Media

Why do people seek to consume sports media, and what is the nature of that experience psychologically? On TV, only sports (and in a very different way, news) is live and unrehearsed with the outcome unknown. This is very different from the rather predictable, formulaic nature of most entertainment programming and advertising. Motivations for watching sports are many, including emotional (entertainment, arousal, self-esteem, escape), cognitive (learning, aesthetic), and social (release, companionship, group affiliation) (Raney, 2006). In this section we examine several aspects of the sports media consumption experience, with the major focus being on the medium of television.

Sports Media Consumption as a Social Event

More often than for other TV programming, part of the reality of the experience of sports media consumption involves the presence of others (Wann,

Melnick, Russell, & Pease, 2001). Friends gather at someone's home or patrons congregate in a sports bar to watch a big game. Often the game seems more enjoyable in a group than it would be watching alone, with the presence of others rooting for the same team somehow seeming more important than that of coviewers when watching a movie, a sitcom, or the news (Wenner & Gantz, 1998). The expression of emotion, discussed later, may be part of the reason. Also, watching with a group partially recreates the stadium situation of watching the event in a crowd.

One interesting aspect of the social reality of TV sports viewing is the eating and drinking that accompany the viewing. People eat and drink more watching sports than watching other events on TV, especially when viewing in groups, but the range of what they consume is fairly narrow. The food is most often junk food, snacks, or perhaps hot dogs, and the drink is typically soft drinks or beer. In short, we eat and drink the same sort of substances at home that we might consume if we were in attendance live at the event. It would seem somehow odd to sip coffee and peck at croissants while watching the Chicago Bears and the Green Bay Packers, or to savor a fine red wine while watching the heavyweight boxing championship fight.

One thorny issue in regard to food and drink involves the advertising and promotion of alcohol at university athletic contests. As colleges and universities become increasingly concerned about binge drinking and the role of alcohol in crimes like rape and domestic violence, the lucrative advertising contracts between breweries and university athletic departments have attracted closer scrutiny. Although most schools do not sell alcohol in their athletic facilities, and many prohibit fans from bringing alcohol into the games, those same fans often see lots of beer advertising inside the stadium or coliseum. Although some schools have taken principled stands and refused to accept such advertising, that stand comes as a substantial cost in giving up badly needed revenue. What is your school's policy on alcohol advertising and college sports?

Sports is the type of television most often consumed in a social context. Who one watches sports with and how much one enjoys the game help determine the nature of the viewing experience. For example, depending on whether one watches a sporting event alone, with a group, or with one's family or significant other, different uses and gratifications will be involved (Bonds-Raacke & Harris, 2006). Wenner and Gantz (1998) identified five levels of motivation for watching sports, with decreasing amounts of emotional involvement. First is the fanship dimension, focusing on the thrill of victory and identifying strongly with the players. Second, the learning dimension involves acquiring information about the game and the players. Third, the release dimension involves "letting off steam," relaxing, and eating and drinking. Fourth, companionship involves watching in order to be in the company of others who are watching; such motivations are especially important in the case of family or significant others. Finally, the fifth dimension, which is the least emotionally involving, involves watching to pass the time or because one is bored.

Competitiveness and Cooperation

Obviously, one of the major psychological dimensions of sports is competition and the striving toward victory. Part of the perceived reality of TV sports also involves this desire to win, a value reinforced by media. This strong competitive drive can easily overshadow the learning of teamwork and cooperation. The natural socialization process of child development often involves identification with and support for certain sports teams and individuals. Who this will be is often, although not necessarily, determined by geographical considerations. We most often root for the local team, our school team, or the team our family has supported, perhaps for generations. Still, major teams have fans all over. The hapless Chicago Cubs have supporters who have never been near Wrigley Field, and Roman Catholics throughout North America cheer for the University of Notre Dame's football team.

Competition may also come in the form of nation versus nation in international competition. The World Cup, with one team per nation, becomes a national competition, during which the business life of certain countries in Western Europe and South America takes a de facto holiday. When the Toronto Blue Jays made the baseball World Series in 1992, all Canada celebrated, in spite of the fact that there were no Canadians on the team. The first-time entry of independent former Soviet and Yugoslav nations like Lithuania, Estonia, Croatia, and Slovenia into the 1992 Olympics was a time of intense national pride. Such sports nationalism can occasionally degenerate into antisocial extremes. For example, Colombian soccer star Andrés Escobar was assassinated upon returning home from the World Cup in 1994, apparently by an angry fan upset with his weaker-than-expected performance.

Reward in sports is generally for winning, with very little kudos and few endorsement dollars for coming in second, much less third, or tenth. In carrying so many more sports into so many lives, television has certainly, at least indirectly, encouraged competitiveness. With the star mindset that focuses on individuals, television lavishes attention and acclaim on the winner, whereas it often virtually ignores everyone else. This helps to construct a reality for viewers that coming in first is all that is important. Athletes are not celebrated after the game for doing their best or being good sports. In addition, sports metaphors carry over into our speech and thinking in many other areas of life, such as relationships. A fellow goes on a date and "scores," "gets to first base," or "strikes out." A woman complains that men see women as "conquests" or "trophies."

Often the star mentality of television and the entertainment business in general affects the presentation of sports in the media. Individual plays of the superstars are exalted and glorified by the sportscasters more than, for example, displays of fine teamwork. Coverage tends to focus on the outstanding individual athlete, much as coverage of religion tends to focus on the pope or stories about government focus on the President. This extolling of the individual may subtly undermine the importance of teamwork and cooperation for the viewer, especially the young viewer.

A very different, and subtler, way that competitiveness can manifest itself in the sports viewer is in the accumulation and exhibition of copious, seemingly endless, sports trivia and statistics. Sportscasters encourage this through their endless recitation of such information during radio and TV broadcasts, in part probably to fill the time when there is no play or commercial to air. The computer has made it even easier to amass and retrieve such figures. Such statistics have become part of the reality of media sports. Even young children seemingly unable to remember much in school may recite voluminous facts about RBIs, passes completed, and shooting percentages.

Sports Violence

Although the appeal of violent sports goes back to ancient times (Guttman, 1998), one recent concern is how the media, especially television, tend to focus heavily on, even glorify, the occasional brawl or fight on the field. In a sense, this is a secondary competition to the primary one being played. Although no sportscaster celebrates or even condones serious tragedies like player or fan deaths, camera and media attention immediately shift routinely to any fight that breaks out either in the stands or on the field. When results are reported later on the evening news, it is more likely the brawl, not a play from the game, which is chosen as the sound bite of the evening. Even if fighting is clearly condemned by the sportscaster, which is often not the case, the heavy coverage given to the fight conveys a subtle agenda-setting. The perceived reality to the viewer, especially a young one, may be that the winner of the brawl is to be admired as much as the winner of the game itself, because temper tantrums, rudeness, and racket-hurling are more photogenic and newsworthy than self-control and playing by the rules.

Do people really enjoy watching sports violence? Avid sports fans do enjoy watching rough and even violent sporting events, especially under certain conditions (Gunter, 2006). Inherently more violent people enjoy sports violence more than mild-mannered people. The more one dislikes the victim of the violence, the more that violence is enjoyed. Violence that is morally sanctioned—that is, presented as acceptable or even necessary—is enjoyed more and seen as more acceptable than violence presented as unfair or out of line (Beentjes, van Oordt, & van der Voort, 2002). Such moral sanction may come from several sources, including the rules and customs of the game, the tone of the commentary of the sportscaster or sportswriter, and even the reactions of other fans. The more of these conditions that are present, the more the viewer enjoys the violence. Overall, however, the higher the level of violence is in a game, the greater the fan enjoyment, especially for men (Bryant, Zillmann, & Raney, 1998).

Sometimes sports competition has had some extreme and tragic consequences. In 1969, Honduras and El Salvador fought the so-called "soccer war," precipitated by a particularly bitter soccer game. In 1985 in Brussels, 39 people died and around 450 were injured following tensions and violence among fans attending a championship soccer game between Liverpool, from the UK, and Juventus, an Italian team. Such incidents have caused fans to be screened with metal detectors, nations to exchange information on the most violent fans, and heavily armed soldiers to stand guard in stadiums, between the seating areas for fans of opposing teams. These security measures have come to be part of the reality of big-time sports, although those watching on TV need not be so inconvenienced.

Emotional Benefits

Although there are clear health benefits from participating in sports, benefits from consuming sports through media are somewhat less clear. Obviously, physical health and fitness are not enhanced by watching ball games on TV, and may even be hindered if watching takes up time that the viewers might otherwise spend exercising. Emotionally, the picture is a little less clear. Tension reduction or emotional release—catharsis—may result from physical activity, where we release stress through muscular and aerobic exercise. Some psychologists in the psychodynamic tradition, dating back to Sigmund Freud, argue that catharsis may also be achieved through substitute activities. Although research has not supported the value of a cathartic release of aggressive feeling through watching sports, there is still widespread belief among the general public that such a process exists (Scheele & DuBois, 2006). See Chapter 9 for further discussion of catharsis via media consumption.

Clearly there is often a lot of emotion felt while consuming media sports (David, Horton, & German, 2008). Zillmann, Bryant, and Sapolsky (1979) proposed a disposition theory of sportsfanship to describe such feelings. The enjoyment we experience emotionally from witnessing the success or victory of a competing individual or team increases with the degree of positive sentiments we feel toward that party. Similarly, the more we care about a team or individual's success, the worse we feel when we witness a failure or defeat. Thus, it is hard to become emotionally involved, or sometimes stay interested at all, in watching a game between two teams that we know or care little about.

There are also physical changes associated with these emotions. In a study of Spanish fans watching their national team in the World Cup final in 2010, van der Meij et al. (2012) found that both testosterone and cortisol (the "stress chemical") were higher while viewing the match than in the same people on a control day, although neither level increased after the final victory by the Spaniards. Cortisol secretion during the match was higher among men than women and younger fans than older ones, although some of these differences were apparently explained by different levels of fan enthusiasm, suggesting the need to look at individual differences in responses to sports viewing.

Still, feelings about the competitors are not the only determinants of the emotional response to sports. As with any drama, the degree of perceived conflict is crucial in the experiencing of suspense. A game that is close in score and hard-fought in character evokes both more positive and more negative emotion, regardless of team loyalty, than one where the final victor is never in doubt or one where the participants appear not to be trying very hard (Knobloch-Westerwick, David, Eastin, Tamborini, & Greenwood, 2009). A strong affective predisposition toward one team or the other is necessary in order to experience much suspense. A close basketball game between archrivals settled at the final buzzer carries the viewer along emotionally throughout its course. A game whose outcome is already known is less likely to be of interest in its entirety. How many ball games are ever rerun on television? How many people watch a prerecorded game when they already know the final score?

Gender Roles and Bias

Throughout the history of media sports, male sports have received much more coverage than female sports, which received only 5% of all local sports coverage in 1989 and only 8.7% by 1999; ESPN SportsCenter's figures were even worse, with only 2.2% of its coverage being of women's sports (Duncan, 2006). Also, attendance at men's events is higher than at women's events. The nature of the relationship between coverage and fan interest is complex, however. Does the heavier media coverage of male sports merely reflect the reality of greater fan interest in men's sports, for whatever reason, or is the greater media coverage a *cause* of greater fan interest in men's sports?

Some major media sports such as American football and baseball are virtually male only, without parallel female teams for the media to cover. In other sports, such as pro golf, tennis, soccer, and basketball, there are parallel women's leagues and competitions. Only in professional tennis and the Olympics does the media coverage of women's competition even approach that of men, however, and both of these cases are fairly unusual, in that competition for both sexes occurs in the same structured event. The Olympics and Wimbledon, for example, include both men's and women's matches, whereas PGA and LPGA or NBA and WNBA competitions are separate and unequal events. In the reporting that does occur about female athletes, the coverage is asymmetrical, with women being described in less powerful and success-oriented language (Duncan, 2006; Eastman & Billings, 2000). They are more likely than men to be called by their first names and have their strengths described ambivalently; for example, "small but so effective," "big girl," "favorite girl next door," "her little jump hook." They are also more likely to be described in terms of their attractiveness and sexuality, while male athletes are described primarily in terms of their strength and athleticism (Baroffio-Bota & Banet-Weiser, 2006; Kane, 1996).

Curiously, the increase in sports participation by girls and the modest increase in broadcasting of women's sports has not translated into comparably larger audiences for professional women's sports. The male model of boys participating in sports and through that developing interest in watching sports has not been replicated for girls. Girls and women are watching more sports on television but much of what they watch is men's sports. Whiteside and Hardin (2011) noted this phenomenon and studied it. They concluded that women's sports viewing patterns were more a function of a woman's role in the family. For example, if one's husband or children are watching football, it is likely to capture Mom's interest as well.

The Olympics are an instructive and somewhat atypical instance. Both the Summer and Winter Games are heavily covered by television, often with both live coverage and extended edited excerpts broadcast a few hours later, at more convenient local times. Women's events receive nearly as much coverage as men's events, though overall number of minutes and quality of coverage still favors the men (Billings & Eastman, 2003). Interest in women's Olympic sports has been high for many years, and superstar athletes such as Jackie Joyner-Kersee, Mia Hamm, Bonnie Blair, Sarah Hughes, Kristi Yamaguchi, Mary Lou Retton, and Dorothy Hamill have become genuine heroes and every bit as popular as the men.

Sportscasting and sports reporting is probably the last and most stubborn bastion of male supremacy in the journalism industry. Although female news anchors and reporters, meteorologists, and even editors are increasingly common and accepted, the female sportscaster or sports reporter (covering men's sports) is still highly exceptional. Not until 1993 was the first woman pro baseball announcer hired (Sherry Davis, by the San Francisco Giants). It is unclear whether this absence reflects a true public dislike or distrust of women reporting men's sports or is merely an unfounded industry fear they will alienate viewers. It seems the problem is deeper than highly publicized but bogus pseudo-issues such as the awkwardness of sending female sportscasters into men's locker rooms for postgame interviews. (No reporters of either gender are allowed into women's locker rooms after the games; couldn't that model work for the men as well?)

Although not nearly as dichotomous as in the past, greater encouragement is given to boys than to their sisters to participate in all kinds of sports. Less obviously, the same asymmetry applies to media consumption of sports. Boys are encouraged by their parents, particularly their fathers, to watch games on TV as well as to play catch and shoot baskets in the yard. Both playing sports and watching sports on TV have become part of the male gender socialization role. The boy who is not particularly interested in spending his time this way, but whose father is, often receives subtle or not-so-subtle messages that such lack of interest does not measure up, perhaps calling into question his masculinity. Consuming media sports together has become a part of the reality of many father–son relationships, and, increasingly, some father–daughter ones as well.

One advantage for men watching sports is that this is probably the one arena where they are most free to express positive emotion to each other. Men watching a ball game together, somewhat like the players themselves, may relatively freely express feelings and even touch one another. In mainstream Anglo North American society this is practically the only time when many men feel comfortable publicly embracing. Many heterosexual men may never in their lives hug another man outside their family (perhaps inside it, too), except in the context of playing or watching sports. For this reason, if for no other, sports are important.

In the past, girls were often given messages, especially after reaching puberty, that participation in sports was tomboyish and unfeminine and could be a serious liability in attracting a man. In recent decades, however, this has changed considerably, and girls and women are increasingly allowed to be athletic and sexy at the same time. Less and less is it considered surprising or awkward for women to watch ball games or to know more about sports than men, although TV audiences for most sporting events are still a majority male. Another important variable in media coverage may be whether a sport is "lean" or "nonlean" (Harrison & Fredrickson, 2003). In lean sports such as gymnastics, diving, or cross-country, weight and appearance are more important for success, whereas in nonlean sports like basketball, tennis, golf, track and field, volleyball, or softball, they are less relevant (see Creedon, 1994 for a collection of readings about women, sports, and the media).

Racial Bias

Although a large majority of American players in the NFL and NBA, as well as lesser but substantial numbers in other sports and the Olympics, are African American, their numbers are far smaller among front office personnel and head coaches. A few content analysis studies of play-by-play broadcasting suggest that racial stereotypes are sometimes being at least subtly reinforced by sportscasting. For example, Jackson (1989), looking at NFL and NCAA men's college football commentary, found that 65% of comments about African American football players pertained to physical size or ability, compared to 17% for White players. On the other hand, 77% of comments about White football players stressed their intelligence, leadership, or motivation, and only 23% of comments about African American players did (63% vs. 15% for basketball players). Similar findings occur for European sports media, where athletes of African, Asian, or Latin American descent are often admired for their "natural athleticism" and are described in terms of group stereotypes more often than White Europeans, for instance "Latin temperament," "Pakistani religious fanaticism," or "superior African muscularity" (Blain, Boyle, & O'Donnell, 1993). Sometimes the "myth of natural physicality" of the Black athlete subtly appears in sports reporting, as does the association of African-American manhood with criminality and drugs or the commodification and marketing of the Black street hip-hop world (Grainger, Newman, & Andrews, 2006).

Hero Worship

Media coverage of sports has enhanced, or at least altered, the perceived reality of the hero. Sports stars have long been heroes emulated by youth, but the age of television, and to a lesser extent other media, has changed this role somewhat. On the one hand, LeBron James is seen by many more people on television than was previously possible. On the other hand, the close scrutiny of television shows the faults as well as the nobler aspects of a potential hero.

Children emulate their TV sports heroes in all sorts of ways. A child may imitate not only his hero's great shooting but also his temper tantrums or drug use. Nor is emulation of athletes limited to children. Long-time golfers reported that play on golf courses slowed noticeably after major golf tournaments began to be televised in the 1960s. This occurred primarily because amateur golfers started bending down to line up their putts and imitating other behaviors they saw among the pros on TV, no matter that the amateurs may not have understood what they were looking for when lining up that putt. They'd just seen Jack Nicklaus do it.

Fans develop significant parasocial relationships (see Chapter 2) with sports figures. Sometimes this can be very traumatic, as seen in the outpouring of grief following the crash death of NASCAR driver Dale Earnhardt, Sr. in 2001. Rapidly expanding from its Southeastern U.S. base to become one of the fastest growing North American sports, NASCAR adherents are very loyal, especially to their favorite drivers. Earnhardt was a true hero to many, and his death was a troubling loss to countless fans.

One particular area of concern in regard to hero worship has been the use of drugs by sports stars and the resulting effects on youth (Donohew, Helm, & Haas, 1989). The widespread use of cocaine by baseball and basketball stars in the 1980s seemed somehow worse than such use by other citizens, even by other public figures, because sports figures are heroes to youth. This has caused persons and institutions like the commissioner of baseball, the NCAA, and the NBA to be tougher on drug users among their athletes than they might otherwise be. The hero status is often used more directly to discourage drug use, as when Earvin "Magic" Johnson was hired to do an antidrug testimonial PSA, several years before he tested positive for HIV and became a spokesperson for AIDS awareness and safer sex (see Close-Up 6.5).

Close-Up 6.5: Sports Heroes with the AIDS Virus

Starting in the 1990s, there were increasing numbers of revelations of sports heroes who tested positive for HIV, the AIDS virus. Perhaps the most celebrated case was pro basketball's superhero Earvin "Magic" Johnson, who resigned from the Los Angeles Lakers at the height of his career in late 1991, announcing that he had tested positive for HIV. A widely recognized athlete of extraordinary talent, as well as a positive role model for youth, Johnson's announcement was greeted with a massive outpouring of public sympathy. Moreover, he was appointed to a Presidential advisory committee on AIDS policy and embarked on a heavy schedule of speaking engagements to youth about the importance of safe sex and traditional values. Receiving heavy media coverage for several weeks, Johnson admitted that he had been quite promiscuous as a single man before his recent marriage, and it was this activity that had presumably infected him. Interestingly, this violation of traditional morals did not seem to significantly impair his superhero status (including lucrative commercial endorsements), as happened when 1980s Olympic diver medalist Greg Louganis revealed he was gay and HIV-positive. See Casey et al. (2007) for a meta-analysis of studies of the effect of Magic's announcement.

In the wake of Magic Johnson's revelations, the media carried a number of stories about the sexually promiscuous lifestyles of some male professional athletes, and many athletes became vocally concerned about possible physical contact with HIV-infected opponents during football or basketball games. Still, there seemed to be considerable moral ambiguity about such behavior; during this same period, former basketball great Wilt Chamberlain publicly boasted of having had sex with 20,000 different women. Although clearly practicing exceptionally unsafe sex, to say nothing of the moral issues, Chamberlain did not lose his hero status. Even a celibate but gay superstar athlete probably would not have been treated half as well.

A very different situation occurred around the early 1992 revelation by retired tennis great Arthur Ashe that he was HIV positive, as a result of a blood transfusion with tainted blood during heart surgery in the early 1980s. Although Ashe had known of his infection for over 3 years, he only chose to reveal the fact publicly after a USA Today reporter had discovered the information and told Ashe that he intended to make it public. Unlike Johnson, Ashe was retired and no longer a public figure, and had acquired the HIV virus through means above moral reproach. Although public response to Ashe's announcement and his death in early 1993 was uniformly sad and sympathetic, the question remains about whether the privacy of Ashe and his wife and daughter or the public's right to know was more important.

A substantial benefit of hero status is lucrative product endorsement contracts for the major stars. For Olympic athletes this is often a critical part of their financial support, allowing them to pursue an amateur career. For wealthy professional athletes it is more like the icing on the already rich cake. These endorsement campaigns lead to an even greater media presence because that person becomes familiar as a spokesperson in advertising for that product. Sometimes a single individual may endorse several different products in different classes. A certain wholesome and unblemished status is required, however. After NBA star Latrell Sprewell assaulted and threatened his coach in December 1997, he was immediately dropped from his Converse shoe endorsement contract. When former Romanian Olympic gymnast hero Nadia Comăneci emigrated to the United States, the fact that she was openly and unapologetically living with a man married to someone else apparently rendered her worthless to advertisers. After Olympic medal-winner Marion Jones admitted to steroid use, she lost her medals and her endorsement potential.

Another aspect of emulating athletic heroes is seen in the area of fashion. Thanks to the influence of television, we not only want to act like the stars but we want to dress like them as well. Dress of different sports becomes chic at different times and places. Jogging clothes at one time became high fashion, not only for non-jogging adults but also for infants who could not even walk! Clothing manufacturers make large sums selling high-fashion clothes for tennis, skiing, or bicycling to folks who have never taken part in those sports and who have no intention of ever doing so. Some people wanting to learn to ski first buy the latest ski fashions and only later the skis and poles.

In spite of television's enhancement of sports heroes, some (e.g., Rader, 1984) have argued that modern sports heroes can never be on the same pedestal as past stars like Willie Mays, Johnny Unitas, Jesse Owens, or Stan Musial. The huge salaries and fast-track living now seem to separate star athletes from the rest of us and encourage their narcissistic and hedonistic tendencies, rather than the righteous and humble characteristics that we used to at least think our heroes possessed. The intrusive eye of television focuses on a ballplayer not only when he makes that glorious play, but also when he is petulantly fuming on the sidelines or selfishly proclaiming that he cannot make ends meet on a mere $2 million a year. No matter that all of us have our selfish and petulant moments; we like to think that true heroes do not, and the age of television makes it harder to maintain that fiction.

Cyber Sports

With the advent of computer-mediated communications has come several new arenas for sport. Fantasy sports (Lomax, 2006) can involve board games (APBA, Strat-O-Matic), simulation games, Internet-based leagues, rotisserie or pool leagues, and single-season or keeper (open-ended time frame) leagues. These involve media to varying degrees and the issues of importance are still evolving, with very little scientific study to date. Some issues to be resolved include determining criteria for success, development of player ratings, and communication and education about the sport.

Sports video games account for over 30% of video game sales, and some, like *Madden NFL*, are consistent industry best-sellers (D. Leonard, 2006). Team sports games (football, baseball, soccer, basketball) are very popular. Extreme sports games, such as the popular *Tony Hawk's Underground* skateboarding game or *Sunny Garcia Surfing* are also popular. Some sports games are quite realistic in their representation of the sport and others are unabashedly cartoonish. One issue with both types is racial stereotyping, involving both the direct play and extensions like *NFL Street*, which takes football to the street and to the world of hip-hop music.

Finally, there is the role of the Internet in sports participation, marketing, coverage, and branding (Mahan & McDaniel, 2006). Sometimes traditional media outlets like ESPN or *Sports Illustrated* extend their coverage through their websites. Sometimes cyber outlets offer more play-by-play coverage, as, for example, when NBC can broadcast several hours of daily Olympic highlights on its network affiliates but offer 24-hour coverage of all events through its website. Satellite radio such as Sirius XM in the United States can deliver more sports coverage. Of course, along with this coverage on the Internet, radio, or TV can come promotion of the events and marketing of ancillary products. For example, the small sportswear manufacturer Under Armour (UA) has used web marketing to compete effectively with traditional companies like Nike or Reebok in ways that would have never been possible before the Internet.

It is not yet clear what the fan experience of cyber sports is like. On the one hand, there are numerous opportunities for participation, such as websites and games, but much of it has a far more individual character than watching a ball game in a stadium or even with a group of friends at home.

Conclusion

When media report sporting events, they are doing more than reflecting the reality of those events. Television in particular has changed the very sports themselves. Television has also changed the way that our minds consider these sports and the way our hearts react to them. TV sports is a world all its own, a world often only imperfectly related to the sports in the field. When people think of sports, they are most likely to think first of watching television. The perceived reality of sports acquired through television is thus what sports become for most people. Just as media are our knowledge source about groups of people, social values, or products for sale, so they tell us about sports, how to play them, how to watch them, and how to feel about them. The very high level of coverage also sets a clear agenda that sports are important. Sports fans consider what the sportscaster says, not what they observe with their own senses, as authoritative; this is why people take their radios and even their small televisions to the stadium, so they can know what is "really happening." See Billings (2011) for a series of papers on recent thinking about sports media.

Now let us turn to a second media domain which plugs very centrally into our emotions, namely the world of music.

Music

Listening to popular music on radio, CD, music video, or MP3 player is one of the most preferred leisure activities among adolescents and young adults worldwide, occupying between 2½ and 5 hours per day for the average teen (Strasburger & Wilson, 2002). Since the advent of rock and roll in the 1950s, the latest artists, whether Elvis Presley, The Beatles, Pink Floyd, Metallica, Eminem, Lady Gaga, or Amy Winehouse, have been immensely popular with teens but thought scandalous by their parents.

Popular music has also always been associated with dancing, in recent history going back at least to the Charleston in the 1920s, which raised parents' eyebrows in its time. Rock music has always been associated with movement, particularly dancing but also screaming, clapping, stomping, and even what some concerned onlookers have called "rioting." Sexually suggestive movements associated with music have been particularly threatening to some. When Elvis appeared on *The Ed Sullivan Show* in the 1950s, he was only photographed from the chest up, so that his gyrating hips would not unduly arouse teens. Taking a broad historical perspective, Ehrenreich (2006) argues that this strong association between movement and music has actually been much more the rule than the exception throughout history. In fact she notes that the sedentary custom of sitting quietly and listening to music, with parallel newly sedentary behaviors for theater and worship, only began in Europe in the early nineteenth century. Rock music's debt to various African American musical traditions like blues, jazz, gospel, hip hop, and country is also seen in its emphasis on movement, always stronger in African musical and worship traditions than in European.

Pop musicians have often also been at the forefront of fashion. When The Beatles came on the pop music scene in 1963, their "long" hair created an immense stir, but within a few years much of the male population was wearing their hair at least that long, with The Beatles themselves sporting much longer hair. Punk and heavy metal rockers may have scandalized people in the early 1980s by wearing earrings, but 15 to 20 years later body piercings in all sorts of places were widespread. Music performances and award ceremonies are common venues for everything from fashions that are merely avant garde to those which are truly outrageous, such as Lady Gaga's appearance at the 2010 MTV Video Music Awards wearing a dress made of meat.

Beginning in the early 1980s, recorded music developed a visual component. Music Television (MTV) began in 1981 (MTV Europe in 1987) by playing promotional videos made by the record companies. Discovering that these video ads had very wide appeal, the cable channel played more and more music videos and grew until it became a youth icon, becoming both a barometer and a leading trend-setter in the youth culture market. Some have argued that the demand for access to international popular culture was a major impetus for the democratic revolutions in Eastern Europe between 1989 and 1991, that it was not so much the failure of Marxist systems but rather the inability of these systems to deliver Big Macs, Levis, and rock music. Karl Marx in his political theory never anticipated the problem that "I want my MTV" could create for decision makers in socialist countries (Orman, 1992, p. 282).

In later years MTV has evolved to include other kinds of teen-oriented programming, such as the stunt program *Jackass* and its annual spring break marathon. Other music video-oriented channels, notably VH-1 and Black Entertainment Television (BET), arose to provide more music video programming (although in recent years, as with MTV, these networks devote little of their schedules to music videos). About half of all music videos are performance videos, where the singer or group performs a song in a studio or concert setting. A concept video, on the other hand, tells a story, which may go beyond the lyrics of the song. Concept videos contain many special visual effects and also make heavy use of sex, dance, and sometimes violent themes.

The heavy influence of American and British bands and soloists has been a major factor in the ascendance of English as the worldwide language of popular culture. Though there is also much rock music in numerous other languages, it is a fact that international stars need to record in English to break into the U.S. market. Whereas South Americans, Europeans, or Africans will listen to music sung in languages they don't understand, it is commonly believed that North Americans will not do so.

There are, however, increasing cross-national and cross-genre influences, with almost every musical style becoming more international (Hutcheon, 2002). Formerly very local music has now found wider audiences: Indian sitar music, Jamaican reggae, Brazilian samba, Irish Celtic ballads, Louisiana Cajun and zydeco, and Caribbean salsa are listened to worldwide. New hybrid styles are continually emerging and finding large audiences. For example, Afro-Colombian cumbia blends African percussion, European melodies, and Andean flutes and accordions. Nigerian Afrobeat combines traditional African music with American funk. There are even several Islamic heavy metal bands in Morocco, Egypt, Pakistan, Lebanon, and other Muslim countries (LeVine, 2008). See Close-Up 6.6 for examples of how music has political power in Africa.

The advent of the Internet has also opened up new possibilities for preserving, sharing, archiving, and commenting on music. Music from earlier analog formats has been converted into digital files and made available on the

---

Close-Up 6.6: African Pop Music and Democracy

Ivory Coast pop music has long been quite political. Following a 1999 coup led by General Robert Gueï, the overthrow of the previous president was announced by reggae superstar Alpha Blondy performing a song and then introducing the new president. Singer Tiken Jah Fakoly was even more identified with the revolution, having been an advisor to Gueï's forces. The singers also acted as liaisons between media and law enforcement agencies (H. Lee, 2000). Ivorian anthems have been used by political forces elsewhere. For example, Fakoly's "We've Had It" was taken up by protesters in Madagascar and his "The Country's in Trouble" became the opposition anthem in Chad's 2000 election (Médioni, 2002). Nigerian singer Fela Anikulapo Kuti, founder of the Afrobeat style, found an international audience before his death in 1997. His son Femi Kuti founded a movement against corruption and regularly writes editorials in song, most of which are censored in his native Nigeria. Afro-funk singer Angélique Kidjo emerged as the most popular person in her native Benin in a poll asking who they would prefer as president. Not interested in politics, she has nonetheless integrated Afro-Brazilian and African traditions to support democracy in Africa, as well as entertaining large international audiences (Médioni, 2002).

Internet, along with ample opportunity for commenting in blogs. For example, there are numerous Brazilian music websites, including Loronix to preserve "forgotten music" and offer chance for comment, and Toque Musical ("Musical Touch") to offer a chance to hear and comment on rare or forgotten albums (Fullerton & Rarey, 2012).

Uses and Gratifications of Popular Music

Popular music, indeed all music, centrally appeals to the emotions in many different ways (Strasburger & Wilson, 2002). There are many uses and gratifications that we receive from music. For one thing, it is physiologically arousing. The body is "pumped up" in response to many kinds of music, although individual tastes vary greatly. Music can induce pleasant mood states of different sorts, and it can reduce feelings of anxiety and generally lift the spirits. Indeed, music is frequently used as a tool for mood management and mood repair (Chen, Zhou, & Bryant, 2007; Knobloch, 2003; Knobloch & Zillmann, 2002).

Music is also used to fill silence and supply background noise, either at home or while driving a car. Thus it can relieve boredom. It also has a social function, being a natural background to or a part of talking with friends, partying, or other recreation. Sometimes it is difficult to definitively separate social and solitary uses of music (Roberts & Christenson, 2001). Teens may often listen to music by themselves but for reasons that serve social relationships ("quasi-social" uses). For example, music may remind one of an absent friend and relieve loneliness or serve to strengthen one's social identification with others who like the same music.

Music can also serve to help define one's self-identity and facilitate one's entry into groups. Within a high school, for example, one group listens to rap, another to heavy metal, another to country music, and so on. The music can be an agent of socialization bringing the teen into the subculture by influencing how he/she dresses and acts. This musical culture is not necessarily restricted to one's culture of origin. Many popular American musical genres (e.g., jazz, blues, rock, gospel, rap, hip hop) have their origins in the African American community but have wide appeal beyond that subculture. Many continue to be amazed at the current popularity of rap, given its urban Black origins, with affluent White suburban teens. Sometimes even the same genre of music has different divisions within it; for example, "redneck" and "blue-neck" political partisans within country music (Willman, 2005), or Christian punk and secular punk.

Finally, music in adolescence, along with dancing and other movement, serves as a marker of separation from adults. Part of its appeal is frankly that adults dislike it and don't understand it. This phenomenon repeats itself with rap and heavy metal today, as it has in the past with rock and roll in the 1950s or the Charleston in the 1920s. Even something as simple as a teen turning on the radio or CD in the car or house serves as a separation from parents. If the music is on, he doesn't have to talk to them.

Music is powerful material, and anything powerful can potentially be threatening. See Close-Up 6.7 for some examples of how music has threatened the status quo throughout history and Close-Up 6.8 for how music has even been used to torture.

Content

Though it probably will not surprise you, the most common theme in music lyrics over the last 70 years is being in love, although the lyrics are more sexually explicit now than they used to be, for example, expressing love as lust (Hansen & Hansen, 2000). There was an increase in violent and misogynistic themes starting in the 1990s, especially in rap, punk, and heavy metal. Increasingly these themes became more mainstream, as seen when bad-boy rapper Eminem received Grammy awards in the early 2000s. The advent of music videos in the early 1980s offered a new outlet for women to be presented as sex objects and ornamental decorations, much as they had long been portrayed in many other entertainment genres and advertising. Music videos also provided more opportunities for the intertwining of sexual and violent themes.

Close-Up 6.7: Music As a Threat (Taruskin, 2001)

Music has often been a threatening force and can sometimes produce a violent reaction. Perhaps the most extreme example of a backlash against music was seen in the brutal Taliban regime in Afghanistan (1996–2001), which sought out musical instruments, cassette tapes and videos, and cassette players and burned them in public pyres. Musicians caught playing were beaten with their instruments and then imprisoned. Other puritanical authoritarian regimes have also opposed music. Believing it had hypnotic or addictive effects, theocratic ruler Ayatollah Khomeini banned music from TV and radio in Iran after the Islamic Revolution of 1979.

Such extremes have also been seen in Western secular and church traditions. Plato's *Republic* was highly suspicious of music, seeing it as taking hold of the soul. In the history of Christianity there have been many religious leaders and traditions suspicious of music, including such diverse company as St. Augustine, St. John Chrysostom, the Massachusetts Puritans, and various conservative Protestant groups.

Music also derives power and threat from its culture of association. For many years the music of German composer Richard Wagner was not performed in Israel (by custom, not by law). When composer Daniel Barenboim broke this taboo in 2001, the decision was very controversial and many Israelis found his choice insensitive.

Close-Up 6.8: Music as Torture (Pellegrinelli, 2009)

Although music has long been used in warfare to rally troops and distract the enemy, sometimes it goes beyond that to become a weapon of torture. In the U.S. invasion of Panama in 1989, forces helped drive dictator Manuel Noreiga out of hiding in the Vatican Embassy by blasting Van Halen and Metallica at high volumes from multiple boom boxes. In the early days of the Iraq War in 2003, U.S. forces exposed captives to prolonged loud music, including Metallica's "Enter Sandman" and Barney the Dinosaur's theme song "I Love You." The next year, in the second battle of Fallujah, AC/DC's "Shoot to Thrill" was used to flush out insurgents. Even long before the age of electronic media, the Mexican army band played loud music the night before their attack on the Alamo in 1836. In recent years several professional music research and musicology societies have passed resolutions condemning the use of music as torture.

One content concern with popular music has been the promotion of drug use. Roberts, Henriksen, and Christenson (1999) analyzed the lyrics from the 1,000 most popular songs in 1996 and 1997. They found that 17% of the songs overall had reference to alcohol and 18% to illicit drugs. With rap, however, figures were much higher (47% for alcohol and 63% for illicit drugs). More importantly, any mention of negative consequences of drug use was rare; only 9% of songs mentioning alcohol mentioned any negative consequences of its use. Tobacco was rarely mentioned, although more often in rap and hip hop than other genres. These antisocial themes were generally higher in music videos than in the lyrics themselves, especially in rap videos (DuRant et al. 1997). For example, Jones (1997) found the following percentages of themes in rap videos: guns 59%, drug use 49%, profanity 73%, grabbing 69%, alcohol use 42%, and explicit violence 36%.

Content analysis does not tell the whole story, however. The interpretation of that content is important, and people of different ages do not always interpret lyrics in the same way (Hansen & Hansen, 2000). For example, in response to lyrics which are quite sexually explicit, teens see less sex and more love where adults see only sex (Rosenbaum & Prinsky, 1987). Girls often see a sexy woman as a powerful figure, whereas boys see her as an erotic plaything. Children will interpret a video more literally than a teen or adult will. Often teens do not fully understand the lyrics (Desmond, 1987; Greenfield et al., 1987; Strasburger & Wilson, 2002). Lyrics may also mean different things in different times. For example, a popular mainstream hit from 1968, "Young Girl" by Gary Puckett and the Union Gap, today sounds like a creepy pedophile anthem ("Young girl, get outta my mind, my love for you is way outta line, better run girl").

There may also be a socially positive side to even fairly extreme lyrics. For example, some have argued that rap music has a positive social role, being a voice for very marginalized and disenfranchised groups, empowering young Black males and drawing broader society's attention to their plight (Krohn & Suazo, 1995; McDonnell, 1992). These lyrics or videos probably serve to prime ideas and as cues to retrieve related knowledge, however. If a teen watches lots of videos that portray women as sexual playthings, for example, that will prime gender-role memories and attitudes consistent with that type of schema. This in turn will guide future attention and information processing, directing attention toward exemplars that confirm such beliefs and away from those which are inconsistent with it. For example, Gan, Zillmann, and Mitrook (1997) found that sexually enticing rap videos primed a negative stereotype of African American women for White viewers, and that this negative schema was subsequently used to evaluate other Black women in more negative ways.

Effects

Parallel to popular judgments about media violence, people often take an extreme position on popular music, either damning it as the cause of all moral decline in society or dismissing the criticisms as "no big deal." Although it is difficult to do well-controlled research on causative effects of music consumption, we do know something about its effects (see Levitin, 2006, for a fascinating look at how the brain processes music, and Allen et al., 2007, for a meta-analysis of effects of music on behavior).

First of all, there is clear research support for arousal; that is, music does arouse us emotionally, even though specific tastes differ greatly and what is pleasant for one person may be highly aversive for another. The tempo of music differentially affects skin conductance, with fast-paced music consistently causing greater arousal than slower-paced music, which in turn arouses more than silence (Dillman Carpentier & Potter, 2007). Music also can clearly affect mood (Ballard & Coates, 1995). Although a possible causative role is not entirely clear, there is some evidence that a preference for heavy metal music, in particular, may be a marker for alienation, psychiatric disorders, risk-taking, or substance abuse in adolescence (Strasburger & Wilson, 2002), in that heavy metal is disproportionately preferred by teens with these conditions. In an interesting study looking at effects of listening to opera, Balte, Avram, Miclea, and Miu (2011) found that listening to an excerpt from Puccini's *Tosca* elicited positive emotion and arousal, as measured by heart rate, respiration rate, and skin conductance. Following that, reading a synopsis of the opera's sad plot before listening to the music a second time led to decreased positive emotion but continued high arousal. This was moderated somewhat by listening to the excerpt a third time while watching a subtitled film of the segment.

Different music lyrics can elicit different sorts of behaviors. Listening to music with aggressive lyrics can lead to more aggressive cognitions, emotions, and behaviors (Anderson, Carnagey, & Eubanks, 2003). On the other hand, people listening to music with prosocial lyrics leave larger tips in restaurants and donate more to a charitable organization (Greitemeyer, 2009a, 2009b, 2011a; Jacob, Guéguen, & Boulbry, 2010). Listening to prosocial lyrics was also associated with a decrease in state hostility, which led to reduced aggression (Greitemeyer, 2011b). Such findings suggest great untapped potential for positive effects of music on society.

Reactions to music can also depend on one's prior knowledge, experiences, and prejudices. Fried (1996, 1999) conducted a couple of very interesting experiments on the reactions of adults of various ages to music lyrics. The lyrics to an obscure 1960s Kingston Trio folksong "Bad Man's Blunder" were pretested and shown to be not recognized as a folk song and to be equally credible as country or rap music. The lyrics, very similar to the controversial Ice T "Cop Killer" rap of 1992, tell of a young man who intentionally shoots and kills a police officer and shows no remorse for it. The written lyrics were identified as being from an artist named "D. J. Jones" and were then shown to European American and Hispanic adults in public places like malls and coffee shops. The key manipulation was that half were told it was a country music song and half that it was a rap song, two genres identified as surprisingly similar by some text analyses (Armstrong, 1993; Noe, 1995). Participants were then asked to rate the lyrics on seven attitude scales, such as "I find these lyrics offensive" and "This song promotes violence, riots, and civil unrest," from which a composite score was created.

Results showed that adults over 40 rated the lyrics much more negatively when they were identified as rap than when the same lyrics were identified as country. For adults under 40, however, there was no difference as a function of the genre attribution and much more positive ratings overall. A second analysis, partitioned by whether the participants had children instead of by age, showed that adults with children rated the alleged rap lyrics more negatively than the alleged country lyrics, but that ratings by adults without children showed no difference. Clearly the reactions are not only to the presented lyrics but also to prior knowledge and attitudes about the musical genre. In the case of older adults and adults who are parents, rap was far more negative. Fried (1999) offers several possible explanations for these findings. One invokes a subtle racism, in which the rap music is associated with urban Black culture, which has negative associations, especially with violence, for White and Hispanic parents. Another factor is familiarity, with the less familiar being more threatening. The older adults were probably less familiar with rap as a genre than with country. In any case, these studies show that we bring considerable cognitive and emotional baggage to our response to music.

There is also evidence of desensitization effects of music. For example, exposure to violent rap videos can lead to greater acceptance of violence in dating situations and lower academic aspirations for young African American teens and college students (Johnson, Adams, Ashburn, & Reed, 1995; Johnson, Jackson, & Gatto, 1995). Watching rock videos with antisocial themes led to greater liking for antisocial behavior (Hansen & Hansen, 1990b). See Chapter 9 for a discussion of densensitization in relation to other kinds of violent media.

See Close-Up 6.9 for an example of the use of music in attempts to gain international influence.

Music as a Memory Cue

Music turns out to be an excellent cue to memory, with melody providing an additional possible retrieval route beyond the words themselves. In many societies, extensive oral traditions have been handed down for generations through music, with the melodies serving to help encode the verbal information and preserve it in the collective memory (D. C. Rubin, 1995). Marketers have long known that musical jingles can aid memory for products advertised (Yalch, 1991). Songs can also be powerful cues for remembering the events of one's life (Cady, Harris, & Knappenberger, 2008; Schulkind, Hennis, & Rubin, 1999). People strongly associate certain songs with, for example, their senior

Close-Up 6.9: Pop Music in the Service of Diplomacy

Who is the largest distributor of Arabic-language popular music in the Middle East? It is Radio Sawa ("Together"), and it will probably surprise you to know that Radio Sawa is funded by the U.S. government in its efforts to woo the hearts and minds of young adult Arabs. Radio Sawa is the successor to the Voice of America Arabic service, a 7-hour daily news service on shortwave radio that was little more than U.S. political propaganda, with little popular appeal even for those few who could receive it. Designed by Norman Pattiz after intense local market research, Radio Sawa broadcasts on FM and sometimes AM with a 24-hour format of eclectic popular music from the Arab world, the United States, and elsewhere. There are also two hourly news segments (a 10-minute segment with correspondent reports and a 5-minute headline segment), as well as PSAs on topics like drugs, drunk driving, and AIDS. In an attempt to win local appeal, announcers use local Arab dialects and broadcast local news, weather, and traffic reports. Of course, the most controversial aspect is the news, this being a part of the world with a high level of distrust and dislike of the U.S. government. Radio Sawa, with headquarters in Dubai, is broadcast to Jordan, Qatar, the United Arab Emirates, Kuwait, Bahrain, Djibouti, and Cyprus, with access from these places to Iraq, Egypt, Palestine, and elsewhere (Gubash, 2002). What do you think of Lady Gaga and Kanye West being an integral part of the U.S. diplomatic message to the Arab world?

year in high school, a long road trip with friends, or driving to work at a certain job. The popularity of oldies radio stations and classic rock in general is no doubt due to the highly effective triggering of personal memories by these songs. Cady et al. (2008) found that, when college students were presented with a list of songs popular during certain eras of their lives (e.g., preschool, middle school, high school), most could easily recall a personal memory associated with the songs. For the most part these were very pleasant memories, with the earliest ones being the most pleasant and the more recent ones being more vivid.

Sometimes music memories enter our consciousness without being invited or perhaps even wanted. These melodic memories of a song "stuck in our head" are called Involuntary Musical Imagery (IMAs) or, more informally, "earworms" (Bailes, 2007; Beaman & Williams, 2010; Liikkanen, 2008; Williamson et al., 2011). Earworms occur spontaneously and are hard to control, occurring most often in times of low alertness and low demands on our attention. Sometimes a very long-forgotten earworm may emerge into consciousness, for example when someone remembers an advertising jingle from decades earlier.

Earworms are very common; 92% reported experiencing them at least weekly and 26% "several times a day" (Liikkanen, 2008). They are most often some very familiar song, often triggered by some cue that elicits that melody. Women and younger people report earworms more often than men and older people. They are often experienced as pleasant but at times may be annoying.

Sports and music elicit strong emotional responses, but perhaps nothing taps into deeper emotions than one's religion. Overt expressions of religion in media are, however, surprisingly scarce, perhaps deemed potentially too emotionally explosive. We now turn to the media's portrayal, often very awkward and understated, of religion.

Religion

For people of faith, perhaps nothing elicits a more fundamental positive emotional response than appeals to one's deeply held religious beliefs or a more negative emotional response than an attack on that faith or what is seen as an unfair distortion of it. Even among nonbelievers, religion is often a highly emotion-laden topic. Throughout history, extremely positive actions have been carried out in the name of religion, such as the centuries of education and social services offered by church entities and church members. Sadly, strongly negative actions have been carried out as well, from the Crusades and the Inquisition to the New York, London, and Madrid radical Islamic terrorist attacks.

Gallup polls consistently show the United States to be by far the most religious industrialized country in the world (over 90% of Americans believe in God; over 40% attend religious services weekly), yet religion is perhaps the most touchy and neglected area in American media, perhaps because journalists are afraid of the emotion associated with it. When Beatle John Lennon said offhandedly in 1966 that their group was more popular than Jesus, many were highly offended. Even subsequent clarifications of satirical intent and a sort of apology failed to mollify critics. Out of fear of controversy, religion often becomes invisible in mainstream media, especially in television and popular movies. Let us examine several aspects of religion in the media, including religion in entertainment and news, religious media, and effects of media on religion more broadly.

Religion in Entertainment

Generally speaking, religion plays almost no role in the lives of characters in American entertainment TV series or movies. They hardly ever mention going to church or believing in God, nor do they mention that they do not go to church or do not believe in God. It appears that producers are loath to offend anyone, either by identifying their favorite TV characters with a particular faith or by saying that they have no faith. Action-adventure shows make virtually no mention of religion either, with the occasional exception of having an extreme religious fanatic or terrorist as a villain. Nonetheless, one many derive religious moral lessons from just about any film or TV program (see R. S. J. Leonard, 2006, for a set of examples).

This absence of religious themes probably reflects (1) TV producers' and writers' relative lack of involvement with religion themselves, compared to most Americans, and, most importantly, (2) an implicit belief that religion is a very touchy subject and one in relation to which people are easily offended. Perhaps program makers fear that Protestants and Jews would stop watching *Modern Family* if the Pritchetts and Dunphys were identified as Catholic or that atheists and agnostics would lose interest in *How I Met Your Mother* if Ted and Barney became born-again Christians.

In a content analysis of 100 episodes of U.S. prime-time network entertainment TV, Skill, Lyons, and Larson (1991) found only 5% of the characters with an identifiable religious affiliation, compared to 89% of the U.S. population. Over half of those identified characters were Roman Catholic, with the rest Protestant, cult members, or New Age adherents. There were no Jews, Muslims, or other religions represented. A large proportion of those few that were represented appeared on a few episodes of particular shows, particularly a few nonspecific "God" shows like *Touched by an Angel*.

By most estimates, the prime-time show on American TV that takes religion the most seriously is the irreverent animated sitcom *The Simpsons* (Pinsky, 2007). Unlike almost any other TV family, the Simpsons attend church weekly, pray before meals, self-identify as Christians, and generally find spiritual issues important in their lives. To be sure, the sharp-edged show satirizes the foibles of religion, as it does just about everything else, but Homer and Marge and the kids return to God in prayer and trust time and again. They attend Springfield Community Church (no denomination specified). Neighbor Ned Flanders is a somewhat rigid evangelical Christian, but he is more rounded than the totally hypocritical caricature that many evangelical Christians in entertainment are reduced to. If Bart Simpson prays before dinner, "Rub-a-dub-dub, thanks for the grub," he is not unlike many of our own children. When Marge tells God she will be a better person and give the poor something they really like, not just old lima beans and canned pumpkin, it strikes a familiar chord.

Why do the producers of *The Simpsons* believe they can endow their sitcom family with a spiritual dimension when almost no other TV writers do? Is there something about the animated format that makes this less risky? Perhaps not coincidentally, two other fairly religious sitcoms are also animated, the very edgy *South Park* and *Family Guy*, which both feature Jesus as an occasional character and have had plot lines dealing with Mormonism, Judaism, and various shades of Christianity.

Except for explicitly religious programming such as Christian broadcasting, religious professionals are greatly underrepresented on U.S. television. When they are shown, they are often, at best, saintly but shallow characters, and, at worst, vicious hypocrites hiding behind their clerical collars. The fanatical cult preacher archetype is typically very extreme and very evil. Such characters have to be very perverted so as not to evoke any sympathy or any criticisms about the program saying negative things about a real man or woman of God. The unexpected success of the show *Touched by an Angel* in the mid-1990s brought the public's interest in spiritual themes to the networks' notice, even if in a somewhat generic and non-specific form. The networks were still wary, however, following a 1980s conservative Christian campaign against *NYPD Blue* that scared away enough advertisers to force the network to sell ad time for a top-rated show at bargain-basement rates.

Religion in the News

Although in general religious news has traditionally been underreported in the United States relative to its importance, a look at what is reported reveals some interesting trends. Religious news that is centered on an individual person receives relatively heavier coverage, following the star model of political and entertainment news coverage (see Chapter 7). Most often the focus is either on Roman Catholicism, whose colorful pageantry and identifiable individual newsmakers (especially the Pope) make good photogenic copy, or on Protestant fundamentalist preachers, whose dogmatic theology and contentious political activism make good controversy-ridden stories, especially when centered on a charismatic individual. Groups of mainline Protestants politely discussing multiple points of view on social welfare or Reform Jews examining different degrees of support for Israel may be just as important but they are less photogenic and newsworthy. Media dealing with religious themes have considerable power to both promote peace and incite violence, and there is ample evidence of their having done both (Mitchell, 2012).

Some major changes in religious news coverage appeared in 1987 with the onset of several televangelism scandals. The revelation that popular TV evangelist Jim Bakker had had a sexual liaison with a secretary several years before was sharply at odds with his pious image. This was followed by discoveries of financial mishandling of Bakker's PTL Ministries funds and of the extravagant lifestyle of Bakker and his wife Tammy Faye. The subsequent tryst of televangelist Jimmy Swaggart and a prostitute further tarnished the image. Unlike earlier religious stories, these were widely reported in the media and the participants were widely ridiculed by comedians. The media apparently decided that in this case comedy about religion, even scathing and derisive comedy, was acceptable, though it was almost unprecedented in the United States. Apparently these cases and the pathetic individuals brought down were considered to be sufficiently lacking in sympathy that comic skewering would not be unduly offensive.

Religion is sometimes simplistically presented as the entire basis for what are actually much more complex social problems (in e.g., Northern Ireland,

Palestine, Lebanon, and India and Pakistan); in other cases the importance of religion is missed altogether. A prime example is the role of religion in the revolutions that brought down the communist regimes of Eastern Europe between 1989 and 1991. In Poland, the Roman Catholic Church had been the only legal forum for political discussion for years and, as such, had been the focus of dissent. Neighboring and rebellious Lithuania, the only former Soviet republic with a majority Roman Catholic population, was the first to challenge Moscow and demand its independence. In Romania, the revolt against the brutal regime of Nicolae Ceauçescu began with a protest after a reformed church service in Timişoara, a western city near the border with less-censored, already-democratizing Hungary. The protesters were gunned down, but an outraged Romanian nation responded with a force that ended in the televised execution of the hated dictator and his wife on Christmas Day, 1989.

Perhaps most dramatic, however, was the situation in the old German Democratic Republic (GDR), where 40% of the officially atheistic country were practicing Lutherans, ironically a much larger percentage than in free West Germany. The weekly protests in Leipzig that led to the fall of the GDR government and its hated symbol, the Berlin Wall, in November 1989 had actually begun the previous summer with a weekly Monday night prayer meeting at a Lutheran church. Its numbers grew weekly, from a handful of members who quietly picketed after the prayer meeting to a mass protest of thousands filling the streets. The church was given so much credit for the peaceful revolution that the Leipzig city government later hung a huge banner that read "We thank you, church."

In the U.S. media, very little was said about the role of religion in these democratic revolutions. Why not? It was probably not a conspiracy of silence, but rather simply an oversight by journalists for whom religion was not very important in their own lives. Perhaps they were also not used to seeing politics and religion interact in this very different way than they do in the United States. Another possible factor was some uneasiness regarding how to present the role of religion to a society used to having the religious sphere completely separate from the secular sphere.

In a somewhat different type of situation, religious dimensions of the news are sometimes ignored or underplayed when they become politically uncomfortable. For example, when the U.S. media were patriotically drumming up support for wars against Iraq in 1991 and in 2003, much was made of Iraqi leader Saddam Hussein's admittedly brutal dictatorship, but few stories mentioned that he did allow considerable freedom of religion and that Iraq was one of the few Arab nations with a sizable Christian minority. Moreover, U.S. ally Saudi Arabia rigidly forbade the practice of any religion but Islam, even to the extent of not allowing Christian and Jewish U.S. soldiers stationed there to privately practice their own faith.

In a provocative book called *God's Politics: Why the Right Gets It Wrong and the Left Doesn't Get It* (2005), political activist and Christian writer Jim Wallis argues that the American political right has for many years co-opted Christianity and defined only a small number of issues like abortion and gay marriage as "moral issues." On the other hand, the political left has for many years rejected all faith-based efforts as politically suspect and a tool of the right. Consequently, in U.S. politics, the right has been allowed to identify its views as the only authentic Christianity. Journalists tended to buy into this and people came to believe that only people on the right (i.e., Republicans) had faith and only those on the left (i.e., Democrats) had a social conscience. Wallis tells the right to start accepting issues like poverty, unjust wars, and massively uneven distributions of wealth as moral issues. Likewise, he tells the left to acknowledge some moral decline in society and to not be afraid to talk publicly about one's faith. He tells both sides to listen to each other and seek common ground. For example, maybe the reason children do not have such strong parental guidance in terms of values is that both parents are having to work long hours at low-paying jobs that provide no benefits.

People listened. In the 2008 Presidential campaign, unlike any that had come before, Democrats talked a lot about their faith, and Republicans mentioned moral imperatives in social issues. Sometimes candidates got in trouble for doing so. Barack Obama had to disavow his former pastor's saying some unpopular things, but few doubted Obama's personal faith. This could be the beginning of a major new way to look at religion, politics, and media. See Chapter 8 for further discussion of politics and media.

Why have mainstream media been so reluctant to cover religious news and religious dimensions of secular news? Hoover (1998) suggests six mistaken beliefs. First is the belief that, as societies become more modern and advanced, they necessarily become more secular and less religious; this tenet seems to be widely believed in American intellectual life, in spite of poll numbers showing the country is a blatant counterexample. Second is the belief that religion is fundamentally a private matter and thus largely outside the realm of public discourse, including the realm of journalism. Third, religion makes claims outside the empirical realm of what is knowable and concrete. Journalism is "all about verification and sources, but religion is fundamentally unverifiable" (Hoover, 1998, p. 29). Fourth, religion is thought to be complex and thus hard to cover in brief media sound bites. Fifth, religion is controversial and coverage, however careful and objective, is likely to offend someone. Finally, there is the misunderstanding that the First Amendment to the U.S. Constitution, forbidding the establishment of a state church, somehow mandates the complete separation of church and state in public discussion. It does not; it merely says that the state may not establish a state church.

Religious Media

In the United States—but in few other places in the Western world—explicitly religious programming is a thriving business (Bruce, 1990; Peck, 1992).

Consistent with the separation of religion from other aspects of American life, it is produced and distributed totally separately from other television programming. Religious books are sold in separate bookstores from secular books, religious music is typically recorded by different artists and marketed separately from other music, and religious television is produced by religious networks. Although largely a U.S. phenomenon, there is some international growth of TV evangelism, especially in Latin America and most notably in Guatemala, the first majority Protestant country in Latin America. Increasingly, religious groups of all sorts are turning to the Internet as a domain for some of their more creative ministries (Campbell, 2010)

Although there was some Christian broadcasting in the early days of radio and television, the modern electronic church really began with Billy Graham's TV specials, starting in 1957. These were later followed by Rex Hubbard, Oral Roberts, Jerry Falwell, Robert Schuller, Jimmy Swaggart, Pat Robertson's *700 Club*, and Jim and Tammy Bakker's *PTL Club*. These programs had a variety of formats and their emphases were also quite varied, including Robertson and Bakker's talk-show format, Falwell's emphasis on politics, and Roberts' focus on spiritual healing. All except Schuller were theologically evangelical or fundamentalist, with a heavy emphasis on evangelism (Hoover, 1988). In spite of its evangelistic emphasis, however, Christian TV attracts few nonbelievers, and in fact serves mainly to reinforce the existing beliefs of its viewers (Fore, 1987).

Effects of Television on Religion

Finally, there are some who have argued that the mere presence of television as a medium has altered all religion in subtle but profound ways, so much so that the perceived reality of religion will never be the same again. In his provocative critique of 1980s popular culture, *Amusing Ourselves to Death*, Neil Postman (1985) argued that television had radically reshaped practically everything about our lives. One domain that was greatly changed was religion, in ways that go far beyond the Sunday morning church broadcasts and TV evangelists. Postman argued that, because TV is, at heart, entertainment, the preacher is thus the star performer, and "God comes out as second banana" (p. 117). Although Christianity has always been "a demanding and serious religion," its TV version can acquire its needed share of the audience "only by offering people something they want" (p. 121), which is hardly historical Biblical Christianity. Furthermore, Postman argues, TV is such a fundamentally secular medium that religious TV necessarily uses many of the same symbols and formats (e.g., *The 700 Club* was modeled after *Entertainment Tonight*).

Thus, TV preachers are stars who are attractive and affluent, just like movie stars. Worship on TV is not participatory; the audience can sit at home and absorb, but does not have the communal worship experience of group singing, praying, or liturgy. Although a church may be considered holy ground where

---

Close-Up 6.10: Is Walmart Our Media Values Gatekeeper?

The growing economic power of retail giant Walmart and other discount chains has led to concern about their influence on public values and taste. In 2003, Walmart alone accounted for over 50% of the sales of best-selling albums/CDs, over 60% of best-selling DVDs, and 40% of the best-selling books. Over one-third of all music was sold through the big chains, with Walmart accounting for 20% of the total. Because they sell so many of the best-selling items, Walmart and other chains do not carry a broad assortment, a policy that leaves music, books, or films that are of limited or esoteric tastes, as well as anything at all controversial, left behind. For example, they sell no albums with parental warning labels, a policy that excludes most rap and hip hop artists. They also sell huge amounts of Christian music, videos, and books. The *VeggieTales* videos of animated vegetables teaching Bible and morality lessons only received widespread exposure after Walmart started selling them. The publisher of the *Left Behind* series of apocalyptic Christian novels credits Walmart with turning one of its novels into the best-selling book in the country. Country music sells well at Walmart, as do Christian writings and popular books by politically conservative authors. Is this trend a positive development in "controlling smut," as some have argued, or a disturbing market force steering us toward a politically conservative, rural-oriented, evangelically Christian–flavored popular culture (Kirkpatrick, 2003)?

---

people act with reverence, there is no comparable sacred space when watching church on TV at home, where one can sit in dirty underwear drinking beer and eating pizza during the sermon without offending anyone.

Postman (1985) argued that, as more and more religious services are broadcast on TV and as pastors become more sophisticated in the use of electronic media, the "danger is not that religion has become the content of television shows but that television shows may become the content of religion" (p. 124). Pastors become concerned about providing the kind of worship conducive to television, even if the service is not being televised. Congregations subtly expect to be entertained, even amused. Worship services have jazz music, rap liturgy, and computerized multimedia presentations. One church ran a full-page ad touting its contemporary Saturday evening service, called "Church Lite," for college students who wanted to sleep in on Sunday. Other churches use Sunday school curricula like "The Gospel According to the Simpsons" or "The Gospel According to Harry Potter." One of your book's authors (RJH) recently attended a high-tech Christian wedding, complete with multi-screen video montages of the couple in their courtship, ending with a 20-foot-high projected sonogram of the baby the couple was expecting. A Baptist church in Arkansas hired Wacky World Studios in Tampa for a $279,000 makeover of a former chapel into "Toon Town," with buzzers and confetti that explode during joyful celebrations like baptisms; the Sunday school attendance doubled (Labi, 2002). Is this a creative reaching out to people in mission or selling one's soul on the altar of popular culture? The answer is not always obvious.

Places of worship no longer have a particularly sacred character, because one can worship through TV while at home. One congregation worships regularly in a former roller rink, another in an old laundromat, while yet another rents space on Sunday mornings in a large university classroom. There is little sense of the sacred, as is found most strikingly in the magnificent medieval cathedrals of Europe. Thus, behavior in houses of worship is often no different from behavior anywhere else. Has television contributed to this change? For a recent text on media and religion, see Stout (2011); for a stimulating set of readings about media, religion, and society see Hoover and Lundby (1997).

In a very different type of popular culture threat to religion, some have argued that the big retail chains such as Walmart have an undue but unrecognized control over religious media and popular culture more generally; see Close-Up 6.10.

Conclusion

For most people few events elicit more emotion than an exciting ball game between two teams they care about, listening to a song that they really love or hate, or having our most cherished religious beliefs affirmed or attacked. The emotions triggered by media can be very powerful, and they are a fundamental part of the media experience.

Chapter 7

News

Setting an Agenda about the World

Q: In 2002 Bill O'Reilly spoke of "100,000 abductions of children by strangers every year in the U.S." How many were there, in fact?

A: According to the U.S. Office of Juvenile Justice, only 115 (Glassner, 2010).

Q: How often do teens and young adults get their news from social networking sites?

A: According to 2011 surveys, 38% of those under 30 get their news "regularly or sometimes" through Facebook, Twitter, or other social networking sites. For high school students, the figure was 76% (Loth, 2012).

Q: How many children are frightened or upset by news stories on television?

A: Thirty-seven percent of children between kindergarten and sixth grade, according to a survey of their parents by Cantor and Nathanson (1996).

If there is one area of media that people are most likely to uncritically accept as reflecting reality rather than constructing it, that area is probably the news. People watch, read, or listen to news in order to find out what happened in the world that day. However, their perceived reality may still diverge quite dramatically from the real world, where much more happened than can be reported in any day's news program, publication, or website. Even the most earnest attempt to accurately and fairly represent the day's events requires producers and editors to select which items to cover, how prominently to cover them, and in what manner to cover them. The typical daily newspaper, for example, only selects 25% of the daily Associated Press (AP) wire service material to print (McCombs, 1994).

These choices necessarily involve some agenda setting (see Chapter 2); that is, telling us what to think about, what is important (Dearing & Rogers, 1996; McCombs & Reynolds, 2009; McCombs & Shaw, 1993). Agenda setting does not necessarily mean that media tell us *what* to think, although some sources quite unashamedly do that. The news is not a reflection of the day; it is a "set of stories constructed by journalists about the events of the day" (McCombs, 1994, p. 11). When the months-long U.S. Presidential primary elections are given massive media coverage, for example, the public receives the implicit but unmistakable message that these campaigns are important. When a prominent celebrity has a substance abuse meltdown, the extensive media coverage tells us we should care about that. Likewise, when stories receive little coverage, the implicit message communicated is that they are not important. Those in power know this well. For example, when the besieged Assad government in Syria closed its borders to reporters during the uprising of 2012, it was hoping that this limiting of news coverage would cause the world to forget about the atrocities being committed within its borders. See Brosius and Kepplinger (1990), Edelstein (1993), McCombs and Reynolds (2009), and Sheafer and Weimann (2005) for different measures of agenda setting in regard to news.

The form of the narrative of the news can subtly set an agenda and tell us what is important. For example, Anker (2005) examined American news coverage of the September 11, 2001, terror attacks and argued that they strongly fit a narrative of melodrama, meaning heavy use of emotionality, clear demarcation of good and evil, and salient unambiguous roles of victim, villain, and hero. Anker argued that this type of coverage has certain consequences, such as ensuring that the public sees the issue in very stark and moralistic good and evil terms, and sees the power of the state as necessary and good to fight a terrible evil. Those who question its tactics are thus open to charges of lack of patriotism. The agenda can even be set by the use of a compelling metaphor. See Close-Up 7.1 for an example of how a metaphor has driven popular thought and even foreign policy in dealing with terrorism.

Close-Up 7.1: How a Metaphor Shaped a Decade of Thinking and Foreign Policy (Kruglanski, Crenshaw, Post, & Victorioff, 2007; Lakoff, 2009)

When U.S. President George W. Bush spoke on September 12, 2001, he framed the terrorism problem as war: "The deliberate and deadly attacks which were carried out yesterday against our country were more than acts of terror. They were acts of war." Linguist George Lakoff (2009) and Kruglanski et al. (2007) argue that this metaphor has been accepted unquestioningly and should be examined.

What are the implications of using this war metaphor to think about terrorism? First of all, it frames terrorism as a national security problem, where each side's interest, perhaps even their very existence, is threatened. Second, it becomes a zero-sum game, in which "victory" is only possible for one side, not both. It also requires national unity, such that the solution is seen only in military terms and dissent is seen an unpatriotic. The expansion of executive powers, including restrictions of civil liberties and brutal interrogation practices, is accepted.

How does the war metaphor not fit the problem of terrorism? Unlike in traditional wars, the opposition (Al Qaeda) is not a state, though it sometimes takes refuge in weak states. Second, victory is hard to define. It is not clear when the enemy is defeated, there is not likely to be a surrender by either side, and the "war" will likely drag on indefinitely, accompanied by increasing dissent among a weary population. Third, military force does not fundamentally weaken terrorism, though it may cause temporary setbacks. Nor does it decrease motivation or morale to resist, and it may even increase them. It also obscures the serious grievances of those drawn to terrorism, encourages stereotyping of Arabs and Muslims, diverts resources from other needs, and damages civil liberties.

If there are problems with the war metaphor of terrorism, what are the alternatives? One suggested alternative is "fighting crime"—seeing terrorism as fundamentally a problem of law enforcement, given that acts of terrorism invariably break some laws. This metaphor is generally the one used by Israel, the UK after the 2005 rail station bombings, and the U.S. after the first World Trade Center bombings in 1993. Some advantages of the fighting crime metaphor include more focus on bringing to justice perpetrators who have violated particular laws. It is also less likely to incite discrimination against whole groups and is a less overwhelming financial commitment. The cost of mistakes and "collateral damage" is generally less. Also, police work is more suited than military operations to understanding local culture and cultivating community relationships as information sources. In addition, it is easier to get international cooperation for law enforcement than for "war." Since 2009, President Barack Obama has quietly partially moved rhetoric toward using this metaphor.

A second alternative metaphor is "disease containment," in which terrorist ideology is seen like a disease spreading to vulnerable people. This metaphor suggests addressing issues like the origin and boundaries of the outbreak, its methods of transmission, who is most at risk, and how to contain the threat and inoculate the population. Methods of propagation through radical imams or the Internet suggest counterterrorism strategies of eliminating social conditions that leave people vulnerable to terrorists' appeals.

In conclusion, Kruglanski and colleagues and Lakoff recommend that no single metaphor should guide all counterterrorism efforts. Furthermore, we need to recognize how metaphors guide thought and policy. Each metaphor highlights certain aspects of the situation and obscures others, and we need more political and policy debate on the metaphors themselves.

News programming is put in an especially tricky position by the economic realities of the media industry. Even though news divisions are separate from entertainment divisions at most television networks, and news has the explicit function of informing rather than entertaining, the success of news is determined by ratings every bit as much as is the success of a sitcom or drama series, and that increases the pressure to entertain. Similarly, a newspaper, website, or magazine must try to maximize its advertising revenue, which is closely related to the number of readers or subscriptions sold. In deciding what news to include, pressures clearly exist to tell people what they want to hear and what will entertain them, in order to keep them coming back and to keep advertisers happy. If the public does not want to hear that its leaders are conducting an unjust war or if major advertisers do not care to see news coverage of studies showing their product to be harmful, those pressures are unlikely to be ignored (Lee & Solomon, 1991; Steyer, 2002).

Understanding the psychology of media news requires an examination of the nature of the medium itself, as it transmits news. After some introductory comments on recent trends in coverage and consumption, this chapter examines what news is, in a psychological sense, and how the perceived reality about world events is constructed from reading or watching news reports. The rest of the chapter examines effects of consuming news, including effects on memory, decision making, evaluation of risk, and foreign policy. We conclude with a look at the blending of news and entertainment in the docudrama.

Thinking about contemporary news coverage requires us to take a close look at television news, which has its roots in the movie newsreel of the early to mid-20th century. With such news shorts, which were shown in theaters before feature films, the audience experienced an immediacy in relation to distant world events, which, although initially delayed several weeks, had never been possible before. This use of moving visuals to convey the news brought about the new technique of montage—the juxtaposition of images for dramatic effect. Reporters and editors reassemble the ingredients of the reality to best express what they perceive as the essence of that reality. Montage allows the telling of a news story using many of the dramatic narrative techniques from drama and fiction writing, making the event more compelling and entertaining. Do such techniques open the door for other elements of fiction to enter as well?

Although news has been on television from the early days of the medium, the TV coverage of John F. Kennedy's assassination and funeral in November 1963 firmly established television as a serious player—and for many years the predominant player—in news coverage. All other programming was preempted for three days as the country sat glued to its TV sets. There was a further unexpected surprise when the assassination of the alleged assassin, Lee Harvey Oswald, by Jack Ruby was captured on live TV from the basement of the Dallas police station! In the next five years, the U.S. TV news audience jumped 50%, the sharpest increase ever. By 1977, 62% of all adult Americans watched at least one TV newscast per weekday, making television the major source of news in the United States. More recently, however, the network share has fallen. In the 1990s, the audience for national news on the three major U.S. networks fell from 60 to 30% (Farhi, 2001), with much of the loss going to cable news channels like CNN, MSNBC, and Fox News, and, increasingly since 2000, Internet news sources. However, local TV newscasts, including weather and sports, remain popular and are critical for local stations in establishing their unique identity in the community, given that the large majority of programming is either network produced or syndicated, both of which are identical regardless of the local station. See Close-Up 7.2 for further discussion of weather reports and reporters.

One interesting recent trend is for increasing numbers of people, especially young adults and teens, to get their news from late-night comedy programs like *The Tonight Show*, *Saturday Night Live Weekend Update*, *The Daily Show*

Close-Up 7.2: TV Weather Forecasts: More than Telling If It Will Rain

An indispensable part of all local news shows, as well as some national ones, is the weather forecaster. The Weather Channel and weather.com website draw huge audiences, especially in times of threatening weather. Although all U.S. weathercasters use essentially the same data—those gathered by the National Weather Service—clearly not all weathercasts are equal. High quality computer graphics now allow even small local stations to give a weathercast of high accuracy and technical quality.

Although weathercasts are often seen as the frivolous or soft side of the news, often the subject is deadly serious. Forecasts and warnings of tornadoes, hurricanes, and floods can mean the difference between life and death. The National Weather Service issues the watches, warnings, and advisories, but it is the local TV weathercaster, who nowadays almost always has college-level training in meteorology, who offers critical interpretation as to how strongly to advise taking precautionary measures. During weather emergencies, often a station's whole local weather crew is in the studio tracking multiple computers and data to keep us safe. A wrong judgment call in such a situation can have tragic consequences, and excessively shrill calls of crises that do not materialize risk the public not taking warnings seriously. As global warming continues to produce more extremes of temperature and precipitation, weathercasters' roles will only increase in importance (Zhao, 2009).

with Jon Stewart, and *The Colbert Report*. In 2000, over one-third of Americans under 30 reported such shows to be their *primary* source for news and almost 80% said they sometimes or regularly got political information from such entertainment sources (Williams & Delli Carpini, 2002). It is sobering to think that large numbers of citizens are getting their news primarily from parodies of the news! These shows are discussed in more detail later in the chapter.

Many other news consumers are finding Internet blogs useful sources of news, even though many of these are extreme in viewpoint and not subject to the institutional quality control present in mainstream media (Vraga, Edgerly, Wang, & Shah, 2011). Newsmaker appearances on entertainment talk shows, though often criticized by traditional news media as inauthentic, are often "repackaged" later by those same media as hard news (Edy & Snidow, 2011); for example, the President's comment on *The Tonight Show* may appear on news channels the next day.

Social media sites such as Facebook and Twitter have come to play a prominent role in world events. For example, they were critical in organizing people and sharing information in the "Arab Spring" movements of 2011, particularly in the Tahrir Square protests leading to the fall of the Hosni Mubarak regime in Egypt. Any act of repression today is likely to be captured and photographed by someone's mobile phone and widely shared. Although not immune to government control, social media are difficult to muzzle, particularly where there is a large number of well-educated citizens, who are often technologically ahead of those who would suppress them. Social media are very democratic, being freely available to anyone with Internet access. Indeed, 76% of U.S. high school students and 38% of those under 30 reported turning in 2011 to Facebook, Twitter, and other social networking sites for news (Loth, 2012).

One significant change in recent decades has been a precipitous drop in the amount of international news coverage in the United States, in part due to budget-cutting reductions of expensive foreign correspondents. Between 1989 and 1995 alone, the number of minutes of stories on the ABC, NBC, and CBS evening news broadcasts from foreign correspondents dropped from 4,032 to 1,991. What is filling this space? In 1995, the network evening news broadcasts spent 1,591 minutes on the O. J. Simpson murder trial, compared to 418 minutes on the bombing of the Oklahoma City federal building, and 318 minutes on the civil war in Bosnia (Moeller, 1999). These figures are for the most respected mainline news sources; this trend of tabloid coverage is far stronger on some cable channels, such as Fox News or HLN. Think about the agenda that is being set regarding what is important.

The fastest-growing news source in recent years has been the Internet. The web pages for various newspapers, networks, wire services, television stations, and other sources are read by millions daily. There is some indication that this may be taking place primarily at the expense of newspapers, although some of the most widely visited sites are newspaper sites, some of which (e.g., *The New York Times*) have e-mailing services available with news summaries and links to complete stories. Increasingly, Internet-only news sites such as the *Huffington Post* are taking larger shares as well. Internet sites are less constrained than either newspapers or television in terms of the amount of material than can be published, since they are not limited to a certain number of pages or minutes of air time. Most of the same biases of use found in traditional print or broadcast media hold true for Internet news sources; for example, men tend to read more stories about achievement and performance and women more about social or interpersonal topics (Knobloch-Westerwick & Alter, 2007). See Gunter (2003) and Tewksbury (2003) for discussions of Internet news.

TV news reporters, especially network and local news anchors, become trusted friends in our lives. They may be a part of our mealtimes, almost like having the news anchor as a regular dinner or breakfast guest. We invite them into our homes through our choice to turn on the TV to a particular channel. It is not unusual for people to audibly respond to an anchor's greeting, such as responding "Hi, Brian" to NBC news anchor Brian Williams as he signs on with "Good evening." They become substitute friends in a sort of parasocial interaction (Giles, 2002; Klimmt, Hartmann, & Schramm, 2006), as discussed in Chapters 2 and 3. This is why the change of network news anchors is still such a "big deal," even in the age of declining viewership; it was a major news story in itself when Katie Couric was selected as the first female CBS news anchor, and again later when she left the anchor chair.

There is a sense of solidarity with the anchors. As one person explained about his relationship with long-time CBS anchor Walter Cronkite, "I grew up watching him. I guess I expect him to be there when I turn on the news. We've been through a lot together, Walter and me" (Levy, 1982, p. 180). That feeling of having "been through a lot together" captures very well why news anchors are far more important people in our lives than merely folks who read us the day's events. In recent years some of these important personalities (e.g., Rachel Maddow, Bill O'Reilly, Sean Hannity, and Glenn Beck) have become increasingly partisan. Even with local news, if the anchor gets married or the sportscaster has a baby, that event is one of the news stories that evening. We have no comparable relationships with newspaper or Internet editors or writers.

What Is News?

Jamieson and Campbell (1992, p. 31) defined hard news as: "any report of an event that happened or was disclosed within the previous 24 hours and treats an issue of ongoing concern." The event itself need not be recent, although it usually is, but it must at least involve some new revelation or previously unknown connection. Revelations that Abraham Lincoln may have suffered from depression, that DNA evidence confirmed that Thomas Jefferson fathered children with a slave, or of the discovery of the asteroid crater that probably led to the extinction of the dinosaurs 65 million years ago have all been news in recent years.

In contrast to hard news are human interest stories, which touch universal concerns and are less tied to place and time. Sometimes called "soft news," these features have a narrative structure closer to fiction and are most prevalent on so-called "slow news days" (such as weekends) and may include anything from a farmer in west Texas who planted 1950s Cadillacs tail-fin-upward in his field, to the heartwarming story of a poor Mississippi sharecropper whose nine children have all graduated from college (most with advanced degrees), to the mildly titillating story of a brothel madam with a master's degree.

Primary Characteristics of a Newsworthy Event

What characteristics do stories which receive a lot of news coverage have? Jamieson and Campbell (1992) identified five qualities of a newsworthy event. They need not all be present in every story, but no doubt several of them will be present for each hard news story. The more of these characteristics a story has, the more likely it is to be heavily covered in the news. An understanding of these qualities goes a long way toward explaining something most of us have wondered about at one time or another, namely why certain events receive so much coverage and certain others so little. No one has decreed that news stories must have these characteristics; rather, they have evolved naturally.

Personalization

First, a newsworthy story is personalized—it is about individuals. This allows audiences to identify with the person and can help make a dauntingly complex event easier to comprehend. It also lends itself well to photography and the interview format, which works well with TV, print, or Internet, but it may be at the cost of oversimplifying (and possibly distorting) complex events and overemphasizing "stars" such as the political head of state, the Pope, a serial killer, a movie or sports star, or a terrorist looking for a media platform. It is basically an entertainment model extended to news. Such an individual frame for a news story may actually lead readers to hold more polarized opinions than those reading the same story with a group frame (Boyle et al., 2006; Keum et al., 2005).

Another negative consequence of this highly individualistic framing of news stories is a failure to consider systemic issues. For example, pathological crimes such as Presidential assassination attempts and school shootings are usually covered through the frame of the demented criminal versus the threatened, vulnerable victim (Hoerl, Cloud, & Jarvis, 2009). While there certainly is a lot of truth to such a narrative in many, if not most, such cases, other important dimensions may be missed. For example, it took several years after the 1999 Columbine High School shootings and similar crimes of that era for public schools to seriously come to terms with the problems of bullying and its consequences, and to take serious steps to combat destructive behavior long considered normal (Hoerl, 2002). As long as the crimes were seen only through the frame of a demonic monster versus an innocent and vulnerable victim, such systemic problems are unlikely to receive much attention.

Drama and Conflict

Second, a newsworthy event is dramatic and conflict-filled, even violent, again following the pattern of entertainment TV. Amateur videos of police beating protesters make for more exciting news images and copy than politicians debating economic policy. This emphasis on conflict helps to ensure coverage of opposing views, but on the negative side may overemphasize the confrontational and violent nature of the story. Very infrequent violent events may be assumed by viewers to be the norm. Nonviolent events may be neglected, and very important issues which are not conducive to drama, conflict, or personalization may be underreported. Complex and protracted economic stories like the Eurozone currency crisis are always a challenge to cover and often tend to be framed in terms of specific events like protests against a government's austerity policy or a story of an individual who lost his job. See Close-Up 7.3 for discussion of how a less dramatic but very important story of the 1980s was covered (or not).

Close-Up 7.3: News Coverage of Nuclear War Threats of the 1980s

Although a potentially cataclysmic danger for over sixty years, the threat of nuclear war does not have many of the characteristics of a newsworthy story. Rubin and Cummings (1989) conducted a content analysis of network news coverage of three stories in 1983, related to the nuclear threat at the last high point of the Cold War. The first story was the new scientific theory of nuclear winter, which proposed that a nuclear war would trigger enough fires to send up enough smoke, dust, and soot to block 95% of the sun's light in many latitudes, soon to be followed by a huge disruption of the growing season and the possible destruction of all humanity. The second event was the televising of a fictional ABC TV movie *The Day After* about a Soviet nuclear attack on the rural Midwest; this became the highest-rated TV movie up to that time. Embraced by the antinuclear movement and attacked by Cold War conservatives, its impact was weaker than either side predicted (Scholfield & Pavelchak, 1985). The third story was the public commenting by members of the Reagan administration about the possibility of winning a limited nuclear war.

Compared to what one might expect about their importance, Rubin and Cummings (1989) found coverage of these three stories to be minimal; they offered four possible explanations for this. It may be that TV journalism had accepted that life could not survive a nuclear exchange; additional evidence was thus uncritically embraced and ignored. The nuclear winter story and the message of *The Day After* were "not so much displaced ... as smothered by uncritical acceptance" (Rubin & Cummings, 1989, p. 49). A second, more paternalistic, possibility is that TV news had decided that viewers were not emotionally able to handle any more discussion of this threatening issue. Third, it is possible that TV journalism had decided that nuclear weapons were here to stay and thus should not be politicized by arousing controversy. In support of such a view is the fact that the network cut a line from *The Day After* which stated that the justification for the fictional Soviet attack was the U.S. movement of Pershing missiles in Europe, and also the fact that there was very little questioning of the Reagan administration's assumptions about nuclear war. Finally, the paltry coverage may have been due to the fact that TV had acquired only a limited inventory of images for communicating the horror of nuclear war, namely computer graphics, file footage of Hiroshima and Nagasaki, Pentagon film of old missile tests, and scenes of everyday life with a voiceover intoning the consequences of nuclear war. In conclusion, the "coverage of these events in 1983 was fatalistic, overly respectful of government, visually unimaginative, and politically neutralized" (p. 56).

There is reason to think that the emphasis on conflict has escalated more broadly in recent years. In a very provocative and, sadly, prophetic book, *The Argument Culture: Stopping America's War of Words*, Georgetown University sociolinguist Deborah Tannen (1998) argued that American society at all levels had become more confrontational and argumentative in recent decades, reflected in the contentiousness seen in the press, politics, the legal system, and even in family and interpersonal relationships. At least for the press, Tannen traced much of this back to Watergate in the 1970s, when investigative journalism had indeed played a strongly, and constitutionally critical, adversarial role in rooting out the scandal in the Nixon administration. She worried that the mindset has never really changed and news media, as well as office holders, continue to believe they must attack and challenge at every opportunity. Thus one sees, for example, candidates for office or nominees for appointed positions being subject to intense and unprecedented scrutiny of all aspects of their personal lives. Sometimes this is so unpleasant that highly qualified people withdraw from consideration rather than subject themselves and their families to such treatment. The rapid increase in acrimony on cable news and talk radio in the new millennium is further disturbing evidence of this. By 2010 all sides in Washington seemed to have lost interest in political compromise and seemed to seek only to further their own interest and the election of their candidates.

Action

The third characteristic of a newsworthy event is that it contains action and some observable occurrence. This often becomes the "hook" on which to hang what is essentially a more abstract story. For example, trends in inflation or unemployment are covered by interviews with specific consumers expressing their views on rising prices and lack of job prospects. Important stories that do not have such a convenient hook or discrete encapsulating event receive less attention. For example, the dramatic shift in the Third World over the last 50 years from domestic food production to export agriculture is a profound change, but is seldom mentioned in the news because it is not easily symbolized by discrete events.

The action chosen as the frame can have serious consequences. For example, framing a news story on Moroccan immigration to Spain using the theme of the growth of crime led to more negative responses toward immigrants than the same story framed in more positive terms, of the economic contributions of immigrants (Igartua & Cheng, 2009).

Novelty and Deviance

The fourth characteristic of hard news is that it is novel or deviant. Contrary to the "late-breaking news" metaphor, most news is not particularly surprising. For example, much political and economic news is covered by the normal beat reporters who know in advance that certain speeches will be made, votes taken, or meetings held. Events outside this predictable range of news will stand a better chance of being covered if they are novel, with chances of coverage increasing as the events get more and more strange and bizarre. A junkie being shot to death in New York City may not be big news, but it is big news when a Sunday school teacher is killed in a satanic ritual in rural Saskatchewan.

An event may be deviant in different senses (Shoemaker, Chang, & Brendlinger, 1987; Shoemaker, Danielian, & Brendlinger, 1987). Statistical deviance refers purely to the frequency of an event, with highly unusual events being the most deviant. Normative deviance involves the violation of social and legal norms. Pritchard and Hughes' (1997) analysis of homicide reports found that normative deviance was a more important component of newsworthiness than statistical deviance.

Finally, potential for social change deviance refers to how much the existing status quo is threatened, a type of deviance involved in major terrorist events like the 1995 Oklahoma City federal building bombing, the September 11, 2001, attacks on the World Trade Center and the Pentagon, or the 2003 Madrid and 2005 London transit bombings.

Link to Ongoing Themes

Last, events are more likely to receive news coverage if they are linked to themes of ongoing current interest. Some of these themes are deep-seated, even archetypal, at least within a given society. For example, appearance versus reality has always been a common theme in Western literature and drama. News stories about deception and hypocrisy make good copy; the Watergate scandal (1972–1974), which eventually led to the resignation of President Richard Nixon, was one of the hottest news stories in U.S. history. Second, big versus little is a powerful theme, nicely captured by some of the crusading stories on 60 *Minutes*, *Dateline*, or *20/20*. Closely related is good versus evil, a moral framework often imposed on news stories (e.g., the brave consumer vs. the evil polluting corporation, righteous America versus the evil dictator). A fourth theme is efficiency versus inefficiency, commonly used in stories such as exposés of government or corporate waste or mismanagement. Finally, the unique versus routine highlights the unusual. New movements emerging in the U.S. in recent years have made use of these classic themes, for example the Tea Party movement casts government as evil, hypocritical, and inefficient.

Besides these underlying, archetypal themes we also have cyclical themes, such as political cycles and seasonal, holiday, and weather themes. For example, we know we will see the Pope saying midnight mass on Christmas, the groundhog in Punxsutawney, Pennsylvania looking for his shadow every February 2, stories about Ireland around March 17, and local news reporters in the spring in the Midwest telling us how to protect ourselves from tornadoes. Such events appear in the news because they fit the cyclical themes, in spite of having few of the other characteristics of newsworthy events.

Secondary Characteristics of a Newsworthy Event

Besides the five basic characteristics of newsworthy events, there are four other more specific, pragmatic characteristics that are required for a story to receive extensive coverage.

Inoffensiveness

A story must be inoffensive or at least not blatantly offensive. Sometimes such concerns about taste keep a story from receiving coverage it might otherwise deserve. For example, the press was very slow to pick up on reporting on the

AIDS epidemic in the early 1980s, in part because it was reluctant to mention the most common way to acquire the disease at the time, namely, anal intercourse by gay men (Meyer, 1990). After the terrorist attacks of 2001, the U.S. press only very cautiously addressed the issues of how U.S. foreign policy might have contributed to a climate spawning radical Islamic terrorism. Mainstream media concluded that most of the country did not want to hear that American foreign policy might be at least partially responsible for the climate that produced those horrible events. Issues like child pornography and human trafficking probably receive less coverage than they warrant because of media concerns about the public being offended by specific depictions of how victims are treated.

Credibility

Second, a serious story must be perceived as credible. An occurrence so bizarre that readers or viewers would not believe it is less likely to be reported, at least by the mainstream press (Meyer, 1990). Although this requirement may sometimes have the salutary effect of weeding out tabloid-style oddities such as alien abductions or Elvis sightings, it may also have a less benign effect, such as when news media self-censor a story that they do not believe their public would accept or want to hear, such as a report that a very popular and respected leader has been involved in corruption. Sometimes a news story cries out for more questioning of its credibility than it receives; see Close-Up 7.4 for a detailed example of an outrageous claim that many news sources passed on uncritically, without question.

Close-Up 7.4: Anatomy of an Unchecked Rumor (Friedman, 2010)

In late 2010 CNN's Anderson Cooper interviewed Republican Presidential primary candidate Michele Bachmann and asked her where the Republicans proposed cutting the federal budget. Instead of answering, she noted that President Obama was about to leave on a state visit to India, which was "expected to cost the taxpayers $200 million a day" for his entourage of 2000 people renting 870 rooms in five-star hotels. This was later repeated by Rush Limbaugh and Glenn Beck, who upped the tab to two *billion* dollars, 34 warships, and 3000 people. Cooper decided to check out these facts, strongly suspecting that the President was not likely to be traveling with 10% of the U.S. Navy or spending more per day than the war in Afghanistan or 20 times more than Bill Clinton's trip to Africa in 1998! Although the White House does not release the exact cost of such trips for security reasons, it did decry Bachmann's figures as "absurd." Cooper found that the rumor had started as a quote from some unnamed provincial official in Maharashtra state in India. This anonymous Indian quote, which offered no source for these figures, was picked up by the Drudge Report online and then made its way to conservative talk radio. Why had no one before Cooper checked the facts on this?

Sound Bites

Third, a story must be packageable in small pieces, fit for a very brief TV news story or a short piece online or in print. A story that fits this packaging demand is much more likely to receive coverage than one that does not. The importance of this sound bite requirement is often underappreciated by those wishing their work would receive more coverage, such as scientists and others who are not very skilled in explaining their work to journalists in small, easy-to-digest pieces. Although the sound bite is often seen as a creation of television, some have argued that the pithy sound bite, whether or not it was actually uttered by its supposed author, has actually been with us for a long time (Wernick, 1996). For example, Louis XIV's *L'état, c'est moi* ("I am the state"), Julius Caesar's *Veni, vidi, vici* ("I came, I saw, I conquered"), or Harry Truman's "The buck stops here" have a lot in common with Nancy Reagan's "Just say no to drugs" or the Occupy movement's "We are the 99%" references. Sound bites have become increasingly important as the length of TV news stories has been decreasing; the average length of a TV news story about a U.S. Presidential election campaign declined from 43 seconds in 1968 to 9 seconds in 1988 (Hallin, 1992). Although television news deals in very short pieces, some media offer alternatives, especially the Internet and even newspapers, which over the last century have printed longer stories with more interpretation rather than simply reporting the facts (Barnhurst & Mutz, 1997).

The Local Hook

A final secondary characteristic of newsworthiness is the local hook, the connection of the story to the community of the reader, viewers, or listeners. At the local level, a newspaper or TV or radio station will be much more likely to cover a national or international event if it has a local angle (e.g., a local resident caught in a foreign uprising, the closing of a local plant because of Mexican economic policy). On a national level, the hook in the United States may be a current policy debate in Washington or the presence of U.S. troops abroad. Sadly, some very important stories are downplayed or missed altogether because of the lack of an obvious local hook. U.S. media in particular are notorious for extensive foreign coverage during an immediate crisis, but very little before or after. Consequently, for the average person foreign crises seem to emerge suddenly out of nowhere, because they have not been aware of some smoldering issues. Also, after the immediate crisis, the all-important follow-up period receives little coverage. For example, the Afghanistan invasion during the fall of 2001 to oust the Taliban regime received extensive coverage, but the subsequent period of "nation-building" did not. The press had moved on to covering the invasion of Iraq to oust Saddam Hussein. Attention reverted from Iraq back to Afghanistan after U.S. troops were withdrawn from Iraq but more were committed to Afghanistan. See Close-Up 7.5 for an extended example of American news coverage from the same part of the world a generation earlier.

This strong desire to play up a local connection and make the story relevant to readers can sometimes end up distorting the news (Goldberg, 2002). For example, when the media discovered the problem of the homeless, the homeless individuals actually interviewed were very articulate, very needy, usually White, often professional people down on their luck. In short, they were very

---

Close-Up 7.5: Coverage of the Iran Hostage Crisis

The fact that Iran's 1979 Islamic revolution came as a surprise to many Americans was in part attributable to the almost total lack of coverage from Iran prior to that time (it represented 1% of international news stories on US TV from 1972–1977; Beeman, 1984; Mowlana, 1984). From November 1977 to January 1979, U.S. reporting on Iran increased, notably in relation to the autocratic pro-Western ruler's visit to Washington in 1977 and a demonstration against him. After his overthrow in January 1979, TV served as the major communication between the exiled Islamic leader Ayatollah Khomeini in Paris and a fragile caretaker government in Tehran. Although American media covered the return of Khomeini to Iran in February, coverage increased dramatically after the Iranian seizure of dozens of American hostages at the U.S. embassy in Tehran in late 1979, comprising nearly one-third of all international news stories in 1980. Television, and to a lesser extent newspapers, became major channels of communication between the two governments, as all diplomatic and commercial channels had been broken. A failed rescue attempt in 1980 and the safe return of the hostages on Ronald Reagan's Inauguration Day in January 1981 received heavy coverage, but the few subsequent stories on Iran originated elsewhere, or occasionally from correspondents from other nations who were stationed in Iran (Larson, 1986).

much like the majority audience (Hodgetts, Cullen, & Radley, 2005). Never mind that the majority of the homeless had substance abuse or major mental illness problems and were often people of color. In another example, when AIDS started to receive wide coverage in the late 1980s, it was the relatively few heterosexual, non-drug-user AIDS victims who were interviewed. Just as with the homeless issue, the media believed that viewers would be more interested in the problem (which would therefore gain higher ratings) if they felt it was a personal threat. Thus the media chose "representative" individuals most like the majority audience in order to make the story connect with the most viewers. The result, however, was that many people were far more worried about contracting AIDS or becoming homeless than was warranted. At the same time, less attention was paid to the underlying systemic problems of what to do with the homeless mentally ill after state institutions closed and how to stop the spread of HIV among intravenous drug users and gay men not practicing safe sex.

The surest way to obtain coverage of one's activities is to imbue them with these nine primary and secondary newsworthy characteristics. The more of these an event has, the more likely the media will be to show interest in covering it. For example, the double murder trial of former football legend and sometime actor O. J. Simpson in 1995 had all of the newsworthy characteristics. It focused on one person who was greatly admired but was accused of committing a shockingly violent act. It related to many central cultural themes—big vs. little, right vs. wrong, appearance vs. reality. The fact that the entire trial was televised also helped to ensure saturation coverage for several months. See Close-Up 7.6 for an interesting explanation from Aristotle for the public fascination with the Simpson trial.

Close-Up 7.6: Aristotle's Explanation for the Interest in the O. J. Simpson Trial

Although written around 400 BC, Aristotle's *Rhetoric* offers some arguments about three elements needed to move an audience. Although Aristotle was talking about theater, Stonehill (1995) argued that these elements (*pathos*, *logos*, and *ethos*) also fit television and help to explain the intense public fascination with events like the O. J. Simpson trial of 1995. *Pathos*, the emotional appeal, was very high in this murder case, with overtones of sex, race, and deceit. *Logos*, the intellectual component, appeared in the whodunit mystery but also in other questions, such as why a low-speed car chase occurred and what all the DNA evidence meant. Finally, *ethos* is charisma, celebrity, or authority, which was of course very high in the case of a trial of a previously loved and respected athlete and movie star. Stonehill even argued that this case might be one of the highest ever on these three Aristotelian dimensions. However, not long after the Simpson trial had faded from view, other high-profile events captured the media's and the public's attention. The death of Britain's Princess Diana in August 1997 and the Clinton–Lewinsky sex scandal of 1998 likewise went off the charts in terms of *pathos*, *logos*, and *ethos*—and press coverage. Aristotle was right!

Terrorists very often know all about how to stage a newsworthy event. This is why they are particularly fond of large public symbolic targets, like the Pentagon, the World Trade Center, railroad stations or airports, and government buildings, especially in well-known places like New York, London, Paris, or Washington. They know there will be more reporters there and thus more news coverage, as well as more damage and deaths due to the denser population.

Now that we have seen what makes a newsworthy event, we examine how the media create the story that is news.

News Media as Creating a Perceived Reality

As discussed in Chapter 1, mass communication mediates between the audience and some objective reality out there in the world. In Western culture, at least, we assume that such an external reality exists. However, what appears in the media are the news writers' and producers' interpretations of that reality, as seen through both their choice of topics and the amount of coverage they give to them (i.e., agenda setting). Although the choices of media coverage are usually motivated by a sincere desire to present news stories to the public in the most complete and accurate way possible, there are occasional instances when the construction of reality goes beyond the bounds of what most would consider acceptable (see Close-Up 7.7).

Close-Up 7.7: When News Reporters Become Newsmakers

In their desire to make "an invisible truth visible, dramatic, and entertaining" (Bogart, 1980, p. 235), media have occasionally gone too far. In 1966, CBS helped to finance an armed invasion of Haiti in exchange for exclusive TV rights for the event; the invasion was aborted by U.S. Customs. The next year a U.S. soldier cut off the ear of a dead Vietcong soldier; it later came out in his court martial that he did so after being offered a knife on a dare by a TV news camera operator

(Lewy, 1978). There were numerous accounts of TV news crews in the 1960s arranging for protest demonstrations or drug parties to be staged again if the original event was not caught on camera. Janet Cooke lost her Pulitzer Prize in 1981 after admitting that her article, "Jimmy's World" was not based on a real Jimmy, but rather on different people who contributed to the fictional composite Jimmy.

NBC faked a crash test in 1993 to show that a car it believed to be dangerous would explode. In 1998, Stephen Glass, writer for the *New Republic* and other magazines, was found to have fabricated all or parts of dozens of investigative journalism articles, even including a totally fictitious story about a cult that worshiped George Bush, Sr. (Lacayo, 2003). Writer Jayson Blair and two editors lost their jobs at *The New York Times* in 2003 after numerous articles of Blair's turned out to be fabricated or plagiarized from other sources.

At other times, news journalists may become newsmakers in more positive ways. For example, Egyptian President Anwar Sadat's historic trip to Israel in 1977 was arranged not by the United Nations or U.S. State Department diplomats, but by CBS News anchor Walter Cronkite. It was Cronkite who persistently called Sadat and Israeli Prime Minister Menachem Begin to arrange their eventual meeting (Weymouth, 1981).

Manipulation of News

Aside from the constraints of being newsworthy, sometimes other forces inside or outside of government impinge on journalists and affect the reality of the news they create. Even in a thriving democracy with constitutional guarantees of a free press, there are always some limits on content. For example, release of classified information is not permitted, nor is libel or slander, obscenity, or language inciting people to violence.

Direct Censorship

In totalitarian nations with prior censorship, material must be submitted to government or military censors for advance approval before being aired or published, or sometimes the government owns and controls all news media. In such cases, a very selective piece of reality may be offered, so much so that history may be substantially rewritten. For example, Russian citizens' views of the West during the Cold War years (1945–1990) were very heavily colored by unflattering news stories about American crime, racism, homelessness, and imperialism that appeared in the Soviet press. Even if very little in these stories was actually untrue, one's overall perception was grossly distorted if, for example, crime was believed to be the rule rather than the exception.

Direct censorship can come in other ways. For example, Azerbaijan's government owns the printing company all newspapers must use; it refuses printing to those it doesn't like. Malaysia and Singapore have laws forbidding discussion of topics that are deemed potentially divisive (such as religion, interethnic violence, or anything that might make the government look bad). Belarus evicted the newspaper *Pahonya* from its offices and moved it to a building with no water or sewage service. Later, the tax auditors levied a large fine against the paper (Martz, 1998).

Intimidation

Sometimes journalists are bullied by forces which may or may not be connected to any government. For example, when the editor of Tijuana's newspaper *Zeta* wrote against the local drug cartel, he was visited by a team of assassins. Although he survived and continued to write, not everyone would have had the courage to do so. When Zairian freelance writer Jean Mbenga Muaganvita wrote a series of articles on then-strongman President Mobutu Sese Seko, he was arrested and held incommunicado, and soldiers raped his 14-year-old daughter when they searched his home (Martz, 1998). Noted Colombian investigative journalist Fabio Castillo was fired by Bogota's *El Espectador* after implicating a government minister in a bank corruption scandal. Although the paper claims he was dismissed purely for financial reasons, the fact that the minister under suspicion mysteriously received an advance copy of the article before publication suggests otherwise (Rosenberg, 2003). Many journalists have been killed in recent years in Algeria, Mexico, Colombia, Cambodia, and other places.

Blocking Access

Certain news stories may be effectively censored purely through blocking the access of the media to the scene of the story. For example, during the apartheid era in South Africa, journalists were often forbidden to enter the Black townships. Similar policies by the Israeli government have sometimes kept the press out of the West Bank during times of Palestinian unrest. Recently the Syrian government of Bashir Assad has largely closed off the country to foreign journalists in the hopes that the world will forget about his repressive policies. In these cases, the governments involved clearly hoped that public attention would wane if compelling images could no longer be obtained for publication or broadcast.

One of the clearest and most controversial examples of blocking press access has come in the coverage of recent regional wars. Working on the conventional (although dubious) wisdom that unrestricted press coverage lost the Vietnam War for the United States, Britain in 1982 and the United States in 1983 forbade the press from accompanying troops in the island wars in the

Falklands/Malvinas and Grenada, respectively (Strobel, 1997). The same policy was followed by the United States in the 1989 invasion of Panama to oust dictator Manuel Noriega. Only much later did the public learn that casualties were far higher than originally reported, and of the nearly total destruction of a large, poor neighborhood in Panama City.

One of the most widespread and pervasive cases of censorship through blocking access was exercised by the United States, Saudi Arabia, and their coalition allies in the six-week 1991 Persian Gulf War to oust Iraq from its occupation of Kuwait. Reporters were put in pools, ostensibly to protect them and prevent allied forces from being overwhelmed by reporters. Stories were subject to military censorship, supposedly to prevent the leaking of troop movement information. Sometimes stories were held up for days, and in some instances the Pentagon actually announced the story first at its briefings. There were total blackouts at the start of the air and ground campaigns, as well as a ban on photos of coffins of killed U.S. soldiers arriving home. Media were also used to help confuse the Iraqis. For example, reporters were frequently taken to the area near the southern Kuwaiti border with Saudi Arabia but not to the western border area where the real build-up for the ground invasion was occurring. Pools were taken to cover practice maneuvers for an apparent sea assault on Kuwait, an assault that never came but was rather used to divert attention from the planned ground thrust from the west.

Journalists were probably themselves highly supportive of the coalition effort, being determined not to allow themselves to be the scapegoats for a lost war (think Vietnam), and they were not going to allow themselves to be called unpatriotic. This concern may not have been unrealistic—the little independent coverage that did occur sometimes elicited angry cries of traitor. Media coverage of the Gulf War continued to be debated and analyzed for many years (Greenberg & Gantz, 1993; Iyengar & Simon, 1993; Mowlana, Gerbner, & Schiller, 1993: Zelizer, 1992).

Indirect Censorship

In some nations, it is an official crime to broadcast material that is in any way against the interests of the state. Such vague legislation is available for use according to the political whims of the current rulers. In other cases, the government and large business interests are so close that politically suspect TV stations and newspapers cannot find the advertising they need to survive. Even in most democratic countries, the government issues licenses for TV and radio stations. Sometimes these are withheld or delayed for political reasons. Some countries require journalists to be licensed, a practice consistently condemned by the International Press Institute as threatening freedom of the press. In other cases, the supply and distribution of newsprint is controlled by the government and may be allotted according to political considerations.

Manipulation by Timing

Sometimes "bad news" may be released at a time guaranteed to receive less coverage than average. For example, U.S. President Gerald Ford's 1974 pardon of ex-President Richard Nixon for any Watergate-related crimes was announced on a Sunday morning, after the Sunday morning TV news talk shows and newspaper distribution but before most people arrived home from church. In 1992, President George H. W. Bush pardoned Iran-contra defendants on Christmas Day, when most people were busy with family activities. Several Presidents have issued pardons to convicted felons during their last hours in office. These unpopular policies were deliberately announced at times likely to receive the least possible coverage and attention. Often, government sources strategically leak stories about upcoming policy to gauge public reaction (a practice known as a "trial balloon"). If the reaction is negative, the policy need never be officially announced and the government will not be blamed for proposing it.

Media Self-Censorship

Sometimes censorship is self-imposed by the media, often due to pressure or fear of pressure from advertisers or the public. The largest commercial TV networks give limited attention to major corporate changes involving themselves or to any story reflecting unfavorably on their parent company, such as ABC TV and Disney (Lee & Solomon, 1991; Steyer, 2002); see also the discussion of this sort of censorship in Chapter 1. Magazines that accept tobacco advertising publish fewer stories about the health risks of smoking than do magazines that do not accept tobacco ads (Strasburger & Wilson, 2002). Advertiser pressure can lead to self-censorship. For example, the *San Jose Mercury News* published a lengthy consumer story on "how to buy a car," including tips on negotiating with dealers and information on dealer incentives and money holdbacks and how customers could use the invoice to figure the actual cost of the car. In response, the Santa Clara County Motor Car Dealers' Association pulled $1 million of advertising. The editor published a letter apologizing for the article and extolling the paper's long-standing partnership with the local car dealers. There were no subsequent in-depth stories dealing with auto dealership issues (Lieberman, 2000).

Sometimes media are in possession of information that they choose not to reveal for some reason. Sometimes this may be military information about troop movements, but it may also be information that some government official has lied. The press may conclude (rightly or wrongly) that the public just does not want to hear, or would not believe, certain highly negative news about their country or government. For example, when the Soviet Union shot down a South Korean commercial airliner in 1983, the Kremlin made the predictable Cold War charge that it was an American spy plane.

Although this claim was widely reported in the United States, it was practically never taken seriously there. In a careful analysis of the coverage of this issue by *Time, Newsweek,* and *U.S. News & World Report,* Corcoran (1986) concluded that all three publications, with an estimated combined readership of around 50 million, followed a virtually identical Reagan administration party line of anti-Soviet diatribe and paranoia (see also Entman, 1991). Outside of the United States (e.g., in reputable British publications like *The Guardian*) available evidence supporting the theory that the airliner was on a spy mission was fully examined and seen to be a credible explanation, though it was never definitively confirmed or discredited. Why was this perspective not heard in the United States? It was not due to government censorship but rather, perhaps, to the press sensing that the U.S. public did not want to seriously consider (or maybe would not believe) such a claim.

In the Watergate scandal of the early 1970s, the press chose to call President Nixon and other high U.S. government officials liars only after a considerable period of time and the emergence of very compelling evidence. In the mid-1980s, the press was very hesitant to directly expose the very popular President Reagan's misinformation about Soviet involvement in Nicaragua. Only after the revelation in late 1986 that the Reagan administration had been sending arms to Iran with the profits being diverted to the Nicaraguan right-wing contra rebels did the press seem to give itself permission to seriously criticize the President. The Washington press corps long knew of the Reagan administration's disinformation campaign in attributing a Berlin disco bombing in 1985 to Libya's Muammar Gaddafi, but said nothing. More recently, U.S. news outlets reporting the mistreatment of prisoners by U.S. soldiers in the 2004 Abu Ghraib Iraq prison scandal tended to follow the Bush administration "party line," in spite of strong objections to such framing from the political opposition (Rowling, Jones, & Sheets, 2011). Such behavior on the part of some U.S. soldiers (called "torture" by many) was a major threat to the positive national identity of the nation. Apparently the press was reluctant to stray too far from the official positive (or at least less negative) spin that the Bush administration put on the event.

Consolidation of News-Gathering Organizations

Although not exactly manipulation of news as such, another factor impacting the perceived reality of world events is the increasing consolidation of news-gathering organizations. Skyrocketing costs, plus the undeniable logic of efficiency, mandates a pooling of resources. Clearly, not every newspaper, news magazine, website, or TV or radio station can afford to have its own reporter in every potential news spot in the world.

This consolidation, however, has reduced news gatherers to a very small club. In terms of newspapers, most news copy in most newspapers comes from a very few sources, most often the wire services of AP, Reuters, and Agence

France-Presse (AFP). Only a very few large dailies, such as *The New York Times* and *Los Angeles Times*, have their own wire service. In terms of television, the U.S. commercial networks of ABC, NBC, CBS, Fox, and CNN have enormous influence worldwide. A few other major networks, such as the BBC and ITN in the United Kingdom and Brazil's TV Globo, take large pieces of the remaining pie. These few sources have enormous impact on our perceived reality of distant events. For example, even in nations ruled by stridently anti-American regimes, a large percentage of the news copy comes from the AP wire service.

A small number of sources is not in and of itself cause for alarm. Large organizations like the AP or CNN take great pains to present diverse and balanced viewpoints, and it is strongly in their interest to be perceived by all as fair and unbiased. Still, the potentially enormous influence of any of these sources on people's knowledge worldwide is sobering, especially in light of the recent popularity of cable channels and websites with a very openly partisan agenda.

Another consequence of the financial realities of international news reporting is a greatly decreased number of foreign bureaus and correspondents. For example, by 1996 CBS was down from a high of 20 to four major foreign bureaus (Tokyo, Moscow, Tel Aviv, London), with ABC having eight, NBC seven, and CNN 20. Although this reduction does not preclude a news anchor or Washington correspondent from reading a foreign story accompanied by visuals from file footage or freelance or government sources, the number of minutes of news stories on the three major broadcast networks from correspondents posted at foreign bureaus fell from 4,032 to 2,763 just between 1989 and 1994 (Strobel, 1997). Although 45% of news time on U.S. network news was international in the 1970s, only 13.5% was international by 1995 (Moisy, 1997).

As the number of reporters in the field has gone down, there is increasing sharing of reporters and content across TV channels, Internet sites, and other outlets. A lesser known trend is the increasing use of "video news releases" (VNRs). These are prepared by the newsmakers, often in prepackaged "news story" format and made available to news outlets. Although these outlets are free to use these as they choose, including editing or ignoring them, tight budgets and reduced staff make it tempting to present these VNRs largely unedited and often without the public realizing their source, even if explicitly identified in the news story (Tewksbury, Jensen, & Coe, 2011).

"Disguising" the News as Entertainment

Increasingly news appears in forums that are not even part of news departments; that is, as soft news, which is becoming increasingly intertwined with hard news, especially on cable and Internet sources (Coe et al., 2008). For example, television shows like *The View, Entertainment Tonight, Inside Edition,* and the late-night talk shows are produced by entertainment, not news, divisions, yet they frequently contain interviews and other material amplifying some current news story. Magazines like *People* or *Us* are similar, and even established Internet news sites like MSNBC contain a large proportion of gossipy stories. What is the effect of such entities in conveying the news? Baum (2002) found that such programs do effectively communicate news, particularly to people who are otherwise relatively uninvolved politically and low consumers of news media.

One highly successful television format has been "fake news" shows like *The Daily Show with Jon Stewart* and *The Colbert Report* (Baym, 2005; Trier, 2008a, 2008b). These shows have the format of a news show and are actually based on the day's events, complete with the host reading the news, followed by reports from (fake) correspondents and interviews with (real) newsmakers. Events are regularly parodied, and venal or hypocritical newsmakers are sometimes ruthlessly taken to task, often by shameless editing to make them look as bad as possible. Stewart regularly has political candidates and office-holders, other newsmakers, and famous entertainers as guests. Intriguingly, he often conducts serious and probing interviews which, not infrequently, are at least as enlightening as comparable efforts on real news programs. Occasionally, a fake news show can actually take the lead in forcing legislative attention on a real problem. For example, an obviously outraged Jon Stewart once almost singlehandedly shamed the U.S. Congress into passing legislation restoring the health benefits of the 9/11 first responders. In a content analysis of fake news shows in 2005, Brewer and Marquardt (2007) found that more than half of the news stories covered politics, many focusing on issues, and a substantial minority addressed news media themselves. Although the audience can learn considerable information from *The Daily Show*, they still acquire more information from traditional news shows (Kim & Vishak, 2008).

Of course, being comedians, Stewart and Colbert do not have to adhere to any of the ethical norms of journalism (Borden & Tew, 2007). They regularly take quotes from newsmakers out of context and make fun of them, "report" outrageous events that never happened, and are not constrained to present a fair representation or even to check the accuracy of what is reported. When Stewart regularly framed his reports about the Iraq War with a "Mess-O-Potamia" background slide, he was not being biased, simply entertaining. Nonetheless, such shows may have something to say about journalistic ethics. Stewart and Colbert "do not inhabit the role of journalists but, rather, adopt the performance of journalists to draw attention to lapses in journalistic integrity" (Borden & Tew, 2007, p. 311).

Stewart has used his fame to encourage a higher ethical standard of news journalism. Most notably, he used a 2004 guest appearance on CNN's *Crossfire* to criticize that program for "hurting America" with its strident adversarial format. He called the show's protagonists "partisan hacks" and said "You have a responsibility to public discourse and you failed miserably" (Baym, 2005).

Does fake news have higher standards than real news? Some credit Stewart's critique for leading to the subsequent demise of *Crossfire.*

What about the partisanship of entertainment news? In an interesting study of perceived partisanship of news sources, Coe et al., (2008) found that liberal partisans saw more bias in the traditionally conservative sources like *Fox News* or *The O'Reilly Factor*, while conservatives saw more bias in *The Daily Show.* In other words, we see bias in sources we strongly disagree with and fail to notice biases consistent with our own (Reid, 2012). Not only that, people also seek out news sources which they believe to be ideologically compatible with themselves, even on topics not particularly prone to partisan bias, such as crime reports or travel stories (Iyengar & Hahn, 2009).

The fake news trend may be catching on in other ways. For example, evangelical Christian Joel Kilpatrick started the website larknews.com as a spoof on Christian news. It even has a "Prayer/Gossip" line and t-shirt sales ("You suck, which is why you need Jesus," "Jesus Loves You … But Then Again He Loves Everybody"). Stories have included "Holy Spirit Neglects to Show Up at Revival," "Christians Planning to be Offended by Next Eminem Album," "Church Measures Attendance by Weight," "'Do Not Pray' Lists Prove Popular," "Home Schooler Spends Three-Day Suspension in Backyard Tent," and "Group Starts Ministry to Men with Pony Tails" (Van Biema, 2008).

Now that we have looked at how the media mediate between the reality of the news and the reports we receive, let us examine some effects of news coverage.

Effects of News Coverage

Long after the events reported in the news, what is primarily remembered is the media coverage. "The reality that lives on is the reality etched in the memories of the millions who watched rather than the few who were actually there" (Lang & Lang, 1984, p. 213). Here we consider the impact and effects of consuming news coverage, including the importance of different points of view, memory for the news, effects on decision making and other behaviors, effects of crime coverage, and the effect of news reporting on foreign policy.

The Impact of Different Points of View

Part of the reason that people in different nations tend to perceive the same situations so differently is that the reality they construct in response to news is so different (Schmitt, Gunther, & Liebhart, 2004). Not only does the reporting of such events in the media vary in different places, but, even more basically, interpretation of the same events differs depending on the knowledge, motivations, and experiences of those who hear or see the news (David, 2009). To illustrate, let's look at a few examples.

The Caucasian and African American audience responded quite differently to news reports of Hurricane Katrina damage in 2005. Blacks overwhelmingly blamed the federal government and were not affected by whether or not a news story contained pictures of victims and, if so, what race they were. White readers, however, attributed less government blame overall, but even this was lessened by the inclusion of pictures of victims (Ben-Porath & Shaker, 2010). Similarly, Israeli Arabs perceive news very differently than their Jewish neighbors (Tsfati, 2007). Different groups of people also choose to read about different people; in a study of online news stories selected to read, African American readers disproportionately read more stories about Blacks, while White readers showed no comparable differences (Knobloch-Westerwick, Appiah, & Alter, 2008).

The actual framing of the news can have a great impact. For example, the 2011 popular uprising in Egypt which ultimately led to the overthrow of Hosni Mubarak was framed by government newspapers as "a conspiracy against the Egyptian state," while independent news sources and social media framed it as "a revolution for freedom and social justice" (Hamdy & Gomaa, 2012). That same dichotomy has appeared in the somewhat longer and less tractable conflict against the Assad regime in Syria. Social media allows the publication of material in frames that would have been very difficult to use in authoritarian regimes until recently. The potential impact of the greater variety of framing of public events now possible through social media is hard to overestimate (Lim, 2012; Nisbet, Stoycheff, & Pearce, 2012). Someone reading everything framed the same way would get a very different idea of events than someone who only read everything framed in the opposite way.

Many of the most intractable and chronic world conflicts have at their heart a gigantic divergence in point of view, a chasm that causes the two sides to interpret reports of the same events totally differently. They also consistently fail to appreciate how differently other people view the same events. For example, during the Cold War (1945–1990), the Soviet Union and Western nations viewed each other through their own mirror-image biases (Hirschberg, 1993). Israelis and Palestinians on the West Bank, Tutsis and Hutus in Rwanda, Serbs and Albanians in Kosovo, and Christians and Muslims in Lebanon see themselves as besieged and oppressed by each other. In the 1990s, when the West moved to expand NATO, that development looked very threatening to Moscow, which saw it as an aggressive move. From the Russian perspective, it looked like preparation for war to the east. When the United States moved hundreds of thousands of troops to the Persian Gulf and invaded two countries (Afghanistan in 2001 and Iraq in 2003) to remove unfriendly regimes, neighboring countries quite reasonably wondered if they would be next, even if that concern seemed ridiculous to many Americans. See Close-Up 7.8 for a more extended example of the sharply divergent points of view of Islam and the West on political, social, and religious issues.

Close-Up 7.8: The Cognitive Gulf between Islam and the West

Islam as a religion is very poorly understood in the West, a fact especially troubling to Muslims, given its position, with Christianity and Judaism, as one of the three related monotheistic Abrahamic faiths (Easterbrook, 1989; Shaheen, 2008; see also Chapter 4). Events of the last 30 years, particularly the unprecedented Muslim migration to the West and the heightened Islamist terrorist threat of the new millennium, bring a new urgency to bridging this gap. There are some fundamental differences in the faiths and associated cultures that both sides would do well to better understand. It is very much against the dictates of Islam to criticize the theology of Judaism or Christianity, which are seen as part of the foundations of Islam, although considerable criticism of Western politics is permitted. In a similar vein, it is acceptable for Christians to make gentle jokes about Jesus, but in Islam there exist strong proscriptions against discussing the personal life of the prophet Mohammed or even having any pictorial representations of him. This explains the worldwide Muslim outrage at the Danish publication of a cartoon picturing Mohammed as a terrorist. Intellectual debate and disagreement about the prophet's actions is quite acceptable but anything personal or disrespectful is not. Finally, Islam is no more monolithic than is Christianity, and Muslims are understandably offended when Western media portray a radical Islamic terrorist as a typical Muslim.

There is also a fundamental difference between Islam and the West in the relationship between church and state. Most Muslim countries accept some degree of theocracy, although the degree varies. Thus insulting Mohammed is an insult to all Muslim nations and all Muslims, even those not actively practicing their faith. This is somewhat like nonreligious Jews' abhorrence of anti-Semitism, although there is no real parallel in Christianity, which has much less nonreligious cultural identity than does either Judaism or Islam.

One of the most basic beliefs in Western Europe and especially in North America is the separation of church and state, a belief whose deep ideological character and ramifications are not well understood by Muslims. In the West, it is unacceptable for one person's religious beliefs to infringe on another person's political freedom. Although it is a political belief, this tenet is highly ideological, almost religious in character, especially in the United States. Furthermore, the Western democratic tradition of free speech is also something like a religious belief to most people in the United States and the European Union.

> The treatment of women is seen in the West as a political right, not a religious decision, although most Western religions support equality of the sexes as well. When Muslim news stories of violence against women tend to blame the victim and downplay responsibility of the perpetrator (Halim & Meyers, 2010), this does not sit well in Western eyes and ears.

Memory for the News

News offers an interesting case to test people's memories in a real-world setting, with obvious applied as well as theoretical import (McCombs & Reynolds, 2009; Meeter, Murre, & Janssen, 2005). News stories in all media are most typically fairly short, self-contained pieces, which happen to be very useful units for experimental research on memory.

Schneider and Laurion (1993) studied metamemory for radio news, finding that people's assessment of what they had remembered from news was fairly accurate. In the case of television, however, the information involves more than the verbal content. The simultaneous presence of both visual and auditory information provides the potential of their either (a) complementing or (b) interfering with each other in the processing of and memory for news content. In general, memory for visual content is better than memory for verbal content (Graber, 1990), and memory is better if there is a close fit between the video and the audio component, such as when the video illustrates exactly what is being described by the reporter (Fox, 2004). When the relationship is less clear or when the video and audio portions evoke different previous information in the viewer's memory, comprehension and memory for the new information suffers (Fox et al., 2004; Grimes, 1990, 1991; Mundorf, Drew, Zillmann, & Weaver, 1990). Children may be especially vulnerable. Otgaar, Candel, Merckelbach, and Wade (2009) found that 7–8-year-old Dutch children's exposure to a false newspaper report about UFO abductions in the Netherlands led to 70% of those children later falsely "remembering" themselves as having been abducted by aliens.

Whether you are in a good or bad mood can affect what you remember from the news. German high school students read either a news story about a soccer match won by the German national team or a depressing article about child soldiers in Congo. Their memory for six subsequent news articles was affected by the tone of the first article. Students reading about the soccer victory recalled more positive than negative information from the subsequent articles, while those reading about the child soldiers in Congo recalled more negative than positive information from subsequent articles (Baumgartner & Wirth, 2012).

Memory for persons in the news can also be affected by the viewers' social attitudes. For example, Whites are more likely to identify an African

American, rather than a White person, as a criminal suspect (Gibbons, Taylor, & Phillips, 2005; Oliver & Fonash, 2002; Oliver, Jackson, Moses, & Dangerfield, 2004), and people generally are more interested in, aroused by, and better remember news stories about their own ethnic group (Fujioka, 2005b). As predicted by cultivation theory, Whites who watch more local TV news on which a disproportionate number of African Americans are presented as criminals were more likely to perceive Blacks as violent (Dixon, 2008a) or poor (Dixon, 2008b), or to identify race-unidentified perpetrators as Black (Dixon, 2007). People more skeptical about the Iraq War were better able to remember that early claims supporting the war had later been retracted than were those less critical of the war, who more often failed to remember that the early supporting claims had been retracted (Lewandowsky, Stritzke, Oberauer, & Morales, 2005). Assuming the video and audio portions are congruent, children remember news presented in a televised form better than news presented in a radio or print form, even if the print form contains illustrations (Walma van der Molen & van der Voort, 2000).

The rapid rise of strident partisan news sources in recent years has raised some issues about the effects of such sources on learning from news reports. An interesting study by Feldman (2011) suggests that the impact may be more complicated than first imagined. She had people read a neutral, a "pro," or an "anti" news article about a proposal to allow undocumented immigrant children in the U.S. to gain legal status. Overall, the opinionated versions neither enhanced nor interfered with learning from the article. However, a more careful analysis revealed why this null finding was the case. Perceptions of bias prompted readers to attend more closely and increase the processing resources devoted to comprehending and remembering the news story content, thus enhancing learning. However, at the same time, the perceived opinionated perspective of the article also drew attention away from the content to focus more on the source, thus interfering with processing of the content itself. These two competing effects cancelled each other out to leave an overall null effect.

How the visual and auditory content of newscasts might interact and possibly interfere with each other is an important theoretical and practical issue. A particularly interesting type of case is an emotionally intense visual shot, the sort that frequently accompanies news stories about wars, accidents, famines, or riots. The effect on memory turns out to be complex. An emotionally intense image such as a shot of the bloody, disfigured body of an accident or war victim, actually inhibits memory for verbal information presented just prior to that picture (Christianson & Loftus, 1987; Loftus & Burns, 1982; Newhagen & Reeves, 1992). However, material presented during or after the intense image is remembered shortly afterward, as well as or, in the case of material presented after the image, sometimes even better than, material not accompanied by an intense image. Apparently, what happens cognitively is that the intense emotional image disrupts the rehearsal in working memory of the immediately preceding information, much as a moderate head injury can produce retroactive amnesia for events just preceding the impact. However, the intense picture is itself highly memorable and may enhance memory for following related information by serving as an organizational schema for construction of a memory representation. Thus, a TV news editor deciding whether and when to show a bloody shot of accident victims should recognize that the decision has ramifications for viewers' memory of material from the story.

Some of the most distressing events ever to be broadcast on television were the terrorist attacks of September 11, 2001. Thanks to a fortuitous longitudinal study of dream content in progress from August to December 2001, researchers were able to document an increase in troubled dream content after 9/11. These included threats or specific reference to events of that day. The authors argued for a causal connection between the disturbing news footage shown repeatedly on television in those days and the disturbed dreaming (Hartmann & Basile, 2003; Propper, Stickgold, Keeley, & Christman, 2007).

Effects of News on Attributions and Decision Making

Comprehension of news media has implications beyond memory. How the news is reported can affect our knowledge about the topic. For example, Gibson and Zillmann (1994) found that readers of a magazine news story about carjacking evaluated the problem as both more serious and more frequent if the story contained an extreme example (a victim killed during the crime) as compared to a less extreme example (a victim injured little or not at all). Brown and Siegler (1992) found that the amount of media coverage of a country predicted people's rated knowledge of that country and their estimate of its population. Countries receiving more media coverage were believed to be more populous than those receiving less coverage. Gibbons, Lukowski, & Walker (2005) found that merely being exposed repeatedly to initially unbelievable headlines over time led readers to find them more believable. Readers of news continually update their mental models of the content being described, for example drawing causal inferences from material mentioned (Blanc, Kendeou, van den Broek, & Brouillet, 2008; Blanc, Stiegler-Balfour, & O'Brien, 2011). Viewers' goals in watching TV news and their expertise on the topic affect how carefully and systematically they extract information from a news story (Tewksbury, 1999). For example, people relatively high in need for cognition enjoy the cognitive processing of news stories, regardless of their level of skepticism or trust of the source (Tsfati & Cappella. 2005).

Another issue is the effect of media publicity on juror decision making. There are two general concerns here. One relates to specific pretrial publicity about a case. Jurors' exposure to information about a particular case affects verdicts. For example, lurid pretrial information about a rape or murder case increases the likelihood of a conviction vote. This knowledge is not erased by a judge's direction to disregard the information.

A second concern involves general pretrial publicity and jurors' exposure to information about other cases involving similar issues. To test this second type of effect, Greene and Wade (1987) asked students to read a news magazine story about either (1) a heinous crime—the rape of an elderly woman—or (2) a miscarriage of justice—the wrongful conviction of a man for a rape to which someone else later confessed. A third group of students was not given any story to read. In a second phase of the study, which was presented as an unrelated experiment, the research participants acted as jurors, reading an excerpt from a different court case and deciding on a verdict. Reading about the prior case did affect their verdicts. Compared to the control group, twice as many (20% vs. 10%) who had read of the unrelated heinous crime said that the defendant in the second case was definitely guilty. Although 57% of those reading about the prior miscarriage of justice called the new defendant probably not guilty, only 25% did so after reading about the heinous crime, probably due to having that example available in their memory (Tversky & Kahneman, 1973). In the real world, jurors' prior exposure to such examples is all but impossible to control, because such cases receive wide media coverage. A powerful example can do much to drive future information processing and behavior (Zillmann, 2002).

Responses to Crime Coverage in Media

Several provocative books address the question of the effect of media coverage of crimes on the public perception of different dangers, most notably Barry Glassner's (1999) *The Culture of Fear: Why Americans Are Afraid of the Wrong Things*, Daniel Gardner's (2008) *The Science of Fear: Why We Fear the Things we Shouldn't—and Put Ourselves in Greater Danger*, and Joel Best's (1999) *Random Violence: How We Talk about New Crimes and New Victims*.

How News Distorts the Reporting of Dangers

Best (1999) identified three unwarranted, yet widely believed, assumptions about so-called "random" violence. First of all, violence is believed to be patternless, with everyone equally likely to be a victim. However, the facts are otherwise. Young adult men, especially if they are young men of color, are much more likely to be victims of violent crime than anyone else (except for women as rape victims). Second, violence is seen to be pointless; that is, perpetrated for no apparent reason. On the contrary, there is almost always some motive for violent crimes, although the rare exceptional cases where there is not receive heavy coverage and seem particularly threatening. Finally, violent crime is perceived to be getting worse, while in fact most violent crime rates in the United States have been falling since the early 1990s. If violent crime rates are falling and violent crime is not patternless or pointless, why do most people believe otherwise?

One reason is that very often in crime reporting scenarios substitute for facts. Vivid cases are reported without reference to a base rate of incidence for that type of crime. The vivid case is thus made to appear typical, even to represent an "epidemic." For example, Glassner (1999, 2010) looks at the crime of "road rage," trendy in the 1990s, when we started hearing about people being shot at on the freeway for no apparent reason and people thus became afraid of what might happen when they were driving their daily commute. Looking at base rates instead of vivid cases, Glassner found that five drivers died from road rage crimes in the years 1993 to 1998, amounting to less than one-thousandth of the 250,000 road deaths from 1990 to 1997; 85 times as many motorists died as a result of accidents caused by drunk drivers. Yet all the distraction about "road rage" kept us from looking at related systemic problems like increasingly long commutes and inadequate investment in highway infrastructure.

Since the 1960s, the volume of commercial air flights has more than doubled but the accident rate is down 85%, with the probability of dying in an aircraft crash about one in 4 million. Yet people are typically much more afraid to fly than to drive, which is statistically far more dangerous. Gardner (2008) estimated that 1,600 additional motor vehicle deaths occurred in the United States in the months after the 9/11 attacks, as people turned to driving out of heightened fear of the still-safer flying.

The chance of being killed by a coworker at work is about one in 2 million—even less if you are not in either of the two particularly dangerous occupations of taxi driving or mining. The chance of a child being killed at school was actually less in 2000, after highly covered tragedies like the Columbine High massacre in 1999, than it was in 1990. The chance of dying in a terrorist attack is less than one in 10,000, while the chance of dying of cancer or heart disease is one in 3 (Gardner, 2008).

One of the biggest fears of the 1970s was the fear of tainted Halloween candy. Glassner (1999) cites a 1985 article which concluded that there had been no confirmed deaths or serious injuries from strangers' candy and only a few reports of minor cuts from sharp objects in candy bags, most of which were hoaxes. The only two documented cases of deaths from Halloween candy were one case in which candy was laced with heroin by the child's family to fool police about the cause of the child's death and another in which the child's father poisoned candy with cyanide to collect life insurance money on his child.

One of the most sensationalized crimes is child abduction. One USA Today headline screamed "MISSING CHILDREN: A FEARFUL EPIDEMIC," while the CBS program 48 Hours set up a mock abduction to show how easily children could be lured out of a mall store by a stranger needing help finding his dog, even though there was no evidence such a crime had ever happened, and in 2002 Bill O'Reilly spoke of "100,000 abductions of children by strangers every year in the U.S.," although the U.S. Office of Juvenile Justice reported only 115 such abductions (Glassner, 2010). That is 115 too many but hardly an epidemic.

Although a few celebrated cases have received publicity on the local or national news, most missing children are runaways, not kidnap victims, and most of the small minority that are true abductions are by noncustodial parents in child custody disputes. In fact, only 1.3% of child abductions are by nonfamily members ("Numbers," 2001). Nevertheless, parents drag their children to the mall to be fingerprinted or to have dental identification implants, with apparently no thought to the fear and insecurity they might be inducing by telling their child that this is being done in case they are abducted and murdered, so that their remains can be identified!

There are other impacts of such reporting, beyond the fear induced in the public. Typically some vicious stranger is blamed for the crime, with no mention of bad policies creating conditions that increase its likelihood. Thus we worry about encountering the crazed gunman on the freeway or a violent robber, but don't think much about policies that allow anyone to buy a deadly weapon at a gun show without a background check or about the lack of a social support network that leaves inner-city youth with nowhere to turn to but drugs and crime. Sometimes there are major financial interests that stand to benefit from the status quo. For example, large political donations from pharmaceutical companies may discourage elected officials' criticism of prescription drug abuse, especially when it is easier to focus on illicit drugs, whose purveyors have no powerful legislative lobby.

Thus, just as there are threats that we worry about too much, there may be others that we do not worry about enough. Although we worry a lot about illegal drugs, we think much less about the mixing of alcohol and prescription drugs, which is very common in drug overdose cases. The abuse and overdose of prescription drugs sends more adolescents to emergency rooms than the use of cocaine, heroin, marijuana, and LSD combined. Drug abuse by physicians and the elderly are huge problems, though their full extent is unknown. In terms of drugs and rape, the fact that alcohol is involved in a very large number of date rapes sometimes gets lost in the hysteria over the "date-rape drug epidemic." A study of U.S. newspaper coverage of intimate partner violence in 2002 and 2003 found that, although two-thirds of victims report alcohol being a factor in their battering, only 6% of the news reports mentioned the batterer as being under the influence of alcohol and only 2% mentioned him as being under the influence of other drugs (Carlyle, Slater, & Chakroff, 2008). An important part of the story was left out.

In relation to violence, Glassner also argues that we are worrying about the wrong things. Although middle-class communities generally remain very safe places, some poor communities are extremely dangerous. The chronically high violent crime rate in minority communities receives far less media attention than a single sensational crime in a middle-class suburb. The easy availability of guns in the United States has led to far higher rates of death from handguns than elsewhere. More teen suicide attempts succeed today than formerly because more (60%) use guns.

Is there a cost to inducing disproportionate fear in children by overreacting to extremely rare crimes like child abduction? Many fewer children walk to school or play outside than a generation or two ago, often out of parents' disproportionate fears of abduction and other crimes. This contributes to poorer fitness and greater obesity. One of your authors (RJH) once noted another dad at a parent soccer meeting for a second-grade team speak out strongly against putting children's names on the back of their soccer jerseys because "then someone could call him by name and kidnap him."

Another instance of our worrying about the wrong things concerns medical risk. For example, in almost all cases, the danger from not receiving a vaccine is far larger than the extremely unlikely outcome of an extreme side effect caused by the vaccine. Before 1949, 7,500 children died from whooping cough and 265,000 were sick annually, whereas the actual deaths from DPT vaccine were zero or almost zero (Glassner, 1999). During a vaccine scare in the UK that led to a 40% drop in immunizations, 100,000 whooping cough cases appeared over 8 years. Japan had a tenfold increase in cases and a threefold increase in deaths after a temporary ban on the vaccine. See Offit (2011) for an excellent and detailed look at the history and costs of the anti-vaccine movement. Recently many have looked at an apparently large increase in the diagnosis of autism and worried of a possible link to childhood immunizations; see Close-Up 7.9 for some reassurance that even the perceived increase is questionable.

Close-Up 7.9: Why there Isn't Really an Autism Epidemic

The experimental psychologist married couple Morton Gernsbacher and Hill Goldsmith are parents of an autistic son, and they are also very concerned about the popular and, in their view, unfounded belief that there has been an "epidemic" of autism in the last 30 years. Why do they believe that the large increase in diagnosed cases does not indicate an increased prevalence of autism? The major reason is a change in diagnostic criteria. Before 1980 diagnoses were based on individual doctors' criteria, with the first formal diagnostic criteria appearing in the American Psychiatric Association's DSM-III in 1980, in which six mandatory criteria were presented; only if all six were present and the patient judged to show "a pervasive lack of responsiveness to other people" would someone be diagnosed as autistic. The 1994 revision (DSM-IV) expanded the criteria list to 16, but only half had to be present, and the person judged to show only "a lack of spontaneous seeking to share ... achievements with other people," for an autism diagnosis. More changes are expected with the release of DSM-V in 2013.

Another major change in 1994 involved the expansion of the categories of autism from two to five, two of the new ones being Asperger's disorder and pervasive developmental disorder not otherwise specified (PDDNOS), milder varieties of autism which together account for nearly three-quarters of current diagnoses (Chakrabarti & Fombonne, 2001). Gernsbacher, Dawson, and Goldsmith (2005) argued that an alleged 273% increase in autism in California from 1987 to 1998 and misleading numbers reported by schools to the Department of Education are entirely accounted for by the changes in diagnostic criteria for autism spectrum disorders (Gernsbacher et al., 2005). Thus we must be careful when we hear of "epidemics" of new diseases in the press.

Sometimes proposed steps to promote safety, based on what appear to be strong and legitimate grounds, may have the opposite effect due to a failure to consider base rates. For example, periodically one hears calls for requiring the use of child safety seats in airplanes for children under two. Although this might occasionally save a child's life, it most likely would cost far more, because the extra expense of buying another ticket (infants currently fly free on their parent's lap) would cause many parents to use the much more dangerous travel mode of driving instead. Finally, calls to allow disconnection of airbags in cars have often followed the very rare deaths of children, usually infants, in car seats in the front seat. In fact, airbags have saved many lives, and allowing motorists to disconnect them would almost surely cost lives, whereas the risk to children can be easily dealt with by putting them, especially infants in car seats, in the back seat, where there is no risk of an airbag injury.

The same sorts of concerns come into play in responding to health news. For example, a 2011 report advising against routine use of PSA screening for prostate cancer was met with considerable public opposition. A careful study of the causes of this reaction showed an excessive reliance on anecdotal evidence and personal experience ("My friend was screened and it caught his cancer"), as well a misinterpretation of data and inadequate understanding of base rates and false positives (Arkes & Gaissmaier, 2012).

Why, in the late 20th century, was there a jump in the proportion of the American public who believed crime to be the "most important problem" facing the country, from 5 to 52%? From looking at TV news broadcasts and crime statistics from 1978 to 1998, Lowry, Nio, and Leitner (2003) concluded that changes in network TV news accounted for four times as much of the variance in public perceptions as did actual crime rates! One of the best individual predictors was the sheer amount of time devoted to crime stories. Employing the cultivation theory perspective, Romer, Jamieson, and Aday (2003) and Slater and Rasinski (2005) found that the amount of exposure to crime-ridden local TV news was a good predictor of the amount of fear and concern about crime. People recalled media examples very readily, especially for classes of events in which one's life experience was limited, such as murders, drug busts, and courtroom trials (Busselle & Shrum, 2003). Those lower in quantitative literacy were especially likely to be overly influenced by compelling exemplars (Gibson, Callison, & Zillmann, 2011; Zillmann, Callison, & Gibson, 2009). Members of the public commenting in a news story may actually have even more influence on viewers than so-called experts or politicians, although pre-existing attitudes are also an important factor (Lefevere, de Swert, & Walgrave, 2012).

Can these media effects be counteracted? Exposure to base-rate information (e.g., information about population increasing faster than associated crime rates) led to lower levels of apprehension and perceived victimization risk among men (though not among women) compared to those receiving only frequency information, such as reports of increasing numbers of crimes over time (Berger, 1998, 2000). In a study of estimated risks of terrorist events, Fischhoff, Gonzalez, Lerner, and Small (2005) found that a fear-inducing manipulation led participants to raise their perceived likelihood of risks, though an anger manipulation actually caused them to reduce the risk estimates. Inducing fear and raising estimated likelihoods of negative events may not always be bad. For example, Slater, Hayes, and Ford (2007) found that adolescents' increased attention to news coverage of alcohol-related vehicle accidents led to increased judgments of likelihood of such accidents. This is of course the logic behind showing gory films of traffic accidents in driver education classes.

Although everyone loves to complain about it, does sensationalist news reporting still actually appeal to people? In an interesting study of channel-switching, Lang et al. (2005) found that a major reason that news viewers change the channel is a decrease in physiological arousal. However, this may not be the whole story. Vettehen, Nuijten, and Peeters (2008) found that the more sensationalist aspects a news story had (as defined by both negative content and various production techniques like background music and close camera zooms), the higher the emotional arousal. This arousal then increased people's liking for the story but only up to a point. Apparently we prefer a moderate level of arousal more than either very low or very high arousal. Thus it would appear that increasing sensationalism raises arousal, which in turn increases liking up to a point, after which it starts to decrease. For example, a news story that is extremely graphic or disturbing may not be liked as much as one that is only moderately so. Clearly, the way crimes are reported has a huge influence on the way we think about specific crimes and the likelihood of we ourselves being victimized.

Occasionally there is one particular news event whose coverage triggers unusually strong responses in the public. Perhaps the most striking of this sort in recent years were the September 11, 2001 terrorist attacks (Marshall et al., 2007; Schlenger et al., 2002; Silver et al., 2002; Torabi & Seo, 2004). There were strong correlations between exposure to TV coverage of the 9/11 attacks and the diagnosis of anxiety and other symptoms of posttraumatic stress disorder (PTSD) in viewers throughout the United States (Marshall et al., 2007). This was not limited to those geographically near the attacks and also was not explainable in terms of the media coverage exacerbating symptoms already present. Marshall and colleagues argue that the cognitive notion of relative risk appraisal (Slovic, Finucane, Peters, & MacGregor, 2004) is important to understanding media effects in such cases. Persons are continually making relative judgments of risk of various outcomes, and these judgments are very intuitive and involve emotional responses to the situation. Assessments of the relative risk of terrorism may be particularly high because such events are high on both dimensions of risk: dread risk, which arises in response to catastrophic and uncontrollable events (nuclear war, major toxin accidents) and unknown risk, in which a person does not know when he or she is exposed or how he or she might be injured. Because the media reports necessarily stress these two factors (an unprecedented catastrophic event that could happen anywhere), the assessment of risk among the public would be especially high. This would the explain the unusually high level of diagnosis of anxiety disorders and PTSD observed after 9/11. For reactions to the London bombings of July 7, 2005, see G. C. Rubin, Brewin, Greenberg, Simpson, & Wessely (2005); for reactions to the Palestinian intifada in Israel, see Bleich, Gelkopf, & Solomon (2003).

Suicides: Triggered by News?

A very different approach to studying the effects of news stories was taken by sociologist David Phillips (Bollen & Phillips, 1982; D. P. Phillips, 1977, 1984; D. P. Phillips & Carstensen, 1986), who used archival data to study the role of media news in triggering suicides. This research examined the hypothesis that news coverage of suicides encourages others to take their own lives.

The basic method Phillips used was to examine correlations of media reports of suicides with changes in the rates of actual suicides. For example, Phillips and Carstensen (1986) examined seven years of such relationships by looking at 12,585 actual teenage suicides in relation to TV news reports and feature stories about suicide. They found that there was a significant increase in suicides 0 to 7 days after such a news story. This increase was correlated ($r = .52$) with the number of news programs carrying the story. This correlation was significant only for teen, not adult, suicides, and was stronger for girls than for boys. The experimenters concluded that the news stories (either general feature stories or reports of actual suicides) do in fact trigger teen suicides. Phillips and Carstensen discussed and refuted several possible alternative explanations of their findings, although the findings remain controversial. Romer, Jamieson, and Jamieson (2006) supported a suicide contagion effect with more recent reports, while others dispute this explanation (Joiner, 1999; Kessler, Downey, Milavsky, & Stipp, 1988).

How Media Affect Foreign Policy

News media, especially television, can even affect foreign policy and foreign relations (Gilboa, 2002; Larson, 1986; Naveh, 2002). The transnational character of media news-gathering necessarily involves it in policy-making issues. The sharing of wire service stories and TV footage is common. Reporters in a foreign locale depend on local facilities to transmit news stories home, and often they must cope with local censorship or interference with such coverage. Governments sometimes try to manipulate the perceived reality by limiting the coverage. For example, Saudi Arabian authorities have prevented Western reporters from covering repression of women there.

Diplomatic Negotiations

The presence of the press makes private or secret negotiations between governments more difficult. Diplomats negotiating sensitive issues must also consider the implicit third party of public opinion in the negotiations. With television, it is especially hard to keep secret talks secret. Although such public scrutiny has probably placed some highly desirable curbs on corruption and extralegal activity, it has also made legitimate secret negotiations in the public interest much harder to keep secret.

Compelling Images

The availability of relevant and appropriate video material affects the choice of stories. This clearly leads to overcoverage of some photogenic issues and undercoverage of others that are less so, thus covertly setting the agenda. It also favors coverage from places where networks or wire services have correspondents on site, which historically for U.S. media has meant primarily Western Europe, with many other places covered firsthand only if there is a current crisis or American military involvement.

A particularly compelling visual image can galvanize world opinion and may affect foreign policy decisions. The picture of a lone person standing in front of a line of tanks in Tiananmen Square in Beijing in 1989 helped to increase the world's condemnation of the Chinese government's squelching of the prodemocracy movement. In the late 1960s, Pulitzer Prize-winning photos of a Vietcong prisoner as he was being shot in the head and a naked little girl running from an explosion were thought to help turn U.S. public opinion against the Vietnam war.

Some have worried that the policy of sending American military forces to oversee relief efforts in Somalia in 1992 to 1993 was a direct response to the grotesque images of starving children broadcast worldwide. Although such images probably played a role, Strobel (1997) argued that the media more likely followed the agenda of government rather than set it. The power of media, especially television, to convey emotions and a sense of intimacy may be necessary for government action, but it is not in itself sufficient in the absence of government resolve. Although the U.S. government appeared to be sending troops to Somalia in response to press and public outcry, there were also grisly images from Bosnia, Rwanda, and other places around the same time that did not result in U.S. military intervention. Strobel argued that in these cases there existed a clear government policy against intervention—a position absent in relation to the Somalia situation—thus the press coverage had less policy impact; see Gilboa (2002) for a discussion of research on the nature and impact of media on foreign policy decisions.

Media and Government

In fact, television networks and major wire services usually follow or reinforce government policy, at least implicitly (Larson, 1984). This happens not so much out of slavish conscious adherence to official policy, but rather because of the fact that so many sources for most stories are inside governments. Also, the newsworthiness of individual people ensures that reporters will follow policy makers and spokespersons more than they will follow abstract trends and background. For example, summit meetings between world leaders are heavily covered in the press, even when it is all but certain that little of substance will emerge. Media sometimes even participate in foreign policy by serving as a direct channel of communications between government officials or policy elites in different nations. An example is CBS news anchor Walter Cronkite's pivotal role in bringing Israel's Begin and Egypt's Sadat together in 1978 (see Close-Up 7.7). In some crisis situations media may actually know more than governments and may thus reverse the usual government-to-media flow of news. During the 1991 Persian Gulf War, both U.S. President George H. W. Bush and Iraqi leader Saddam Hussein reportedly watched CNN (along with the rest of us!) to learn what was happening in the war. Furthermore, they both used the network to send messages to the other side, since that was the fastest and most reliable means of communication.

Policy problems may be created or exacerbated by the lack of media attention to basic processes of social and cultural change in developing nations. The bias in international news coverage by U.S. sources toward greater coverage of developed nations and those of obvious current geopolitical importance has long been known. Western Europe, Japan, and Russia receive heavy coverage in the United States, whereas Africa, Latin America, and much of Asia have traditionally been largely invisible (Larson, McAnany, & Storey, 1986;

McAnany, 1983). Only in a crisis or when events thrust the United States into immediate involvement does the focus shift to such places, as was seen in Iran in 1979 (see Close-Up 7.5), Iraq in 1990 and 1991, Somalia in 1992, Bosnia in 1993, Rwanda in 1995, Afghanistan in 2001, Iraq (again) in 2003, and (briefly) Libya in 2011. Thus the perceived reality often comes across as heavily ahistorical, with no background provided for understanding the puzzling present events. Crises seem to pop up out of nowhere, and the public often has little understanding of why they have occurred.

The Vietnam War

Media can change public perceptions about foreign affairs, particularly when they convey new visual information and when such information is repeatedly presented over a long period of time. The dramatic change in U.S. public opinion about the Vietnam War from 1965 to 1969 is perhaps the most compelling example. In addition to being the first war ever lost by the United States, Vietnam was the first televised war. This aspect is sometimes cited as a major reason why the war lost support among the American people to an extent not seen in the United States in modern history. Although there were many other reasons for the lack of public support for the Vietnam War, the fact that the public could see the horrors of war every night while they ate dinner brought home the reality of how violent and deadly it truly was. The romantic ideals that some soldiers had traditionally taken to war, and that some family members back home had clung to, simply could not continue to be embraced. This war (like all others) was hell, but this time everybody could see that firsthand.

The effect of bringing war into our homes through television has been a hotly debated topic, however (Cumings, 1992; Strobel, 1997). Some (e.g., Strobel, as discussed earlier in this chapter) argue that the role of the media in changing public opinion about Vietnam was far less influential than generally believed. Critical media coverage, starting around 1967, followed public opinion, rather than preceded it. The movement in public opinion away from supporting the war occurred similarly for both the Korean (1950–1953) and Vietnam (1963–1975) wars and was more due to increases in U.S. casualties and a prolonged stalemated situation than to the nature of news coverage (Strobel, 1997). Although the worry that news coverage influences neutral people is widespread, such influence may be less than we believe. Even if the media influence opinion less than is often believed, the fact that many policy makers firmly believe in that influence can itself affect policy, most notably in the restriction and censorship of reporting on military operations post-1980, in order to avoid "another Vietnam."

Iraq and Afghanistan

Even though post-Vietnam war coverage was greatly censored, both by governments and military and by self-censorship of the press, the criticism that the press was not being adequately supportive of a national war effort has continued. For example, the George W. Bush administration complained that news coverage of the wars in Iraq and Afghanistan was unfairly negative and eroded national support for those efforts. Was there any truth to these claims? Aday (2010) analyzed all war reports on NBC *Nightly News* and Fox News' *Special Report with Brit Hume* during 2005. It was found that, while both channels focused on a lot of negative stories, overall they both actually under-reported the violence in Iraq and Afghanistan. Moreover, although Fox News was much more sympathetic to the Bush administration than was NBC, both were more positive than events may have warranted. In an analysis of British media coverage of the 2003 Iraq War, considerable support was also found for the elite-driven (i.e., government-supporting) position, but there was also some evidence of some independent and oppositional coverage (Robinson, Goddard, Parry, & Murray, 2009).

Terrorism

Although a terrorist incident is often a highly newsworthy story in terms of the characteristics discussed earlier in this chapter (Weimann & Brosius, 1991), terrorism stories place a difficult set of pressures on the media. Wittebols (1991; see also Herman & Chomsky, 1988; Herman & O'Sullivan, 1989) has distinguished between "institutional" and "grievance" terrorism. Grievance terrorism challenges the powers that be and actively seeks media attention to help advance its cause and publicize its side of the story. For example, radical Islamic suicide bombers or those who shoot abortion providers are grievance terrorists. In contrast, institutional terrorism has the purpose of maintaining the status quo and generally shuns media coverage, even actively threatening those who try to cover it; examples are paramilitary death squads in Colombia or Zimbabwe. Governments are most often complicit in or at least providing implicit support for institutional terrorism.

The most likely trap that media fall into with grievance terrorism is excessive coverage that risks legitimizing or glamorizing the terrorists, a very frequent criticism of coverage of terrorism in the 1970s and 1980s. Since that time, the press has to a degree learned how to handle terrorism and avoid giving the extremists their desired media platform. On the other hand, the media risk with institutional terrorism is failing to cover it at all, or failing to identify those really responsible for it, in cases where such responsibility can even be determined; see Alali and Eke (1991), Kushner (2001), Paletz and Schmid (1992), and Picard (1993) for further examinations of media coverage of terrorism.

Conclusion: Fiction Becomes Reality

The media often become news. The weekly Nielsen ratings top ten is reported in the news. Certain blockbuster TV entertainment shows are news events, receiving coverage across print and broadcast media. For example, the final episodes of *Friends* and *Will and Grace* in May 2006 and *Oprah* in 2011were major news stories. The annual publication of the *Sports Illustrated* swimsuit issue is announced in all media. The releases of blockbuster movies such as the *Harry Potter* films are major news stories. This news coverage effectively serves as highly effective and free advertising, greatly boosting the audiences for the films.

The Docudrama: Fact or Fiction?

Sometimes the line between the genres of media news and fiction becomes blurred. A particularly controversial format is the docudrama, a fictional story based on real events. Although it is certainly not new to take historic events and build a story around them, embellishing where facts are unavailable or undramatic (Shakespeare did it all the time), there is greater concern with TV dramas or movies based on spectacular crimes, political and international figures, and other news stories. Such programming is very popular. On one weekend in January 1993, CBS, NBC, and ABC all premiered TV docudrama movies based on the same story of a teenager who only months earlier had been accused of trying to kill her alleged lover's wife. All three movies did at least reasonably well in the ratings.

Sometimes docudramas so quickly follow the news events they dramatize that they make it difficult to distinguish them from news. In one sweeps week in late May 1993, networks aired TV movies about the first World Trade Center bombing (February 1993), Hurricane Andrew (August 1992), and the siege of the Branch Davidian cult in Waco, Texas (April 1993). The latter script was written and came to the screen in record time. From the initial shootings of federal agents in late February to the final FBI assault on the compound on April 19, the country waited for news of how the siege would play out. All the while, the TV movie was in production, with the script being written and rewritten in response to each day's news. The movie aired on May 23, only 34 days after the real death of its lead character David Koresh and dozens of his followers. For millions of people, that script's interpretation of the Waco events became reality.

There may be limits on what the media believes the public will find acceptable. For example, in contrast to those events of the 90s, it was five or more years after the terrorist attacks of September 2001 before any movies or TV shows based on those events appeared. Entertainment based on events that horrible carries a public relations risk of being perceived as attempting to profit from a catastrophic tragedy. There is also the issue of when the public is ready to watch entertainment based on very recent tragedies. For example, there were several theatrical movies set in the Iraq War released in the 2005–2010 time period, including one Oscar winner (*The Hurt Locker*), but the audiences for such films were modest at best.

Producers are hungry for docudrama deals and have little compunction about changing the facts to suit entertainment needs. For example, when North American peace worker Jennifer Casolo was approached about a contract for a movie about her experiences working in El Salvador in the 1980s and being falsely arrested for being a revolutionary, the producers wanted her permission to make two changes in the story. They wanted her to (1) be guilty instead of innocent, and (2) fall in love with one of her captors. Unimpressed, Ms. Casolo turned down a lucrative offer.

Sometimes details of the story and its marketing are subtly changed for different audiences. For example, the 2001 film *Pearl Harbor* played up the love story and played down the battle scenes for its Japanese debut. A scene where an American major tells his men that, should an upcoming raid on Tokyo not succeed, he would "kill himself and as many Japanese as possible" was deleted. There were also certain changes in language. For example, the phrase "a few less dirty Japs" was softened to "a few less Japs" (Kleiner, 2001).

In fact, the whole genre of the docudrama is merely a continuation of filmed interpretations of the past. In a fascinating study of cinematic stories of American historical events, historian Robert Toplin (1995) argued that famous period films such as *Mississippi Burning, Sergeant York, JFK, Bonnie and Clyde, Patton,* and *All the President's Men* all significantly distort the historical record, yet at the same time convey a fairly accurate sense of time and place to many people who would never be reached by purely historical writing.

Sometimes telling the story accurately risks distorting it in a broader sense. For example, Clint Eastwood's critically acclaimed 2006 film, *Flags of Our Fathers*, about the six men who planted the flag on Mount Suribachi during the Battle of Iwo Jima in World War II (also its companion film, *Letters from Iwo Jima*), was quite accurate historically. In that racially segregated period Whites and African Americans were trained separately and the latter were limited to supportive though still dangerous supply roles; the film portrayed the six heroes as all White, which they actually were, but some, including director Spike Lee, argued that Eastwood should have used a metaphorical "wider-angle lens" to include African American roles in this iconic battle (Altman, 2008).

Although there is often an underemphasis on examining the underlying motivations for the behavior of historical figures (Hoekstra, 1998), the dramas are compelling and make events of the past accessible to many people. How does one balance the distortion of the historical record with the advantage of telling more people an important story? See Close-Up 7.10 for a detailed comparison of fiction and reality in one docudrama.

Limits of Media Influence

In spite of the enormous influence of news media, we must be careful not to attribute an even larger role to media in the perceived reality of our world than is appropriate. Even if news is not quite the preeminent influence it is ' sometimes believed to be, it clearly occupies a major place in the popular imagination. The coverage of news has itself become news, sometimes bigger news than the event being covered. On the eve of the Iowa Presidential caucuses one year, a voter in the studio was asked if she planned to attend the caucus and thus participate in the historical selection of a nominee for President. Her reply was to look around the studio and say, "Oh, I guess so, but I hate to miss all the excitement here." In other words, for her the act of reporting had become the newsworthy event, eclipsing the event being reported. This example suggests the continuation of this discussion in the context of the specific area of politics, which is the subject of Chapter 8.

Close-Up 7.10: Case Study of the Docudrama *Amistad*

Steven Spielberg's film *Amistad* told the previously little-known story of a rebellion by 53 kidnapped Africans aboard a Portuguese slave ship bound for the U.S. in 1839. They killed all but two of their captors. Double-crossed by these two survivors, who kept sailing to America at night instead of back to Africa, the Africans ended up in a Connecticut jail. However, their cause was taken up by Christian abolitionists, who hired ex-President John Quincy Adams to argue their case up to the U.S. Supreme Court, which eventually released them. The movie left out or downplayed certain major protagonists and enhanced the roles of others or combined them into fictional composites. For example, J. Q. Adams's stirring speech to the U.S. Supreme Court never happened, according to *Amistad* historian and film consultant Clifford Johnson. The Africans' earlier attorney Roger Baldwin is portrayed as a more minor and inept character than he in fact was. Abolitionism as a social movement almost disappeared in the film, except for the abolitionist Lewis Tappan, who is played as a hypocrite with a more minor and far less noble role than the historical Tappan had. The central driving role of Christianity in the lives of the abolitionists is largely absent, in keeping with the general invisibility of religion in American popular culture (see Chapter 6). Still, for all its rewriting of history, the film *Amistad* brought this important but previously largely unknown incident to the consciousness of millions in a way that historians could never hope to do (Goldstein, 1998; A. Schneider, 1998).

In a curious footnote to this film, an egregious historical error came to light. The revolt's leader Cinqué, portrayed as a hero in Spielberg's film, has been identified in several sources as having later returned to Africa, and as having become a slave trader himself. In a bit of bibliographic sleuthing, *Amistad* historian Howard Jones traced the historical source of this claim to several history textbooks by Samuel Eliot Morison in the 1950s and 1960s. The sole source cited in these texts is a 1953 novel *Slave Mutiny* by William Owens. Apparently, several historians adopted Morison's interpretation without checking primary sources. Although novelist Owens apparently reported seeing some document somewhere confirming Cinqué's role as a slave trader, researchers at the Amistad Research Institute could find no record of such activity ("Hot Type," 1998).

Chapter 8

Politics

Using News and Advertising to Win Elections

Q: How much is spent on political campaigns in the United States?

A: The 2000 U.S. Presidential election, the most expensive to that date, cost $3 billion in combined expenses for all candidates, parties, and interest groups (Johnston, 2001). In the 2008 Democratic primary campaign, $137 million was spent on TV ads alone, up from $51 million in 2004 ("Numbers," 2008b). According to the Center for Responsive Politics in Washington, 72% of all the political ad spending during the 2010 elections in the U.S. would have been prohibited before the 2010 *Citizens United* Supreme Court ruling removed most limits on contributions to political action committees ("Harper's Index," 2012).

Q: What was the average length of stories on U.S. network TV news during the Presidential campaign of 1968?

A: 42 seconds (Hallin, 1992)

Q: What was the average length in 2000?

A: 7.8 seconds (Lichter, 2001)

Politics and media have long been intimately involved with each other, with media strongly setting the agenda that politics is very important. Although television, and more recently the Internet, have made some drastic changes in the nature of that relationship, the connection itself is not new. Print media have long covered political campaigns, and the level of political rhetoric has sometimes been even more vicious than it is today. For example, the U.S. Presidential campaign of 1884 saw Democrat Grover Cleveland's alleged fathering of an illegitimate child as a major campaign issue ("Hey, man, where's my pa?/Gone to the White House, ha, ha, ha!"). Still, from the first tentative and fragmented radio reporting of Warren Harding's U.S. Presidential victory in 1920 to today's framing of whole campaigns around the use of television and Internet news and advertising, broadcast media have transformed political campaigns beyond recognition, compared to Grover Cleveland's days. Franklin D. Roosevelt (1933–1945) was perhaps the quintessential radio president; his lofty, mellow tones electrified listeners in ways that watching his body in a wheelchair could never do. In recent decades, candidates have been forced to deal with the visual aspect of television, and some of them have done so only grudgingly. For another historical example, see Close-Up 8.1, on the political use of the media by abolitionists in the pre-Civil War United States.

Close-Up 8.1: Abolitionist Media Campaigns in the 19th Century (Jakes, 1985)

One of the major political and philosophical issues in 19th-century America was slavery, a controversy so divisive that it eventually led to the calamitous American Civil War (1861–1865). The Abolitionists successfully used pre-electronic media to gradually turn the nation's thinking against slavery.

Abolitionism was considered a rather extreme position in its early days in the 1820s, in that it advocated the end of all slavery on moral grounds, not merely prohibiting its extension to the new Western territories. The Abolitionists ran their own newspapers and had supporters in the editors' chairs at many publications, such as William Lloyd Garrison's *Liberator*, Frederick Douglass's *North Star*, Horace Greeley's *New York Tribune*, and even a children's newspaper called *The Slave's Friend*. Several books were also tremendously influential. Narratives of escaped slaves became popular in the 1840s, with the preeminent example being Frederick Douglass's autobiography. Far eclipsing all other books in influence, however, was Harriet Beecher Stowe's *Uncle Tom's Cabin* (1852), written more out of religiously motivated concern for the treatment of slaves than out of any political conviction or true egalitarian sentiment (Stowe favored sending freed slaves back to Africa). In fact, the novel was based only on Stowe's one short visit to a Kentucky plantation and contained very condescending portraits of African Americans. Still, it had substantial political impact.

Highly newsworthy events that received wide coverage polarized already strong opinions to help lead the nation to war. Public meetings led by White clergymen or escaped slaves drew increasing crowds. Protests over the Fugitive Slave Law allowing Southern slaveholders to hunt and retrieve runaway slaves in the North occasionally led to dramatic countermeasures, such as the founding of the Underground Railroad to help runaway slaves escape to Canada. Garrison once burned a copy of the U.S. Constitution, calling it "a covenant with death and an agreement with hell." In 1859 Abolitionist John Brown and 21 followers tried unsuccessfully to seize arms from the federal arsenal in northern Virginia. He was caught, tried, and hanged, but coverage of the trial split the country more sharply than ever.

Closing the Distance between the Candidate and the Public

Meyrowitz (1985) argued that television coverage forever changed politics by decreasing the psychological distance between the politician and the voter. Although it was no longer necessary to cross the gulf between oneself and the voters by being an imposing physical presence in a crowd or an accomplished orator, it was imperative to know how to use the more intimate medium of video to one's advantage. Analysts of various political persuasions have acknowledged that U.S. Presidents Ronald Reagan (1981–1989) and Bill Clinton (1993–2001) were highly effective television politicians, as was John F. Kennedy (1961–1963) in an earlier period. Other recent presidents and candidates, such as George H. W. Bush, Gerald Ford, Al Gore, Richard Nixon, John McCain, Michael Dukakis, Jimmy Carter, Bob Dole, John Kerry, and Walter Mondale, have used television less effectively. Political audiences are also not as segmented as they used to be. A candidate cannot deliver one speech to an audience of factory workers and a contradictory address to a group of business leaders, because both will be reported on the evening news and posted on the Internet, especially if reporters perceive any inconsistency. A single unfortunate statement or behavior may have a lasting negative effect through the magic of television transferring that one place to all places, to say nothing of the gaffe being available for all to watch repeatedly on YouTube. Democratic Presidential candidate Edmund Muskie was the frontrunner for his party's nomination in 1972 until he was seen on television shedding a tear in New Hampshire in response to a newspaper editor's unfounded character attack on his wife. This reaction, however noble and loyal, was then interpreted as weakness and may have cost him the nomination. One would hope the public has become more forgiving over time, yet when House Speaker John Boehner shed some tears in 2010 it became frequent fodder for late night comedians' political satire. The public has developed strategies for evaluating the emotional responses of candidates (Bucy & Newhagen, 1999).

Candidates' racist slurs or insensitive comments about some group have costly career effects because of the instant, widespread dissemination of such comments in the media, on YouTube, and the Internet as a whole. In 1990, Texas Republican gubernatorial candidate and political novice Clayton Williams seemed to bring insensitivity to new depths when he commented that bad weather was like rape, "If it's inevitable, just relax and enjoy it," a remark that drew shocked and widespread condemnation. Slow to learn, Williams went on to say that during his youth, crossing into Mexico and "being serviced by prostitutes" was part of a healthy Texas boy's coming of age. Although Williams began over ten points ahead, he became an acute embarrassment to Texas Republicans and lost the election. Internet and new media have only enhanced the possibilities for sharing one's weaknesses and gaffes. In 2011, New York Congressman Anthony Weiner (yes, it's pronounced "ween-er") was forced to resign after first denying and then admitting sending lewd cell phone photos of himself to young women. Not only did this story dominate the news for a week or so but the pictures of his bulging underwear circulated widely on the Internet.

In discussing the infamous Watergate tapes of the 1970s Nixon White House, Meyrowitz (1985) suggested that Nixon always saw those tapes as private conversations rather than as public statements. In private most people on occasion say some things that they would not deem appropriate for a public forum, due to language (e.g., profanity), content (e.g., prejudicial or judgmental comments), or style (e.g., imitation of someone). Limited to the private world, such conversations may not be unusual. As public discourse, however, they appeared highly inappropriate, insensitive, and even shocking. Electronic media technology has broken down that public–private barrier by bringing formerly private discourse into the public world. No longer can a public figure assume that private comments will remain private. Indeed, it seems rather naïve when a public figure seems surprised their comments have been made public.

People process media information, including political information, in multiple ways. The processing may be central, with elaboration and careful consideration of arguments of each candidate, or it may be peripheral, with little elaboration and noting primarily superficial aspects like a candidate's appearance or some lighthearted comment. Central or peripheral processing can be either online, meaning processed while perceiving, or memory-based—thinking about it later. Thus, a person consuming political news is likely processing it in all of these ways at different, or possibly the same, times, and different audience members are processing the same message very differently (Choi, 2011). This is the challenge of measuring effects of political news and advertising.

In this chapter we begin by looking at the news media coverage of political campaigns, including televised candidate debates. Then we examine how politicians can manage the news coverage that their campaigns receive. This is followed by a case study of the media coverage of the closest Presidential election in U.S. history. Next we take a careful look at political advertising, when candidates pay to say exactly what they want. Finally, we briefly look at the cultivation theory thesis that television cultivates politically moderate attitudes in heavy viewers. Politicians consistently hope to use media to create a favorable reality about themselves in the public mind. The examples discussed are primarily from the United States, because that is the area known best to your authors and the one most studied by scholars examining politics and the media. Most of the principles discussed, however, are also applicable elsewhere.

Coverage of Political Campaigns

In most nations of the world, the media strongly set the agenda that politics is a very important concern. In a cross-cultural study of television news in the

United States, Japan, Germany, Russia, Italy, India, Colombia, and China, politics comprised between 25 and 40% of all news stories in each nation— more than economic, social, cultural, military, or crime stories (Straubhaar et al., 1992). Political news can set more subtle agendas as well. For example, people who attended highly to political news were less likely to hold scientifically accurate beliefs about global warming and were less likely to see it as a high risk than were those who attended highly to science and environmental news (Hwang & Southwell, 2009; Southwell & Torres, 2006; Zhao, Leiserowitz, Maibach, & Roser-Renouf, 2011). This was no doubt a reflection of the high degree of scientific consensus about the human causes of global warming and the high level of political rhetoric from some quarters questioning those scientific conclusions.

Although political campaigns, candidates, and issues, especially at the national level, receive heavy media news coverage, a closer look reveals that some political news receives more coverage than others.

What Is Heavily Covered

Certain aspects of political campaigns are inordinately heavily covered and others more lightly covered, in large measure depending on how newsworthy they are, in the sense discussed in Chapter 7. First, major pronouncements receive press attention, especially formal announcements of intent to run for office or to withdraw from a race. Other types of strong statements, like a strident attack on an opponent, also have high visibility.

Second, any type of major gaffe or blunder, even if substantially inconsequential in the long run, receives wide attention (Baker, 2004). One of the most notorious gaffes historically was President Gerald Ford's statement in the 1976 Presidential debates that Poland was a "free country," not dominated by the Soviet Union. Although this was clearly incorrect at the time (he later claimed he meant the Polish "spirit" could never be dominated), the press did not let the public forget. Vice-Presidential candidate Sarah Palin's comment in a 2008 campaign interview suggesting that she had foreign policy experience because, she "could see Russia from land here in Alaska" produced widespread derision and helped to frame her as an uninformed lightweight (Harp, Loke, & Bachmann, 2010). Even press coverage of candidate spouses tends to disproportionately cover controversies (Shoop, 2010). Sometimes, however, the public may weigh the blunders less heavily than the media. A series of allegations in early 1998 about President Bill Clinton's dalliances with several women received heavy tabloid-style coverage but did not seem to hurt his popularity very much, nor did widespread dissatisfaction with the Iraq War hurt President Bush in the 2004 Presidential contest.

A third aspect of campaigns which receives heavy coverage is the colorful public responses to a political speech or event. Cheering masses and, more especially, angry demonstrations draw cameras. When candidate Barack

Obama spoke to an estimated 200,000 in Berlin in 2008, that cheering crowd provided quite a boost to his campaign. In many countries, rulers of questionable legitimacy regularly pay people to attend a speech and "spontaneously" cheer. Likewise, protests against a leader are carefully orchestrated primarily for the TV cameras, not for the speaker. The democratic protests of 1986 (Philippines), 1987 (South Korea), 1990–1991 (Baltic nations), and 2011 (Tunisia, Egypt, Libya) were televised around the world and eventually forced repressive regimes to yield power. Protesters worldwide routinely have sets of posters and banners in several languages to display as appropriate, depending on which nation's camera crew is present. The world media audience, not the local one, is the most important.

Fourth, meetings of a candidate with important people receive press coverage. This is particularly important for candidates without wide experience in some areas. For example, candidate Barack Obama's July 2008 trip to the Middle East and Europe produced lots of good photo opportunities with American generals in Iraq and Afghanistan, as well as meetings with heads of state in Israel, Germany, Britain, and elsewhere, which were tactically important in burnishing the image of a candidate without much foreign policy experience.

Finally, and probably most importantly, any aspect of a campaign that emphasizes the so-called horse race (who's currently ahead and who's behind in the polls) receives coverage. Poll results are reported widely and promptly, as are predictions by experts and any event that "upsets" the relative standings of the "players." In the 2000 U.S. Presidential campaign coverage, 71% of the TV news stories were concerned with the horse race, rather than the issues (Lichter, 2001). Less than a third mentioned any issue at all (Jamieson & Waldman, 2003). A large majority of TV news election stories are on horse race and superficial campaign events, rather than on substantive issues or a candidate's qualifications (Fox, Angelini, & Goble, 2005). The number of poll-related stories and the relative prominence of such stories have risen greatly in the last 40 years (Craig, 2000), with the agenda increasingly being set that what is important in the campaign is primarily the change in poll results since the last report.

What are the effects of such preoccupation with who is ahead and who is behind? Relatively unknown candidates who are suddenly perceived as serious contenders or even frontrunners receive a rapid and substantial increase in coverage. At least in primary elections, they do not necessarily have to win; a simple "better-than-expected" showing is often enough for a media-framed "victory." Dark horse anti–Vietnam War candidate Gene McCarthy's surprisingly good showing in the New Hampshire Democratic primary in 1968 may have been instrumental in President Lyndon Johnson's surprise decision not to seek renomination himself. Early Republican primary victories, or "better-than-expected" showings, in 2012 by relatively unknown candidates Ron Paul, Herman Cain, Rick Santorum, and Michele Bachmann temporarily catapulted them from the relatively obscure group of minor candidates to being serious contenders.

This heavy coverage of horse races has probably encouraged the proliferation of more and earlier contests. With the New Hampshire Presidential primary happening by law two weeks before the earliest primary of any other state, that state ensures the continued attention and economic development benefits of all the media coverage; in 2012 it occurred in early January, ten months before the general election. Other states, such as Iowa, have attempted an end run by having nonprimary caucuses or statewide straw polls even earlier. These contests end up drawing considerable coverage, far out of proportion to the few delegates (if any) at stake. Most primary states have moved their primaries earlier in recent years in the hope of having some influence before the contest is decided. The primary system has now become so front-loaded that the two major candidates are often effectively chosen by March or April, 7 to 8 months before the general election in November! This extensively protracted campaign period is a major reason for both the rapidly escalating cost of campaigns and the public's increasing weariness of them. They simply last too long, a problem almost everyone acknowledges but no one knows quite how to fix. Most other nations typically have national election campaigns that last no longer than several weeks.

The race aspect that is covered the most heavily of all is, of course, the result of the actual election. There is a lot of concern that knowledge of the results, or predicted results, in the case of network projections of winners, may actually affect the outcome of the election by influencing voters who have not yet gone to the polls. See Close-Up 8.2 for further discussion of this issue.

Close-Up 8.2: Public Opinion Polling and Election Results

Started by newspapers in the 1800s but greatly scientifically improved since 1950, public opinion polls are an integral part of modern political life most everywhere. The famed Gallup Poll began in the 1930s and held a margin of error of 4% in the period from 1936 to 1950, although this had fallen to 0.3% by 1984. It is larger if there are three, instead of two, candidates, as in 1980 when the Carter–Reagan–Anderson contest produced a margin of error of 4.7%.

One of the most notorious blunders in polling history occurred in the *Literary Digest* Presidential poll in 1936. Mailed to auto and phone owners in the heart of the Great Depression, the poll came back favoring Republican Alf Landon, who in fact lost to incumbent Franklin Roosevelt by a landslide. The poll, which was so inaccurate due to a skewed sample of more-affluent-than-average voters, was such a point of disgrace that it helped lead to the demise of the magazine.

One particularly controversial issue concerns the broadcasting of election results and projection of winners before the polls have closed in all states. In the days of paper ballots, no substantive results could be obtained for several hours, but that is no longer the case. Four studies done many years ago assessed U.S. West Coast voters' exposure to election results and projections before they voted (Fuchs, 1966; Lang & Lang, 1968; Mendelsohn, 1966; Tuchman & Coffin, 1971). These studies show only modest exposure to the projections and very small proportions that indicate a change in their vote or a decision not to vote (1–3%). Still, these studies were done before the widespread use of exit polls and, in any case, many elections are decided by very close margins.

Since these studies were done, sampling techniques have improved and networks today take exit polls by asking voters as they leave the polling places which candidate they voted for. Assuming appropriate sampling and truthful responses, exit poll results can project winners with great accuracy before the polls close. Networks, in a race to scoop the competition, routinely declare projected winners in races with only a tiny percentage of the votes counted (often less than 10%). Although this may be scientifically sound, based on representative sampling, it may nonetheless convey a troubling message to viewers. If results can be obtained with only 5% of the votes in, it may not seem to an individual voter that a single ballot can make much difference. The United States has consistently had one of the lowest voter turnout rates in the world, not infrequently less than half of the qualified voters. There is not much incentive to go and vote after you have already heard the results announced on television.

What Is Lightly Covered?

Just as some aspects of political campaigns are heavily covered, others are relatively lightly covered. Candidates' qualifications in intangible, but highly important, areas are relatively difficult for the press to cover. What have candidates gained from being governor of Texas, senator from Arizona, CEO of a financial firm, or first lady for a previous president that would help qualify them to be president? Very abstract issues such as character are in one sense extremely important, but in another sense very difficult to assess. Coverage tends to focus on superficial, though not necessarily completely irrelevant, indicators of integrity (or more often lack thereof), like marital infidelity or questionable business dealings. For example, although there was much talk early in the 1992 Presidential campaign of Democrat Bill Clinton's apparent extramarital affairs some years before, the exact relevance or irrelevance of these to his possible performance as President was never clarified (and perhaps could not be).

Also relatively lightly covered are positions on issues, especially complex ones. Television news especially is ill-suited to detailed presentations of positions on complex issues like the economy. Print media or the Internet can do much better, as in publication of a candidate's lengthy position paper on some issue. However, few people read such reports; they listen instead to a television commentator's 30-second interpretation of it, which may focus on peripheral aspects that are more "newsworthy" than the main argument. Many candidates and incumbents have written scholarly books or papers carefully outlining comprehensive positions on complex issues; such positions may be vitally important to predicting their performance in office, yet such positions are difficult to cover adequately in the media, especially on television. A 200-page treatise on economic issues simply does not translate well to a 15-second news story. Most TV campaign coverage is even shorter than that— the length of an average TV political news story fell from 43 to 8 seconds between 1968 and 2000 (Bucy & Grabe, 2007; Hallin, 1992; Lichter, 2001). There is also some evidence that the use of so-called "image bites" (e.g., seeing video footage of a candidate speaking to someone without hearing his or her words) is increasing over time (Bucy & Grabe, 2007).

Interpretation by the Press

When more abstract issues such as economic policies are covered, they tend to be seriously distorted. For example, early in the 1992 Democratic Presidential primary campaign, major rivals Bill Clinton and Paul Tsongas had both written extensive, detailed, and well-thought-out economic programs. What one heard about these from the media, however, was that Clinton favored a modest income tax reduction for middle-income Americans, whereas Tsongas did not, calling Clinton's proposal a "gimmick." What we did not hear was that, except for that relatively minor point, almost the entire economic programs of both candidates were very similar and each offered a reasoned, viable alternative to the programs of Republican incumbent George H. W. Bush. Similarly, in the protracted 2008 Democratic primary fight between Hillary Clinton and Barack Obama, the press highlighted their few differences rather than their many similarities. Because of the media's highlighting of differences (remember, conflict is more newsworthy), the truth can suffer.

Sometimes the political and general culture of a society will affect how certain aspects of a campaign and other political news are covered. Perhaps the most striking example of this is the response to sex scandals of high officials (see Close-Up 8.3 for a historical view). When reports of President Bill Clinton's dalliances with several women began to surface in early 1998, the domestic and international press did not quite know what to make of it. On the one hand, allegations and rumors were reported in great detail, along with rampant speculation about how the President may have lied about these affairs, possibly to the point of a legally impeachable offense. Even as the media wallowed in this saturation coverage and tabloid-like reporting, a curious thing happened. The President's popularity in the polls actually *increased*, to some of its highest levels. Many constituencies were in a quandary. Opposition Republicans were presented with an opportunity for potential political gain but one with definite risks. If they succeeded in impeaching and removing the Democratic President Clinton, they would have an incumbent President Al Gore (as Vice President, he would be Clinton's replacement) to face in the next election, instead of a less experienced challenger. More liberal constituencies were heavily embarrassed by the apparently sexist, insensitive behavior of their President, who had done more to advance the cause of women than any of his predecessors. It is probably no coincidence that Presidential candidates of the next few years (George W. Bush, Al Gore, Barack Obama, John McCain, and Mitt Romney) were all completely above reproach in terms of marital infidelity. No one wanted to deal with the gossip.

Close-Up 8.3: Promiscuous Presidents: How Much Do We Want to Know?

Although President Bill Clinton's (1993–2001) alleged extramarital adventures received far greater coverage in the late 1990s than had the indiscretions of his predecessors in earlier times, such behavior is hardly unprecedented among U.S. Presidents. With a few exceptions, such as Grover Cleveland's alleged out-of-wedlock child who surfaced in the 1884 campaign, relatively few people knew of such liaisons, and those who did either did not care or chose not to make them issues. For example, John F. Kennedy (1961–1963) and Lyndon B. Johnson (1963–1969) were both long rumored to have had extramarital affairs but the press refrained from pursuing the specifics too aggressively. Somewhat earlier, Warren Harding (1921–1923) and Franklin D. Roosevelt (1933–1945) were known to have mistresses but both also had strong wives highly respected in their own right. Woodrow Wilson (1913–1921) was widowed while in office and later married Edith Bolling Galt, with whom he had been rumored to have had a long-term relationship. The second Mrs. Wilson later acted as de facto President after her husband became physically incapacitated, a condition hidden from the public by Mrs. Wilson. Founding father Thomas Jefferson (1801–1809) was widowed early in life and never remarried but later apparently had a long-term relationship, including children, with one of his slaves, Sally Hemings. It may have been as hard for the public of

Jefferson's time to accept that he had a long-term relationship with a Black slave as to accept that he had children out of wedlock with her.

More potentially controversial, and less well known, are claims that the U.S.'s only bachelor President, James Buchanan (1857–1861), was a homosexual who lived for several years with a senator from Alabama, a disturbing piece of news that, when discovered by his fiancée Anne Cole, allegedly led to her suicide. It is also possible that the married James Garfield, killed after being in office only months, had frequent homosexual flings (Hurst, 1998). If the press had not shown some restraint, how might these stories have played out? Is the public better off knowing or not knowing?

The international press responded to Clinton through their various cultural lenses. Some Middle Eastern countries presented Bill Clinton as a sort of immoral clown totally unfit for his office. They wondered how such a powerful country could permit such an irresponsible person to hold office. On the other hand, many Western European nations wrung their journalistic hands at how a puritanical nation was threatening to destroy a highly successful presidency over details of the incumbent's private life, which should remain private and have no bearing in evaluating his public performance in office. Only a few years earlier, the state funeral of former French President François Mitterrand prominently featured both his wife and his longtime mistress, and his children with each woman, among the mourners. In 2012 François Hollande was elected President of France, in spite of not being married to his longtime partner, with whom he had children.

The increasingly nasty political landscape in the second decade of the new millennium has been a cause for concern. What is the effect on voters of reporters and opposition candidates continuing to harp on long-discredited or irrelevant issues like whether Barack Obama was actually born in the U.S. (he was) or whether Mitt Romney bullied a fellow student in high school (he didn't remember)? An interesting study was done to test the effects on the audience of different types of hosts on political talk shows (Vraga et al., 2012). College students viewed one of three prepared political talk shows with a host and two guests discussing environmental policies such as cap and trade. The three versions contained identical factual information but varied the style of the host. One host (the "correspondent") asked the guest questions but did not critique the responses, using the style of Meet the Press or Face the Nation. A second (the "comic") used humor as he pointedly questioned his guests, using the style of The Daily Show, The Colbert Report, or Real Time with Bill Maher. The third host (the "combatant") used a very aggressive style to elicit information and challenge guests' claims, in the style of Chris Matthews or

Bill O'Reilly. Results showed that the correspondent and his program were seen as the most credible, while the combatant and his program were seen as the least credible. Participants also rated the correspondent's program the highest in information value and the combatant's program led to the lowest level of perceived general media trustworthiness. Interestingly, the three programs did not differ in rated entertainment value.

Political Candidate Debates

An exception to television not dealing well with complex candidate positions might be televised debates between candidates, when there is more time to articulate positions and challenge the opponent. U.S. televised debates began in 1960 with the Presidential candidate debates between John F. Kennedy and Richard Nixon. These quadrennial debates were not repeated in the next three elections but have occurred regularly since 1976; see Hinck (1992), Kraus (1988, 1996), and Minow, LaMay, and Gregorian (2008) for analyses of these debates. Here the candidates have a chance to put forward their positions in more detail than is usual for television and, most importantly, in perhaps the only forum where partisans of the other candidate will actually listen to them.

Still, however, the debates are typically analyzed by both media commentators and the public primarily in terms of superficial appearances and performances. Polls and scholars showed that Kennedy "won" in 1960 with those who watched on TV, while Nixon "won" with those who listened on radio (Kraus, 1996). Gerald Ford "lost" the 1976 debates because of his unfortunate remark about Poland (discussed earlier in this chapter). Reagan "won" the 1980 and 1984 debates because he seemed friendly and trustworthy and stuck to generalities; the only exception was the one debate that he "lost" because he became too bogged down in facts and was perceived as not comfortable, eloquent, or accurate. Bill Clinton "won" the third 1992 debate, which involved talking directly to audience members, a format at which he excelled. Third-party candidate Ross Perot impressed viewers in the first debate with his pithy, down-to-earth, no-nonsense replies; by the third debate, however, his glib aphorisms seemed to many to be shallow, hackneyed, and lacking in substance.

Televised Debate Coverage

The media mediate between the debate itself and the viewers' interpretation of it. There has long been criticism of presidential debate coverage as being too superficial. However, Kraus (1988, 1996) argued that such critics often fail to accept the reality of debates and campaigns. In spite of their stated intent to inform, people expect the debates to produce winners and losers. They are an integral part of a candidate's campaign strategy, designed to produce a winner. The debates are part of a society that loves a contest and expects to be constantly entertained by television. The horse race type of debate coverage has always predominated. In a study of the 1980 debates, Robinson and Sheehan (1983) found that CBS and a newspaper wire service both devoted more space to horse race aspects than to any others, and 55 to 60% of the stories failed to contain even one sentence about an issue.

The specific format of a particular debate is whatever the candidates themselves decide, because they will only agree to what they think will help them. Most of this is not really new. The Lincoln–Douglas debates of 1858 in Illinois are often seen as a prototype of pure political debate, but in fact they were actually much more like today's televised candidate debates than we often realize. Candidate Abraham Lincoln manipulated the press and used the occasion to launch his national platform and campaign for the presidency in 1860. At least today technology allows the accurate recording of a debate; Lincoln and Douglas had to rely on the biased memories of each side.

In a careful review of the 1996 debates and their predecessors, Hart and Jarvis (1997) concluded that, despite their problems, the presidential debates have had a positive influence on the political process. "Debates cut through some of the campaign baloney, ground political discourse a bit, sharpen points of difference, make the candidates at least faintly introspective, and restrain overstatements" (p. 1120). Even if they do not do any of these things to the extent we might hope, they do so to a substantial degree. As for how presidential debates changed between 1960 and 1996, Hart and Jarvis conclude that the major change was decreasing certainty and more tentativeness in statements, and an increasing conviviality and sociability. This may be due to what Hart (1994) called the "phenomenology of affect" engendered by the highly intimate medium of television, whereby everything and everyone on television strives to connect more with the viewer at the emotional level. Candidates have increasingly learned this lesson, though some have learned it better than others.

Effects on Viewers

What are the effects of the debates on the public? To begin with, at least the presidential debates draw large audiences, although far smaller recently than in their early years (60% of homes in 1960 vs. 26% in the last debate of 2000) (Jamieson & Waldman, 2003). They are regularly followed by polls about the candidates' debate performance. Campaign handlers know this and carefully plan to try to make a strong impact first.

One very important function is to activate the electorate through engaging citizens, expanding audiences, and creating interest and discussion among voters. The research is inconsistent in regard to the effects of debates on actual voting. They certainly reinforce and crystallize existing attitudes and may actually influence some votes (Benoit & Hansen, 2004). Although viewers may acquire information about candidate positions from watching debates, that information may not always be accurate. For example, careful studies of a

2002 German general election debate between candidates for Chancellor, Gerhard Schroeder and Edmund Stoiber, found that viewers did in fact learn economic information from the debates but that much of this information was misinformation stemming from candidates' selective presentation of facts (Maurer & Reinemann, 2006). Furthermore, attack statements tended to polarize supporters on both sides (Reinemann & Maurer, 2005). Prior exposure to counterarguments against one's preferred candidate had some success in "inoculating" people against persuasive attempts by the other candidate (An & Pfau, 2004). The framing of the coverage is also important. In a study of postdebate coverage of the 2004 U.S. Presidential debates, Pingree, Scholl, and Quenette (2012) found that a "game-framed" story (who won, who lost) decreased viewers' thinking about issues, while a "policy-framed" story increased such thought, relative to a control group seeing no postdebate story. Overall, debate viewing tends to move partisans of the two candidates further apart, compared to partisans who did not view the debates (Holbert, LaMarre, & Landreville, 2009).

One particularly thorny problem of the televised political debate is how to handle third-party candidates. Presumably one would not want to include any and all fringe candidates, most of whom typically have (at least in the United States) minuscule popular support. In the case of a viable third-party candidacy, however, it becomes awkward. For example, in 1980 centrist independent John Anderson showed strong support in early polls. However, to be included in the televised debates, both major candidates would have had to agree to his participation. Because one did not, it was only a two-way debate, and Anderson's fortunes fell sharply after this exclusion. A different solution was reached in 1992, with populist billionaire third-party candidate H. Ross Perot. Perot had a substantial minority of the electorate supporting him, and Democrat Bill Clinton and Republican George H. W. Bush apparently both thought that the damage to them from Perot's debate presence would be less than the public relations damage if they were to exclude him, so Perot participated in a set of three-way debates. Conventional wisdom was that Perot "hung himself" in this format, to which he was not well suited. When Perot ran again in 1996, incumbent President Clinton and Republican Senator Bob Dole felt strong enough to exclude Perot from the debates.

Following the precedent of the presidential debates, increasing numbers of state and local candidates now conduct televised debates.

Now let us turn to looking at how candidates can use the media news coverage to their advantage.

Candidates' Use of News Media

Campaign strategists devote considerable energy to examining how to use news coverage most effectively to create a positive and electable image of their candidate. This is both much cheaper and more believable than using advertising.

Setting the Agenda

Using the news for political gain can be done in many different ways, some of which are an integral part of the daily life of newsmakers. For example, an elected official may have more or fewer news conferences, depending on the desire for press coverage at the time. An incumbent has considerable advantage over the challenger in such matters (Hopmann, de Vreese, & Albaek, 2011). One of the most famous historical examples of skillfully using the incumbency occurred in early summer 1972. While hopeful Democratic Presidential candidates were squabbling among themselves, Republican candidate and incumbent President Richard Nixon captured media attention with a historic trip to China. His landmark voyage opened up the world's largest country to the West and contrasted sharply with the petty bickering of his Democratic opponents, attacking each other in their primary campaigns. More recently, during the 2012 Presidential campaign, President Barack Obama issued an executive order halting deportation of undocumented young adults who had been brought to the country as children. Predictably, his opponent Mitt Romney criticized this as a political move to woo Latino voters, though Obama responded that the Republican House had blocked an earlier attempt to pass a similar law. See Kiousis, McDevitt, and Wu (2005) and Walgrave and Van Aelst (2006) for preliminary models of political agenda setting.

Candidates help to set an agenda by telling us which issues are important in the campaign. Ronald Reagan in 1980 and 1984 told us that it was important to "feel good" about America, and that struck a responsive chord in a nation weary of inflation, Watergate, and international terrorism. The same appeal by incumbent George H. W. Bush in recession-weary 1992 failed to resonate with voters who did not "feel good" about their economic distress. In 1984 Walter Mondale tried unsuccessfully to argue that honesty was an important issue, even to the point of saying that he might have to raise taxes. It is a reality that, in setting the agenda in terms of issues, candidates must consider not only what they believe is important, but also what they believe the public wants to hear. Sometimes one candidate's agenda can affect his or her opponent's by eliciting certain attitudes (see Close-Up 8.4) or even forcing them to deal with issues they may prefer to avoid (Dunn, 2009). Agenda setting then helps to crystallize political attitudes, which can subsequently affect voting behavior (Kiousis & McDevitt, 2008).

Should candidates talk more about what they have done in the past (retrospective) or what they would do in the future if elected (prospective)? Benoit (2006) performed a content analysis of U.S. Presidential campaign messages from 1948 to 2004. He found no differences between winners and losers in the

Close-Up 8.4: Your Emotions Can Affect Your Political Attitudes

People often have very strong feelings about political candidates and issues, but do these emotions affect our attitudes, and, if so, how? One study found that Americans' emotional responses of anger and anxiety affected attitudes to the Iraq War in opposite directions (Huddy, Feldman, & Cassese, 2007). Those who were angered by news reports of the war showed increased approval of the 2003 invasion, perhaps because their anger and associated heightened physiological arousal caused them to reduce their evaluation of the risk. On the other hand, those who responded with anxiety showed reduced support. Positive emotions can also have their effects. Following the 9/11 attacks, people experiencing the emotions of pride and hope showed greater confidence in institutions (Gross, Brewer, & Aday, 2009). This powerful role for emotion in setting a political agenda gives considerable food for thought in this era of increasingly strident political rhetoric and advertising (Gonzalez-Bailon, Banchs, & Kaltenbrunner, 2012).

primary campaigns in terms of the proportions of retrospective and prospective messages. However, in the general election campaigns, winners, especially if they were incumbents, used a larger proportion of retrospective and smaller proportion of prospective messages. This would suggest that candidates would be advised to talk more about what they have done in the past than what they would do in the future. Perhaps voters find this information more useful because it is a "known quantity," rather than speculative promises.

Framing the Candidates

Candidates sometimes come to have a prevailing image that becomes the frame through which all their actions are viewed.

Pinocchio and Dumbo

In the 2000 U.S. Presidential election, Democrat Al Gore came to have the "lying panderer"—"Pinocchio"—frame, while Republican George W. Bush had the "inexperienced dolt"—"Dumbo"—frame (Jamieson & Waldman, 2003). Bush was seen as more trustworthy and Gore as more knowledgeable. Such frames sometimes evolve from the media's attempt to play amateur psychologist and identify and explore the candidates' characters. All too often, however, deep probing of character and its potential effects on qualifications for office does not occur, leaving a frame with a life of its own, and everyone interpreting a candidate's actions simplistically around it.

Because of the Pinocchio frame, Gore's statements were scrutinized much more carefully than Bush's for possibly misleading information. For example, Gore was often chastised for claiming to having invented the Internet. His actual statement, made in an interview with CNN's Wolf Blitzer, was, "During my service in the U.S. Congress, I took the initiative in creating the Internet" (Jamieson & Waldman, 2003, p. 48), reflecting that he had in fact played a large role in securing funding for expanding that new system. Once the word *invented* became attached to that statement, however, there was no correcting it. On the other hand, George Bush's malapropisms like "misunderestimate" were given much more attention than Gore's. Bush's, but not Gore's, speech errors were front-page news, as was his poor performance on an impromptu quiz involving naming world leaders.

Because of the well-known and validated principle of the confirmation bias, we tend to seek, notice, and remember information consistent with our prior beliefs about the candidate and forget or ignore information incongruent with those same beliefs. This bias applies to both journalists and the public. This much greater intentional exposure to political messages we agree with than to those we disagree with also reinforces what some have called the "political self" (Knobloch-Westerwick & Meng, 2011).

These frames were reinforced not only by many journalists but also by comedians. Late-night comedians continually poked fun at Bush's intelligence and speech errors and at Gore's exaggerations and stiffness. Since the early nineties, TV comedy and talk shows have become increasingly important formats, not only for what they say about the candidates but also as expected venues for the candidates to visit. In recent elections, visiting Jay Leno, David Letterman, MTV, and even Jon Stewart's *The Daily Show* have been as necessary as visiting the Iowa caucuses and the New Hampshire primary. Some have argued that this development only goes to show that political news, and perhaps news more generally, has become subordinate to entertainment and just another part of television's overriding aim of entertaining its audience (P. Taylor, 2000).

Changing Frames

Sometimes for various reasons a frame may no longer be desirable and cease to be useful. One of the most dramatic illustrations of this occurred in the U.S. in 2001. Although the dim, inexperienced "Dumbo" image of George W. Bush persisted several months into his presidency, the terrorist attacks of September 11 changed all that. Suddenly, we did not want Dumbo leading us in those tragic times, when difficult decisions had to be made. Overnight, press descriptions of Bush changed radically. His speech errors were no longer noted. He was now described with language like "eloquent" and "thoughtful," and as a "strong leader." Many wrote about how the President had been transformed by September 11, but there are some good arguments that it was actually journalists who had been transformed (Jamieson & Waldman, 2003). Comedians also changed; Bush was the butt of 32% of all late-night jokes in 2001 up until September 11, but only 4% thereafter. Although the predominant frame for George Bush before the attacks was Dumbo, afterwards we did not want to think of our leader in that way, so the idealized frame of the wise and strong leader took hold. Using the confirmation bias, reporters and the public noted Bush's statements and behaviors that fit this new image and neglected those congruent with the old Dumbo frame.

Creating Pseudo-Events

One way to increase news coverage beyond what is routinely expected is to create "pseudo-events" to capture media coverage and, in effect, produce many hours of free advertising. One of the most creative and successful examples was when Bob Graham ran for governor of Florida in 1978. Although he began as an unknown state legislator with 3% name recognition and 0% of the projected vote, he overcame this largely due to his "work days" project. During the campaign he worked for 100 days doing different jobs around the state, one job per day, apparently to learn the demands and needs of different sectors of the electorate. These were heavily covered by the media and worked greatly to Graham's advantage, in spite of the obvious self-serving motivation behind them. He defused some of the predictable criticism of opportunistic gimmickry by dressing appropriately and actually working a full eight hours on each job. The first nine days were done before the media were invited in, so Graham had time to fine-tune his program. Photos from the work days were of course used in his campaign advertising, but, more importantly, they were also widely covered as news. In his campaign speeches he made references to insights he had gained from these days, and he continued making them intermittently after becoming governor, all in all confirming the impression that he had actually learned from the project and was not merely dealing in transparent political grandstanding. It was a brilliant example of the use of news media for one's own political gain; no amount of paid advertising could have bought what Graham gained for free in the news coverage.

Some new opportunities for pseudo-events appeared in the United States beginning in 1992, with the advent of "talk-show politics." Candidates Clinton, Bush, and Perot were all interviewed on MTV, *Larry King Live*, and other entertainment talk shows. In fact, these programs opened new avenues for the candidates to present themselves as "real people" who were very approachable. Lasting images were created during some of these appearances. When amateur musician Bill Clinton donned sunglasses and played the saxophone with the band on the *Arsenio Hall Show*, the contrast between the energetic and hip young baby-boomer candidate and the aging and cautious George H. W. Bush and the stodgy and curmudgeonly Ross Perot was striking.

Creating pseudo-events can backfire, however. In 1988, modest-sized Democratic candidate Michael Dukakis sat in a tank to try to project a "strong on defense" image, but instead looked more like a small turtle sticking his head out of a large shell. Likewise, Ivy Leaguer George H. W. Bush's occasional attempts to don cowboy boots and eat pork rinds to appear like a "true Texan" did not always ring true. His son George W. Bush, who actually grew up in Texas, came across more believably in this role.

Dealing with Attacks from the Opponent

In the 1992 Democratic primary campaign, candidate Bill Clinton had been accused of an extramarital affair that allegedly occurred years before. The forum he chose to respond to this was a 60 Minutes TV newsmagazine interview where he and his wife Hillary admitted that there had been "problems" in their marriage but said that those had been worked through and they were thoroughly reconciled. It was a masterful combination of confession and avoidance of admitting critical information. Clinton's story of how his daughter Chelsea hugged him after hearing of the accusations melted people's hearts. They were ready to forgive, interpreting what they saw on TV as sincere repentance and love for family. Shortly after the interview, the alleged affair ceased to be a campaign issue. It is hard to imagine how it could have been so effectively refuted and defused in a traditional press conference or interview. Later, when confronted with other allegations of personal and real estate scandal, Clinton apparently forgot his own lesson and did not meet the criticism so directly. When Barack Obama was embarrassed by the publication of his former pastor Jeremiah Wright's apparently racist and unpatriotic comments in 2008, he confronted it directly by publishing a lengthy and thoughtful paper about issues of race in America, defusing the criticism while at the same time contributing something positive to discussion of a major unspoken campaign issue.

How a political candidate responds to attacks from the opposition can be very important. An attack left unchallenged may be assumed by the electorate to be true, a mistake made by John Kerry in not responding more directly to the infamous and false "Swift Boat" allegations from the Vietnam War in the 2004 campaign. On the other hand, an overly vicious or petty response may actually engender support for the opponent. An incumbent has less flexibility than a challenger in handling attacks. In some cases, rather than "dignifying" an attack with a response, it may be better to ignore or brush it off, as challenger Ronald Reagan did with his oft-repeated "Well, there you go again" response to President Jimmy Carter in the 1980 debates.

There always exists the danger of a backlash of sympathy for the opponent if an attack is perceived as too unfair or mean-spirited. This tends to keep potential mudslinging in check. However, sometimes this fear may also suppress useful dialogue. For example, in the historic 2008 Democratic primary, which pitted the first serious female candidate, Hillary Clinton, against the first serious African American candidate, Barack Obama, the candidates and other challengers meticulously avoided any criticism that might suggest women or African Americans were not qualified for the office. Similarly, Obama made little mention of Republican John McCain's advanced age (72) in the general election campaign. At the same time, all candidates were squarely attacked for their policies, a sure sign they were being taken seriously. If a candidate is not attacked by opponents, the perception is of a less-than-serious candidate. If a candidate is far ahead in the polls, he or she usually refrains from attacking the opponent at all, because an attack only tends to legitimatize that opponent.

The Need to Be Taken Seriously

For lesser-known candidates, the most difficult aspect of their campaign is convincing the media to take them seriously. If the public and the media do not perceive someone as having a realistic chance of winning, acceptance or rejection of that candidate's stand on issues or of the candidate themselves is largely irrelevant. Although polls showed that large numbers of Americans favored the positions of moderate independent candidate John Anderson in the 1980 Presidential race, less than 10% eventually voted for him, largely because they felt that he had no chance of winning. In 1992, early summer polls showed Ross Perot's support to be substantial enough to conceive of his winning the presidency. However, his support gradually eroded, although he still acquired a larger share of the November vote (around 20%) than any other third-party candidate in modern times. When he ran again in 1996, he failed to do as well. Because no one other than a Republican or Democrat has been elected President of the United States since 1848, people perceive such an outcome as highly unlikely, a social perception that can quickly become a self-fulfilling prophecy.

Religious Discourse and Politics

As discussed in Chapter 6, there has always been an uneasy relationship between religion and popular culture, especially in the United States. In American politics, lip service has traditionally been paid to a vague civil religion, with occasional references to God, but until fairly recently, not much explicit "God talk." Every U.S. President, except Roman Catholic John Kennedy, has adhered to some sort of Protestant Christian faith, though that has varied widely from Jimmy Carter's born-again Southern Baptist faith to Thomas Jefferson's deism. In an interesting analysis of inaugural and State of the Union addresses from 1933 to 2005, Coe and Domke (2006) found an increase in explicit references to God by Presidents, starting with Ronald Reagan in 1980, with instances being particularly high for Reagan and George W. Bush. This change probably reflects the rise of Christian conservatives' political power. Because of the very recent breakdown of the Republican–Christian alliance and the Democrats' rediscovery of talking about faith (see Chapter 6), this issue will be a very interesting one to follow in the future (see Wallis, 2005 for further discussion).

Case Study: Press Coverage of the 2000 U.S. Presidential Election

The historic 2000 Presidential election on November 7 was the closest race in U.S. history. Republican George W. Bush and Democrat Al Gore were virtually tied in electoral votes the morning after the election. For the next 36 days, the outcome was uncertain, as the controversy swirled around the count in the state of Florida. The election was only finally decided on December 12, when a close decision by the U.S. Supreme Court favored the claims of George Bush. After this decision, Al Gore conceded; but it will probably never be definitively established which candidate actually won Florida, where the margin determining the outcome of the popular vote was within a hundredth of 1%, with the winner receiving the entire electoral vote. The role of the press in covering this election and the postelection process was carefully examined in an illuminating book by Jamieson and Waldman (2003), *The Press Effect*.

Election Night Coverage

When networks make projections that turn out to be accurate (as most do), they tend to take credit for their skill. However, when they have to retract their projections, as they did repeatedly with the 2000 Florida Presidential returns, they tended to blame "bad data," even though all networks were drawing on basically the same data, from the Voter News Service (VNS).

Premature Overconfident Projections

On election evening, the networks projected Florida first for Gore and later reversed themselves and called it for Bush. Around 10:15 p.m. Eastern Time they retracted both and placed the state (and thus the whole election) back into the "too-close-to-call" category. Several smaller states were also very close and undecided until well into the next day or days. At 2:20 a.m. the networks called the election for Bush, but retracted this call at 3:50 a.m.

As more returns came in and the election results became increasingly uncertain—the opposite of the usual trend—reporters and pundits struggled in their interpretation. There were numerous discussions about "egg on their faces" and "eating crow," as well as extended discussions about possible scenarios ("if Gore wins these three states, he could still lose Florida and win ..."). Some of this was accompanied by startlingly low-tech graphics, scribbled on paper by network analysts and anchors with crayons, and held up to the camera!

Framing the Electoral Uncertainty

Jamieson and Waldman (2003) argue that, during the next five weeks, the prevailing frame for discussing the outcome of the election gradually came to increasingly favor Bush over Gore, although the objective data coming in over that time did not necessarily do so. The three possible frames, each drawing on true information, would be that (1) Gore had won the popular vote and was ahead in the electoral vote, and the final outcome in the Electoral College was uncertain; (2) Bush was ahead in the key state that would decide the final electoral vote and thus was the presumed victor unless Gore's campaign proved otherwise; or (3) neither candidate was ahead nor held an advantage over the other. In the news coverage over those five weeks (especially the influential Sunday morning network news shows), the bias favoring the second frame, with Bush as presumed victor, gradually emerged, as Bush's campaign people managed the media more effectively than Gore's. (See Wicks (2001) for discussion of the idea of framing of news events.)

How did they do this? First of all, Republicans began to frame the postelection hand recount as flawed and unfair. The Bush camp framed the initial machine count, which showed him ahead by a few hundred votes out of several million cast, as legitimate, and the subsequent statewide hand recount as suspect and unreliable. The latter was always referred to by Republicans as a "recount" rather than a "full count," "complete count," or "hand count." Attempts to force a recount were described as attempts to "overturn the results." Also, the Bush campaign talked openly of challenging Gore's winning results in other close states like New Mexico, Oregon, Wisconsin, and Iowa, but Gore's camp did not aggressively do likewise.

Perhaps the most telling reframing related to the decisions about the legitimacy of the overseas absentee ballots, which came in late and had to be counted by hand. Gore attempted to have those strictly evaluated, with those not meeting specified criteria (such as containing a postmark no later than Election Day) thrown out, while the Bush campaign framed those ballots as "military ballots" (which only some of them were) and questioned the patriotism of those trying to "disenfranchise" the voting of our "brave men and women defending our country." Both sides insisted on strict adherence to the law only when it favored their candidate. In the case of the absentee ballots, whose legitimacy was decided very idiosyncratically by each county, the Bush frame casting Gore's adherence to the law as an attack on the patriotism of the military was adopted by the news media, which came to see Gore's moves as illegitimate and as a desperate attempt to overturn the election results favoring Bush. Thus, 680 questionable votes were accepted and counted, even though some had no postmark or a postmark after Election Day, and in some cases were from people who had already voted. These may well have determined the election, with Bush's final certification of victory reflecting only a 537-vote margin.

The frame of Bush as the apparent winner and Gore as the stubborn loser had become the prevailing network news frame by late November. Frequent photo shots of Bush supporters holding "Sore Loserman" signs parodying the Democratic "Gore Lieberman" placards supported this frame. When Bush started naming people to his cabinet but Gore did not, the perception of the inevitability of a Bush victory was further reinforced. Implications of "stealing the election" were raised in relation to Bush only three times in the five weeks of Sunday news shows, but 12 times in connection with Gore. Also, 20 out of 23 times the word "concession" appeared in a question over these weeks, it was applied to Gore.

The contest finally ended 36 days after the election, when the U.S. Supreme Court ruled to halt the further counting of votes, arguing that the petitioner Bush would be "irreparably harmed" by continuing the count, thereby "casting a cloud upon what he claims to be the legitimacy of his election" (Jamieson & Waldman, 2003, p. 127). The vote was 7–2 that there were constitutional problems with the state-court-mandated recount and 5–4 to halt the count and declare Bush the victor. After the ruling in Bush vs. Gore, Al Gore promptly conceded the election, his legal recourse exhausted.

Once Bush had been declared the victor, and especially after he assumed office on January 20, 2001, the press seemed eager to assert his legitimacy and downplayed any consideration of the possibility that the wrong man may have assumed the Presidency. In fact, in 2001 there were two largely unknown recounts of the Florida votes, designed to answer the question for the historical record. The first, by the *Miami Herald*, *USA Today*, and Knight-Ridder, produced eight alternative sets of results, depending on the standard used to judge the acceptability of ballots; five of these favored Bush and three favored Gore. The second, more comprehensive, recount was conducted by the Associated Press, *The New York Times*, the *Washington Post*, and the *Wall Street Journal*. This count produced 44 separate results, 22 favoring Bush and 22 favoring Gore! Because these were not available until shortly after the terrorist attacks of September 11, 2001, their release did not receive much attention by a press and country too traumatized from terrorism to consider it might have made a mistake at the last Presidential inauguration. The fact remains, though, that we will never definitively know which candidate received more votes in Florida and thus actually "won" the election. It truly was "too close to call," but that is not an option when a country needs a winner to assume office.

Now that we have considered a candidate's use of news for political advantage, let us consider the most directly partisan form of political media, namely political advertising. Although political advertising has much in common with advertising in general (see Chapter 5), there are also some important differences (Thorson, Christ, & Caywood, 1991).

Political Advertising

One of the major political issues of our time is the rapidly escalating cost of running for office, due in large part to the increased purchase of television time and hiring of media consultants. This trend was greatly accelerated in the U.S. by the 2010 Supreme Court decision *Citizens United vs. Federal Election Commission*, which essentially removed all limits on campaign spending by political action committees, which are not formally linked to candidates and which can be formally disavowed if their claims are determined to have gone too far, but which nonetheless support them. Although the political process has always been unduly influenced by the wealthy, that trend has since 2010 accelerated to an alarming degree (Frank, 2012). Although the arguments of the campaign finance reform debate are outside the scope of this book, we want to examine the purposes and effects of political advertising, the aim of which is to affect the perceived reality of a candidate in our minds.

Purposes

Name Recognition

A primary purpose for lesser-known candidates and those campaigning outside of their previous constituency (e.g., a senator or governor running for President) is simply awareness and recognition of their name. Voters must have heard of a candidate before they can be expected to have any image of or attitude to that candidate. Name recognition is the perennial problem of "dark horse" challenger candidates for any office. In this sense, the goal of political advertising is not unlike the goal of advertising for a new product on the market.

Agenda Setting

Political advertising can also set the agenda on issues by conveying to us what issues we should feel are particularly important (Schleuder, McCombs, & Wanta, 1991). Obviously candidates emphasize those issues on which they believe they are strongest. For example, an incumbent president with several foreign policy successes but economic problems at home will try to position foreign policy as a major issue in the campaign, whereas the opposing candidate may try to direct the agenda toward domestic economic issues. Sometimes such decisions are not so clear-cut. For example, Democrats in 2008 had to decide whether to make age an issue in regard to Republican John McCain, who, if he had won, would have been the oldest president ever elected. On the one hand, they stood to gain if voters became concerned that 72 was too old to begin the job. On the other, they stood to lose if voters perceived them to be too mean-spirited and unfairly attacking a nice older gentleman (and decorated veteran) fully capable of functioning competently in office. For better or worse, Democrats chose not to make age an issue, the same choice they had made running against Ronald Reagan in 1980 (age 69) and 1984 or against Bob Dole (age 72) in 1996.

If a viewer is primed by prior exposure to a story about the economy (for example), associations from that initial concept activate related information in memory, causing it to reach a more conscious level than information about other topics (Collins & Loftus, 1975; Schleuder et al., 1991). Thus when it comes to processing later information, such as a political ad, the agenda is set that this issue is important. Either a prior ad or a news story could serve this priming function. A candidate must therefore be concerned about an ad appearing immediately following a news story that inadvertently sets a different agenda. For example, a candidate vulnerable on economic issues would not want his or her ad to follow a news story about gloomy economic indicators.

Sometimes an agenda of a different sort is set by political advertising, perhaps in ways not intended by the creators of the ads. Certain social, ethnic, or racial groups may be marginalized simply by their non-appearance in advertising. For example, a careful analysis of television advertising in the Guatemalan Presidential election of 2007, in which a Mayan candidate (Rigoberta Menchu) competed for the first time, showed that ads for all candidates, including Menchu, showed few indigenous peoples, and only in minor roles like background crowd members (Connolly-Ahern & Castells i Talens, 2010). One would never know from seeing these commercials that a majority of the population of Guatemala was indigenous Maya, who had long been politically marginalized.

Image-Building

Political advertising also seeks to express an image of a candidate, or perhaps reinforce, soften, or redefine an existing image. This construction of an image is done especially effectively by television, which communicates nonverbal as well as verbal behaviors. One effective way to communicate an image is through eliciting emotional responses in the viewer (Englis, 1994). Another is to cultivate a candidate's particular image of morality (Page & Duffy, 2009). The widespread use of media consultants testifies to the importance of image-building. Polls are continually taken by a candidate's campaign staff to determine what issues voters are concerned about and what aspects of their own and their opponent's campaign attract or trouble them. The candidate's image is then tailored accordingly.

Some studies of candidate image have focused on general affective traits or personality or social attributes, and compared the image a voter has with actual voting behavior (Andersen & Kibler, 1978; Nimmo & Savage, 1976). More situational approaches have demonstrated a relationship between voters' ratings of candidate behaviors and voting preference (Husson, Stephen, Harrison, & Fehr, 1988). Another approach has been to study how voters use their cognitive schemas to form an image of a candidate, which subsequently affects their evaluation (Garramone, Steele, & Pinkleton, 1991). Lau (1986) argued that there are four general schemas that people use to process political information: candidate personality factors, issues, group relations, and party identification. Many voters fairly consistently use one of these schemas more than the others. There are limits, of course, to what a media campaign can do; an urban candidate may never look comfortable and convincing astride a horse making a political ad for the rural West. Also, one cannot assume that all voters will understand an ad in the same way. The image that different members of the public construct in response to the same ad may be strikingly different because of their unique experiences and political predilections. What one viewer sees as a sincere interest in the common people looks to another to be offensively hokey and opportunistic.

Issue Exposition

Occasionally, ads develop a candidate's position on issues. Such appeals are most conducive to lengthy print or Internet ads but few voters will read such material. Of course, due to the mass nature of media communication, even a minuscule percentage of the population reading a newspaper ad might be considered a success for the candidate. If the issue appeal is simple, even a TV spot can effectively communicate a candidate's position (Just, Crigler, & Wallach, 1990).

Fund-Raising

Finally, ads may be used to raise money. Barack Obama was incredibly successful raising money from many small donors over the Internet in 2008. Although ads are a major expense, they may also bring in money. Of course, they also do so indirectly by keeping the candidate's name in the public consciousness, a prerequisite for any successful fund-raising.

Appeals in Political Advertising

Political ads use most of the same types of appeals discussed in Chapter 5, on advertising. Various psychological appeals are quite common. Basic appeals to security come out in the "strong national defense" and "law and order" appeals.

Fear appeals can be especially powerful in political advertising. For example, in George H. W. Bush's infamous Willie Horton ad of the 1988 Presidential campaign, viewers were encouraged to fear that Democratic opponent Michael Dukakis would let dangerous criminals go free, citing the example of Massachusetts felon Willie Horton, who had been released on parole and then committed murder. The fact that Horton was an African American subtly played to White fears about Black criminality and may have reinforced racist stereotypes of African American men. Fear appeals, in general, are most often used by incumbents, playing on voters' fear of the unknown quantity of what the challenger's work in office would be like.

Patriotic appeals are particularly common in political advertising, with certain national symbols like the flag very commonly present, even for regional and local races. Other patriotic symbols like familiar public buildings, monuments like the Statue of Liberty, and national historical symbols are also widely used.

Family and affiliation appeals are seen in the typical family campaign ad photo of a candidate with smiling supportive spouse and children, as if being married or a parent somehow qualified one to hold public office. It is interesting and ironic that an occupation virtually guaranteed to take enormous amounts of time away from family is so heavily "sold" with such family appeals. Using only pure logic, one might argue that an appeal from an unmarried, childless candidate who could say, "I have no family responsibilities; I'll spend all my time in office working for you" would be the most successful. However, such an appeal would probably be a dismal failure.

Testimonials are often used, sometimes from famous endorsers such as a senator or President plugging for the local candidate, sometimes by the man or woman in the street saying how much they trust a candidate to look after their interests if elected. A popular President or other office holder of one's party is eagerly sought for testimonial purposes; an unpopular one may be an embarrassing liability for a party's candidates for other offices; Republican candidates tried to keep their distance from the relatively unpopular incumbent George W. Bush in 2008.

Sometimes certain types of appeals are effective with particular demographic groups. For example, a study of American TV ads targeting Latinos found that these ads were very positive in nature and tended to focus on this group, encouraging their identification with the candidates and inviting them to see their political role as valued and important (Connaughton & Jarvis, 2004). Although most people learn something from political advertising, those who are more politically aware learn even more, especially when it comes to making inferences beyond what is explicitly stated in the ad. However, the least politically aware may actually be the most susceptible to persuasion by the ads (Valentino, Hutchings, & Williams, 2004). See Close-Up 8.5 for some examples of ads with various appeals from the American Presidential election of 2008.

Close-Up 8.5: Sample Political TV Ads from the 2008 U.S. Presidential Campaign (Mottola & Margolis, 2009).

McCain (Republican) Ad #1: Positive inspirational appeal

Announcer: "It was a time of uncertainty, hope, and change: the summer of love. Half a world away, another kind of love … of country. [Visual of Vietnam War] John McCain, shot down, bayoneted, tortured. Offered early release, he said, "No." He'd sworn an oath. Home, he turned to public service. His philosophy: before party, polls, and self—America. A maverick, John McCain tackled campaign reform, military reform, spending reform. He took on Presidents, partisans, and popular opinions. He believes our world is dangerous, our economy in shambles. John McCain doesn't always tell us what we hope to hear. Beautiful words cannot make our lives better. But a man who has always put his country and her people before self, before politics, can. Don't hope for a better life. Vote for one. McCain" (Mottola & Margolis, 2009, p. 112).

McCain Ad #2: Attack ad

Announcer: "*Education Week* says Obama hasn't made a significant mark on education. That he's elusive on accountability. A staunch defender of the existing public school monopoly. Obama's one accomplishment? Legislation to teach comprehensive sex education to kindergarteners. Learning about sex before learning to read? Barack Obama. Wrong on education. Wrong for your family" (p. 115).

Note: The major claim of this ad (sex education in kindergarten) was not true and provoked a backlash against McCain.

Obama (Democrat) Ad #1: Inspirational

Obama: "We want an end to this war. And we want diplomacy and peace. Not only can we save the environment, we can create jobs—and opportunity. We're tired of fear, we're tired of divisions. We want something new. We want to turn the page. [Cheering] The world as it is, is not the world it has to be" (p. 126).

Obama Ad #2: Attack on McCain's wealth

Obama: "Maybe you're struggling just to pay the mortgage on your home. But recently, John McCain said, the fundamentals of our economy are strong. Hum. Then again, that same day when asked how many houses he owns? McCain lost track. He couldn't remember. Well, it's seven. Seven houses. And here's one house America can't afford to let John McCain move into [visual of White House]" (p. 128).

As voters absorb political information from a variety of sources, including media news stories and political advertising, there is subsequently considerable source confusion about where that information came from (Johnson, 2007). For example, Yegiyan and Grabe (2007) found that, a week after exposure to political news stories, conventional political ads, or "news-like" political ads, people showed considerable confusion about the source of the information; in particular, they incorrectly remembered the information in news-like ads to have come from news stories. Given the greater general credibility of news over advertising sources, it is easy to see how such source confusion could work to a candidate's advantage.

Negative Advertising

The issue of how stridently and directly to attack the opponent in advertising is a major question that all political campaigns must deal with. Attacks on the opposition may be highly effective *if* they are perceived as fair. Regardless of their factual merit, or lack thereof, if the ads are perceived as mean-spirited "cheap shots," they can boomerang disastrously (Garramone, 1984, 1985). Fear of such a scenario sends shivers up the spines of all politicians and often causes them to not take chances in this area, as seen in the Democrats' decision not to make John McCain's or Ronald Reagan's age an issue. Nonetheless, negative political advertising continues to be widely used (Geer, 2006; West, 2005).

It is not clear whether or how much negative advertising has increased in recent years. By some counts (Kaid & Johnston, 1991), negative advertising increased in the 1980s over the 1970s to about one-third of the TV ads in the Presidential campaigns. On the other hand, the Campaign Discourse Mapping Project (Jamieson & Waldman, 1997) concluded that attack ads had been roughly constant in percentage since 1960. Some argue that the outrage at negative advertising that was common in an earlier era has become much more muted since the late eighties, as voters have apparently accepted some degree of mudslinging and even falsifying the opponent's record as normal (Jamieson, 1992). Still others argue that it is not even conceptually clear what constitutes a negative political ad (Richardson, 2001).

Attacks may be strong without being direct or even mentioning the opponent by name. For example, one of the most notorious historical instances was incumbent President Lyndon Johnson's 1964 TV ad (withdrawn after one airing due to complaints) showing a little girl in a field of daisies. Suddenly an atomic bomb explodes and we hear Johnson's voiceover: "These are the stakes: to make a world in which all God's children can live, or go into the dark" (cited in Devlin, 1987). Republican candidate Barry Goldwater was never mentioned, but the ad clearly played on viewers' fears of his hawkishness.

Does negative advertising work? The answer seems to be yes and no. Research suggests that negative ads are remembered well, even though they are generally disliked (Garramone, 1984; Garramone, Atkin, Pinkleton, & Cole, 1990; Klein & Ahluwalia, 2005; Lau, Sigelman, Heldman, & Babbitt, 1999; Meffert, Chung, Joiner, Waks, & Garst, 2006; Newhagen & Reeves, 1991; Phillips, Urbany, & Reynolds, 2008). This finding is quite consistent with the widespread negative attitudes about political attack advertising and the popular perception that such ads apparently work (Kaid & Boydston, 1987). Negative emotional ads are remembered better than positive emotional ads, perhaps due to their greater use of automatic, as opposed to controlled, cognitive processing (Lang, 1991, 2000) and peripheral rather than central processing (Kahneman, 2011; Petty et al., 2002). There is also evidence that negative ads engender cynical attitudes (Schenk-Hamlin, Procter, & Rumsey, 2000). It may also be important whether the negative message is embedded in a positive or negative context. Messages that contrast with their context are recalled better (Basil, Schooler, & Reeves, 1991). This negative attitude toward attack ads may have two undesired effects for the candidate: it may erode support among current partisans, and it may lead opposing partisans to draw up defenses to strengthen their position (J. M. Phillips et al., 2008). See Close-Up 8.6 for an examination of a celebrated 2008 case in which intended political satire was widely interpreted as a vicious attack.

Close-Up 8.6: When Is It Satire and When Is It Just Plain Mean?

During the U.S. Presidential campaign of 2008, the *New Yorker* magazine published what turned out to be an extremely controversial cover illustration. The cartoonish drawing showed Michelle and Barack Obama dressed as Muslim terrorists fist-bumping each other in the Oval office. She carried a machine gun and sported a large Afro. He was dressed in a caftan and turban with a portrait of Osama bin Laden on the wall and an American flag burning in the fireplace. Although editor David Remnick and artist Barry Blitt professed surprise and disbelief at the critical offense taken, Harvard social psychologist Mahzarin Banaji (2008) argued that they should not have been. The magazine claimed that the drawing was a satirical piece attempting to skewer the political far right's attempt to distort Obama's record and exploit racial and religious prejudice by depicting the future President as a Muslim apologist for Islamic terrorism. However, Banaji argued the simple associative power of the image (Obama = terrorist) far overshadowed the intended, more intellectual appeal of satirizing the far right. For example, she says, would anyone seriously find a cartoon of an older man and young teen boy fist-bumping after having enjoyed sex to be a satirical condemnation of pedophilia? She concludes that "it is the moral responsibility of the artist to know about how art is received by its intended audience" (p. B13).

Whether negative ads directly affect voting behavior is less clear. It may depend what the source of the negative message is, whether the focus is issue- or person-oriented, at what point in the campaign they are used, and what sort of response is made to the negative attack. In a study of effects of ads in the 1996 Presidential general election campaign, Kaid (1997) concluded that negative ads did affect voters' image of the candidate in intended ways, and that this in turn affected voting behavior. In a study of a U.S. Senate race, Lemert, Wanta, and Lee (1999) found that attack ads by a Republican candidate, coupled with a pledge from the Democrat not to use negative advertising, led to a lower voting rate by Republicans but not Democrats. Negative ads, in the framework of comparing the two candidates directly, may be the most effective way to produce attack advertising. Studies have shown that negative comparative ads reduce preference for the targeted candidate without much backlash against the sponsoring candidate (Pinkleton, 1998), and that negative ads stimulate voter turnout (Goldstein & Freedman, 2002) and are more effective than positive ads in reinforcing commitment of prior supporters (J. M. Phillips et al., 2008). Finally, in yet another example of the third-person effect (defined in Chapter 2), people believe strongly that negative ads affect other people and other political parties more than themselves and their party (Gardikiotis, 2008; Hoffner & Rehkoff, 2011; Wei & Lo, 2007).

Sometimes there are other negative influences besides advertising and news. See Close-Up 8.7 for a discussion of a popular political documentary film that influenced the political landscape in the 2004 U.S. Presidential election.

Close-Up 8.7: The Effect of a Documentary Film on Political Perceptions: The Case of *Fahrenheit 9/11*

All sorts of influences may affect political attitudes and perceptions, including some surprising ones. One unusual event in the 2004 U.S.

Presidential campaign between incumbent George W. Bush and challenger Massachusetts Senator John Kerry was the release of Michael Moore's polemical documentary *Fahrenheit 9/11*. Although Moore had long been known for hard-hitting documentaries in the classic muckraking tradition, including the previous *Bowling for Columbine* and *Roger and Me*, *Fahrenheit 9/11* drew his largest audience and became the most-seen documentary in U.S. film history, competing with blockbuster summer films. *Fahrenheit 9/11* was a scathing portrayal of the Bush administration and seemed designed to evoke strong anger against George W. Bush. It used accepted historical and news footage but put them together in creative ways. One of the most famous scenes was the shot of the President reading a story to a group of children just after he had heard the World Trade Center had been attacked. The film was praised as a brilliant political documentary and decried as a grossly unfair and biased piece of propaganda. It may have been both.

What effect did viewing this film have? Communications researchers Lance Holbert and Glenn Hansen (2006, 2008; see also Holbert, Hansen, Caplan, & Mortensen, 2007) attempted to answer this question. Examining Bush and Kerry supporters who either had or had not seen *Fahrenheit 9/11*, Holbert and Hansen found that anger toward Bush after seeing the film mediated impressions of his performance in the televised debates. Those who saw the film (both Bush and Kerry supporters) increased their anger toward Bush and this led them to rate his debate performance as poorer. Holbert and Hansen argue that a potent emotional stimulus such as this film can have a crucial role in forming political opinion.

Effects of Political Advertising

The effects of political ads, as well as other forms of political communication in media, can be many. The study of such effects has come from the perspectives of political science, advertising, social psychology, and communication. In spite of the prevalent perception that the overriding intent of political ads is to cause attitude change in people, relatively few political ads actually change anyone's mind, in the sense of causing them to switch loyalties from one candidate to another (Blumler & McQuail, 1969; Cwalina, Falkowski, & Kaid, 2000). This is not to say that they are ineffective, however. Political ads frequently help crystallize existing attitudes by sharpening and elaborating them. For example, perhaps someone was slightly leaning toward Mitt Romney for President in 2012 because of his experience in the private sector and as Governor of Massachusetts. Political advertising for Romney may help flesh out that attitude by providing more information about his positions, past performance as a governor, and general intangible impressions about him. Similarly, political advertising may reinforce existing attitudes in voters, keeping in the fold voters who are leaning toward a candidate but not strongly committed. Such reinforcement is more likely to translate into voting on Election Day and greater resistance to an opposing candidate's attempts to change that attitude. There is also evidence that political advertising, at least on a local level, leads to more political information-seeking through television, the Internet, and social contacts (Cho, 2008, 2011). Political strategists are always concerned about reinforcing "soft" support from voters who are leaning toward their candidate but not strongly committed. Many ads are targeted at such people to help ensure that they turn out on Election Day.

Occasionally political advertising may actually convert a voter from one candidate to another, but this is fairly rare and did not increase substantially with the advent of television (see Berelson, Lazarsfeld, & McPhee, 1954; Lazarsfeld, Berelson, & Gaudet, 1948, for pre-TV studies). Of course, because some elections are decided by a tiny fraction of the vote, such swing votes are not unimportant.

Reactions to political advertising may also depend on the connection that the voter feels with the candidate (Alwitt, Deighton, & Grimm, 1991). Such an attitudinal bond may be based on an objective belief ("I support her program for the economy") or on a subjective emotion ("I feel good about him") criterion. Sometimes the two may be opposed—there may be intellectual agreement with the candidate's positions on issues but passionate opposition on more emotional levels, or vice versa. Also, an image-oriented ad may have a different impact than an issue-oriented ad. For example, Geiger and Reeves (1991) found that candidates were evaluated more favorably after issue ads than image ads, but visual memory for the candidate was better following an image ad. Of course, it is very difficult to evaluate the effects of political ads in isolation, as virtually all voters are also exposed to political news stories, personal conversations, and other influences. See Faber (1992), Jamieson (1992), Johnson-Cartee and Copeland (1997), and Kaid and Holtz-Bacha (1995) for reviews of political advertising and its effects.

Television as Cultivator of Political Moderation

Before leaving the topic of politics and media, let us examine the argument of one group of researchers who believe that television, in a very general sense, shapes our political attitudes and perceived reality about politics in some subtle ways. Using cultivation theory, Gerbner, Gross, Morgan, and Signorielli (1982, 1984) examined the relationship between television viewing in general and political attitudes. Using data gathered for several years by the National Opinion Research Center in their General Social Surveys, Gerbner et al. (1984) looked at the correlation between the amount of TV viewing (and other media use) and political self-designation on a liberal–moderate–conservative dimension.

Frequent TV viewers were most likely to label themselves as politically moderate, whereas frequent newspaper readers labeled themselves conservative and heavy radio listeners labeled themselves liberal. This relationship was quite consistent within various demographic subgroups, especially so for the conservatives and the moderates. Among light viewers, there was consistently greater difference of opinion between liberals and conservatives on several different specific issues than there was between the liberal and conservative heavy viewers. Gerbner and colleagues (1982, 1984; see also Morgan et al., 2009) argued that television, with its mass-market appeal, avoids extreme positions that might offend people and thus by default it cultivates middle-of-the-road perspectives.

Heavy and light viewers may use information differently. In a study of the 2000 Bush–Gore U.S. Presidential election, Cho (2005) found that high TV news viewers were more likely than low TV news viewers to decide on a candidate based on image perception and were less likely to vote based on policy issues.

This sort of cultivation is not limited to North American culture, although the specific effects may differ in different places. For example, Morgan and Shanahan (1991, 1995) found that Argentine adolescents who were heavy TV viewers were more likely to agree that people should submit to authority, approve of limits on freedom of speech, and believe that poor people are to blame for their own poverty. In a country having recently come out from under a repressive military dictatorship, it appeared that television "cultivates views that provide legitimacy to authoritarian political practices" (Morgan & Shanahan, 1991, p. 101). See Morgan (1990) for other applications of cultivation theory in international settings. For an interesting comparison of the 1988 Presidential elections in France and the United States, see the readings in Kaid, Gerstle, and Sanders (1991). For a comparison of effects of political advertising in France, Germany, and Poland, see Cwalina et al. (2000).

Television may interact with political ideology in other ways to subtly support or undercut existing structures in a society. The social and commercial realities of television may sometimes produce politically strange bedfellows. See Close-Up 8.8 for an interesting example.

Close-Up 8.8: Television and Ideology: A Brazilian Case Study

Does television serve to indoctrinate or perpetuate political and social ideologies? The question is a complex one with no easily generalizable answer. The Brazilian telenovela (soap opera) is an instructive example.

In many developing countries television is controlled largely by the economic elites, often with close political ties to right-wing ideologies. This was true in military-ruled Brazil in the 1970s, when the huge Globo communications network thrived and rose to become the world's fourth largest TV network of the time, after the big three in the United States. Globo came to be acclaimed for its high-quality programming, which was exported to dozens of countries. The most popular shows, both domestically and for export, were the telenovelas, evening soap operas which typically aired for an hour six nights a week for a period of several months.

During the 1980s, however, the content of some of the novelas came to reflect some politically leftist themes. For example, *Isaura the Slave* was set in colonial Brazil and strongly condemned racism and slavery. *Malu, Woman* showed the struggles of a divorced woman and had a strong feminist message. *Roque Santeiro* told of a small town controlled by political bosses who stopped at nothing to maintain power. *Wheel of Fire* told of a business executive who repented of past corruption. It featured characters who were torturers, rulers, and guerrillas during the years of military rule (1964–1985).

Formerly shunning television as a tool of the capitalist elites, leftist artists like *Roque Santeiro*'s author Dias Gomes, then a self-described Marxist, realized the potential of television, particularly through a large and powerful corporation like TV Globo, to reach far more people than theater, films, or print media could ever hope to. At the same time, Globo's corporate executives began realizing the immense profitability of television programs that deal with some of these progressive themes (Amaral & Guimarães, 1994; Bacchetta, 1987).

Conclusion

Our perceived reality of the political world is largely a product of the media. The role of media in politics will continue to be hotly debated. The loudest critics some years ago decried how TV was corrupting the democratic process and reducing political discourse to banal superficialities. The same concern is directed toward the Internet today. There is a consistent historical trend of people being the most critical of the newest medium or newest uses of old media. "If one goes back through the history of press criticism, a distinct pattern emerges: the most modern medium is always regarded as the most issueless, the most frivolous—first in print, then daily press, then radio, then television … [the] newest medium attracts the loudest complaints" (Robinson & Sheehan, cited in Kraus, 1988, p. 88). Predictably, in recent years there have been loud criticisms of candidates' using talk-show TV formats in campaigning. An even louder outcry about the political use of the Internet has also arisen recently (Jacques & Ratzan, 1997; Selnow, 1997; Whillock, 1997; Wojcieszak & Mutz, 2009), in spite of its considerable promise in increasing civic engagement of voters, especially young ones (Verser & Wicks, 2006; Xenos & Moy, 2007).

What is certain, however, is that media do create a political world that is the basis for most of our perceived political knowledge and subsequent political behavior, most notably voting. That role is not likely to change, so it behooves us to understand it better. Specific media uses will evolve, such as increased use of the Internet by candidates. However, it is still media which offer the interpretation of political events and candidates, allowing us to construct our reality of these candidates. Even entertainment media may affect political attitudes; see Close-Up 8.9. The almost-tied 2000 U.S. Presidential election, the true outcome of which will never be known, reminds us of the potentially very high stakes, and of the importance of constructing that political reality in a responsible fashion.

Close-Up 8.9: Watching *The West Wing* Makes People Like Their Real Presidents

It is not only political news and political advertising that affect our political attitudes and help construct our political reality. A clever study by Holbert et al. (2003) showed that entertainment may also prime political attitudes. The show they chose was NBC's drama *The West Wing* (1999–2006), set in the White House of a sympathetic fictional President played by Martin Sheen. Using a pretest–posttest design, they found that Missouri students who watched an episode of *The West Wing* in February 2002 afterward showed an increase in perception of positive character traits of both then-sitting President George W. Bush and former President Bill Clinton. Apparently watching and thinking about a positive example of a President, even a fictional one, helped cause them to see the real Presidents more positively.

Chapter 9

Violence
Watching All That Mayhem Really Matters

Q: How many murders has the average child seen on TV by the time he or she finishes elementary school?

A: Eight thousand, plus 100,000 other acts of violence (Huston et al., 1992). If they happened to have seen the film *Die Hard 2*, they saw 264 murders in that movie alone! According to a 2007 study, there was one instance of violent, sexual, or profane content every 4.8 minutes on TV programming between 7 and 9 p.m. ("Numbers," 2007).

Q: In a poll, what percentage of parents said they were "somewhat concerned" or "very concerned" that their children were watching too much violent content on TV?

A: 80% (Kaiser Family Foundation, 2007b)

Q: How often is torture portrayed on American television?

A: Although there were only an average of four torture scenes per year before 2001, there have been more than 100 per year since then, 67 alone in the first five seasons of the popular Fox show *24* (Holcomb, 2007).

Q: How much violence is in G-rated movies?

A: According to a 2000 survey of 74 G-rated Hollywood films, at least one character was injured in 46 of the films and someone was killed in half of them. Overall the films contained 9.5 minutes of violence, with the worst being 1998's *Quest for Camelot*, with 24 minutes of violence, nearly 30% of the entire movie! Also very violent was Disney's *Mulan*, in which hundreds, if not thousands, were killed in battle scenes. However, none of these films contained any sex or profanity.

Although specific frequency figures depend on our precise operational definition of violence, the reality of media, especially television and film in the United States, Japan, India, and elsewhere, is a highly violent world. About two-thirds of American prime-time TV programs and 90% of the movies on TV contain some sort of violence (*National Television Violence Study*, 1997;

Smith, Nathanson, & Wilson, 2002). On U.S. television, there are 7.9 violent acts per hour in programming aimed at children, compared to 4.7 violent acts per hour in adult prime-time programs. Even without counting the cartoon violence, there are still 6.3 violent incidents per hour on children's TV (Carlsson-Paige, 2008), much of which is trivialized, glamorized, and sanitized (Wilson, Smith et al., 2002). Considerable violence even occurs in programming we do not immediately associate with aggression, such as news, music videos, and even commercials aimed at children. Also, about two-thirds of the most popular video games contain acts of violence (Smith, Lachlan, & Tamborini, 2003).

How about the response that media violence only reflects an imperfect world that is very violent? Yes, there is violence in the real world but much less than is portrayed in the media. According to FBI statistics, only about 13% of real crimes are violent, but 87% of crimes on live-action TV entertainment are. With murder, the contrast is even stronger; only 0.2% of all crimes reported to the FBI are murders, whereas 50% of the crimes on TV are murders (Bushman & Anderson, 2001; Oliver, 1994). We have already seen in Chapter 7 how the sensationalist news reporting of grisly but unusual crimes leads to people hugely overestimating their occurrence in reality.

Consistent with the definition of most, though not all, researchers, "violence" is defined here as behavior intended to cause physical harm or pain to another individual. Excluded from this definition are accidental injury, vandalism of property, and various behaviors sometimes called "psychological," "relational," or "verbal" aggression, including emotional abuse and the "alternative aggressions" often used by girls to intimidate other girls by threatening to withdraw relationships (Simmons, 2002). These issues are all very important and deserve serious study in regard to media images. However, they have not received much research attention as yet (though see Coyne & Archer, 2004, 2005; Coyne & Whitehead, 2008; Martins & Wilson, 2012), whereas the effects of physical violence have been the subject of intense research scrutiny for the last half century. Although the term is not always used precisely or uniformly, "aggression" is the internal motivation behind violent behavior; the behavior may be observed directly, while the motive of aggression must be inferred from those acts.

Media violence on television has long been a contentious political issue, and there has probably been more psychological research on the topic of violence than on all other topics in this book put together—by some estimates at least 3,000 to 4,000 studies by the 1990s alone (Grossman & deGaetano, 1999; Huston et al., 1992). This chapter makes no claim to comprehensively review all of that literature; thorough reviews and discussions in varying detail are available elsewhere (see Anderson, Berkowitz et al., 2003; Christensen & Wood, 2007; Donnerstein & Smith, 1997; Dubow & Miller, 1996; Geen, 1994; Huston et al., 1992; Kirsh, 2006; J. P. Murray, 1999; National Television Violence Study, 1997; Paik & Comstock, 1994; Potter, 1999; Smith & Donnerstein, 1998; Sparks, Sparks, & Sparks, 2009).

This research has most often been conducted within the theoretical frame-works of social cognition and cultivation theories (see Chapter 2), although other perspectives have also been useful. Often the discussion of the scientific issues has been clouded and colored by the economic interest or ideological perspectives of those involved, and much of the popular writing on the topic has taken the form of either (1) polemical and unfounded media bashing (e.g., "It's all the media's fault,"), or (2) a defensive apologia to support one's economic self-interest (e.g., "It's all just make-believe"). Either of these positions blatantly ignores the large body of research that is readily available. In addition, in these types of arguments, crucial distinctions between diverse types and contexts of violence and between different populations are often lacking.

In considering the effects of media violence on society, we must not make the mistake of imagining media to be the only factor, or even the major factor, which contributes to violence in society. Negative social conditions like poverty, racism, crowding, drugs, parental neglect, weakened family values, availability of weapons, and the underclass subculture doubtlessly contribute far more than television, movies, or video games. Negative family or peer role models also have substantial effects. However, even if media violence is responsible for only 5 to 15% of societal violence, as estimated by some researchers (Sparks & Sparks, 2002; Strasburger, 1995), that is still very important. Because of the nature of mass communication, even a very small effect of media can be substantial. For example, suppose a violent movie incites 0.001% of viewers to act more violently. Although the percentage may be minuscule, 0.001% of an audience of 20 million is still 200 people!

We approach the study of media violence in this chapter by looking at the various effects of the violent view of the world presented in media. This study of the perceived reality of media violence focuses on the psychological processes involved and the weight of the evidence supporting the existence of those effects. Later in the chapter we look at individual differences among those who are attracted to or repelled by media violence and longitudinal studies probing for long-term effects. Then we look at one of the newest areas of concern: violent video games. Finally, we address the question of what may be done to provide balance to this perceived reality of violence. As we will see, most of the public concern and scientific study of the perceived violent reality of media centers on the effects of viewing televised violence.

Effects of Media Violence

The effect that many think of first is behavioral, when people imitate or model violent behavior that they see on the screen. However, this is only one of several effects. The research on the different effects has been driven by diverse theoretical frameworks; for example, studies of behavioral effects have most often been heavily influenced by social learning/cognitive theory, and studies of attitudinal effects often draw on cultivation theory (see Chapter 2). This section examines various effects of media violence in turn and the evidence supporting each of them. We begin with what is perhaps the most immediate effect, the idea that watching violence induces fear.

Fear

Much of the research on fear responses to violent media comes from the laboratory of Joanne Cantor (1996, 1998a, 2002, 2006, 2009), who concludes that "transitory fright responses are quite typical, that enduring and intense emotional disturbances occur in a substantial proportion of children and adolescents, and that severe and debilitating reactions affect a small minority of particularly susceptible individuals of all ages" (Cantor, 1996, p. 91). Overall, there is a correlation between the amount of television viewed and the prevalence of symptoms of psychological trauma like anxiety, depression, and posttraumatic stress (Singer, Slovak, Frierson, & York, 1998).

Fear-Inducing Images

Different categories of stimuli and events differentially produce fear responses in viewers of different ages. Distortions of natural forms (e.g., monsters and mutants) are very scary to preschoolers but typically less so to older children. Depictions of dangers and injuries (e.g., assaults, natural disasters) are more scary to older elementary school children than they are to preschoolers. This is in part because the older children are cognitively able to anticipate danger and its possible consequences and thus be fearful before the actual event occurs. The older the child, the more able he or she is to think abstractly and be frightened by watching situations of endangerment to others. Sometimes two siblings viewing together may be afraid of very different aspects of a movie; or one, not necessarily the younger, may be afraid while the sibling is not. For example, consider two brothers watching a movie about a benevolent alien visiting from outer space. The preschooler may be afraid of the fantastic form of the alien, while the older child may be afraid during the scenes in which he recognizes that the friendly alien or sympathetic humans may be in potential danger from others. Alternatively, the younger child may not be afraid at all—in fact, he may love the cute little alien—and may not be able to think abstractly enough to understand why his brother is afraid of the potential danger.

Responses to Fear

Cantor and Oliver (1996; see also Cantor, 1998a, 2002, 2006, 2009) identify some principles for predicting fear responses in children. First, the older the child, the more a character's behavior, relative to appearance, is important in predicting fear responses, although all children will be more fearful of an ugly than an attractive character. Second, as children grow older they become more responsive to realistic dangers and less responsive to fantasy dangers in the media. Third, and closely related, the older the child, the more able he or she is to be afraid of increasingly abstract dangers. In fact, very young children tend not to be very afraid of abstract threats. For example, fear responses to a 1980s TV movie about nuclear war in the heartland of the United States found young children to be the least afraid and adults the most afraid (Scholfield & Pavelchak, 1985), with the number of parental reports of their children discussing the movie with them increasing with the age of the child (Cantor, Wilson, & Hoffner, 1986).

When they are afraid of watching something scary, preschoolers tend to cope by using noncognitive strategies like eating, drinking, covering their eyes, or clutching a beloved object. School-age children tend to use and respond well to cognitive strategies like verbal explanations, reminders of the unreality of the situation, or instructions to think about the danger in a new, less threatening way, provided that the explanation is at an appropriate level. It is, however, quite difficult to totally reason away a strong media-induced fear in a young child. Interestingly, one study (Paavonen, Roine, Pennonen, & Lahikainen, 2009) indicated that parents may not always be comforting to children who encounter scary media. In fact, Paavonen and colleagues discovered that parental coviewing of scary TV actually increased TV-related fears among children, indicating that mere parental presence is not always effective at reducing fears. The authors suggest that what may be most important in reducing children's fears of media violence is the nature and quality of the discussion that accompanies coviewing. Others (Carroll, 2009) have speculated that, in attempting to comfort children frightened by media (by, say, cuddling them), parents may sometimes actually be reinforcing the frightened reaction.

Several studies (Cantor & Oliver, 1996; Harrison & Cantor, 1999; Hoekstra, Harris, & Helmick, 1999) found that practically all young adults were readily able to remember an incident of being extremely scared by a movie as a child or teen. Such memories, and perhaps some of the effects as well, are long lasting. Some effects reported are general fear or anxiety, specific fears (e.g., fear of swimming after seeing *Jaws*), sleep disturbances, and nightmares (see Close-Up 9.1 for some actual memories reported by Cantor's participants). These kinds of effects may also translate into perceptions of the world. For example, one investigation (Riddle, Potter, Metzger, Nabi, & Linz, 2011) found that most college students sampled could remember a specific, graphic instance of media violence they had viewed between the ages of 5 and 23. Further, those who had vivid memories of the gory media (usually movies) tended to overestimate the prevalence of real-world violent crimes.

Sometimes self-reports may not be a completely adequate measure of induced fear. For example, Sparks, Pellechia, and Irvine (1999) found that

Close-Up 9.1: Memories of Being Scared by Movies Seen as a Child

Cantor, in her research on the inducement of fear by violent media, has interviewed and tested hundreds of young adults about their memories of being scared by a movie seen in childhood. Here are two actual accounts of these experiences (Cantor, 1998b, pp. 9–10).

After the movie [Jaws], I had nightmares for a week straight. Always the same one. I'm in a room filled with water with ducts in the walls. They would suddenly open and dozens of sharks would swim out. I felt trapped with no place to go. I would usually wake up in a sweat. Occasionally I'll still have the exact same dream. The movie didn't just affect me at night. To this day I'm afraid to go to the ocean, sometimes even a lake. I'm afraid that there will be a shark even if I know deep down that's impossible.

I watched [Friday the 13th, Part II] when I was 14 years old and it scared me so much that I couldn't sleep for a whole month. I was scared of the name Jason and I hated standing under a thatched roof. At night I needed a night light so I could see everything around me. I was very conscious of the smallest little noise, I had nightmares about knives, chain-saws, blood, screams, and hockey masks. I was very jumpy. This kind of slaughter film still has these effects on me.

certain "repressor" personality types reported low levels of negative emotion in response to watching a 25-minute segment from the horror film *When a Stranger Calls* but high levels of physiological arousal, as measured by skin conductance. In a similar vein, Peck (1999, as cited in Cantor, 2002) discovered that in general women's verbal reports of fear in response to watching scary scenes from *A Nightmare on Elm Street* were more intense than men's, but in some cases men's physiological responses were more intense than women's, especially if the victim in the scene was male. Thus, it is possible that in some circumstances some people either cannot or do not accurately report the fear they experienced, and we cannot assume that self-reports of fear completely reflect their internal emotion.

Brain Correlates

Some exciting newer work with brain imaging suggests that our brains respond differently to violent and nonviolent stimuli (Murray et al., 2006). Children aged 8 to 13 watched an 18-minute video segment, either violent (boxing in

Rocky IV) or nonviolent (from a National Geographic documentary or the children's literacy TV program *Ghostwriter*), while functional magnetic resonance imaging (fMRI) mapped their brain activity. Although both videos activated certain brain regions routinely involved in visual and auditory processing, only the violent film activated parts of the amygdala and right cerebral cortex involved with arousal, threat detection, and unconscious emotional memory. This suggests a neural basis for the fear response to violent video. It also suggests that areas such as the right hemisphere and amygdala, known to be involved with other kinds of emotional responding, are also active while watching violent media. Such emotional memories often endure long after the associated cognitive memories have faded, explaining, for example, why someone might be afraid of swimming in the ocean years after watching *Jaws* (Cantor, 2006).

Clearly, violent media do induce fear in viewers. Further, the type of image that induces the most fear varies greatly with the age and cognitive developmental level of the viewer. However, any expression of fear by a child should be taken seriously by the parent or caretaker, not ignored, and never belittled. Even if the danger is very unreal or even silly from an adult perspective, the child's fear is very real, and that is what both parents and children must address. See Cantor (1998b) for an excellent guide for parents on this subject.

Modeling

Research on modeling comes primarily out of social cognitive theory (see Chapter 2), which applies principles of learning to social situations.

How Modeling Works

From the modeling/social learning/social cognitive perspective, people see a violent act in the media and later, as a result, behave more violently themselves than they otherwise would. For this to happen, first, the relevant behavior of the model must be attended to. For example, a child must notice and pay attention to a violent horror movie like *Saw*. Second, the model behavior must be retained and encoded into memory in some form; this usually occurs as the behavior is being analyzed and interpreted through cognitive processing. Using the earlier example, the child would need to think about the events in the *Saw* movie, perhaps even days after it was viewed. Whether the learned behavior is later actually produced by the viewer will depend on many factors, such as motivation and the strength of prevailing inhibiting factors. Thus, the hypothetical child viewer mentioned earlier might reenact some of the punching seen in the movie while playing with friends.

The process of modeling may actually teach new behaviors, much as one might learn a new athletic skill by watching a coach demonstrate it. When a teenager opens fire on his classmates a few days after seeing a film with a similar scene in it, he may not have known or thought to behave that way before seeing the film. This would appear to be a particularly troublesome example of the common phenomenon called observational learning. A well-documented example is the notorious New Bedford gang rape case of the mid-1980s, when several men raped a woman on a pool table in a bar (later the basis of the movie *The Accused* in which a character played by Jodie Foster was gang raped on a pinball machine). The rapists had recently seen a movie with a barroom gang rape scene in a nearby theater. See Close-Up 9.2 for the story of some especially tragic cases in which legal charges were filed against media for teaching violent behaviors.

Close-Up 9.2: Are Media Criminally Liable for Effects of Violent Content?

From time to time, lawyers defending violent crime perpetrators who appear to have been affected by television have used rather creative defenses, which inevitably come up against First Amendment freedom of speech issues. For example, in 1977, Ronald Zamora, 15, killed his 82-year-old neighbor in a robbery attempt after she discovered Zamora and threatened to call the police. What was particularly unusual was that the defense attorney argued for temporary insanity at the time of the crime, arguing that Zamora was "suffering from and acted under the influence of prolonged, intense, involuntary, subliminal television intoxication" (Liebert & Sprafkin, 1988, p. 127). He further argued that the shooting was a TV-learned conditioned response to the stimulus of the victim's threatening to call the police. Television was thus an accessory to the crime. In the end, however, the jury failed to accept this reasoning, and Zamora was convicted on all counts and sentenced to life.

A second case involved 9-year-old Olivia Niemi, who in 1974 was assaulted and raped with a bottle by three older girls and a boy. Four days before, a TV movie, *Born Innocent*, had been aired, showing a scene of a girl being raped with a toilet plunger. Olivia's mother then sued NBC for $11 million for alleged negligence in showing the movie in prime time. Her lawyer argued for vicarious liability and claimed that the movie had incited the children to criminal activity. After a series of appeals and countersuits, the case was finally thrown out when a judge ruled that the plaintiff had to prove that the network had intended its viewers to imitate the violent sexual acts depicted. However, when NBC aired *Born Innocent* as a rerun, it aired at 11:30 p.m. with most of the critical rape scene edited out (Liebert & Sprafkin, 1988).

More often, however, it is not the specific behavior itself that is learned from the media. A second process by which modeling can work is when watching media violence produces *disinhibition*; that is, it reduces the normal inhibitions most people have against acting violently or accepting violence. For example, watching a movie with scenes of street fighting might produce disinhibition by weakening a viewer's usual proscriptions against fighting. The viewer already knows how to fight, and the medium cannot be blamed for teaching that behavior. However, TV may be breaking down the normal inhibitions that we would otherwise have against engaging in such violence. Thus, actual violent behavior may occur in the future with less provocation than would have been necessary to evoke it prior to the disinhibition.

Disinhibition may also occur through the teaching of more accepting attitudes toward violent behavior. Although most people are raised with the general belief that violent behavior is bad (specific circumstances when it might be acceptable may vary), exposure to repeated media violence may break down these attitudinal inhibitions against thinking violence is acceptable. This change toward a more accepting attitude about the appropriateness of using violence to settle disputes may subsequently and indirectly lead to violent behavior, although such an unequivocal causal connection is very difficult to demonstrate empirically.

Most of the concern with modeling effects of media violence assumes that persons may become violent in their own behavior in a somewhat different way than the media model; that is, the effect generalizes beyond the specific behavior demonstrated in the media. A person who watches a war movie may be disinhibited from violent behavior generally and may subsequently punch or kick another person, but they will not necessarily start shooting with an AK-47 exactly as a character in the movie did. This generalized type of modeling is far more common than the modeling of a very specific behavior.

Sometimes the nature or timing of the response can be taught through media. For example, Grossman (1996; Grossman & DeGaetano, 1999) argues that violent TV and movies, and especially violent video games, train children to shoot rapidly without thinking at the appearance of certain stimuli. The normative behavior in many video games is to shoot as soon as some target appears, with the fastest reaction being the best one. Thus, Grossman argues that the child playing video games is learning to shoot first and ask questions later. Does this learned shooting behavior transfer to other situations? Grossman cited one of the boys charged in relation to 1998 Jonesboro, Arkansas, schoolyard shootings who had little if any experience shooting real guns but a lot of experience playing video games. He and his buddy were good enough shots to hit 15 people with 27 shots from a distance of 100 yards. Research on video games is discussed later in this chapter.

There are other, even more indirect, ways in which modeling may occur. Viewing violence may alter the general emotional responsiveness of the viewer, which could in turn lead to violent behavior. It may also raise the overall arousal level, which could prime the person for (among other behaviors) violence.

Now let us turn to some of the research done to test the modeling hypothesis and to identify the conditions under which modeling occurs.

Basic Social Learning and Field Research

The best-known early research studying modeling of media violence was social psychologist Albert Bandura's Bobo doll studies (Bandura, 1965; Bandura, Ross, & Ross, 1963; see also Hicks, 1965). In a typical Bobo doll study testing modeling, Bandura had young children watch someone else behave aggressively toward a large plastic inflatable doll known as Bobo the Clown. The child's own behavior with the Bobo doll was subsequently observed. Studies of this type consistently demonstrated that children imitated violent behavior previously observed in a live model. Most importantly for our purposes, the same effect was found when the violent model was on film rather than live (Bandura et al., 1961; J. P. Nelson, Gelfand, & Hartmann, 1969; Rosencrans & Hartup, 1967; Walters & Willows, 1968). Many laboratory studies have replicated these effects over the years and have demonstrated generalization to other behaviors. For example, participants who had seen a series of violent films were more likely to respond negatively in an "unrelated" study to a research assistant who had written insulting comments on a questionnaire they had completed (Zillmann & Weaver, 1999).

Although these experimental studies were groundbreaking, they were not without criticism. They were primarily attacked for being too artificial and of questionable application to the real world. However, later research moving away from the laboratory also found corroborative evidence for modeling (Huesmann, Lagerspetz, & Eron, 1984; Joy, Kimball, & Zabrack, 1986; Lefkowitz, Eron, Walder, & Huesmann, 1977; Leyens, Camino, Parke, & Berkowitz, 1975). It also should be noted that the rates of violent crimes rose in societies following the introduction of television, with its steady diet of violence. For example, although the homicide rate for White Americans and Canadians rose 93% and 92% respectively between 1945 and 1974, it declined by 7% in the same period for White South Africans, living in comparable economic conditions except for the lack of television, which was not introduced in South Africa until 1975 (Centerwall, 1989, 1992; Joy, Kimball, & Zabrack, 1986). After the introduction of TV, the homicide rate rose there as well. Centerwall (1989) rules out other explanations like economics, age, firearms availability, and civil unrest as accounting for these changes. Thus, there is evidence that modeling media violence is not purely an artificial laboratory phenomenon.

Sensitization

Sensitization is a sort of reverse modeling effect, whereby viewers react so strongly to seeing violence and have such a traumatized perceived reality that they are actually *less* likely to imitate it as a result. This is most likely to occur with very extreme violence and might be the reaction, for example, of someone who has never previously seen anything stronger than a G-rated Disney movie, when he or she sees a graphically violent R-rated film. The behavioral tendency away from violence might arise from the arousal of anxiety about the violence and/or the arousal of empathy for the victim of the violence. Hoffner and Levine (2007) concluded from a meta-analysis that, relative to others, people high in the "personal distress" and "empathic concern" measures of empathy showed less enjoyment of fright and violence. Using a different conceptualization of empathy, Tamborini, Stiff, and Heidel (1990) found that people who most dislike watching graphic violence (i.e., those who are most sensitized) were those who score high in measures of empathy such as "fictional involvement," and "humanistic orientation." That is, these people can easily imagine themselves in the position of the victim of the violence and vicariously experience the negative emotions that person would feel. Someone who cannot easily do this would also be aroused but would be more likely to enjoy the violence, because the negative emotions would not be so strongly felt.

It is likely that the strongest sensitization effects come from very graphic violence that is clearly understood as real (i.e., the news). Sometimes producers face a difficult decision as to whether or not to air an extremely violent scene from a news story (see Close-Up 9.3 for some especially compelling

Close-Up 9.3: Extremely Violent News Images

Sometimes television networks and stations or print media are faced with a difficult decision about whether to show a graphically violent news photograph. One of the most agonizing decisions came in July 2003 after the deaths of deposed Iraqi dictator Saddam Hussein's sons Oday and Qusay in an assault by the U.S. military on a fortified house in Mosul, Iraq. At this point, Iraq was occupied by U.S. and UK forces but Saddam was still alive and in hiding. The two sons were notorious, hated and feared for perpetrating crimes of incredible cruelty. Although the United States generally had a policy of not releasing photographs of people killed in military action, it decided that at least the Iraqi public needed concrete evidence that the hated brothers were really dead. Thus the gruesome photos of the dead brothers were published.

Another Iraq War image issue arose when an Islamist website offered video footage of terrorists slowly sawing off the head of a captured 26-year-old American contractor. Although nearly all networks declined to run the video in its entirety, most did describe the scene quite graphically, arguing that it was necessary to fully communicate the horror of the act. In 2011, the White House struggled with the notion of releasing a photo of the body of Osama bin Laden as proof that he really had been captured and killed. Ultimately, President Barack Obama decided that the image was too gruesome, and the news media was denied access to it.

Decades earlier, in 1968, an AP photographer working in Saigon during the Vietnam War captured a disturbing photo of a Vietcong operative being executed at point-blank range. The photo (and accompanying TV news footage) appeared in media outlets around the world. The photographer later won a Pulitzer Prize for the image.

Sometimes cameras fortuitously happen to capture a gruesome image. Local media photographers covering a routine 1987 news conference by Pennsylvania State Treasurer Budd Dwyer caught the unexpected image of Dwyer putting a pistol in his mouth and pulling the trigger, killing himself instantly. Network news, TV stations, and newspapers then faced the decision of whether to run the grisly sequence. Most TV stations chose not to air the tape or did so only to the point of Dwyer placing the gun in his mouth. A few TV stations and newspapers carried pictures of what happened after that, saying it was "an important historical event" and should be covered. In a 1993 case, a Florida woman being interviewed by a television crew in a park in broad daylight was suddenly accosted and shot several times by her estranged husband. Although the photos later provided important legal evidence, networks were faced with the decision of whether or not to air the footage on the news. Many (including CNN) did so.

The public has a right to know, but how much does the public have a need or right to know and see explicitly? The answer is obviously an ethical and policy question, although one study suggested a positive effect of learning at least some gory details. College students who read a newspaper report of a wife-battering incident rated it as more serious and rated the batterer more negatively if the victim's injuries were described in detail, compared to a situation in which they were not explicitly described (Pierce & Harris, 1993). These descriptions, however, were much less graphic than the pictorial images described above.

examples). Once in a while they may be unable legally to block the image, for example if it comes in a political ad, which legally may not be censored.

Although product and political advertisers are generally reluctant to risk offending the public, once in a while a great while a political candidate may wish to do so. For example, in the fall 1992 U.S. election campaigns, several antiabortion candidates for Congress and other offices chose to air photos of what they said was an aborted fetus. Their explicit goal was to offend viewers, in order to convince them that abortion really is offensive. Such tactics are risky, however, because viewers might be even more offended by a decision to use such an image.

Although sensitization effects are hard to study scientifically for ethical reasons (e.g., we cannot show young children highly graphic violence), general sensitization effects are probably not too widespread and probably do not occur nearly as often as their opposite, desensitization, which is discussed in the next section.

In general, situations in which sensitization effects might seem present can often be interpreted equally plausibly as leading to desensitization. For example, people have argued that daily news broadcasts of the Vietnam War sensitized us to the horrors of war and eroded public support for that conflict, in contrast to previous wars. On the other hand, others have argued that the same news broadcasts desensitized us to war, and thus we are now not as bothered by seeing images of other conflicts (see Chapter 7). See Close-Up 9.4 for a brief history of the treatment of the Vietnam War in films.

Close-Up 9.4: Hollywood Goes to War

The 1966 pro-Vietnam War film *The Green Berets* starred John Wayne in a stylized epic with good guys and bad guys. Two years later, for many, such a simplistic approach to Vietnam rang very hollow and false. Shortly after *The Green Berets*, sentiment in the United States turned completely around, and whatever glory there had ever been in the Vietnam War had all but disappeared. The 1974 Oscar-winning documentary *Hearts and Minds*, by Peter Davis, was very graphic and carried such a strong antiwar message that some newspapers refused to publish reviews of the film. Although the last U.S. troops left Vietnam in 1973 and Saigon fell in 1975, there were no commercially successful film images of Vietnam before 1978, when *The Deer Hunter* and *Coming Home* picked up seven Oscars between them. Both of these films (along with *Apocalypse Now* in 1979) carried a strong antiwar message and reflected the country's disgust with the war in Vietnam, a wound that had only begun to heal.

That healing proceeded slowly until 1986, when Oliver Stone's graphic and realistic *Platoon* and Sylvester Stallone's live-action comic book *Rambo: First Blood Part II* appeared. Both were huge successes, but *Platoon* was the greater commercial gamble, having taken years to acquire the necessary funding. The Pentagon refused to help the producers, although it enthusiastically aided the makers of the heroic

Top Gun, on the grounds that it wanted to ensure a realistic portrayal of the military! Widely hailed as a critical success and winner of that year's Best Picture Oscar, *Platoon* astounded everyone with by also becoming a huge commercial success. It was then followed by a spate of realistic Vietnam films such as *Gardens of Stone, Casualties of War, The Hanoi Hilton*, and *Full Metal Jacket*, none of which achieved critical or commercial success close to that of *Platoon*.

By 1988, the wounds of Vietnam had healed enough to allow the production and modest commercial success of the first Vietnam War TV series, *Tour of Duty*, and big-screen comedy, *Good Morning, Vietnam*. A comedy about Vietnam would have been unthinkable much before that time. Not too long after they were followed by another Oliver Stone antiwar film, *Born on the Fourth of July*, the biographical story of gung-ho soldier turned antiwar protester Ron Kovic.

A contrast can also be made between the World War II films *The Longest Day* and *Saving Private Ryan*. *The Longest Day*, produced in 1962, depicts the D-Day invasion of Normandy as difficult, but manageable by brave and smooth-talking leaders. *Saving Private Ryan*, released 36 years later, sought to portray the same event in a much more realistic way. In the latter film, the horrors of war are graphically depicted, with mass fear and confusion among troops, widespread death, and severed body parts. Although difficult to watch, many (including some Normandy veterans) praised the film for its realism (Wallace, 1998).

Desensitization

Although the primary concern of public debate about the effects of media violence typically involves the inciting of violent behavior, there may be far more pervasive attitudinal effects, especially in the area of *desensitization*. The basic principle here is that viewing a steady diet of violence in the media makes us less sensitive to it, more jaded, and less aroused and bothered by it. We become so used to seeing people wasted, blown apart, or impaled that it no longer particularly troubles us. For example, after seeing a violent TV show, sixth graders were less sensitive to violent images in a subsequent film than were children who had seen a nonviolent film first (Rabinovitch, McLean, Markham, & Talbott, 1972). Desensitization is typically measured experimentally through physiological or attitudinal measures.

How Desensitization Works

Desensitization may be seen as a straightforward example of classical conditioning (see Figure 9.1). The normal, unlearned responses to being

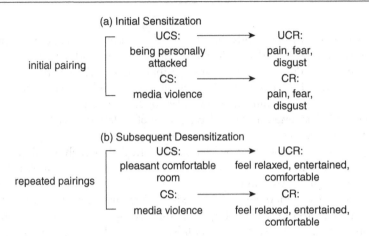

Figure. 9.1 Desensitization as classical conditioning.

physically hurt include pain, fear, and disgust. The first time one sees media violence, it probably evokes such negative emotional responses due to its similarity to real violence (Figure 9.1a). Such a single occurrence may actually produce sensitization, as discussed previously.

What happens with repeated viewing of violence in comfortable surroundings is quite different, however (Figure 9.1b). Suppose, for example, that the normal, unlearned response to sitting at home in one's easy chair is feeling relaxed and happy. When this is repeatedly paired with violence on TV, vicarious violence in a pleasant home context gradually becomes associated with that situation and itself comes to be seen as entertaining, pleasant, and even relaxing. The natural association of filmed violence with real-life violence is weakened as the new association of video violence with recreation is strengthened. We repeatedly see violence without experiencing pain or hurt ourselves, and thus the normal negative responses to it weaken. Given what we know about classical conditioning in psychology, it is unlikely that such frequent and repeated exposure to stimuli could not have a substantial effect. In the adolescent subculture, part of the male gender-role socialization has been for a boy to desensitize himself so that he can watch graphic violence and not appear to be bothered by it (Harris, Hoekstra et al., 2000; Mundorf, Weaver, & Zillmann, 1989; Zillmann & Weaver, 1996; Zillmann et al., 1986). Demonstrating desensitization to violence thus becomes a way to impress peers or a date.

Consequences of Desensitization

What are the implications of people becoming desensitized to violence in the media? Becoming jaded with respect to news of war and violence will cause such stories not to bother us so much. Even if we never come actually to like violence or behave violently ourselves, we may come to not really be bothered by it deeply; it does not seem all that serious. This has important implications for behavior. For example, Drabman and Thomas (1974, 1976) had 8- to 10-year-old children watch a violent or nonviolent film and later watch younger children at play. When the younger children started to get rough, the older children who had watched the nonviolent film called an adult sooner than did the older children who had watched the violent film, thus showing some generalization of the desensitization effect. In a more recent study, Krahé and colleagues (2011) found that habitual exposure to media violence in college students correlated positively with factors such as pleasant arousal and negatively with factors such as sweating while watching a violent movie clip. Interestingly, these correlations were not present while students watched sad or funny film clips, suggesting a desensitization effect specific to violence.

One of the major areas of concern with desensitization has to do with tolerance of violence toward women. Male college students who viewed a series of slasher horror movies later showed less empathy and concern for victims of rape (Linz, Donnerstein, & Penrod, 1984). Sexual violence is one of the major current concerns among media researchers studying violence; we examine this aspect of violence in some detail in Chapter 10.

Cultivation

Another type of attitudinal effect in regard to violence is *cultivation*. As discussed in Chapter 2, cultivation theory argues that the more exposure a person has to television, the more that person's perception of social realities will match what is presented on TV (Gerbner, Gross, Morgan, Signorielli, & Shanahan, 2002; Morgan et al., 2009). In fact, cultivation theory was originally developed in regard to studying media violence. In contrast to modeling, cultivation attributes a more active role to the viewer, who is interacting with the medium, not being passively manipulated by it. Nevertheless, there is a coming together of the outlook of the viewer and that of the medium whereby the person's perceived reality gradually approaches that of the media world.

Cultivation theory is best known through research on the cultivation of attitudes related to violence (Gerbner, Gross, Signorielli, & Morgan, 1986; Morgan et al., 2009; Riddle et al., 2011). Such studies show that frequent viewers believe the world to be a more dangerous and crime-ridden place than infrequent viewers believe it to be. The world of TV portrays about 50% of characters being involved in violence each week, compared to less than 1% of the population *per year* in real life (Bushman & Anderson, 2001). This cultivation effect could be due either to media teaching that this is what the world is like or to the fact that more fearful people are drawn to watching more TV. If it is the former—and cultivation theorists believe it is—media can induce a general mindset about the existence of violence in the world, separate from any effects it might have in teaching violent behavior.

Finally, cultivation theory speaks of media teaching the role of the victim. From watching a heavy diet of crime and action-adventure, viewers learn what it is like to be a victim of violence, and this role becomes very real to them, even if it is completely outside of their own life experience.

The effects of media violence just discussed are not presented as an exhaustive list but rather as general classes into which most proposed effects fall. Occasionally an effect falls outside of these classes, however; see Close-Up 9.5 for some interesting evidence of violent media causing amnesia in viewers.

Important Interactive Factors

Now that we have looked at the major effects of watching media violence, it is time to examine important moderating variables that affect how much the violent behavior will be modeled or how strongly induced the attitudinal effects of desensitization, cultivation, or fear will be. Consistent with the conditional effects model discussed in Chapter 2, it should be understood that

---

Close-Up 9.5: Do Violent Images Cause Amnesia?

Amnesia is not typically on the list of effects of media violence, but evidence for just such an effect has been offered (Christianson & Loftus, 1987; Newhagen & Reeves, 1992). It has been known for some time that a physical injury to the brain can result in a loss of memory for events immediately preceding the impact (retrograde amnesia). For example, the shock of one's head flying against the headrest in an auto collision may lead to amnesia for events immediately preceding the impact. It is as if the brain had not yet had time to transfer the event from working memory to long-term memory. Loftus and Burns (1982) demonstrated that such an effect may also occur solely from the mental shock of seeing graphic violence on the screen. Research participants saw a two-minute film of a bank robbery, either a violent or nonviolent version. In the violent version the fleeing robbers shot their pursuers and in the street they hit a young boy in the face, after which he fell, clutching his bloody face. The nonviolent version was identical up to the point of the shooting, at which point the camera cut to the interior of the bank. Measured using both recall and recognition measures, people seeing the nonviolent version of the film remembered the number on the boy's T-shirt better than those seeing the violent film, although the shirt was shown for the same amount of time in both. A second study ruled out the possibility that the effect could have been due to the unexpectedness or surprising nature of the shooting.

individual differences are important to models of media violence effects. Thus these effects models do not apply to everyone the same way under all circumstances. Numerous important variables such as modeling or desensitization heighten or lessen effects.

Model Attributes

First, several characteristics of the violent model are important. People are more likely to imitate or be disinhibited by viewing the violent behavior of an attractive, respected, prestigious model (such as a movie superhero) than by viewing that of a model without such qualities. Also, the more deeply we identify and empathize with a model, the more likely we are to imitate that person (Huesmann et al., 1984; Huesmann, Moise-Titus, Podolski, & Eron, 2003). These points suggest that violence by the characters we admire and identify with is a stronger influence than violence by the bad guys. For example, when a heroic character shoots a bad guy point blank in the chest, there may be more of a lasting impact on the viewer than when a villain performs a similar act. This kind of effect has important ramifications for assessing the implications of viewing action-adventure and police shows.

Reinforcement of Violence

Whether or not the violence is reinforced in the plot is also a very important moderating variable. One of the central principles of operant conditioning, and indeed of all psychology, reinforcement occurs when some event follows a response and increases the likelihood of that response occurring again. The connection (contingency) between the response and the reinforcement is learned; thus the response is made in anticipation of receiving the reinforcement. A dog learns to fetch a stick because he is reinforced with a treat when he performs the act. A girl does her homework each night because she is reinforced by being allowed to watch TV after she is finished. A police officer is reinforced for using excessive force by catching the bad guy and sending him to prison and earning a promotion for himself. After the learning has occurred, responses continue to be made for some period of time without the reinforcement, until they gradually diminish and are finally extinguished altogether.

If acting violently appears to pay off for the violent character (in money, power, social recognition, relationship status, etc.), the violent behavior is thus reinforced in the context of the story. Research suggests that reinforced violence is more likely to desensitize or be modeled than nonreinforced or punished violence (e.g., Bandura, 1965). Krcmar and Cooke (2001) found that 4- to 7-year-olds thought unpunished violence in a video clip was more acceptable than punished violence. In a typical TV story line, violence by the hero is more likely to be rewarded (reinforced) than is the violence of the villain, although the latter may have been reinforced for much of the show.

Model characteristics and reinforcement suggest that a particularly troubling type of violent perpetrator is the violent child or teen character. Content analyses show that, compared to adult models, violent child models in media are more attractive to children and less likely than adults to be punished or to experience other negative consequences of the violence (Wilson, Colvin, & Smith, 2002); both of these characteristics make modeling by young viewers more likely.

Interestingly, King and Hourani (2007) found that viewers of horror films with alternative endings strongly preferred the "traditional" ending in which the evil antagonist is punished and destroyed over a "teaser" ending in which the evildoer revives, perhaps setting the stage for a sequel. People not only liked the traditional ending better but, surprisingly, found it less predictable, perhaps reflecting the large number of teaser endings and sequels for recent horror movies. This result held for viewers strongly motivated by gore and thrill factors, as well as the general population.

Finally, sometimes media do not necessarily reinforce specific behaviors but rather reinforce certain values about the use of violence. For example, characters in action-adventure TV shows and movies frequently use violence to settle interpersonal disputes. As such, they subtly reinforce the value that violent behavior is a realistic and morally acceptable manner of dealing with conflict, a value that may become part of the viewer's perceived reality. Children seeing a fantasy movie clip ending in violence later rated a different story with violence as more morally correct than children seeing the same clip but without the violence (Krcmar & Curtis, 2003). In sports, when sportscasters legitimize on-field violence as necessary or regrettably acceptable in the context in which it occurred, or when an athlete receives only a slap on the wrist for assaulting another player, such treatment reinforces violence as a way of dealing with the stresses of the game (Bryant et al., 1998).

Perceived Reality

Another important moderating factor is whether the violence is seen as real or make-believe, that is, the degree of perceived reality (van der Voort, 1986). There is some evidence of stronger effects for violence perceived as real than for violence perceived as unrealistic. Although children's cartoons are by far the most violent genre of TV show, cartoon violence is also the most stylized and unrealistic. Other than very young children, few people believe that someone could survive falls from high cliffs or being flattened under an anvil. However, although cartoon violence is generally perceived as less realistic than live-action violence, and in many instances is less likely to induce fear or desensitization or be imitated, numerous moderating factors are important, including how graphic the violence is and whether it is perceived as humorous (Kirsh, 2006).

In understanding the perceived reality of violent media, it is always important to consider the viewer's cognitive understanding of television at any given time (see e.g., Cantor, 1998b, 2002; Kirsh, 2006). For example, a very young child might think that a violent death on a police drama actually shows someone dying, rather than merely an actor pretending to die. Children who believe such staged violence to be real are often more disturbed by it than those who understand the convention of acting. The greater the perceived realism of media violence, the more likely that aggressive behavior will increase (Huesmann et al., 2003). Continuing this line of reasoning, the most difficult forms of TV violence for children to deal with are probably news and documentaries, because violence on these programs is real and not staged.

Beyond the issue of perceived realism, the whole issue of how the viewer interprets the violence is very important; such variables often account for more of the statistical variance in studies than stimulus factors (e.g., amount of violence) manipulated by the experimenter (Potter & Tomasello, 2003).

Personality Characteristics of the Viewer

Research has generally found larger modeling and attitudinal effects in people more naturally inclined toward violence in terms of personality (Kirsh, Olczak, & Mounts, 2005; Scharrer, 2005), although this result has not been found consistently (e.g., Huesmann, Eron, Lefkowitz, & Walder, 1984), perhaps due to trait aggression being a complex, multifactor construct (Scharrer, 2005). Violence in the media may reinforce dispositional violent tendencies already present in the viewer, even if it is not the cause of those tendencies. The more such tendencies are reinforced, the more likely they are to manifest themselves in behavior. Regrettably, the lack of a uniform effect on viewers has often been used to argue that there is no substantial impact from media violence. As suggested previously, however, a modeling effect on even a tiny percentage of the population may be cause for serious concern. The fact that people less naturally inclined toward violence do not respond as strongly as those more inclined toward violence is not an argument that media violence has no effect!

Another important factor in moderating the effects of media violence may be the thoughts that one has in response to viewing it (Berkowitz, 1984). Those thoughts may focus on the suffering of the victim, the triumph of the violent person, the relation of the violence to one's own experience, and so on. Depending on the nature of these thoughts, their mediating role in facilitating violent behavior may vary substantially. For example, someone who is overwhelmed by the suffering of the victim is probably less likely to behave violently than one who identifies strongly with a heroic and attractive character like James Bond (McCauley, 1998). Even preschoolers exposed to one violent cartoon give more aggressive story endings than children seeing a nonviolent cartoon or still picture. See Krcmar and Kean (2005), and Goldstein (1998) for discussions of individual differences in reactions to TV violence.

Arousal

The variable of arousal level of the viewer is important in understanding media violence and viewer behavior. Studies in past decades have revealed that a person who is already physiologically aroused, for whatever reason, is more likely to engage in violence after seeing a violent media model than is a nonaroused person (Tannenbaum, 1971, 1980). The arousal may come from the film itself, given that violent films tend to be emotionally arousing and exciting, or it may come from some prior and unrelated source, such as the manipulation in some experiments of making one group of participants angry before exposing them to a violent media model (e.g., Berkowitz, 1965; Hartmann, 1969; Zillmann, 1978). This issue of the interaction of arousal and a violent model becomes important when considering sexual violence, which is examined in Chapter 10.

Age and Gender

In terms of age and gender, modeling effects typically increase up to about ages 8 to 12 and slowly decrease thereafter. After this age, children have developed their own viewing schemas and are better able to separate video experience from reality. Although boys consistently both watch more violent media and are themselves more violent than girls, there is no clear evidence of a stronger modeling effect as such on either boys or girls, at least not before about age 10 (Hearold, 1986; Kirsh, 2006).

Context of Violence

One moderating variable that has not yet been studied very extensively is the embedding of graphic violence in a humorous context. For example, violent characters can utter humorous wisecracks, a laugh track can accompany violent scenes, and acts of violence can be presented as having humorous consequences. Sometimes technical or editing devices can serve to reinforce violence in such a context. For example, when the hero in the 1994 film *Natural Born Killers* drowned his girlfriend's father in a fish tank and killed her mother by tying her to a bed, dousing her in gasoline and burning her alive, a background laugh track encouraged us to see this brutality as humorously entertaining, reinforcing positive responses within the viewer. A similarly gruesome scene played out in the 2008 Batman movie *The Dark Knight*, when the Joker made a pencil "disappear" by ramming the eye socket of a mafioso onto it. One empirical study of the effects of viewing wisecracking heroes and villains in a violent action film (*The Hitman*) found a different pattern of results in men and women (King, 2000). The presence of humor in the hero increased distress in women but not in men, while the participants' reactions to a subsequent nonfiction film showed no such effect.

This embedding of violence in comedy is a specific instance of the broader situation of violent behavior being reinforced by virtue of its occurrence in a context that is overall very reinforcing. For example, because viewers may choose to identify more with the glamorous opulence of shows like *The O.C.* or *Mad Men* than with the gritty seediness of the *CSI* shows, the violence on the former shows may have a greater effect, even if it is less frequent or less graphic. However, this effect may be mitigated by the fact that the more realistic shows may have a greater impact than the less realistic ones due to their closer connection to the viewers' own experiences. Thus we see that many factors are at work in producing modeling effects.

We turn now to a final alleged psychological effect of violence: catharsis.

Catharsis

The notion of *catharsis* extends all the way back to Aristotle's *Poetics*, in which he spoke of drama purging the emotions of the audience and leading to a ritual purification (Scheele & DuBois, 2006). In modern times, however, the notion was developed largely in psychoanalytic theory, with emphasis on the purging more than the purifying function. According to Freud, the *id*, *ego*, and *superego* are locked in battle, with anxiety resulting from id impulses trying to express themselves and, in so doing, coming into conflict with the moralistic superego. Threatening unconscious impulses like sex and aggression are repressed from consciousness but may cause anxiety when they creep back. These repressed impulses and the anxiety that they produce may be dealt with directly by overt sexual or violent behavior or indirectly through some sublimated substitute activity, such as watching others act sexually or violently onscreen.

The emotional release called catharsis comes from venting the impulse (i.e., expressing it directly or indirectly). This emotional purging has been a notoriously difficult concept to operationally define and test, but it has continued to have a lot of intuitive appeal and anecdotal support (e.g., people report feeling better after watching a scary movie).

Catharsis theory, however, does make one very clear prediction about the effect of screen violence on behavior, a prediction that is eminently testable and exactly opposite to the prediction of modeling theory. Whereas modeling predicts an *increase* in violent behavior after watching media violence, catharsis theory predicts a *decrease* in such behavior (Feshbach, 1955). If the substitute behavior of watching the violence provides the emotional release that would normally result from actually acting violently, then violent behavior should decrease after watching media violence. For example, catharsis theory would predict that a girl who is angry at her sister and then watches a violent cartoon would be less likely to actually hurt her sister than if she hadn't watched the cartoon.

Thus, the catharsis and modeling theories are clearly and competitively testable. When such tests have been done, modeling theory has been consistently supported (e.g., Siegel, 1956), whereas catharsis theory has received little support. In spite of consistent failures to be supported by scientific evidence over many years (Bushman, Baumeister, & Stack, 1999; Geen & Quanty, 1977; Zillmann, 1978), catharsis continues to occupy a prominent though undeserved place in the conventional wisdom about the effects of media violence. Indeed, many intuitively believe that consuming violent media prevents them from behaving aggressively. Unfortunately research evidence does not support this belief, and in fact supports just the opposite.

Later refinements of catharsis theory have been proposed (Feshbach & Singer, 1971). It may be that the media violence elicits fantasizing by the viewer, and that fantasizing, rather than the media violence per se, is what leads to catharsis. Another version of catharsis theory argues that watching media violence reduces one's arousal level, and thus one is less prone to violence. There is evidence that a reduction in arousal level is associated with decreased violent behavior. Third, media violence may elicit an inhibition response, which puts a brake on tendencies toward violent behavior. This is very similar to a sensitization hypothesis. None of these explanations, however, has offered a serious challenge to the overall conclusion that viewing media violence leads to increases in violent behavior.

Who Watches Media Violence and Why?

Another approach to studying media violence has been to examine what attracts viewers to violence and why some are attracted to it much more than others (W. Goldstein, 1998; Sparks & Sparks, 2000). What is it that is appealing about violence as entertainment? Some answers that have been suggested are its novelty, sensory delight, and the violation of social norms. It also may have some social utility, for example in allowing the display of mastery of threats or dependence on a loved one (Zillmann & Weaver, 1996).

Social Factors

In a historical sense, very violent films, especially horror films, have generally been the least popular during wartime and have shown very strong popularity during times of overall peace accompanied by high degrees of social unrest. In his book *The Monster Show*, cultural historian David Skal (1993) traces the history of horror movies in the U.S. throughout the 20th century, pointing out that these films often reflect cultural angst that precedes and follows wars. For example, in the 1930s films such as *The Black Cat* (1935) and *King Kong* (1933) may have foreshadowed Nazi atrocities and the leveling of large cities by a tyrannical force. The 1937 French film *J'Accuse* even used maimed World War I veterans as actors portraying monsters who were reincarnated war dead (see also Fahy, 2010, for a further discussion of motivations behind consuming horror media).

In terms of gender socialization in adolescents, Zillmann and Weaver (1996) developed and tested a model of the role of social motives in consuming horror films. Specifically, they argued that preadolescent and adolescent boys use horror films to develop mastery over fear and to perfect their displays of fearlessness and protective competence. Girls, on the other hand, use the same films to develop their displays of fearfulness and protective need. Although girls actually enjoy the films less than boys do, both find them socially useful as they practice the very traditional gender roles in dating, whereby the boy is the fearless protector and the girl the dependent and fearful companion. The boy's expression of boredom or amusement in response to graphic violence is thus a statement of his apparent mastery over fear. This mastery then may actually mediate a feeling of pleasure. This pleasure, however, was much greater in the presence of a fearful young female companion than in the presence of a fearless female companion who expressed less dependence. Young men, compared to women, are much more desirous that their date not know how scared they felt while watching a scary movie (Harris et al., 2000).

Individual Differences

Several researchers have examined the relationship between personality factors and preference for violent media (e.g., Haridakis, 2002; Slater, Henry, Swaim, & Cardador, 2004). Empathy, discussed earlier in this chapter, is one of the most-studied traits in this regard. Empathy is itself a multidimensional construct (Davis et al., 1987; Zillmann, 2006a) which tends to be negatively associated with a preference for violent media. Tamborini (1996) developed a complex cognitive-motivational model of empathy as a predictor of reactions to viewing violence. Empathy may be evoked to different degrees by certain editing techniques and formal features. For example, extended close-ups of faces encourage empathic responses more than rapid-fire, wide-angle camera shots. Raney (2002; see also Raney & Bryant, 2002) argues that the elicitation of empathy may evoke sympathy for the victim of violence, which in turn predicts lesser enjoyment of the violence.

Another personality variable studied in relation to violent media consumption is *sensation seeking* (Zuckerman, 1994, 1996, 2006), the "seeking of varied, novel, complex, and intense sensations and experiences, and the willingness to take physical, social, legal, and financial risks for the sake of such experience" (Zuckerman, 1996, p. 148). Sensation seeking is positively correlated with a preference for viewing violence (Krcmar & Greene, 1999), although the relationship is tempered by the degree of alienation experienced and by the fact that high sensation seekers tend to prefer real-life over vicarious media experiences and thus tend to be lighter-than-average TV viewers overall (Slater, 2003; Slater et al., 2004). High sensation seekers also tend to prefer to view more intense images (e.g., graphic violence or sex) and to experience higher levels of arousal than do low sensation seekers (Zuckerman, 2006).

Another individual difference variable studied is the level of *psychoticism* (a personality trait thought by some to be related to a predisposition for mental illnesses like schizophrenia). Men (though not women) scoring high in psychoticism found violence a more acceptable way to solve an interpersonal problem after seeing very violent contemporary action films like *Total Recall* and *Die Hard 2*, though not after seeing "old-style," less graphic action or horror-film violence (Zillmann & Weaver, 1997). This suggests that personality factors can interact with certain kinds of violence but not others.

Perhaps the most dramatic individual difference variable comes in the area of psychopathology. Although there have been few studies of effects of media violence on people with particular diagnosed psychiatric disorders, one interesting recent study showed significantly different psychophysiological and behavioral responses in boys ages 8 to 12 who had been diagnosed with one of the disruptive behavioral disorders (DBD), which include attention deficit hyperactivity disorder (ADHD), oppositional defiant disorder (ODD), and conduct disorders (Grimes, Anderson, & Bergen, 2008). Compared with a control group not diagnosed with DBD, the boys with DBD showed several differences while watching three violent movie clips—less physiological arousal but more frequent anger in their facial expressions, though the two groups did not differ in their verbal reports of anger. Grimes and colleagues (2008) claim this may be because they were not cognitively processing the film thoroughly enough to respond with appropriate autonomic reactions; they were not interpreting social cues accurately enough to direct their anger in a mature fashion. They argue that the responses of such people are what we should worry about more than effects of violent media on the population as a whole.

Longitudinal Studies

Although literally hundreds of studies have shown some negative psychological effects of media violence, most of those have been short term and conducted in a laboratory setting, often using the methodology of showing participants a film or film clip and subsequently measuring their behavior or attitudes in some way. Although these findings are important, they do not directly address the long-term cumulative effects of watching hundreds of hours of violent television and movies as recreation throughout one's childhood. There have been a few studies that have addressed this issue, most notably those by Rowell Huesmann and Leonard Eron and their colleagues. Because of their long-range view, such longitudinal studies are especially powerful in understanding the real-world effects of media violence.

Longitudinal studies over as long as 30 years in the United States and Finland provided the first evidence of a causal relationship between real-world viewing of TV violence through childhood and violent behavior as a child and a young adult (Eron & Huesmann, 1984; Eron, Huesmann, Lefkowitz, & Walder, 1972; Huesmann & Eron, 1986; Lefkowitz et al., 1977; Pitkanen-Pulkkinen, 1981). Through careful design and control of other variables, Eron and colleagues (1972) as well as Lefkowitz and colleagues (1977) concluded that they could rule out other plausible third variables, such as dispositional violence, as being the cause of both violent TV viewing and violent behavior. Strikingly, Huesmann and Eron's research has shown that the amount of television watched at age 8 was one of the best predictors of criminal behavior at age 30, even after controlling for individual aggressiveness, IQ, and socio-economic status. Those who were heavy TV viewers in preadolescence were also more likely to more severely punish their own children many years later than were those who watched less TV during the critical years of ages 8 to 12. Watching more TV in adolescence did not seem to matter.

In a three-year longitudinal study, Huesmann, Lagerspetz, and Eron (1984) further explored the role of several intervening variables on the relationship between viewing media violence and violent behavior in U.S. and Finnish children in elementary school. The study collected data from the children, their parents, the children's peers, and the school. Data gathered included measures of TV viewing, attitudes, behaviors, ratings of self and others, and family demographics.

As had been found in many other studies, there was a positive correlation between violent TV viewing and peer-rated aggression, which was stronger for boys than for girls and for Americans than for Finns. The overall level of violent behavior was also higher in the U.S. children. One of the most striking results for both samples was the strong correlation of violent behavior and self-rated identification with violent TV models, especially in boys. The best predictor of later violent behavior was the interactive product of violent viewing and identification with violent characters. There was no evidence that violent TV affects only those children naturally more predisposed to violent behavior or that children who fantasize more were affected any differently. In addition, neither parents' level of violent behavior nor parents' TV viewing had any effect on children's level of violence.

More recent longitudinal research presents the strongest evidence yet that exposure to media violence from ages 6 to 10 predicts violent behavior in young men and women in early adulthood (Huesmann et al., 2003). Following up on children first tested between 1977 and 1978 (Huesmann & Eron, 1986), all of the same persons who could be found (about 60% of the original sample) were tested as young adults over three years. Data were obtained on their adult TV violence viewing and their adult aggressive behavior, the latter obtained from self-reports, spouse/significant other reports, and archival crime and traffic-violation data. Results showed that childhood TV violence viewing was a significant predictor of adult aggressive behavior. These effects were strongest if there was strong viewer identification with the aggressive model and if the perceived realism of the violence was high. Unlike the earlier longitudinal studies, this study found predictive effects for both men and women. The effects persisted even when the factors of socioeconomic status and intellectual ability were controlled. These results were replicated by another, 17-year longitudinal study of 700 children (Johnson, Cohen, Smailes, Kasen, & Brook, 2002).

Putting this All Together: Making Sense of the Body of Research

Although the evidence from longitudinal and other studies has consistently supported the existence of significant negative effects of viewing media violence, studies that look at multiple contributors to societal violence typically estimate that media account for 10 to 15% of the variance in the dependent measure (Perse, 2001; Perse & Lambe, 2013; Sparks & Sparks, 2002). Some critics tend to dismiss the media component in the face of the 85 to 90% of the variance attributable to other factors. In fact, however, this 10 to 15% range is neither surprising nor insignificant. In any complex social behavior, there are naturally going to be multiple causes. In the case of inter-personal violence, there are numerous known strong causes such as parental behavior, poverty, drugs, gangs, absent parents, and easy access to weapons, all of which clearly contribute greatly to this problem. Thus, it would be surprising, indeed completely incredible, to expect media to account for half of societal violence! The importance of media violence is further demonstrated when we realize that media may be one of the easier causes of societal violence to control. There are also some good reasons to think the contribution of media to societal violence may be, if anything, underestimated by these studies (Perse, 2001).

Nevertheless, there are some critics who argue that the negative effects of media violence are less widespread and serious than most researchers argue. Although some of these critics have obvious self-interest (e.g., television network executives or movie producers) and others may be engaging in the third-person effect (see Chapter 2), there are a few who offer more reasoned arguments. Grimes, Anderson, and Bergen (2008) offer the most careful and articulate of these arguments, contending that media "causationist" researchers, as they call them, are in fact driven by ideology rather than science. Another argument they make is that one cannot generalize the negative effects beyond very specialized populations, which they acknowledge may be strongly adversely affected.

However, reaching the clearest conclusion about the mass of research on the effects of media violence requires a convergent evidence approach. Any study taken by itself is subject to some criticism in terms of methodology, interpretation, or validity. When looking at the big picture, however, the weight of the evidence clearly falls on the side of violent media having several negative behavioral and attitudinal effects, especially modeling and desensitization. Typically these effects are not uniform and they are frequently moderated by other variables, but they do seem to be causal in nature. According to one estimate (Grossman & DeGaetano, 1999), of the 3,500 research studies conducted between 1950 and 1999 studying the effects of watching media violence, all but 18 (i.e., 99.5%) show negative effects of consuming violent entertainment. When the large majority of thousands of studies, using a wide variety of methodologies, point in the same direction in terms of results, this cannot be discredited by pointing to particular flaws or limitations of experimental design in individual studies. Further, a 1993 American Psychological Association report summed up the research in this area by saying this:

> Nearly four decades of research on television viewing and other media have documented the almost universal exposure of American children to high levels of media violence...[T]here is absolutely no doubt that higher levels of viewing violence on television are correlated with increased acceptance of aggressive attitudes and increased aggressive behavior.
>
> American Psychological Association, 1993, pp. 32–33)

The strength of these conclusions has only increased in subsequent years (Bushman & Anderson, 2001).

A useful way to look at effects of media violence is in terms of risk and protective factors (Kirsh, 2006). Strong negative effects will only be observed in someone who exhibits or is exposed to multiple risk factors. Some of these risk factors are demographic (being male, young, living in high-violence environments, heavy exposure to media violence, using drugs, being in gangs). Others are personality and mental health factors (high alienation, proneness to violence, hopelessness, high sensation seeking, lacking social support, being angry, having been diagnosed with a DBD, being low in empathy). Finally, there are risk factors in the media itself (violence is reinforced, realistic, perpetrated by admired characters with whom one identifies). The alienated youth who starts shooting classmates has not merely watched bloody movies, he almost surely has multiple risk factors to a high degree. It is thus quite understandable that most people watching violent media do not show clear ill effects. However, given the mass audience, serious negative effects on a few individuals are still cause for great concern.

Just as there are risk factors which push a child toward experiencing more negative reactions to watching media violence, so are there protective factors which may reduce the likelihood of exhibiting negative effects. Like the risk factors, some of these are dispositional attributes of the person, such as low sensation seeking, high empathy, low violence proneness, slowness to anger, and generally easy temperament. There are also protective factors in the environment, such as positive engaged parenting, mediation from parents about media, safe and nonviolent surroundings, absence of drugs and gangs, and lower exposure to screen violence. Parents aiming to protect their children from negative effects of media violence should seek to minimize as many of the risk factors and maximize as many of the protective factors as possible, keeping in mind that the risk will never be zero.

No one but the most strident media basher seriously argues that violence in media is to blame for *all* societal violence. However, the conclusion of "no effects" or "no clear picture yet" from the research is simply not tenable scientifically, although it is, surprisingly, the view that is increasingly presented in popular news reporting.

Research versus the Public Perception

Bushman and Anderson (2001) conducted a meta-analysis of over 200 studies on the effects of media violence, collectively involving over 43,000 participants. They concluded that the evidence for negative effects of media violence is strong and its strength is increasing, especially in the post-1990 research. Overall, effects are larger for experimental than correlational studies, as one would naturally expect, though the trend is the same. Interestingly enough, however, during this same period, when the research evidence on the negative effects of media violence was becoming stronger, the popular news reporting of the same research erroneously suggested that these effects were becoming weaker.

What are some possible reasons for this serious deviation from reality? Huesmann (2010) argues some may be unwilling to embrace the fact that violent media like video games are related to real-life aggression, due to a misguided concern that this acceptance may lead to limits on freedom of expression. Bushman and Anderson (2001) suggest three additional explanations. First, certain segments of the media and entertainment industries have a substantial vested interest in denying a strong link between media violence and violent behavior, given that they make enormous profits from selling violent entertainment (Hamilton, 1998). Television networks, movie studios, cable channels, and sometimes also print media outlets are part of the same huge conglomerates, which are under considerable pressure to maintain or increase their audience size for their advertisers. A second reason suggested by Bushman and Anderson is what they call a "misapplied fairness doctrine." One of media's strongest abiding principles is balance and fairness—presenting all sides of an issue. This causes media to look very hard for an opposing view (e.g., pro vs. con opinions on the negative effects of media violence), even when evidence on one side of an issue is weak. The resulting presentation of both sides of this issue leaves the reader/viewer with the mistaken impression that research opinion is more or less evenly divided on the issue. This laudable attempt to be fair ends up obscuring the fact that, although there are two sides of opinion on the issue (whether violent media do or do not cause violent behavior), the overwhelming majority of scientific opinion comes down on the negative effects side. Finally, Bushman and Anderson argue that the research community has often failed to advocate its position with strength and clarity. Researchers are by training very cautious and conservative about overgeneralizing the effects of their research, and most have no training and little or no experience in talking to the press. We return to this communication issue in Chapter 12.

Violent Video Games

One of the newer forms of media violence, video games, is causing great concern among both scholars and parents. In 2008, the release of the very violent *Grand Theft Auto IV* set an all-time record for first-day sales for any entertainment release ($310 million), far surpassing the previous record of $220 million for the last Harry Potter book in 2007 ("Numbers," 2008a). However, that record was broken (or tied, depending on how the numbers are tabulated) the next year when *Call of Duty: Modern Warfare 2*, also highly violent, was released (Itzkoff, 2009). Unlike TV or movie violence, video games are interactive and allow players to participate in the violence as aggressors themselves (Grodal, 2000). Over 83% of 8- to 18-year-olds have their own video game console, and 56% have two or more systems (Rideout, Robert, & Foehr, 2005). Video games are particularly popular with college students, with about 70% reporting playing them at least "once in a while." Although men and women play video games equally often, in terms of uses and gratifications, men are more likely to play for fun (45%) and women because they're bored (33%). The kinds of games played by males and females may also differ. In a study of 13-year-olds, Kutner and Olson (2008) found that the most popular video game among boys was *Grand Theft Auto*; among girls, it was *The Sims* (although *Grand Theft Auto* was the second most popular choice among girls). While gamers can play many video games alone, gaming is more social for men, with 51% of men but only 34% of women believing that gaming improves their friendships, contrary to the alienated social misfit image sometimes associated with video games (Weaver, 2003b). In fact, many gaming systems now allow players to interact online, playing against living opponents they may never meet. Interestingly, more women than men (60% vs. 40%) reported playing computer and online games like *Diamond Mine* and *Tetris* (Weaver, 2003b).

Probably the major concern with video games is the high level of violence. For example, *Grand Theft Auto* allows gamers to commit carjacking and murder police officers as they drive through a virtual criminal playground. You can pick up a prostitute and take her to a dark alley. She takes your money (as the car rocks excitedly) but you can get it back by killing her. In *Postal*, you become a paranoid psychopath and kill hostile people, with no penalty for shooting innocent bystanders. Once you have wounded someone, you can stand above them while they beg for mercy, and then shoot them (Crockett, 2002). *Quake* features a machine that consumes humans and spits them out in bits and pieces. A French video game by BMG Interactive called on players to become Public Enemy No. 1 by stealing, murdering, and drug trafficking. The largest police union in Paris called for the game to be banned (J. T. Hamilton, 1998). In *Carmageddon*, players knock down and kill innocent pedestrians. In *Duke Nukem*, the shooter shoots posters of scantily clad women and then moves on to murdering female prostitutes, who are often naked and tied to columns, pleading "Kill me, kill me." In *Outlaw Golf*, players build their skill by punching their caddies in the stomach and smashing car windows.

Media violence research and its theories have guided the more recent research on the effects of playing violent video games. Following predictions from social learning theory (Bandura, 2002), game players learn shooting behaviors from playing the video game and imitating violent characters in the game. Children behave more aggressively after playing a violent video game than a nonviolent one (C. A. Anderson & Morrow, 1995; Bartholomew & Anderson, 2002; Bushman & Anderson, 2002; Kirsh, 1998; Lightdale & Prentice, 1994). Results from a meta-analysis of over 80,000 participants indicated that engaging in "active" violent media such as video games was associated with risk-taking behaviors in real life (Fischer, Greitemeyer, Kastenmuller, Vogrincic, & Sauer, 2011). Playing violent video games also raises the overall arousal level, thus raising physiological indicators like heart rate and priming the person to behave violently with relatively less provocation than would otherwise be the case (C. A. Anderson & Dill, 2000; C. A. Anderson et al., 2004; Ballard & Wiest, 1996; Fleming & Rickwood, 2001; Panee & Ballard, 2002). In addition, playing violent video games can elicit hostile expectations, leading one to expect that others will respond aggressively (Bushman & Anderson, 2002; Eastin & Griffiths, 2006). It also heightens negative emotions in a way that is similar to possessing high trait hostility (Barlett, Harris, & Baldassaro, 2007; Kirsh, Olczak, & Mounts, 2005). Participants playing a violent video game with the "blood on" condition show more hostility and arousal (Barlett, Harris, & Bruey, 2008) and more physically aggressive intentions (Farrar, Krcmar, & Nowak, 2006) than those playing the same game with the blood option off.

Reinforcement matters, too. When violent game actions are rewarded in the game, hostile emotions, aggressive thoughts, and aggressive behavior all increase; when the violent actions are punished, only hostile emotion increases (Carnagey & Anderson, 2005). Technologically more advanced games have stronger effects on arousal than do older games (Ivory & Kalyanaraman, 2007). An fMRI study (Weber, Ritterfeld, & Mathiak, 2006) found that brain activation during violent video game play was remarkably similar to real-life experiences when behaving violently and dealing with violence.

Sherry (2001) and Anderson and Bushman (2001) independently conducted meta-analyses of 25 to 35 studies conducted between 1975 and 2000 on the effects of violent video game play on violent behavior. Results showed a consistent effect that playing violent video games led to more violent behavior. The results were stronger for fantasy and realistic-violence games than for sports games, with larger effect sizes for studies with better methodologies (Anderson et al., 2003). Another study (Kutner & Olson, 2008), focusing on middle school students, found positive correlations between children who played M (mature)-rated video games and real-life problem behaviors such as aggression, bullying, delinquency, and school problems.

Violent video games also increase physiological arousal and aggressive affect and cognitions. Interestingly, Sherry (2001) found that the effects became weaker the longer the games were played, unlike findings from TV violence research exposure. An extensive meta-analysis published in 2010 that examined 136 studies (with over 130,000 participants) concluded, "The evidence strongly suggests that exposure to violent video games is a causal risk factor for increased aggressive behavior, aggressive cognition, and aggressive affect and for decreased empathy and prosocial behavior" (Anderson et al., 2010, p. 151). Commenting on the results of this meta-analysis, Huesmann (2010) said, "violent video games stimulate aggression in the players in the short run and increase the risk for aggressive behaviors by players later in life. The effects occur for males and females and for children growing up in Eastern or Western cultures" (p. 179). See Anderson et al. (2003), Griffiths (1999), Bensley and Van Eenwyk (2001), Lee and Peng (2006), Sherry (2007), and Weber, Ritterfeld, and Kostygina (2006) for reviews of the literature on the effect of playing violent video games on violent behavior, and Bushman and Anderson (2002) for the development and testing of the general aggression model to account for effects of violent video games.

One type of video game causing particular concern is the first-person shooter, in which the player controls interactive guns that he or she has to learn to hold, aim, and fire at a moving target. These account for a little over a quarter of video game sales. In the case of the Nintendo Wii platform, playing the game also involves physically making many of the motions a real-life shooter would perform. *The House of the Dead* has players fire at zombies and monsters that attack. *Time Crisis* has a kickback function to simulate the feel of a real weapon. The player also has a foot pedal that can control when the character takes cover to reload or steps out to shoot. In PlayStation's *Operation Desert Storm*, the player shoots Iraqi soldiers. Home video systems are increasingly able to add features to approach the arcade game level of realism. For example, some games have a built-in vibrating system called a rumble pack, which vibrates the controller whenever a bullet is fired. One can clearly expect these games to become even more graphically violent and realistic in coming years, with improvements in technology. The games may even become more easily customizable, allowing players to scan in photos of a school, neighborhood, or "enemies." Even back in 1999, the computer of one of the Columbine High assassins contained a customized version of *Doom*,

Close-Up 9.6: Who Shoots Better, Soldiers or Video Gamers?

In studying historic battles, military psychologist David Grossman (1996) discovered that there was often more posturing than killing. For example, 90% of the muskets picked up from dead and dying soldiers at the Battle of Gettysburg in 1863 were loaded, over half of them with multiple loads. This was surprising, considering that it took 19 times as long to load a musket as to fire one. Such findings suggest that there was a lot of loading and posturing by basically decent young soldiers who could not bring themselves to actually fire their weapons. Another study found that only 15 to 20% of World War II soldiers could bring themselves to actually fire at an exposed enemy soldier. Once the army discovered this, they set out to improve this record through training involving classical and operant conditioning, desensitization, and a heavy dose of brutalization. Such efforts worked. In the Korean War, 55% of the soldiers were willing to fire, and over 90% did so in the Vietnam War.

Grossman (1996; Grossman & DeGaetano, 1999) argues that we are doing the same thing with video games and violent movies, except that we start training shooters much younger. Teaching people to shoot immediately in response to the sight of the enemy is not always good soldiering or good police behavior, but it is successful video game play. Associating brutal killing with entertainment greatly lessens the distress and inhibitions we normally have about such behavior, and that is what is going on all the time with teens consuming a steady diet of violent video game play as regular amusement. "We have raised a generation of barbarians who have learned to associate violence with pleasure, like the Romans cheering and snacking as the Christians were slaughtered in the Colosseum" (Grossman, 1996, p. 5).

into which the killer had scanned photos of his school and classmates he despised so he could practice killing them.

Do first-person shooter games teach anything more than military and police training do? See Close-Up 9.6 for some surprising research from military psychology about how eager and effective soldiers have (or haven't) been in battle.

Helping Children Deal with Violent Media

Given the concerns identified by the research, as well as the impossibility of totally shielding our children from violent media, what can we do to help mitigate these negative effects, especially on children? Possible solutions arise in several different areas, which we will examine in turn.

Institutional Solutions

Given the probable negative effects and influences of violent media, what can a parent do, short of prohibiting viewing or game-playing altogether?

The V-Chip

Prohibition would not be totally successful because children see violent TV at friends' homes and may rent violent movies. Even as the V-chip mandated by the Telecommunications Act of 1996 has become standard practice (Price, 1998), it must be programmed in each TV set to block out the violent shows, as determined by the rating. To the surprise of its proponents, the V-chip has been used very little. The reasons for this are not completely clear, but it is probably due to a combination of ignorance of its presence, lack of knowledge about how to program and implement it, a reluctance to block out a large number of programs of possible interest to the parents, tech-savvy kids' ability to get around the technology, and questionable criteria for blocking programs (Kunkel et al., 2002).

Television Content Ratings

First implemented in the late 1990s in the U.S. as a parallel to the more familiar MPAA movie rating systems, TV ratings attempt to specify appropriate viewing ages (e.g., TV-14—not suitable for children under 14), sometimes giving information as to the nature of the questionable content (sex, language, violence). These ratings continue to be the subject of criticism and refinement in an attempt to make them more useful. One criticism is that the ratings may lack uniformity because networks voluntarily set the ratings for each show themselves. As with movie ratings, indications are that sex, more than violence, drives the ratings (Leone, 2002).

Mediation and Media Literacy Training

Although mitigating the effects of TV violence has not been the major thrust of the research in this area, there have been some interesting findings that speak to this issue.

Classroom Training

Huesmann, Eron, Klein, Brice, and Fischer (1983) developed a treatment designed to change children's attitudes about violent TV. One hundred sixty-nine first and third graders who watched a lot of violent TV were exposed to two treatment sessions over two years. The first session involved showing children TV film clips and having them discuss the violence and alternative nonviolent, realistic ways that the problems could have been solved. Neither the treatment session nor a control session discussing other aspects of TV had any effect on the children's own violent behavior or on their belief about the reality of TV violence.

However, a second intervention nine months later with the same group had children develop arguments about the negative effects of TV violence, write a paragraph on the topic, and make a group video with everyone reading his or her essay. This treatment (but not the control) led to reduced violent behavior and a weaker relationship between aggression and violent TV viewing. In terms of attitudes, the treatment had a substantial effect on children's responses to two questions ("Are television shows with a lot of hitting and shooting harmless for kids?" and "How likely is it that watching a lot of television violence would make a kid meaner?"). The mitigation effect was strongest in children who identified least with the violent characters, suggesting the important role of identification with the aggressive model.

More recently, Robinson, Wilde, Navracruz, Haydel, and Varady (2001) tested a six-month training session for third and fourth graders and their parents, designed to reduce television, video, and video game use. Children were encouraged to watch no TV or video for 10 days and stay on a one-hour-per-day regimen thereafter. Children also received lessons on various aspects of media literacy and parents were encouraged to help their children follow the schedule and to encourage the family to do likewise. Compared to a control group, the experimental group showed less peer-rated aggression and observed verbal aggression.

Systematic Desensitization

A somewhat different approach taken by Wilson and Cantor and their colleagues draws on an application of classical conditioning. They used systematic desensitization techniques to reduce children's fear reactions to scary media presentations (Wilson, 1987, 1989; Wilson & Cantor, 1987; Wilson, Hoffner, & Cantor, 1987). For example, before watching a scary movie about lizards, children of ages 5 to 10 did one of the following: (1) saw a live lizard; (2) saw the experimenter touch a live lizard; or (3) had no exposure to a live lizard. The group in which the experimenter modeled touching the lizard experienced the most reduction in negative emotional reactions and interpretations while viewing the scary video (Wilson, 1989).

The successes of Huesmann and Wilson and their colleagues in mitigating the effects of TV violence through training is encouraging, if for no other reason than that it shows that this antisocial learning is subject to alteration by new learning. This is especially encouraging because violence as a dispositional behavior trait is known to be remarkably stable over time (Huesmann, Eron, Lefkowitz, & Walder, 1984; Olweus, 1979).

Personality Development

Another approach to mitigating negative effects of media violence is suggested by the individual differences research of Tamborini and his colleagues (Tamborini, 1996; Tamborini & Stiff, 1987; Tamborini, Stiff, & Heidel 1990; Tamborini, Stiff, & Zillmann, 1987; see also McCauley, 1998). If certain types of personalities (e.g., highly empathic) find graphic violence distasteful and disturbing, and others (e.g., sensation seeking) find it pleasantly arousing, cultivating empathic qualities in one's children and discouraging sensation seeking should presumably help in ensuring that they will not find viewing violence to be pleasurable. Similarly, encouraging psychological identification with the victims rather than the perpetrators of violence should decrease the enjoyment level of violent TV. Anything to lower the risk factors or raise the protective factors will help lessen the negative effects of media violence on children

See Cantor and Wilson (2003) for a thorough review of strategies to reduce negative effects of media violence in children.

Conclusion

What, then, may we conclude from this mass of research on media violence inside and outside of the laboratory? Although no single study by itself is definitive in establishing the deleterious effect of TV violence on children, the evidence overall strongly converges on the conclusion that media violence does have harmful effects, especially on children, primarily in three areas. After exposure to media violence, there is an increase in fear, violent behavior, and desensitization (Anderson et al., 2003; Bushman & Anderson, 2001; Dubow & Miller, 1996; Kirsh, 2006). The laboratory research has generally yielded stronger conclusions than the field studies, which is exactly what would be expected. The majority of opinions clearly conclude that there is strong evidence of these three negative effects.

Although most of the longitudinal field studies have shown a significant positive correlation between viewing televised violence and subsequent aggressive behavior, such correlations have typically been small in magnitude (e.g., Pearson r correlations between 0.15 and 0.30, statistically accounting for 2 to 9% of the variance). The fact that this correlation is small should not be surprising, however. Social cognitive theory, for example, would predict such a modest effect, because television is after all only a small part of the matrix of influences in people's lives (Perse & Lambe, 2013). It is clearly one of those influences, however, and no doubt an important one.

The effects of media violence do not fall equally on all viewers. Some people are affected more than others, and some portrayals of violence and some shows have more effect than others. The more risk factors that are present and the fewer protective factors, the greater the negative effects on viewers. In proposing policy—either legislative regulation or industry guidelines—such issues must be considered. All violence is not equally harmful to all people. This is also the challenge to those implementing the V-chip and industry ratings.

A final issue that complicates policy-setting questions is the fact that violent themes are very widespread in media. Certainly most prevalent in entertainment TV programming, films, and videogames, violence is also widespread in cartoons, news, song lyrics, sports, and other places we do not always think about when discussing media violence (see Close-Up 9.7). The debate over the effects of media violence has been strident and heated and will probably continue at that level. Predictably, the television and film industries in general have questioned the conclusions of much of the behavioral research. Although the negative effects of TV may not be quite as widespread or serious as suggested by the strongest critics, they are not nearly as benign as suggested by the apologists. We have not yet seriously addressed one of the types of media violence causing the greatest concern today: sexual violence. We examine this issue and research on the problem in detail in the next chapter, after a consideration of sex in the media.

Close-Up 9.7: Other Media Support for Violence

When we talk of violence in media, we typically think of television entertainment, movies, and possibly news. However, there are many other media messages that violence is cool, okay, or at least not too bad. Consider the following:

Music

Popular music, especially rap and heavy metal, have many violent themes. A very popular song on the U.S. pop charts in late 1997 was "Smack My Bitch Up" by the dance band Prodigy. A popular gangsta rap lyric, "Know the Game," from Mobb Deep, said, "Hitman for hire, who's the next to expire/Shoot it up in black attire, hit you wit the rapid fire/The stainless bisket will leave your brain smoking/Your whole frame broken and clothes soaken, head blown open" (Bullard, 1998). According to a content analysis, 15% of music videos (29% of rap videos) contained violence, most of it sanitized and not punished (Smith & Boyson, 2002).

Sports

In a December 1997 practice, Golden State Warriors' leading scorer Latrell Sprewell assaulted Coach P. J. Carlesimo by throttling him, and, a few minutes later, yelling, "I'm going to kill you. You better get me off this team, or that's what I'm going to do." Although this earned him the longest NBA suspension in history (1 year) and the immediate loss of a lucrative endorsement contract with Converse, there was still much discussion in the press about how Carlesimo had "provoked" Sprewell and was "insensitive." Sprewell's suspension was later shortened, but even so, he was punished more severely than other NBA hotheads, such as basketball superstar Charles Barkley, who earlier had spat on a fan and thrown a man through a plate-glass window. Still, many wondered what other job would allow someone to return to work at all after assaulting the boss and threatening to kill him.

Advertising

A Minnesota physician examined the commercials shown during 15 baseball playoff and World Series games in 1997. He found 104 violent commercials, 67% of them promoting movies or other TV programs. Half of them showed guns and about one-quarter showed knives (Colburn, 1997).

Chapter 10

Sex

Is Tuning In Turning Us On?
Sexuality through a Media Lens

Q: What percentage of prime-time broadcast TV shows contain sexual content?

A: Seventy-seven percent, with 70% of all TV programs containing sexual content (Kaiser Family Foundation, 2005).

Q: How many sexual references does the average U.S. child see per year?

A: Nearly 15,000 sexual references, innuendoes, and jokes per year. Only 16% of the scenes and 15% of the shows mention any concerns regarding abstinence, birth control, or consequences of sex like pregnancy or STDs (Kunkel, Eyal et al., 2007). According to one study, there was a 96% increase in sexual scenes on television between 1998 and 2005 ("Numbers," 2005).

Q: Although violent men are sexually aroused by viewing an explicit rape or sexual assault scene, nonviolent heterosexual men are generally not sexually aroused by watching a rape scene unless what occurs in the scene?

A: If the woman is portrayed as enjoying and being sexually turned on by being raped, nonviolent men are also aroused by it (Malamuth, 1984; Malamuth & Check, 1983).

Q: What percentage of parents believe that exposure to sexual content in media contributes "a lot" to children becoming involved in real-life sexual situations before they are ready?

A: Fifty-five percent, with an additional 30% believing that such content "somewhat" contributes to this risk (Kaiser Family Foundation, 2007b).

Some of our major sources of information about sex are from the media (Chia, 2006; Sutton, Brown, Wilson, & Klein, 2002). Everything from the mildest innuendo on a network sitcom to the most explicit pornographic Internet video can contribute to our perceived reality of what sex is all about and what people expect from it. According to one Time/CNN poll (Stodghill, 1998), 29% of U.S. teens identified television as their principal source of information about sex, up from 11% in 1986. Somewhat more (45%) mentioned friends as the major source, but only 7% cited parents and 3% sex education. In a 2005 poll, 51% of young teens (13–16 years of age) indicated that they received information about sex from TV and movies. Another 34% said they got sex information from magazines, and 19% indicated that they had obtained sex information from the Internet (Topline Report NBC/People, 2005).

Yet another study found that 29% of boys rated pornography as their *most significant* source of sex education (Check, 1995). In other studies, 90% of Toronto boys and 60% of girls (mean age 14) had seen at least one pornographic movie, and 43% of U.S. males saw at least one sex magazine in a year (Russell, 1998). One of the newest media sources of sex is the Internet, which, in addition to numerous pornography sites, has informational sex sites that are widely visited (Cooper, 1998; S. N. Wilson, 2000). We are continually learning more about sex and modifying our constructed reality of its nature. How we act on that information may have serious consequences for our lives and the lives of others. In this chapter we first examine how sex is presented in the media and then turn to research on the effects of exposure to that material. Toward the end of the chapter, we focus on one of the most controversial varieties of media sex, namely sexual violence.

The Nature of Sex in Media

Whenever we speak of sex in the media, we must clarify what we are including in that term. There is a class of media often explicitly labeled erotic, pornographic, or sexually explicit, which comprises magazines, videos, films, and Internet websites. These materials have typically been marketed separately from nonsexual media and have been at least somewhat restricted to children, although this is becoming increasingly difficult, especially with the Internet.

Definitional Issues

Pornography brought in $13 billion in the United States in 2006 (IT Facts, 2007), far more money than professional sports, performing arts, theater, or all other Internet commerce. In 2001, video porn alone brought in around $4 billion per year, with 11,000 new titles released annually (compared to only 400 from Hollywood), and 750 million video/DVD rentals per year ("Naked Capitalists," 2001). An estimated 100,000 adult pornographic websites take in around $1 billion annually, and porn films are ordered by business travelers in hotel rooms 10 times as often as standard films (Sigesmund, 2003). Interestingly, however, changes in Internet usage patterns are increasingly providing financial challenges to the pornography industry. Specifically, YouTube-type porn sites seem to be leading to pornography piracy and user-submitted videos that can be accessed without fees, which in turn leads to less traffic on pay porn websites (Chiang, 2009). Of course, that doesn't mean that there is less interest in online pornography—it just seems that it is becoming easier, and cheaper, to locate as the Internet matures.

Pornography can be difficult to define; an Associate Supreme Court justice once famously said, "I know it when I see it" (see Close-Up 10.9 for further discussion of pornography and politics). However, traditionally, pornographic media have been recognized as being for sexual purposes only and without recognized literary or artistic merit, although there are a few signs that pornography is becoming more mainstream (Sigesmund, 2003). Porn film stars are becoming more widely known, and several recent feature films have dealt with the porn industry (*The People vs. Larry Flynt, Boogie Nights, The Girl Next Door, Wonderland*), while TV series like Fox's *Skin* and documentary series like HBO's *Pornucopia* and Showtime's *Family Business* feature porn producers as major characters. More than any other medium, however, the widespread, private availability of pornography on the Internet has spread its influence. Interestingly enough, as the new technology has spread sexually explicit media in unprecedented ways, some traditional sex media, especially magazines, have fallen on hard times. Most sex magazines have lost at least 10% of their circulation per year since the mid-1990s. For example, *Penthouse*'s publishing has fallen from 5 million copies a month to less than 150,000 (Audit Bureau of Circulations, 2012; Sigesmund, 2003).

Defining Sexual Violence

Scholars have found it helpful to distinguish between sexually violent material, which portrays rape and other instances of physical coercion and harm to persons in a sexual context, and nonviolent sexual material, which may or may not depict degradation, domination, subordination, or humiliation. Nonviolent and nondegrading material typically depicts a couple having intercourse with no indication of violence or coercion. Research has consistently shown more negative effects from viewing sexual violence than from the nonviolent, nondegrading material, with intermediate results from the nonviolent degrading material. Child pornography portrays minors and, although in most countries it is illegal to produce, distribute, and in some cases possess, it still circulates widely through foreign magazines, personal distribution, and especially the Internet (Jenkins, 2001). For obvious ethical reasons, there has been little scientific research on the effects of child pornography, though see Paul and Linz (2008) for a creative attempt to measure effects of showing participants "barely legal" photos of women who appear to be minors.

Of course, sex occurs in many other media outlets besides these explicitly sexual materials. For example, it is rampant in advertising, certainly for products like mouthwash, perfume, cologne, and aftershave, but also for tires, automobiles, and faucets (see Chapter 5). Sex in media is not limited to explicit portrayals of intercourse or nudity, but rather may include any representation that portrays or implies sexual behavior, interest, or motivation. Indeed, the most common category of sex in media is talking about sex, the sort of dialogue rampant on sitcoms and dramas like *Glee, Grey's Anatomy*,

The Big Bang Theory, Two and a Half Men, or *Desperate Housewives.* Although much of this chapter deals with explicit sexual materials, we consider sexual talk as well, which can also convey strong messages about sex. Because the term "pornographic" is highly value-laden but scientifically imprecise, from here on we will generally refer to such materials as "sexually explicit."

History of Sex in Media

Sexual themes in fiction have been around as long as fiction itself. Ancient Greek comedies were often highly sexual in content, for example Aristophanes' *Lysistrata,* an antiwar comedy about women who withhold sex from their husbands to coerce them to stop fighting wars. Literary classics like Chaucer's *Canterbury Tales* and Shakespeare's *The Taming of the Shrew* are filled with sexual double entendres and overtly sexual themes, some of which are missed today due to the archaic language and the classic aura around such works. Throughout history, the pendulum has swung back and forth in terms of how much sexual expression is permitted in literature, art, and entertainment at any given time and how explicit it may be.

Since the advent of electronic media, standards have usually been more conservative for movies, radio, and television than for print, because it is easier to keep sexually oriented print media from children than it is radio or TV. The issue is more complex with movies, because although there is a movie ratings system in place (see Close-Ups 1.2 and 10.1), it is not always enforced. With the advent of widespread cable and digital technology, a sort of double standard has arisen, with greater permissiveness for video and premium cable channels than for network television, using the logic that premium cable and DVDs are invited into the home, whereas broadcast network programming is there uninvited whenever a TV set is present. Of course, the most difficult access issue is the ready availability of sex on the Internet and how to restrict its availability to minors. Pornography filters have some success, although they raise free speech issues and sometimes unintentionally restrict nonsexual sites (e.g., breast cancer information); also, entrepreneurs of sexually explicit websites are usually one step ahead of the screeners in designing ways to avoid the filters.

Close-Up 10.1: Sex, Movie Censorship, and the Hays Code

Most moviegoers in the U.S. today are familiar with the film rating system employed by the Movie Picture Association of America (MPAA), in which films are given the ratings G, PG, PG-13, R, and NC-17 (see also Close-Up 1.2). What is probably less known to modern movie audiences is the surprising history that predates the use of these ratings.

Almost as soon as movies began to be produced, there was concern about their content, particularly as it related to sex. There may have been good reason to be worried. You may think of old movies as generally tame and "family friendly," but many films in the 1920s to mid-1930s were anything but. In this era before much regulation was in place, movie producers often pushed the envelope with racy content such as graphic violence, adultery, promiscuity, out-of-wedlock births, rape, and prostitution. No one pushed the envelope more than writer and performer Mae West. In movies such as *She Done Him Wrong* (1933) and *I'm No Angel* (1933), West sang seductive numbers like "A Man What Takes His Time," alluding to the benefits of sexual foreplay. She also purred snappy one-liners including, "It's not the men in your life that matters, it's the life in your men," and "When I'm good, I'm very good, but when I'm bad, I'm better." This sort of innuendo, combined with themes of organized crime, prostitution, and even brief glimpses of nudity and lesbian relationships, delighted some and outraged others (Black, 1994; Doherty, 1999).

Interestingly, even when some of the most scandalous early movies were made, there was a detailed film censorship policy in place. Formally called the "Motion Picture Production Code of 1930," it became better known as the "Hays Code" after Will Hays, who at the time was president of the Motion Picture Producers and Distributors of America (MPPDA). The Hays Code contained very specific dos and don'ts relating to topics like vulgarity (e.g., "the name Jesus Christ should never be used except in reverence"), costume (e.g., "nudity is never permitted"), and location (e.g., "brothels and houses of ill fame, no matter of what country, are not proper locations for drama"). Later additions to the Code forbid depictions of seduction, rape, venereal disease, scenes of actual childbirth, and miscegenation (sex relationships between the Black and White races).

Despite this specificity, the MPPDA (which would later become the MPAA mentioned above) was at first a largely symbolic organization constructed by the big movie studios as a way to quell talk of government censorship. Thus, the Hays Code was rarely followed or enforced. However, as movies became particularly edgy in the early 1930s, there was increased opposition from various fronts, including religious leaders, the Roosevelt administration, and academics, who began to report on the negative effects of viewing provocative movies. Seeing the writing on the wall (and wanting to avoid outside governmental censorship, or worse—box office boycotts), Hays and the MPPDA by 1934 had begun to enforce the Code (Doherty, 1999; Skal, 1993). The turnaround was profound: "Now truly under the Code, the landscape of American cinema underwent a tectonic shift. In a matter of months, the genres, tones, and textures of pre-Code Hollywood were erased from the screen" (Doherty, 1999, p. 331).

The Hays Code was strictly enforced throughout most of the rest of the 1930s, 40s, and 50s, giving rise to squeaky-clean movies starring performers such as Shirley Temple and Judy Garland. It wasn't until the 1960s that the Code was replaced with the current MPAA rating system, although by that time the Code was again largely being ignored by producers, as audiences seemed to demand more sophisticated movie fare.

Media Sex Today

Content analyses of media show that sexual innuendoes and, less often, behaviors are common, very frequently occurring in a humorous context. In 2004 and 2005, 70% of overall U.S. TV prime-time general entertainment programming contained sexual talk or behaviors, with an average of 5.0 sexual scenes per hour (Kaiser Family Foundation, 2005). The rates were even higher in the more specific TV categories of movies (92%), comedies (87%), and soap operas (85%) (Kaiser Family Foundation, 2005). More of the programs contained talk about sex (68%) than actual sexual behavior (35%), though intercourse was depicted or strongly implied in 11% of the shows, up from 7% eight years earlier (Kaiser Family Foundation, 2005; Kunkel et al., 2007). Only 14% of the shows mentioned any concerns with abstinence, birth control, or consequences of sex like pregnancy or STDs (Kaiser Family Foundation, 2005). Mentions of such concerns are rising slowly over time, from only 1 to 5% in the early 1990s, but the depiction of sex as behavior without serious consequences remains a major distortion of reality in the media presentation of sex.

A longitudinal meta-analysis of 25 content analyses from 1975 to 2004 for sexual content appearing on U.S. prime-time broadcast network programming (NBC, ABC, CBS, and Fox) found a decrease in the frequency per hour for passionate kissing, touching, and intercourse from the early 1990s to 2004 (Hetsroni, 2007). Interestingly, however, the amount of sex talk steadily increased from 1999 to 2004. Media references to premarital and extramarital sexual encounters far outnumber references to sex between spouses, by a ratio of at least 6 to 1 (Greenberg & Hofschire, 2000) and as high as 32 to 1 in R-rated movies (Greenberg, Brown, & Buerkel-Rothfuss, 1993). A 1995 content analysis of soap operas showed some increase since the 1970s and 80s of themes of negative consequences of sex and rejection of sexual advances (Greenberg & Busselle, 1996). The frequency of nonmarital intercourse and prostitution also increased between 2000 and 2004 (Hetsroni, 2007).

We have clearly come a long way from the early 1950s, when network censors required Lucy and Ricky Ricardo on *I Love Lucy* to have twin beds and refer to her expectant state as "having a baby," never as "pregnant," but there are still firm lines that no network or mainstream cable TV shows dare cross, such as frontal nudity, explicit sexual intercourse, or use of the notorious "F-word."

Standards for television are more conservative than for radio, which is in turn more conservative than the recording industry. These differences are especially clear in terms of music lyrics. When Mick Jagger and the Rolling Stones appeared on *The Ed Sullivan Show* in the 1960s, they had to change the line "Let's spend the night together" to "Let's spend some time together." When Jagger performed this line, he did so with exaggerated gestures, rolled eyes, and body language to communicate his attitude to the censoring. Concern has continued ever since, such as when a song moves from the more permissive radio to the more conservative television, as in the case of MTV. Some of the strongest rap and heavy metal lyrics never even make it to the radio version of a song, but are widely available to youth on CD or via the Internet.

Sex in media is one area in which we clearly tolerate some limits on freedom of speech, and that fact is generally accepted. The sharp differences of opinion come in deciding just where those limits should be. Few are arguing that a network sitcom should show frontal nudity or child prostitutes, although it is highly unlikely that the producers would ever care to do so. One important issue in discussion of where the limits should be is the age of the consumer. There is far more concern about the effects of sexual media on children than on adults. Even a highly libertarian person probably does not want a 6-year-old surfing porn sites on the Internet, whereas even a morally conservative person would be less alarmed about adults viewing X-rated videos than young children seeing them. The whole area of the effects of sexual media on children is a difficult area to study for ethical reasons; however, there are some ingenious ways to probe their effects without actually presenting children with stimuli that many of their parents would object to (see Close-Up 10.2).

Close-Up 10.2: Studying Effects of Sexual Media on Children

One empirical question we would like to know the answer to is almost impossible to study for ethical reasons: What is the effect of sexual media on children? What parent would approve of his or her young child watching pornography, or even an R-rated movie, for research purposes? Nevertheless, we all know that children do see sexual media. One clever methodology to examine this question involves the use of the retrospective method, which entails questioning adults about their memories of watching sexual content as children. The researchers are not exposing children to any questionable stimuli, but merely asking people about material they have already seen a long time ago on their own. Cantor, Mares, and Hyde (2003) asked 196 college students to remember an exposure to sexual media between the ages of 5 and 12 or during the teen years. Almost 92% could do so, 39% remembering something seen between the ages of 5 and 12 and 61% at age 13 or over. Most often (79%) the content was R or NC-17 rated movies, and 80% were viewed with someone else (only 17% with parents, however). Disgust, shock/surprise, interest, and embarrassment were the most common emotional responses remembered (21% to 25% each), with sexual arousal (17%) and avoidance (14%) the most common physical reactions.

Memories from younger ages (5–12) tended to focus on salient sensory aspects like nudity, kissing, and "sexual noises," while the memories from older ages focused on dialogue or themes like rape or same-sex sexual behavior. Overall, men's memories were more positive and more likely to focus on physical aspects than women's. Although there is no way to verify the accuracy of these students' memories, the vividness of memories years after the exposure testifies in itself to the powerful effect of seeing this sexual content relatively early in life.

Explicit sexual materials have traditionally been designed by and for heterosexual men. As such, they have a distinctly macho and hypermasculinized orientation. Although all varieties of heterosexual intercourse are shown, there is typically little emphasis on associated foreplay, afterplay, cuddling, relationships, or tenderness in general. Women are typically seen as eagerly desiring and participating in intercourse, often with hysterical euphoria (see Chapter 4 for a discussion of the sexualization of females in the media). There is little presentation of any consequences of sex or the relational matrix within which most people experience it.

Recently there has been some increase in sexual materials with more emphasis on relationship, pre- and postcoital behaviors, and the woman's point of view generally, developed primarily to be marketed to women (Mosher & Maclan, 1994; Senn & Desmarais, 2004). However, these comprise only a minuscule part of the worldwide porn market. Although men are much more active seekers and users of sexual material than women, this cannot necessarily be attributed to greater intrinsic male interest in explicit sexual media; it may merely reflect the pornography industry's extreme slant to the traditional male perspective.

Media are clearly major sources of information about sexual issues that we use to construct our reality of what sexuality and sexual behavior and values are all about (Fabes & Strouse, 1984, 1987; Kunkel et al., 2007; Strouse & Fabes, 1985; Sutton et al., 2002). To better understand this perceived reality, let us examine some effects of viewing sex in the media. How do we change after exposure to such material?

Effects of Viewing Media Sex

Although many people might wish it otherwise, sex—even very explicit sex—does sell, though see Close-Up 10.3 for an interesting exception. Sexually oriented print, broadcast, and Internet media are highly profitable, and this fact has ramifications for all media. However, this economic issue is not the focus of this book, and we turn now to the various psychological effects (see Gunter, 2001; Harris & Barlett, 2009; Linz & Malamuth, 1993; Mundorf, Allen, D'Alessio, & Emmers-Sommer, 2007; Oddone-Paolucci, Genuis, & Violato, 2000 for reviews of the literature on the effects of viewing sexual media).

Arousal

The most straightforward effect of sex in media is sexual arousal, the drive that energizes or intensifies sexual behavior. Sexually oriented media do arouse

---

Close-Up 10.3: Does Sex on TV Help Sell Products?

Bushman (2005) showed 336 adults ages 18 to 54 a TV show containing one of four possible content conditions: violence, sex, violence and sex, or neither violence nor sex. All groups saw the same 12 commercials embedded in the program. Those who had seen programs with violence or sex were less likely to remember the advertised brands and showed less interest in buying or selecting a coupon for that brand. This held for both men and women, of all ages, regardless of their preference for content with sex or violence.

What if the sex is in the ad itself? Parker and Furnham (2007) showed viewers either sexual or nonsexual ads in the context of a sexual (*Sex and the City*) or nonsexual (*Malcolm in the Middle*) TV program. People remembered more content from the commercials in the nonsexual program, although there was no difference in the recall of sexual and nonsexual ads. Overall, men recalled sexual ads better and women the nonsexual ads.

people, especially men, both in terms of self-ratings of arousal level and physiological measures such as penile engorgement (Eccles, Marshall, & Barbaree, 1988; Lohr, Adams, & Davis, 1997), vaginal changes (Sintchak & Geer, 1975), and body temperature (Abramson, Perry, Seeley, Seeley, & Rothblatt, 1981). See Chivers, Seto, Lalumiere, Laan, & Grimbos (2010), for a meta-analysis of sexual media consumption and the agreement between self-report and physiological measures of arousal. Overall, men tend to be more aroused by sexual media than women are (Malamuth, 1996; Murnen & Stockton, 1997), although there is some evidence that women may be more aroused by sexual media developed by and for women that does not portray sex from an extreme hypermasculine fantasy point of view (Mosher & Maclan, 1994; Quackenbush, Strassberg, & Turner, 1995). Sexual violence is particularly arousing to sex offenders and much less so to other men, unless the victim is portrayed as being aroused by the assault; this issue is discussed in more detail later in the chapter.

Sexual arousal to stimuli not naturally evoking such a response may be learned through classical conditioning, discussed earlier, in Chapters 5 and 9. This process could account for the vast individual differences in the specific stimuli that arouse people sexually. Through our different experiences, we have all been conditioned to different stimuli through their associations with those we are attracted to and/or love. Because of its association with a particular person, someone may be aroused by a certain perfume or cologne, type of clothing or food, or specific behaviors.

Contrary to what one might expect, the degree of arousal is not necessarily highly correlated with the degree of explicitness of the media. Sometimes one is actually more aroused by a less sexually explicit story than a more explicit one. Censoring out a sex scene may sometimes actually make a film more arousing, because sexual arousal is highly individual, and some viewers prefer to "fill in" their own fantasies. When people are allowed to use their own imaginations to construct the ending of a romantic scene, they are more likely to construct a scenario that is more arousing to them personally than if they view someone else's idea of what is arousing. There is some validity to the old truism that the most important sex organ is the brain.

Attitudes and Values

Some of the major effects of media sex are on attitudes and values. In exploring sexual attitudes and values, we now turn to several specific value issues.

Sexual Details in the News

How explicit should the media be in reporting news of sex-crime trials? When is the public's right to know overtaken by its right to standards of good taste? When does reporting turn into voyeurism? Consider some true examples.

1. A small city is the scene of a child sexual molestation trial of a prominent businessman accused of abusing two 13-year-old boys. Each day's court proceedings are reported in great detail in front-page stories in the local newspaper, always identifying the accused, though never the boys. Sexually oriented entertainment involving pornography and alcohol in the man's home was described in detail, along with extensive direct quotes from the victims' testimony: "He rubbed our butts in the shower," "He called me to where he was sitting and told me to play with his penis," "He also made me and [the other boy] lay on the floor and have oral sex with each other while he watched." Other episodes such as the man asking the boys to reach inside his underwear and squeeze his penis were also explicitly described.

    Predictably, this coverage provoked some community comment, although even the most outraged people nevertheless always seemed to read the articles thoroughly. Although no one defended the abuse that had occurred, some argued that young readers should not be exposed to such explicit descriptions in the newspaper. Others countered, however, by saying that such events are serious and need to be reported in detail to show everyone how horrible they are and thus increase commitment to ensure that they do not happen again.

2. In a somewhat similar 2012 case, Pennsylvania State University football coach Jerry Sandusky was on trial for multiple counts of child sexual abuse. One victim testified that he had been anally raped in the basement of Sandusky's home, screaming for help while Sandusky's wife was upstairs. When another witness testified, it was widely reported that Sandusky had been seen naked in locker room showers holding young boys while a "skin-on-skin slapping sound" was heard (Belson, 2012).

3. In the early 1990s there were two celebrated date-rape trials of men of some notoriety. In the first, John, Robert, and Ted Kennedy's nephew, William Kennedy Smith, was accused of raping a single mother at the Kennedy estate in Palm Beach, Florida. In the second trial, boxing heavyweight champion Mike Tyson was accused of raping a Miss Black America contestant whom he had met and invited to his hotel room. Both trials were broadcast on cable (with faces of victims blanked out) and were heavily covered in all the news media. In both trials, the basic legal question was whether there was consent. Viewers heard questions like, "Did you ejaculate into her mouth?" and "Did you have an erection?" and the answers to them.

4. In 2011, New York Congressman Anthony Weiner was caught in a "sexting" scandal in which it was revealed that he had been using his Twitter account to send sexually explicit photos of himself to a college student. Initial waffling and denials by Weiner only led to additional media coverage, including (eventually) the photos being published online and in some newspapers. Weiner resigned soon after.

5. One of the most celebrated cases of sexually explicit language in the news came with the release in September 1998 of U.S. President Bill Clinton's grand jury testimony about his alleged affair with White House intern Monica Lewinsky. The critical legal, and potentially impeachable, question here was whether the President had perjured himself in grand jury testimony about the specific sexual behaviors. The videotapes and news commentary on them had the look of both high political drama and sleazy tabloid reporting. Parents were in a quandary as to how to explain these matters to their children. Many lamented the depth to which news reporting had fallen, but no one quite knew what to do about it. Such a story involved the leader of the free world in a possibly impeachable offense and thus could not be ignored.

Although such sexually explicit language as occurred in these news stories would not be acceptable on prime-time entertainment programming, because these stories were news, their use was not covered by entertainment standards. Still, however, it caused some concern, especially insofar as many people watch TV news and read the newspaper for entertainment purposes.

Premarital Sex

Sex before marriage, often shortly after one's first meeting, seems to be the norm in TV and film entertainment today. However, there is somewhat of a double standard depending on whether adolescents or adults are involved. Often for teens, but seldom for adults, the choice of whether to have sex is a difficult or complex decision. Traditional values are far more likely to be affirmed in the end if the story lines involve youth. A teenager may consider having sex with a boyfriend or girlfriend and discuss it openly with family and friends. In the end, however, the teenager may decide that he or she is not ready, choosing to abstain. Even when the decision is affirmative, however, there is considerable moralizing and prior discussion of the behavior, often with parents. Moreover, sometimes there is clear regret afterwards. In such cases, traditional values are more or less affirmed.

In contrast to the moral angst of teen decisions about premarital sex in entertainment media, between adults it appears to be a nonissue. Dramatic TV shows and movies seem to presuppose a norm of early sexual activity on the part of adult dating couples, usually with little if any concern about either moral propriety or protection against pregnancy or sexually transmitted diseases. Premarital sex between adults is portrayed as routine and noncontroversial with little indication of either party struggling with the decision. In fact, there is seldom any discussion by either party about whether it is right or whether it is too soon in the relationship. Only in story lines with adolescents does it seem to be considered a moral or developmental issue. Premarital sex is thus treated fairly conservatively in regard to teens and very permissively in regard to adults. For example, on *Glee*, an entire episode was devoted to whether couples Kurt and Blaine and Rachel and Finn were going to have sex. In contrast, even the nerdy single adult characters on *The Big Bang Theory* seem to have sex fairly often. See Close-Up 10.4 for a very unusual case in which a sitcom story line involving the consequences of premarital sex caused a national political furor.

Close-Up 10.4: The Vice President versus Murphy Brown

On May 18, 1992, the sitcom *Murphy Brown* aired its season finale, featuring the birth of a baby to single female news anchor Murphy Brown. The day after the TV birth, then-U.S. Vice President Dan Quayle made a political speech lamenting the nation's poverty of values. In this speech he referred to the bad example set by character Murphy Brown in "having a child alone, mocking the importance of fathers, by bearing a child alone, and calling it just another lifestyle choice" ("Dan Quayle vs. Murphy Brown," 1992, p. 20). The comment highlighted the depth of emotion evoked by a sitcom portrayal. President George H. W. Bush, network executives, political leaders and columnists, and of course many humorists, commented extensively on the issue in subsequent weeks. What was it about Murphy Brown having a baby that inspired so much emotion? Why didn't these critics complain about all of the sex on soap operas or, for that matter, all of the real children born out of wedlock every day to single parents far less prepared than the affluent Murphy Brown character?

Although Quayle's detractors chided him for making such a big deal out of a sitcom plot, they too may have missed the point. So what if Murphy Brown is not a real person and no one ever had actual sex to produce that fictitious baby? A TV character has a reality and an impact on real people that most real people do not. In some sense, both the Vice President and his critics were affirming the thesis of this book.

The story did not end there. The fall premiere episode of *Murphy Brown* had fictitious new mom Murphy watching a real news report of Dan Quayle criticizing her moral example. Her TV office was besieged with reporters asking for reactions. Although staying secluded for a while, Murphy eventually made an on-air editorial response to the Vice President. Subsequent news reports told of the fictional program's response to the real criticism by Quayle. Quayle even sent a real baby gift of a stuffed Republican elephant to the fictitious baby. Fantasy and reality had seldom become so blurred.

Extramarital Sex

Although less frequent than premarital sex, extramarital sex is also not unusual in TV and film and is especially common in soap operas. Depending on the situation, it may be treated comically or seriously. If treated humorously, it may discourage taking seriously the consequences of marital infidelity. If treated seriously, it may either carry the implicit message that adultery is okay, or at least that it does not have terribly serious consequences, or it may convey the message that adultery has serious repercussions for all concerned. The effect on viewers may be very different in these two cases.

In thinking about portrayals of extramarital sex, the first shows that come to mind are soap operas, in which adultery is a frequent theme, even an accepted way of life for many of the characters. In terms of values, both approval and condemnation come through at different times. A sympathetic character who is trapped in an unhappy marriage uses an affair as a relatively healthy outlet for her needs. The inevitable pain and hurt resulting from the adultery may or may not be dealt with in the plot line. Buerkel-Rothfuss and Mayes (1981) found that college students' heavy viewing of soap operas was positively correlated with higher estimates of the percentages of people having affairs, divorces, abortions, and illegitimate children, although it was unrelated to their perception of how many people were happily married. The perceived reality constructed from such shows apparently depends not only on the program content, but also on the viewer's motives and uses of the medium, as well as parental values and parent–child discussion and coviewing (Carveth & Alexander, 1985; Greenberg et al., 1982; Perse, 1986).

Just as extramarital affairs are presented as common, sometimes marital sex is actually denigrated. For example, one episode of the old family sitcom *Married... with Children* had the father eye his wife dressed very seductively and say, "Geez, if I weren't married to you, I'd really be turned on about now!" The message is clear: sex within marriage is boring, uninteresting, or otherwise devalued. The good stuff lies elsewhere.

AIDS Education and Birth Control

Although we accept great amounts of implied or semi-explicit sex on TV, even after the onset of AIDS in the mid-1980s, birth control ads were for a long time felt to be too controversial for most U.S. television audiences, though such ads had appeared regularly in magazines for years. It is as if the action of having sexual intercourse is acceptable if done in the heat of a passionate moment, but that planning for it is somehow unseemly or dirty. This communicates a potentially dangerous reality! The teen pregnancy rate is higher in the United States than in any other industrialized country, and such rates elsewhere fell dramatically after media campaigns that included televised birth control ads. It is an interesting paradox that all sorts of nonmarital sex, at least some of which would clearly be against the personal values of most Americans, were considered acceptable for story content, but that the use of birth control, a practice consistent with the values and practice of most citizens, was seen as too controversial to advertise or to even mention in story lines. Thus, we see another paradox of fairly extreme permissiveness in regard to nonmarital media sex coexisting with extreme conservatism in regard to birth control and protection. Why are premarital and extramarital sex so acceptable, while birth control and a reasonable concern about acquiring sexually transmitted diseases are perceived as unseemly?

The spread of HIV and AIDS has heightened the discussion of such issues. As AIDS moved beyond the gay community and drug culture in the late 1980s, the general population became concerned and even alarmed. The introduction of AIDS education into schools suggests that fear of AIDS (and death) was gradually becoming stronger than fear of exposing children to sexual information. In terms of media, the advertising of condoms had cautiously crept into some cable channels like MTV by the 1990s, but it is still rare. In terms of entertainment programming, story lines continued to portray very casual attitudes toward nonmarital sex and its consequences, especially among adults. Although there have recently been increasing numbers of story lines indicating some concern about AIDS or the use of protection (so-called safe sex), that is still much more the exception than the rule (Kaiser Family Foundation, 2005).

One concern is a desensitization to certain expressions of sexuality deemed by others to be inappropriate. For example, sitcoms showing teenagers considering being sexually active may disinhibit and thus weaken family-taught values against premarital sex. Fashion ads that sell clothing by showing a scantily clad woman being physically dominated by a man may desensitize readers to violence toward women.

Sometimes the media may actually change one's values or attitudes, rather than merely desensitizing or reinforcing existing ones. For example, if a teen boy watches his favorite sitcom character consider having sex, the teen viewer may approach his own girlfriend about making their relationship sexual. This kind of modeling is especially likely to happen if the TV characters demonstrating certain values are respected characters with whom viewers identify. Sexual promiscuity by a prostitute character is less likely to influence the values of a viewer than promiscuity by a character who is a respected suburban wife and mother.

Comedic vs. Serious Sex

Another concern about the effects on values and attitudes is that sexually oriented media may encourage people not to take sexual issues seriously. When the sex magazine *Hustler* had a regular cartoon called *Chester the Molester* featuring a child molester and *Family Guy* has a recurring pedophile character, many argue that this is an inappropriately light treatment of an extremely serious subject. A *Penthouse* story "Soothing Private Ryan" featured a barmaid putting a condom over the private's privates, in a spoof of the serious war movie *Saving Private Ryan*. One article in a sex magazine aimed at male teenagers was entitled "Good Sex with Retarded Girls." Although few would be likely to argue that sex should never be comedic, there are for most people some sexual subjects, for example child sexual abuse, that do not seem appropriate for light treatment.

Sometimes a comedic treatment of sex can send a serious message. When the father on *Married... with Children* chastised his daughter for receiving a bad grade, upon closer scrutiny he was relieved because "at least it was in sex education." Ironically, this sexually permissive sitcom confirmed a very conservative, and in this case scientifically unsupported, belief that having more knowledge about sex and contraception leads to promiscuity. Even mainstream ads communicate sexual values. When a car ad features two women discussing whether men drive big cars to compensate for the size of their penises ("I wonder what he's got under the hood"), they send a message about what is important about men in the eyes of women. A pizza commercial shows a couple with the wife saying, "The pizza will be here in 30 minutes. What do we do till then?" and the husband saying he has an idea. Then the ad cuts to another scene with the man in his bathrobe and the woman saying, "Now what do we do for the other 28 minutes?" What is the message being communicated about (especially male) sexuality?

Attitudes toward Women

One type of sexual value of particular concern involves men's attitudes toward women. One of the major criticisms of traditional pornography is that it is anti-women in an ideological sense. It is usually women, not men, who are the playthings or victims of the opposite sex. Although this concern spans the gamut of sexual content in media, it is particularly leveled at sexual violence. What are teenage boys who are first learning about sex going to think that women want when they see a picture of a jackhammer in a woman's vagina as the opening photo to a story called "How to Cure Frigidity"? When *Hustler* magazine runs a photo spread of a gang rape turning into an orgy, showing the women appearing to be aroused by the assault, what is being taught about women and their reactions to forcible sex? Can a boy resist the temptation to click on Internet links to see *Live Asian Sluts* or *Farm Girls: Bizarre Barnyard Sex*?

Several studies have shown effects on attitudes and values about sex as a result of exposure to nonviolent sexually explicit materials. After seeing slides and movies of beautiful female nudes engaged in sexual activity, men rated their own partners as being less physically endowed, although they reported undiminished sexual satisfaction (Weaver, Masland, & Zillmann, 1984). In another study, men reported loving their own mates less after seeing sexually explicit videos of highly attractive models (Kenrick, Gutierres, & Goldberg, 1989). Men who saw a pornographic video responded more sexually to a subsequent female interviewer than those seeing a control video, although this result only held for men holding traditional gender schemas (McKenzie-Mohr & Zanna, 1990). Some of these results mirror those of a 1980 study in which men who watched a single episode of *Charlie's Angels* rated real women as less attractive than did men in a control group who had not seen the show before making ratings (Kenrick & Gutierres, 1980). All of these studies showed significant attitude changes after a very limited exposure to sexual media.

Using a paradigm of showing participants weekly films and testing them 1 to 3 weeks later, Zillmann and Bryant (1982, 1984) found that participants watching sexually explicit films overestimated the frequency of sexual practices like fellatio, cunnilingus, anal intercourse, sadomasochism, and bestiality, relative to perceptions of a control group seeing nonsexual films. This may reflect the cognitive heuristic of availability, whereby we judge the frequency of occurrence of various activities by the ease with which we can generate examples (Kahneman, 2011; Taylor, 1982; Tversky & Kahneman, 1973, 1974). In line with cultivation theory, vivid media instances thus lead to an overestimation of such behavior in the real world and a perceived reality at odds with actual reality.

Using the same methodology as in their 1982 and 1984 studies, Zillmann and Bryant (1988a, 1988b) found effects of this perceived reality on attitudes about real people. Participants seeing the explicit films reported, relative to a control group, less satisfaction with the affection, physical appearance, sexual curiosity, and sexual performance of their real-life partners. They also saw sex without emotional involvement as being relatively more important than the control group did. In addition, they showed greater acceptance of premarital and extramarital sex and lower evaluation of marriage and monogamy. They also showed less desire to have children and greater acceptance of male dominance and female submission. Results generally did not differ for men versus women or college students versus nonstudents.

The sexual material need not be explicit or graphic to affect attitudes. Bryant and Rockwell (1994) found that, compared to controls, teenagers who watched a heavy diet of highly sexual prime-time programs showed an influence on their judgments of the degree of sexual impropriety or of how much the victim had been wronged, although these effects were greatly attenuated by a clear and well-defined family value system, active critical viewing, and open discussion within the family.

Internet Sex

Internet pornography has become of major interest to researchers (see Griffin-Shelley, 2003 for a review). Two early experimental studies (Barak & Fisher, 1997; Barak, Fisher, Belfry, & Lashambe, 1999) failed to find a consistent effect of amount of Internet sex exposure on any of several measures of misogynistic attitudes. Later work, however, has shown clearer effects. In an extensive correlational study investigating the effect of Internet pornography on adolescent male attitudes, a significant correlation was found between the amount of Internet pornography viewed and recreational sexual attitudes, which included items such as "It is OK to have sexual relationships with more than one partner," but this effect depended some on the degree of realism of the pornography (Peter & Valkenburg, 2006). When the sexual actions on the Internet website looked as though they could happen in real life, teenage boys were more likely to have more liberal attitudes toward sex. Similarly, Lo and Wei (2005) found that exposure to Internet pornography was significantly correlated with attitudes toward extramarital sex and sexually permissive behavior; as the viewing amount increased, so did more accepting attitudes of infidelity, as well as the amount of self-reported sexual behavior by participants.

Adolescents' self-reported exposure to explicit Internet sex over one year was correlated with more thoughts about sex, as well as increased perceived sexual arousal (Peter & Valkenburg, 2008). Further, a survey of college students found that viewing sexually explicit material on the Internet was significantly correlated with masturbating online, sending and receiving pornography online, and seeking new people online (Boies, 2002). The same study also sought the uses and gratifications for viewing pornography on the Internet, and responses indicated that men (more than women) use this form of media to sexually arouse themselves, to satisfy sexual needs, to fulfill sexual fantasies, and to satisfy curiosity about new sexual techniques (Boies, 2002).

Behavioral Effects

Another large class of effects of sexual media consists of effects on behavior—how consuming sexual media leads to changes in actual sexual behaviors. Research on some of these behavioral effects are discussed in this section.

Teaching New Behaviors

Sexual media may actually teach new behaviors. As part of sex therapy, a couple may buy a sex manual like The Joy of Sex in order to learn new sexual positions or behaviors that they had not tried before. New behaviors are not always so benign, however. One issue of Penthouse contained a series of photographs of Asian women bound with heavy rope, hung from trees, and sectioned into parts. Two months later an 8-year-old Chinese girl in Chapel Hill, North Carolina, was kidnapped, raped, murdered, and left hanging from a tree limb (The New York Times, 1985, cited in Department of Justice, 1986, p. 208). Thankfully, such cases are not commonplace; definitively demonstrating a causal relationship between exposure to the media and acting the behavior is difficult, but the juxtaposition is nonetheless disturbing.

Disinhibition of Known Behaviors

Erotic material may also disinhibit previously learned behaviors, as when the viewing of TV's treatment of premarital sex reduces a viewer's inhibition against engaging in such behavior. Watching a rape scene in which a woman is portrayed as enjoying being assaulted may weaken some men's moral prohibitions against committing such a crime. This is of particular concern given some evidence suggesting that a surprisingly large number of college men reported that they might commit rape if they were sure they would not be caught (Check, 1985).

Sex Crimes

One of the main concerns about a behavioral effect of viewing sexually explicit materials is that such viewing may lead to sex crimes. There have been many studies that have looked at rates of crimes like rape, sexual assault, indecent exposure, and child sexual molestation, relative to changes in the availability of sexually explicit materials. Drawing scientifically sound general conclusions has been difficult, however. Court (1977, 1982, 1984) argued that there is in fact a correlation between availability of sexually explicit materials and certain sex crimes. Court claimed that earlier studies, especially the Kutchinsky (1973) study claiming a drop in reported sex crimes in Denmark after liberalization of pornography restrictions in the 1960s, were not really valid, due to an inappropriate lumping of rape with nonviolent acts of voyeurism, indecent exposure, and gay sex.

Most Western nations have experienced both a large increase in the availability of sexually explicit media and a rise in reported rapes in the last 40 years. However, Court (1984) presented some data from two Australian states that showed a sharp increase in rape reports in South Australia, but not Queensland, after state pornography laws were liberalized in South Australia in the early 1970s. A downturn in reported rapes occurred temporarily in Hawaii between 1974 and 1976 during the imposition of restraints on sexually explicit media. For an interesting apparent counterexample, see Close-Up 10.5.

Close-Up 10.5: Pornography in Japan

Japan is an interesting and unusual case of a society with wide availability of sexual media, but very low rape rates (Diamond & Uchiyama,1999). Sexual themes in art and society go back centuries to ancient religious fertility objects and wood block prints called *ukiyo-e*. Although some restriction and censorship occurred after the Meiji Restoration in 1868, and even more under the U.S. occupation that began in 1945, sexuality continued to be a strong theme of Japanese society and not one particularly associated with shame or guilt. Although there are specific restrictions in Japan on showing pictorial representations of pubic hair or adult genitalia, there is less compartmentalization of sexual media to certain types of magazines, bookstores, or theaters, than occurs in the United States. There has even been a surge of popularity in recent years of "elder-porn," series with names like *Maniac Training of Lolitas* and *Forbidden Elderly Care*, which star actors into their 70s and have been immensely popular with the aging population of Japan (Toyama, 2008). Why, then, is the incidence of reported rapes so much lower in Japan than elsewhere (2.4 per 100,000 vs. 34.5 in the United States, 10.1 in England, and 10.7 in Germany)? Abramson and Hayashi (1984) argued that the answer may lie in cultural differences. Japanese society emphasizes order, obligation, cooperation, and virtue, and one who violates social norms is the object of shame. Others have suggested that rape in Japan is more likely to be group instigated, perpetrated by juveniles, and greatly underreported by victims (Goldstein & Ibaraki, 1983).

Firmly establishing a causal relationship between the availability of sexually explicit media and the frequency of rape is extremely difficult, due to the many other relevant factors that cannot be controlled, including the different varieties of sexual material, changes in social consciousness about reporting sexual assaults, and changing norms that sanction such behavior.

Although some have argued from the evidence that an increase in sex crimes follows greater availability of pornography (Court, 1984) and others have argued that there is no such demonstrated relationship (Kutchinsky, 1991), there has been no recent support for the idea that greater availability of sexually explicit media decreases the rate of sex crimes. Recent experimental studies (Vega & Malamuth, 2007) and reviews (Bauserman, 1996; Malamuth, Addison, & Koss, 2000) have concluded that there is an association between the heavy consumption of pornography, especially violent pornography, and the perpetration of sex crimes.

Interference with Cognitive Processing

Although there has been very little study of the effects of sexual media on information processing, at least one recent study suggests that watching sexy pictures really can make young men think less clearly. See Close-Up 10.6.

Close-Up 10.6: Does Watching Women in Bikinis Really Make Men Stupid?

Believe it or not, three Belgian researchers (Van den Bergh, Dewitte, & Warlop, 2008) conducted several studies to examine this question. In one, young men either watched a series of landscapes or a series of pictures of women in bikinis or lingerie. In another they were given a series of either T-shirts or bras to examine and evaluate. In a third they watched a video of either a group of men or bikini-clad young women running across landscapes. Afterwards all the men were given a choice of receiving 15 euros immediately or bargaining for more over a longer period of time. In each case the men exposed to the sexual media or clothing settled for a less lucrative bet and chose not to negotiate for a better deal. Apparently the bikinis had made them more impulsive and less thoughtful, seeking more immediate gratification rather than holding out for what would probably be a better deal.

Adolescent Socialization

Teenagers who watch a heavy diet of television with sexual content were twice as likely to engage in sexual intercourse over the following year as teens who were light viewers of sexual content, even after controlling for other possible factors (Collins, Elliott et al., 2004). Heavy TV viewing of sexual content was also associated with other non-coital sexual behaviors (heavy petting, deep kissing, etc.). These findings were the same regardless of whether the sexual content was explicitly shown in behavior or only discussed in dialogue. In another, longitudinal study on adolescents, a relationship was found between heavy exposure to sexual media (music, movies, TV, and magazines) at ages 12–14 and having had sexual intercourse by ages 14–16 (Brown et al., 2006). One study even found that heavy exposure to sexual content on television predicted teen pregnancy, even when controlling for other variables like low grades and deviant behaviors (Chandra et al., 2008). Of course, the causative relation works both ways: more sexually active adolescents seek out more sex in the media, and those exposed to more sex in media gradually become more sexually active themselves (Bleakley, Hennessy, Fishbein, & Jordan, 2008).

On the other hand, sexual content in media can have positive effects of increasing knowledge and instigating information seeking. For example, after an episode of the medical drama ER with three minutes on emergency contraception, 51% of viewers reported talking with others about the issue, 23% sought information from another source, and 14% talked to their doctor about it (Kaiser Family Foundation, 2002). After an episode of Friends that portrayed a pregnancy resulting from condom failure, about two thirds of viewers aged 12 to 17 reported learning that condoms could fail and most remembered that six months later (Collins et al., 2003). After airing several episodes of a character dealing with an HIV diagnosis in 2001, the soap opera *The Bold and the Beautiful* displayed the National STD and AIDS Hotline toll-free phone number. During the time periods when those episodes aired (and immediately afterward), the number of calls to the hotline increased significantly (Kennedy, O'Leary, Beck, Pollard, & Simpson, 2004).

Cybersex

Communicating online and masturbating (Ferree, 2003), as well as viewing sexual images on the Internet while masturbating, have behavioral consequences for the user as well as the user's partner and family. Results from an online survey of those affected by their significant other's frequent cybersex found that such behavior was a contributing factor in separation and divorce. Furthermore, the majority of these couples abstained from having sexual intercourse, resulting from the (usually female—97%) partner's feelings of isolation and lower self-esteem from not feeling as attactive as the online models, and anger from being lied to (Schneider, 2001). If the user and partner had children, 14% of those children had seen pornographic images or the user masturbating, while 11% of children were adversely affected by the images and users' cybersex behavior (Schneider, 2003).

Catharsis

Another alleged effect of media sex is catharsis, that emotional release so important to psychodynamic models of personality (e.g., Freud; Scheele & DuBois, 2006). Applied to sex, the catharsis argument says that consuming media sex relieves sexual urges, with the erotic film or magazine acting (perhaps in conjunction with masturbation) as a sort of imperfect substitute for the real thing. A catharsis argument was used some years ago by civil libertarians to support appeals for lessening restrictions on sexually explicit material (Kutchinsky, 1973). However, the research support for catharsis as a function of viewing media sex is basically nonexistent (Bushman, Baumeister, & Stack, 1999; Department of Justice, 1986). In fact, exposure to sexual media typically energizes the sex drive and leads one to do more, not less, to try to satisfy it. However, as we saw with the violence research on catharsis (see Chapter 9), the popular belief in this scientifically discredited process remains strong.

Context of Sexuality

The perceived reality of media sex and the effects of sex in media also depend on the context of the sexual images and the context in which the person sees it, all of which can make an enormous difference in the experience of consuming sexually explicit media. One of the relevant contextual variables is the degree of playfulness or seriousness of the material. For example, a documentary on rape or a tastefully done TV drama on incest may be considered perfectly acceptable, whereas a far less explicit comedy with the same theme may be highly offensive and considered too sexual. What is really the concern in such cases is not the sex as such, but rather the comedic treatment of it.

A second contextual consideration is the artistic worth and intent. We react very differently to a sexually explicit drawing by Picasso versus one in *Hustler* magazine. Shakespeare, Chaucer, *The Song of Solomon* in the Bible, and serious sex manuals like *The Joy of Sex* are seen to have serious literary or didactic intentions, and thus the sex therein is considered acceptable, perhaps even healthy. One interesting issue in this regard is how to respond to something of clear artistic worth that was written at a time when standards were different to those of today. For example, should Rhett Butler's forcing his attentions on Scarlett O'Hara in *Gone with the Wind* be seen as rape or as the noncontroversial romantic moment that it appeared to be in 1939? In fact, a man continuing to press his sexual desires against a woman who has clearly stated her wish that he stop is today legally defined as rape; however, this was a common theme in films in the mid-20th century.

The relation and integration of sex with the overall plot and intent of the piece is another important contextual factor. A sex scene, even a mild and nonexplicit one, may be offensive if it appears to be thrown in merely to spice up the story, without intrinsic connection to the plot. Something far more explicit may find greater acceptance if it is necessary and central to the story line. Sex scenes in a story about a prostitute may be much less gratuitous than comparable scenes in a story about a female corporate executive. Sex, of course, is not the only common gratuitous factor in media; TV shows and movies frequently insert, for example, car chases and rock video sequences only tangentially related to the plot.

The context of the viewing also influences the experience and effect of sex in the media. Watching an erotic film may elicit different reactions, depending on whether you watch it with your parents, your grandparents, your children, by yourself, in a group of close same-sex friends, or with your significant other. It can be seen as more or less erotic or arousing, and more or less entertaining, appropriate, or offensive. For example, watching a movie that is more sexual than you had realized with a first date might be quite embarrassing, whereas it might be quite enjoyable and arousing if seen with a longtime partner. In a study asking college students to rate the degree of hypothetical discomfort from watching various types of movies with different coviewers, by far the most uncomfortable situation was watching an R-rated sexually explicit movie with one's parents (Harris & Cook, 2011).

The cultural context is also important. Some cultures do not consider female breasts to be particularly erotic or inappropriate for public view.

We recognize these cultural differences and thus, at least after the age of 14, most readers do not consider topless women from some exotic culture in *National Geographic* photos to be the slightest bit erotic, sexual, or inappropriate. Even in Western culture, standards have changed. In much of the 19th century, knees and calves were thought to be erotic, and a bare-kneed woman would be as scandalous, even as sexually arousing, as would a topless woman today. As societies go, North America is overall a bit more conservative with regard to allowable sexual expression than many Western European or Latin American cultures but far more permissive than most Islamic and East Asian cultures.

Messages about sexuality are often, though by no means always, presented in a context of romance, especially so in song lyrics and TV and movie entertainment; much less so in the case of pornography. Romance, however, has its own media skewing. There are prevalent myths about romance which emanate from song lyrics of virtually every genre and era, as well as from love stories in TV and movies (Galician, 2004, 2007). To the extent that these drive people's search for mates and evaluation of relationships, they may be using very unrealistic, even impossible, standards. Contrary to popular belief, it is not only women who like romantic movies or who are affected by romantic myths (Harris et al., 2004). See Close-Up 10.7 for the 12 media myths of romance.

Close-Up 10.7: Media's Myths of Romance

Related to sexuality is romance, which is also the subject of interesting and sometimes less-than-helpful media messages. Mary-Lou Galician (2004, 2007) argues that the media perpetuate 12 myths of romance which lead young viewers to expect very unrealistic outcomes from relationships. These myths are rampant in song lyrics, movie plot lines, TV shows, Internet quizzes, and self-help magazine articles:

1. Your perfect partner is cosmically predestined, so nothing/nobody can ultimately separate you.
2. "Love at first sight" exists and is highly desirable.
3. Your true "soul mate" should know what you're thinking or feeling without you having to tell him or her.
4. If your partner is truly "meant for you," sex is easy and wonderful.
5. To attract and keep a man, a woman should look like a model or centerfold.
6. The man should not be shorter, weaker, younger, poorer, or less successful than the woman.
7. The love of a good and faithful true woman can change a man from a "beast" into a "prince."

8. Bickering and fighting a lot mean that a man and a woman really love each other passionately.
9. All you really need is love, so it doesn't matter if you and your partner have very different values.
10. The right mate "completes you," filling your needs and making your dreams come true.
11. In real life, actors are often like the romantic characters they portray.
12. Since mass media portrayals of romance aren't "real," they don't really affect you.

All of these are myths, in terms of people's real lives and what the research shows (a perusal of most social psychology textbooks will verify the falsehood of most of these myths). How many of them do you (perhaps secretly) believe and how do these affect how you look at relationships? Where did you get these ideas, anyway? Look to the media.

Finally, the expectations we have about the appearance of media sex affect our perception. Sex is less offensive and shocking if it is expected than if it appears as a surprise. Seeing a video of an orgy on a pornographic website is less shocking than suddenly encountering explicit sex in *Newsweek*. The stimulus may be similar, but the perceived experiential reality of the fact of seeing it would differ considerably in the two cases.

We now examine that potent combination of sex and violence in the media: sexual violence.

Sexual Violence

Although neither sex nor violence in the media is new, the integral combination of the two has become more prevalent in recent decades. As discussed previously, cable, digital, and Internet technology have greatly expanded the ability to privately and conveniently view all sorts of sexually explicit material. Whereas many people would not have been comfortable seeking out and visiting theaters that showed such films, the chance to view such material safely and privately in one's own home or hotel room makes it much more accessible. Another old familiar genre, the horror film, has evolved into showing frequent and extensive scenes of violence against women in a sexual context (see readings in Weaver & Tamborini, 1996). These films are widely viewed by teens and preteens, in spite of their R ratings.

A major concern beyond the sex or violence in themselves is the way the two appear together. The world constructed in the mind of the viewer of such materials can have some very serious consequences. Let us turn now to examining some of the effects of viewing sexual violence.

Erotica as Stimulator of Aggression

Links between sex and aggression have long been speculated upon, particularly in the sense of sexual arousal facilitating violent behavior. The research has been inconsistent, however, with some studies showing that erotic materials facilitate aggression (Baron, 1979; Donnerstein & Hallam, 1978) and others showing that they inhibit it (Donnerstein, Donnerstein, & Evans, 1975; White, 1979). The resolution of this issue apparently concerns the nature of the material. Sexual violence and unpleasant themes typically facilitate aggression, whereas nonviolent, more loving and pleasant soft-core explicit materials may inhibit it (Sapolsky, 1984; Zillmann, Bryant, Comisky, & Medoff, 1981). Individual differences such as overall aggression levels also no doubt play a role in whether sexual aggression is perceived as sexually arousing (Kingston & Malamuth, 2011).

How the Woman Is Portrayed

Men who see films with scenes of sexual violence later showed a more callous attitude toward rape and women in general, especially if the women victims were portrayed as being aroused by the assault. In terms of sexual arousal, men were aroused by the sexual violence only if the victim was shown to be aroused, and not if she was not so portrayed (Malamuth, 1984).

Individual Differences in Male Viewers

Convicted rapists were aroused by both rape and consenting sex, whereas men in a control group were aroused only by the consenting sex (Abel, Barlow, Blanchard, & Guild, 1977; Quinsey, Chapman, & Upfold, 1984). An important exception to this occurred if the victim was portrayed as enjoying the rape and coming to orgasm; in this case nonrapist U.S. and Japanese college men, though not women, were equally or more aroused by the rape than by the consenting sex (Malamuth, Heim, & Feshbach, 1980; Ohbuchi, Ikeda, & Takeuchi, 1994). Malamuth and Check (1983) had men listen to an audiotape of a sexual encounter of (1) consenting sex; (2) nonconsenting sex in which the woman showed arousal; or (3) nonconsenting sex in which she showed disgust. When the woman showed disgust, both dispositionally violent and nonviolent men were more aroused, in terms of both self-report and penile engorgement, by the consenting than the nonconsenting (rape) scene. However, when the woman was portrayed as being aroused, the nonviolent men were equally aroused by both the consenting and nonconsenting versions, whereas the violent men actually showed more arousal to the nonconsenting (rape) version. Analogous results were obtained using video stimuli (Malamuth, 1981). Using a similar design, Bushman, Bonacci, van Dijk, and Baumeister (2003) discovered that men scoring high in narcissism found a rape scene preceded by affection between the parties more entertaining and more sexually arousing than low narcissists did.

Some situational variables can affect arousal as well. For example, ordinary men were more aroused than usual by a rape scene if they had been previously angered by a female confederate (Yates, Barbaree, & Marshall, 1984). Also, alcohol consumption can decrease sensitivity to victim distress and thus allow greater arousal to sexual violence (Norris, George, Davis, Martell, & Leonesio, 1999). Alcohol can even affect women's judgments. Women reading an eroticized rape description while intoxicated were less likely than a sober control group to label coercive sex events as rape (Davis, Norris, George, Martell, & Heiman, 2006). Shope (2004) found that men who used pornography, especially if they also abused alcohol, were more likely than nonusers to batter their partners.

Can such effects transfer to new situations? Donnerstein and Berkowitz (1981; see also Donnerstein, 1980) showed men a sexually violent film in which a woman was attacked, stripped, tied up, and raped. In one version of the film, the woman was portrayed as enjoying the rape. Afterward, participants were given a chance to administer electric shocks to a confederate who had earlier angered them. Men who had seen the film in which the woman appeared to enjoy being raped administered more shocks to a female confederate, though not to a male. This suggests that the association of sex and violence in the film allows violent behavior to be transferred to a new situation.

Most of this research has been conducted on men. However, a few studies examining women and sexually violent media have shown behavioral effects of increased aggression toward other women (Baron, 1979) and desensitization effects of trivialization of rape and acceptance of rape myths and more traditional gender-role attitudes (Malamuth, Check, & Briere, 1986; Mayerson & Taylor, 1987; Schwarz & Brand, 1983; Zillmann & Bryant, 1982).

In a meta-analysis of studies examining the relationship of exposure to pornography and the acceptance of rape myths, Allen, Emmers, Gebhardt, and Giery (1995) conclude that experimental studies show a consistent positive effect between pornography exposure and rape myth acceptance, while nonexperimental studies show only a very small positive or nonexistent effect. The relationship was consistently stronger with violent than nonviolent erotica, although some experimental studies obtained effects from both (see the section entitled "Press Coverage of Sexually Violent Crimes" later in this chapter for further discussion of rape myths).

Sexual Violence: Conclusions

Several conclusions emerge from the sexual violence research (see Pollard, 1995, for a review). The most critical aspect of the sexually violent film is whether the woman is shown as enjoying and being aroused by the assault. Far more undesirable effects occur in men if the woman is shown as aroused than if she is seen to be terrorized. This media portrayal of women as being turned on by rape is not only a highly unrealistic and distasteful deviation from reality, but also a potentially dangerous one. For example, imagine how a sexually inexperienced young man might behave with a real woman if his primary model for sexual behavior has been violent pornography. A second important conclusion is that sexually violent media affect men differently, depending on their propensity to use force in their own lives. Convicted rapists and other men prone to use violence in their own lives are more likely to become aroused or even incited to violence by sexually violent media, even more so if the woman is portrayed as being aroused by the assault.

Slasher Films

The studies discussed so far in this section used very sexually explicit materials that would be considered hard-core pornography. However, sexual violence is by no means confined to material generally considered pornographic.

Sex + Violence in Mainstream Movies

Hundreds of mainstream R-rated films are readily available to teenagers anywhere, especially on DVD. There are the highly successful series like *Halloween, Child's Play, Friday the 13th, Scream, Nightmare on Elm Street, Scary Movie, The Ring, Saw,* and *I Know What You Did Last Summer,* as well as many single films like *The Texas Chainsaw Massacre* (1974 or 2003 version) and *The Blair Witch Project.* Many are extremely violent with strong sexual overtones. Some have noted a trend toward stronger, less victimized female characters in recent films like *Urban Legend, I Know What You Did Last Summer,* and *The Bride of Chucky.* Even the 1995 James Bond movie *Goldeneye* featured a villainess who seduces Bond, only to alternately pull a gun on him or throw him against a wall and kiss or embrace him passionately. Such seduction scenes show very violent mutual battering as a sort of foreplay. In some countries, rape and other acts of violence against women are even more standard entertainment fare (see Close-Up 10.8).

Close-Up 10.8: Rape to Sell, Indian Style

The nation producing the largest number of movies annually is India. Some of these use rape scenes as major audience draws. The great Indian epics *Mahabharata* and *Ramayana* have demure heroines who are nearly raped but who are rescued just in time from their attackers by their own virtue. This theme also appears in Indian movies featuring the same type of heroine. But the women characters who are portrayed as more independent, corrupt, immoral, or even morally ambiguous must suffer their fate, which is more typically blamed on their lifestyle rather than on the attacker. One film, *Crime Time*, advertised: "See first-time underwater rapes on Indian screen." One popular Indian actor, Ranjeet, has enacted over 350 rape scenes in 19 years of film acting (Pratap, 1990). There is some call for change. The chair of the Central Board of Film Certification announced his intent in 1990 to force producers to remove much of the titillation from the rape scenes, but filmmakers lobbied for his removal from the post. Curiously, verbal suggestiveness is more frowned upon than overt violence. A 1993 movie *Khalnayak* (Evil One) stirred up controversy when prominent film actress Madhuri Dixit clutched her breast while singing "What's Beneath My Blouse?" (Maier, 1994).

Although most of these films have R ratings in the United States, others are released unrated to avoid the accompanied-by-parent restriction of R-rated movies. Because few restrictions apply in stores or on the Internet, the rating is not a major issue. The viewing of such films is widespread among youth. Oliver (1993) found that punitive attitudes toward sexuality and traditional attitudes toward women's sexuality were associated with high school students' greater enjoyment of previews of slasher films.

The major concern with such films is the juxtaposition of erotic sex and violence. For example, the 2007 horror hit *Hostel: Part II* is set in a mysterious Slovakian spa where rich people can pay large sums of money to experience the thrill of torturing and killing someone. Three young American women in Rome are lured eastward to become the next victims. One scene in the film shows a woman suspended upside down and naked, and being tortured with a sickle. Another shows her head being sliced open with a circular saw, while a third shows two vicious dogs eating her various body parts. Other scenes in recent horror films include a naked woman strung up in a meat locker and sprayed with cold water that turns to ice (*Saw III*), the organs of a woman disemboweled by a truck shining in the sun (*The Devil's Rejects*), and six young women spelunkers being tormented by creepy men/monsters, with one left standing in a pool of blood reaching up to her chin (*The Descent*; Keegan, 2006).

Effects of Viewing Slasher Films

A series of studies starting in the 1980s examined the effects of viewing slasher films (Linz, Donnerstein, & Penrod, 1984; Linz, Donnerstein, & Adams, 1989).

Male college students were initially screened to exclude those who had prior hostile tendencies or psychological problems. The remaining men in the experimental group were shown one standard Hollywood R-rated film per day over one week. All of the films were very violent and showed multiple instances of women being killed in slow, lingering, painful deaths in situations associated with erotic content. Each day the participants completed questionnaires evaluating the film, as well as some personality measures. These ratings showed that the men became progressively less depressed, less annoyed, and less anxious in response to the films during the week. The films themselves were gradually rated over time as more enjoyable, more humorous, more socially meaningful, less violent and offensive, and less degrading to women. Over the week, the violent episodes in general and rape episodes in particular were remembered as occurring less and less frequently. A similar study by Krafka, Linz, Donnerstein, and Penrod (1997) tested women and did not find the same effects on perception.

Although these data provide clear evidence of desensitization in men, there is still the question of whether there is generalization from the films to other situations. To answer this question, the same people participated in what they thought was an unrelated study (Krafka et al., 1997; Linz et al., 1984; Weisz & Earls, 1995). For these experiments, participants observed a mock rape trial at a law school and evaluated it. Compared to control groups seeing nonsexual violent or sexually explicit nonviolent films, both men and women who had seen the sexually violent films, regardless of whether a man or a woman was the rape victim, rated the female rape victim in the trial as less physically and emotionally injured. These results are consistent with those of Zillmann and Bryant (1984), who found that jurors' massive exposure to sexually explicit media, even nonviolent, resulted in shorter recommended prison sentences for a rapist. Such findings show that the world we construct in response to seeing such movies can not only be at odds with reality but can also have very serious consequences when actions are taken in response to believing that such a world is reality.

Although a majority of these studies have been done with male participants viewing women as the sex object, gender is obviously a very important variable (Clover, 1992; Grant, 1996; Pinedo, 1997), and men and women see these films quite differently. In an interesting text analysis of students' writing about the most memorable slasher film they had seen, Nolan and Ryan (2000) found that men wrote more about fear of strangers and rural landscapes, while women wrote more about betrayed intimacy, stalkings, and spiritual possession.

Slasher Films: Conclusions

Not surprisingly, these studies (see Donnerstein, Linz, & Penrod, 1987, for a review) have caused considerable concern among the public, as well as considerable scientific concern. Some of the major effects have not been replicated in later work (Linz & Donnerstein, 1988), and there have been some methodological (Weaver, 1991) and content (Sapolsky & Molitor, 1996) criticisms.

The sharp distinction that Linz and Donnerstein have made between the effects of violent and nonviolent pornography has been questioned by some. Zillmann and Bryant (1988c) argued that Linz and Donnerstein were too quick to cite failures to reject the null hypothesis as support for the harmlessness of nonviolent pornography. Further, Check and Guloien (1989) found that men exposed to a steady diet of rape-myth-supporting sexual violence reported a higher likelihood of committing rape themselves, compared to a no-exposure control group; however, the same result was found for a group exposed to nonviolent pornography. There is considerable controversy, both scientific and political (see Close-Up 10.9), about the use and interpretation of data from particular studies; see Pollard (1995) for a review of pornography and sexual aggression. Although there is some difference of opinion over how serious the effects of nonviolent sexual media are, there is little dispute about the serious effects of sexual violence, especially if it shows the woman as being aroused by being attacked.

Close-Up 10.9: The Pornography Commissions, Or Why Science and Politics Don't Mix

A commission was established by U.S. President Lyndon Johnson in 1967 to analyze (1) pornography control laws, (2) the distribution of sexually explicit materials, and (3) the effects of consuming such materials, and (4) to recommend appropriate legislative or administrative action. It funded more than 80 research studies on the topic, providing an important impetus to the scientific study of sexually explicit material. The final report, three years later, recommended stronger controls on distribution to minors but an abolition of all limits on access by adults. The latter recommendation was based on the majority conclusion that "there was no evidence that exposure to or use of explicit sexual materials play a significant role in the causation of social or individual harms such as crime, delinquency, sexual or nonsexual deviancy or severe emotional disturbance" (Commission on Obscenity and Pornography, 1970, p. 58). Although the composition of the commission was criticized for being overloaded with anticensorship civil libertarians, its majority conclusions were rejected anyway by the new administration of Richard Nixon, who declared, "so long as I am in the White House there will be no relaxation of the national effort to control and eliminate smut from our national life" (Eysenck & Nias, 1978, p. 94).

Fifteen years later during the Reagan administration, a second commission was formed. U.S. Attorney General Edwin Meese charged this commission to assess the nature, extent, and impact of pornography on U.S. society, and to recommend more effective ways to contain the spread of pornography, clearly stating a political position. One of the major conclusions of the commission dealt with the effect of sexual violence: "the available evidence strongly supports the hypothesis that substantial exposure to sexually violent materials bears a causal relationship to antisocial acts of sexual violence, and for some subgroups, possibly the unlawful acts of sexual violence" (Department of Justice, 1986, p. 40).

Groups like these commissions typically have both a scientific and a political agenda (Einsiedel, 1988; Paletz, 1988; Wilcox, 1987). Sometimes, even if there is relative consensus about the scientific conclusions, there is strong disagreement about the policy ramifications. For example, Linz, Donnerstein, and Penrod (1987) took exception to some of the conclusions drawn by the 1986 commission about those researchers' own work demonstrating deleterious effects of sexual violence. Linz and colleagues (1987) argued that the commission's call for strengthening obscenity laws was not an appropriate policy change based on the research, because it ignored the strong presence of sexually violent themes in other media not covered by such laws.

Such political–scientific adventures are not unique to the United States. During the same period, the Longford (1972) and Williams (1979) commissions in Great Britain issued reports, followed a few years later by the Fraser commission in Canada (Special Committee on Pornography and Prostitution, 1985). The major conclusion of these commissions was that there is a lack of conclusiveness in the research to date. Do such commissions serve a useful purpose?

Mitigating the Negative Effects of Sexual Violence

The results from the research showing strong desensitization effects are disturbing, especially given the widespread viewing of horror films by children and young teens and the overall increase in sexually violent media. Can anything be done to lessen these effects?

Malamuth, Heim, and Feshbach (1980) offered an extensive debriefing, complete with information on the horrible reality of rape and the complete unreality of portrayals of the victim enjoying it. They even included a discussion of why the myth of women enjoying rape was so prevalent in sexually violent media. Other studies included evaluations of such debriefing sessions and showed that, compared to a control group not in the experiment, debriefed people showed less acceptance of rape myths (Donnerstein & Berkowitz, 1981;

Malamuth & Check, 1980). Some studies have developed and evaluated more extensive pre-exposure training procedures to attempt to lessen the desensitizing effects of sexual violence (Intons-Peterson & Roskos-Ewoldsen, 1989; Intons-Peterson, Roskos-Ewoldsen, Thomas, Shirley, & Blut, 1989; Linz, Donnerstein, Bross, & Chapin, 1986; Linz, Fuson, & Donnerstein, 1990). These studies have typically shown mitigating effects on some measures and not on others. Linz and colleagues (1990) found that men were most strongly affected by the information that women are not responsible for sexual assaults perpetrated upon them. There is evidence that desensitization can be reduced by introducing information about rape myths and the inaccuracy of media portrayals after people have seen some of the sexually violent media. At least some participants were more impressed with such arguments after they had felt themselves excited and aroused by the film and had seen specific examples illustrating the points of the debriefing or mitigation information. In the context of having seen such a film, the specific points of the sensitization training had greater impact. A meta-analysis of these studies concluded that the education and debriefing of these studies largely eradicated any harmful effects of viewing the material, and in fact often left participants with less antisocial attitudes that those they held before participation (Mundorf et al., 2007).

Using a different approach to mitigating negative effects, Wilson, Linz, Donnerstein, and Stipp (1992) measured the effect of seeing a prosocial movie about rape. They found that, compared to a control group, people viewing the film generally showed heightened awareness and concern about rape. However, not all groups were so affected. Unlike women and young and middle-aged men, men over 50 had their preexisting attitudes reinforced and actually blamed women more for rape after seeing the film. This suggests that the attitudes and experiences of the target audience must be carefully considered with any intervention.

Although the discussion of sexual violence so far has dealt with the effects of fictional portrayals, there is another type of material which is part of our exposure to sexually violent content, namely news coverage of sexually violent crimes.

Press Coverage of Sexually Violent Crimes

The way that the press covers crimes like rape can subtly support rape myths. For example, even severe violence may sometimes be described in terms of passion or love. When a man kills his ex-wife and her boyfriend, the press may call it a "love triangle." When a man shoots and kills several coworkers, including a woman that refused to date him, it is called a "tragedy of spurned love." When a man kidnaps, rapes, and strangles to death his estranged wife, the press reports that he "made love to his wife, and then choked her when he became overcome with jealous passion" (Jones, 1994). Does *love* really have anything to do with such crimes?

Benedict (1992) identified several problems with the newspaper coverage of sex crimes. To begin with, there is often a gender bias of the writers, reporters, and editors covering such crimes. Reporters who cover rape cases are two or three times more likely to be male than female, usually crime and police reporters. There is also a gender bias of language, with women more likely than men to be described in terms of their physical appearance and sexuality. Some rape myths are subtly supported by descriptions of rape as being a crime due to unfulfilled sexual need. Less often do we encounter rape presented as an act of torture, although that perspective is more likely to be used in reporting of wartime rapes. For example, when mass rapes of Bosnian women occurred in the Bosnian civil war of the mid-1990s, they were reported as acts of war and torture, and there was no description of the victims' attractiveness or dress or flirtatious behavior.

In her content-analysis studies of numerous newspaper reports of several high-profile rape cases, Benedict (1992) identified two common rape narratives, both of which distort and trivialize the crime. The most common "story" is the *vamp*, a sexy woman who incites the lust of a man, who then cannot control himself and rapes her. A second narrative is the *virgin*, the pure and innocent woman attacked by a vicious monster. Benedict identifies several factors that increase the likelihood that the press will use the vamp narrative; that is, blame the victim. She is more likely to be described in terms of the vamp narrative if (1) she knew the assailant, (2) no weapon was used, (3) she was young and pretty, (4) her behavior showed deviation from traditional sex roles, and (5) she was of the same or a lower-status race, class, or ethnic group as the rapist. The more of these conditions there were in a particular case, the more likely it was that the reporting would conform to the vamp narrative; the fewer of them there were, the more likely it was that the case would be reported using a virgin narrative.

Why does such bias occur? Benedict blames in part the habitual pressure of deadlines, but also our heavy emphasis on victims of crimes. While this reflects genuine empathy for victims, it also taps into a desire of reporters and the public to reassure themselves that such acts will not happen to them because they don't behave like that. Thus, the behaviors and attributes of the victim are highlighted. There is less emphasis on the rapist, especially in the vamp narrative, and not much examination in either narrative of the societal forces that drive some men to behave in such violent ways. These biases can have consequences. A Texas grand jury in 1993 refused to indict a man for rape because his quick-thinking victim had convinced him to use a condom; only a public outcry forced a reconsideration of the decision.

Conclusion

What may we conclude from the research on the effects of viewing sexual media and the perceived reality of such media? First, it is useful to make a distinction between violent and nonviolent sexual media, although this distinction may not be quite as important as Linz and Donnerstein have argued. While there are some negative effects of nonviolent erotica, especially on attitudes toward women (Weaver, 1991; Zillmann & Bryant, 1984, 1988a, 1988b), the research is particularly compelling in the case of sexual violence. Sexual violence is arousing to sex offenders, naturally violent men, and sometimes even to other men if the woman is portrayed as being aroused by the attack. For reviews and meta-analyses of results of numerous experimental studies on the effects of viewing sexually explicit media, see Allen, D'Alessio, and Brezgel (1995), Allen et al. (1995), Bauserman (1996), Gunter (2001), Harris and Barlett (2009), Malamuth and Impett (2001), Mundorf et al. (2007), Oddone-Paolucci et al. (2000), and Pollard (1995). Repeated exposure to sexual violence may lead to desensitization with respect to violence against women in general, and greater acceptance of rape myths. Not only does this suggest that the combination of sex and violence together is worse than either one separately, but it also matters what the nature of the portrayal is. If the woman being assaulted is portrayed as being terrorized and brutalized, negative effects on normal male viewers are less than if she is portrayed as being aroused or achieving orgasm through being attacked. Perhaps more than any other topic discussed in this book, this is an extremely dangerous reality for the media to create and for us to accept as real. There is nothing arousing or exciting about being raped, and messages to the contrary do not help teenage boys understand the reality of how to relate to girls and women, nor do they help young girls learn about what it is reasonable to expect from boys.

Not all the themes of sexual aggression against women are limited to specifically sexual material or even to very violent movies. These images are also found in mainstream television. As discussed in Chapter 4, many years ago a story line of the soap opera *General Hospital* focused on the rape of one main character, Laura, by Luke. Although Laura first felt humiliated, she later fell in love with Luke and married him, in a fairy-tale wedding seen by 30 million viewers in 1981. Although Laura and Luke went through a lot in 25 years, including death and resurrection, extramarital affairs, marriages to other people, and several children with serious problems, in 2006 Laura was revived from a four-year coma just in time to marry Luke again, in a gala reunion wedding, before promptly returning to her catatonic state.

Sexually violent images also appear in media other than film and TV, including detective magazines (Dietz, Harry, & Hazelwood, 1986), music videos (Hansen & Hansen, 1990a; Zillmann & Mundorf, 1987), and music lyrics (Christenson, 1992). The reality of some of these media is that men dominate and brutalize women. Moreover, the women are sometimes portrayed as being sexually turned on by being raped or tortured. What is the cost of this message about how men treat women, especially for those in the audience who may not realize that this picture deviates so significantly from reality?

As a final thought on this emotionally charged subject, we need to be aware of our own biases and ideology which we bring to the topic. Even the scientific research can be directed, in part, by the researchers' ideology (see Close-Up 10.10). Just as people believe that other people are influenced more by media in general than they are themselves—the so-called third-person effect (Gunther, 1991; Perloff, 2002)—so people believe that others are influenced more by sexual media than they are (Gunther, 1995). This is also exactly what people believe about the effects of advertising (Gunther & Thorson, 1992) and news coverage (Gunther, 1991; Perloff, 1989). It always affects the other person but not me.

Close-Up 10.10: Normative Pornography Theories

Two of the most prominent researchers on sexual media, Daniel Linz and Neil Malamuth (1993), have talked about how various normative theories have guided research and may be lurking behind the scientific evidence. First is the *conservative-moralist theory*. This position, very prominent in Anglo-American history and culture, sees public portrayals of sex as disgusting and offensive. However, they are at the same time arousing, and are seen as very threatening if the sex occurs outside of monogamous relationships. There is an implicit belief that a heavy emphasis on sexual gratification and permissiveness leads to behavior that undermines moral beliefs about women and sexuality, and ultimately to the decay of family and other traditional societal structures. This position tends to encourage research on sexual arousal, what materials produce it, and how exposure to sexual materials undermines traditional attitudes and can affect later reactions.

A second normative theory is the *liberal theory*, which endorses the idea that sexual depictions trigger fantasies but that these fantasies are not acted out and thus no one is hurt. They may even be socially beneficial, through liberating a person's excessive prudishness. Liberals believe that if sexual behavior (and the viewing of it) is kept private, then the government should not restrict or regulate what is best left to the marketplace of ideas, which will adjust on its own to changing social standards. The liberal theory tends to value more highly research on physical and behavioral effects of sexual media in the real world, as opposed to research conducted in the laboratory. It would also favor media literacy education, and counteracting antisocial messages with competing messages rather than through legislative restriction.

The third and most recent normative theory is *feminist theory*, which views pornography as a powerful socializing agent that promotes the sexual abuse of women and the social subordination of women as a group. Feminist-inspired research tends to focus on the arousal, or lack of it, of women in rape scenes. It also tends to look more at attitudes than behaviors, including differences between men with or without a propensity to rape.

Linz and Malamuth recognize that each normative theory has inspired some useful research, but they stress that we must recognize researchers' ideological positions when we evaluate their conclusions and the contributions of their studies to the matrix of media effects research overall.

Chapter 11

Socially Positive Media
Teaching Good Things to Children (and the Rest of Us)

Q: What is the most watched educational television program of all time?
A: *Sesame Street*, on the air continuously with new episodes since 1969.

Q: What was the effect of NBC *Today* anchor Katie Couric undergoing a colonoscopy on national television in March 2000?
A: According to a study in the *Archives of Internal Medicine*, colonoscopy rates in the United States jumped over 20% after the nation saw the inside of Katie's bowels on TV. With colon cancer almost always curable if detected early but still the second leading cause of cancer deaths, Katie undoubtedly saved many lives. Incidentally, this was not a shameless publicity stunt; Couric's husband had recently died at 42 from colon cancer, and Katie was determined to save others the heartbreak that her family had suffered (Bjerklie, 2003).

Q: How did Twitter affect the relationship between Planned Parenthood and the Susan G. Komen for the Cure breast cancer advocacy group?
A: When the Komen foundation decided to stop providing funding for Planned Parenthood in 2011 (due at least in part to concerns about Planned Parenthood providing abortion services), Twitter exploded with over 1.3 million tweets, many of them opposing the decision. This kind of negative reaction caused the Komen foundation to reverse course and continue funding Planned Parenthood programs for breast cancer screenings and education (Belluck, Preston & Harris, 2012).

Much of this book has focused on rather problematic perceived realities gleaned from the media: worlds of excessive violence, deception, stereotyping, sexual promiscuity, or tabloid news reporting. However, we must not lose sight of the fact that the power of media can also be used in very positive ways. In this chapter we examine some of this potential, when the media are intentionally used to produce or encourage socially positive ("prosocial") outcomes. We begin by looking at prosocial children's television, programming specifically designed to help kids to learn or to be better people in some way. Next, we look at social marketing, with a focus on public service media campaigns to teach improved health behaviors. Finally, we examine the use of entertainment media such as prime-time television and movies to teach explicit prosocial lessons and healthy behavior.

Prosocial Children's Television

Given children's massive exposure to media, primarily television, it is inconceivable that they are not learning anything from it. In fact, throughout this book we have been examining what children learn from media. Here, however, we focus on some specific projects explicitly designed to teach kids prosocial behaviors and attitudes through television (see Close-Up 11.1 for a discussion of prosocial video games).

Although there had been some specifically educational children's shows on the U.S. commercial networks since TV debuted (e.g., *Kukla, Fran, and Ollie*; *Romper Room*; *Captain Kangaroo*), by the mid-1960s there was increased interest in developing more children's television programming that would be commercial-free, explicitly educational, socially positive, and of high technical quality. Towards this end, in the United States, National Educational

---

Close-Up 11.1: Can Playing Video Games have Positive Effects?

Although there is considerable evidence of the negative outcomes of playing video games (see Chapter 9), recent research by at least one psychology laboratory suggests that not all video games are created equal. Building on previous studies investigating prosocial effects associated with music, Tobias Greitemeyer and his colleagues in Europe have discovered some positive outcomes from playing video games in which players provide help to others within the game. For example, as compared to those who played a "neutral" video game (*Tetris*), participants who played "prosocial" video games (*Lemmings, City Crisis*) in which they rescued other characters were more likely to help real people in real-life situations, including a person they believed was being harassed (Greitemeyer & Osswald, 2010). In other studies, those who had just played prosocial video games reported more prosocial thoughts (Greitemeyer & Osswald, 2011), more feelings of empathy, and less *schadenfreude* (pleasure at others' misfortune) than those who had just played a neutral video game (Greitemeyer, Osswald, & Brauer, 2010). When compared to the number of violent video games on the market, there are no doubt fewer with prosocial elements. However, there could be important implications from this line of research for those who design and buy video games.

Television (NET) began in 1954, followed by the Corporation for Public Broadcasting (CPB), founded in 1967, and eventually the Public Broadcasting Service (PBS) in 1970. The CPB was created by a 1967 act of Congress that also established National Public Radio (NPR). The artistic and technical quality of children's programming greatly improved during this period, particularly with the founding of the Children's Television Workshop (CTW, later known as Sesame Workshop) in 1968, initially supported by both public and private funds (Stewart, 1999).

Sesame Street

Sesame Street, one of the most important television shows of all time in terms of viewership and research, saw its debut in 1969. Designed from the beginning to be "hip and fast and funny," the show was a hit from the start (Stewart, 1999, p. 113). Although there would be periodic struggles with the U.S. government over funding (Davis, 2008), even President Richard Nixon was a fan of the early show, writing to CTW: "The many children and families now benefiting from 'Sesame Street' are participants in one of the most promising experiments in the history of that medium...This administration is enthusiastically committed to opening up opportunities for every youngster, particularly during his first five years of life, and is pleased to be among the sponsors of your distinguished program" (Ferretti, 1970, p. 79).

Although it was only the first of several such shows, *Sesame Street* is still by far the most successful and popular young children's show worldwide; it is seen in well over 100 countries with about 20 different adaptations, from Kuwait to Turkey to Sweden to China. As appropriate, it has been translated into many languages but is always locally produced and adapted to local culture (Fisch, 2004; Gettas, 1990; Gikow, 2009). Its original stated purpose was to provide preschoolers with an enriched experience leading to prereading skills. With its urban, multicultural setting, the program was especially targeted at so-called disadvantaged children who often entered school less prepared for reading than were their suburban peers. However, the show would come to appeal to children across the social spectrum. Regular characters like Big Bird, Cookie Monster, Oscar the Grouch, and Bert and Ernie have become part of almost everyone's childhood.

What the Show Is Like

The technical quality of *Sesame Street* has been consistently very high throughout its years, using a combination of live action, animation, and puppetry, with much humor and lots of movement. There is a pleasing mixture of human and Muppet characters. Recognizing that commercials are familiar and appealing to young children, *Sesame Street* draws on many of the technical characteristics of ads (e.g., "This program has been brought to you by the letter H and the number 6"). In later years the influence of music videos became apparent, with the use of that format within the show. Many segments are short, so as to not lose even the youngest viewers' interest. In fact, even some infants under 1 year old are regular watchers. Practically all people under 40 in many societies of the world have had some exposure to *Sesame Street*, and many have had very heavy exposure. In many markets the show is on three or more times per day on PBS affiliates and their digital subchannels, and much more is available on DVD and online. All of this has combined to make *Sesame Street* by far one of the most watched TV shows, educational or otherwise, in history.

There is also much wordplay and satire to amuse adults watching with their children or listening in the background. A rock band of insect puppets sings about nutrition in the song "Hey Food," which just happens to sound a lot like The Beatles' "Hey Jude." There was also "Letter B," a take on another Beatles song, "Let it Be." More recently, there was a playful parody of HBO's popular *True Blood* called "True Mud." There is also spoofing of the show's own network, PBS. The segment "Monsterpiece Theater" featured a smoking jacket–attired Cookie Monster ("Good evening, I'm Alastair Cookie") introducing classics about numbers and letters, including "The Old Man and the C" and "1 Flew over the Cuckoo's Nest." Children are introduced to operatic music at the all-bird "Nestropolitan Opera" with conductor Phil Harmonic and lead tenor Placido Flamingo. Popular adult stars frequently put in guest appearances, too: Neil Patrick Harris, Katy Perry, Julia Roberts, Paul Simon, Robin Williams, and news anchors like Anderson Cooper, Brian Williams, and Barbara Walters have all visited *Sesame Street*. Even Supreme Court justice Sonia Sotomayor once stopped by to mediate a conflict between Goldilocks and one of the Three Bears. Adults who had earlier watched the show as preschoolers frequently have the feeling, seeing *Sesame Street* as adults, that there are a lot of nuances that they missed, in contrast to shows like *Barney and Friends* or *Teletubbies*, which have little intrinsic appeal to adults. This appeal is not accidental; children get more out of *Sesame Street* if their parents watch and discuss it with them, and the producers know that.

The intentional use of a multiracial, multiethnic, multiclass, and increasingly gender-balanced cast ensemble has set a valued social model for children as well; it provides far more diverse and positive multicultural modeling than most of what is offered by commercial television. Among the human characters on the show, there have always been substantial numbers of women and members of diverse ethnic groups; they go about the business of being human, not particularly identifying as members of some social group. Sometimes the teaching is more focused. For example, there is a heavy draw from various Hispanic cultures, including Spanish and bilingual English-Spanish songs, such as "Somos Hermanos/We are Brothers." On one occasion the *Sesame Street* characters took a trip to the Crow Reservation in Montana to learn about that particular Native American culture. There have also been visits to Louisiana to learn about Cajun culture and food and zydeco music.

Effects of Watching Sesame Street

Besides being the most watched young children's TV show of all time, *Sesame Street* has also been the most extensively evaluated show, in terms of scientific research, generating according to one estimate over 1,000 studies (Fisch, 2004). We turn now to some of the effects of watching *Sesame Street* (Fisch, 2002, 2004; Fisch & Truglio, 2000; Huston et al., 1990).

As most parents know very well, children's attention and interest level while watching *Sesame Street* is typically high; preschoolers really do like the show. In terms of more substantive effects on learning, there is solid evidence for short-term effects, in the sense of vocabulary growth and the acquisition of prereading skills and positive social skills and attitudes, such as showing evidence of nonracist attitudes and behavior (D. R. Anderson, 1998; Ball & Bogatz, 1970; Huston & Wright, 1998; Rice, Huston, Truglio, & Wright, 1990). Those who watched *Sesame Street* also spent more time reading and doing other educational activities and needed less remedial instruction (Fisch, Truglio, & Cole, 1999; Zill, 2001). Longer-term effects are less clear, with some early studies showing that the advantages of watching *Sesame Street*, compared to a control group not watching it, disappear after a few months or years (Bogatz & Ball, 1971). However, later longitudinal research showed that heavy viewing of *Sesame Street* in the preschool years is positively correlated with later school grades in English, math, and science, even with early language ability and parental education level controlled (Huston, Anderson, Wright, Linebarger, & Schmitt, 2001; Huston & Wright, 1998).

Some interesting qualifications of these effects have been found. The positive effects are stronger if combined with parental discussion and teaching (Cook et al., 1975). This suggests that, among other functions, the program can serve as a good catalyst for informal media literacy education within the family. (See Chapter 12 for a closer look at media literacy.) Another interesting finding is that, at least initially, *Sesame Street* helped higher socioeconomic status children more than lower socioeconomic status children, although both groups improved significantly (Ball & Bogatz, 1970). However, this result should not have been unexpected, because any kind of intervention generally most helps those who are most capable or advantaged to begin with and thus more able to take full advantage of what it has to offer.

There have also been positive social effects. Minority children watching *Sesame Street* showed increased cultural pride, confidence, and interpersonal cooperation (Greenberg, 1982) and more prosocial free play (Zielinska & Chambers, 1995). Also, after two years of watching *Sesame Street*, White children showed more positive attitudes toward children of other races (Bogatz & Ball, 1971; Christensen & Roberts, 1983).

Although very widely praised, *Sesame Street* does have its critics (e.g., Healy, 1990; Winn, 2002), who mostly fault its encouragement of passivity and short attention span, as well as its slighting of language skills, through the necessarily highly visual nature of television. However, these criticisms are mostly general criticisms of television, with little recognition of the differential quality of programming. See D. R. Anderson (1998) for a careful discussion and refutation of specific claims of these critics, and Close-Up 11.2 for hypotheses about the effects of TV in general on reading.

Sesame Street is still going strong in its sixth decade. New material is continually being created, but there is also heavy recycling of old material,

---

Close-Up 11.2: Does Television Interfere with Reading?

A common concern of many parents is that their children watch too much television and do not read enough. Koolstra, van der Voort, and van der Kamp (1997) identified various hypotheses about the effect of watching TV on reading and looked at the support for each of them. *Facilitation hypotheses* argue that watching television facilitates or encourages reading. Not widely held, only a few small pieces of evidence support it, namely learning to read from reading subtitles on TV (*on-screen reading hypothesis*—see Close-Up 1.4) and reading a book either reviewed on or directly based on a TV show after watching the show (*book-reading promotion hypothesis*—see Close-Up 11.4). Both of these, however, apply to only very restricted, specific contexts.

More widely believed and scientifically studied is some sort of *inhibition hypothesis*, with TV watching reputed to have a negative impact on reading. There are four variations of inhibition hypotheses. First, the *passivity hypothesis* argues that TV causes children to become more mentally lazy and less prepared to invest the mental effort necessary for reading. Although it is true that TV requires less mental effort than reading (Salomon, 1984, 1987), viewers are far from totally passive. A second variety of inhibition hypothesis is *concentration-deterioration*, which says that TV weakens a child's ability to concentrate. The *reading depreciation (antischool) hypothesis* argues that TV leads children to expect school to be as entertaining as Sesame Street or Barney and Friends and, when it is not, they lose motivation. Finally, the *displacement hypothesis* argues that television hurts reading but only when it takes away time from reading.

Although not all the research is entirely consistent (Koolstra & van der Voort, 1996; Koolstra et al., 1997; Mutz, Roberts, & van Vuuren, 1993; Ritchie, Price, & Roberts, 1987), the displacement and reading depreciation hypotheses appear to have the most support. If children watch TV instead of reading, it may induce more negative attitudes about reading and diminish their reading skills (Koolstra et al., 1997).

> If they watch TV *in addition* to reading, there is probably no detrimental effect on reading. Regarding fantasy play, watching nonviolent TV programs does not interfere with children's fantasy play, but violent shows reduce fantasy play (van der Voort & Valkenburg, 1994). Overall, TV appears to stimulate day dreaming but reduce creative imagination (Valkenburg & Van der Voort, 1994).

and old and new segments appear together in the same show. Preschoolers are not bothered by reruns; in fact, familiarity often makes them more attractive. Although often at the forefront of dealing with social issues (see Close-Up 11.3), there are some areas about which *Sesame Street* has remained silent. For example, there is generally little treatment of mainstream religion or religious holidays, and there are no openly gay or lesbian characters (despite rumors about Bert and Ernie's relationship[1]).

Other CTW/Sesame Workshop Projects

In the fall of 1971, CTW launched a second major program, *The Electric Company* (TEC), which used much of the successful *Sesame Street* format but was aimed at improving the reading skills of older children (around second grade). TEC was heavily used in schools as well as at home. Evaluative research (Ball & Bogatz, 1973) found that viewing TEC led to improved scores on a reading test battery in children who had watched in school, but there was no improvement in a control group who had merely watched TEC at home. This suggests that the show was helpful in teaching reading, but primarily so in conjunction with the experiences offered in the classroom by the teacher and the curriculum. Never as popular as *Sesame Street*, TEC later operated in reruns until it was finally canceled in 1986, only to be revived in 2009 for a few seasons.

There have been other CTW/Sesame Workshop projects (e.g., *Ghostwriter*, *Square One TV*), as well as independently produced prosocial programs that have shown up on PBS, like *Where in the World is Carmen Sandiego?*, *Mister Rogers' Neighborhood*, *Barney and Friends*, *Arthur*, and *Caillou*. Many of these kinds of shows have produced demonstrable positive effects. For example,

---

1   For years, comedians, bloggers and others have been speculating, and joking, that the *Sesame Street* characters Bert and Ernie might be more than roommates. One independent filmmaker even made a spoof called *Ernest and Bertram* in 2002, about the two characters being outed as a gay couple in the press. Sesame Workshop did not respond kindly to the film, ordering screenings stopped under charges of copyright infringement. An official at Sesame Workshop at the time said that Bert and Ernie "do not portray a gay couple, and there are no plans for them to do so in the future. They are puppets, not humans" (Maerz, 2010, ¶14).

Close-Up 11.3: *Sesame Street* Deals with Difficult Issues

One of the most remembered segments in the history of *Sesame Street* is the death of Mr. Hooper in 1983. When the human actor playing Mr. Hooper passed away, the producers decided to have the character die as well. They used the segments around his death to teach three specific points they believed all viewers would accept: (1) Mr. Hooper died; (2) he is not coming back; and (3) he will be missed. In order not to offend any viewers with particular religious beliefs (or lack of them) in regard to any afterlife or reasons for the death, no mention was made of heaven or hell. Evaluation research showed that half of preschool viewers' parents reported discussing death with their child after watching the critical episode.

A few years later the show dealt with the human characters Luis and Maria falling in love, getting married, and having a baby. Teaching goals for this sequence were for the children to understand that: (1) people can love each other even when they argue; (2) a baby grows inside its mother's body; and (3) the baby can move inside the womb.

In response to increased concern about children's poor eating habits, in the 2000s Cookie Monster started eating vegetables and encouraging children to do likewise, which required a major evolution in his character.

Provocative topics are not new to *Sesame Street*. Reflecting the times, one early episode from 1969 even had Grover learning rules of civil disobedience (Conan, 2009).

Sometimes the program's planned campaigns did not work, however. For example, a 1990s proposal to deal with divorce through Snuffy and Alice's parents divorcing was scrapped and never aired after a pilot version showed that young viewers did not understand that the parents still loved their children and that the children would continue to see their dad after the divorce (Fisch et al., 1999).

when preschoolers watch Barney, the cheery purple dinosaur that anyone over 6 loves to hate, they show better manners than a control group not watching Barney's show on manners (Singer & Singer, 1998). A more recent study (Penuel et al., 2012) revealed that, in comparison to a control group, preschoolers who were exposed to in-class media clips from shows like *Sesame Street* and *Super Why!* showed enhanced prereading skills relating to letters and sounds. In fact, a number of studies indicate that children are quite able to pick up the intended curriculum of educational shows, whether it be related to academic or social skills (Kirkorian & Anderson, 2011). In a move some may find ironic, television has even been used to teach children about literature and to encourage reading (see Close-Up 11.4). In light of increased difficulties in obtaining funding for such shows, some have criticized the newer programs, especially, for being more entertaining than educational, a situation brought about by increasing economic pressures to attract an audience as public television increasingly relies on corporate funding. For reviews of these

---

Close-Up 11.4: Using Television to Encourage Reading

Using a television show to encourage reading? Surely that is a contradiction in terms and a waste of time? The producers of a few popular PBS shows think otherwise. The children's book review show, *Reading Rainbow*, hosted by *Roots* and *Star Trek: The Next Generation's* LeVar Burton, reads stories to children, accompanied by compelling illustrations and live-action photography, followed by LeVar's visit to a setting described in the story. Near the end of the show other books are read or reviewed in briefer fashion. Does it matter? Sales of books featured on *Reading Rainbow* jumped 150 to 900% and a survey of librarians found that 82% reported children asking for books featured on *Reading Rainbow* (Fisch, 2002; Wood & Duke, 1997).

Super Why!, a more recent animated PBS offering, follows the adventures of Whyatt and his friends, who become super hero-like "Super Readers," complete with capes and alter egos (Whyatt transforms into Super Why). After saying, "Calling all Super Readers! To the Book Club!", the Super Readers become physically immersed in the plot of a book, reading along the way to address real-life kid issues like sharing, offering help to others, or making friends. Other recent PBS children's shows that encourage reading such as *Martha Speaks* and *Word World* are also designed to inspire book sales and library visits.

Can the same phenomenon happen with adults? Although acclaimed novelist Toni Morrison won a Nobel Prize in 1993, that was nothing compared to having her novel *Song of Solomon* selected as the second offering of the Oprah Book Club in December 1996. Although Morrison, who seldom watches TV, had never heard of the Oprah Book Club, she quickly realized its importance. Within months, a million copies of her selected novel sold, and paperback sales of her other novels jumped about 25% (Gray, 1998)! When Oprah announced in 2002 that she would be discontinuing her book club, publishers and authors emitted a collective gasp. The first 48 selections on Oprah's Book Club all sold at least 500,000 copies after being featured, and many sold over one million (Sachs, 2002). Oprah revived her book club in 2003, although with selections offered less frequently. That version of the club ended when her daytime show closed its run in 2011. However, in 2012 Oprah again announced that the book club would be reincarnated, as "Oprah's Book Club 2.0." This time, however, discussion would take place on her Oprah Winfrey Network (OWN) cable channel and via Facebook and Twitter. Those who read the book selections in electronic form on e-readers could even see "margin notes" written by Winfrey herself. After the first book selection was made for "2.0," sales of the title surged, indicating that Oprah had not lost her influence on reading (Minzesheimer, 2012).

kinds of programs and their effects, see Calvert and Wilson (2011), Chen (1994), Fisch (2002), and Mares and Woodard (2001).

Commercial TV Contributions

The 1990 Children's Television Act, which required all broadcast stations in the United States to provide educational programming for children, was clarified by the 1996 interpretation of this law by the FCC, which required each station to provide a minimum of three hours a week of educational and informational programming for children (Kunkel, 1998). At least one extensive study (Calvert & Kotler, 2003), has found many overall positive effects associated with the Children's Television Act, one of which has been a substantial increase in commercial educational programming for children. The most extensive single project has been the cable channel Nickelodeon's investment in new children's programs (Anderson, 1998). The network, along with its sister channels like Nick Jr., has presented preschool shows that have been popular and have shown some promising initial evaluation research results. *Allegra's Window* used puppets and humans to emphasize social problem-solving in a continuous half-hour story. *Gullah Gullah Island* featured a real human family from a little-known American culture, the Gullah of the South Carolina Sea Islands. The shows were presented as part of a commercial-free block. *SpongeBob SquarePants* is an animated show aimed at children but, like *Sesame Street*, it has a subtext of more mature humor that appeals to teens and preteens. So do shows like The Disney Channel's *Phineas and Ferb*, which features imaginative half-brothers who concoct grand schemes like building a time machine. Nickelodeon's *Yo Gabba Gabba!* offers a wacky live host with a crew of cuddly monsters who sing and dance to hip hop music about dancing food and vegetables who want to party in your tummy.

Blue's Clues, aimed at preschoolers, features a human character with an animated dog (Blue) in an animated world. Every episode invites the viewers to help solve the day's mystery, for which Blue has left her paw print in three places as clues. Her human sidekick frequently "needs help" and asks the audience questions and waits for them to answer, in order to more actively involve the child viewer in creative problem solving. The same episode is shown five days in a row, in order to better empower the child to make use of all the clues; research shows that attention is maintained at a high level, at least through three episodes (82% of the time looking at the screen), after which it drops to around the average level of attention to entertainment programming (Anderson et al., 2000). Research also showed that viewers of *Blue's Clues*, compared to a non-viewing control group (or sometimes in comparison to those viewing other shows), performed better on several measures of cognitive development (Anderson et al., 2000; Crawley, Anderson, Wilder, Williams, & Santomero, 1999; Linebarger & Walker, 2005).

Science Shows for Children

Although science shows for children are not new (*Wild Kingdom* and *Mr. Wizard* appeared in the 1950s), one of the earliest modern science shows was the CTW project, *3-2-1 Contact*, which debuted in 1980 with the goal of teaching scientific thinking to 8- to 12-year-olds. It attempted to help children experience the excitement of scientific discovery and to encourage all children, particularly girls and minorities, to feel comfortable with science as an endeavor (Mielke & Chen, 1983).

More recently, the PBS programs *Zooboomafoo, Kratt's Creatures*, and *Wild Kratts* featured naturalists Chris and Martin Kratt, who go romping over the world in their quest to see interesting creatures and teach young viewers how important it is to preserve these species and their habitats. In an animated series on PBS, *Sid the Science Kid* runs experiments and examines topics like the five senses or simple machines. Nickelodeon's *Dino Dan* follows the adventures of the live-action young character Dan as he gathers clues about animated dinosaurs. *DragonflyTV* features Eric, Mariko, and Michael hosting science activities. A somewhat different, very high-energy approach, was taken by *Bill Nye the Science Guy*, another PBS program offering a wide variety of high-tech, high-action science demonstrations, with a generous helping of wisecracks thrown in. There is modeling of conducting experiments in many settings. The commercial offering *Beakman's World* took a similar approach. Both shows effectively counter the image of science as being difficult, stuffy, and generally uncool. Many such shows also include interactive websites where kids can run "experiments" of their own. See Fisch (2002) for an excellent review of educational effects of children's prosocial television programs.

International Contributions

Many nations are getting in on the rush to create high-quality, commercially successful prosocial children's programs. One of the most successful, *LazyTown*, began in one of the world's smallest nations, Iceland, but is now seen in over

110 countries, including the U.S. Its creator Magnús Scheving, a.k.a. "Sportacus" on the show, uses acrobatics and "sports candy," that is, fruits and vegetables, to try to save LazyTown from the temptations of junk food and the plots of villain Robbie Rotten. After a 2004 healthy-eating campaign on *LazyTown*, sales of fruits and vegetables rose 22% in Iceland, so much that the country's president called the program a "brilliant tax-saving phenomenon," in spite of being one of the most expensive children's programs ever, at $800,000 per 25-minute episode. Its combination of live action, puppets, and computer graphics is state-of-the-art technology (Bates, 2008).

A hugely popular program for preschoolers in South Korea and over 80 other countries (though not yet in the U.S.) is Choi Jong Il's *Pororo the Little Penguin*, about a 3D penguin who lives on a snowy island with six animal friends. Pororo is 4 years old and wants to fly, and wears an aviator hat and goggles. He and his friends have a rich fantasy life (Veale, 2008).

Channel One

One of the most controversial efforts in prosocial children's TV has been Channel One News, a service of daily news for secondary school students. Offered directly to schools at no charge since 1990, Channel One was in about 40% of all middle and high schools in the United States by 1997 (Bachen, 1998), with an audience of approximately 6 million adolescents in 8,000 schools by 2009 ("About Channel One News," 2009). Channel One has been controversial since its inception, primarily because of its inclusion of two minutes of commercials, the revenues of which support the 10 minutes of news in the program. Although commercials are hardly new to teenagers, the "captive audience" nature of the in-school setting has caused particular concern. Evaluation research (see Bachen, 1998, for a review) suggests a small positive effect of learning about events in the news. Some research shows that students report a greater desire to buy the advertised products, relative to a control group (Greenberg & Brand, 1993), and that children tended to remember advertising more than news after watching Channel One (Austin, Chen, Pinkleton, & Johnson, 2006). Interestingly, another potential but seldom-expressed concern about Channel One is the possibility of abuse by some future producers, who might choose to set a particular political agenda or offer a very biased view of the news to this young captive audience.

Teen Programs

Beginning in the late 1950s and into the 60s, when the Baby Boom generation started entering adolescence, advertisers saw in teenagers a very lucrative new marketing opportunity. In the U.S. this translated into the first TV shows aimed directly at teenagers, with sitcoms like *The Many Loves of Dobie Gillis*, *The Patty Duke Show*, *The Monkees*, and *Gidget*. In the 1970s and 80s, an interesting television genre became popular with older children and teens. Somewhat ahead of their time, these shows took on controversial topics several times a year in the late afternoon hours. ABC *Afterschool Specials* and CBS *Schoolbreak Specials* presented dramatized stories of serious topics like racism, suicide, teen pregnancy, drug use, and homosexuality.

Compared to decades past, the proliferation of cable channels in the new millennium has resulted in greater amounts of programming targeted at preteens ("tweens") and early adolescents. These programs, particularly prevalent on the Nickelodeon and Disney cable channels (and their various sister channels), are the most extensive attempts ever on commercial TV to develop older children's programming. Such shows as *Hannah Montana, Drake & Josh, iCarly, That's So Raven,* and *The Suite Life of Zack & Cody* are immensely popular with 11- to 15-year-olds and have launched the movie careers of several hot young actors, including Zac Efron, Miley Cyrus, and Shia LeBoeuf. These shows model behavioral scripts of dealing with difficult situations common for that age range; for example, bullying, trying to be popular, maintaining friendships, and relating to parents and siblings. They present interesting and humorous characters in amusing situations, but with a refreshing lack of bad language, sexual overtones, or violence. See Close-Up 11.5 for a look at how one set of movies portrayed teen friendships.

Close-Up 11.5: Teen Friendships in *Harry Potter*

Some of the most popular books and movies of recent years have been J. K. Rowling's seven *Harry Potter* books (1997–2007), all made into highly successful movies (2001–2011). Throughout his 7 years at Hogwarts school (one book per year), Harry's longtime best friends were Ron Weasley and Hermione Granger. This trio hung out together in and out of school. One interesting aspect of Harry's support system was that, of his two best friends, one was a boy, and one was a girl. Hermione was not Harry's girlfriend, though there was some periodic attraction between Hermione and Ron. Although it is perhaps surprising that a teen boy would have a girl as a close friend, this is actually a very common configuration in TV shows, books, and movies targeted at teens and preteens. For example, the film *Big Fat Liar* (2002) showed 14-year-old Jason and Kaylee going on an adventure in Hollywood together to exact revenge on a ruthless film producer who stole Jason's script idea. Using slightly younger characters in a semi-fantasy setting, *Bridge to Terabithia* (2007) also depicted a strong friendship bond between a boy and a girl.

Although no doubt one reason for these cross-sex friendships is commercial—that is, to attract both the boy and girl audiences—they may also serve a useful prosocial function. This prevalent model communicates that you can have close friends of the opposite sex with no romantic or sexual component, and it is a positive social model for an age when preoccupation with coupling is strong. Indeed, some research (Sanborn, 2004) indicates that there can be considerable nonromantic, nonsexual benefits to such cross-sex friendships in childhood, adolescence, and adulthood. It is also interesting that in the world of media, which is saturated with sex and sexual innuendo, there is this common nonsexual model of friendship. Mulholland (2006) has an interesting set of readings on the psychology of *Harry Potter*.

Children's Prosocial Learning from Adult Television

Although children's television is important, a large majority of what children watch is not television produced for children but rather programs produced for a general audience, primarily made up of adults. A content analysis of programming on 18 broadcast network and cable channels found that 73% of the shows included some instance (2.92 incidents per hour) of people sharing or helping each other (S. W. Smith et al., 2006). Can children learn such prosocial attitudes and behaviors from watching them on television? A few studies suggest that they can. Rosenkoetter (1999) had first, third, and fifth graders watch episodes of the family sitcoms *The Cosby Show* and *Full House* and found that the large majority at all ages comprehended the lessons from the *Cosby* episode, and about half did so from the *Full House* episode. How many hours of prosocial sitcoms children watched was a moderate predictor of first graders' actual prosocial behavior, as judged by their parents, although this difference was less pronounced with older children. In a meta-analysis of 34 studies of the positive effects of prosocial TV content, Mares and Woodard (2005) found strong effects of such content on prosocial behaviors, especially altruism. In a study that didn't involve a specific TV show, Potts and Swisher (1998) exposed children ages 5 to 8 to a safety educational videotape, in which child actors engaged in dangerous recreational behavior from which they suffered injuries, later enacting alternative safe behaviors. Watching this video decreased the children's willingness to take physical risks and increased their identification of injury hazards, as measured by pre- and posttests. Other studies have shown that virtual reality technology can be used to teach compassion and empathy (Gillath, McCall, Shaver, & Blascovich, 2008). For a good review of the possible prosocial effects of media, particularly with regard to children, see Mares, Palmer, and Sullivan (2011).

Now let us turn from specific programming for children to the use of media more broadly to further prosocial aims. We begin by looking at the general area of social marketing.

Media Use in Social Marketing

A traditionally underemphasized but currently booming area in the world of marketing is *social marketing*. Sometimes difficult to define, the general goal of social marketing is to use media to promote behaviors that lead to improved health or wellbeing (Quinn, Ellery, Thomas, & Marshall, 2010). This can involve the selling of socially and personally positive actions to ensure or improve one's health or safety, such as avoiding tobacco and drunk driving (Backer, Rogers, & Sopory, 1992; Brown & Walsh-Childers, 2002; Flay & Burton, 1990). Thus, many social critics, researchers, and practitioners long concerned with selling products are now turning their attention to selling healthy, safe, and socially positive lifestyles. Mass media are a major, although not the only, component of a social marketing campaign.

Although theory building in this area has not been extensive, some researchers have offered possible theoretical foundations for social marketing. For example, Manrai and Gardner (1992) developed a model to explain how the differences between social and product advertising predict a consumer's cognitive, social, and emotional reactions to social advertising. Hornik and Yanovitzky (2003) argued that a theory of prosocial media effects is essential in designing such campaigns. Dutta (2007) suggested some directions for including cultural variables in theory development in regard to health communication, Southwell (2005) proposed a multilevel model of memory to look at memory for health ads, and Dunlop, Wakefield, and Kashima (2008) proposed a model looking at types of emotional responses to health communication.

Obstacles to Social Marketing

Although selling good health or safety is in many ways not unlike selling soap or automobiles, there are some challenges that are particularly acute for social marketing that don't apply to the selling of products. Social and product advertising differ in several important ways, most of which mean that there are greater obstacles facing public health and other social advertisers, as compared to commercial advertisers (Goldberg, 1995; Manrai & Gardner, 1992). First, social ideas tend to have a higher degree of both shared benefits and shared responsibilities than products, whose use is most often entirely an individual choice. For example, some (perhaps most) of the benefits of recycling household waste will be to society, not to the individual. Consequently, individuals may view society, not themselves, as also having much (or most) of the responsibility for the problem. Thus, motivating behavior with respect to the social message will be more difficult than selling a product, which has clear benefits to the individual.

Second, the benefits that do exist with social marketing tend to be delayed or intangible. Often there is a great physical, or at the very least psychological, distance between the consumer and the product. Selling cologne can stress how much sexier you will be for that big date tonight. Selling the idea of quitting smoking has a much less immediate payoff. Teen smokers think much more about looking cool with their friends today than about dying from lung cancer or emphysema in 30 or 40 years. Young, healthy adults do not typically feel much urgency to sign an organ donor card; psychologically the need is very distant. With social marketing, consumers are often not all that opposed to the message and may even support it; they simply do not feel the immediacy of it and thus are not particularly motivated to make much effort to act on the message.

Third, social marketing campaigns are often very complex, compared to what is typically involved in commercial marketing. Particularly with regard to health, the beliefs, attitudes, and motives for unhealthy practices tend to be deeply rooted and highly emotion-laden and thus rigidly resistant to change. For example, efforts to convince women to self-examine their breasts for lumps flies against their enormous fear of cancer and the potential damage to their sexual self-image by the contemplation of possible breast surgery. Convincing people to wear seatbelts when they have driven for 50 years without doing so is not easy. People are particularly resistant to change if anxieties occur in response to unrealistic but prevalent fears, such as the irrational fear of being declared dead prematurely in order for the doctors to acquire organs for transplantation (Harris, Jasper, Lee, & Miller, 1991; Shanteau & Harris, 1990). The complexity of the interaction of individual motives for behavior, the social context of that behavior, and the specific prosocial appeals can be very difficult to unravel in conceptual and theoretical terms (Yanovitzky & Bennett, 1999).

Fourth, unlike product advertising, social marketing messages frequently face strong opposition. This opposition may be social, as in the adolescent peer group that encourages and glamorizes smoking and tanned bodies, or it may be organized and institutional, as when tobacco companies threaten to withdraw advertising from magazines that carry articles about the dangers of smoking. Social marketing campaigns tend to be poorly funded compared to product advertising, and they often face opposing forces that hold enormous economic and political power. For example, the Tobacco Institute, oil companies, the pharmaceutical industry, and the National Rifle Association have been tremendously powerful lobbies quick to oppose media messages against smoking, alternative energy sources, prescription drug abuse, or gun controls, respectively. Public service announcements (PSAs), whether print or broadcast, tend to be poorer in technical quality and appear less frequently than commercial ads because of lower budgets. Although radio and TV stations air a certain number of unpaid PSAs, they generally do so at times when they are least able to profitably sell advertising. We see many PSAs while watching late-night TV, but there are very few during the Olympics or *American Idol*. Thus, specific demographic groups cannot be targeted by PSAs as well as they can by commercial advertising.

Fifth, social marketers often set unrealistically high goals, such as changing the behavior of 50% of the public. Although a commercial ad that affects 1 to 10% of consumers is considered hugely successful, social marketers have often failed to fully appreciate that an ad that affects even a very small percentage of a mass audience is a substantial accomplishment. Persons preparing social marketing campaigns are often less thoroughly trained in advertising, media, and marketing than those conducting product ad campaigns. A couple of meta-analyses of mediated health campaigns (Parcell, Kwon, Miron, & Bryant, 2007; Snyder, 2007) show significant, though modest, effect sizes for such campaigns, with the highest effect sizes approaching 0.30 but most in the 0.05 to 0.25 range, depending on the subject of the campaign and whether one is looking at behavioral or attitudinal/knowledge outcomes.

Finally, social marketing appeals are often aimed at the 15% or so of the population that is least likely to change. These may be the least educated, most traditional, or oldest segments of the population, precisely the people least likely to stop smoking or overeating, or to start wearing seatbelts, exercising, or requesting medical checkups. Just as political media strategists target advertising at the few undecided voters, so social marketing might best target those people most receptive to attitude and behavior change in the intended direction, rather than the group that is least likely ever to change at all.

Considering the Audience

Knowing the audience well and targeting it as specifically as possible is as helpful in selling health or safety as it is in marketing toothpaste, beer, or political candidates. Choosing a realistic audience, not those least likely to change, and setting realistic goals and targets are useful. Trying to see the issue from the audience's point of view will make for a more convincing message. Frequently social marketers are fervently convinced of the rightness of their message and fail to see how anyone else could view the issue differently. Self-righteousness tends not to be convincing.

The attitudes, desires, motivations, and reasonable beliefs of the audience may be used to drive the character of the message. A serious consideration of the kinds of psychological appeals that will be the most effective in motivating the particular target audience will be helpful. For example, when adolescents are targeted, given their strong sense of invulnerability and their habit of looking to other people for approval and comparison, forcing them to focus on the message and elaborate its meaning more deeply can be successful in reducing risk-taking behavior (Greene, Krcmar, Rubin, Walters, & Hale, 2002). If the goal of a social marketing campaign is a reduction in binge drinking in college students, there could be important differences in the motivations of "light," "medium" and "heavy" binge drinkers (Deshpande & Rundle-Thiele, 2011). To focus an appeal on the notion that some behavior (e.g., binge drinking, drug use, driving recklessly) is stupid, when in fact it appears adaptive within the target person's world, or part of the framework of his or her personality (e.g., as a sensation seeker), is not likely to be convincing (Morgan, Palmgreen, Stephenson, Hoyle, & Lorch, 2003; Nell, 2002; Stephenson, 2003). In cases when the approval and influence of peers is especially critical, such as in teens' decision to start smoking, those seeking to promote healthier alternatives must understand the complexities of how this peer influence operates (Gunther, Bolt, Borzekowski, Liebhart, & Dillard, 2006; Paek & Gunther, 2007). Perceived realism and relevance to one's life are also important (Andsager, Austin, & Pinkleton, 2001), as is the nature of the specific language used in the appeal (Miller, Lane, Deatrick, Young, & Potts, 2007) and the personality of members of the target audience (Lang, Chung, Lee, Schwartz, & Shin, 2005).

When designing social marketing for children, it is vitally important to consider the age of the child in the target group. For example, in testing antismoking posters, Peracchio and Luna (1998) found that 7- to 8-year-olds responded best to a picture of a dirty sock labeled "gross" next to an ashtray full of cigarette butts labeled "really gross." The 9- to 10-year-olds responded best to pictures of dead insects with a message saying smoking is chemically equivalent to spraying yourself in the face with insecticide, while 11-year-olds responded best to a poster of a car's tailpipe with written copy asking why you would smoke if you wouldn't suck car exhaust. Even adolescents and college students may respond differently to the same PSAs (Lang et al., 2005; Paek, 2008). See Close-Up 11.6 for a fascinating media campaign using comic books to help children avoid land mines.

Demographic factors may also affect viewers' response to a PSA. For instance, Meirick (2008) found that people would infer that the predominant

---

Close-Up 11.6: Using Superman and Wonder Woman to Teach Land Mine Avoidance in Central America

How can children in war-torn lands be taught how to avoid the lethal land mines that remain dangerous long after a war has ended? A part of the Organization of American States (OAS) Assistance Program for Demining in Central America involved the distribution of over 600,000 copies of special *Superman y la Mujer Maravilla* comic books in schools in Honduras, Guatemala, and Nicaragua. In this collaborative project of UNICEF, D.C. Comics, and the U.S. Army's Southern Command, Superman grabs Diego just before he steps on an antipersonnel mine, while Wonder Woman (*la Mujer Maravilla*) saves little Gabriela from a mine in a stream where she is washing clothes. A similar comic book had been successful in alerting children to land mines in the former Yugoslavia in 1996 (Mesmer, Baskind, & Lerdau, 1998).

gender, age, and ethnic groups present in antidrug PSAs were the predominant target of the PSA. The more of those groups the viewer belonged to, the more he or she self-identified as the intended audience.

Emphasizing specific behaviors that the audience may be able to change one small step at a time is often more useful than a general exhortation aimed at changing general attitudes. People may know very well that they should stop smoking, lose weight, or start wearing seat belts. What they most need are more specific, realistic behaviors that can be successfully used to meet that end. Often, existing motivation may be harnessed and channeled to build confidence in taking appropriate, specific actions.

Merely exhorting people to stop smoking may be of limited use. Showing a PSA of a young child smoking and talking about how cool he looks, just like Daddy, might reach the smoking parent more effectively. In one study, a workshop in which teens not only discussed and analyzed but also actually wrote and produced antismoking messages was more effective than a workshop in which they merely analyzed cigarette and antismoking ads (Banerjee & Greene, 2006). Further, if people are told that many others are also engaging in the bad behavior it may boomerang by legitimatizing the unwanted behavior; see Close-Up 11.7.

Close-Up 11.7: Convincing People Not to Steal Petrified Wood from a National Park

Social psychologist Robert Cialdini (2003) has discovered that some types of appeals are more effective than others in discouraging environmental theft. He performed a very clever field experiment in Arizona's Petrified Forest National Park, which suffers a loss of 14 tons of petrified wood each year due to stealing by visitors. Cialdini tested the relative effectiveness of two types of signs posted at entrances to visitor walking paths. The *descriptive-norm* appeal read, "Many visitors have removed petrified wood from the Park, changing the natural state of the Petrified Forest" and was accompanied by pictures of three visitors taking wood. The *injunctive-norm* sign stated, "Please don't remove the petrified wood from the Park, in order to preserve the natural state of the Petrified Forest" and was accompanied by a picture of one person stealing a piece of wood with a red circle and bar over his hand. Results showed that theft of specially marked pieces of petrified wood over five weeks was higher (7.9%) in the vicinity of the descriptive-norm signs than it was around the injunctive-norm signs (1.7%). Why the difference? Cialdini argued that the descriptive-norm approach, although trying to impress on visitors the enormity of the theft problem, in fact may have legitimatized it by suggesting "everybody does it." This was exactly the problem with the very popular "social norms" approach to curbing binge drinking in the 1990s and 2000s; by stressing how many people are doing it, the PSAs actually legitimatized the behavior they were trying to eliminate.

Positive Effects of Social Marketing

In spite of the obstacles, a spate of research has shown that social marketing media campaigns do have some clear positive effects. The first kind of effect is an altered perceived reality that includes a heightened awareness of the problem. Virtually everyone in North America is aware of the health dangers of smoking, driving drunk, and not wearing seat belts; such was not the case 40 years ago. Unlike 20 or 30 years ago, most people today are also aware of the need to recycle and sign organ donor cards, largely due to media publicity.

A second positive effect is making the problem more salient, thereby increasing receptivity to other, later influences in the same direction. Even though a particular PSA may not immediately send a person to the doctor to check a suspicious mole for possible melanoma, that person may pay more attention to a later message on that topic and perhaps be a little more careful about excessive exposure to the sun. An eventual behavioral change may actually be a cumulative effect of several influences. This, of course, makes it very difficult to scientifically measure precise effects of particular media campaigns.

A third effect is stimulating later conversation with one's family, friends, or doctor. Publicity about the dangers of smoking may encourage dinner table conversation between parents and teenagers who are being encouraged by peers to smoke. Although a decision not to smoke may result more from the personal interaction than directly from the message, the latter may have partially laid the groundwork for the former. Sometimes such conversation may not have the desired effect, however. For example, David, Cappella, and Fishbein (2006) found that teens discussing anti-marijuana ads actually had stronger pro-marijuana attitudes after discussing the ads in an online chat room than did teens who had not had the online chat opportunity. Also, the attitudes were not affected by the strength of the anti-marijuana arguments in the ads.

Sometimes media publicity may help create an overreaction. In the early 1990s, pediatricians were being warned against overdiagnosing Lyme disease. A high level of media publicity over the preceding few years was leading patients to ask about this illness and physicians to be quick to diagnose it. In the psychological realm, the explosion in the 1990s of the "recovery" of repressed memories relating to child sexual abuse in adults, based only on very common and nonspecific symptoms (sometimes accompanied by some widely publicized celebrity "victims"), led to huge overdiagnosis of child sexual abuse effects. This in turn resulted in highly divisive controversies in the counseling field (Loftus & Ketcham, 1994).

A fourth effect of social marketing campaigns is self-initiated information seeking in individuals (Afifi & Weiner, 2006). People may seek additional information on some topic as a result of their interest being piqued by media coverage of that issue. They might ask their doctor about it on their next visit, they might search the Internet for information, or they may read a newspaper article on the topic that they would have passed by before. Sometimes sick people seek additional information and sometimes they do not, and the reasons for this may be complex (Rains, 2008; Zhao & Cai, 2008). For example, in a study of breast cancer patients, Lee, Hwang, Hawkins, and Pingree (2008) found that negative emotion (feeling bad about one's illness) was correlated with greater health information seeking in those with high health self-efficacy, that is, those who felt in control of their situation. On the other hand, negative emotion was negatively correlated with health information seeking in those low in health self-efficacy. Thus feeling bad may work in opposite directions, depending on the degree of control the individual feels they have over a given condition.

Finally, prosocial media campaigns can reinforce positive existing attitudes and behavior, such as encouraging the ex-smoker to try hard not to succumb or reinforcing someone's feeling that he or she really should see a doctor about some medical condition. Often people know what they should do but need a little encouragement to actually do it. For example, newspaper coverage of youth advocacy efforts against smoking contributed to a decline in smoking among those exposed to those news stories (Niederdeppe, Farrelly, Thomas, Wenter, & Weitzenkamp, 2007).

Next we examine one of the major domains of social marketing campaigns—public health.

Public Health Media Campaigns

Breslow (1978) identified three methods of risk-factor intervention in public health campaigns. *Epidemiological intervention* involves identifying the characteristics correlated with increased frequency of the disease and taking steps to alter those characteristics. For example, cardiovascular risk factors like smoking, obesity, cholesterol level, physical inactivity, and hypertension are first identified, followed by screening people using blood pressure and blood chemistry tests.

Environmental intervention involves changing the environment in a healthier direction. Legislation restricting smoking in public places, reducing industrial emissions into the air or water, and adding fluoride to drinking water illustrate such interventions. Adding air bags to cars, substituting canola oil for coconut oil in fried foods, and selling lower-fat milk also manipulate the environment. Although sometimes harder to implement politically, such changes often yield huge improvements in health over time.

The third type of intervention, *educational programming*, often involves media and is of most concern for our purposes. Such programs may aim to alter the perceived reality by providing more information or providing an impetus for changing behavior and thereby making a change in the knowledge base. Often changes in knowledge are easier to produce than changes in behavior. For example, even though most smokers are well aware that smoking is bad for their health, their own perceived reality, at least at an emotional level, is that they will not themselves develop lung cancer (the kind of cognitive dissonance discussed in Chapter 2).

All three types of interventions must keep in mind the culture and demographics of the target population (Deshpande & Rundle-Thiele, 2011; Ilola, 1990). For example, an AIDS prevention campaign would (or at least should) take a very different form if targeted at North American gay men, intravenous drug users, or health care workers, or African heterosexual women without much social power to resist their partners' requests for intercourse. See Close-Up 11.8 for some interesting examples of health media campaigns designed specifically for various African cultures. See also Maibach and Parrott (1995) for a set of readings on psychological and communications considerations in designing health messages, and Brown and Walsh-Childers (2002) for a review of health effects of media messages.

Close-Up 11.8: Striking Examples of Prosocial Media from Africa

1. A popular comic book and video character in Zambia and several other African countries is 12-year-old Sara, a girl whose adventures include outwitting her greedy uncle who tries to steal her school fees, rescuing a friend who is about to be sexually molested, escaping from older women attempting genital mutilation, and making a smokeless cooking stove for her mother. The UNICEF-produced series has become very popular and provides a role model for empowering adolescent girls in societies that have not always valued education for girls (Bald, 1998).

2. After West African villagers in impoverished Sanankoroba, Mali, saw news on their battery-powered televisions of massive ice storm damage in Eastern Canada in January 1998, they took up a collection and sent about US$66 to their sister city of Sainte-Élisabeth, Quebec. Although the per capita income of Sainte-Élisabeth was about 75

times that of Sanankoroba, the Malians appreciated the Quebeckers' donations to them after floods in 1995 and 1997 and cited the Malian proverb that, "If you cannot share the meager resources you have today, you will not know how to part with a centime of the wealth you have tomorrow" ("Friend in Need," 1998).

3. In another uplifting story from Mali, Malian singer Oumou Sangaré sings "More and more we live in a world ruled by individualism, a selfish world," and "Let us fight for women's literacy/Women, let us fight together for our freedom, so we can put an end to this social injustice." Sangaré's message combines traditional Malian music with a sort of blues style that has made her immensely popular worldwide, causing her traditional countrymen to listen seriously to a message they had long been closed to (Rothenberg, 1998).

Cardiac Risk Reduction Projects

A very clear and consistent finding from studies of public health social marketing campaigns is that mass media campaigns are most successful when used in conjunction with other types of intervention (see Solomon & Cardillo, 1985, for a discussion of the components of such campaigns). A good example of such a campaign is the extensive and relatively well-controlled project conducted by Stanford University to reduce the instance of coronary heart disease and related factors (Farquhar et al., 1990; Schooler, Chaffee, Flora, & Roser, 1998; Schooler, Flora, & Farquhar, 1993; Schooler, Sundar, & Flora, 1996). This project involved three central California towns, each with a population of 12,000 to 15,000. Two of the towns received multimedia campaigns over a two-year period about the risks of coronary heart disease (CHD). One of these towns also received intensive interventions targeted at the high-risk population. These interventions involved both media messages and cooperation from the medical community. Health screenings were held, specific behavior-modification programs were set up, and people's attempts to reduce high-risk behaviors and characteristics were monitored.

Changes in both knowledge and behavior were monitored in the experimental towns and in the control town, which received no media campaign and no intervention. Results showed that media campaigns by themselves produced some increases in knowledge but only very modest, if any, changes in behavior or decreases in the overall percentage of at-risk people. Only when media campaigns were coupled with specific behavioral interventions and health monitoring were significant improvements and reduction of the numbers in the at-risk population seen. Similar results were found with other projects, such as a six-city study in Minnesota (Luepker et al., 1994).

Even more dramatic success came in the North Karelia project in rural Eastern Finland, which had one of the highest CHD rates in the world. Along with media campaigns and medical intervention, environmental interventions were also instituted, including restrictions on smoking, selling more low-fat dairy foods, and the substitution of mushrooms for fat in the local sausage. After four-and-a-half years of the project, there were dramatic reductions in systolic blood pressure and stroke incidence (McAlister, Puska, & Solonen, 1982).

This project had local and national government cooperation and combined what Wallack, Dorfman, Jernigan, and Themba (1993) labeled *downstream* and *upstream* marketing. Downstream efforts involve attempts to change consumers' behavior (e.g., stopping smoking, starting to exercise, seeking medical checkups, using designated drivers), while upstream efforts work at changing the conditions that produce or encourage the unhealthy behaviors (e.g., restricting tobacco sales to minors, prohibiting smoking in some places, stopping the sale of high-fat meat, raising the drinking age, forcing insurance companies to pay for mammograms). Downstream marketing, which has been the predominant approach in social marketing, is often limited in what it can accomplish without some upstream changes as well (Goldberg, 1995).

Even the riches of health information on the Internet are of limited value in isolation. For example, Gustafson and colleagues (2008) studied newly diagnosed breast cancer patients and tested the relative efficacy of a control group, an Internet-only group, and a group with Internet access plus additional support and decision and analysis tools. The group with the comprehensive resources did better in terms of quality of life and social support than either the control group or the Internet-only group, even though numerous high-quality medical websites were available. Other research has shown that the thoroughness of websites and user motivation are critical factors in the perceived source credibility of health websites (Dutta-Bergman, 2004).

AIDS Awareness Campaigns

One of the most pressing public health issues of the last generation has been HIV-AIDS. Worldwide, nations and organizations have taken a variety of media approaches to try to increase general awareness and knowledge and to change risky behaviors, especially in high-risk target groups like gay men, intravenous drug users, and heterosexuals with multiple sex partners. A content analysis of 127 AIDS-awareness PSAs televised in the United States in 1988 showed that most were directed at general audiences, rather than targeted at high-risk audiences. They tended to use rational rather than emotional appeals and emphasized the acquisition of information rather than change of behavior (Freimuth, Hammond, Edgar, & Monahan, 1990). A similar content analysis of 317 television PSAs in 33 different countries from 1991 to 1994 found the major emphasis was on general facts and nonbehavioral content, targeted at a general, poorly defined heterosexual audience (D. Johnson & Rimal, 1994).

Taking an experimental approach, Flora and Maibach (1990) measured people's cognitive involvement with the AIDS issue and exposed them to either a rationally based or an emotionally based PSA. Results showed that emotional appeals were more memorable than rational ones, especially for people relatively less involved psychologically with the content of the message. Information on prevention in conjunction with modeling and a chance for cognitive rehearsal of the prevention information was the most successful message (Maibach & Flora, 1993). Emotional appeals were also more effective than cognitive appeals in stimulating a desire to learn more about AIDS. For an analysis of Australian media messages about AIDS, see Tulloch, Kippax, and Crawford (1993); for an evaluation of the U.S. government's AIDS media campaign by the Centers for Disease Control and Prevention, see Ratzan, Payne, and Massett (1994).

Sometimes particular high-risk target groups react differently to AIDS spots than the general public does (Baggaley, 1988). In general, prevention programs targeted at gay White men have been the most successful in changing risky behaviors (Coates, 1990; Stall, Coates, & Hoff, 1988; Witte, 1992), whereas more general appeals and messages targeted at other groups have been less successful. Especially in the developing world, changes in longstanding and deep-rooted social customs are required to slow the spread of AIDS. For example, in parts of central Africa, where AIDS is spread primarily from men to women by heterosexual intercourse, polygamy and multiple sex partners for men are condoned, and women have little social power to resist their husbands' sexual advances or to insist on condom use. Such behaviors and attitudes may be extremely resistant to change, but will have to be altered before the spread of AIDS can be contained. In recent years there is some encouraging evidence that the spread of HIV-AIDS in southern and eastern Africa has finally started to decline, due partly to more effective media campaigns, but primarily to the greatly increased numbers of HIV-positive patients receiving antiretroviral drugs in countries like Botswana and South Africa.

Sometimes circumstances allow the use of a celebrity to advance the cause of some pro-health topic, as when a celebrity's public admission of dealing with a certain illness or health issue captures considerable press attention. One of the most celebrated and influential cases came with basketball great Magic Johnson's announcement in 1991 that he was HIV positive. Casey and colleagues (2007) performed a meta-analysis of studies reporting the effects of Johnson's revelation that he was HIV positive, having contracted the illness through promiscuous heterosexual behavior. Results showed significant gains in adults' feelings of vulnerability to HIV and children's and adults' knowledge of HIV infection, more positive perception of people with AIDS, and increased numbers of people seeking HIV testing. So Magic's announcement of his condition probably did save many lives.

Although the use of PSAs and other media-based campaigns, especially if coupled with medical or environmental interventions and specific behavioral tips, can be useful in increasing knowledge and sometimes in changing behavior, the sell is a difficult one. Another, very different use of media for prosocial ends comes in using entertainment media to convey these prosocial messages in the context of captivating fictional stories. We now turn to this type of media.

Entertainment-Education Media

Entertainment media may sometimes be explicitly and intentionally used for socially positive purposes within a society. Many such entertainment-education (E-E) campaigns have been implemented in dozens of nations worldwide, and they are especially prevalent in developing countries (Sherry, 2002; Singhal, Cody, Rogers, & Sabido, 2004; Singhal & Rogers, 1999). Some of these projects have been carefully evaluated and have shown impressive successes, which has contributed to their popularity throughout the world. Interestingly enough, this type of media is relatively unknown in much of North America and Europe, but even there it is starting to appear in a somewhat covert fashion.

Sample E-E Programs

In many developing countries, radio and television have long been seen as tools for development and positive social change, rather than merely vehicles for entertainment. The earliest concerted effort in this direction began in 1975, when the giant Mexican network Televisa began to produce several series of programs, many in the very popular genre of telenovelas (soap operas). These programs were explicitly designed to promote gender equality, adult literacy, sexual responsibility, and family planning (Brown, Singhal, & Rogers, 1989; Rogers & Singhal, 1990; Singhal & Rogers, 1989b), though they were first and foremost entertainment. The shows were very popular and viewers often requested the services promoted by the programs (Lozano, 1992).

Televisa's Descendants

Televisa's model of communicating prosocial messages through entertainment was emulated elsewhere. In 1987, Kenya aired the prosocial soap opera *Tushariane* ("Let's Discuss"), designed to promote family planning; it became the most popular show in the history of Kenyan TV (Brown & Singhal, 1990). The Nigerian soap opera *Cock Crow at Dawn* encouraged the adoption of modern agricultural practices (Ume-Nwagbo, 1986). Televisa's *Sangre Joven* ("Young Blood") telenovela of the early 1990s dealt with family planning, AIDS, and drug abuse. Jamaica produced a family planning radio soap opera,

Naseberry Street, which reached 40% of the Jamaican population from 1985 to 1989 (Rogers & Singhal, 1990). The Peruvian Amazon's ¡*Bienvenida Salud!* ("Welcome, Health!") combined a radio drama with popular music, local news, contests, and listener letters and testimonials (Sypher, McKinley, Ventsam, & Valdeavellano, 2002).

Rwanda, Tanzania, and Botswana

The Rwandan radio drama *Musekeweya* ("New Dawn") is a sort of Romeo-and-Juliet story of Tutsi and Hutu villages on the brink of conflict but saved from it by improved communication. This was launched in 2007 to try to lead to reconciliation and avoidance of a repeat of the calamitous 1994 Hutu–Tutsi civil war and genocide (Phillips, 2007). The Tanzanian radio soap opera *Twende na Wakati* ("Let's Go with the Times") featured a promiscuous truck driver who contracted HIV. His wife then left him to set up her own business and was "rewarded" by not contracting AIDS. This program reached 55% of the population from 1993 to 1998, with 82% of those saying they had changed their behavior to reduce the chance of HIV infection (Rogers et al., 1999). A somewhat similar radio program in Botswana, called *Makgabaneng* ("We Fall and We Rise"), featured storylines like people falling in love and discussing HIV testing before marriage, and couples with one HIV-positive and one HIV-negative partner. Results from one study (Pappas-DeLuca et al., 2008) indicated that those who had listened to the show, particularly frequent listeners, were more willing to get tested for HIV and to talk to a partner about testing.

Soul City

One of the most ambitious E-E projects was the South African TV, radio, and public health campaign *Soul City* (Singhal & Rogers, 1999), which dealt with a range of themes, including HIV prevention, maternal and child health, domestic violence, and alcohol abuse. It used a multifaceted approach, with its prime-time TV segment becoming South Africa's top-rated television show and its radio drama airing daily in eight different languages. Very importantly, public health materials were widely distributed along with the broadcasts. *Soul City* was very successful in generating discussion and in furthering information-seeking, and the show also led to impressive increases in reported condom use and commitment to tell one's partner of HIV infection. Before *Soul City*, only 3% agreed that one's HIV-positive status should not be kept secret from one's partner, but afterward 75% agreed the partner should be told. The show also introduced the behavior of banging kitchen pots as a community signal that domestic violence is taking place, and as a way of identifying abusers and showing support for victims (Singhal et al., 2004).

Hum Log and Jasoos Vijay

Another impressive commercial success was the Indian TV drama *Hum Log* ("We People"), which debuted in 1984. It became the most popular program in the history of Indian TV and also had substantial social impact (Brown & Cody, 1991; Singhal & Rogers, 1989a, 1989c). Although it was a commercial entertainment program, *Hum Log* also had the overt purpose of advancing the status of women through dealing with such issues as wife battering, the dowry system, and the political and social equality of women and men. At the end of every episode, a famous Indian film actor gave a 30- to 50-second summary of the episode and appropriate guides to action. *Hum Log* encouraged women to work outside of the home and to make their own decisions.

Evaluation research (Brown & Cody, 1991) found *Hum Log's* impact to be substantial, though complex and not always what was expected. For example, many women viewers identified with Bhagwanti, the family matriarch and traditional woman, rather than with her more independent daughters Badki and Chutki, at least in part because of concern over the difficulties that the younger women's more independent stance had brought to them. There is an interesting parallel between the effects of *Hum Log* and the 1970s U.S. sitcom *All in the Family*, in which more traditional viewers identified with the bigoted Archie Bunker and found him to be a more positive figure than the producers had envisioned (Vidmar & Rokeach, 1974). This phenomenon of some viewers identifying with the intended negative role models has been observed in several nations and has come to be known as the "Archie Bunker effect" (Singhal & Rogers, 1999).

A more recent Indian program, *Jasoos Vijay*, featured a famous Indian actor as a detective who solves mysteries while trying to provide information and reduce the stigma of HIV/AIDS. Each episode ended with a cliff-hanger plot twist, followed by an epilogue by a famous actor. Viewers were encouraged to respond to these epilogues (Singhal et al., 2004). Evaluation of *Jasoos Vijay* found that 16% of the audience reported changing their sexual behavior in the months following the show (Singhal et al., 2004). Even if there was some self-reporting bias here, the effect is impressive. E-E campaigns have shown such clear effects, when well implemented. The basic entertainment function provides interesting characters with whom the public develops parasocial relationships (Papa et al., 2000; Sood, 2002; see Chapter 2 for further discussion of parasocial media relationships).

The narrative form may be an especially good format for inserting persuasive messages (Slater & Rouner, 2002). A good E-E program can increase a viewer or listener's sense of self-efficacy—their beliefs about their ability to exercise control over events that affect their lives (Bandura, 1997). These beliefs can then lead to prosocial behaviors such as using condoms, seeking medical advice, or taking control over one's reproductive health. It can also contribute to a sense of collective efficacy—the belief in joint capabilities for forging individual self-interests into a shared agenda (Bandura, 1995). For example, after watching an E-E soap opera involving characters dealing with abdominal pain and cervical cancer screenings, Thai-American women indicated that they were more likely than a control group to discuss Pap tests with doctors and friends (Love, Mouttapa, & Tanjasiri, 2009). More dramatically, when viewers of a *Soul City* story on wife battering gather in front of a neighborhood batterer's home and bang their pans in censure, a behavior seen in the series, collective efficacy is achieved (Singhal & Rogers, 2002).

Conclusions

In considering the effectiveness of entertainment-education media in developing countries, Rogers and Singhal (1990; see also Singhal & Rogers, 1999, 2002; Singhal et al., 2004) drew several conclusions:

1. Placing an educational message in an entertainment context can draw a mass audience and earn large profits, which can then be used to support the prosocial campaign.
2. The educational message cannot be too blatant or too much of a hard sell, or the audience will reject it.
3. The effect of the media message in such programs is enhanced by specific supplementary tips about behavior change.
4. The repetition of prosocial themes in a telenovela has a greater effect than a one-shot media PSA campaign. A continuing series like *Soul City* will generally have greater impact than a one-episode story on *ER*.
5. Prosocial campaigns are most successful if the media, government, commercial sponsors, and public health organizations work together; see Bouman (2002) for discussion of various management models for E-E campaigns.

E-E in the United States

Although few broad-based, popular E-E campaigns have been promulgated in the United States (see the discussion of *Afterschool Specials* earlier in this chapter, for example), elements of E-E have appeared on American entertainment television from time to time. One of the earliest was the designated driver campaign of the late 1980s (Rosenzweig, 1999). Professor Jay Winsten of the Harvard School of Public Health worked with NBC and over 250 writers, producers, and TV executives over six months to try to incorporate what was then a new idea—the "designated driver"—into TV plot lines. By 1994, the designated driver message had appeared on 160 prime-time shows and had been the main topic of 25. Two-thirds of the public had noted the mention of designated drivers in TV shows, and just over half of young adults reported they had served as a designated driver. By the late 1990s, the drunk-driving fatality rate had fallen by one-third from 10 years earlier, in part due to greater use of designated drivers. This concept achieved acceptance in part due to a subtle entertainment-education campaign and in part due to changing societal values about the use and abuse of alcohol (see Close-Up 11.9).

As another example, consider when *ER*'s Dr. Mark Greene, concerned about overuse of antibiotics and left brutally honest by his brain surgery, walked into his hospital waiting room and told the patients there not to expect antibiotics for the flu, after which half of them left. Another episode of *ER* used a plot line about morning-after contraception; subsequent research showed that 6 million of the show's 34 million viewers had learned about morning-after contraception from watching the show (Rosenzweig, 1999).

Unbeknownst to many viewers, these plot lines (along with those in many other shows, including *Numb3rs* and *24*) were written by, or with the cooperation of, the Centers for Disease Control and Prevention (CDC), which since 1998 has had an entertainment-education department to assist teleplay writers in placing positive health messages in their scripts for popular TV shows. Viewers do find the information from such shows helpful. A Kaiser Family Foundation study found that one third of *ER* viewers reported learning something from the show that had been helpful in making health care decisions in their own families ("Going Hollywood," 2007; Stolberg, 2001).

One of the most carefully evaluated cases (also mentioned in Chapter 10) involved the 2001 HIV subplot on the daytime soap opera *The Bold and the Beautiful* (*B&B*), which reached about 4.5 million households at the time. Written in collaboration with the CDC, this week-long sequence had an attractive young man test positive for HIV. He told his doctor that he had always used condoms with recent sexual partners (all women). He also disclosed his HIV-positive status to all of his partners, including the woman he planned to marry. Moreover, he worked to overcome emotional obstacles and interpersonal issues and tried to live a full and productive life. Immediately after each episode, a toll-free phone number for the CDC's national AIDS and HIV hotline appeared on the screen. Call attempts to the HIV hotline increased dramatically just after the airing of the *B&B* episode on these days,

---

Close-Up 11.9: Media Values about Substance Abuse

Some very deeply held values center around substance use and abuse, but even these can change, albeit slowly. In regard to alcohol, the most widely abused drug, the United States has seen decreasing acceptance of alcohol abuse since the mid-1980s. Although social drinking has been modestly reduced, levels remain high and alcoholism as a disease and a social problem is still rampant. Attitudes toward excessive drinking are somewhat less tolerant than they once were, however. The drunk is not so much an object of humor as of pity or disgust. Portrayals of drinking on TV have had to take note of this, at least implicitly. There are still concerns, however, one of the biggest being binge drinking among college students. This is perhaps encouraged by, for example, university newspaper stories about people celebrating their 21st birthdays by visiting several bars until they pass out, or by ads showing a fellow passed out on the bathroom floor with "Happy 21st" written below. Is this just reporting reality or is it legitimizing dangerous antisocial behavior?

Attitudes toward smoking have changed far more dramatically. Like many early TV characters, Lucy and Ricky Ricardo in the old *I Love Lucy* show of the 1950s smoked cigarettes regularly, sometimes at the specific request of Philip Morris, the tobacco company sponsor. For the most part, however, regular characters on TV series have not smoked since the 1960s, clearly out of a health concern over possible negative effects on youth of seeing admired TV characters smoking (one notable exception is the throwback show *Mad Men*, which is set in the 1960s). Although this certainly reflects the great decline in the percentage of adult smokers since 1960, it may have also contributed to that decline. Even among teens, smoking is much less cool than it used to be, and television may be part of the reason for that. Curiously, however, the same trend is not apparent in movies, where characters smoke far more frequently; this is probably to some extent due to product placement agreements with tobacco companies (see Chapter 5).

Finally, most TV shows today are careful not to show illicit drug use by respected characters. Adults or teens may occasionally be shown using drugs, but it is nearly always presented as wrong. This mindset even carries over into news. As the Baby Boom generation coming of age in the 1960s and 1970s began to move into leadership positions, however, reactions began to change. In the 1992 Presidential campaign, Democratic candidate Bill Clinton admitted to trying marijuana once as a graduate student in 1969. This was widely covered in the media (especially his rather curious disclaimer that he "didn't inhale"[2]). However, the public did not hold this transgression against Clinton; he won the election. In a subsequent presidential election, youthful marijuana use was apparently a nonissue.

---

2 When questioned later about the apparently self-serving "I didn't inhale" comment, Clinton explained that, having never smoked tobacco, he did not know how to inhale. This explanation, however, received very little attention in the copious news coverage of this issue.

and these were not explained by typical daily time trends in calls. For example, on one day there were less than 200 calls every hour until the hour just after the show, when there were 1,840 (Kennedy et al., 2004)! This suggests an enormous, and in the United States largely untapped, potential prohealth role for entertainment-education programming.

An organization that the CDC often cooperates with is Hollywood, Health, and Society, which is affiliated with the University of Southern California. One collaboration involved spreading the word about BRCA gene mutation and the risk of breast cancer in women. Storylines were woven into two scripted dramas (*ER* and *Grey's Anatomy*) in the fall of 2005. Both stories involved characters learning they had the gene mutation and struggling with the idea of having preventative mastectomies before cancer inevitably set in. Results from one study (Hether, Huang, Beck, Murphy, & Valente, 2008) indicated that this sort of repeated exposure (multiple episodes, multiple shows) was more associated with positive outcomes (like understanding that getting a second opinion is important) than watching just one show.

E-E or Social Marketing?

In examining explicit public health media campaigns, Flay and Burton (1990; see also Brown & Einsiedel, 1990) identified seven steps for such a campaign to be maximally effective:

1. Develop and use high-quality messages, sources, and channels.
2. Disseminate effectively to the most appropriate target audience.
3. Gain and keep the attention of the audience.
4. Encourage favorable interpersonal communication about the issue after exposure to the message.
5. Work for behavior changes, as well as changes in awareness, knowledge, and attitudes.
6. Work for broader societal changes.
7. Obtain knowledge of campaign effectiveness through evaluation research.

Interestingly enough, all of these apply just as well to E-E as to traditional public health media campaigns, and in fact some aims may be better met through E-E than through traditional social marketing PSA campaigns. For example, people will pay more attention to gripping entertainment media than to PSAs and will talk more about them later. The audiences for E-E messages are potentially huge. Of course, there are ethical issues of concern, particularly in the case of messages not everyone would agree with. For example, if *Modern Family* had a script strongly supporting or opposing the right to abortion, large numbers of viewers would likely be incensed. Still, the E-E path is probably one that deserves a closer look in Western countries. Indeed, one study showed that even just thinking about a popular and sympathetic gay character like Will Truman on *Will and Grace* can do a lot toward increasing a person's acceptance of homosexuals (Bonds-Raacke et al., 2007). This suggests a huge potential role for entertainment media in promoting social change.

Conclusion

A recurring theme throughout this chapter, indeed throughout the entire book, is that the effects of the media depend on more than their content. A perceived reality is constructed by viewers, readers, or listeners as their minds interact with the media message. Media exhortations to treat other people better or live a healthier lifestyle are more effective if combined with behavioral interventions providing specific tips on lifestyle change and support for efforts to do so.

This idea is not unlike research findings on how children and adults survive traumatic life experiences in general (e.g., Leavitt & Fox, 1993). The ones who survive and grow, rather than succumb to defeat and trauma, are those who have support in the rough times, those who can talk over the troubling events, and those who have countervailing positive influences to partially balance strong negative ones. It is almost a truism that media may be a force for ill or good. Much writing and research has focused on the ill effects of TV or the Internet. Media are with us to stay, however; we cannot isolate our children from these influences. However, we can take steps to make that interaction a more positive, even rewarding, experience than it would otherwise be.

Do media merely reflect the state of society or do they serve as a catalyst for changing and even improving it? Clearly they do in some sense mirror society, but they can and do serve as a catalyst for change. How this change occurs is of great importance, but it is also difficult to study. The cultivation theory approach (see Chapter 2) has been particularly useful here (e.g., Morgan et al., 2009): Television and other media cultivate a worldview through the interaction of the viewer and the content presented. The social reality presented in media gradually becomes the reality for the viewer. If that media world includes, as normal features, the regular use of seatbelts, sunscreen, bike helmets, condoms, and designated drivers, that world will be adopted by viewers and will improve their lives.

Of course, media in fact send many mixed messages on health issues, such as when PSAs stress using condoms and not smoking, on the one hand, and at the same time respected characters in movies smoke and have casual, unprotected intercourse. No wonder many young people are confused about what is normal. In the final analysis, we must remember that, given the economic realities of media, whatever sells the best will be what we see the most of. For example, the recent fad for so-called "reality shows" offers up a quite unrealistic, even unhealthy, slice of life, yet these shows draw large numbers of viewers (see Close-Up 11.10).

Close-Up 11.10: Reality Shows Show the Worst Side of Reality

MTV's notorious reality show *Jackass* featured stunts like having a group of guys kick their friend in the groin for the amusement of the audience (there were disclaimers of "Don't try this at home"). Another show featured diving into a sewage holding tank ("poo-diving"). *Jackass* was so popular that it became a series of movies, starting in 2002. Along the same lines, *Fear Factor* had contestants perform stunts like eating live slugs or dunking their head into a tankful of snakes.

By 2005, out-of-control brides became common as a reality show subcategory on cable channels. Relatively tame programs like *Say Yes to the Dress*, which followed brides making decisions about their wedding gowns, were supplemented by shows like *Bridezillas*, which featured self-centered, pouting, and sometimes violent brides-to-be. Perhaps the worst of this genre was *Bridalplasty*, in which brides competed for their dream gown and the perfect plastic surgery for their wedding day.

The *Survivor*-style reality shows which gained popularity in the early 2000s relied on entertaining audiences by placing groups of people in competition with each other to survive on a desert island. Daily reckonings for whom to "vote off the island" kept fans riveted for weeks. An African version of the show *Big Brother* was very popular but was condemned by governments and religious leaders in several African nations for its explicit sexual content ("Malawi bans *Big Brother Africa*," 2003). Perhaps the pinnacle (or pit) of this genre was *Temptation Island*, where faithful couples were surrounded by beautiful opportunities to be unfaithful to their partners while the audience cheered them on. The show *Who Wants to Marry a Millionaire?* presented a handsome young man as a millionaire to be the object of several women's competing affections. The "punch line" was the women's reactions when they found out he wasn't really a millionaire. On one occasion, producers were in some difficulty when inadequate background checks failed to discover one real life "hunk" being "sold" to competing women in fact had a criminal record for domestic battering.

How real are reality shows, anyway? On ABC's *The Dating Experiment* the producers wanted a contestant to like one of her "suitors" whom she did not, so they asked her who her favorite celebrity was. "Oh, I really love Adam Sandler," she said. Sandler's name was replaced with the name of the suitor before the clip appeared on the show. On *Joe Millionaire* a contestant and his date disappeared offstage while "lusty noises and captions" were edited in. A contestant on *The Amazing Race* appeared to be kicked out of a cab after browbeating the driver. In fact the driver had had an accident and the vehicle could not continue, but facile editing made it look like a hostile altercation (Poniewozik, 2006).

Many have argued that the values communicated by such shows are unhealthy and distressing. In some anxious people they may even trigger anxiety attacks (McCook, 2003). They affect our views of the world; those who watch more reality dating shows are more likely to expect real dating to be similar (Ferris, Smith, Greenberg, & Smith, 2007). Marling (2002) has argued that a class bias is at work here: we like to watch lower-class "trailer park trash" demean themselves while we smugly sit back and watch, and comfort ourselves that we would never stoop so low. Or have we already stooped that low by watching? As a contrast to the shows discussed here, see Close-Up 4.3 for a description of a very early reality show.

Chapter 12

Responding to Media

Getting Our Two Cents In

Q: How popular is Facebook?

A: As of early 2012, Facebook had over one billion users worldwide, who spend an average of 5 to 7 hours each month on the site, posting over 300,000 status updates every minute and sharing 4 billion pieces of content per day (Gustin, 2012; Wilson, Gosling, & Graham, 2012).

Q: How much of television can be considered educational TV?

A: According to former FCC chairman Nicholas Johnson, "All of it. The only question is, what is it teaching?" (quoted in Liebert & Schwartzberg, 1977, p. 170).

Q: How many text messages do young people send?

A: The average teen surveyed for 2010 Nielsen research sent over 3,000 text messages every month (Turkle, 2011)!

Q: What popular entertainers have earned Ph.D.s?

A: Comedian and actor Bill Cosby has a doctorate in education from the University of Massachusetts Amherst. Actress Mayim Bialik has a doctorate in neuroscience from UCLA. Actor Robert Vaughn earned a Ph.D. in Communications from the University of Southern California and later published his dissertation as a book. The doo-wop rock group Sha Na Na has exceptionally well-educated members: Rob Leonard is Professor of Linguistics at Hofstra University, George Leonard teaches humanities at San Francisco State University, Dennis Greene has an M.S. from Harvard and a law degree from Yale, and teaches at the University of Dayton, Bruce Clarke teaches literature and science at Texas Tech, Alan Cooper is Provost and Professor of Jewish Studies at the Jewish Theological Seminary, and Rich Joffe earned a Ph.D. but is now an antitrust lawyer (Norton, 2008).

In this book we have examined the way in which the perceived reality that we create from media often deviates substantially from the real world; that distortion can have all sorts of effects. Although media are certainly not the only sources of knowledge about the world, our perceived reality of what the world is like is often far more heavily influenced by the media than we realize. As we have seen throughout this book, media greatly affect our attitudes and behavior, especially when we implicitly assume that the world of the media faithfully reflects the real world.

In this final chapter we turn our attention to various ways that we can actively respond to the rapidly evolving media landscape. One major need is to expand and improve media literacy, both in terms of formal curricula in the schools and elsewhere, and in terms of better mediation in the home. Another type of response to media involves the often overlooked but surprisingly effective tactics of sharing views with media and advocating changes. This can be in the form of individual concerns or corporate actions like boycotts or lawsuits. We also look at the problems in the process of communicating important research results to the public. Journalists and scientists often do not speak each other's language, have different goals, and little or no training in how to communicate with each other effectively. Finally, we conclude with some integrative thoughts on mass communication and the world it creates.

Media Literacy

In a 2004 interview, filmmaker George Lucas aptly suggested the great need for media education:

> When people talk to me about the digital divide, I think of it not being so much about who has access to what technology as who knows how to create and express themselves in this new language of the screen. If students aren't taught the language of sound and images, shouldn't they be considered as illiterate as if they left college without being able to read or write? Unfortunately, most learning institutions find that idea very difficult to swallow. They consider the various forms of non-written communication as some type of therapy or art.
>
> ("Media Deconstruction," 2012, p. 2)

There is a critical need for greater media literacy in modern society. Media literacy may be defined as a set of critical thinking skills involving the "ability to access, analyze, evaluate, and process media" (Steyer, 2002, p. 195). Its goals are to teach people to use media consciously and selectively and to think critically about media messages and images. Media literacy may be conceptualized in different ways, including as a public policy issue, an educational curriculum issue, a responsible parenting issue, or as an area of scholarly inquiry from a variety of disciplinary perspectives (Christ & Potter, 1998). See Potter (2001) for a comprehensive formulation of media literacy, Potter (2004) for a more theoretical approach, and Jeong, Cho, and Hwang (2012) for a meta-analysis of media literacy intervention programs.

Consistent with recent theory and research on mass communication, the contemporary emphasis in media literacy is more on the empowerment of consumers than on protection from some monolithic, pernicious influence. Realistically, no one can be completely shielded from media and popular culture, nor should we want to be; media are omnipresent, enduring, and often very useful and rewarding parts of our lives. Rather, we must learn to live not only with traditional print and electronic media, but also with all the rapidly evolving new technologies of mass, personal, and computer-mediated communication, especially the Internet, social media, and other aspects of cyberspace. In all of this, the purpose of media literacy is to give us more control over our interpretations of media (Potter, 2001).

Scholars identify different types of media literacy. Meyrowitz (1998), for example, suggests three. Media *content literacy* focuses on characters, themes, information, behaviors, and so on. Media *grammar literacy* looks at learning the formal features of each particular medium. For example, as children mature and experience more TV, they acquire the knowledge of how to interpret the cuts, fades, dissolves, and general montage techniques used in the editing of film or TV. Very young children may misinterpret things that they see on television because they fail to understand these techniques. The third type of literacy, *medium literacy*, involves learning the specific conventions, modalities, and processing requirements for using each particular medium. Different media require the use of different sensory modalities and parts of the brain. Specific conventions of visual literacy require different skills and understanding than does purely verbal media (Messaris, 1994, 1997, 1998). For example, in contrast to radio and print, television to some extent and more especially some computer-mediated communications, such as hypertext on the Internet, are notoriously nonlinear in character.

Media literacy interventions can have two broad categories of intended outcomes: *media-relevant* and *behavior-relevant* (Jeong et al. 2012). Media-relevant outcomes include *knowledge*, for example knowing the techniques that advertising uses to persuade (Buijzen, 2007). A second outcome is *criticism*, for instance understanding the persuasive intent of ads (Austin, Pinkleton, Hust, & Cohen, 2005). A third type of outcome is *influence*—understanding that media affect audiences in a variety of ways, from cultivating world beliefs to changing attitudes to teaching behaviors (Duran, Yousman, Walsh, & Longshore, 2008). The final media-relevant outcome is the outcome of *realism*, referring to the understanding that media represent, to varying degrees, factual and/or social reality (Austin, Pinkleton, & Funabiki, 2007). Behavior-relevant outcomes include understanding the consequences of performing a behavior or holding particular attitudes about it, for example knowing that accepting the assumptions of a certain type of political ad could lead to voting against one's own interest (Banerjee & Greene, 2006, 2007). These types of outcomes also include perceptions of one's own self-efficacy (perceived ability to perform some behavior) and the perception of the behaviors of others in regard to media (Austin et al., 2005).

Media literacy can be carved up in a different way, into four interrelated dimensions, each of which must be developed, and each of which can be thought of as a continuum (Potter, 2001). The *cognitive* dimension involves thinking, knowledge, and mental processes, drawing heavily on one's knowledge structures. Some examples of such knowledge are understandings of formal features of a medium (e.g., that a TV exterior shot of a house followed by a cut to an interior shot suggests that the room pictured is inside the house) or media structural understandings, like knowing that companies buy commercial time on TV shows in order to sell products. The *emotional* dimension concerns the emotional response to media. For example, we understand that suspenseful movies make us anxious, and understand the techniques used to evoke and manipulate such feelings (e.g., scary music, certain editing techniques). The *aesthetic* dimension involves appreciating the content from an artistic point of view, for example understanding conventions of particular program genres or appreciating the style of a certain director. Finally, the *moral* dimension concerns comprehension of the underlying values portrayed by a particular medium, show, or episode. For example, action-adventure shows and movies frequently confirm the myth of redemptive violence (see Chapter 9)—that the use of violence is acceptable against "bad guys"—and soap operas may convey sexual values which provide that considerable promiscuity is acceptable.

Finally, media literacy may be segmented by particular media content, such as advertising literacy, violence literacy, or news literacy. There may be important differences across areas. For example, some have argued that advertising literacy that focuses on conceptual knowledge of advertising is of limited success, because we most often process ads on a more emotional level, using relatively little cognitive elaboration (Rozendaal, Lapierre, Reijmersdal, & Buijzen, 2011). Thus a child may have extensive knowledge about advertising but that may not be brought to bear in processing claims from a particular ad, because largely emotion-based peripheral processing is used to interpret the ad. For advertising, it may be that media literacy stressing unconscious and affective processes is more effective. One study showed that having children speaking their thoughts aloud while watching ads increased their critical processing of both cognitive and emotional thoughts (Rozendaal, Buijzen, & Valkenburg, 2012). Overall, media literacy interventions have been successful in teaching about topics of violence (Cantor & Wilson, 2003; Scharrer, 2006; Webb, Martin, Afifi, & Kraus, 2010), body image and sexuality (Allen, d'Alessio, Emmers, & Gebhardt, 1996; Richardson, Paxton, & Thomson, 2009; Wilksch & Wade, 2009; Yamamiya, Cash, Melnyk, Posavec, & Posavec, 2005), advertising (Livingstone & Helsper, 2006), news (Loth, 2012), and health promotion (Bergsma & Carney, 2008).

Of course, the effectiveness of media literacy interventions is also influenced by several moderating variables (Jeong et al., 2012). For example, the agent or source of the teaching and the setting in which it occurs may be factors. The source may be a teacher, a parent, a peer, or the author of a curriculum (Webel, Okonsky, Trompeta, & Holzemer, 2010). Also, the audience is important. A program for children of a certain age will be more effective if it deeply understands the cognitive processing skills and psychological needs of children of that age.

Curriculum Development

Numerous attempts have been made to develop curricula for use in schools to help children become more critical viewers of television. These programs have been more widespread in places like Australia, Canada, and the United Kingdom than they have in the United States, where media literacy has sadly often been seen as a "frill" and one of the first programs to be cut in times of budget problems and "back-to-basics" movements in education. For reviews and evaluation of some of these projects, see Brown (1991), Buckingham (1993, 1998, 2003), and Potter (2001). Such curricula have been developed by school districts, universities, religious organizations (e.g., the U.S. Catholic Conference, the Media Action Research Center), private companies (e.g., The Learning Seed Co., Television Learning, Ltd.), the United Nations/ UNESCO, and other governmental or nongovernmental organizations (e.g., the Scottish Film Council, Western Australia Ministry of Education, National Congress of Parents and Teachers).

An example of an early program was developed by Dorothy and Jerome Singer and their colleagues at Yale University starting in the late 1970s. They offered eight lessons to be taught twice a week over a 4-week period to third-, fourth-, and fifth-grade children. Topics included reality and fantasy on TV, camera effects, commercials, stereotypes, identification with TV characters, and violence and aggression. Evaluation studies showed sizable increases in knowledge in the experimental group, particularly at immediate testing. The program was then extended to kindergarten, first-, and second-grade children; extensive pilot testing suggested that such children could be taught considerable amounts about the nature of television through such a curriculum (Singer & Singer, 1981, 1983; Singer, Singer, & Zuckerman, 1981; Singer, Zuckerman, & Singer, 1980).

A more recent example is an 18-lesson, 6-month classroom intervention for third and fourth graders (Robinson, Saphir, Kraemer, Varady, & Haydel, 2001). This program was designed to reduce television, videotape, and video game use, which would thus lead to fewer effects of those media on the children. It succeeded in doing so, and also in reducing the number of children's reports of requests to parents to purchase advertised toys, especially in the children who reduced their TV and video use more. However, it did not affect the parental reports of toy purchase requests, compared to a control group. Still, this suggests that it is possible to reduce television and video consumption and such reductions can have other positive effects.

These projects, as well as most others that have been developed, have focused primarily on television. A recent meta-analysis (Jeong et al., 2012) looked at 51 evaluative media literacy studies and concluded that they were generally effective, especially those which did not try to evaluate too many components in one project. The need for media literacy for computer-mediated communications continues to be a current, pressing issue.

What Can Be Done in the Home?

Media education should not be limited only to the classroom, however. As we have seen throughout this book, whatever the negative effects of media on children, they can be mitigated, and perhaps even redirected to become positive changes, through positive interaction and dialogue in the home. Such *parental mediation*, as it is called, can take any of three general forms (Nathanson, 1999). *Active mediation* involves talking with children about television. This mediation may be either positive (e.g., endorsement of content) or negative (e.g., criticism of content). It may be fully intended as mediation (strategic mediation) or thought of by those doing it only as incidental conversation (nonstrategic mediation) (Buerkel-Rothfuss & Buerkel, 2001). It also starts very early in life, as early as the first year (Barr, Zack, Garcia, & Muentener, 2008; Fidler, Zack, & Barr, 2010). Resources are available to help; for example, Niemiec and Wedding's (2008) book on using films to build virtues and character strengths.

Restrictive mediation involves setting rules and limits on media use or screen time, a strategy used by most parents at least occasionally. This could come in the form of preventing viewing certain programs, websites, or disallowing media use outside certain allowed hours. In other families it takes the form of limits on overall TV viewing or screen time. The final form of parental mediation is *coviewing*, that is, watching television with children. Most scholars agree that coviewing TV with young children is very helpful, though admittedly not always realistic, especially as the child grows older.

These mediation categories are not mutually exclusive and in fact often coexist. For example, parents may prevent children from watching certain shows and may coview others with them, while making both positive and negative active mediation comments. All of these types of mediation probably occur in all families at some point, but parents would be well advised to recognize the mediation they do and be more intentional about it. Restrictive mediation is the most common type of parental mediation overall in all social classes but especially so among lower-income parents (Warren, 2005).

Although it is seldom possible to do all the mediation one might like, even occasional mediation by parents can be helpful. As the family watches television together or discusses shows previously watched, conversation may occur about deceptive advertising, stereotyped group portrayals, antisocial values, or excessive sex or violence. Parents may offer factual comments ("Those people are really actors and that isn't real blood") or evaluative comments ("That man is mean. People don't like people who act like that") appropriate to the age of the child (Buijzen, 2007; Nathanson, 2004). Parents can also question children about their reactions to what is on TV, thus better understanding the perceived reality constructed by the child (e.g., "Do you think most grown women look that that model?"). They may comment about their own reactions, thus providing a balance to what may be a skewed media portrayal. For example, parents could voice their concern about a violent scene and share that they remember being scared by such scenes as a child (Nathanson & Yang, 2003). They do need to talk, however. It is unfortunate that parents often do not talk to their children as much while they are watching television together as while they are reading or playing with toys (Nathanson & Rasmussen, 2011); these can be important missed opportunities.

Parental mediation has measurable effects. The quality of family interaction, especially for children around 11 years old, can actually be improved by television viewing, when it is seen as an important family activity involving interaction and discussion (Johnsson-Smaragdi, 1983). Negative active mediation can induce a mistrust of television, lower levels of aggression and skepticism toward television news, while positive active mediation is related to positive attitudes toward television and improved understanding of cognitively complex material (Austin, 1993, 2001; Austin, Bolls, Fujioka, & Engelbertson, 1999; Austin, Pinkleton, & Fujioka, 2000; Nathanson, 1999, 2004). A study of parental mediation with children following extensive news coverage in the Netherlands of the assassination of filmmaker Theo van Gogh in 2004 found that active mediation had some effect in reducing fear, worry, and anger in young children, but not older ones, and that restrictive mediation was not helpful and was sometimes even counterproductive (Buijzen, Walma van der Molen, & Sondij, 2007). Sibling coviewing, without parents, may have some positive effects, for example in reducing fearful responses to suspenseful programs (Wilson & Weiss, 1993), although how helpful that is for the younger child obviously depends heavily on what the older siblings say.

Television may be used as a catalyst for discussion of important issues within the family. Although it is often difficult for parents and children to discuss topics like sex or drugs, it may be easier in the context of discussing a TV program on such a theme. Even if the program is not particularly well done or consistent with the family's values, it may still serve as a relatively nonthreatening catalyst for discussion. Parents should take advantage of such opportunities. Television need not be an antisocial medium that isolates one family member from another (a "shut-up-so-I-can-listen" model). It can also be an activity that brings them together to watch as a family, but also to talk about the content and other topics that it leads to (a "hey-look-at-this" model). It can help family members to understand each other's reactions to many topics and situations. It can be a stimulus to cognitive, emotional, and personal growth. All of this is not to say that it always *will* be such a positive influence, just that it *can* be. The more carefully programs are selected and the more intentional the parent is about discussing the content, the better the outcome.

Austin, Roberts, and Nass (1990; see also Desmond, Singer, & Singer, 1990; Nathanson, 1999) developed and tested a model of how parent–child communication about TV and its portrayals can affect children's construction of reality. Social, cultural, and family structure variables also have a role in determining the effect of family interactions on the impact of TV on children (Greenberg, Ku, & Li, 1992; Wright, St. Peters, & Huston, 1990). For excellent general books to help parents guide their children through the decisions and challenges of television, see Chen (1994) or Steyer (2002). For help with the specific issue of dealing with fear induced in children by violent media, see Cantor (1998b). See Levin and Kilbourne (2009) for help in dealing with the overly sexualized popular culture or Lindstrom (2011) for dealing with advertising. For a broader approach helping parents to deal not only with media but also other potentially toxic aspects of popular culture, see the excellent book by Carlsson-Paige (2008).

Media literacy must involve new computer-mediated communication as well as the traditional media. Parents need to know what their children are doing on Facebook and Twitter as well as what they are watching on TV. They need to talk about rules for uploading and downloading videos from the Internet just as much as they need to talk about what TV shows are permitted. In the year 2006 alone, the number of videos viewed on YouTube jumped tenfold, from 10 million to 100 million per day (Cloud, 2006–2007). Parents need to talk about video games their kids play as much as they need to talk about music they listen to. Compared to the past, today's child or teen has such completely different ways of managing his or her own entertainment and media use that sometimes it is difficult for the parents to even understand what their child is doing. Not only that, but younger and younger children are using new media. In 2011 almost one-third of children under 2 had televisions in their bedrooms, and 12% of children ages 2–4 used computers every day (Lewin, 2011). Social class is a factor; children from lower income families (under $30,000) were much more likely than those from higher income families (over $75,000) to have their own TVs (64% vs. 20%) but much less likely to have smart phones or tablets with multiple apps (Lewin, 2011).

One final point regarding parental mediation and discussion of media within the family should be stressed. It is difficult to have much mediation of any sort if the children or teens are usually watching TV or using computers in the privacy of their own rooms. Keeping the major media hardware in public areas of the home is an important way for parents to keep some control over what children watch, but it also allows for many more opportunities for parental mediation. If parents lament their child or teen's amount of TV or computer time and the particular content chosen, they have contributed greatly to that problem by allowing personal television sets or computers in bedrooms. Although many parents relent and allow this in response to the frustration of dealing with arguments among kids over what to watch or whose turn it is on the computer, such disagreements can themselves be positive opportunities for learning valuable negotiation skills. Of course, in this age of smart phones and Internet-ready tablets, keeping children off the Internet is a more difficult challenge than ever.

Most of this book has been concerned with the perceived reality that we construct through the interaction of our minds with the stimulus material from media. If we want to actually change the media itself, however, we can sometimes do that as well. Although not a major focus of this book, this issue is worth examining briefly as a complement to our basic thesis.

Influencing the Media

Very often when we critically examine media we are left with the feeling that there is much that we do not like, for whatever reason, but little we can do about that state of affairs other than to choose not to use that medium. However, just as we cognitively interact with the media in understanding it, so can we behaviorally interact with it to help effect change in desired ways. Commercial and political interests have long been doing this, and it behooves concerned and interested individual media consumers to learn to do likewise.

Individual Efforts

Individual complaints do have disproportionate impact, in that those who receive them assume that each complaint represents a similar view of many others who did not complain. Certain types of letters, e-mails, or blog entries are more effective than others. A reasoned, logically argued case has a lot more impact than an angry tirade. For example, one brand of club cocktails once advertised in Ms. magazine with the slogan "Hit me with a Club." The company received over 1,000 letters of protest, arguing that the ad implied acceptance of violence toward women. They responded that such a connection was never intended or imagined, yet editors were concerned enough by the letters to withdraw the ad (Will, 1987). Complaints do make a difference! Letters from a Michigan homemaker and her supporters concerned about negative family values once caused Kimberly-Clark, McDonald's, and other sponsors to pull their ads from Married... with Children. Protests from some parents about the marketing of thong underwear with the words Eye Candy and Wink Wink to 10-year-old girls convinced Abercrombie and Fitch to stop selling these items (Carlsson-Paige, 2008).

Jamieson and Campbell (1992) suggested three types of particularly effective arguments to pursue when writing to a network, TV or radio station, business, or publication. First, a claim of inaccuracy or deception elicits immediate concern. Publishing or broadcasting inaccurate information is not generally acceptable, and a quick correction may avoid a loss of credibility and possible legal trouble as well. Second, a claim that an item violates community standards or general good taste causes concern. The press is loath to offend, for example, with overly explicit sex, violence, or raunchy language. A sufficient number of people with such concerns may lead to the fear of lost advertising dollars, the lifeblood of the enterprise. See Close-Up 12.1 for an example of a marketing campaign that offended people and was withdrawn due to their complaints. Third, a claim of lack of balance or fairness is taken seriously. This includes obvious concerns like lack of fairness in covering a political campaign or the use of a misleading ad, but also claims such as unfairly stereotyping some group or unfairly exploiting the cognitive immaturity of children to encourage them to request certain products from their parents.

Once in a great while the efforts of a single individual can result in a major policy change or in the founding of organizations intended to counter the effects of heavy media use. For example, in the 1960s John F. Banzhaf III persuaded the FCC that the Fairness Doctrine required television to run antismoking ads to counter cigarette ads on TV at the time (tobacco ads were discontinued in the U.S. in 1971). Pete Shields, who lost a son to a handgun homicide, and Sarah Brady, whose husband Jim was permanently brain-damaged

Close-Up 12.1: Case Study of a Marketing Campaign Killed by Complaints

In 2011 JCPenney and Forever 21 began marketing shirts to young girls featuring the slogans "I'm too pretty to do homework, so my brother has to do it for me" and "Allergic to Algebra." Various women's groups and the progressive Internet movement Credo Action mobilized a writing and petition-signing campaign against what they claimed were sexist messages. Their message was heard; JCPenney CEO Myron Ullman responded to Credo, "JCPenney used this incident as a 'teachable moment' for our buying teams ... [who] fully understand their responsibility in upholding the integrity of our company and share with you their commitment to ensuring better merchandise decisions in the future. We agree that the 'Too Pretty' T-shirt does not deliver an appropriate message, and we have immediately discontinued its sale... we would like to apologize to our customers." Public complaints do make a difference.

This was not the first such sexist marketing gaffe. A 1992 talking Barbie doll whined "Math class is tough," before Mattel modified its message. Other questionable messages on girls' T-shirts have included "Future Trophy Wife" and "Who Needs Brains When You Have These?" both of which were killed by complaints from the public.

in the assassination attempt on President Reagan in 1981, became active media advocates in gun control lobbying efforts. Documentary filmmaker Morgan Spurlock recorded his one-month experiment of surviving, though just barely, on McDonald's for three meals a day in the film *Super Size Me*. Millionaire heart-attack victim Phil Sokolof took out large newspaper ads pressuring big food corporations to change their practice of cooking in cholesterol-rich tropical oils. This campaign and the ensuing media coverage helped cause 12 large food corporations to begin using healthier oils within two years. Sokolof then directed his campaign at McDonald's, to encourage them to reduce the fat content in their burgers (Dagnoli, 1990).

The advent of the Internet has opened up all sorts of new possibilities for individual media action. One particularly compelling recent example is the story of the wildly popular "Kony 2012" video on YouTube. Back in 2003, a recent film studies graduate, Jason Russell, was traveling in Uganda "looking for a story to tell" when gunmen shot at the truck in front of him. This was his introduction to the ruthless guerilla group called the Lord's Resistance Army and its leader Joseph Kony. Russell spent the next several years researching this group and making the video. When it was finally posted on YouTube and Vimeo and linked to Facebook and Twitter in 2012, it attracted more than 50 million hits, especially unusual for a long half-hour video on a very gruesome and unpleasant topic. It didn't hurt that celebrities like Oprah Winfrey, Rihanna, and Ryan Seacrest posted supportive comments. The video informed people about a conflict few knew existed and raised millions of dollars for Russell's organization Invisible Children. Never mind that his information was somewhat dated by 2012, as the LRA had left Uganda for even more chaotic locales, and the number of child soldiers was then way below the 30,000 implied in the film. In fact, Russell made no claims to have produced a balanced academic film; his stated purpose was to raise consciousness and outrage about Kony and the LRA. "We view ourselves as the Pixar of human rights stories" (Kron & Goodman, 2012). He got people's attention.

An excellent first outlet for media concerns, especially local issues, is the editorial page of a local newspaper. Most are delighted to print letters to the editor or even guest columns. To find out about some larger media organizations and governmental and consumer agencies, search the Internet for websites which provide addresses, phone numbers, and e-mail addresses where agencies may be contacted. Another possibility is starting a blog or posting to an existing one. Do some research first; most blogs are read by very few people, although a few are disproportionately influential.

Group Efforts

People working together can often have more impact than single individuals. One community method is the boycott, whereby people refrain from buying some product or using some publication or station until desired changes are made. Even the threat of a boycott sends chills up the spines of advertisers, publications, businesses, and radio and TV stations. Newspapers have gone out of business when certain key economic interests have pulled their advertising. Nestlé changed its infant formula marketing campaign many years ago in response to a public outcry and boycott. Convenience stores have stopped selling sex magazines in response to public complaints and the threat of boycott. Two single dads in Washington, DC, picketed local stores and the corporate headquarters of the manufacturer of *Grand Theft Auto*; this campaign eventually led to the DC government banning sales of M-rated video games to children (Carlsson-Paige, 2008).

A grassroots organization called Citizens' Campaign for Commercial-Free Schools identified all forms of commercialism in 30 Seattle schools and persuaded the Seattle school district to rescind a new policy selling wall space in schools to advertisers. Five years later, the group succeeded in influencing the district to pass a comprehensive anticommercialism policy prohibiting most kinds of advertising and commercial activities in Seattle schools (Carlsson-Paige, 2008). A similar group persuaded Boston mass transit to ban ads in subways for video games rated M (mature) or AO (adults only). Fear of adverse and organized public reaction is a major reason that U.S. television stations are so slow to accept condom ads, even in the age of AIDS, when a majority of public opinion favors such ads.

In occasional cases a group may file legal action against a media organization. For example, when the FCC periodically reviews applications of radio and television stations for renewal of their broadcast licenses, the opportunity arises to challenge such renewals. Although the actual failure to renew is extremely rare in the United States, such pressure may have substantial effects on subsequent station policy. For example, civil rights groups in the 1960s used this approach to force broadcasters to become more responsive to African American concerns in their communities. Sometimes the mere threat of legal or legislative action is enough to produce the desired change. For example, consumer groups like the now-defunct Action for Children's Television (ACT) put pressure on the broadcast industry's National Association of Broadcasters (NAB) to limit the allowable number of minutes of commercials per hour on children's television. Their appeals to the FCC to regulate such numbers led to the NAB limiting commercial time itself, a move it apparently considered preferable to government-mandated regulation.

Certain organizations have established themselves as watchdogs on certain kinds of issues. For example, the National Parent–Teacher Association (PTA) has at different times monitored children's advertising and violent and sexual content on television. Resulting public awareness, as well as the latent threat of a boycott, has probably had some subtle effects. Many local citizens' groups protesting pornography have pressured convenience stores to stop selling sex magazines or put pressure on sponsors of very violent or sexual television programs. For example, a boycott of Pepsi once led to the company's cancellation

---

**Close-Up 12.2: Movie Sanitizers: Welcome Influence
or Artistic Intrusion?**

There are several options available for viewers who want to watch
movies without the full measure of violence, sex, or rough language.
A Utah company called Cleanflicks offers cleaned-up versions of over
100 Hollywood films. A different approach is taken by MovieMask,
ClearPlay, and Family Shield Technologies, all of which offer software
loaded onto home computers or a box on the television. This software
offers several levels of editing to remove as much or as little offending
material as the viewer desires. Although most changes involve removing
questionable material, sometimes other avenues are taken, such as when
MovieMask gave Kate Winslet a digital corset for the nude sketching
scene in *Titanic*, or replaced the swords in *The Princess Bride* with what
looked like *Star Wars* lightsabers (Lyman, 2002). Many Hollywood
directors have decried such editing on artistic grounds. Is this unfair
tampering with an artistic work or a long-overdue option welcomed by
parents? What do you think?

---

of its sponsorship of a Madonna video and tour. See Close-Up 12.2 for a very
different approach to "cleaning up" the airwaves.

Sometimes follow-up monitoring is necessary, recognizing that unwanted
regulation may sometimes be creatively circumvented. For instance, the
Children's Television Act of 1990 required TV stations to increase the number
of hours of educational programming to children. In response to this, some
stations redefined existing cartoons and syndicated sitcom reruns as "educational." For example, in its license renewal application, one station described
the *G.I. Joe* cartoon as "presenting a fight against an evil that has the capabilities of mass destruction of society" ("School of Hard Knocks," 1992, p. 32).
Truly educational shows like news shows for children ran at 5:30 in the morning, whereas newly defined "educational" programs like *The Jetsons* and *Leave
It to Beaver* reruns retained the better time slots. By 1997, public dissatisfaction with such ruses pressured the FCC to clarify the 1990 law with an exact
number of hours and clearer specification of what programming was considered educational (Steyer, 2002). However, after 2001 the pendulum again
swung back in the free-market, laissez-faire direction.

Another opportunity for public input comes in public hearings about pro-
posals for mergers and corporate takeovers (see Close-Up 12.3). Before such
consolidations are approved, hearings are conducted to air public concerns. In
many cases strong public concern has prevented, delayed, or modified a proposed merger or takeover.

Close-Up 12.3: Some Hidden Costs of Media Consolidation

In recent decades there has been a tremendous consolidation within the media and entertainment industries. Does this consolidation matter in terms of the news we receive and the entertainment choices we have? There is evidence it does. For example, in 1998 ABC news (owned by Disney) prepared a major investigative report on abuses of labor and safety practices at Walt Disney World (Steyer, 2002). The story was either killed by Disney executives or self-censored by ABC before it aired, as were other stories about large executive compensation (no one wanted to offend very well-paid Disney chairman Michael Eisner), lax screening procedures that allowed the hiring of pedophiles at the theme parks, and even a feature about the hit movie *Chicken Run*, produced by Disney rival DreamWorks (Mayer, 2000).

Media consolidation can also affect local markets in surprising ways. For example, a late-night train derailment in Minot, North Dakota in 2002 spilled large amounts of toxic anhydrous ammonia. When emergency responders called the seven local radio stations to have them alert the public, there was nobody present at six of the seven stations, which were all owned by Clear Channel and were operating by broadcasting prerecorded material from corporate headquarters without any local on-air staff in the middle of the night (Collum, 2008).

Sometimes social science research itself may have an important impact on policy making. For example, the laboratory research finding that people could not perceive or be affected by backward audio messages (see Close-Up 5.8) led several states to withdraw pending legislation requiring record companies to put warning labels on album jackets (Vokey & Read, 1985). Research played a role in developing, and later modifying, the set of age-based content ratings first used for TV programs in the United States in 1997 (Cantor, 1998a). Research on sexual violence (discussed in Chapter 10) has tremendous potential to impact legal, policy, filmmaking, and even lifestyle issues. For a careful discussion of how research on sexual violence may be used to effect legal and policy change, see Penrod and Linz (1984) and Linz, Turner, Hesse, and Penrod (1984).

Before such research can have much impact on public opinion or public policy, however, the findings from that research must somehow be communicated to the world beyond the scientific community. This act in itself can often affect the perceived reality about that issue in the minds of the public. Unfortunately, crossing the gap from scientists to the public can sometimes be a communications minefield.

Communicating Media Research Findings to the Public

In the reporting of science to the general public, the scientist's "truth" and the reporter's "news" are often quite different. For example, an editor may not consider a particular background feature story about pornography research as newsworthy because the paper has already carried two stories that week on that particular topic. The scientist looking at the same situation may not be convinced of the overlap, given that one article was a story about citizens seeking better curbs on pornographic websites and the other was a feature about a woman who acted in pornographic videos, neither of which at all overlaps with a report of behavioral research on effects of pornography.

In their desire to fairly present all sides of an issue, journalists may disproportionately emphasize controversy and thus inadvertently play up and legitimatize a fringe position given little credibility in the scientific community. As discussed in Chapter 7, conflict and controversy are highly newsworthy. For example, subliminal advertising greatly intrigues and even alarms the general public, whereas the research community has long realized that its feared effects are at most vastly overrated, and are probably nonexistent (see Chapter 5). Such a topic may make for compelling journalism, but it is bad science. As discussed in Chapter 9, attempts to be fair and balanced in the treatment of media violence research have led to the mistaken view in the popular press that the research community is evenly split or undecided on whether violent media have negative effects. The perceived reality of readers in response to such stories may be significantly at variance with the scientific reality. Also, journalists and scientists use language in very different ways.

> To the academician, the language of the reporter is excessively casual, trivializing, and simple-minded, if not downright wrong or silly. To the journalist, the language of the academician is excessively passive, technical, and complicated, if not downright wordy or pompous. Academic language strives to be informative and accurate. To the reporter, though, the result sounds like nit-picking; it encumbers the research with so many qualifications and exceptions that the results seem meaningless
>
> (Tavris, 1986, p. 25).

It is not unusual to encounter the impression that social science is inferior, immature science. Not surprisingly, this feeling is common among the relatively few journalists trained in science. More surprising, however, is that this view is also not unusual among social scientists themselves, some of whom see themselves as doing work that is inferior to that of their colleagues in physics or biology. If many social scientists do not see themselves as true scientists, is it surprising that others do not perceive them that way?

This collective feeling of inferiority may stem from the fact that social science is by its very nature probabilistic, not deterministic. One can never predict for sure the effect on a particular person of seeing a violent movie, in the sense that one can predict with absolute certainty that $2 + 2 = 4$. One particular burden of social science is the challenge of communicating uncertainty in a world that seeks and values deterministic answers (Friedman, Dunwoody, & Rogers, 1999). Too often discussion of statistical uncertainty comes across to the public as a wishy-washy lack of commitment, which falsely conveys an impression of inconclusiveness of the scientific research.

As advances in neuroscience, genetics, and other interfaces of biology and psychology become more prominent and of more interest to the public, new challenges and possibilities for misinterpretation will emerge. Conrad (2001) examined news coverage of genetics and mental illness research over a 25-year period and found a dominant frame he called "genetic optimism." This frame had three elements: a gene for every disorder exists, that gene will be found, and this is good. This frame has the effect of encouraging people to believe in overly simplistic and optimistic solutions for mental illness, such as there being a discrete gene that in and of itself causes the disorder, and that dealing with this gene will effectively treat the illness. In another example of a very complex research field, Thompson and Nelson (2001) discuss research on early brain development and the challenges of communicating those findings to the public. Researchers, including social science researchers, have not always been very successful at, or even interested in, communicating the results of their research to the public. Sometimes the few highly respected scientists who do so very well are actually scorned by their professional colleagues (Diamond, 1997; Ferris, 1997). They are certainly not rewarded by the academic profession, which primarily rewards the obtaining of research grants and publication of scholarly research papers in scientific journals. Even writing textbooks is held in relatively low esteem in terms of professional advancement (no professors ever write textbooks before they have tenure!), and talking to the press and the public is often not valued at all, possibly even scorned. Professors and research-ers typically receive no training at all in their doctoral programs or elsewhere in how to speak with the press, and often have no clue how to talk to reporters about their work in a way that gives the journalist something he or she can use in writing a story. Sometimes the opportunities we do get and the end products from such interviews are not particularly enlightening or encouraging to anyone, nor are they likely to make us eager to seek out more such opportuni-ties. See Close-Up 12.4 for a personal example.

In spite of all this, however, social science stories still hold great interest for many readers and journalists. Dunwoody (1986) found that newspaper editors actually reported a preference for social science topics over those in physical science. However, the reverse preference was found in reporters. Thus, there may often be a situation of an editor selecting a social science topic but assign-ing it to a reporter who has less interest in it and thus may not treat it as science, resulting in more sloppy treatment than would be given a "real science" story. One study showed that neither journalists nor scientists believed that media do a good job communicating scientific information to

**Close-Up 12.4: One of Your Authors' Appearance on the
Today Show: Did this Advance the Cause of Understanding
Research on Romance and Media?**

As media researchers, we are occasionally contacted by the media for our views on various aspects of topics discussed in this book. Perhaps the one with the most exposure was my (RJH's) 2008 appearance on NBC's *Today* show, on a Valentine's Day-themed story. A producer called me about my research on young adults' moviegoing experiences, in this case watching romantic movies (Harris et al., 2004). This was a complex pair of studies asking people to retrospectively recall and evaluate an experience watching a romantic movie on a date. We looked at how that experience had affected the relationship, how men and women viewed it differently, and how they would fantasize about their own lives interacting with the movie. A producer and photographer came from New York and spent over an hour setting up a fake "office" in a seminar room (my real office was too small for all their equipment). Once this was completed, they taped about a 15-minute interview in which they asked me good questions and I tried to communicate as best I could and in terms everyone could understand what we had found in our research.

The story that appeared on the air a few days later was something else again. Although the whole piece lasted 6 to 8 minutes, very long for a TV news story, I was on air for about 30 seconds and basically said that men like romantic movies, though not as much as women do. Obviously our published paper contained results a bit more sophisticated and complex than that, though I guess I should be grateful that the brief appearance did not distort what I said or make me look totally stupid or incoherent. After my short statement, Matt Lauer and Meredith Vieira bantered a bit about their opinions, while the several minutes remaining were entirely devoted to an argument between two people, a woman identified as a therapist and a man identified only as a "relationship expert." While the woman made some thoughtful comments, the man consistently countered with multiple ways of basically stating that real men wouldn't be caught dead watching romantic films. What the producers wanted was controversy, shouting back and forth, and my academic piece was only a small chunk of evidence for one side. I ended up not thinking that I had contributed anything substantial to the viewers' understanding of the topic. Should I have declined this interview? Should I accept such offers in the future? This experience left me pessimistic about the worth of doing so, although I have no doubt that any producer could easily find someone with fewer scruples than I willing to talk to them if I would not.

the public (Chappell & Hartz, 1998). Indeed, sometimes the impression conveyed in the popular press is entirely opposite to the state of the research, as described in Chapter 9 in relation to popular press coverage of conclusions from media violence research (Bushman & Anderson, 2001).

Does any of this matter? There are increasing cries about the dangers of scientific illiteracy. See Mooney and Kirshenbaum (2009) for a particularly cogent and compelling argument about this issue. Science is presented so poorly in the media, and it is so shamelessly manipulated by some political interests, that the general nonscientific public has little understanding of either the general principles by which science proceeds or of specific findings in fields of a particular scientific endeavor. About 46% of the American public holds young-earth-creationist views of the formation of the earth, in spite of a total lack of scientific support (Mooney & Kirshenbaum, 2009). The debate over global warming being caused, at least in part, by human activity, is largely settled in the scientific community but appears to the public to still be a matter of scientific debate, thanks to scientifically irresponsible political demagoguery. Valuable time in dealing with this issue is being lost while the public confuses a political issue with a scientific one.

Conclusion: Revisiting Mass Communication

Throughout most of this book, we have focused on the perceived reality of the receiver of media input. It is even more magical to appear in the media, especially on television. Because it is a very intrusive medium, being on television makes someone either very excited or very uncomfortable, or perhaps both. The importance seems to be more in the act of merely being on TV than in what one does there. People are very eager to look perfectly foolish singing a song off key (*American Idol*), undergoing psychotherapy (*Dr. Phil*), or exposing personally embarrassing information on a daytime talk show. Over the years we have seen shows featuring people in the real world, often doing very strange things (e.g., *Candid Camera*, *America's Funniest Home Videos*, *Amazing Race*, and *Survivor*). On the other hand, social media are proving to have some very important prosocial uses probably never imagined at their inception; see Close-Up 12.5 for how Facebook has helped diagnose rare diseases. Interestingly, the use of video technology does not seem to have removed the magic of being on TV, even though children now grow up seeing themselves frequently on the TV screen and perhaps on YouTube as well. Being broadcast on TV is still special.

For all sorts of reasons discussed in this book, it is becoming increasingly difficult to know exactly where mass media stop and personal media begin, or to identify the boundary between entertainment or popular culture and mass media. We have taken a broad view of what constitutes media, and, as such, have considered films, video games, and various computer-mediated communications, as well as the traditional print and broadcast media. It seems likely

> ### Close-Up 12.5: Crowdsourcing and Medical Diagnosis through Social Media (Park, 2012)
>
> After a woman kept having seizures and numerous doctors had been unable to diagnose her problem, she and her husband created a Facebook page in June 2012 describing her symptoms, medical history, and test results, and including a plea for help. In less than a week she was receiving a thousand posts a day from around the world. Thanks to this online help, her doctors carried out further testing for a very rare tumor on the adrenal gland, a condition previously dismissed as too rare to be worth seriously considering. Similar online crowdsourcing has solved other baffling medical diagnosis mysteries, often identifying conditions which are eminently treatable.

that such an inclusive scope of what is considered media will continue to be useful and probably necessary in the future. See Delwiche and Henderson (2012) for readings on how digital technology has produced what has come to be called "participatory cultures."

One of the earliest major manifestations of this new communications technology integration appeared in the worldwide fax revolution by Chinese students, a response to the 1989 Tiananmen Square massacre and subsequent government crackdown in which the estimated 10,000 fax numbers in China were jammed for weeks with reports from abroad about what had really happened in Beijing (Ganley, 1992). Much of the communication among those sending the fax messages was by e-mail. Taped newscasts out of Hong Kong (which was not yet part of China) circulated widely on the 2 million or more VCRs in China. The democratic uprising in China was suppressed but it would never again be possible to so totally isolate a society from the news of its own oppression, as evidenced, for example, by the difficulty the Chinese had in blocking news of the 2008 protests over Tibet just before the opening of the Beijing Olympics. Indeed, the technology revolution has been a major factor in the opening up of China in the last two decades. Electronic information in all its forms is not easily controlled, although the Chinese government never seems to stop trying to do so.

Skilled use of the Internet has come to be a common prerequisite for any grassroots social movement, from the Zapatista Army of National Liberation in Chiapas, Mexico (Wolfson, 2012), to the International Campaign for Justice in Bhopal, still fighting for justice for the victims of the catastrophic 1984 gas leak from the Union Carbide plant in Bhopal, India (Pal & Dutta, 2012). Facebook is given major credit for the Egyptian grassroots movement that ousted longtime President Hosni Mubarak in 2011, with the country's 5 million users creating 14,000 new pages in just 2 weeks, following the start of the protests in January 2011 (Wilson et al., 2012). Social media and e-mail have sometimes been almost the only sources of information from inside Syria during its internal conflict.

Cell phone technology, including smart phones, may be changing more lives faster than any other invention. For example Kenya seems to have mastered the art of bringing wireless communication to the masses, with the lowest cell phone charges in Africa. Phones and phone services have been rapidly falling in price, with calls in mid-2012 costing less than 3 cents a minute within the country and 4 cents for international numbers. Beyond that, a mobile banking platform called M-Pesa allows over 60% of Kenyans to use text messages to pay rent or utility costs, buy groceries, or even send money to relatives in isolated villages. In 2011 over $11 billion moved over the mobile network in this poor nation (Murray, 2012).

Still, however, grandiose claims about new technologies revolutionizing the lives of everyone on the planet may be somewhat premature. Although there are encouraging examples of marginalized people having voices on the Internet (e.g., Mitra, 2004), they may be more the exception than the rule for the poor majority of the planet. In fact, many believe that new communications technologies will only widen the gap between the rich and the poor. Consider, for example, Wresch's (1996) look at two Namibian men, one rich and one poor. The poor man, Negumbo, has no skills, no job, and no electricity. Newspapers cost one tenth of his daily wage, on days that he manages to find work. Few in his neighborhood have TV, and it is all in English, a language he does not understand. His news sources are largely limited to one radio station that broadcasts in his language. He has been nowhere but his village in northern Namibia and the capital, Windhoek.

The rich Namibian man, Theo, is president of his own computer company, drives a BMW, speaks three languages, and is wired into the world via mobile phone, e-mail, and the Internet. He also makes at least yearly trips to Germany and the United States and has a buyer in California who sends him a weekly shipment. He can come home and watch American sitcoms, Mexican soap operas, or a variety of movies on his TV (but no Namibian movies—there aren't any). Even as the information revolution wires Theo into more and more places, his countryman Negumbo becomes more and more isolated. Developing countries like Namibia are becoming increasingly divided by information as well as income, and it is not at all clear that technology will bridge this gap anytime soon.

All of this brings us back to the question of why study the psychology, especially cognitive psychology, of the media? At heart media offer an experience that emerges from the interaction of our minds with the content of the communication. Media affect our minds: they give us ideas, change our attitudes, and show us what the world is like or what it can be like. Our mental constructions (i.e., our perceived reality) then become the framework around which we interpret the totality of experience. Thus, media consumption and effects are very much cognitive phenomena.

In one sense, media production is a creation, a fabrication, and performing in media is pretending, taking a role. But Picasso once said, "Art is a lie that makes us realize truth"—and one might say the same about media. To borrow from Oscar Wilde: life imitates media, and media imitate life. After a while, it becomes hard to tell which is which.

References

Abel, G. G., Barlow, D. H., Blanchard, E. B., & Guild, D. (1977). The components of rapists' sexual arousal. *Archives of General Psychiatry, 34,* 895–903.

Abelman, R., Atkin, D. J., & Lin, C. A. (2007). Meta-analysis of television's impact on special populations. In R. W. Preiss, B. M. Gayle, N. Burrell, M. Allen, & J. Bryant (Eds.), *Mass media effects research: Advances through meta-analysis* (pp. 119–135). Mahwah, NJ: Erlbaum.

Abernethy, A. M. (1992). The information content of newspaper advertising. *Journal of Current Issues and Research in Advertising, 14*(2), 63–68.

About Channel One news (2009, December 16). Retrieved from http://www.channelone.com/about/faq/

Abramson, P. R., & Hayashi, H. (1984). Pornography in Japan: Cross-cultural and theoretical considerations. In N. M. Malamuth & E. Donnerstein (Eds.), *Pornography and sexual aggression* (pp. 173–183). Orlando, FL: Academic Press.

Abramson, P. R., Perry, L., Seeley, T., Seeley, D., & Rothblatt, A. (1981). Thermographic measurement of sexual arousal: A discriminant validity analysis. *Archives of Sexual Behavior, 10*(2), 175–176.

Aday, S. (2010). Chasing the bad news: An analysis of 2005 Iraq and Afghanistan war coverage on NBC and Fox News Channel. *Journal of Communication, 60,* 144–164.

Afifi, W. A., & Weiner, J. L. (2006). Seeking information about sexual health: Applying the theory of motivated information management. *Human Communication Research, 32,* 35–57.

Ahn, W.-K., Brewer, W. F., & Mooney, R. J. (1992). Schema acquisition from a single example. *Journal of Experimental Psychology: Learning, Memory, and Cognition, 18,* 391–412.

Alali, A. O., & Eke, K. K. (Eds.) (1991). *Media coverage of terrorism: Methods of diffusion.* Newbury Park, CA: Sage.

Alesandrini, K. L. (1983). Strategies that influence memory for advertising communications. In R. J. Harris (Ed.), *Information processing research in advertising* (pp. 65–82). Hillsdale, NJ: Erlbaum.

Allen, M., D'Alessio, D., & Brezgel, K. (1995). A meta-analysis summarizing the effects of pornography II: Aggression after exposure. *Human Communication Research, 22,* 258–283.

Allen, M., D'Alessio, D., Emmers, T., & Gebhardt, L. (1996). The role of educational briefings in mitigating effects of experimental exposure to violent sexually explicit material: A meta-analysis. *Journal of Sex Research, 33,* 135–141.

Allen, M., Emmers, T., Gebhardt, L., & Giery, M. A. (1995). Exposure to pornography and acceptance of rape myths. *Journal of Communication, 45*(1), 5–26.

Allen, M., Herrett-Skjellum, J., Jorgenson, J., Ryan, D. J., Kramer, M. R., & Timmerman, L. (2007). Effects of music. In R. W. Preiss, B. M. Gayle, N. Burrell, M. Allen, & J. Bryant (Eds.), *Mass media effects research: Advances through meta-analysis* (pp. 263–279). Mahwah, NJ: Erlbaum.

Alperstein, N. (1991). Imaginary social relationships with celebrities appearing in television commercials. *Journal of Broadcasting and Electronic Media*, 35, 43–58.

Alter, A. (2012, June 29). Your e-book is reading you. *Wall Street Journal* (U.S. Edition), p. D1.

Altman, A. (2008, June 23). Debating Iwo Jima. *Time*, p. 42.

Alwitt, L. F., Deighton, J., & Grimm, J. (1991). Reactions to political advertising depend on the nature of the voter-candidate bond. In F. Biocca (Ed.), *Television and political advertising: Psychological processes* (Vol. 1, pp. 329–350). Hillsdale, NJ: Erlbaum.

Amaral, R., & Guimarães, C. (1994). Media monopoly in Brazil. *Journal of Communication*, 44(4), 26–38.

American Psychological Association (1993). Violence and youth: Psychology's response, Vol. 1, summary report of the American Psychological Association Commission on violence and youth.

An, C., & Pfau, M. (2004). The efficacy of inoculation in televised political debates. *Journal of Communication*, 54, 421–436.

Andersen, P. A., & Kibler, R. J. (1978). Candidate valence as a predictor of voter preference. *Human Communication Research*, 5, 4–14.

Anderson, B., Fagan, P., Woodnutt, T., & Chamorro-Premuzic, T. (2012). Facebook psychology: Popular questions answered by research. *Psychology of Popular Media Culture*, 1, 23–27.

Anderson, C. A., Berkowitz, L., Donnerstein, E., Huesmann, L. R., Johnson, J. D., Linz, D. et al. (2003). The influence of media violence on youth. *Psychological Science in the Public Interest*, 4, 81–110.

Anderson, C. A., & Bushman, B. J. (2001). Effects of violent video games on aggressive behavior, aggressive cognition, aggressive affect, physiological arousal, and prosocial behavior: A meta-analytic review of the scientific literature. *Psychological Science*, 12, 353–359.

Anderson, C. A., Carnagey, N. L., & Eubanks, J. (2003). Exposure to violent media: The effects of songs with violent lyrics on aggressive thoughts and feelings. *Journal of Personality and Social Psychology*, 84, 960–971.

Anderson, C. A., Carnagey, N. L., Flanagan, M., Benjamin, A. J., Eubanks, J., & Valentine, J. C. (2004). Violent video games: Specific effects of violent content on aggressive thoughts and behavior. *Advances in Experimental Social Psychology*, 36, 199–249.

Anderson, C. A., & Dill, K. E. (2000). Video games and aggressive thoughts, feelings, and behavior in the laboratory and in life. *Journal of Personality and Social Psychology*, 78, 772–790.

Anderson, C. A., & Morrow, M. (1995). Competitive aggression without interaction: Effects of competitive versus cooperative instructions on aggressive behavior in video games. *Personality and Social Psychology Bulletin*, 21(10), 1020–1030.

Anderson, C. A., Shibuya, A., Ihori, N., Swing, E. L., Bushman, B. J., Sakamoto, A. et al. (2010). Violent video game effects on aggression, empathy, and prosocial behavior in Eastern and Western countries: A meta-analytic review. *Psychological Bulletin*, 136(2), 151–173.

Anderson, D. R. (1998). Educational television is not an oxymoron. *The Annals of the American Academy of Political and Social Science*, 557, 24–38.

Anderson, D. R., Bryant, J., Wilder, A., Santomero, A., Williams, M., & Crawley, A. M. (2000). Researching *Blue's Clues*: Viewing behavior and impact. *Media Psychology*, 2, 179–194.

Anderson, D. R., & Burns, J. (1991). Paying attention to television. In J. Bryant & D. Zillmann (Eds.), *Responding to the screen: Reception and reaction processes* (pp. 3–25). Hillsdale, NJ: Erlbaum.

Anderson, D. R., & Field, D. E. (1991). Online and offline assessment of the television audience. In J. Bryant & D. Zillmann (Eds.), *Responding to the screen: Reception and reaction processes* (pp. 199–216). Hillsdale, NJ: Erlbaum.

Anderson, D. R., Fite, K. V., Petrovich, N., & Hirsch, J. (2006). Cortical activation while watching video montage: An fMRI study. *Media Psychology*, 8, 7–24.

Anderson, D. R., & Kerkorian, H. L. (2006). Attention and television. In J. Bryant & P. Vorderer (Eds.), *Psychology of entertainment* (pp. 35–54). Mahwah, NJ: Erlbaum.

Andreasen, M. S. (1994). Patterns of family life and television consumption from 1945 to the 1990s. In D. Zillmann, J. Bryant, & A. C. Huston (Eds.), *Media, children, and the family: Social scientific, psychodynamic, and clinical perspectives* (pp. 19–36). Hillsdale, NJ: Erlbaum.

Andsager, J. L., Austin, E. W., & Pinkleton, B. E. (2001). Questioning the value of realism: Young adults' processing of messages in alcohol-related public service announcements and advertising. *Journal of Communication*, 51(1), 121–142.

Anker, E. (2005). Villains, victims, and heroes: Melodrama, media, and September 11. *Journal of Communication*, 55, 22–37.

Appel, M. (2008). Fictional narratives cultivate just-world beliefs. *Journal of Communication*, 58, 62–83.

Appel, M., & Richter, T. (2010). Transportation and need for affect in narrative persuasion: A mediated moderation model. *Media Psychology*, 13, 101–135.

Appiah, O. (2002). Black and white viewers' perception and recall of occupational characters on television. *Journal of Communication*, 52, 776–793.

Apter, M. J. (1982). *The experience of motivation: The theory of psychological reversals*. San Diego, CA: Academic Press.

Arkes, H. R., & Gaissmaier, W. (2012). Psychological research and the prostate-cancer screening controversy. *Psychological Science*, 23, 547–553.

Armstrong, E. G. (1993). The rhetoric of violence in rap and country music. *Sociological Inquiry*, 63, 64–84.

Armstrong, G. B., Neuendorf, K. A., & Brentar, J. E. (1992). TV entertainment, news, and racial perceptions of college students. *Journal of Communication*, 42(3), 153–176.

Armstrong, J. (2011, May 20). The rise and fall and rise again of Black TV. *Entertainment Weekly*, p. 21.

Asamen, J. K., & Berry, G. L. (2003). The multicultural worldview of children through the lens of television. In E. L. Palmer & B. M. Young (Eds.), *The faces of televisual media: Teaching, violence, selling to children* (pp. 107–123). Mahwah, NJ: Erlbaum.

Atkin, C., Greenberg, B., & McDermott, S. (1983). Television and race role socialization. *Journalism Quarterly*, 60(3), 407–414.

Attardo, S. (1997). The semantic foundations of cognitive theories of humor. *Humor*, 10, 395–420.

Aubrey, J. S. (2007). Does television exposure influence college-aged women's sexual self-concept? *Media Psychology*, 10, 157–181.

Aubrey, J. S., & Harrison, K. (2004). The gender-role content of children's favorite television programs and its links to their gender-related perceptions. *Media Psychology*, 6, 111–146.

Audit Bureau of Circulations (2012). Consumer magazines. Retrieved from http://abcas3.accessabc.com/ecirc/magform.asp

Austin, E. W. (1993). Exploring the effects of active parental mediation of television content. *Journal of Broadcasting & Electronic Media*, 37, 147–158.

Austin, E. W. (2001). Effects of family communication on children's interpretation of television. In J. Bryant & J. A. Bryant (Eds.), *Television and the American family* (2nd ed., pp. 377–395). Mahwah, NJ: Erlbaum.

Austin, E. W., Bolls, P., Fujioka, Y., & Engelbertson, J. (1999). How and why parents take on the tube. *Journal of Broadcasting & Electronic Media*, 43, 175–192.

Austin, E. W., Chen, Y., Pinkleton, B. E., & Johnson, J. Q. (2006). Benefits and costs of Channel One in a middle school setting and the role of media-literacy training. *Pediatrics*, 117, 423–433.

Austin, E. W., Pinkleton, B. E., & Fujioka, Y. (2000). The role of interpretation processes and parental discussion in the media's effects on adolescents' use of alcohol. *Pediatrics*, 105, 343–349.

Austin, E. W., Roberts, D. F., & Nass, C. I. (1990). Influences of family communication in children's television-interpretation processes. *Communication Research*, 17, 545–564.

Austin, E. W., Pinkleton, B. E., & Funabiki, R. P. (2007). The desirability paradox in the effects of media literacy training. *Communication Research*, 34, 483–506.

Austin, E. W., Pinkleton, B. E., Hust, S., & Cohen, M. (2005). Evaluation of an American legacy foundation/Washington State Department of Health media literacy pilot study. *Health Communication*, 18, 75–95.

Bacchetta, V. (1987). Brazil's soap operas: "Huge dramas where the country portrays itself". *Latinamerica Press*, 19(9), 5–6.

Bachen, C. M. (1998). Channel One and the education of American youths. *The Annals of the American Academy of Political and Social Science*, 557, 132–147.

Backer, T. E., Rogers, E. M., & Sopory, P. (1992). *Designing health communication campaigns: What works?* Newbury Park, CA: Sage.

Baggaley, J. P. (1988). Perceived effectiveness of interactional AIDS campaigns. *Health Education Research: Theory and Practice*, 3, 7–17.

Baggett, P. (1979). Structurally equivalent stories in movie and text and the effect of the medium on recall. *Journal of Verbal Learning and Verbal Behavior*, 18, 333–356.

Bailes, F. (2007). The prevalence and nature of imagined music in the everyday lives of music students. *Psychology of Music*, 35, 555–570.

Baker, K. (2004, April/May). The shriek heard round the world: When does a single gaffe sink a campaign? *American Heritage*, 34–36.

Bald, M. (1998, May). Africa's wonderchild. *World Press Review*, 45, 22.

Ball, S., & Bogatz, G. A. (1970). *The first year of Sesame Street: An evaluation*. Princeton, NJ: Educational Testing Service.

Ball, S., & Bogatz, G. A. (1973). *Reading with television: An evaluation of The Electric Company*. Princeton, NJ: Educational Testing Service.

Ballard, M. E., & Coates, S. (1995). The immediate effects of homicidal, suicidal, and nonviolent heavy metal and rap songs on the mood of college students. *Youth & Society*, 27, 148–169.

Ballard, M. E., & Wiest, J. R. (1996). Mortal Kombat: The effects of violent video game play on males' hostility and cardiovascular responding. *Journal of Applied Social Psychology*, 26(8), 717–730.

Balter, R. (1999). From stigmatization to patronization: The media's distorted portrayal of physical disability. In L. L. Schwartz (Ed.), *Psychology and the media: A second look* (pp. 147–171). Washington, DC: American Psychological Association.

Balteş, F. R., Avram, J., Miclea, M., & Miu, A. C. (2011). Emotions induced by operatic music: Psychophysiological effects of music, plot, and acting. *Brain and Cognition*, 76, 146–157.

Banaji, M. R. (2008, August 1). The science of satire. *The Chronicle Review*, p. B13.

Bandura, A. (2009). Social cognitive theory of mass communication. In J. Bryant and M. B. Oliver (Eds.), *Media effects: Advances in theory and research* (3rd ed., pp. 94–124). New York: Taylor and Francis.

Bandura, A. (1965). Influence of models' reinforcement contingencies on the acquisition of imitative responses. *Journal of Personality and Social Psychology*, 1, 585–595.

Bandura, A. (1977). *Social learning theory*. Englewood Cliffs, NJ: Prentice-Hall.

Bandura, A. (1995). Exercise of personal and collective efficacy. In A. Bandura (Ed.), *Self-efficacy in changing societies* (pp. 1–45). New York: Cambridge University Press.

Bandura, A. (1997). *Self-efficacy: The essence of control*. New York: Freeman.

Bandura, A. (2001). Social cognitive theory of mass communication. *Media Psychology*, 3, 265–299.

Bandura, A. (2002). Social cognitive theory of mass communication. In J. Bryant & D. Zillmann (Eds.), *Media effects* (2nd ed., pp. 121–153). Mahwah, NJ: Erlbaum.

Bandura, A., Ross, D., & Ross, S. A. (1961). Transmission of aggression through imitation of aggressive models. *Journal of Abnormal and Social Psychology*, 63, 575–582.

Bandura, A., Ross, D., & Ross, S. A. (1963). Imitation of film-mediated aggressive models. *Journal of Abnormal and Social Psychology*, 66, 3–11.

Bandura, A., & Walters, R. H. (1963). *Social learning and personality development*. New York: Holt, Rinehart & Winston.

Banerjee, S. C., & Greene, K. (2006). Analysis versus production: Adolescent cognitive and attitudinal responses to antismoking interventions. *Journal of Communication*, 56, 773–794.

Banerjee, S., & Greene, K. (2007). Antismoking initiatives: Effects of analysis versus production media literacy interventions on smoking-related attitude, norm, and behavioral intention. *Health Communication*, 22, 37–48.

Bannon, L. (1995, October 24). Bazaar gossip: How a rumor spread about subliminal sex in Disney's Aladdin—schoolyards, churches buzz over supposed smut, but who started it all?—Evangelical actors play role. *Wall Street Journal*.

Barak, A., & Fisher, W. A. (1997). Effects of interactive computer erotica on men's attitudes and behavior toward women: An experimental study. *Computers in Human Behavior*, 13, 353–369.

Barak, A., Fisher, W. A., Belfry, S., & Lashambe, D. R. (1999). Sex, guys, and cyber-space: Effects of Internet pornography and individual differences on men's attitudes toward women. *Journal of Psychology and Human Sexuality*, 11, 63–91.

Barcus, F. E. (1983). *Images of life on children's television*. New York: Praeger.

Barlett, C. P., & Gentile, D. A. (2012). Attacking others online: The formation of cyberbullying in late adolescence. *Psychology of Popular Media Culture*, 1, 123–135.

Barlett, C. P., Harris, R. J., & Baldassaro, R. (2007). Longer you play, the more hostile you feel: Examination of first person shooter video games and aggression during video game play. *Aggressive Behavior*, 33, 486–497.

Barlett, C. P., Harris, R. J., & Bruey, C. (2008). The effect of the amount of blood in a violent video game on aggression, hostility, and arousal. *Journal of Experimental Social Psychology*, 44, 539–546.

Barlett, C. P., Rodeheffer, C. D., Baldassaro, R., Hinkin, M. P., & Harris, R. J. (2008). The effect of advances in video game technology and content on aggressive cognitions, hostility, and heart rate. *Media Psychology*, 11, 540–565.

Barlett, C. P., Smith, S. J., & Harris, R. J. (2006). The interference effect of men's handling of muscular action figures on a lexical decision task. *Body Image*, 3, 375–383.

Barnhurst, K. G., & Mutz, D. (1997). American journalism and the decline in event-centered reporting. *Journal of Communication*, 47(4), 27–53.

Baroffio-Bota. D., & Banet-Weiser, S. (2006). Women, team sports, and the WNBA: Playing like a girl. In A. A. Raney & J. Bryant (Eds.), Handbook of sports and media (pp. 485–500). Mahwah, NJ: Erlbaum.

Baron, R. A. (1979). Heightened sexual arousal and physical aggression: An extension to females. Journal of Research in Personality, 13, 91–102.

Barr, R. Zack, E., Garcia, A., & Muentener, P. (2008). Infants' attention and responsiveness to television increases with prior exposure and parental interaction. Infancy, 13, 30–56.

Bartholomew, B. D., & Anderson, C. A. (2002). Effects of violent video games on aggressive behavior: Potential sex differences. Journal of Experimental Social Psychology, 38(3), 283–290.

Bartsch, A. (2012). As time goes by: What changes and what remains the same in entertainment experience over the life span? Journal of Communication, 62, 588–608.

Bartsch, R. A., Burnett, T., Diller, T. R., & Rankin-Williams, E. (2000). Gender representation in television commercials: Updating an update. Sex Roles, 43, 735–743.

Basil, M. D. (1994). Secondary reaction-time measures. In A. Lang (Ed.), Measuring psychological responses to media (pp. 85–98). Hillsdale, NJ: Erlbaum.

Basil, M., Schooler, C., & Reeves, B. (1991). Positive and negative political advertising: Effectiveness of ads and perceptions of candidates. In F. Biocca (Ed.), Television and political advertising: Psychological processes (Vol. 1, pp. 245–262). Hillsdale, NJ: Erlbaum.

Bateman, T. S., Sakano, T., & Fujita, M. (1992). Roger, me, and my attitude: Film propaganda and cynicism toward corporate leadership. Journal of Applied Psychology, 77, 768–771.

Bates, T. (2008, May 26). Hip hero. Time, p. 55.

Battles, K., & Hilton-Morrow, W. (2002). Gay characters in conventional spaces: Will and Grace and the situation comedy genre. Critical Studies in Media Communication, 19(1), 87–106.

Baum, M. A. (2002). Sex, lies, and war: How soft news brings foreign policy to the inattentive public. American Political Science Review, 96, 91–109.

Baumgartner, S. E., & Wirth, W. (2012). Affective priming during the processing of news articles. Media Psychology, 15, 1–18.

Bauserman, R. (1996). Sexual aggression and pornography: A review of correlation research. Basic and Applied Social Psychology, 18, 405–427.

Baym, G. (2005). The Daily Show: Discursive integration and the reinvention of political journalism. Political Communication, 22, 259–276.

Beagles-Roos, J., & Gat, I. (1983). Specific impact of radio and television on children's story comprehension. Journal of Educational Psychology, 75, 128–137.

Beaman, C. P., & Williams, T. I. (2010). Earworms (stuck song syndrome): Towards a natural history of intrusive thoughts. British Journal of Psychology, 101, 637–653.

Becker, A. E. (2004). Television, disordered eating, and young women in Fiji: Negotiating body image and identity during rapid social change. Culture, Medicine and Psychiatry, 28, 533–559.

Beeman, W. O. (1984). The cultural role of the media in Iran: The revolution of 1978–1979 and after. In A. Anno & W. Dissayanake (Eds.), The news media and national and international conflict (pp. 147–165). Boulder, CO: Westview Press.

Beentjes, J. W. J., van Oordt, M. N., & van der Voort, T. H. A. (2002). How television commentary affects children's judgments on soccer fouls. Communication Research, 29, 31–45.

Belkin, L. (2001, March/April). Primetime pushers. Mother Jones, pp. 30–37.

Belluck, P., Preston, J., & Harris, G. (2012, February 3). Cancer group backs down on cutting off Planned Parenthood. New York Times. Retrieved from http://www.nytimes.com

Belson, K. (2012, June 12). Former coach testifies against Sandusky. *New York Times*. Retrieved from http://www.nytimes.com

Benedict, H. (1992). *Virgin or vamp: How the press covers sex crimes*. New York: Oxford University Press.

Benoit, W. L. (2006). Retrospective versus prospective statements and outcome of the Presidential elections. *Journal of Communication*, 56, 331–345.

Benoit, W. L., & Hansen, G. J. (2004). Presidential debate watching, issue knowledge, character evaluation, and vote choice. *Human Communication Research*, 30, 121–144.

Ben-Porath, E. N., & Shaker, L. K. (2010). News images, race, and attribution in the wake of Hurricane Katrina. *Journal of Communication*, 60, 466–490.

Bensley, L., & Van Eenwyk, J. (2001). Video games and real life aggression: Review of the literature. *Journal of Adolescent Health*, 29(4), 244–257.

Ben-Zeev, A., Scharnetzki, L., Chan, L. K., & Dennehy, T. C. (2012). Hypermasculinity in the media: When men "walk into the fog" to avoid affective communication. *Psychology of Popular Media Culture*, 1, 53–61.

Berelson, B. R., Lazarsfeld, P. F., & McPhee, W. N. (1954). *Voting*. Chicago: University of Chicago Press.

Bergen, L., Grimes, T., & Potter, D. (2005). How attention partitions itself during simultaneous message presentations. *Human Communication Research*, 31, 311–336.

Berger, C. R. (1998). Processing quantitative data about risk and threat in news reports. *Journal of Communication*, 48(3), 87–106.

Berger, C. R. (2000). Quantitative depictions of threatening phenomena in news reports. *Human Communication Research*, 26, 27–52.

Bergsma, L. J., & Carney, M. E. (2008). Effectiveness of health-promoting media literacy education: A systematic review. *Health Education Research*, 23, 522–542.

Berkowitz, L. (1965). Some aspects of observed aggression. *Journal of Personality and Social Psychology*, 2, 359–369.

Berkowitz, L. (1984). Some effects of thoughts on anti- and prosocial influences of media events: A cognitive neoassociation analysis. *Psychological Bulletin*, 95, 410–427.

Bernard, P., Gervais, S. J., Allen, J., Campomizzi, S., & Klein, O. (2012). Integrating sexual objectification with object versus person recognition: The sexualized-body-inversion hypothesis. *Psychological Science*, 23, 469–471.

Berry, G. L. (1980). Television and Afro-Americans: Past legacy and present portrayals. In S. B. Withey & R. P. Abeles (Eds.), *Television and social behavior* (pp. 231–247). Hillsdale, NJ: Erlbaum.

Berry, V. T. (1992). From *Good Times* to *The Cosby Show*: Perceptions of changing televised images among black fathers and sons. In S. Craig (Ed.), *Men, masculinity, and the media* (pp. 111–123). Newbury Park, CA: Sage.

Bessenoff, G. R. (2006). Can the media affect us? Social comparison, self-discrepancy, and the thin ideal. *Psychology of Women Quarterly*, 30, 239–251.

Best, J. (1999). *Random violence: How we talk about new crimes and new victims*. Berkeley, CA: University of California Press.

Bever, T., Smith, M., Bengen, B., & Johnson, T. (1975). Young viewers' troubling responses to TV ads. *Harvard Business Review*, 53(6), 109–120.

Bhat, S., Leigh, T. W., & Wardlow, D. L. (1998). The effect of consumer prejudices on ad processing: Heterosexual consumers' responses to homosexual imagery in ads. *Journal of Advertising*, 27(4), 9–29.

Bickham, D. S., Wright, J. C., & Huston, A. C. (2001). Attention, comprehension, and the educational influences of television. In D. G. Singer & J. L. Singer (Eds.), *Handbook of children and the media* (pp. 101–119). Thousand Oaks, CA: Sage.

Bilandzic, H. (2006). The perception of distance in the cultivation process. *Communication Theory*, 16, 333–355.

Billings, A. C. (Ed.) (2011). *Sports media: Transformation, integration, and consumption*. New York: Routledge.

Billings, A. C., & Eastman, S. T. (2003). Framing identities: Gender, ethnic, and national parity in network announcing of the 2002 Winter Olympics. *Journal of Communication*, 53, 569–585.

Bird, S. E. (Ed.). (1996). *Dressing in feathers: The construction of the Indian in popular culture*. Boulder, CO: Westview Press.

Bird, S. E. (1999). Gendered construction of the American Indian in popular media. *Journal of Communication*, 49(3), 61–83.

Bischoff, R. J., & Reiter, A. D. (1999). The role of gender in the presentation of mental health clinicians in the movies: Implications for clinical practice. *Psychotherapy*, 36(2), 180–189.

Bissell, K. L., & Zhou, P. (2004). Must-see TV or ESPN: Entertainment and sports media exposure and body-image distortion in college women. *Journal of Communication*, 54, 5–21.

Bjerklie, D. (2002, August 12). Label reform. *Time*, p. 4.

Bjerklie, D. (2003, July 28). No title. *Time*, p. 73.

Black, G. D. (1994). *Hollywood censored: Morality codes, Catholics, and the movies*. New York: Cambridge University Press.

Blain, N., Boyle, R., & O'Donnell, H. (1993). *Sport and national identity in the European media*. Leicester, UK: Leicester University Press.

Blanc, N., Kendeou, P., van den Broek, P., & Brouillet, D. (2008). Updating situation models during reading of news reports: Evidence from empirical data and simulations. *Discourse Processes*, 45, 103–121.

Blanc, N., Stiegler-Balfour, J. J., & O'Brien, E. J. (2011). Does the uncertainty of information influence the updating process? Evidence from the reading of news articles. *Discourse Processes*, 48, 387–403.

Blatt, J., Spencer, L., & Ward, S. (1972). A cognitive developmental study of children's reactions to television advertising. In E. A. Rubinstein, G. A. Comstock, & J. P. Murray (Eds.), *Television and social behavior: Television in everyday life: Patterns of use* (Vol. 4, pp. 452–467). Washington, DC: U.S. Government Printing Office.

Bleakley, A., Hennessy, M., Fishbein, M., & Jordan, A. (2008). It works both ways: The relationship between exposure to sexual content in the media and adolescent sexual behavior. *Media Psychology*, 11, 443–461.

Bleich, A., Gelkopf, M., & Solomon, Z. (2003). Exposure to terrorism, stress-related mental health symptoms, and coping behaviors among a nationally representative sample in Israel. *Journal of the American Medical Association*, 290, 612–620.

Block, C. (1972). White backlash to Negro ads: Fact or fantasy? *Journalism Quarterly*, 49(2), 253–262.

Blumler, J. G., & McQuail, D. (1969). *Television in politics: Its uses and influences*. Chicago: University of Chicago Press.

Blumler, J. G., McLeod, J. M., & Rosengren, K. E. (Eds.). (1992). *Comparatively speaking: Communication and culture across space and time*. Newbury Park, CA: Sage.

Boese, A. (2006). *Hippo eats dwarf: A field guide to hoaxes and other B.S.* Orlando: Harcourt.

Bogart, L. (1980). Television news as entertainment. In P. H. Tannenbaum (Ed.), *The entertainment functions of television* (pp. 209–249). Hillsdale, NJ: Erlbaum.

Bogatz, G. A., & Ball, S. (1971). *The second year of Sesame Street: A continuing evaluation*. Princeton, NJ: Educational Testing Service.

Bogle, D. (1973). *Toms, coons, mulattoes, and bucks: An interpretive history of blacks in American films.* New York: Viking Press.

Boies, S. C. (2002). University students' uses of and reactions to online sexual information and entertainment: Links to online and offline sexual behaviour. *The Canadian Journal of Human Sexuality,* 11, 77–89.

Bollen, K. A., & Phillips, D. P. (1982). Imitative suicides: A national study of the effects of television news stories. *American Sociological Review,* 47, 802–809.

Bolls, P. D., & Lang, A. (2003). I saw it on the radio: The allocation of attention to high-imagery radio advertisements. *Media Psychology,* 5, 33–55.

Bolls, P. D., Lang, A., & Potter, R. F. (2001). The effects of message valence and listener arousal on attention, memory, and facial muscular responses to radio advertisements. *Communication Research,* 28, 627–651.

Bonds-Raacke, J. M., Cady, E. T., Schlegel, R., Harris, R. J., & Firebaugh, L. C. (2007). Remembering gay/lesbian media characters: Can Ellen and Will improve attitudes toward homosexuals? *Journal of Homosexuality,* 53(3), 19–34.

Bonds-Raacke, J. M., & Harris, R. J. (2006). Autobiographical memories of televised sporting events watched in different social settings. *Psychological Reports,* 99, 197–208.

Borah, P. (2011). Conceptual issues in framing theory: A systematic examination of a decade's literature. *Journal of Communication,* 61, 246–263.

Bordeaux, B. R., & Lange, G. (1991). Children's reported investment of mental effort when viewing television. *Communication Research,* 18, 617–635.

Borden, S. L., & Tew, C. (2007). The role of journalist and the performance of journalism: Ethical lessons from "fake" news (seriously). *Journal of Mass Media Ethics,* 22, 300–314.

Botta, R. A. (1999). Television images and adolescent girls' body image disturbance. *Journal of Communication,* 49(2), 22–41.

Boucher, E. M., Hancock. J. T., & Dunham, P. J. (2008). Interpersonal sensitivity in computer-mediated and face-to-face conversations. *Media Psychology,* 11, 235–258.

Bouman, M. (2002). Turtles and peacocks: Collaboration in entertainment-education television. *Communication Theory,* 12, 225–244.

Bower, A. (2002, May 6). Fast-food networks. *Time,* p. 161.

Boyle, M. P., Schmierbach, M., Armstrong, C. L., Cho, J., McCluskey, M., McLeod, D. M., et al. (2006). Expressive responses to news stories about extremist groups: A framing experiment. *Journal of Communication,* 56, 271–288.

Bradley, S. D., & Meeds, R. (2002). Surface-structure transformations and advertising slogans: The case for moderate syntactic complexity. *Psychology & Marketing,* 19, 595–619.

Bradley, S. D., & Meeds, R. (2004). The effects of sentence-level context, prior word knowledge, and need for cognition on information processing of technical language in print ads. *Journal of Consumer Psychology,* 14, 291–302.

Breslow, L. (1978). Risk factor intervention for health maintenance. *Science,* 200, 908–912.

Bretl, D. J., & Cantor, J. (1988). The portrayal of men and women on U.S. television commercials: A recent content analysis and trends over 15 years. *Sex Roles,* 18, 595–609.

Brewer, P. R., & Marquardt, E. (2007). Mock news and democracy: Analyzing *The Daily Show. Atlantic Journal of Communication,* 15(4), 249–267.

Brewer, W. F., & Nakamura, G. V. (1984). The nature and functions of schemas. In R. S. Wyer & T. K. Srull (Eds.), *Handbook of social cognition* (pp. 119–160). Hillsdale, NJ: Erlbaum.

Brosius, H. B. (1993). The effects of emotional pictures in television news. *Communication Research,* 20, 105–124.

Brosius, H.-B., & Kepplinger, H. M. (1990). The agenda-setting function of television news: Static and dynamic views. *Communication Research,* 17, 183–211.

Brown, A. S., & Logan, C. (Eds.). (2005). *The psychology of The Simpsons*. Dallas, TX: Benbella.

Brown, D., & Bryant, J. (1983). Humor in mass media. In P. E. McGhee & J. H. Goldstein (Eds.), *Handbook of humor research* (Vol. 2). New York: Springer-Verlag.

Brown, J. A. (1991). *Television "critical viewing skills" education: Major media literacy projects in the United States and selected countries*. Hillsdale, NJ: Erlbaum.

Brown, J. D., & Einsiedel, E. F. (1990). Public health campaigns: Mass media strategies. In E. B. Ray & L. Donohew (Eds.), *Communication and health: Systems and applications* (pp. 153–170). Hillsdale, NJ: Erlbaum.

Brown, J. D., L'Engle, K. L., Pardun, C. J., Guo, G., Kenneavy, K., & Jackson, C. (2006). Sexy media matter: Exposure to sexual content in music, movies, television, and magazines predicts Black and White adolescents' sexual behavior. *Pediatrics, 117*, 1018–1027.

Brown, J. D., & Walsh-Childers, K. (2002). Effects of media on personal and public health. In J. Bryant & D. Zillmann (Eds.), *Media effects* (2nd ed., pp. 453–488). Mahwah, NJ: Erlbaum.

Brown, N. R., & Siegler, R. S. (1992). The role of availability in the estimation of national populations. *Memory & Cognition, 20*, 406–412.

Brown, W. J., Basil, M. D., & Bocarnea, M. C. (2003). Social influence of an international celebrity: Responses to the death of Princess Diana. *Journal of Communication, 53*, 587–605.

Brown, W. J., & Cody, M. J. (1991). Effects of a prosocial television soap opera in promoting women's status. *Human Communication Research, 18*, 114–142.

Brown, W. J., & Singhal, A. (1990). Ethical dilemmas of prosocial television. *Communication Quarterly, 38*, 268–280.

Brown, W. J., Singhal, A., & Rogers, E. M. (1989). Pro-development soap operas: A novel approach to development communication. *Media Development, 36*(4), 43–47.

Brownstein, A. (2001, February 23). A battle over a name in the land of the Sioux. *The Chronicle of Higher Education, 47*, pp. A46–A49.

Bruce, S. (1990). *Pray TV: Televangelism in America*. London: Routledge.

Bruno, K. J., & Harris, R. J. (1980). The effect of repetition on the discrimination of asserted and implied claims in advertising. *Applied Psycholinguistics, 1*, 307–321.

Bryant, J., Aust, C. F., Bryant, J. A., & Venugopalan, G. (2001). How psychologically healthy are America's prime-time television families? In J. Bryant & J. A. Bryant (Eds.), *Television and the American family* (2nd ed., pp. 247–270). Mahwah, NJ: Erlbaum.

Bryant, J., & Bryant, J. A. (2001). *Television and the American family* (2nd ed.). Mahwah, NJ: Erlbaum.

Bryant, J., & Holt, A. M. (2006). A historical overview of sports and media in the United States. In A. A. Raney & J. Bryant (Eds.), *Handbook of sports and media* (pp. 21–43). Mahwah, NJ: Erlbaum.

Bryant, J., & Miron, D. (2004). Theory and research in mass communication. *Journal of Communication, 54*, 662–704.

Bryant, J., & Oliver, M. B. (Eds.) (2009). *Media effects: Advances in theory and research* (3rd ed.). New York: Taylor & Francis.

Bryant, J., & Raney, A. A. (2000). Sports on the screen. In D. Zillmann & P. Vorderer (Eds.), *Media entertainment: The psychology of its appeal* (pp. 153–174). Mahwah, NJ: Erlbaum.

Bryant, J., & Rockwell, S. C. (1994). Effects of massive exposure to sexually oriented prime-time television programming on adolescents' moral judgment. In D. Zillmann, J. Bryant, & A. C. Huston (Eds.), *Media, children, and the family: Social scientific, psychodynamic, and clinical perspectives* (pp. 183–195). Hillsdale, NJ: Erlbaum.

Bryant, J., Zillmann, D., & Raney, A. A. (1998). Violence and the enjoyment of media sports. In L. A. Wenner (Ed.), *MediaSport* (pp. 252–265). London: Routledge.

Buchholz, M., & Bynum, J. (1982). Newspaper presentation of America's aged: A content analysis of image and role. *The Gerontologist, 22*, 83–88.

Buckingham, D. (1993). *Children talking television: The making of television literacy*. London: Falmer.

Buckingham, D. (1998). Media education in the UK: Moving beyond protectionism. *Journal of Communication, 48*(1), 33–43.

Buckingham, D. (2003). *Media education: Literacy, learning, and contemporary culture*. Cambridge, UK: Polity/Blackwell.

Bucy, E. P., & Grabe, M. E. (2007). Taking television seriously: A sound and image bite analysis of Presidential campaign coverage, 1992–2004. *Journal of Communication, 57*, 652–675.

Bucy, E. P., & Newhagen, J. E. (1999). The emotional appropriateness heuristic: Processing televised Presidential reactions to the news. *Journal of Communication, 49*(4), 59–79.

Buerkel-Rothfuss, N. L., & Buerkel, R. A. (2001). Family mediation. In J. Bryant & J. A. Bryant (Eds.), *Television and the American family* (2nd ed., pp. 355–376). Mahwah, NJ: Erlbaum.

Buerkel-Rothfuss, N. L., & Mayes, S. (1981). Soap opera viewing: The cultivation effect. *Journal of Communication, 31*, 108–115.

Buijzen, M. (2007). Reducing children's susceptibility to commercials: Mechanisms of factual and evaluative advertising interventions. *Media Psychology, 9*, 411–430.

Buijzen, M., & Valkenburg, P. M. (2004). Developing a typology of humor in audiovisual media. *Media Psychology, 6*, 147–167.

Buijzen, M., & Valkenburg, P. M. (2008). Observing purchase-related parent-child communication in retail environments. *Human Communication Research, 34*, 50–69.

Buijzen, M., Walma van der Molen, J. H., & Sondij, P. (2007). Parental mediation of children's emotional responses to a violent news event. *Communication Research, 34*, 212–230.

Bullard, S. (1998). Gangstawulf: Examining the allure of violence in lyric form. *Teaching Tolerance, 7*(1), 16–19.

Bureau of Labor Statistics (2010). American time use survey. Retrieved from http://www.bls.gov/tus/

Burke, R. R., DeSarbo, W. S., Oliver, R. L., & Robertson, T. S. (1988). Deception by implication: An experimental investigation. *Journal of Consumer Research, 14*, 483–494.

Bushman, B. J. (1998). Effects of television violence on memory of commercial messages. *Journal of Experimental Psychology: Applied, 4*, 291–307.

Bushman, B. J. (2005). Violence and sex in television programs do not sell products in advertisements. *Psychological Science, 16*, 702–708.

Bushman, B. J., & Anderson, C. A. (2001). Media violence and the American public: Scientific facts versus media misinformation. *American Psychologist, 56*, 477–489.

Bushman, B. J., & Anderson, C. A. (2002). Violent video games and hostile expectations: A test of the general aggression model. *Personality and Social Psychology Bulletin, 28*, 1679–1686.

Bushman, B. J., Baumeister, R. F., & Stack, A. D. (1999). Catharsis, aggression, and persuasive influences: Self-fulfilling or self-defeating prophecies? *Journal of Personality and Social Psychology, 76*, 367–376.

Bushman, B. J., Bonacci, A. M., van Dijk, M., & Baumeister, R. (2003). Narcissism, sexual refusal, and aggression: Testing a narcissistic reactance model of sexual coercion. *Journal of Personality and Social Psychology, 84*, 1027–1040.

Bushman, B. J., & Phillips, C. M. (2001). If the television program bleeds, memory for the advertisement recedes. *Current Directions in Psychological Science, 10*, 43–47.

Busselle, R., & Bilandzic, H. (2009). Measuring narrative engagement. *Media Psychology*, 12, 321–347.

Busselle, R. W., & Shrum, L. J. (2003). Media exposure and exemplar accessibility. *Media Psychology*, 5, 255–282.

Cady, E. T., Harris, R. J., & Knappenberger, J. B. (2008). Using music to cue autobiographical memories of different lifetime periods. *Psychology of Music*, 36(2), 157–177.

Calvert, S. L. (1988). Television production feature effects of children's comprehension of time. *Journal of Applied Developmental Psychology*, 9, 263–273.

Calvert, S. L., & Kotler, J. A. (2003). Lessons from children's television: The impact of the Children's Television Act on children's learning. *Journal of Applied Developmental Psychology*, 24(3), 275–335.

Calvert, S. L., Kotler, J. A., Zehnder, S. M., & Shockey, E. M. (2003). Gender stereotyping in children's reports about educational and informational television programs. *Media Psychology*, 5, 139–162.

Calvert, S. L., & Wilson, B. J. (Eds.). (2011). *The handbook of children, media, and development*. Malden, MA: Wiley-Blackwell.

Cameron, G. T., & Frieske, D. A. (1994). The time needed to answer: Measurement of memory response latency. In A. Lang (Ed.), *Measuring psychological responses to media* (pp. 149–164). Hillsdale, NJ: Erlbaum.

Campbell, H. A. (2010). *When religion meets new media*. New York: Routledge.

Cantor, J. (1996). Television and children's fear. In T. M. Macbeth (Ed.), *Tuning in to young viewers: Social science perspectives on television* (pp. 87–115). Thousand Oaks, CA: Sage.

Cantor, J. (1998a). Ratings for program content: The role of research findings. *The Annals of the American Academy of Political and Social Science*, 557, 54–69.

Cantor, J. (1998b). *"Mommy, I'm scared": How TV and movies frighten children and what we can do to protect them*. San Diego: Harcourt Brace.

Cantor, J. (2002). Fright reactions to mass media. In J. Bryant & D. Zillmann (Eds.), *Media effects* (pp. 287–306). Mahwah, NJ: Erlbaum.

Cantor, J. (2006). Why horror doesn't die: The enduring and paradoxical effects of frightening entertainment. In J. Bryant & P. Vorderer (Eds.), *Psychology of entertainment* (pp. 315–327). Mahwah, NJ: Erlbaum.

Cantor, J. (2009). Fright reactions to mass media. In J. Bryant & M. B. Oliver (Eds.), *Media effects: Advances in theory and research* (3rd ed., pp. 287–303). New York, NY: Routledge.

Cantor, J., Mares, M. L., & Hyde, J. S. (2003). Autobiographical memories of exposure to sexual media content. *Media Psychology*, 5, 1–31.

Cantor, J., & Nathanson, A. I. (1996). Children's fright reactions to television news. *Journal of Communication*, 46(4), 139–152.

Cantor, J., & Oliver, M. B. (1996). Developmental differences in responses to horror. In J. B. Weaver & R. Tamborini (Eds.), *Horror films: Current research on audience preferences and reactions* (pp. 63–80). Mahwah, NJ: Erlbaum.

Cantor, J., & Wilson, B. J. (2003). Media and violence: Intervention strategies for reducing aggression. *Media Psychology*, 5, 363–403.

Cantor, J., Wilson, B. J., & Hoffner, C. (1986). Emotional responses to a televised nuclear holocaust film. *Communication Research*, 13, 257–277.

Caplan, S. E. (2005). A social skill account of problematic Internet use. *Journal of Communication*, 55, 721–736.

Capsuto, S. (2000). *The uncensored story of gay and lesbian images on radio and television*. New York: Ballantine Books.

Carlson, S. (2003, August 15). Can Grand Theft Auto inspire professors? *The Chronicle of Higher Education*, 49, pp. A31–A33.

Carlsson-Paige, N. (2008). *Taking back childhood: Helping your kids thrive in a fast-paced, media-saturated, violence-filled world*. New York: Hudson Street Press.

Carlsson-Paige, N., & Levin, D. E. (1990). *Who's calling the shots? How to respond effectively to children's fascination with war play and war toys*. Philadelphia: New Society.

Carlyle, K. E., Slater, M. D., & Chakroff, J. L. (2008). Newspaper coverage of intimate partner violence: Skewing representations of risk. *Journal for Communication*, 58, 168–186.

Carnagey, N. L., & Anderson, C. A. (2005). The effects of reward and punishment in violent video games on aggressive affect, cognition, and behavior. *Psychological Science*, 16, 882–889.

Carroll, L. (2009, October 21). Mom and dad make scary movies even scarier: Kids who watch TV with their parents get even more freaked out. Retrieved from http://www.msnbc.com

Carveth, R., & Alexander, A. (1985). Soap opera viewing motivations and the cultivation process. *Journal of Broadcasting & Electronic Media*, 29, 259–273.

Casey, M. K., Allen, M., Emmers-Sommer, T., Sahlstein, E., DeGooyer, D., Winters, A. M. et al. (2007). The impact of Earvin "Magic" Johnson's HIV-positive announcement. In R. W. Preiss, B. M. Gayle, N. Burrell, M. Allen, & J. Bryant (Eds.), *Mass media effects research: Advances through meta-analysis* (pp. 363–375). Mahwah, NJ: Erlbaum.

Cassata, B., Anderson, P., & Skill, T. (1980). The older adult in daytime serial drama. *Journal of Communication*, 30, 48–49.

Cassata, M., & Irwin, B. J. (1997). Young by day: The older person on daytime serial drama. In H. S. Noor Al-deen (Ed.), *Cross-cultural communication and aging in the United States* (pp. 215–230). Mahwah, NJ: Erlbaum.

Celluloid Closet, The (1995). [Documentary film.] Written by V. Russo, R. Epstein, J. Friedman, & S. Wood. Columbia Tristar Home Video.

Center for the Study of Women in Television and Film. (2012). It's a man's (celluloid) world: On-screen representations of female characters in the top 100 films of 2011. San Diego: M. Lauzen. Retrieved from http://www.wif.org/

Centerwall, B. S. (1989). Exposure to television as a risk factor for violence. *American Journal of Epidemiology*, 129, 643–652.

Centerwall, B. S. (1992). Television and violence: The scale of the problem and where to go from here. *Journal of the American Medical Association*, 267, 3059–3063.

Chakrabarti, S., & Fombonne, W. (2001). Pervasive developmental disorders in pre-school children. *Journal of the American Medical Association*, 285, 3093–3099.

Chandler, D. (1997). Children's understanding of what is "real" on television: A review of the literature. *Journal of Educational Media*, 23, 65–80.

Chandra, A., Martino, S. C., Collins, R. L., Elliott, M. N., Berry, S. H., Kanouse, D. E., & Miu, A. (2008). Does watching sex on television predict teen pregnancy? Findings from a national longitudinal survey of youth. *Pediatrics*, 122(5), 1047–1054.

Chang, C. (2004). Country of origin as a heuristic cue: The effects of message ambiguity and product involvement. *Media Psychology*, 6, 169–192.

Chappell, C. R., & Hartz, J. (1998, March 20). The challenge of communicating science to the public. *The Chronicle of Higher Education*, 45, p. B7.

Charlton, T., Gunter, B., & Hannan, A. (Eds.). (2002). *Broadcast television effects in a remote community*. Mahwah, NJ: Erlbaum.

Check, J. V. P. (1985). *The effects of violent and nonviolent pornography*. Ottawa: Department of Justice for Canada.

Check, J. V. P. (1995). Teenage training: The effects of pornography on adolescent males. In L. Lederer & R. Delgado (Eds.), *The price we pay: The case against racist speech, hate propaganda, and pornography* (pp. 89–91). New York: Hill & Wang.

Check, J. V. P., & Guloien, T. H. (1989). Reported proclivity for coercive sex following repeated exposure to sexually violent pornography, nonviolent pornography, and erotica. In D. Zillmann & J. Bryant (Eds.), *Pornography: Research advances and policy considerations* (pp. 159–184). Hillsdale, NJ: Erlbaum.

Chen, L., Zhou, S., & Bryant, J. (2007). Temporal changes in mood repair through music consumption: Effects of mood, mood salience, and individual differences. *Media Psychology, 9*, 695–713.

Chen, M. (1994). *The smart parent's guide to kids' TV*. San Francisco: KQED Books.

Chia, S. C. (2006). How peers mediate media influence on adolescents' sexual attitudes and sexual behavior. *Journal of Communication, 56*, 585–606.

Chiang, O. J. (2009, August 5). The challenge of user-generated porn. *Forbes*. Retrieved from http://www.forbes.com/2009/08/04/digital-playground-video-technology-e-gang-09-ali-joone.html

Chivers, M. L., Seto, M. C., Lalumiere, M. L., Laan, E., & Grimbos, T. (2010). Agreement of self-reported and genital measures of sexual arousal in men and women: A meta-analysis. *Archives of Sexual Behavior, 39*, 5–56.

Cho, J. (2005). Media, interpersonal discussion, and electoral choice. *Communication Research, 32*, 295–322.

Cho, J. (2008). Political ads and citizen communication. *Communication Research, 35*, 423–451.

Cho, J. (2011). The geography of political communication: Effects of regional variations in campaign advertising on citizen communication. *Human Communication Research, 37*, 434–462.

Chock, T. M. (2011). Is it seeing or believing? Exposure, perceived realism, and emerging adults' perceptions of their own and others' attitudes about relationships. *Media Psychology, 14*, 355–386.

Choi, Y. J. (2011). Do central processing and online processing always concur? Analysis of scene order and proportion effects in broadcast news. *Applied Cognitive Psychology, 25*, 567–575.

Christ, W. G., & Potter, W. J. (1998). Media literacy, media education, and the academy. *Journal of Communication, 48*(1), 5–15.

Christensen, P. N., & Wood, W. (2007). Effects of media violence on viewers' aggression in unconstrained social interaction. In R. W. Preiss, B. M. Gayle, N. Burrell, M. Allen, & J. Bryant (Eds.), *Mass media effects research: Advances through meta-analyses* (pp. 145–168). Mahwah, NJ: Erlbaum.

Christenson, P. G. (1992). The effects of parental advisory labels on adolescent music preferences. *Journal of Communication, 42*(1), 106–113.

Christenson, P. G., Henriksen, L., & Roberts, D. F. (2000). *Substance use in popular prime-time television*. Washington, DC: Office of National Drug Control Policy.

Christenson, P. G., & Roberts, D. F. (1983). The role of television in the formation of children's social attitudes. In M. J. A. Howe (Ed.), *Learning from television: Psychological and educational research* (pp. 79–99). London: Academic Press.

Christianson, S., & Loftus, E. F. (1987). Memory for traumatic events. *Applied Cognitive Psychology, 1*, 225–239.

Chung, J. E. (2011). Mapping international film trade: Network analysis of international film trade between 1996 and 2004. *Journal of Communication, 61*, 618–640.

Cialdini, R. B. (2003). Crafting normative messages to protect the environment. *Current Directions in Psychological Science, 12*(4), 105–109.

Clark, C. (1969). Television and social controls: Some observation of the portrayal of ethnic minorities. *Television Quarterly, 8*(2), 18–22.

Cloud, J. (2006–2007, December 25–January 1). The YouTube gurus. *Time*, p. 66–74.

Clover, C. J. (1992). *Men, women, and chainsaws: Gender in the modern horror film*. Princeton, NJ: Princeton University Press.

Coates, T. J. (1990). Strategies for modifying sexual behavior for primary and secondary prevention of HIV disease. *Journal of Consulting and Clinical Psychology*, 58, 57–69.

Coe, K., & Domke, D. (2006). Petitioners or prophets? Presidential discourse, God, and the ascendancy of religious conservatives. *Journal of Communication*, 56, 309–330.

Coe, K., Tewksbury, D., Bond, B. J., Drogos, K. L., Porter, R. W., Yahn, A., et al. (2008). Partisan use and perceptions of cable news programming. *Journal of Communication*, 58, 201–219.

Cohen, J. (2001). Defining identification: A theoretical look at the identification of audience with media characters. *Mass Communication & Society*, 4, 245–264.

Cohen, J. (2004). Parasocial breakup from favorite television characters: The role of attachment styles and relationship intensity. *Journal of Social and Personal Relationships*, 21, 187–202.

Cohen, J. (2006). Audience identification with media characters. In J. Bryant & P. Vorderer (Eds.), *Psychology of entertainment* (pp. 183–198). Mahwah, NJ: Erlbaum.

Colburn, D. (1997, October 13). Violent TV ads common on post-season baseball. *Manhattan Mercury* (Washington Post syndication), p. A7.

Cole, J. (2000). *Surveying the digital future*. Los Angeles: UCLA Center for Communication Policy.

Colfax, D., & Steinberg, S. (1972). The perpetuation of racial stereotypes: Blacks in mass circulation magazine advertisements. *Public Opinion Quarterly*, 35, 8–18.

Collins, A. M., & Loftus, E. F. (1975). A spreading activation theory of semantic processing. *Psychological Review*, 82, 407–428.

Collins, J. (1998, March 30). Talking trash. *Time*, pp. 63–66.

Collins, R. L., Elliott, M. N., Berry, S. H., et al. (2003). Entertainment television as a healthy sex educator: The impact of condom-efficiency information in an episode of *Friends*. *Pediatrics*, 112, 1115–1121.

Collum, D. D. (2008, March). Blocking the big mouths. *Sojourners*, p. 38.

Commission on Obscenity and Pornography. (1970). *The report of the Commission on Obscenity and Pornography*. New York: Bantam.

Common Sense Media. (2011). Zero to eight: Children's media use in America. Retrieved from http://www.commonsensemedia.org

Comstock, G., Chaffee, S., Katzman, N., McCombs, M., & Roberts, D. (1978). *Television and human behavior*. New York: Columbia University Press.

Comstock, J., & Strzyzewski, K. (1990). Interpersonal attraction on television: Family conflict and jealousy on primetime. *Journal of Broadcasting and Electronic Media*, 34(3), 263–282.

Conan, N. (2009, November 12). On Sesame Street, "c" is for controversy. Retrieved from http://www.npr.org/templates/story/story.php?storyId=120355663

Conklin, J. E. (2008). *Campus life in the movies: A critical survey from the silent era to the present*. Jefferson, NC: McFarland.

Connaughton, S. L., & Jarvis, S. E. (2004). Invitations for partisan identification: Attempts to court Latino voters through televised Latino-oriented political advertisements, 1984–2000. *Journal of Communication*, 54, 38–54.

Connolly-Ahern, C., & Castells i Talens, A. (2010). The role of indigenous peoples in Guatemalan political advertisements. *Communication, Culture & Critique*, 3, 310–333.

Conrad, P. (2001). Genetic optimism: Framing genes and mental illness in the news. *Culture, Medicine and Psychiatry*, 25, 225–247.

Conway, J. C., & Rubin, A. M. (1991). Psychological predictors of television viewing motivation. *Communication Research*, 18, 443–463.

Cook, G. (1992). *Discourse of advertising.* London: Routledge.

Cook, T. D., Appleton, H., Conner, R. F., Shaffer, A., Tabkin, G., & Weber, J. S. (1975). *Sesame Street revisited.* New York: Sage.

Coontz, S. (1992). *The way we never were: American families and the nostalgia trap.* New York: Basic Books.

Coontz, S. (1997). *The way we really are: Coming to terms with America's changing families.* New York: Basic Books.

Cooper, A. (1998). Sexuality and the Internet: Surfing into the new millennium. *CyberPsychology and Behavior*, 1(2), 187–193.

Corcoran, F. (1986). KAL 007 and the evil empire: Mediated disaster and forms of rationalization. *Critical Studies in Mass Communication*, 3, 297–316.

Coulson, M., Barnett, J., Ferguson, C. J., & Gould, R. L. (2012). Real feelings for virtual people: Emotional attachments and interpersonal attraction in video games. *Psychology of Popular Media Culture*, 1, 176–184.

Court, J. H. (1977). Pornography and sex crimes: A re-evaluation in the light of recent trends around the world. *International Journal of Criminology and Penology*, 5, 129–157.

Court, J. H. (1982). Rape trends in New South Wales: A discussion of conflicting evidence. *Australian Journal of Social Issues*, 17, 202–206.

Court, J. H. (1984). Sex and violence: A ripple effect. In N. M. Malamuth & E. Donnerstein (Eds.), *Pornography and sexual aggression* (pp. 143–172). Orlando, FL: Academic Press.

Coyne, S. M., & Archer, J. (2004). Indirect, relational, and social aggression in the media: A content analysis of British television programs. *Aggressive Behavior*, 30, 254–271.

Coyne, S. M., & Archer, J. (2005). The relationship between indirect aggression on television and in real life. *Social Development*, 14, 324–336.

Coyne, S. M., & Whitehead, E. (2008). Indirect aggression in animated Disney films. *Journal of Communication*, 58, 382–395.

Craig, R. (2000). Expectations and elections: How television defines campaign news. *Critical Studies in Media Communication*, 17, 28–44.

Crawley, A. M., Anderson, D. R., Wilder, A., Williams, M., & Santomero, A. (1999). Effects of repeated exposures to a single episode of the television program Blue's Clues on the viewing behaviors and comprehension of preschool children. *Journal of Educational Psychology*, 91, 630–637.

Creedon, P. J. (Ed.). (1994). *Women, media, and sport: Challenging gender values.* Thousand Oaks, CA: Sage.

Crockett, S. A., Jr. (2002, August 23). For young fans, the name of the video game is gore. http://www.washingtonpost.com/wp-dyn/articles/A55183-2002Aug23.html

Croteau, D., & Hoynes, W. (1992). Men and the news media: The male presence and its effect. In S. Craig (Ed.), *Men, masculinity, and the media* (pp. 154–168). Newbury Park, CA: Sage.

Cruea, M., & Park, S.-Y. (2012). Gender disparity in video game usage: A third-person perception-based explanation. *Media Psychology*, 15, 44–67.

Cumberbatch, G., & Negrine, R. (1991). *Images of disability on television.* London: Routledge.

Cumings, B. (1992). *War and television.* New York: Verso.

Cuperfain, R., & Clarke, T. K. (1985). A new perspective on subliminal perception. *Journal of Advertising*, 14(1), 36–41.

Cwalina, W., Falkowski, A., & Kaid, L. L. (2000). Role of advertising in forming the image of politicians: Comparative analysis of Poland, France, and Germany. *Media Psychology*, 2, 119–146.

D'Haenens, L. (2001). Old and new media: Access and ownership in the home. In S. Livingstone & M. Bovill (Eds.), *Children and their changing media environment: A European comparative study* (pp. 53–84). Mahwah, NJ: Erlbaum.

d'Ydewalle, G., & De Bruycker, W. (2007). Eye movements of children and adults while reading subtitles. *European Psychologist*, 12(3), 196–205.

d'Ydewalle, G., Praet, C., Verfaillie, K., & Van Rensbergen, J. (1991). Watching subtitled television: Automatic reading behavior. *Communication Research*, 18, 650–666.

d'Ydewalle, G., & Van de Poel, M. (1999). Incidental foreign-language acquisition by children watching subtitled television programs. *Journal of Psycholinguistic Research*, 28, 227–244.

Dagnoli, J. (1990, April). Sokolof keeps thumping away at food giants. *Advertising Age*, 3, 63.

Dahl, M. (2011). Why watching "The Office" makes us cringe. http://bodyodd.msnbc.com/_news/2011/04/14/6472696. Retrieved 4/15/2011

Dal Cin, S., Gibson, B., Zanna, M. P., Shumate, R., & Fong, G. T. (2007). Smoking in movies, implicit associations of smoking with the self, and intentions to smoke. *Psychological Science*, 18, 559–563.

Dall, P. W. (1988). Prime-time television portrayals of older adults in the context of family life. *The Gerontologist*, 28, 700–706.

Dalton, M. A., Ahrens, M. B., Sargent, J. D., Mott, L. A., Beach, M. L., Tickle, J. J. et al. (2002). Relation between adolescent use of tobacco and alcohol and parental restrictions on movies. *Effective Clinical Practice*, 5, 1–10.

Dan Quayle vs. Murphy Brown (1992, June 1). *Time*, p. 50.

David, C. C. (2009). Learning political information from the news: A closer look at the role of motivation. *Journal of Communication*, 59, 243–261.

David, C., Cappella, J. N., & Fishbein, M. (2006). The social diffusion of influence among adolescents: Group interaction in a chat room environment about antidrug advertisements. *Communication Theory*, 16, 118–140.

David, P., Horton, B., & German, T. (2008). Dynamics of entertainment and affect in a Super Bowl audience. *Communication Research*, 35, 398–420.

Davies, M. M. (1997). *Fake, fact, and fantasy: Children's interpretations of television reality.* Mahwah, NJ: Erlbaum.

Davis, K. C., Norris, J., George, W. H., Martell, J., & Heiman, J. R. (2006). Men's likelihood of sexual aggression: The influence of alcohol, sexual arousal, and violent pornography. *Aggressive Behavior*, 32, 581–589.

Davis, M. (2008). *Street gang: The complete history of Sesame Street.* New York: Viking.

Davis, M. H., Hull, J. G., Young, R. D., & Warren, G. G. (1987). Emotional reactions to dramatic film stimuli: The influence of cognitive and emotional empathy. *Journal of Personality and Social Psychology*, 52, 126–133.

Davis, R. H. (1983). Television health messages: What are they telling us? *Generations*, 3(5), 43–45.

Davis, R. H., & Davis, J. A. (1985). *TV's image of the elderly.* Lexington, MA: Lexington Books/D. C. Heath.

Day, D. M., & Page, S. (1986). Portrayal of mental illness in Canadian newspapers. *Canadian Journal of Psychiatry*, 31, 813–816.

De Bruycker, W., & d'Ydewalle, G. (2003). Reading native and foreign language television subtitles in children and adults. In J. Hyönä, R. Radach, & H. Deubel (Eds.), *The mind's eye: Cognitive and applied aspects of eye movement research* (pp. 671–684). Amsterdam: Elsevier Science BV.

Dearing, J., & Rogers, E. (1996). *Agenda setting.* Thousand Oaks, CA: Sage.

Delwiche, A., & Henderson, J. J. (Eds.) (2012). *The participatory cultures handbook.* New York: Routledge Taylor & Francis.

Department of Justice. (1986). Final report of the attorney general's commission on pornography. Nashville, TN: Rutledge Hill Press.

Derrick, J. L., Gabriel, S., & Hugenberg, K. (2009). Social surrogacy: How favored television programs provide the experience of belonging. *Journal of Experimental Social Psychology, 45,* 352–362.

Deshpande, A., Menon, A., Perri, M., & Zinkhan, G. (2004). Direct-to-consumer advertising and its utility in health care decision-making: a consumer perspective. *Journal of Health Communication, 9,* 499–514.

Deshpande, S., & Rundle-Thiele, S. (2011). Segmenting and targeting American university students to promote responsible alcohol use: A case for applying social marketing principles. *Health Marketing Quarterly, 28*(4), 287–303.

Desmond, R. (1987). Adolescents and music lyrics: Implications of a cognitive perspective. *Communication Quarterly, 35*(3), 276–284.

Desmond, R., & Carveth, R. (2007). The effects of advertising on children and adolescents: A meta-analysis. In R. W. Preiss, B. M. Gayle, N. Burrell, M. Allen, & J. Bryant (Eds.), *Mass media effects research: Advances through meta-analysis* (pp. 169–179). Mahwah, NJ: Erlbaum.

Desmond, R., Singer, J. L., & Singer, D. G. (1990). Family mediation: Parental communication patterns and the influences of television on children. In J. Bryant (Ed.), *Television and the American family* (pp. 293–309). Hillsdale, NJ: Erlbaum.

Detenber, B. H., & Reeves, B. (1996). A bio-informational theory of emotion: Motion and image size effects on viewers. *Journal of Communication, 46*(3), 66–84.

Dettwyler, K. A. (1995). Beauty and the breast: The cultural context of breast-feeding in the United States. In P. Stuart-Macadam & K. A. Dettwyler (Eds.), *Breastfeeding: Biocultural perspectives* (pp. 167–215). Hawthorne, NY: De Gruyter.

Devlin, L. P. (1987). Campaign commercials. In A. A. Berger (Ed.), *Television in society* (pp. 17–28). New Brunswick, NJ: Transaction Books.

Diamond, J. (1997, May). Kinship with the stars. *Discover,* pp. 44–49.

Diamond, M., & Uchiyama, A. (1999). Pornography, rape, and sex crimes in Japan. *International Journal of Law and Psychiatry, 22,* 1–11.

Dick, K. (2006). This film is not yet rated. [Documentary film.]

Dietz, P. E., Harry, B., & Hazelwood, R. R. (1986). Detective magazines: Pornography for the sexual sadist? *Journal of Forensic Sciences, 31*(1), 197–211.

DiFranza, J. R., Richards, J. W., Jr., Paulman, P. M., Wolf-Gillespie, N., Fletcher, C., Jaffe, R. D., et al. (1991). RJR Nabisco's cartoon camel promotes Camel cigarettes to children. *Journal of the American Medical Association, 266,* 3149–3152.

DiFranza, J. R., & Tye, J. B. (1990). Who profits from tobacco sales to children? *Journal of the American Medical Association, 263,* 2784–2787.

Dillard, J. P., Weber, K. M., & Vail R. G. (2007). The relationship between the perceived and actual effectiveness of persuasive messages: A meta-analysis with implications for formative campaign research. *Journal of Communication, 57,* 613–631.

Dillman Carpentier, F. R., Brown, J. D., Bertocci, M., Silk, J. S., Forbes, E. E., & Dahl, R. E. (2008). Sad kids, sad media? Applying mood management theory to depressed adolescents' use of media. *Media Psychology, 11,* 143–166.

Dillman Carpentier, F. R., & Potter, R. F. (2007). Effects of music on physiological arousal: Explorations into tempo and genre. *Media Psychology, 10,* 339–363.

Dimmick, J. (2003). *Media competition and coexistence: The theory of the niche.* Mahwah, NJ: Erlbaum.

Dine Young, S. (2012). *Psychology at the movies*. Chichester, UK: Wiley-Blackwell.

Distefan, J. M., Gilpin, E. A., Sargent, J. D., & Pierce, J. P. (1999). Do movie stars encourage adolescents to start smoking? *Preventive Medicine, 28*, 1–11.

Dixon, T. L. (2007). Black criminals and white officers: The effect of racially misrepresenting law breakers and law defenders on television news. *Media Psychology, 10*, 270–291.

Dixon, T. L. (2008a). Crime news and racialized beliefs: Understanding the relationship between local news viewing and perceptions of African Americans and crime. *Journal of Communication, 58*, 106–125.

Dixon, T. L. (2008b). Network news and racial beliefs: Exploring the connection between national television news exposure and stereotypical perceptions of African Americans. *Journal of Communication, 58*, 321–337.

Dixon, T. L., & Linz, D. (2000). Overrepresentation and underrepresentation of African Americans and Latinos as lawbreakers on television news. *Journal of Communication, 50*(2), 131–154.

Dobrow, J. R., & Gidney, C. L. (1998). The good, the bad, and the foreign: The use of dialect in children's animated television. *The Annals of the American Academy of Political and Social Science, 557*, 105–119.

Doherty, T. (1999). *Pre-code Hollywood: Sex, immorality, and insurrection in American cinema 1930–1934*. New York: Columbia University Press.

Dominick, J. R., & Rauch, G. E. (1972). The image of women in network TV commercials. *Journal of Broadcasting, 16*, 259–265.

Donnerstein, E. (1980). Aggressive erotica and violence against women. *Journal of Personality and Social Psychology, 39*, 269–277.

Donnerstein, E., & Berkowitz, L. (1981). Victim reactions in aggressive erotic films as a factor in violence against women. *Journal of Personality and Social Psychology, 41*, 710–724.

Donnerstein, E., Donnerstein, M., & Evans, R. (1975). Erotic stimuli and aggression: Facilitation or inhibition? *Journal of Personality and Social Psychology, 32*, 237–244.

Donnerstein, E., & Hallam, J. (1978). Facilitating effects of erotica on aggression against women. *Journal of Personality and Social Psychology, 36*, 1270–1277.

Donnerstein, E., Linz, D., & Penrod, S. (1987). *The question of pornography: Research findings and policy implications*. New York: Free Press.

Donnerstein, E., & Smith, S. L. (1997). Impact of media violence on children, adolescents, and adults. In S. Kirschner & D. A. Kirschner (Eds.), *Perspectives on psychology and the media* (pp. 29–68). Washington, DC: American Psychological Association.

Donohew, L., Helm, D., & Haas, J. (1989). Drugs and (Len) Bias on the sports page. In L. A. Wenner (Ed.), *Media, sports, and society* (pp. 225–237). Newbury Park, CA: Sage.

Doob, A. N., & Macdonald, G. E. (1979). Television viewing and fear of victimization: Is the relationship causal? *Journal of Personality and Social Psychology, 37*, 170–179.

Douglas, S. J. (1994). *Where the girls are: Growing up female with the mass media*. New York: Times Books.

Douglas, S. J. (1997, October 25). Mixed signals: The messages TV send to girls. *TV Guide*, pp. 24–29.

Douglas, W. (2001). Subversion of the American television family. In J. Bryant, & J. A. Bryant (Eds.), *Television and the American family* (2nd ed., pp. 229–246). Mahwah, NJ: Erlbaum.

Dow, B. J. (2001). Ellen, television, and the politics of gay and lesbian visibility. *Critical Studies in Media Communication, 18*(2), 123–140.

Drabman, R. S., & Thomas, M. H. (1974). Does media violence increase children's toleration of real-life aggression? *Developmental Psychology, 10*, 418–421.

Drabman, R. S., & Thomas, M. H. (1976). Does watching violence on television cause apathy? *Pediatrics*, 57, 329–331.

Dubow, E. F., & Miller, L. S. (1996). Televised violence viewing and aggressive behavior. In T. M. Macbeth (Ed.), *Tuning in to young viewers: Social science perspectives on television* (pp. 117–147). Thousand Oaks, CA: Sage.

Dudo, A., Brossard, D., Shanahan, J., Scheufele, D. A., Morgan. M., & Signorielli, N. (2011). Science on television in the 21st century: Recent trends in portrayals and their contributions to public attitudes toward science. *Communication Research*, 38, 754–777.

Duncan, M. C. (2006). Gender warriors in sport: Women and the media. In A. A. Raney & J. Bryant (Eds.), *Handbook of sports and media* (pp. 231–252). Mahwah, NJ: Erlbaum.

Dunlop, S., Wakefield, M., & Kashima, Y. (2008). Can you feel it? Negative emotion, risk, and narrative in health communication. *Media Psychology*, 11, 52–75.

Dunn, S. W. (2009). Candidate and media agenda setting in the 2005 Virginia gubernatorial election. *Journal of Communication*, 59, 635–652.

Dunwoody, S. (1986). When science writers cover the social sciences. In J. H. Goldstein (Ed.), *Reporting science: The case of aggression* (pp. 67–81). Hillsdale, NJ: Erlbaum.

Duran, R. L., Yousman, B., Walsh, K. M., & Longshore, M. A. (2008). Holistic media education: An assessment of the effectiveness of a college course in media literacy. *Communication Quarterly*, 56(1), 49–68.

Durant, R. H., Rich, M., Emans, S. J., Rome, E. S., Allred, E., & Woods, E. R. (1997). Violence and weapon carrying in music videos: A content analysis. *Archives of Pediatric & Adolescent Medicine*, 151, 443–448.

Durkin, K. (1985a). Television and sex-role acquisition 1: Content. *British Journal of Social Psychology*, 24, 101–113.

Durkin, K. (1985b). Television and sex-role acquisition 2: Effects. *British Journal of Social Psychology*, 24, 191–210.

Dutta, M. J. (2007). Communication about culture and health. *Communication Theory*, 17, 304–328.

Dutta-Bergman, M. J. (2004). The impact of completeness and web use motivation on the credibility of e-health information. *Journal of Communication*, 54, 253–269.

Easterbrook, G. (1989, February 20). Satanic Verses as Muslims see it. p. *Manhattan Mercury*, A5.

Eastin, M. S., & Griffiths, R. P. (2006). Beyond the shooter game: Examining presence and hostile outcomes among male game players. *Communication Research*, 33, 448–466.

Eastman, H., & Liss, M. (1980). Ethnicity and children's preferences. *Journalism Quarterly*, 57(2), 277–280.

Eastman, S. T., & Billings, A. C. (2000). Sportscasting and sports reporting: The power of gender bias. *Journal of Sport and Social Issues*, 23, 192–213.

Eccles, A., Marshall, W. L., & Barbaree, H. E. (1988). The vulnerability of erectile measures to repeated assessments. *Behavior Research and Therapy*, 26, 179–183.

Edelstein, A. S. (1993). Thinking about the criterion variable in agenda-setting research. *Journal of Communication*, 43(2), 85–99.

Edy, J. A., & Snidow, S. M. (2011). Making news necessary: How journalism resists alternative media's challenge. *Journal of Communication*, 61, 816–834.

Ehrenreich, B. (2006). *Dancing in the streets: A history of collective joy*. New York: Metropolitan Books.

Einsiedel, E. F. (1988). The British, Canadian, and U.S. pornography commissions and their use of social science research. *Journal of Communication*, 38(2), 108–121.

Eisenberg, D. (2002, September 2). It's an ad, ad, ad, ad world. *Time*, pp. 38–41.

Elliott, S. (2002a, April 16a). Campaign spotlight: State Farm aims for where you live. *The New York Times*. Retrieved April 16, 2002, from http://ads.nyt. com/ia.ad/ia-court08/courttv2.html/4-16-02

Elliott, S. (2002b, May 14). The ad within the ad. *The New York Times*. Retrieved May 14, 2002, from http://www.ads.nyt.com/ia.ad

Ely, M. P. (2001). *The adventures of Amos 'n' Andy: A social history of an American phenomenon*. Charlottesville, VA: University of Virginia Press.

Englis, B. G. (1994). The role of affect in political advertising: Voter emotional responses to the nonverbal behavior of politicians. In E. M. Clark, T. C. Brock, & D. W. Stewart (Eds.), *Attention, attitude, and affect in response to advertising* (pp. 223–247). Hillsdale, NJ: Erlbaum.

Entman, R. (1990). Modern racism and the images of Blacks in local television news. *Critical Studies in Mass Communication, 7*, 332–345.

Entman, R. (1991). Framing U.S. coverage of international news: Contrasts in the narratives of the KAL and Iran Air incidents. *Journal of Communication, 42*(1), 6–27.

Entman, R. (1992). Blacks in the news: Television, modern racism, and cultural change. *Journalism Quarterly, 69*, 341–361.

Entman, R. (1993). Framing: Toward clarification of a fractured paradigm. *Journal of Communication, 43*(4), 51–58.

Entman, R. (1994a). Representation and reality in the portrayal of Blacks on network television news. *Journalism Quarterly, 71*, 509–520.

Entman, R. (1994b). African Americans according to TV news. *Media Studies Journal, 8*, 29–38.

Eron, L. D., & Huesmann, L. R. (1984). The control of aggressive behavior by changes in attitudes, values, and the conditions of learning. In *Advances in the study of aggression* (pp. 139–171). Orlando, FL: Academic Press.

Eron, L. D., Huesmann, L. R., Lefkowitz, M. M., & Walder, L. O. (1972). Does television violence cause aggression? *American Psychologist, 27*, 253–263.

Esslin, M. (1982). *The age of television*. San Francisco: Freeman.

Eveland, W. P., Jr., Cortese, J., Park, H., & Dunwoody, S. (2004). How web site organization influences free recall, factual knowledge, and knowledge structure density. *Human Communication Research, 30*, 208–233.

Eveland, W. P., Jr., & Dunwoody, S. (2001). User control and structural isomorphism or disorientation and cognitive load? Learning from the web versus print. *Communication Research, 28*, 48–78.

Eveland, W. P., Jr., & Dunwoody, S. (2002). An investigation of elaboration and selective scanning as mediators of learning from the Web versus print. *Journal of Broadcasting & Electronic Media, 46*, 34–53.

Eveland, W. P., Jr., Seo, M., & Marton, K. (2002). Learning from the news in campaign 2000: An experimental comparison of TV news, newspapers, and online news. *Media Psychology, 4*, 353–378.

Everts, S. (2012, August 3). How advertisers convinced Americans they smelled bad. *Smithsonian*. Retrieved from http://www.smithsonianmag.com

Ex, C. T. G. M., Janssens, J. M. A. M., & Korzilius, H. P. L. M. (2002). Young females' images of motherhood in relation to television viewing. *Journal of Communication, 52*(4), 955–971.

Eyal, K., & Cohen, J. (2006). When good Friends say goodbye: A parasocial breakup study. *Journal of Broadcasting and Electronic Media, 50*, 502–523.

Eysenck, H. J., & Nias, N. K. B. (1978). *Sex, violence and the media*. New York: Harper.

Faber, R. J. (1992). Advances in political advertising research: A progression from if to when. *Journal of Current Issues and Research in Advertising, 14*(2), 1–18.

Fabes, R. A., & Strouse, J. S. (1984). Youth's perception of models of sexuality: Implications for sexuality education. *Journal of Sex Education and Therapy, 10*, 33–37.

Fabes, R. A., & Strouse, J. S. (1987). Perceptions of responsible and irresponsible models of sexuality: A correlational study. *Journal of Sex Research, 23*, 70–84.

Fabrikant, G. (2004, September 23). CBS is fined $550,000 for Super Bowl incident. *New York Times*.

Facebook (2012, June 10). Newsroom key facts. Retrieved from http://newsroom.fb.com/content/default.aspx?NewsAreaId=22

Fahy, T. (Ed.) (2010). *The philosophy of horror*. Lexington, KY: University of Kentucky Press.

Farhi, P. (2001, June). Nightly news blues. *American Journalism Review*, 32–37.

Farquhar, J. W., Fortmann, S. P., Flora, J. A., Taylor, B., Haskell, W. L., Williams, P. T., et al. (1990). Effects of communitywide education on cardiovascular disease risk factors: The Stanford five-city project. *Journal of the American Medical Association*, 264, 359–365.

Farrar, K. M., Krcmar, M., & Nowak, K. L. (2006). Contextual features of violent video games, mental models, and aggression. *Journal of Communication*, 56, 387–405.

Feaster, F., & Wood, B. (1999). *Forbidden fruit: The golden age of the exploitation film*. Baltimore: Midnight Marquee Press.

Feldman, L. (2011). The effects of journalist opinionation on learning from the news. *Journal of Communication*, 61, 1183–1201.

Ferguson, D. A., & Perse, E. M. (2000). The World Wide Web as a functional alternative to television. *Journal of Broadcasting & Electronic Media*, 37, 31–47.

Ferrante, C. L., Haynes, A. M., & Kingsley, S. M. (1988). Image of women in television advertising. *Journal of Broadcasting & Electronic Media*, 32, 231–237.

Ferree, M. C. (2003). Women and the web: Cybersex activity and implications. *Sexual and Relationship Therapy*, 18, 385–393.

Ferretti, F. (1970, February 9). *Sesame Street* plan may alter public-TV form. *New York Times*.

Ferris, A. L., Smith, S. W., Greenberg, B. S., & Smith, S. L. (2007). The content of reality dating shows and viewer perceptions of dating. *Journal of Communication*, 57, 490–510.

Ferris, T. (1997, April 4). The risks and rewards of popularizing science. *The Chronicle of Higher Education*, p. 43.

Feshbach, N. D. (1988). Television and the development of empathy. In S. Oskamp (Ed.), *Television as a social issue* (pp. 261–269). Newbury Park, CA: Sage.

Feshbach, N. D., & Feshbach, S. (1997). Children's empathy and the media: Realizing the potential of television. In S. Kirschner & D. A. Kirschner (Eds.), *Perspectives on psychology and the media* (pp. 3–27). Washington, DC: American Psychological Association.

Feshbach, S. (1955). The drive-reducing function of fantasy behavior. *Journal of Abnormal and Social Psychology*, 50, 3–11.

Feshbach, S., & Singer, R. (1971). *Television and aggression*. San Francisco: Jossey-Bass.

Festinger, L. (1957). *A theory of cognitive dissonance*. Stanford: Stanford University Press.

Fidler, A. E., Zack, E., & Barr, R. (2010). Television viewing patterns in 6- to 18-month olds: The role of caregiver-infant interactional quality. *Infancy*, 15, 176–196.

Fine, C. (2010). *Delusions of gender: How our minds, society, and neurosexism create difference*. New York: W.W. Norton.

Fink, J. S., & Kensicki, L. J. (2002). An imperceptible difference: Visual and textual constructions of femininity in *Sports Illustrated* and *Sports Illustrated for Women*. *Mass Communication & Society*, 5, 317–339.

Fisch, S. M. (2002). Vast wasteland or vast opportunity: Effects of educational television on children's academic knowledge, skills, and attitudes. In J. Bryant & D. Zillmann (Eds.), *Media effects* (pp. 397–426). Mahwah, NJ: Erlbaum.

Fisch, S. M. (2004). *Children's learning from educational television: Sesame Street and beyond*. Mahwah, NJ: Erlbaum.

Fisch, S. M., & Truglio, R. T. (Eds.) (2000). *"G" is for growing: Thirty years of research on children and "Sesame Street."* Mahwah, NJ: Erlbaum.

Fisch, S. M., Truglio, R. T., & Cole, C. F. (1999). The impact of *Sesame Street* on preschool children: A review and synthesis of 30 years' research. *Media Psychology*, 1, 165–190.

Fischer, P., Greitemeyer, T., Kastenmuller, A., Vogrincic, C., & Sauer, A. (2011). The effects of risk-glorifying media exposure on risk-positive cognitions, emotions, and behaviors: A meta-analytic review. *Psychological Bulletin*, 137, 367–390.

Fischer, P. M., Schwartz, M. P., Richards, J. W., Goldstein, A. O., & Rojas, T. H. (1991). Brand logo recognition by children aged 3 to 6 years. *Journal of the American Medical Association*, 266, 3145–3148.

Fischhoff, B., Gonzalez, R. M., Lerner, J. S., & Small, D. A. (2005). Evolving judgments of terror risk: Foresight, hindsight, and emotion. *Journal of Experimental Psychology: Applied*, 11, 124–139.

Fitch, M., Huston, A. C., & Wright, J. C. (1993). From television forms to genre schemata: Children's perceptions of television reality. In G. L. Berry & J. K. Asamen (Eds.), *Children and television: Images in a changing sociocultural world* (pp. 38–52). Newbury Park, CA: Sage.

Flay, B. R., & Burton, D. (1990). Effective mass communication strategies for health campaigns. In C. Atkin & L. Wallack (Eds.), *Mass communication and public health* (pp. 129–146). Newbury Park, CA: Sage.

Fleming, M. J., & Rickwood, D. J. (2001). Effects of violent versus nonviolent video games on children's arousal, aggressive mood, and positive mood. *Journal of Applied Social Psychology*, 31(10), 2047–2071.

Flora, J. A., & Maibach, E. W. (1990). Cognitive responses to AIDS information: The effects of issue involvement and message appeal. *Communication Research*, 17, 759–774.

Fonda, D. (2003, June 30). Baby, you can drive my car. *Time*, pp. 46–48.

Fonda, D. (2004, June 7). Food ads: Kill the messenger? *Time*, p. 87.

Fore, W. F. (1987). *Television and religion: The shaping of faith, values, and culture*. Minneapolis, MN: Augsburg.

Fox, J. R. (2004). A signal detection analysis of audio/video redundancy effects in television news video. *Communication Research*, 31, 524–536.

Fox, J. R., Angelini, J. R., & Goble, C. (2005). Hype versus substance in network television coverage of Presidential election campaigns. *Journalism & Mass Communication Quarterly*, 82, 97–109.

Fox, J. R., Lang, A., Chung, Y., Lee, S., Schwartz, N., & Potter, D. (2004). Picture this: Effects of graphics on the processing of television news. *Journal of Broadcasting & Electronic Media*, 48, 646–674.

Frank, T. (2012, April). It's a rich man's world: How billionaire backers pick America's candidates. *Harper's Magazine*, pp. 22–27.

Freimuth, V. S., Hammond, S. L., Edgar, T., & Monahan, J. L. (1990). Reaching those at risk: A content-analytic study of AIDS PSAs. *Communication Research*, 17, 775–791.

Fried, C. B. (1996). Bad rap for rap: Bias in reactions to music lyrics. *Journal of Applied Social Psychology*, 26, 2135–2146.

Fried, C. B. (1999). Who's afraid of rap: Differential reactions to music lyrics. *Journal of Applied Social Psychology*, 29, 705–721.

Friedman, S. M., Dunwoody, S., & Rogers, C. L. (Eds.) (1999). *Communicating uncertainty: Media coverage of new and controversial science*. Mahwah, NJ: Erlbaum.

Friedman, T. L. (2010, November 18). When the next crazy lie surfaces, let's not repeat it. *Manhattan Mercury*, p. A7. (*New York Times* wire.)

Friend in need (1998, May). *World Press Review*, p. 32.

Frith, K., Shaw, P., & Cheng, H. (2005). The construction of beauty: A cross-cultural analysis of women's magazine advertising. *Journal of Communication*, 55, 56–70.

Fuchs, D. A. (1966). Election-day radio-television and Western voting. *Public Opinion Quarterly*, 30, 226–236.

Fujioka, Y. (1999). Television portrayals and African American stereotypes: Examination of television effects when direct contact is lacking. *Journalism & Mass Communication Quarterly*, 76, 52–75.

Fujioka, Y. (2005a). Black media images as a perceived threat to African American ethnic identity: Coping responses, perceived public perception, and attitudes toward affirmative action. *Journal of Broadcasting & Electronic Media*, 49, 450–468.

Fujioka, Y. (2005b). Emotional TV viewing and minority audiences: How Mexican Americans process and evaluate TV news about in-group members. *Communication Research*, 32, 566–593.

Fullerton, L., & Rarey, M. (2012). Virtual materiality: Collectors and collection in the Brazilian music blogosphere. *Communication, Culture, & Critique*, 5, 1–19.

Funabiki, J. (1992). Asian invasion clichés recall wartime propaganda. *Extra!* 5(5), 13–14.

Furnham, A., Bergland, J., & Gunter, B. (2002). Memory for television advertisements as a function of advertisement–programme congruity. *Applied Cognitive Psychology*, 16, 525–545.

Furnham, A., Gunter, B., & Walsh, D. (1998). Effects of programme context on memory of humorous television commercials. *Applied Cognitive Psychology*, 12, 555–567.

Fussell, J. A. (2000, September 21). Horror show. *Kansas City Star*, p. E1.

Gabbard, G. O., & Gabbard, K. (1999). *Psychiatry and the cinema* (2nd ed.). New York: Psychiatric Press.

Galician, M.-L. (2004). *Sex, love, and romance in the mass media: Analysis and criticism of unrealistic portrayals and their influence*. Mahwah, NJ: Erlbaum.

Galician, M.-L. (2007). "Dis-illusioning" as discovery: The research basis and media literacy applications of Dr. Fun's Mass Media Love Quiz and Dr. Galician's Prescriptions. In M.-L. Galician & D. L. Merskin (Eds.), *Critical thinking about sex, love, and romance in the mass media* (pp. 1–20). Mahwah, NJ: Erlbaum.

Gamson, J. (1995, Fall). Do ask, do tell: Freak talk on TV. *The American Prospect*.

Gan, S. L., Zillmann, D., & Mitrook, M. (1997). Stereotyping effect of black women's sexual rap on white audiences. *Basic and Applied Social Psychology*, 19(3), 381–399.

Ganahl, D. J., Prinsen, T. J., & Netzley, S. B. (2003). A content analysis of prime time commercials: A contextual framework of gender representation. *Sex Roles*, 49, 545–551.

Ganley, G. D. (1992). *The exploding political power of personal media*. Norwood, NJ: Ablex.

Gantz, W. (2001). Conflicts and resolution strategies associated with television in marital life. In J. Bryant & J. A. Bryant (Eds.), *Television and the American family* (2nd ed., pp. 289–316). Mahwah, NJ: Erlbaum.

Gantz, W., Wang, Z., & Bradley, S. D. (2006). Televised NFL games, the family, and domestic violence. In A. A. Raney & J. Bryant (Eds.), *Handbook of sports and media* (pp. 365–381). Mahwah, NJ: Erlbaum.

Gardikiotis, A. (2008). Group distinctiveness, political identification, and the third-person effect: Perceptions of a political campaign in the 2004 Greek national election. *Media Psychology*, 11, 331–354.

Gardner, D. (2008). *The science of fear: Why we fear the things we shouldn't—and put ourselves in greater danger*. New York: Dutton.

Gardner, D. M., & Leonard, N. H. (1990). Research in deceptive and corrective advertising: Progress to date and impact on public policy. *Current Issues and Research in Advertising*, 12, 275–309.

Gardner, M. P., & Houston, M. J. (1986). The effects of verbal and visual components of retail communications. *Journal of Retailing*, 62, 64–78.

Garramone, G. M. (1984). Voter responses to negative political ads. *Journalism Quarterly*, 61(2), 250–259.

Garramone, G. M. (1985). Effects of negative political advertising: The role of sponsor and rebuttal. *Journal of Broadcasting and Electronic Media*, 29(2), 147–159.

Garramone, G. M., Atkin, C. K., Pinkleton, B. E., & Cole, R. T. (1990). Effects of negative political advertising on the political process. *Journal of Broadcasting and Electronic Media*, 34, 299–311.

Garramone, G. M., Steele, M. E., & Pinkleton, B. (1991). The role of cognitive schemata in determining candidate characteristic effects. In F. Biocca (Ed.), *Television and political advertising: Psychological processes* (Vol. 1, pp. 311–328). Hillsdale, NJ: Erlbaum.

Garry, M., Strange, D., Bernstein, D. M., & Kinzett, T. (2007). Photographs can distort memory for the news. *Applied Cognitive Psychology*, 21, 995–1004.

Geen, R. G. (1994). Television and aggression: Recent developments in research and theory. In D. Zillmann, J. Bryant, & A. C. Huston (Eds.), *Media, children, and the family: Social scientific, psychodynamic, and clinical perspectives* (pp. 151–162). Hillsdale, NJ: Erlbaum.

Geen, R. G., & Quanty, M. B. (1977). The catharsis of aggression: An evaluation of a hypothesis. In L. Berkowitz (Ed.), *Advances in experimental social psychology* (Vol. 10, pp. 1–37). New York: Academic Press.

Geer, J. G. (2006). *In defense of negativity: Attack ads in Presidential campaigns*. Chicago: University of Chicago Press.

Geiger, S. F., & Reeves, B. (1991). The effects of visual structure and content emphasis on the evaluation and memory for political candidates. In F. Biocca (Ed.), *Television and political advertising: Psychological processes* (Vol. 1). Hillsdale, NJ: Erlbaum.

Geiger, S., & Reeves, B. (1993a). The effects of scene changes and semantic relatedness on attention to television. *Communication Research*, 20, 155–175.

Geiger, S., & Reeves, B. (1993b). We interrupt this program . . . Attention for television sequences. *Human Communication Research*, 19, 368–387.

Geiogamah, H., & Pavel, D. M. (1993). Developing television for American Indian and Alaska native children in the late 20th century. In G. L. Berry & J. K. Asamen (Eds.), *Children & television* (pp. 191–204). Newbury Park, CA: Sage.

Geis, F., Brown, V., Jennings, J., & Porter, N. (1984). TV commercials as achievement scripts for women. *Sex Roles*, 10(7/8), 513–525.

Gelb, B. D., & Zinkhan, G. M. (1985). The effect of repetition on humor in a radio advertising study. *Journal of Advertising*, 14(4), 13–20.

Gerbner, G. (1997). Gender and age in prime-time television. In S. Kirschner & D. A. Kirschner (Eds.), *Perspectives on psychology and the media* (pp. 69–94). Washington, DC: American Psychological Association.

Gerbner, G., Gross, L., Morgan, M., & Signorielli, N. (1981). Health and medicine on television. *New England Journal of Medicine*, 305(15), 901–904.

Gerbner, G., Gross, L., Morgan, M., & Signorielli, N. (1982). Charting the mainstream: Television's contributions to political orientations. *Journal of Communication*, 32(2), 100–127.

Gerbner, G., Gross, L., Morgan, M., & Signorielli, N. (1984). Political correlates of television viewing. *Public Opinion Quarterly*, 48, 283–300.

Gerbner, G., Gross, L., Morgan, M., Signorielli, N., & Shanahan, J. (2002). Growing up with television: Cultivation processes. In J. Bryant & D. Zillmann (Eds.), *Media effects: Advances in theory and research* (2nd ed., pp. 43–67). Mahwah, NJ: Erlbaum.

Gerbner, G., Gross, L., Signorielli, N., & Morgan, M. (1986). *Television's mean world: Violence profile, No. 14–15*. Philadelphia: Annenberg School of Communication, University of Pennsylvania.

Gerbner, G., & Signorielli, N. (1979). *Women and minorities in television drama (1969–1978)*. Philadelphia: Annenberg School of Communication, University of Pennsylvania.

Gernsbacher, M. A., Dawson, M., & Goldsmith, H. H. (2005). Three reasons not to believe in an autism epidemic. *Current Directions in Psychological Science*, 14, 55–58.

Gettas, G. J. (1990). The globalization of Sesame Street: A producer's perspective. *Educational Technology Research and Development*, 38(4), 55–63.

Ghosh, B. (2012, May 21). The god of big things. *Time*, pp. 40–45.

Gibbons, J. A., Lukowski, A. F., & Walker, W. R. (2005). Exposure increases the believability of unbelievable news headlines via elaborate cognitive processing. *Media Psychology*, 7, 273–300.

Gibbons, J. A., Taylor, C., & Phillips, J. (2005). Gender and racial stereotypes in the mass media. In W. R. Walker & D. J. Herrmann (Eds.), *Cognitive technology: Essays on the transformation of thought and society* (pp. 149–171). Jefferson, NC: McFarland.

Gibson, R., Callison, C., & Zillmann, D. (2011). Quantitative literacy and affective reactivity in processing statistical information and case histories in the news. *Media Psychology*, 14, 96–120.

Gibson, B., & Maurer, J. (2000). Cigarette smoking in the movies: The influence of product placement on attitudes toward smoking and smokers. *Journal of Applied Social Psychology*, 30, 1457–1473.

Gibson, R., & Zillmann, D. (1994). Exaggerated versus representative exemplification in news reports: Perception of issues and personal consequences. *Communication Research*, 21, 603–624.

Gikow, L. A. (2009). *Sesame Street: A celebration—40 years of life on the street*. New York: Black Dog & Leventhal.

Gilboa, E. (2002). Global communication and foreign policy. *Journal of Communication*, 52, 731–748.

Giles, D. (2002). Parasocial interaction: A review of the literature and a model for future research. *Media Psychology*, 4, 279–305.

Gillath, O., McCall, C., Shaver, P. R., & Blascovich, J. (2008). What can virtual reality teach us about prosocial tendencies in real and virtual environments? *Media Psychology*, 11, 259–282.

Gilly, M. C. (1988). Sex roles in advertising: A comparison of television advertisements in Australia, Mexico, and the United States. *Journal of Marketing*, 52, 75–85.

Givens, S. M. B., & Monahan, J. L. (2005). Priming mammies, jezebels, and other controlling images: An examination of the influence of mediated stereotypes on perceptions of an African American woman. *Media Psychology*, 7, 87–106.

Glantz, S. A., Mitchell, S., Titus, K., Polansky, J. R., Kaufmann, R. B., & Bauer, U. E. (2011, July 13). MMWR, 60, 909–913. Retrieved from http://www.cdc.gov/mmwr

Glassner, B. (1999). *The culture of fear: Why Americans are afraid of the wrong things*. New York: Basic Books.

Glassner, B. (2010, January 22). Still fearful after all these years. *The Chronicle Review*, pp. B11–B12.

Going Hollywood: CDC keeps medical TV real (2007, April 20). Associated Press. Retrieved from http://www.msnbc.msn.com

Gold, J., & Gold, I. (2012). The "Truman Show" delusion: Psychosis in the global village. *Cognitive Neuropsychiatry*.

Goldberg, B. (2002). *A CBS insider exposes how the media distort the news*. Washington, DC: Regnery.

Goldberg, M. (1988, February 20). Take two doses for Kildare and Casey and don't call me in the morning. *TV Guide*, pp. 12–13.

Goldberg, M. E. (1995). Social marketing: Are we fiddling while Rome burns? *Journal of Consumer Psychology*, 4, 347–370.

Goldenberg, J. L., Goplen, J., Cox, C. R., & Arndt, J. (2007). "Viewing" pregnancy as an existential threat: The effects of creatureliness on reactions to media depictions of the pregnant body. *Media Psychology*, 10, 211–230.

Goldstein, J. H. (1998). Why we watch. In J. H. Goldstein (Ed.), *Why we watch: The attractions of violent entertainment* (pp. 212–226). New York: Oxford University Press.

Goldstein, K., & Freedman, P. (2002). Campaign advertising and voter turnout: New evidence for a stimulation effect. *Journal of Politics*, 64, 721–740.

Goldstein, S., & Ibaraki, T. (1983). Japan: Aggression and aggression control in Japanese society. In A. Goldstein & M. Segall (Eds.), *Aggression in global perspective*. New York: Pergamon Press.

Goldstein, W. (1998, April 10). Bad history is bad for a culture. *The Chronicle of Higher Education*, 44, p. A64.

Gonzales, A. L., & Hancock, J. T. (2008). Identity shifts in computer-mediated environments. *Media Psychology*, 11, 167–185.

González-Bailón, S., Banchs, R. E., & Kaltenbrunner, A. (2012). Emotions, public opinion, and U.S. Presidential approval rates. *Human Communication Research*, 38, 121–143.

Goodin, S. M., Van Denburg, A., Murnen, S. K., & Smolak, L. (2011). "Putting on" sexiness: A content analysis of the presence of sexualizing characteristics in girls' clothing. *Sex Roles*, 65, 1–12.

Goodman, E. (1999, June 1). Our culture can make any woman anywhere feel insecure. *Manhattan Mercury*, p. A5.

Gorn, G. I., Goldberg, M. E., & Kanungo, R. N. (1976). The role of educational television in changing intergroup attitudes of children. *Child Development*, 47, 277–280.

Gornstein, L. (1997, April 13). Advertising finding its way into movies. *Manhattan Mercury*, p. C5.

Grabe, M. E., Lombard, M., Reich, R. D., Bracken, C. C., & Ditton, T. B. (1999). The role of screen size in viewer experiences of media content. *Visual Communication Quarterly*, 6(2), 4–9.

Graber, D. A. (1990). Seeing is remembering: How visuals contribute to learning from television news. *Journal of Communication*, 40(3), 134–155.

Grainger, A., Newman, J. I., & Andrews, D. L. (2006). Sport, the media, and the construction of race. In A. A. Raney & J. Bryant (Eds.), *Handbook of sports and media* (pp. 447–467). Mahwah, NJ: Erlbaum.

Grant, B. K. (Ed.). (1996). *The dread of difference: Gender and the horror film*. Austin, TX: University of Texas Press.

Graves, S. B. (1980). Psychological effects of black portrayals on television. In S. B. Withey & R. P. Abeles (Eds.), *Television and social behavior* (pp. 259–289). Hillsdale, NJ: Erlbaum.

Graves, S. B. (1996). Diversity on television. In T. M. Macbeth (Ed.), *Tuning in to young viewers: Social science perspectives on television* (pp. 61–86). Thousand Oaks, CA: Sage.

Gray, P. (1998, January 19). Paradise found. *Time*, pp. 63–68.

Green, M. C., & Brock. T. C. (2000). The role of transportation in the persuasiveness of public narratives. *Journal of Personality and Social Psychology*, 79, 701–721.

Green, M. C., & Brock, T. C. (2002). In the mind's eye: Transportation-imagery model of narrative persuasion. In M. C. Green, J. J. Strange, & T. C. Brock (Eds.), *Narrative impact: Social and cognitive foundations* (pp. 315–341). Mahwah, NJ: Erlbaum.

Green, M. C., Brock. T. C., & Kaufman, G. F. (2004). Understanding media enjoyment: The role of transportation into narrative worlds. *Communication Theory*, 14, 341–327.

Green, M. C., Hilken, J., Friedmann, H., Grossman, K., Gasiewski, J., Adler, R., et al. (2005). Communication via instant messenger: Short- and long-term effects. *Journal of Applied Social Psychology*, 35, 445–462.

Green, M., Kass, S., Carrey, J., Herzig, B., Feeney, R., & Sabini, J. (2008). Transportation across media: Repeated exposure to print and media. *Media Psychology*, 11, 512–539.

Greenberg, B. S. (1982). Television and role socialization. In D. Pearl, L. Bouthilet, & J. Lazar (Eds.), *Television and behavior: Ten years of scientific progress and implications for the eighties: Vol. 2. Technical reviews*. Rockville, MD: National Institute of Mental Health.

Greenberg, B. S. (1988). Some uncommon television images and the Drench Hypothesis. In S. Oskamp (Ed.), *Television as a social issue* (pp. 88–102). Newbury Park, CA: Sage.

Greenberg, B. S., & Atkin, C. (1982). Learning about minorities from television: A research agenda. In G. Berry & C. Mitchell-Kernan (Eds.), *Television and the socialization of the minority child* (pp. 215–243). New York: Academic Press.

Greenberg, B. S., & Brand, J. E. (1993). Television news and advertising in schools: The Channel One controversy. *Journal of Communication*, 43(1), 143–151.

Greenberg, B. S., & Brand, J. E. (1994). Minorities and the mass media: 1970s to 1990s. In J. Bryant & D. Zillmann (Eds.), *Media effects: Advances in theory and research* (pp. 273–314). Hillsdale, NJ: Erlbaum.

Greenberg, B. S., Brown, J. D., & Buerkel-Rothfuss, N. L. (Eds.). (1993). *Media, sex, and the adolescent*. Cresskill NJ: Hampton Press.

Greenberg, B. S., & Busselle, R. W. (1996). Soap operas and sexual activity: A decade later. *Journal of Communication*, 46(4), 153–160.

Greenberg, B. S., & Gantz, W. (Eds.). (1993). *Desert Storm and the mass media*. Cresskill, NJ: Hampton Press.

Greenberg, B. S., & Hofschire, L. (2000). Sex on entertainment television. In D. Zillmann & P. Vorderer (Eds.), *Media entertainment: The psychology of its appeal* (pp. 93–111). Mahwah, NJ: Erlbaum.

Greenberg, B. S., Ku, L., & Li, H. (1992). Parental mediation of children's mass media behaviors in China, Japan, Korea, Taiwan, and the United States. In F. Korzenny & S. Ting-Toomey (Eds.), *Mass media effects across cultures* (pp. 150–172). Newbury Park, CA: Sage.

Greenberg, B. S., Mastro, D., & Brand, J. E. (2002). Minorities and the mass media: Television into the 21st century. In J. Bryant & D. Zillmann (Eds.), *Media effects: Advances in theory and research* (2nd ed., pp. 333–351). Mahwah, NJ: Erlbaum.

Greenberg, B. S., Neuendorf, K., Buerkel-Rothfuss, N., & Henderson, L. (1982). The soaps: What's on and who cares? *Journal of Broadcasting*, 26(2), 519–535.

Greene, E., & Wade, R. (1987). Of private talk and public print: General pre-trial publicity and juror decision-making. *Applied Cognitive Psychology*, 1, 1–13.

Greene, K., Krcmar, M., Rubin, D. L., Walters, L. H., & Hale, J. L. (2002). Elaboration in processing adolescent health messages: The impact of egocentrism and sensation seeking on message processing. *Journal of Communication*, 52, 812–831.

Greenfield, P. M. (1984). *Mind and media*. Cambridge, MA: Harvard University Press.

Greenfield, P. M., & Beagles-Roos, J. (1988). Radio vs. television: The cognitive impact on different socioeconomic and ethnic groups. *Journal of Communication*, 38(2), 71–92.

Greenfield, P. M., Bruzzone, L., Koyamatsu, K., Satuloff, W., Nixon, K., Brodie, M., et al. (1987). What is rock music doing to the minds of our youth? A first experimental look at the effects of rock music lyrics and music videos. *Journal of Early Adolescence*, 7, 315–330.

Greenfield, P. M., Farrar, D., & Beagles-Roos, J. (1986). Is the medium the message? An experimental comparison of the effects of radio and television on imagination. *Journal of Applied Developmental Psychology*, 7, 201–218.

Greenfield, P. M., Yut, E., Chung, M., Land, D., Kreider, H., Pantoja, M., et al. (1993). The program-length commercial: A study of the effects of television/toy tie-ins on imaginative play. In G. L. Berry & J. K. Asamen (Eds.), *Children and television: Images in a changing sociocultural world* (pp. 53–72). Newbury Park, CA: Sage.

Greenwald, A. G., Spangenberg, E. R., Pratkanis, A. R., & Eskenazi, J. (1991). Double-blind tests of subliminal self-help audiotapes. *Psychological Science, 2,* 119–122.

Gregory, S. (2003a, May 19). Lacrosse at 11! *Time.*

Gregory, S. (2003b, June 9). Taking it inside. *Time.*

Greitemeyer, T. (2009a). Effects of songs with prosocial lyrics on prosocial thoughts, affect, and behavior. *Journal of Experimental Social Psychology, 45,* 186–190.

Greitemeyer, T. (2009b). Effects of songs with prosocial lyrics on prosocial behavior: Further evidence and a mediating mechanism. *Personality and Social Psychology Bulletin, 35,* 1500–1511.

Greitemeyer, T. (2011a). Exposure to music with prosocial lyrics reduces aggression: First evidence and test of the underlying mechanism. *Journal of Experimental Social Psychology, 47,* 28–36.

Greitemeyer, T. (2011b). Effects of prosocial media on social behavior: When and why does media exposure affect helping and aggression? *Current Directions in Psychological Science, 20,* 251–255.

Greitemeyer, T., & Osswald, S. (2010). Effects of prosocial videogames on prosocial behavior. *Journal of Personality and Social Psychology, 98*(2), 211–221.

Greitemeyer, T., & Osswald, S. (2011). Playing prosocial video games increases the accessibility of prosocial thoughts. *The Journal of Social Psychology, 151*(2), 121–128.

Greitemeyer, T., Osswald, S., & Brauer, M. (2010). Playing prosocial video games increases empathy and decreases schadenfreude. *Emotion, 10*(2), 796–802.

Griffin-Shelley, E. (2003). The Internet and sexuality: A literature review—1983–2002. *Sexual and Relationship Therapy, 18,* 354–370.

Griffiths, M. (1999). Violent video games and aggression: A review of the literature. *Aggression and Violent Behavior, 4*(2), 203–212.

Grimes, T. (1990). Audio-video correspondence and its role in attention and memory. *Educational Technology, Research, and Development, 38,* 15–25.

Grimes, T. (1991). Mild auditory-visual dissonance in television news may exceed viewer attentional capacity. *Human Communication Research, 17,* 268–298.

Grimes, T., Anderson, J. A., & Bergen., L. (2008). *Media violence and aggression: Science and ideology.* Thousand Oaks, CA: Sage.

Grodal, T. (2000). Video games and the pleasures of control. In D. Zillmann & P. Vorderer (Eds.), *Media entertainment: The psychology of its appeal* (pp. 197–213). Mahwah, NJ: Erlbaum.

Gross, K., Brewer, P. R., & Aday, S. (2009). Confidence in government and emotional responses to terrorism after September 11, 2001. *American Politics Research, 37,* 107–128.

Gross, L. (1984). The cultivation of intolerance: Television, blacks, and gays. In G. Melischek, K. E. Rosengren, & J. Stappers (Eds.), *Cultural indicators: An international symposium* (pp. 345–364). Vienna: Austrian Academy of Sciences.

Grossman, D. (1996). *On killing: The psychological cost of learning to kill in war and society.* New York: Little Brown.

Grossman, D., & DeGaetano, G. (1999). *Stop teaching our kids to kill.* New York: Crown.

Gubash, C. (2002). U.S. woos Arabs with pop music. Retrieved July 25, 2002 http:/ www.msnbc.com/news/784495.asp

Gunter, B. (1986). *Television and sex-role stereotyping.* London: Libbey.

Gunter, B. (2001). *Media sex: What are the issues?* Mahwah, NJ: Erlbaum.

Gunter, B. (2003). *News and the net.* Mahwah, NJ: Erlbaum.

Gunter, B. (2006). Sport, violence, and the media. In A. A. Raney & J. Bryant (Eds.), *Handbook of sports and media* (pp. 353–364). Mahwah, NJ: Erlbaum.

Gunter, B., & Svennevig, M. (1987). *Behind and in front of the screen: Television's involvement with family life.* London: Libbey.

Gunter, B., Furnham, A., & Griffiths, S. (2000). Children's memory for news: A comparison of three presentation media. *Media Psychology, 2,* 119–146.

Gunter, B., Furnham, A., & Pappa, E. (2005). Effects of television violence on memory for violent and nonviolent advertising. *Journal of Applied Social Psychology, 35,* 1680–1697.

Gunther, A. C. (1991). What we think others think: Cause and consequence in the third-person effect. *Communication Research, 18,* 355–372.

Gunther, A. C. (1995). Overrating the X-rating: The third-person perception and support for censorship of pornography. *Journal of Communication, 45*(1), 27–38.

Gunther, A. C., & Storey, J. D. (2003). The influence of presumed influence. *Journal of Communication, 53,* 199–215.

Gunther, A. C., & Thorson, E. (1992). Perceived persuasive effects of product commercials and public-service announcements: Third-person effects in new domains. *Communication Research, 19,* 574–596.

Gunther, A. C., Bolt, D., Borzekowski, D. L. G., Liebhart, J. L., & Dillard, J. P. (2006). Presumed influence on peer norms: How mass media indirectly affect adolescent smoking. *Journal of Communication, 56,* 52–68.

Gustafson, D. H., Hawkins, R., McTavish, F., Pingree, S., Chen, W. C., Volrathongchai, K., et al. (2008). Internet-based interactive support for cancer patients: Are integrated systems better? *Journal of Communication, 58,* 238–257.

Gustin, S. (2012, May 21). The $100 billion question. *Time,* p. 14.

Guttmann, A. (1986). *Sports spectators.* New York: Columbia University Press.

Guttmann, A. (1998). The appeal of violent sports. In J. Holdstein (Ed.), *Why we watch: The attractions of violent entertainment* (pp. 1–26). New York: Oxford University Press.

Haberstroh, J. (1994). *Ice cube sex: The truth about subliminal advertising.* Notre Dame, IN: Cross Cultural.

Haines, E. (2011, August 1). Budget targets leisure travelers with car ad deals. Retrieved from http://hosted2.ap.org

Hajjar, W. J. (1997). The image of aging in television commercials: An update for the 1990s. In H. S. Noor Al-deen (Ed.), *Cross-cultural communication and aging in the United States* (pp. 231–244). Mahwah, NJ: Erlbaum.

Halim, S., & Meyers, M. (2010). News coverage of violence against Muslim women: A view from the Arabian gulf. *Communication, Culture & Critique, 3,* 85–104.

Hallin, D. C. (1992). Sound bite news: Television coverage of elections, 1968–1988. *Journal of Communication, 42*(2), 5–24.

Hamdy, N., & Gomaa, E. H. (2012). Framing the Egyptian uprising in Arabic language newspapers and social media. *Journal of Communication, 62,* 195–211.

Hamilton, A. (1998, March 23). World watch. *Time Digital, 3*(1), 68–69.

Hamilton, J. T. (1998). *Channeling violence: The economic market for violent television programming.* Princeton, NJ: Princeton University Press.

Hamilton, W. L. (2003, March 30). Toymakers study troops, and vice versa. *The New York Times.*

Han, S., & Shavitt, S. (1994). Persuasion and culture: Advertising appeals in individualistic and collectivistic cultures. *Journal of Experimental Social Psychology, 30,* 326–350.

Hansen, C. H., & Hansen, R. D. (1990a). The influence of sex and violence on the appeal of rock music videos. *Communication Research, 17,* 212–234.

Hansen, C. H., & Hansen, R. D. (1990b). Rock music videos and antisocial behavior. *Basic and Applied Social Psychology*, 11(4), 357–369.

Hansen, C. H., & Hansen, R. D. (2000). Music and music videos. In P. Vorderer & D. Zillmann (Eds.), *Media entertainment: The psychology of its appeal* (pp. 175–196). Mahwah, NJ: Erlbaum.

Haridakis, P. M. (2002). Viewer characteristics, exposure to television violence, and aggression. *Media Psychology*, 4, 323–352.

Harp, D., Loke, J., & Bachmann, I. (2010). First impressions of Sarah Palin: Pit bulls, politics, gender performance, and a discursive media (re)contextualization. *Communication, Culture & Critique*, 3, 291–309.

Harper's Index (2012, March). *Harper's Magazine*, p. 11.

Harris, R. J. (1981). Inferences in information processing. In G. H. Bower (Ed.), *The psychology of learning and motivation* (Vol. 15, pp. 82–128). New York: Academic Press.

Harris, R. J., & Barlett, C. P. (2009). Effects of sex in the media. In J. Bryant & M. B. Oliver (Eds.), *Media effects: Advances in theory and research* (3rd ed.). Mahwah, New York: Taylor & Francis.

Harris, R. J., & Karafa, J. A. (1999). A cultivation theory perspective of worldwide national impressions of the United States. In Y. Kamalipour (Ed.), *Images of the U.S. around the world: A multicultural perspective* (pp. 3–17). Albany, NY: SUNY Press.

Harris, R. J., Dubitsky, T. M., & Bruno, K. J. (1983). Psycholinguistic studies of misleading advertising. In R. J. Harris (Ed.), *Information processing research in advertising* (pp. 241–262). Hillsdale, NJ: Erlbaum.

Harris, R. J., Garner-Earl, B., Sprick, S. J., & Carroll, C. (1994). Effects of foreign product names and country-of-origin attributions on advertisement evaluations. *Psychology & Marketing*, 11, 129–144.

Harris, R. J., Hoekstra, S. J., Sanborn, F. W., Scott, C. L., Dodds, L., & Brandenburg, J. D. (2004). Autobiographical memories for seeing romantic movies on a date: Romance is not just for women. *Media Psychology*, 6, 257–284.

Harris, R. J., Hoekstra, S. J., Scott, C. L., Sanborn, F. W., Karafa, J. A., & Brandenburg, J. D. (2000). Young men's and women's different autiobiographical memories of the experience of seeing frightening movies on a date. *Media Psychology*, 2, 245–268.

Harris, R. J., Jasper, J. D., Lee, B. J., & Miller, K. E. (1991). Consenting to donate organs: Whose wishes carry the most weight? *Journal of Applied Social Psychology*, 21, 3–14.

Harris, R. J., Pounds, J. C., Maiorelle, M. J., & Mermis, M. M. (1993). The effect of type of claim, gender, and buying history on the drawing of pragmatic inferences from advertising claims. *Journal of Consumer Psychology*, 2, 83–95.

Harris, R. J., Schoen, L. M., & Hensley, D. (1992). A cross-cultural study of story memory. *Journal of Cross-cultural Psychology*, 23, 133–147.

Harris, R. J., Sturm, R. E., Klassen, M. L., & Bechtold, J. I. (1986). Language in advertising: A psycholinguistic approach. *Current Issues and Research in Advertising*, 9, 1–26.

Harris, R. J., Trusty, M. L., Bechtold, J. I., & Wasinger, L. (1989). Memory for implied versus directly asserted advertising claims. *Psychology & Marketing*, 6, 87–96.

Harris, R. J., & Cook, L. G. (2011). How content and co-viewers elicit emotional discomfort in moviegoing experiences: Where does the discomfort come from and how is it handled? *Applied Cognitive Psychology*, 25, 850–861.

Harris. R. J., Cady, E. T., & Tran, T. Q. (2006). Comprehension and memory. In J. Bryant & P. Vorderer (Eds.), *Psychology of entertainment* (pp. 71–84). Mahwah, NJ: Erlbaum.

Harrison, K. (1997). Does interpersonal attraction to thin media personalities promote eating disorders? *Journal of Broadcasting & Electronic Media*, 41, 478–500.

Harrison, K. (2000). The body electric: Thin-ideal media and eating disorders in adolescents. *Journal of Communication*, 50(3), 119–143.

Harrison, K., & Cantor, J. (1997). The relationship between media exposure and eating disorders. *Journal of Communication*, 47(1), 40–67.

Harrison, K., & Cantor, J. (1999). Tales from the screen: Enduring fright reactions to scary media. *Media Psychology*, 1, 97–116.

Harrison, K., & Fredrickson, B. L. (2003). Women's sports media, self-objectification, and mental health in black and white adolescent females. *Journal of Communication*, 53, 216–232.

Harrison, K., Taylor, L. D., & Marske, A. L. (2006). Women's and men's eating behavior following exposure to ideal-body images and text. *Communication Research*, 33, 507–529.

Hart, R. P. (1994). *Seducing America: How television charms the modern voter*. New York: Oxford University Press.

Hart, R. P., & Jarvis, S. E. (1997). Political debate: Forms, styles, and media. *American Behavioral Scientist*, 40, 1095–1122.

Hartmann, D. P. (1969). Influence of symbolically modelled instrumental aggression and pain cues on aggressive behavior. *Journal of Personality and Social Psychology*, 11, 280–288.

Hartmann, E., & Basile, R. (2003). Dream imagery becomes more intense after 9/11/01. *Dreaming*, 13, 61–66.

Harwood, J., & Giles, H. (1992). "Don't make me laugh": Age representations in a humorous context. *Discourse & Society*, 3, 403–436.

Hartmann, T., & Goldhoorn, C. (2011). Horton and Wohl revisited: Exploring viewers' experience of parasocial interaction. *Journal of Communication*, 61, 1104–1121.

Hatfield, E., Cacioppo, J. T., & Rapson, R. L. (1992). Primitive emotional contagion. In M. S. Clark (Ed.), *Review of personality and social psychology: Vol. 14. Emotions and social behavior*. Newbury Park, CA: Sage.

Hatfield, E., Cacioppo, J. T., & Rapson, R. L. (1993). Emotional contagion. *Current Directions in Psychological Science*, 2, 96–99.

Hausknecht, D., & Moore, D. L. (1986). The effects of time compressed advertising of brand attitude judgments. *Advances in Consumer Research*, 13, 105–110.

Hawkins, R. P., & Pingree, S. (1981). Uniform messages and habitual viewing: Unnecessary assumptions in social reality effects. *Human Communication Research*, 7, 291–301.

Hawkins, R. P., & Pingree, S. (1990). Divergent psychological processes in constructing social reality from mass media content. In N. Signorielli & M. Morgan (Eds.), *Cultivation analysis* (pp. 35–50). Newbury Park, CA: Sage.

Hawkins, R. P., Kim, Y. H., & Pingree, S. (1991). The ups and downs of attention to television. *Communication Research*, 18, 53–76.

Hawkins, R. P., Pingree, S., & Adler, I. (1987). Searching for cognitive processes in the cultivation effect: Adult and adolescent samples in the United States and Australia. *Human Communication Research*, 13, 553–577.

Hawkins, R. P., Pingree, S., Hitchon, J., Radler, B., Gorham, B. W., Kahlor, L., et al. (2005). What produces television attention and attention style? Genre, situation, and individual differences as predictors? *Human Communication Research*, 31, 162–187.

Hayes, D., & Birnbaum, D. W. (1980). Preschoolers' retention of televised events: Is a picture worth a thousand words? *Developmental Psychology*, 16, 410–416.

Haynes, E., & Rich, N. (2002, April). "Obsessed fans!" YM [Your Magazine], 50, 196–199.

Hazlett, R. L., & Hazlett, S. Y. (1999). Emotional response to television commercials: Facial EMG vs. self-report. *Journal of Advertising Research*, 39(2), 7–23.

Healy, J. (1990). *Endangered minds: Why our children's don't think*. New York: Simon & Schuster.

Hearold, S. (1986). A synthesis of 1043 effects of television on social behavior. In G. Comstock (Ed.), *Public communication and behavior* (Vol. 1, pp. 65–133). Orlando, FL: Academic Press.

Heath, R. L., & Bryant, J. (1992). *Human communication theory and research: Concepts, contexts, and challenges*. Hillsdale, NJ: Erlbaum.

Heath, T. B., Mothersbaugh, D. L., & McCarthy, M. S. (1993). Spokesperson effects in high involvement markets. *Advances in Consumer Research, 20*, 704–707.

Heider, D. (2000). *White news: Why local news programs don't cover people of color*. Mahwah, NJ: Erlbaum.

Heintz-Knowles, K. E. (2001). Balancing acts: Work-family issues on prime-time TV. In J. Bryant & J. A. Bryant (Eds.), *Television and the American family* (2nd ed., pp. 177–206). Mahwah, NJ: Erlbaum.

Henson, L., & Parameswaran, R. E. (2008). Getting real with "tell it like it is" talk therapy: Hegemonic masculinity and the *Dr. Phil* show. *Communication, Culture, & Critique, 1*, 287–310.

Herman, E. S., & Chomsky, N. (1988). *Manufacturing consent: The political economy of the mass media*. New York: Pantheon.

Herman, E. S., & O'Sullivan, G. (1989). *The terrorism industry: The experts and institutions that shape our view of terror*. New York: Pantheon.

Herrett-Skjellum, J., & Allen, M. (1996). Television programming and sex-stereotyping: A meta-analysis. In B. R. Burleson (Ed.), *Communication Yearbook* (Vol. 19, pp. 157–185). Thousand Oaks, CA: Sage.

Hether, H. J., Huang, G. C., Beck, V., Murphy, S. T., & Valente, T. W. (2008). Entertainment-education in a media-saturated environment: Examining the impact of single and multiple exposures to breast cancer storylines on two popular medical dramas. *Journal of Health Communication, 13*(8), 808–823.

Hetsroni, A. (2007). Three decades of sexual content on prime-time network programming: A longitudinal meta-analytic review. *Journal of Communication, 57*, 318–348.

Hetsroni, A., & Tukachinsky, R. H. (2006). Television-world estimates, real-world estimates, and television viewing. *Journal of Communication, 56*, 133–156.

Hicks, D. J. (1965). Imitation and retention of film-mediated aggressive peer and adult models. *Journal of Personality and Social Psychology, 2*, 97–100.

Hilt, M. L., & Lipschultz, J. H. (2004). Elderly Americans and the Internet: E-mail, TV news, information and entertainment websites. *Educational Gerontology, 30*(1), 57–72.

Hinck, E. A. (1992). *Enacting the presidency: Political argument, presidential debates, and presidential character*. Westport, CT: Praeger.

Hinshaw, S. (2007). *The mark of shame: Stigma of mental illness and an agenda for change*. New York: Oxford University Press.

Hirsch, P. M. (1980). The scary world of the nonviewer and other anomalies: A reanalysis of Gerbner et al.'s findings on cultivation analysis, part I. *Communication Research, 7*, 403–456.

Hirschberg, M. S. (1993). *Perpetuating patriotic perceptions: The cognitive function of the Cold War*. Westport, CT: Greenwood.

Ho, E. A., Sanbonmatsu, D. M., & Akimoto, S. A. (2002). The effects of comparative status on social stereotypes: How the perceived success of some persons affects the stereotypes of others. *Social Cognition, 20*, 36–57.

Hodgetts, D., & Chamberlain, K. (2002). "The problem with men": Working class men making sense of men's health on television. *Journal of Health Psychology, 7*, 269–283.

Hodgetts, D., & Rua, M. (2010). What does it mean to be a man today? Bloke culture and the media. *American Journal of Community Psychology, 45*, 155–168.

Hodgetts, D., Cullen, A., & Radley, A. (2005). Television characterizations of homeless people in the United Kingdom. *Analyses of Social Issues and Public Policy, 5*, 29–48.

Hoekstra, S. J. (1998). Docudrama as psychobiography: A case study of HBO's "Stalin." *The Psychohistory Review*, 26, 253–264.

Hoekstra, S. J., Harris, R. J., & Helmick, A. L. (1999). Autobiographical memories about the experience of seeing frightening movies in childhood. *Media Psychology*, 1, 117–140.

Hoerl, K. E. (2002). Monstrous youth in suburbia: Disruption and recovery of the American dream. *Southern Communication Journal*, 67, 259–275.

Hoerl, K. E., Cloud, D. L., & Jarvis, S. E. (2009). Deranged loners and demented outsiders? Therapeutic news frames of Presidential assassination attempts, 1973–2001. *Communication, Culture & Critique*, 2, 83–109.

Hoffner, C. A., & Levine, K. J. (2007). Enjoyment of mediated fright and violence: A meta-analysis. In R. W. Preiss, B. M. Gayle, N. Burrell, M. Allen, & J. Bryant (Eds.), *Mass media effects research: Advances through meta-analysis* (pp. 215–244). Mahwah, NJ: Erlbaum.

Hoffner, C., & Buchanan, M. (2002). Parents' responses to television violence: The third-person effect, parental mediation, and support for censorship. *Media Psychology*, 4, 231–252.

Hoffner, C., & Buchanan, M. (2005). Young adults' wishful identification with television characters: The role of perceived similarity and character attributes. *Media Psychology*, 7, 325–351.

Hoffner, C., Plotkin, R. S., Buchanan, M., Anderson, J. D., Kamigaki, S. K., Hubbs, L. A., et al. (2001). The third-person effect in perceptions of the influence of television violence. *Journal of Communication*, 51(2), 283–299.

Hoffner, C., & Rehkoff, R. A. (2011). Young voters' responses to the 2004 U.S. Presidential election: Social identify, perceived media influence, and behavioral outcomes. *Journal of Communication*, 61, 732–757.

Holbert, R. L., & Hansen, G. J. (2006). Fahrenheit 9/11, need for closure and the priming of affective ambivalence: An assessment of intra-affective structures by party identification. *Human Communication Research*, 32, 109–129.

Holbert, R. L., & Hansen, G. J. (2008). Stepping beyond message specificity in the study of emotion as mediator and inter-emotion associations across attitude objects: Fahrenheit 9/11, anger, and debate superiority. *Media Psychology*, 11, 98–118.

Holbert, R. L., Hansen, G. J., Caplan, S. E., & Mortensen, S. (2007). Presidential debate viewing and Michael Moore's Fahrenheit 9/11: A study of affect-as-transfer and passionate reasoning. *Media Psychology*, 9, 673–694.

Holbert, R. L., LaMarre, H. L., & Landreville, K. D. (2009). Fanning the flames of a partisan divide: Debate viewing, vote choice, and perceptions of vote count accuracy. *Communication Research*, 36, 155–177.

Holbert, R. L., Pillion, O., Tschida, D. A., Armfield, G. G., Kinder, K., Cherry, K. L. et al., (2003). *The West Wing* as endorsement of the U.S. presidency: Expanding the bounds of priming in political communication. *Journal of Communication*, 53(3), 427–443.

Holcomb, J. (2007, June). Tortured logic. *Sojourners*, p. 8.

Hong, S. T., & Wyer, R. S., Jr. (1989). Effects of country-of-origin and product-attribute information on product evaluation: An information-processing experiment. *Journal of Consumer Research*, 16, 175–187.

Hong, S. T., & Wyer, R. S., Jr. (1990). Determinants of product evaluation: Effects of the time interval between knowledge about a product's country of origin and information about its specific attributes. *Journal of Consumer Research*, 17, 277–288.

Hoover, S. M. (1988). *Mass media religion*. Newbury Park, CA: Sage.

Hoover, S. M. (1998). *Religion in the news: Faith and journalism in American public discourse*. Thousand Oaks, CA: Sage.

Hoover, S. M., & Lundby, K. (Eds.). (1997). *Rethinking media, religion, and culture*. Thousand Oaks, CA: Sage.

Hopkins, R., & Fletcher, J. E. (1994). Electrodermal measurement: Particularly effective for forecasting message influence on sales appeal. In A. Lang (Ed.), *Measuring psychological responses to media* (pp. 113–132). Hillsdale, NJ: Erlbaum.

Hopmann, D. N., deVreese, C. H., & Albaek, E. (2011). Incumbency bonus in election news coverage explained: The logics of political power and the media market. *Journal of Communication, 61*, 264–282.

Hornik, R., & Yanovitzky, I. (2003). Using theory to design evaluations of communication campaigns: The case of the National Youth Anti-Drug Media Campaign. *Communication Theory, 13*, 204–224.

Hot type (1998, February 20). *The Chronicle of Higher Education*, p. 44, A22.

Houck, M. M. (2006, July). CSI: Reality. *Scientific American, 295*(1), 85–89.

Howard, T. (2009, August 10). Push is on to end prescription drug ads targeting consumers. *USA Today*. Retrieved from http://www.usatoday.com

Howden, L. M., & Meyer, J. A. (2011). Age and sex composition: 2010, 2010 census briefs. Retrieved from http://2010.census.gov/2010census/data/

Hoy, M. G., Young, C. E., & Mowen, J. C. (1986). Animated host-selling advertisements: Their impact on young children's recognition, attitudes, and behavior. *Journal of Public Policy and Marketing, 5*, 171–184.

Huddy, L., Feldman, S., & Cassese, E. (2007). On the distinct political effects of anxiety and anger. In A. Crigler, M. MacKuen, G. E. Marcus, & W. R. Neuman (Eds.), *The political dynamics of feeling and thinking*. Chicago: University of Chicago Press.

Huesmann, L. R. (2010). Nailing the coffin shut on doubts that violent video games stimulate aggression: Comment on Anderson et al. (2010). *Psychological Bulletin, 136*, 179–181.

Huesmann, L. R., & Eron, L. D. (1986). *Television and the aggressive child*. Hillsdale, NJ: Erlbaum.

Huesmann, L. R., Eron, L. D., Klein, R., Brice, P., & Fischer, P. (1983). Mitigating the imitation of aggressive behaviors by changing children's attitudes about media violence. *Journal of Personality and Social Psychology, 44*, 899–910.

Huesmann, L. R., Eron, L. D., Lefkowitz, M. M., & Walder, L. O. (1984). Stability of aggression over time and generations. *Developmental Psychology, 20*, 1120–1134.

Huesmann, L. R., Lagerspetz, K., & Eron, L. D. (1984). Intervening variables in the TV violence-aggression relation: Evidence from two countries. *Developmental Psychology, 20*, 746–775.

Huesmann, L. R., Moise-Titus, J., Podolski, C. L., & Eron, L. D. (2003). Longitudinal relations between children's exposure to TV violence and their aggressive and violent behavior in young adulthood: 1977–1992. *Developmental Psychology, 39*, 201–221.

Huh, J., & Langteau, R. (2007). Presumed influence of DTC prescription drug advertising. *Communication Research, 34*, 25–52.

Hull, J. D. (1995, January 30). The state of the union. *Time*, pp. 53–75.

Humes, K. R., Jones, N. A., & Ramirez, R. R. (2011). Overview of race and Hispanic origin: 2010. Retrieved from http://2010.census.gov/2010census/data/

Hurst, L. (1998, April). History repeats itself—again. *World Press Review*, pp. 28–29.

Husson, W., Stephen, T., Harrison, T. M., & Fehr, B. J. (1988). An interpersonal communication perspective on images of political candidates. *Human Communication Research, 14*, 397–421.

Huston, A. C., Anderson, D. R., Wright, J. C., Linebarger, D. L., & Schmitt, K. L. (2001). Sesame Street viewers as adolescents: The recontact study. In S. M. Fisch & R. T. Truglio (Eds.), *"G" is for growing: Thirty years of research on children and Sesame Street* (pp. 131–144). Mahwah, NJ: Erlbaum.

Huston, A. C., Donnerstain, E., Fairchild, H. H., Fashbach, H. D., Katz, P., Murray, J. P., et al. (1992). *Big world, small screen: The role of television in American society.* Washington, DC: Americal Psychological Association.

Huston, A. C., & Wright, J. C. (1998). Television and the informational and educational needs of children. *The Annals of the American Academy of Political and Social Science, 557,* 9–23.

Huston, A. C., Wright, J. C., Rice, M. L., Kerkman, D., & St. Peters, M. (1990). The development of television viewing patterns in early childhood: A longitudinal investigation. *Developmental Psychology, 26,* 409–420.

Hutcheon, D. (2002, July/August). Mixing up the world's beat. *Mother Jones,* pp. 74–75.

Huus, K. (2005, April 12). Hair-raising TV spot shunned by broadcasters. Retrieved April 12, 2005, from http://www.msnbc.cm/id/7351263/print/1/displaymode/1098

Hwang, Y., & Southwell, B. G. (2009). Science TV news exposure predicts science beliefs: Real world effects among a national sample. *Communication Research, 36,* 724–742.

Hyler, S. E. (1988). DSM-III at the cinema: Madness in the movies. *Comprehensive Psychiatry, 29,* 195–206.

Hyler, S. E., Gabbard, G. O., & Schneider, I. (1991). Homicidal maniacs and narcissistic parasites: Stigmatization of mentally ill persons in the movies. *Hospital and Community Psychiatry, 42,* 1044–1048.

Igartua, J.-J., & Barrios, I. (2012). Changing real-world beliefs with controversial movies: Processes and mechanisms of narrative persuasion. *Journal of Communication, 62,* 514–531.

Igartua, J.-J., & Cheng, L. (2009). Moderating effect of a group cue while processing news on immigration: Is the framing effect a heuristic process? *Journal of Communication, 59,* 726–749.

Iiyama, P., & Kitano, H. H. L. (1982). Asian-Americans and the media. In G. L. Berry & C. Mitchell-Kernan (Eds.), *Television and the socialization of the minority child* (pp. 151–186). New York: Academic Press.

Ilola, L. M. (1990). Culture and health. In R. W. Brislin (Ed.), *Applied cross-cultural psychology* (pp. 278–301). Newbury Park, CA: Sage.

IMDB (2012). Judge Judy. Retrieved from http://www.imdb.com/title/tt0115227/quotes

Intons-Peterson, M. J., & Roskos-Ewoldsen, B. (1989). Mitigating the effects of violent pornography. In S. Gubar & J. Hoff-Wilson (Eds.), *For adult users only.* Bloomington, IN: Indiana University Press.

Intons-Peterson, M. J., Roskos-Ewoldsen, B., Thomas, L., Shirley, M., & Blut, D. (1989). Will educational materials reduce negative effects of exposure to sexual violence? *Journal of Social and Clinical Psychology, 8,* 256–275.

IT Facts. (n.d.). Retrieved July 5, 2007, from http://www.itfacts.biz/index.php?id=P7960

Itzkoff, D. (2009, November 13). Record sales for Modern Warfare 2, but gaming business declines. *New York Times.*

Ivory, J. D., & Kalyanaraman, S. (2007). The effects of technological advancement and violent content in video games on players' feelings of presence, involvement physiological arousal, and aggression. *Journal of Communication, 57,* 532–555.

Iyengar, S., & Hahn, K. S. (2009). Red media, blue media: Evidence of ideological selectivity in media use. *Journal of Communication, 59,* 19–39.

Iyengar, S., & Simon, A. (1993). News coverage of the Gulf Crisis and public opinion. *Communication Research, 20,* 365–383.

Iyer, E., & Banerjee, B. (1993). Anatomy of green advertising. *Advances in Consumer Research, 20,* 494–501.

Jackson, D. Z. (1989, January 22). Calling the plays in black and white. *The Boston Globe*, pp. A30–A33.

Jacob, C., Guéguen, N., & Boulbry, G. (2010). Effects of songs with prosocial lyrics on tipping behavior in a restaurant. *International Journal of Hospitality Management, 29*, 761–763.

Jacobson, J. (2001, March 16). In brochures, what you see isn't necessarily what you get. *The Chronicle of Higher Education, 47*, A41–42.

Jacques, W. W., & Ratzan, S. C. (1997). The Internet's World Wide Web and political accountability: New media coverage of the 1996 Presidential debates. *American Behavioral Scientist, 40*, 1226–1237.

Jakes, J. (1985, November 2). What? A successful media campaign without TV spots and Phil Donohue? *TV Guide*, pp. 12–15.

Jamieson, K. H. (1992). *Packaging the presidency: A history and criticism of presidential campaign advertising* (2nd ed.). New York: Oxford University Press.

Jamieson, K. H., & Campbell, K. K. (1992). *The interplay of influence: News, advertising, politics, and the mass media* (3rd ed.). Belmont, CA: Wadsworth.

Jamieson, K. H., & Waldman, P. (1997). Mapping campaign discourse: An introduction. *American Behavioral Scientist, 40*, 1133–1138.

Jamieson, K. H., & Waldman, P. (2003). *The press effect: Politicians, journalists, and the stories that shape the political world*. New York: Oxford University Press.

Jenkins, P. (2001). *Beyond tolerance: Child pornography on the Internet*. New York: NYU Press.

Jennings, J., Geis, F., & Brown, V. (1980). Influence of television commercials on women's self-confidence and independent judgment. *Journal of Personality and Social Psychology, 38*(2), 203–210.

Jensen, J. D., & Hurley, R. J. (2005). Third-person effects and the environment: Social distance, social desirability, and presumed behavior. *Journal of Communication, 55*, 242–256.

Jeong, S.-H., Cho, H., & Hwang, Y. (2012). Media literacy interventions: A meta-analytic review. *Journal of Communication, 62*, 454–472.

Jeong, S.-H., & Fishbein, M. (2007). Predictors of multitasking with media: Media factors and audience factors. *Media Psychology, 10*, 364–384.

Jhally, S., & Lewis, J. (1992). *Enlightened racism: The Cosby Show, audiences, and the myth of the American dream*. Boulder, CO: Westview Press.

Johnson, D., & Rimal, R. N. (July, 1994). Analysis of HIV/AIDS television public service announcements around the world. Paper presented at International Communication Association meeting, Sydney, Australia.

Johnson, J. D., Adams, M. S., Ashburn, L., & Reed, W. (1995). Differential gender effects of exposure to rap music on African American adolescents' acceptance of teen dating violence. *Sex Roles, 33*, 597–606.

Johnson, J. G., Cohen, P., Smailes, E. M., Kasen, S., & Brook, J. S. (2002). Television viewing and aggressive behavior during adolescence and adulthood. *Science, 295*, 2468–2471.

Johnson, J. D., Jackson, L. A., & Gatto, L. (1995). Violent attitudes and deferred academic aspirations: Deleterious effects of exposure to rap music. *Basic and Applied Social Psychology, 16*, 27–41.

Johnson, M. K. (2007). Reality monitoring and the media. *Applied Cognitive Psychology, 21*, 981–993.

Johnson-Cartee, K. S., & Copeland, G. A. (1997). *Manipulation of the American voter: Political campaign commercials*. New York: Praeger.

Johnsson-Smaragdi, U. (1983). *TV use and social interaction in adolescence: A longitudinal study*. Stockholm: Almqvist & Wiksell.

Johnston, C. B. (2001, Winter). Screened out. *Wooster*, pp. 51–53.

Joiner, T. E., Jr. (1999). The clustering and contagion of suicide. *Current Directions in Psychological Science, 8*, 89–92.

Jones, A. (1994, March 10). Crimes against women: Media part of problem for masking violence in the language of love. *USA Today*.

Jones, K. (1997). Are rap videos more violent? Style differences and the prevalence of sex and violence in the age of MTV. *Howard Journal of Communication, 8*, 343–356.

Jordan, A. B. (2001). Public policy and private practice. In D. G. Singer & J. L. Singer (Eds.), *Handbook of children and the media* (pp. 651–662). Thousand Oaks, CA: Sage.

Joy, L. A., Kimball, M. M., & Zabrack, M. L. (1986). Television and children's aggressive behavior. In T. M. Williams (Ed.), *The impact of television: A natural experiment in three communities* (pp. 303–360). Orlando, FL: Academic Press.

Jurgensen, J. (2012, July 12). Binge viewing: TV's lost weekends. *The Wall Street Journal*. Retrieved from http://online.wsj.com

Just, M., Crigler, A., & Wallach, L. (1990). Thirty seconds or thirty minutes: What viewers learn from spot advertisements and candidate debates. *Journal of Communication, 40(3)*, 120–133.

Kahle, L. R., & Homer, P. M. (1985). Physical attractiveness of the celebrity endorsers: A social adaptation perspective. *Journal of Consumer Research, 11*, 954–961.

Kahneman, D. (2011). *Thinking fast and slow*. New York: Farrar, Straus and Giroux.

Kaid, L. L. (1997). Effects of the television spots of images of Dole and Clinton. *American Behavioral Scientist, 40*, 1085–1094.

Kaid, L. L., & Boydston, J. (1987). An experimental study of the effectiveness of negative political advertisements. *Communication Quarterly, 35*, 193–201.

Kaid, L. L., & Holtz-Bacha, C. (Eds.). (1995). *Political advertising in Western democracies: Parties and candidates on television*. Thousand Oaks, CA: Sage.

Kaid, L. L., & Johnston, A. (1991). Negative versus positive television advertising in U.S. Presidential campaigns, 1960–1988. *Journal of Communication, 41(3)*, 53–64.

Kaid, L. L., Gerstle, J., & Sanders, K. R. (Eds.). (1991). *Mediated politics in two cultures: Presidential campaigning in the United States and France*. New York: Praeger.

Kaiser Family Foundation. (2002). *The impact of TV's health content: A case study of ER viewers*. Menlo Park CA: Kaiser Family Foundation.

Kaiser Family Foundation (2005). Sex on TV 4. Retrieved from http://www.kff.org/entmedia/upload/Sex-on-TV-4-Full-Report.pdf

Kaiser Family Foundation. (2007a). Food for thought: Television food advertising to children in the United States. Retrieved from http://www.kff.org/entmedia/upload/7618.pdf

Kaiser Family Foundation. (2007b). Parents, children, and media: A Kaiser Family Foundation survey. Retrieved from http://www.kff.org/entmedia/upload/7638.pdf

Kaiser Family Foundation. (2010). Generation M2: Media in the lives of 8- to 18-year-olds. Retrieved from http://www.kff.org/entmedia/

Kamalipour, Y. (Ed.). (1999). *Images of the U.S. around the world: A multicultural perspective*. Albany, NY: SUNY Press.

Kane, M. J. (1996). Media coverage of the post Title IX female athlete. *Duke Journal of Gender Law & Policy, 3*, 95–127.

Kassarjian, H. (1969). The Negro and American advertising: 1946–1965. *Journal of Marketing Research, 6*, 29–39.

Kaveney, R. (2006). *Teen dreams: Reading teen film and television from "Heathers" to "Veronica Mars."* London: I.B. Tauris.

Keegan, R. W. (2006, October 30). The splat pack. *Time*, pp. 66–70.

Kehr, D. (2011, March 4). Goodbye, DVD. Hello future. Retrieved from http://nytimes.com

Kelly, H. (1981). Reasoning about realities: Children's evaluations of television and books. In H. Kelly & H. Gardner (Eds.), Viewing children through television. San Francisco: Jossey-Bass.

Kennedy, M. G., O'Leary, A., Beck, V., Pollard, K., & Simpson, P. (2004). Increases in calls to the CDC national STD and AIDS hotline following AIDS-related episodes in a soap opera. Journal of Communication, 54, 287–301.

Kenrick, D. T., Gutierres, S. E., & Goldberg, L. L. (1989). Influence of popular erotica on judgments of strangers and mates. Journal of Experimental Social Psychology, 25, 159–167.

Kenrick, D. T., & Gutierres, S. E. (1980). Contrast effects and judgments of physical attractiveness: When beauty becomes a social problem. Journal of Personality and Social Psychology, 38, 131–140.

Kern-Foxworth, M. (1994). Aunt Jemima, Uncle Ben, and Rastus: Blacks in advertising, yesterday, today, and tomorrow. Westport, CT: Praeger.

Kessler, R. C., Downey, G., Milavsky, J. R., & Stipp, H. (1988). Clustering of teenage suicides after television news stories about suicides: A reconsideration. American Journal of Psychiatry, 145, 1379–1383.

Keum, H., Hillback, E. D., Rojas, H., De Zuniga, H. G., Shah, D. V., & McLeod, D. M. (2005). Personifying the radical: How news framing polarizes security concerns and tolerance judgments. Human Communication Research, 31, 337–364.

Key, W. B. (1976). Media sexploitation. New York: Signet.

Key, W. B. (1981). The clam-plate orgy. New York: Signet.

Key, W. B. (1989). The age of manipulation. New York: Henry Holt.

Kher, U. (2003, January 27). How to sell XXX. Time, pp. 34–36.

Kilbourne, J. (1995). Slim hopes: Advertising and the obsession with thinness. [Video.] Northampton, MA: Media Education Foundation.

Kilbourne, J. (2010). Killing us softly 4: Advertising's image of women. Northampton, MA: Media Education Foundation.

Kilbourne, W. E., Painton, S., & Ridley, D. (1985). The effect of sexual embedding on responses to magazine advertisements. Journal of Advertising, 14(2), 48–56.

Kim, Y. M., & Vishak, J. (2008). Just laugh! You don't need to remember: The effects of entertainment media on political information acquisition and information processing in political judgment. Journal of Communication, 58, 338–360.

Kimball, M. M. (1986). Television and sex-role attitudes. In T. M. Williams (Ed.), The impact of television: A natural experiment in three communities (pp. 265–302). Orlando, FL: Academic Press.

King, C. M. (2000). Effects of humorous heroes and villains in violent action films. Journal of Communication, 50(1), 5–24.

King, C. M., & Hourani, N. (2007). Don't tease me: Effects of ending type on horror film enjoyment. Media Psychology, 9, 473–492.

King, K. W., & Reid, L. N. (1990). Fear arousing anti-drinking and driving PSAs: Do physical injury threats influence young people? Current Issues and Research in Advertising, 12, 155–175.

Kingston, D. A., & Malamuth, N. M. (2011). Problems with aggregate data and the importance of individual differences in the study of pornography and sexual aggression: Comment on Diamond, Jozifkova, and Weiss (2010). Archives of Sexual Behavior, 40, 1045–1048.

Kintsch, W. (1977). On comprehending stories. In P. Carpenter & M. Just (Eds.), Cognitive processes in comprehension (pp. 33–61). Hillsdale, NJ: Erlbaum.

Kiousis, S., & McDevitt, M. (2008). Agenda setting in civic development. Communication Research, 35, 481–502.

Kiousis, S., McDevitt, M., & Wu, X. (2005). The genesis of civic awareness: Agenda setting in political socialization. *Journal of Communication*, 55, 756–774.

Kirk, R. (2011, July). The body in pain. *Sojourners*, pp. 22–25.

Kirkorian, H. L., & Anderson, D. R. (2011). Learning from educational media. In S. L. Calvert & B. J. Wilson (Eds.), *The handbook of children, media, and development* (pp. 188–213). Malden, MA: Wiley-Blackwell.

Kirkpatrick, D. D. (2003, May 19). Shaping cultural tastes at big retail chains. *New York Times*. Retrieved May 18, 2003, from http://www.nytimes.com/2003/05/18/business/18 MART.html

Kirsh, S. J. (1998). Seeing the world through Mortal Kombat-colored glasses: Violent video games and the development of a short-term hostile attribution bias. *Childhood: Global Journal of Childhood Research*, 5(2), 177–184.

Kirsh, S. J. (2006). *Children, adolescents, and media violence: A critical look at the research.* Thousand Oaks, CA: Sage.

Kirsh, S. J., Olczak, P. V., & Mounts, J. R. W. (2005). Violent video games induce an affect processing bias. *Media Psychology*, 7, 239–250.

Kirzinger, A. E., Weber, C., & Johnson, M. (2012). Genetic and environmental influences on media use and communication behaviors. *Human Communication Research*, 38, 144–171.

Klein, J. G., & Ahluwalia, R. (2005, January). Negativity in the evaluation of political candidates. *Journal of Marketing*, 69, 131–142.

Kleiner, C. (2001, June 4). Disney makes nice to Japan. *U.S. News & World Report*, 46–47.

Klimmt, C., Hartmann, T., & Schramm, H. (2006). Parasocial interactions and relationships. In J. Bryant & P. Vorderer (Eds.). *Psychology of entertainment* (pp. 291–313). Mahwah, NJ: Erlbaum.

Kline, S. (1992). *Out of the garden: Toys, TV, and children's culture in the age of marketing.* New York: Verso.

Knill, B. J., Pesch, M., Pursey, G., Gilpin, P., & Perloff, R. M. (1981). Still typecast after all these years? Sex role portrayals in television advertising. *International Journal of Women's Studies*, 4, 497–506.

Knobloch, S. (2003). Mood adjustment via mass communication. *Journal of Communication*, 53, 233–250.

Knobloch, S., Callison, C., Chen, L., Fritzsche, A., & Zillmann, D. (2005). Children's sex-stereotyped self-socialization through selective exposure to entertainment: Cross-cultural experiments in Germany, China, and the United States. *Journal of Communication*, 55, 122–138.

Knobloch, S., & Zillmann, D. (2002). Mood management via the digital jukebox. *Journal of Communication*, 52, 351–366.

Knobloch-Westerwick, S. (2006). Mood management: Theory, evidence, and advancements. In J. Bryant & P. Vorderer (Eds.), *Psychology of entertainment* (pp. 239–254). Mahwah, NJ: Erlbaum.

Knobloch-Westerwick, S., & Alter, S. (2006). Mood adjustment to social situations through mass media use: How men ruminate and women dissipate angry moods. *Human Communication Research*, 32, 58–73.

Knobloch-Westerwick, S., & Alter, S. (2007). The gender news use divide: Americans' sex-typed selective exposure to online news topics. *Journal of Communication*, 57, 739–758.

Knobloch-Westerwick, S., Appiah, O., & Alter, S. (2008). News selection patterns as a function of race: The discerning minority and the indiscriminating majority. *Media Psychology*, 11, 400–417.

Knobloch-Westerwick, S., David, P., Eastin, M. S., Tamborini, R., & Greenwood, D. (2009). Sports spectators' suspense: Affect and uncertainty in sports entertainment. *Journal of Communication*, 59, 750–767.

Knobloch-Westerwick, S., & Meng, J. (2011). Reinforcement of the political self through selective exposure to political messages. *Journal of Communication*, 61, 349–368.

Kolbe, R. H., & Muehling, D. D. (1992). A content analysis of the fine print in television advertising. *Journal of Current Issues and Research in Advertising*, 14(2), 47–61.

Koolstra, C. M., & Beentjes, J. W. J. (1999). Children's vocabulary acquisition in a foreign language through watching subtitled television programs at home. *Education Technology, Research, and Development*, 47, 51–60.

Koolstra, C. M., & van der Voort, T. H. A. (1996). Longitudinal effects of television on leisure-time reading. *Human Communication Research*, 23, 4–35.

Koolstra, C. M., van der Voort, T. H. A., & van der Kamp, L. J. T. (1997). Television's impact on children's reading comprehension and decoding skills: A 3-year panel study. *Reading Research Quarterly*, 32, 128–152.

Korzenny, F., & Ting-Toomey, S. (Eds.). (1992). *Mass media effects across cultures*. Newbury Park, CA: Sage.

Kosicki, G. M. (1993). Problems and opportunities in agenda-setting research. *Journal of Communication*, 43(2), 100–127.

Kotler, J. A., Wright, J. C., & Huston, A. C. (2001). Television use in families with children. In J. Bryant & J. A. Bryant (Eds.), *Television and the American family* (2nd ed., pp. 33–48). Mahwah, NJ: Erlbaum.

Kottak, C. P. (1990). *Prime-time society: An anthropological analysis of television and culture*. Belmont, CA: Wadsworth.

Krafka, C. L., Linz, D., Donnerstein, E., & Penrod, S. (1997). Women's reactions to sexually aggressive mass media depictions. *Violence Against Women*, 3(2), 148–181.

Kraft, R. N., Cantor, P., & Gottdiener, C. (1991). The coherence of visual narratives. *Communication Research*, 18, 601–616.

Krahé, B., Möller, I., Huesmann, L. R., Kirwil, L., Felber, J., & Berger, A. (2011). Desensitization to media violence: links with habitual media violence exposure, aggressive cognitions, and aggressive behavior. *Journal of Personality and Social Psychology*, 100, 630–646.

Krakowiak, K. M. & Oliver, M. B. (2012). When good characters do bad things. *Journal of Communication*, 62, 117–135.

Kraus, S. (1988). *Televised presidential debates and public policy*. Hillsdale, NJ: Erlbaum.

Kraus, S. (1996). Winners of the first 1960 televised Presidential debate between Kennedy and Nixon. *Journal of Communication*, 46(4), 78–96.

Kraut, R., Patterson, M., Lundmark, V., Kiesler, S., Mukopadhyay, T., & Scherlis, W. (1998). Internet paradox: A social technology that reduces social involvement and psychological well-being? *American Psychologist*, 53, 1017–1031.

Krcmar, M., & Cooke, M. C. (2001). Children's moral reasoning and their perceptions of television violence. *Journal of Communication*, 51(2), 300–316.

Krcmar, M., & Curtis, S. (2003). Mental models: Understanding the impact of fantasy violence on children's moral reasoning. *Journal of Communication*, 53(3), 460–478.

Krcmar, M., & Greene, K. (1999). Predicting exposure to and uses of television violence. *Journal of Communication*, 49(3), 24–45.

Krcmar, M., & Kean, L. G. (2005). Uses and gratifications of media violence: Personality correlates of viewing and liking violent genres. *Media Psychology*, 7, 399–420.

Krohn, F. B., & Suazo, F. L. (1995). Contemporary urban music: Controversial messages in hip-hop and rap lyrics. *ETC: A Review of General Semantics*, 52, 139–155.

Kron, J., & Goodman, J. D. (2012). Online, a distant conflict soars to topic no. 1. *New York Times online*. Retrieved July 10, 2012, from www.nytimes.com/2012/03/09/world/africa/online-joseph-kony

Kruglanski, A. W., Crenshaw, M., Post, J. M., & Victoroff, J. (2007). What should this fight be called? Metaphors of counterterrorism and their implications. *Psychological Science in the Public Interest*, 8, 97–133.

Kubey, R. (1980). Television and aging: Past, present, and future. *Gerontologist*, 20, 16–35.

Kubey, R. (1986). Television use in everyday life: Coping with unstructured time. *Journal of Communication*, 36, 108–123.

Kubey, R., & Csikszentmihalyi, M. (1990). *Television and the quality of life: How viewing shapes everyday experience*. Hillsdale, NJ: Erlbaum.

Kunkel, D. (1988). Children and host-selling television commercials. *Communication Research*, 15(1), 71–92.

Kunkel, D. (1998). Policy battles over defining children's educational television. *The Annals of the American Academy of Political and Social Science*, 557, 39–53.

Kunkel, D., Eyal, K., Donnerstein, E., Farrar, K. M., Biely, E., & Rideout, V. (2007). Sexual socialization messages on entertainment television: Comparison content trends 1997–2002. *Media Psychology*, 9, 595–622.

Kunkel, D., Farinola, W. J. M., Farrar, K., Donnerstein, E., Biely, E., & Zwarun, L. (2002). Deciphering the V-chip: An examination of the television industry's program rating judgments. *Journal of Communication*, 52, 112–138.

Kunkel, D., & Gantz, W. (1992). Children's television advertising in the multichannel environment. *Journal of Communication*, 42(3), 134–152.

Kunkel, D., & McIlrath, M. (2003). Message content in advertising to children. In E. L. Palmer & B. M. Young (Eds.), *The faces of televisual media: Teaching, violence, and selling to children* (pp. 301–325). Mahwah, NJ: Erlbaum.

Kushner, H. W. (2001). *Terrorism in the 21st century*. Newbury Park, CA: Sage.

Kutchinsky, B. (1973). The effect of easy availability of pornography on the incidence of sex crimes: The Danish experience. *Journal of Social Issues*, 29(3), 163–181.

Kutchinsky, B. (1991). Pornography and rape: Theory and practice? *International Journal of Law and Psychiatry*, 14, 47–64.

Kutner, L. & Olson, C. K. (2008). *Grand theft childhood: The suprising truth about violent video games and what parents can do*. New York: Simon & Schuster.

Labi, N. (1999, April 19). Classrooms for sale. *Time*, pp. 44–45.

Labi, N. (2002, December 16). The new Funday School. *Time*, pp. 60–62.

Labre, M. P. (2005). Burn fat, build muscle: A content analysis of *Men's Health* and *Men's Fitness*. *International Journal of Men's Health*, 4, 187–200.

Lacayo, R. (2003, May 19). Hear of glass. *Time*, p. 57.

Lakoff, G. (2009). *The political mind: A cognitive scientists's guide to your brain and its politics*. New York: Penguin.

Lambe, J. L., & McLeod, D. M. (2005). Understanding third-person perception processes: Predicting perceived impact on self and others for multiple expressive contexts. *Journal of Communication*, 55, 277–291.

Lambert, W. E., & Klineberg, O. (1967). *Children's views of foreign peoples: A cross-national study*. New York: Appleton-Century-Crofts.

Lang, A. (1990). Involuntary attention and physiological arousal evoked by structural features and emotional content in TV commercials. *Communication Research*, 17, 275–299.

Lang, A. (1991). Emotion, formal features, and memory for televised political advertisements. In F. Biocca (Ed.), *Television and political advertising: Psychological processes* (Vol. 1, pp. 221–243). Hillsdale, NJ: Erlbaum.

Lang, A. (1994). What can the heart tell us about thinking? In A. Lang (Ed.), *Measuring psychological responses to media* (pp. 99–112). Hillsdale, NJ: Erlbaum.

Lang, A. (2000). The limited capacity model of mediated message processing. *Journal of Communication*, 50, 46–70.

Lang, A., Chung, Y., Lee, S., Schwartz, N., & Shin, M. (2005). It's an arousing, fast-paced kind of world: The effects of age and sensation seeking on the information processing of substance-abuse PSAs. *Media Psychology*, 7, 421–454.

Lang, A., Geiger, S., Strickwerda, M., & Sumner, J. (1993). The effects of related and unrelated cuts on television viewers' attention, processing capacity, and memory. *Communication Research*, 20, 4–29.

Lang, A., Potter, R. F., & Bolls, P. D. (1999). Something for nothing: Is visual encoding automatic? *Media Psychology*, 1, 145–163.

Lang, A., Potter, R. F., & Bolls, P. (2009). Where psychophysiology meets the media: Taking the effects out of mass media research. In J. Bryant and M.B. Oliver (Eds.), *Media effects: Advances in theory and research* (3rd ed., pp. 185–206). New York: Taylor & Francis.

Lang, A., Shin, M., Bradley, S. D., Wang, Z., Lee, S., & Potter, D. (2005). Wait! Don't turn that dial! More excitement to come! The effect of story length and production pacing in local television news on channel changing behavior and information processing in a free choice environment. *Journal of Broadcasting and Electronic Media*, 49, 3–22.

Lang, G. E., & Lang, K. (1984). *Politics and television re-viewed*. Beverly Hills, CA: Sage.

Lang, K., & Lang, G. E. (1968). *Politics and television*. Chicago: Quadrangle Books.

LaRose, R., Lin, C. A., & Eastin, M. S. (2003). Unregulated Internet usage: Addiction, habit, or deficient self-regulation? *Media Psychology*, 5, 225–253.

Larson, J. F. (1984). *Television's window on the world: International affairs coverage on the U.S. networks*. Norwood, NJ: Ablex.

Larson, J. F. (1986). Television and U.S. foreign policy: The case of the Iran hostage crisis. *Journal of Communication*, 36(4), 108–130.

Larson, J. F., McAnany, E. G., & Storey, J. D. (1986). News of Latin America on network television, 1972–1981: A northern perspective on the southern hemisphere. *Critical Studies in Mass Communication*, 3, 169–183.

Larson, M. S. (1989). Interaction between siblings in primetime television families. *Journal of Broadcasting and Electronic Media*, 33(3), 305–315.

Larson, M. S. (2001a). Sibling interaction in situation comedies over the years. In J. Bryant & J. A. Bryant (Eds.), *Television and the American family* (2nd ed., pp. 163–176). Mahwah, NJ: Erlbaum.

Larson, M. S. (2001b). Interactions, activities, and gender in children's television commercials: A content analysis. *Journal of Broadcasting & Electronic Media*, 45, 41–56.

Lasisi, M. J., & Onyehalu, A. S. (1992). Cultural influences of a reading text on the concept formation of second-language learners of two Nigerian ethnic groups. In R. J. Harris (Ed.), *Cognitive processing in bilinguals* (pp. 459–471). Amsterdam: Elsevier/North-Holland Publishing.

Lau, R. R. (1986). Political schemata, candidate evaluations, and voting behavior. In R. R. Lau & D. O. Sears (Eds.), *Political cognition* (pp. 95–126). Hillsdale, NJ: Erlbaum.

Lau, R. R., Sigelman, L., Heldman, C., & Babbitt, P. (1999). The effects of negative political advertisements: A meta-analytic assessment. *American Political Science Review*, 93, 851–875.

Lavaur, J.-M., & Bairstow, D. (2011). Languages on the screen: Is film comprehension related to the viewers' fluency level and to the language in the subtitles? *International Journal of Psychology*, 46, 455–462.

Lavine, H., Sweeney, D., & Wagner, S. H. (1999). Depicting women as sex objects in television advertising: Effects on body dissatisfaction. *Personality and Social Psychology Bulletin*, 25, 1048–1058.

Lawlor, S. D., Sparkes, A., & Wood, J. (1994, July). When Lawrence came out: Taking the funnies seriously. Paper presented at Annual Conference of the International Communication Association, Sydney, Australia.

Lazarsfeld, P. F., Berelson, B., & Gaudet, H. (1948). *The people's choice*. New York: Columbia University Press.

Leaper, C., Breed, L., Hoffman, L., & Perlman, C. A. (2002). Variations in the gender-stereotyped content of children's television cartoons across genres. *Journal of Applied Social Psychology, 32*, 1653–1662.

Leavitt, J. D., & Christenfeld, N. J. S. (2011). Story spoilers don't spoil stories. *Psychological Science, 22*, 1152–1154.

Leavitt, L. A., & Fox, N. A. (Eds.). (1993). *The psychological effects of war and violence on children*. Hillsdale, NJ: Erlbaum.

Lecheler, S., & de Vreese, C. H. (2011). Getting real: The duration of framing effects. *Journal of Communication, 61*, 959–983.

Lee, B., & Tamborini, R. (2005). Third-person effect and internet pornography: The influence of collectivism and internet self-efficacy. *Journal of Communication, 55*, 292–310.

Lee, C.-J., & Niederdeppe, J. (2011). Genre-specific cultivation effects: Lagged associations between overall TV viewing, local TV news viewing, and fatalistic beliefs about cancer prevention. *Communication Research, 38*, 731–753.

Lee, E.-J. (2007). Wired for gender: Experientiality and gender-stereotyping in computer-mediated communication. *Media Psychology, 10*, 182–210.

Lee, H. (2000, June). Reggae power. *World Press Review*, p. 37.

Lee, K. M., & Peng, W. (2006). What do we know about social and psychological effects of computer games? A comprehensive reviews of the current literature. In P. Vorderer & J. Bryant (Eds.), *Playing video games: Motives, responses, and consequences* (pp. 327–345). Mahwah, NJ: Erlbaum.

Lee, M. A., & Solomon, N. (1991). *Unreliable sources: A guide to detecting bias in news media*. New York: Carol.

Lee, S. J. (1996). *Unraveling the "model minority" stereotype: Listening to Asian American youth*. New York: Teachers College Press.

Lee, S. Y., Hwang, H., Hawkins, R., & Pingree, S. (2008). Interplay of negative emotion and health self-efficacy on the use of health information and its outcomes. *Communication Research, 35*, 358–381.

Lefevere, J., de Swert, K., & Walgrave, S. (2012). Effects of popular exemplars in television news. *Communication Research, 39*, 103–119.

Lefkowitz, M. M., Eron, L. D., Walder, L. O., & Huesmann, L. R. (1977). *Growing up to be violent: A longitudinal study of the development of aggression*. New York: Pergamon.

Legrain, P. (2003, May 9). Cultural globalization is not Americanization. *The Chronicle of Higher Education, 49*, pp. B7–B10.

Lemert, J. B., Wanta, W., & Lee, T. T. (1999). Party identification and negative advertising in a U.S. Senate election. *Journal of Communication, 49*(2), 123–134.

Leonard, D. (2006). An untapped field: Exploring the world of virtual sports gaming. In A. A. Raney & J. Bryant (Eds.), *Handbook of sports and media* (pp. 393–407). Mahwah, NJ: Erlbaum.

Leonard, R. S. J. (2006). *Movies that matter: Reading film through the eyes of faith*. Chicago: Loyola Press.

Leone, R. (2002). Contemplating ratings: An examination of what the MPAA considers "too far for R" and why. *Journal of Communication, 52*, 938–954.

Levin, D. E., & Kilbourne, J. (2009). *So sexy so soon: The new sexualized childhood and what parents can do to protect their kids*. New York: Ballantine Books.

Levin, D. T. (2010). Spatial representations of the sets of familiar and unfamiliar television programs. *Media Psychology*, 13, 54–76.

Levin, I. P., & Gaeth, G. J. (1988). How consumers are affected by the framing of attribute information before and after consuming the product. *Journal of Consumer Research*, 15, 374–378.

LeVine, M. (2008). *Heavy metal Islam: Rock, resistance, and the struggle for the soul of Islam*. New York: Three Rivers Press.

Levitin, D. J. (2006). *This is your brain on music: The science of a human obsession*. New York: Penguin.

Levy, M. R. (1982). Watching TV news as para-social interaction. In G. Gumpert & R. Cathcart (Eds.), *Inter/media* (2nd ed., pp. 177–187). New York: Oxford University Press.

Levy, M. R., & Windahl, S. (1984). Audience activity and gratifications: A conceptual clarification and exploration. *Communication Research*, 11, 51–78.

Lewandowsky, S., Stritzke, W. G. K., Oberauer, K., & Morales, M. (2005). Memory for fact, fiction, and misinformation: The Iraq War 2003. *Psychological Science*, 16, 190–195.

Lewin, T. (2011, October 25). Screen time higher than ever for children. *The New York Times*. Retrieved July 18, 2012, from www.nytimes.com/2011/10/25/us/screen-time-higher-than-ever

Lewy, G. (1978, February). Vietnam: New light on the question of American guilt. *Commentary*, 65, 29–49.

Leyens, J., Camino, L., Parke, R., & Berkowitz, L. (1975). The effects of movie violence on aggression in a field setting as a function of group dominance and cohesion. *Journal of Personality and Social Psychology*, 32, 346–360.

Li, X. (2008). Third-person effect, optimistic bias, and sufficiency resource in Internet use. *Journal of Communication*, 58, 568–587.

Lichter, S. R. (2001). A plague on both parties: Substance and fairness in TV election news. *Harvard Journal of Press/Politics*, 6(3), 8–30.

Lieberman, T. (2000, May/June). You can't report what you don't pursue. *Columbia Journalism Review*, 44–49.

Liebert, R. M., & Sprafkin, J. (1988). *The early window: Effects of television on children and youth* (3rd ed.). New York: Pergamon.

Liebert, R., & Schwartzberg, N. (1977). Effects of mass media. *Annual Review of Psychology*, 28, 141–174.

Liebes, T., & Livingstone, S. M. (1992). Mothers and lovers: Managing women's role conflicts in American and British soap operas. In J. G. Blumler, J. M. McLeod, & K. E. Rosengren (Eds.), *Comparatively speaking: Communication and culture across space and time* (pp. 94–120). Newbury Park, CA: Sage.

Lightdale, J. R., & Prentice, D. A. (1994). Rethinking sex differences in aggression: Aggressive behavior in the absence of social roles. *Personality and Social Psychology Bulletin*, 20(1), 34–44.

Liikkanen, L. A. (2008). Music in everymind: Commonality of involuntary music imagery. In K. Miyazaki, Y. Hiragi, M. Adachi, Y. Nakajima, & M. Tsuzaki (Eds.), *Proceedings of the 10th International Conference on Music Perception and Cognition* (pp. 408–412).

Lim, M. (2012). Clicks, cabs, and coffee houses: Social media and oppositional movements in Egypt 2004–2011. *Journal of Communication*, 62, 231–248.

Lindstrom, M. (2011). *Brandwashed: Tricks companies use to manipulate our minds and persuade us to buy*. New York: Crown Business.

Linebarger, D. L., & Walker, D. (2005). Infants' and toddlers' television viewing and language outcomes. *American Behavioral Scientist*, 48(5), 624–645.

Linz, D., & Donnerstein, E. (1988). The methods and merits of pornography research. *Journal of Communication*, 38(2), 180–184.

Linz, D., Donnerstein, E., & Adams, S. M. (1989). Physiological desensitization and judgments about female victims of violence. *Human Communication Research*, 15, 509–522.

Linz, D., Donnerstein, E., Bross, M., & Chapin, M. (1986). Mitigating the influence of violence on television and sexual violence in the media. In R. Blanchard (Ed.), *Advances in the study of aggression* (Vol. 2, pp. 165–194). Orlando, FL: Academic Press.

Linz, D., Donnerstein, E., & Penrod, S. (1984). The effects of multiple exposures to filmed violence against women. *Journal of Communication*, 34(3), 130–147.

Linz, D., Donnerstein, E., & Penrod, S. (1987). The findings and recommendations of the Attorney General's Commission on Pornography: Do the psychological "facts" fit the political fury? *American Psychologist*, 42, 946–953.

Linz, D., Fuson, I. A., & Donnerstein, E. (1990). Mitigating the negative effects of sexually violent mass communications through preexposure briefings. *Communication Research*, 17, 641–674.

Linz, D., & Malamuth, N. (1993). *Pornography*. Newbury Park, CA: Sage.

Linz, D., Turner, C. W., Hesse, B. W., & Penrod, S. D. (1984). Bases of liability for injuries produced by media portrayals of violent pornography. In N. M. Malamuth & E. Donnerstein (Eds.), *Pornography and sexual aggression* (pp. 277–304). Orlando, FL: Academic Press.

Lippert, B. (2003, January–February). What's wrong with this picture? *My Generation*, 48–52.

Livingstone, S., & Helsper, E. J. (2006). Does advertising literacy mediate the effects of advertising on children? *Journal of Communication*, 56, 560–584.

Lo, V. H., & Wei, R. (2005). Exposure to Internet pornography and Taiwanese adolescents' sexual attitudes and behavior. *Journal of Broadcasting and Electronic Media*, 49, 221–237.

Loftus, E. F., & Burns, T. E. (1982). Mental shock can produce retrograde amnesia. *Memory & Cognition*, 10, 318–323.

Loftus, E. F., & Ketcham, K. (1994). *The myth of repressed memory*. New York: St. Martin's Press.

Lohr, B. A., Adams, H. E., & Davis, M. J. (1997). Sexual arousal to erotic and aggressive stimuli in sexually coercive and noncoercive men. *Journal of Abnormal Psychology*, 106, 230–242.

Loken, B., & Peck, J. (2005). The effect of instructional frame on female adolescents' evaluations of larger sized female models in print advertising. *Journal of Applied Social Psychology*, 35, 850–868.

Lomax, R. G. (2006). Fantasy sports: History, game types, and research. In A. A. Raney & J. Bryant (Eds.), *Handbook of sports and media* (pp. 383–392). Mahwah, NJ: Erlbaum.

Lombard, M., Reich, R. D., Grabe, M. E., Bracken, C. C., & Ditton, T. B. (2000). Presence and television: The role of screen size. *Human Communication Research*, 26, 75–98.

Lombard, M., Snyder-Duch, J., & Bracken, C. C. (2002). Content analysis in mass communication: Assessment and reporting of intercoder reliability. *Human Communication Research*, 28, 587–604.

Longford, Earl of (Ed.). (1972). *Pornography: The Longford report*. London: Coronet.

Longmore, P. K. (1985, Summer). Screening stereotypes: Images of disabled people. *Social Policy*, Vol. 15, pp 31–37.

Loth, R. (2012, February 5). What's black and white and re-tweeted all over? *The Chronicle Review of Higher Education*. Retrieved July 17, 2012, from http://chronicle.com/article/Teaching-news-Literacy-in-the/130613

Lovdahl, L. T. (1989). Sex role messages in television commercials: An update. *Sex Roles*, 21, 715–724.

Love, G. D., Mouttapa, M., & Tanjasiri, S. P. (2009). Everybody's talking: using entertainment–education video to reduce barriers to discussion of cervical cancer screening among Thai women. *Health Education Research*, 24(5), 829–838.

Lowry, D. T., Nio, T. C. J., & Leitner, D. W. (2003). Setting the public fear agenda: A longitudinal analysis of network TV crime reporting, public perceptions of crime, and FBI crime statistics. *Journal of Communication*, 53(1), 61–73.

Lozano, E. (1992). The force of myth on popular narratives: The case of melodramatic serials. *Communication Theory*, 2, 207–220.

Luebke, B. (1989). Out of focus: Images of women and men in newspaper photographs. *Sex Roles*, 20(3/4), 121–133.

Luepker, R. V., Murray, D. M., Jacobs, D. R., Mittelmark, M. B., Bracht, N., Carlaw, R., et al. (1994). Community education for cardiovascular disease prevention: Risk factor changes in the Minnesota Heart Health Program. *American Journal of Public Health*, 84, 1383–1393.

Luke, C. (1987). Television discourse and schema theory: Toward a cognitive model of information processing. In M. E. Manley-Casimir & C. Luke (Eds.), *Children and television: A challenge for education* (pp. 76–107). New York: Praeger.

Lundman, R. J., Douglass, O. M., & Hanson, J. M. (2004). News about murder in an African American newspaper: effects of relative frequency and race and gender typifications. *The Sociological Quarterly*, 45, 249–272.

Luscombe, B. (2000, October 9). Laugh track. *Time*, p. 102.

Luyt, R. (2011). Representation of gender in South African television advertising: A content analysis. *Sex Roles*, 65, 356–370.

Lyman, R. (2002, September 19). Hollywood balks at high-tech sanitizers. *New York Times*. Retrieved September 19, 2002, from http://www.nytimes.com/2002/09/19/movies/19CLEA.html

Macbeth, T. M. (1996). Indirect effects of television: Creativity, persistence, school achievement, and participation in other activities. In T. M. Macbeth (Ed.), *Tuning in to young viewers: Social science perspectives on television* (pp. 149–219). Thousand Oaks, CA: Sage.

Madden, N. (2010, January 27). China had 174 million cable TV subscribers in 2009. *Advertising Age*. Retrieved from http://adage.com

Madrigal, R., Bee, C., Chen, J., & LaBarge, M. (2011). The effect of suspense on enjoyment following a desirable outcome: The mediating role of relief. *Media Psychology*, 14, 259–288.

Maerz, M. (2010, October 24). Some *Sesame Street* viewers sense a gay-friendly vibe. *Los Angeles Times*. Retrieved from http://www.latimes.com/

Mahan, J. E., III, & McDaniel, S. R. (2006). The new online arena: Sport, marketing, and media converge in cyberspace. In A. A. Raney & J. Bryant (Eds.), *Handbook of sports and media* (pp. 409–431). Mahwah, NJ: Erlbaum.

Maibach, E., & Flora, J. A. (1993). Symbolic modeling and cognitive rehearsal: Using video to promote AIDS prevention self-efficacy. *Communication Research*, 20, 517–545.

Maibach, E., & Parrott, R. L. (1995). *Designing health messages*. Thousand Oaks, CA: Sage.

Maier, S. (1994, January). India's awakening? *World Press Review*, 41, 29.

Malamuth, N. M. (1981). Rape fantasies as a function of exposure to violent sexual stimuli. *Archives of Sexual Behavior*, 10, 33–47.

Malamuth, N. M. (1984). Aggression against women: Cultural and individual causes. In N. M. Malamuth & E. Donnerstein (Eds.), *Pornography and sexual aggression* (pp. 19–52). Orlando, FL: Academic Press.

Malamuth, N. M. (1996). Sexually explicit media, gender differences, and evolutionary theory. *Journal of Communication*, 46(3), 8–31.

Malamuth, N. M., Addison, T., & Koss, M. (2000). Pornography and sexual aggression: Are there reliable effects and can we understand them? *Annual Review of Sex Research*, 11, 26–91.

Malamuth, N. M., & Check, J. V. P. (1980). Sexual arousal to rape and consenting depictions: The importance of the woman's arousal. *Journal of Abnormal Psychology*, 89, 763–766.

Malamuth, N. M., & Check, J. V. P. (1983). Sexual arousal to rape depictions: Individual differences. *Journal of Abnormal Psychology*, 92, 55–67.

Malamuth, N. M., Check, J. V. P., & Briere, J. (1986). Sexual arousal in response to aggression: Ideological, aggressive, and sexual correlates. *Journal of Personality and Social Psychology*, 50, 330–340.

Malamuth, N. M., Heim, M., & Feshbach, S. (1980). Sexual responsiveness of college students to rape depictions: Inhibitory and disinhibitory effects. *Journal of Personality and Social Psychology*, 38, 399–408.

Malamuth, N. M., & Impett, E. A. (2001). Research on sex in the media: What do we know about effects on children and adolescents? In D. Singer & J. Singer (Eds.), *Handbook of children and the media* (pp. 269–287). Newbury Park, CA: Sage.

Malawi bans *Big Brother Africa*. (2003, August 6). *BBC News*. Retrieved August 6, 2003, from http://www.news.bbc.co.uk

Manrai, L. A., & Gardner, M. P. (1992). Consumer processing of social ideas advertising: A conceptual model. *Advances in Consumer Research*, 19, 15–20.

Mares, M. L., & Woodard, E. H. (2001). Prosocial effects on children's social interactions. In D. G. Singer & J. L. Singer (Eds.), *Handbook of children and the media* (pp. 183–205). Thousand Oaks, CA: Sage.

Mares, M. L., & Woodard, E. H. (2005). Positive effects of television on children's social interactions: A meta-analysis. *Media Psychology*, 7, 301–322.

Mares, M. L., Palmer, E., & Sullivan, T. (2011). Prosocial effects of media exposure. In S. L. Calvert & B. J. Wilson (Eds.), *The handbook of children, media, and development* (pp. 268–289). Malden, MA: Wiley-Blackwell.

Marling, K. A. (2002, May 28). They want their mean TV. *The New York Times*. Retrieved May 28, 2002, from http://www.nytimes.com/2002/05/26/arts/television/26MARL.html

Marshall, R. D., Bryant, R. A., Amsel, L., Suh, E. J., Cook, J. M., & Neria, Y. (2007). The psychology of ongoing threat: Relative risk appraisal, the September 11 attacks, and terrorism-related fears. *American Psychologist*, 62, 304–316.

Martin, M. C. (1997). Children's understanding of the intent of advertising: A meta-analysis. *Journal of Public Policy and Marketing*, 16, 205–216.

Martins, N., & Wilson, B.J. (2012). Social aggression on television and its relationship to children's aggression in the classroom. *Human Communication Research*, 38, 48–71.

Martz, L. (1998, May). Defending the most basic freedom. *World Press Review*, 45, 14–16.

Mastro, D. E., & Behm-Morawitz, E. (2005). Latino representations on primetime television. *Journalism & Mass Communication Quarterly*, 82, 110–130.

Mastro, D. E., Behm-Morawitz, E., & Kopacz, M. A. (2008). Exposure to television portrayals of Latinos: The implications of aversive racism and social identity theory. *Human Communication Research*, 34, 1–27.

Mastro, D. E., Behm-Morawitz, E., & Ortiz, M. (2007). The cultivation of social perceptions of Latinos: A mental models approach. *Media Psychology*, 9, 347–365.

Mastro, D. E., Eastin, M. S., & Tamborini, R. (2002). Internet search behaviors and mood alterations: A selective exposure approach. *Media Psychology*, 4, 157–172.

Mastro, D. E., & Greenberg, B. S. (2000). The portrayal of racial minorities on prime-time television. *Journal of Broadcasting & Electronic Media*, 44, 690–703.

Matabane, P. W. (1988). Television and the black audience: Cultivating moderate perspectives on racial integration. *Journal of Communication*, 38(4), 21–31.

Matas, M., Guebaly, N., Harper, D., Green, M., & Peterkin, A. (1986). Mental illness and the media: Part II. Content analysis of press coverage of mental health topics. *Canadian Journal of Psychiatry*, 31, 431–433.

Maurer, M., & Reinemann, C. (2006). Learning versus knowing: Effects of misinformation in televised debates. *Communication Research*, 33, 489–506.

Mayer, J. (2000, August 14). Bad news: What's behind the recent gaffes at ABC? *The New Yorker*, pp. 30–36.

Mayerson, S. E., & Taylor, D. A. (1987). The effects of rape myth pornography on women's attitudes and the mediating role of sex role stereotyping. *Sex Roles*, 17, 321–338.

McAlister, A. L., Puska, P., & Salonen, J. T. (1982). Theory and action for health promotion: Illustrations from the North Karelia project. *American Journal of Public Health*, 72, 43–50.

McAnany, E. G. (1983). Television and crisis: Ten years of network news coverage of Central America, 1972–1981. *Media, Culture and Society*, 5(2), 199–212.

McCauley, C. (1998). When screen violence is not attractive. In J. H. Goldstein (Ed.), *Why we watch: The attractions of violent entertainment* (pp. 144–162). New York: Oxford University Press.

McCombs, M. E. (1994). News influence on our pictures of the world. In J. Bryant & D. Zillmann (Eds.), *Media effects: Advances in theory and research* (pp. 1–16). Hillsdale, NJ: Erlbaum.

McCombs, M. E., & Ghanem, S. (2001). The convergence of agenda setting and framing. In S. D. Reese, O. Gandy, & A. Grant (Eds.), *Framing in the new media landscape*. Mahwah, NJ: Erlbaum.

McCombs, M. E., & Reynolds, A. (2002). News influence on our pictures of the world. In J. Bryant & D. Zillmann (Eds.), *Media effects: Advances in theory and research* (2nd ed., pp. 1–18). Mahwah, NJ: Erlbaum.

McCombs, M., & Reynolds, A. (2009). How the news shapes our civic agenda. In J. Bryant and M. B. Oliver (Eds.), *Media effects: Advances in theory and research.* (3rd ed., pp. 1–16). New York: Taylor & Francis.

McCombs, M. E., & Shaw, D. L. (1993). The evolution of agenda-setting research: Twenty-five years in the marketplace of ideas. *Journal of Communication*, 43(2), 58–67.

McCombs, M. E., Shaw, D. L., & Weaver, D. (Eds.). (1997). *Communication and democracy: Exploring the intellectual frontiers in agenda-setting theory*. Mahwah, NJ: Erlbaum.

McCook, A. (2003, April 17). "Fear Factor" TV show may be too scary for some. *Reuters. Health on the Web*. Retrieved June 17, 2003, from http://www.reuters.com

McCool, J. P., Cameron, L. D., & Petrie, K. J. (2001). Adolescent perceptions of smoking imagery in film. *Social Science & Medicine*, 52, 1577–1587.

McCutcheon, L. E., Ashe, D. D., Houran, J., & Maltby, J. (2003). A cognitive profile of individuals who tend to worship celebrities. *Journal of Psychology*, 137, 309–322.

McDermott, S., & Greenberg, B. (1985). Parents, peers, and television as determinants of black children's esteem. In R. Bostrom (Ed.), *Communication Yearbook 8*. Beverly Hills, CA: Sage.

McDonnell, J. (1992). Rap music: Its role as an agent of change. *Popular Music and Society*, 16, 89–108.

McIntyre, P., Hosch, H. M., Harris, R. J., & Norvell, D. W. (1986). Effects of sex and attitudes toward women on the processing of television commercials. *Psychology and Marketing*, 3, 181–190.

McKenna, K. Y. A., & Bargh, J. A. (1999). Causes and consequences of social interaction on the Internet: A conceptual framework. *Media Psychology*, 1, 249–269.

McKenna, K. Y. A., & Seidman, G. (2005). Social identity and the self: Getting connected online. In W. R. Walker & D. J. Herrmann (Eds.), *Cognitive technology: Essays on the transformation of thought and society* (pp. 89–110). Jefferson, NC: McFarland.

McKenzie-Mohr, D., & Zanna, M. P. (1990). Treating women as sexual objects: Look to the (gender schematic) male who has viewed pornography. *Personality and Social Psychology Bulletin, 16*, 296–308.

McNeal, J. U. (1999). *The kids' market: Myths and realities.* Ithaca, NY: Paramount Market.

Mead, M. (1973). As significant as the invention of drama or the novel. A famed anthropologist takes a careful look at "An American Family." *TV Guide, 21*, 21–23.

Meadowcroft, J. M., & Reeves, B. (1989). Influence of story schema development on children's attention to television. *Communication Research, 16*, 352–374.

Media deconstruction as an essential learning skill (2012, May). *Connections, 39*, 2–3.

Médioni, G. (2002, July). Stand up, Africa! *World Press Review,* 34–35.

Meeter, M., Murre, J. M. J., & Janssen, S. M. J. (2005). Remembering the news: Modeling retention data from a study with 14,000 participants. *Memory & Cognition, 33*, 793–810.

Meffert, M. F., Chung, S., Joiner, A. J., Waks, L., & Garst, J. (2006). The effects of negativity and motivated information processing during a political campaign. *Journal of Communication, 56*, 27–51.

Meirick, P. C. (2008). Targeted audiences in anti-drug ads: Message cues, perceived exposure, perceived effects, and support for funding. *Media Psychology, 11*, 283–309.

Mendelsohn, H. A. (1966). Election-day broadcasts and terminal voting decisions. *Public Opinion Quarterly, 30*, 212–225.

Merikle, P. M. (1988). Subliminal auditory messages: An evaluation. *Psychology & Marketing, 5*, 355–372.

Merikle, P. M., & Cheesman, J. (1987). Current status of research on subliminal advertising. *Advances in Consumer Research, 14*, 298–302.

Merikle, P. M., & Skanes, H. E. (1992). Subliminal self-help audiotapes: A search for placebo effects. *Journal of Applied Psychology, 77*, 772–776.

Merskin, D. (1998). Sending up signals: A survey of Native American media use and representation in the mass media. *Howard Journal of Communication, 9*, 333–345.

Mesmer, T., Baskind, I., & Lerdau, E. (1998, October). Reflecting on an alliance. *Americas, 50*(5), 52–55.

Messaris, P. (1994). *Visual literacy: Image, mind, and reality.* Boulder, CO: Westview Press.

Messaris, P. (1997). *Visual persuasion: The role of images in advertising.* Thousand Oaks, CA: Sage.

Messaris, P. (1998). Visual aspects of media literacy. *Journal of Communication, 48*(1), 70–80.

Meyer, P. (1990). News media responsiveness to public health. In C. Atkin & L. Wallack (Eds.), *Mass communication and public health: Complexities and conflicts* (pp. 52–57). Newbury Park, CA: Sage.

Meyrowitz, J. (1985). *No sense of place: The impact of electronic media on social behavior.* New York: Oxford University Press.

Meyrowitz, J. (1998). Multiple media literacies. *Journal of Communication, 48*(1), 96–108.

Michel, E., & Roebers, C. M. (2008). Children's knowledge acquisition through film: Influence of programme characteristics. *Applied Cognitive Psychology, 22*, 1228–1244.

Mielke, K. W., & Chen, M. (1983). Formative research for *3-2-1 Contact*: Methods and insights. In M. J. A. Howe (Ed.), *Learning from television: Psychological and educational research* (pp. 31–55). London: Academic Press.

Miller, C. H., Lane, L. T., Deatrick, L. M., Young, A. M., & Potts, K. A. (2007). Psychological reactance and promotional health messages: The effects of controlling language, lexical correctness, and the restoration of freedom. *Human Communication Research*, 33, 219–240.

Miller, M., & Pearlstein, E. (Producers). (2004). *TV revolution*. [Television documentary series.] Hollywood: Bravo.

Mills, J. (1993). The appeal of tragedy: An attitude interpretation. *Basic and Applied Social Psychology*, 14, 255–271.

Mills, J. S., Polivy, J., Herman, C. P., & Tiggemann, M. (2002). Effects of exposure to thin media images: Evidence of self-enhancement among restrained eaters. *Personality and Social Psychology Bulletin*, 28, 1687–1699.

Minow, N. N., LaMay, C. L., & Gregorian, V. (2008). *Inside the presidential debates: Their improbable past and promising future*. Chicago: University of Chicago Press.

Minzesheimer, B. (2012, July 19). Oprah's Book Club 2.0 goes digital to study Cheryl Strayed's 'Wild'. *Chicago Sun Times*. Retrieved from http://www.suntimes.com

Mitchell, J. (2012). *Promoting peace, inciting violence: The role of religion and media*. New York: Routledge.

Mitra, A. (2004). Voices of the marginalized on the Internet: Examples from a website for women of South Asia. *Journal of Communication*, 54, 492–510.

Moeller, S. D. (1999). *Compassion fatigue: How the media sell disease, famine, war, and death*. New York: Routledge.

Moisy, C. (1997, Summer). Myths of the global information village. *Foreign Policy*, 78–87.

Mok, T. (1998). Getting the message: Media images and stereotypes ad their effect on Asian Americans. *Culture Diversity and Mental Health*, 4, 185–202.

Monk-Turner, E., Heiserman, M., Johnson, C., Cotton, V., & Jackson, M. (2010). The portrayal of racial minorities on prime time television: A replication of the Mastro and Greenberg study a decade later. *Studies in Popular Culture*, 32, 101–114.

Mooney, C., & Kirshenbaum. S. (2009). *Unscientific America: How scientific illiteracy threatens our future*. New York: Basic Books.

Moore, D. L., Hausknecht, D., & Thamodaran, K. (1986). Time compression, response opportunity, and persuasion. *Journal of Consumer Research*, 13, 85–99.

Moore, T. E. (1982). What you see is what you get. *Journal of Marketing*, 46(2), 38–47.

Moore, T. E. (1988). The case against subliminal manipulation. *Psychology & Marketing*, 5, 297–316.

Morgan, M. (1982). Television and adolescents' sex-role stereotypes: A longitudinal study. *Journal of Personality and Social Psychology*, 43(5), 947–955.

Morgan, M. (1989). Television and democracy. In I. Angus & S. Jhally (Eds.), *Cultural politics in contemporary America* (pp. 240–253). New York: Routledge.

Morgan, M. (1990). International cultivation analysis. In N. Signorielli & M. Morgan (Eds.), *Cultivation analysis: New directions in media effects research* (pp. 225–247). Newbury Park, CA: Sage.

Morgan, M., & Shanahan, J. (1991). Television and the cultivation of political attitudes in Argentina. *Journal of Communication*, 41(1), 88–103.

Morgan, M., & Shanahan, J. (1992). Comparative cultivation analysis: Television and adolescents in Argentina and Taiwan. In F. Korzenny & S. Ting-Toomey (Eds.), *Mass media effects across cultures* (pp. 173–197). Newbury Park, CA: Sage.

Morgan, M., & Shanahan, J. (1995). *Democracy tango: Television, adolescents, and authoritarian tensions in Argentina*. Cresskill, NJ: Hampton Press.

Morgan, M., Shanahan, J., & Signoriell, N. (2009). Growing up with television: Cultivation processes. In J. Bryant and M. B. Oliver (Eds.), *Media effects: Advances in theory and research* (3rd ed., pp. 34–49). New York: Taylor & Francis.

Morgan, S. E., Palmgreen, P., Stephenson, M. T., Hoyle, R. H., & Lorch, E. P. (2003). Associations between message features and subjective evaluations of the sensation value of antidrug public service announcements. *Journal of Communication*, 53(3), 512–526.

Moriarty, C. M., & Harrison, K. (2008). Television exposure and disordered eating among children: A longitudinal panel study. *Journal of Communication*, 58, 361–381.

Moritz, M. J. (1995). The gay agenda: Marketing hate speech to the mainstream media. In R. K. Whillock & D. Slayden (Eds.), *Hate speech* (pp. 55–79). Thousand Oaks, CA: Sage.

Morley, D. (1988). Domestic relations: The framework of family viewing in Great Britain. In J. Lull (Ed.), *World families watch television* (pp. 22–48). Newbury Park, CA: Sage.

Morris, J. S. (1982). Television portrayal and the socialization of the American Indian child. In G. L. Berry & C. Mitchell-Kernan (Eds.), *Television and the socialization of the minority child* (pp. 187–202). New York: Academic Press.

Moscowitz, L. (2010). Gay marriage in television news: Voice and visual representation in the same-sex marriage debate. *Journal of Broadcasting & Electronic Media*, 54, 24–39.

Mosher, D. L., & Maclan, P. (1994). College men and women respond to X-rated videos intended for male or female audiences: Gender and sexual scripts. *Journal of Sex Research*, 31, 99–113.

Moskalenko, S., & Heine, S. J. (2003). Watching your troubles away: Television viewing as a stimulus for subjective self-awareness. *Personality and Social Psychology Bulletin*, 29, 76–85.

Mottola, C., & Margolis, J. (2009). Advertising. In K. H. Jamieson (Ed.), *Electing the President 2008: The insider's view* (pp. 109–134). Philadelphia, PA: University of Pennsylvania Press.

Mowlana, H. (1984). The role of the media in the U.S.-Iranian conflict. In A. Arno & W. Dissayanake (Eds.), *The news media in national and international conflict* (pp. 71–99). Boulder, CO: Westview Press.

Mowlana, H., Gerbner, G., & Schiller, H. (Eds.). (1993). *Triumph of the image: The media's war in the Persian Gulf—A global perspective*. Boulder, CO: Westview Press.

Muehling, D. D., & Kolbe, R. H. (1999). A comparison of children's and prime-time fine-print advertising disclosure practices. In M. C. Macklin & L. Carlson (Eds.), *Advertising to children: Concepts and controversies* (pp. 143–164). Thousand Oaks, CA: Sage.

Mulholland, N. (Ed.). (2006). *The psychology of Harry Potter*. Dallas, TX: Benbella Books.

Mundorf, N., Allen, M., D'Alessio, D., & Emmers-Sommer, T. (2007). Effects of sexually explicit media. In R. W. Preiss, B. M. Gayle, N. Burrell, M. Allen, & J. Bryant (Eds.), *Mass media effects research: Advances through meta-analysis* (pp. 181–198). Mahwah, NJ: Erlbaum.

Mundorf, N., Drew, D., Zillmann, D., & Weaver, J. (1990). Effects of disturbing news on recall of subsequently presented news. *Communication Research*, 17, 601–615.

Mundorf, N., & Laird, K. R. (2002). Social and psychological effects of information technologies and other interactive media. In J. Bryant & D. Zillmann (Eds.), *Media effects* (2nd ed., pp. 583–602). Mahwah, NJ: Erlbaum.

Mundorf, N., Weaver, J., & Zillmann, D. (1989). Effects of gender roles and self-perceptions on affective reactions to horror films. *Sex Roles*, 20, 655–673.

Münzer, S., & Borg, A. (2008). Computer-mediated communication: Synchronicity and compensatory effort. *Applied Cognitive Psychology*, 22, 663–683.

Murnen, S. K., & Stockton, M. (1997). Gender and self-reported sexual arousal in response to sexual stimuli: A meta-analytic review. *Sex Roles*, 37, 135–153.

Murphy, S. T. (1998). The impact of factual versus fictional media portrayals on cultural stereotypes. *Annals of the American Academy of Political and Social Science*, 560, 165–178.

Murray, E., Lo, B., Pollack, L., Donelan, K., & Lee, K. (2003). Direct-to-consumer advertising: public perceptions of its effects on health behaviors, health care, and the doctor-patient relationship. *Journal of the American Board of Family Practice*, 16, 513–524.

Murray, J. P. (1999). Studying television violence: A research agenda for the 21st century. In J. K. Asamen & G. L. Berry (Eds.), *Research paradigms, television, and social behavior* (pp. 369–410). Thousand Oaks, CA: Sage.

Murray, J. P., Liotti, M., Ingmundson, P. T., Mayberg, H. S., Pu, Y., Zamarripa, F. et al., (2006). Children's brain activations while watching televised violence revealed by fMRI. *Media Psychology*, 8, 25–37.

Murray, M. (2012, July 25). Kenyans use cell phones for everything from buying groceries to paying rent. *NBCNews.com*. Retrieved July 25, 2012, http://worldnews.nbcnews.com/_news/2012/07/24/12909129-kenyans-use-cell-phones-for-everything-from-buying-groceries-to-paying-rent

Mutz, D. C., Roberts, D. F., & van Vuuren, D. P. (1993). Reconsidering the displacement hypothesis. *Communication Research*, 20, 51–75.

Myers, P. N., Jr., & Biocca, F. A. (1992). The elastic body image: The effect of television advertising and programming on body image distortions in young women. *Journal of Communication*, 42(3), 108–133.

Nabi, R.L., & Clark, S. (2008). Exploring the limits of social cognitive theory: Why negatively reinforced behaviors on TV may be modeled anyway. *Journal of Communication*, 58, 407–427.

Naked capitalists (2001, May 20). *The New York Times*. Cited in *Kansas State Collegian*, February 5, 2002.

Nathanson, A. I. (1999). Identifying and explaining the relationship between parental mediation and children's aggression. *Communication Research*, 26, 124–143.

Nathanson, A. I. (2004). Factual and evaluative approaches to modifying children's responses to violent television. *Journal of Communication*, 54, 321–336.

Nathanson, A.I., & Rasmussen, E. E. (2011). TV viewing compared to book reading and toy playing reduces responsive maternal communication with toddlers and preschoolers. *Human Communication Research*, 37, 465–487.

Nathanson, A. I., Wilson, B. J., McGee, J., & Sebastian, M. (2002). Counteracting the effects of female stereotypes on television via active mediation. *Journal of Communication*, 52, 922–937.

Nathanson, A. I., & Yang, M. S. (2003). The effects of mediation content and form on children's response to violent television. *Human Communication Research*, 29, 111–134.

National television violence study (1997). Vols. 1–2. Thousand Oaks, CA: Sage.

Naveh, C. (2002). The role of the media in foreign policy decision-making: A theoretical framework. *Conflict & Communication Online*, 1(2), 1–14.

Neeley, S. M., & Schumann, D. W. (2004). Using animated spokes-characters in advertising to young children. *Journal of Advertising*, 33(3), 7–23.

Nell, V. (2002). Why young men drive dangerously: Implications for injury prevention. *Current Directions in Psychological Science*, 11, 75–79.

Nelson, J. P., Gelfand, D. M., & Hartmann, D. P. (1969). Children's aggression following competition and exposure to an aggressive model. *Child Development*, 40, 1085–1097.

Nelson, M. R. (2002). Recall of brand placements in computer/video games. *Journal of Advertising Research*, 42, 80–92.

Nettelhorst, S. C., & Brannon, L. A. (2012). The effect of advertisement choice on attention. *Computers in Human Behavior*, 28, 683–687.

Neuendorf, K. A. (2002). *The content analysis guidebook*. Thousand Oaks, CA: Sage.

Newhagen, J. E., & Reeves, B. (1991). Emotion and memory responses for negative political advertising: A study of television commercials used in the 1988 Presidential election. In F. Biocca (Ed.), *Television and political advertising: Psychological processes* (Vol. 1, pp. 197–220). Hillsdale, NJ: Erlbaum.

Newhagen, J. E., & Reeves, B. (1992). The evening's bad news: Effects of compelling negative television news images on memory. *Journal of Communication, 42*(2), 25–41.

Niederdeppe, J., Farrelly, M. C., Thomas, K. Y., Wenter, D., & Weitzenkamp, D. (2007). Newspaper coverage as indirect effects of a health communication intervention. *Communication Research, 34,* 382–406.

Nielsen Company. (2010a). Television audience report 2009. Retrieved from http://blog.nielsen.com/nielsenwire/wp-content/uploads/2010/04/TVA_2009-for-Wire.pdf

Nielsen Company. (2010b). What Americans do online. Retrieved from http://blog.nielsen.com/nielsenwire/online_mobile/what-americans-do-online-social-media-and-games-dominate-activity/

Nielsen Company. (2011). The cross platform report, Quarter 1, 2011. Retrieved from http://www.nielsen.com/us/en/insights/reports-downloads/2011/cross-platform-report-q1-2011.html

Niemiec, R. M., & Wedding, D. (2008). *Positive psychology at the movies: Using films to build virtues and character strengths.* Cambridge, MA: Hogrefe.

Nimmo, D., & Savage, R. L. (1976). *Candidates and their images.* Pacific Palisades, CA: Goodyear.

Nisbet, E. C., Stoycheff, E., & Pearce, K. E. (2012). Internet use and democratic demands: A multinational, multilevel model of Internet use and citizen attitudes about democracy. *Journal of Communication, 62,* 249–265.

Nisbett, R. E. (2003). *The geography of thought: How Asians and Westerners think differently . . . and why.* New York: Free Press.

Noe, D. (1995). Parallel worlds: The surprising similarities (and differences) of country-and-western and rap. *The Humanist, 55,* 20–23.

Noice, H., & Noice, T. (2006). What studies of actors and acting can tell us about memory and cognitive functioning. *Current Directions in Psychological Science, 15,* 14–18.

Noice, T., & Noice, H. (1997). *The nature of expertise in professional acting: A cognitive view.* Mahwah, NJ: Erlbaum.

Nolan, J. M., & Ryan, G. W. (2000). Fear and loathing at the Cineplex: Gender differences in descriptions and perceptions of slasher films. *Sex Roles, 42,* 39–56.

Norris, J., George, W. H., Davis, K. C., Martell, J., & Leonesio, R. J. (1999). Alcohol and hypermasculinity as determinants of men's empathic responses to violent pornography. *Journal of Interpersonal Violence, 14,* 683–700.

North Korean movies' propaganda role. (2003, August 18). *BBC News.* Retrieved August 18, 2003, from http://www.news.bbc.co.uk

Norton, I. (2008, June 13). From rock 'n' roll stardom to academe. *The Chronicle of Higher Education, 54,* A6.

Numbers (1997, September 29). *Time,* p. 23.

Numbers (1998, January 19). *Time,* p. 19.

Numbers (1999, May 31). *Time,* p. 29.

Numbers (2005, November 21). *Time,* p. 24.

Numbers (2007, September 24). *Time,* p. 20.

Numbers (2008a, May 26). *Time,* p. 18.

Numbers (2008b, June 16). *Time,* pp. 14–15.

Nussbaum, J. F., & Robinson, J. D. (1986). Attitudes toward aging. *Communication Research Reports, 1,* 21–27.

O'Bryant, S. L., & Corder-Bolz, C. R. (1978). The effects of television on children's stereotyping of women's work roles. *Journal of Vocational Behavior, 12*, 233–244.

Oddone-Paolucci, E., Genuis, M., & Violato, C. (2000). A meta-analysis of the published research on the effects of pornography. In C. Violato, E. Oddone-Paolucci, & M. Genuis (Eds.), *The changing family and child development* (pp. 48–59). Aldershot, UK: Ashgate.

Offit, P. A. (2011). *Deadly choices: How the anti-vaccine movement threatens us all.* New York: Basic Books.

Ohbuchi, K., Ikeda, T., & Takeuchi, G. (1994). Effects of violent pornography upon viewers' rape myth beliefs: A study of Japanese males. *Psychology, Crime, & Law, 1*, 71–81.

Oliver, M. B. (1993). Adolescents' enjoyment of graphic horror. *Communication Research, 20*, 30–50.

Oliver, M. B. (1994). Portrayals of crime, race, and aggression in "reality-based" police shows: A content analysis. *Journal of Broadcasting and Electronic Media, 38*, 179–192.

Oliver, M. B., & Bartsch, A. (2010). Appreciation as audience response: Exploring entertainment gratification beyond hedonism. *Human Communication Research, 36*, 53–81.

Oliver, M. B., & Fonash, D. (2002). Race and crime in the news: Whites' identification and misidentification of violent and nonviolent criminal suspects. *Media Psychology, 4*, 137–156.

Oliver, M. B., Jackson, R. L., Moses, N., & Dangerfield, C. L. (2004). The face of crime: Viewers' memory of race-related facial features of individuals pictured in the news. *Journal of Communication, 54*, 88–104.

Oliver, M. B., & Krakowiak, K. M. (2009). Individual differences in media effects. In J. Bryant and M. B. Oliver (Eds.), *Media effects: Advances in theory and research* (3rd ed., pp. 517–531). New York: Taylor & Francis.

Oliver, M. B., & Raney, A. A. (2011). Entertainment as pleasurable and meaningful: Identifying hedonic and eudaimonic motivations for entertainment consumption. *Journal of Communication, 61*, 984–1004.

Olson, D. R. (1994). *The world on paper.* New York: Cambridge University Press.

Olweus, D. (1979). The stability of aggressive reaction patterns in human males: A review. *Psychological Bulletin, 85*, 852–875.

Onishi, N. (2001, February 12). Maradi journal: On the scale of beauty in Niger, weight weighs heavily. *The New York Times.* Retrieved February 12, 2001, from http://www.nytimes.com/2–1/02/12/world/12NIGE.html?pagewanted=all?ex=982993940&ei=1&en=cd9deca02d8a3726

Oppliger, P. A. (2007). Effects of gender stereotyping on socialization. In R. W. Preiss, B. M. Gayle, N. Burrell, M. Allen, & J. Bryant (Eds.), *Mass media effects research: Advances through meta-analysis* (pp. 199–214). Mahwah, NJ: Erlbaum.

Orecklin, M. (2003, May 19). There's no escape. *Time.*

Orman, J. (1992). Conclusion: The impact of popular music in society. In K. J. Bindas (Ed.), *America's musical pulse: Popular music in twentieth-century society* (pp. 281–287). Westport, CT: Praeger.

Otgaar, H., Candel, I., Merckelbach, H., & Wade, K. A. (2009). Abducted by a UFO: Prevalence information affects young children's false memories for an implausible event. *Applied Cognitive Psychology, 23*, 115–125.

Paavonen, E. J., Roine, M., Pennonen, M., & Lahikainen, A. R. (2009). Do parental co-viewing and discussions mitigate TV-induced fears in young children? *Child: Care, Health, & Development, 35*, 773–780.

Paek, H.-J. (2008). Mechanisms through which adolescents attend and respond to anti-smoking media campaigns. *Journal of Communication, 58*, 84–105.

Paek, H.-J., & Gunther, A. C. (2007). How peer proximity moderates indirect media influence on adolescent smoking. *Communication Research, 34*, 407–432.

Paek, H.-J., Nelson, M. R., & Vilela, A. M. (2011). Examination of gender-role portrayals in television advertising across seven countries. *Sex Roles*, 64, 192–207.

Page, J. T., & Duffy, M. E. (2009). A battle of visions: Dueling images of morality in U.S. political campaign UV ads. *Communication, Culture & Critique*, 2, 110–135.

Paik, H., & Comstock, G. (1994). The effects of television violence on antisocial behavior: A meta-analysis. *Communication Research*, 21, 516–546.

Pal, M., & Dutta, M. J. (2012). Organizing resistance on the Internet: The case of the International Campaign for Justice in Bhopal. *Communication, Culture, & Critique*, 5, 230–251.

Paletz, D. L. (1988). Pornography, politics, and the press: The U.S. attorney general's commission on pornography. *Journal of Communication*, 38(2), 122–136.

Paletz, D. L., & Schmid, A. P. (Eds.). (1992). *Terrorism and the media*. Newbury Park, CA: Sage.

Paley Center for Media (2010). I want my gay TV: The LGBT history of television. Retrieved from http://www.paleycenter.org/i-want-my-gay-tv

Palmgreen, P. (1984). Uses and gratifications: A theoretical perspective. In R. N. Bostrom (Ed.), *Communication Yearbook 8* (pp. 20–55). Newbury Park, CA: Sage.

Panee, C. D., & Ballard, M. E. (2002). High versus low aggressive priming during video game training: Effects of violent action during game play, hostility, heart rate, and blood pressure. *Journal of Applied Social Psychology*, 32, 2458–2474.

Papa, M. J., Singhal, A., Law, S., Pant, S., Sood, S., Rogers, E. M., et al. (2000). Entertainment-education and social change: An analysis of parasocial interaction, social learning, collective efficacy, and paradoxical communication. *Journal of Communication*, 50(4), 31–55.

Papacharissi, Z., & Rubin, A. (2000). Predictors of Internet use. *Journal of Broadcasting and Electronic Media*, 44, 175–196.

Pappas-DeLuca, K. A., Kraft, J., Galavotti, C., Warner, L., Mooki, M., Hastings, P., Koppenhaver, T., Roels, T. H., & Kilmarx, P. H. (2008). Entertainment-education radio serial drama and outcomes related to HIV Testing in Botswana. *AIDS Education and Prevention*, 20(6), 486–503.

Parcell, L. M., Kwon, J., Miron, D., & Bryant, J. (2007). An analysis of media health campaigns for children and adolescents: Do they work? In R. W. Preiss et al. (Eds.), *Mass media effects research: Advances through meta-analysis* (pp. 345–361). Mahwah, NJ: Erlbaum.

Park, A. (2012, August 6). Web MDs: Social media are changing how we diagnose disease. *Time*, p. 16.

Park, H. S., Lee, H. E., & Song, J. A. (2005). "I am sorry to send you SPAM": Cross-cultural differences in use of apologies in e-mail advertising in Korea and the U.S. *Human Communication Research*, 31, 365–398.

Park, J. H., Gabbadon, N. G., & Chernin, A. R. (2006). Neutralizing racial differences through comedy: Asian, black, and white views on racial stereotypes in *Rush Hour 2*. *Journal of Communication*, 56, 157–177.

Parker, E., & Furnham, A. (2007). Does sex sell? The effect of sexual programme content on the recall of sexual and non-sexual advertisements. *Applied Cognitive Psychology*, 21, 1217–1228.

Parkin, K. J. (2006). *Food is love: Advertising and gender roles in modern America*. Philadelphia: University of Pennsylvania Press.

Parks, M. R. (1996). Making friends in cyberspace. *Journal of Communication*, 46(1), 80–97.

Paul, B., & Linz, D. (2008). The effects of exposure to virtual child pornography on viewer cognitions and attitudes toward deviant sexual behavior. *Communication Research*, 35, 3–38.

Paul, B., Salwen, M. B., & Dupagne, M. (2007). The third-person effect: A meta-analysis of the perceptual hypothesis. In R. W. Preiss, B. M. Gayle, N. Burrell, M. Allen, & J. Bryant (Eds.), *Mass media effects research: Advances through meta-analysis* (pp. 81–102). Mahwah, NJ: Erlbaum.

Payne, D. (2003, February 21). In your face. *The Chronicle of Higher Education, 49*, pp. A6–A8.

Pechmann, C., & Stewart, D. W. (1988). Advertising repetition: A critical review of wearin and wearout. *Current Issues and Research in Advertising, 11*, 285–329.

Peck, J. (1992). *The gods of televangelism: The crisis of meaning and the appeal of religious television.* Cresskill, NJ: Hampton Press.

Pecora, N. O. (1997). *The business of children's entertainment.* New York: Guilford.

Pellegrinelli, L. (2009, May 8). Scholarly discord: The politics of music in the war on terrorism. *The Chronicle Review*, pp. B7–B9.

Penrod, S., & Linz, D. (1984). Using psychological research on violent pornography to inform legal change. In N. M. Malamuth & E. Donnerstein (Eds.), *Pornography and sexual aggression* (pp. 247–265). Orlando, FL: Academic Press.

Penuel, W. R., Bates, L., Gallagher, L. P., Pasnik, S., Llorente, C., Townsend, E., Hupert, N., Domínguez, X., & VanderBorght, M. (2012). Supplementing literacy instruction with a media-rich intervention: Results of a randomized controlled trial. *Early Childhood Research Quarterly, 27*(1), 115–127.

Peracchio, L. A., & Luna, D. (1998). The development of an advertising campaign to discourage smoking initiation among children and youth. *Journal of Advertising, 27*(3), 49–56.

Percy, L., & Lautman, M. R. (1994). Advertising, weight loss, and eating disorders. In E. M. Clark, T. C. Brock, & D. W. Stewart (Eds.), *Attention, attitude, and affect in response to advertising* (pp. 301–311). Hillsdale, NJ: Erlbaum.

Percy, L., & Rossiter, J. R. (1983). Mediating effects of visual and verbal elements in print advertising upon belief, attitude, and intention responses. In L. Percy & A. Woodside (Eds.), *Advertising and consumer psychology* (pp. 171–186). Lexington, MA: Lexington Books.

Perego, E., del Missier, F., Porta, M., & Mosconi, M. (2010). The cognitive effectiveness of subtitle processing. *Media Psychology, 13*, 243–272.

Perlmutter, D. D. (2000). Tracing the origin of humor. *Humor, 13*, 457–468.

Perloff, R. M. (1989). Ego-involvement and the third person effect of television news coverage. *Communication Research, 16*, 236–262.

Perloff, R. M. (2002). The third-person effect. In J. Bryant & D. Zillmann (Eds.), *Media effects: Advances in theory and research* (2nd ed., pp. 489–506). Mahwah, NJ: Erlbaum.

Perloff, R. M. (2009). Mass media, social perception, and the third-person effect. In J. Bryant and M. B. Oliver (Eds.), *Media effects: Advances in theory and research* (3rd ed., pp. 252–268). New York: Taylor & Francis.

Perse, E. M. (1986). Soap opera viewing patterns of college students and cultivation. *Journal of Broadcasting & Electronic Media, 30*, 175–193.

Perse, E. M. (2001). *Media effects and society.* Mahwah, NJ: Erlbaum.

Perse, E. M. (2007). Meta-analysis: Demonstrating the power of mass communication. In R. W. Preiss, B. M. Gayle, N. Burrell, M. Allen, & J. Bryant (Eds.), *Mass media effects research: Advances through meta-analysis* (pp. 467–488). Mahwah, NJ: Erlbaum.

Perse, E. M., & Rubin, R. B. (1989). Attribution in social and parasocial relationships. *Communication Research, 16*, 59–77.

Perse, E. M., & Lambe, J. (2013). *Media effects and society* (2nd ed.) New York: Routledge.

Peter, J., & Valkenburg, P. M. (2006). Adolescents' exposure to sexually explicit online material and recreational attitudes toward sex. *Journal of Communication, 56*, 639–660.

Peter, J., & Valkenburg, P. M. (2008). Adolescents' exposure to sexually explicit Internet material and sexual preoccupancy: A three-wave panel study. *Media Psychology*, 11, 207–234.

Peters, J. W. (2011, March 11). The *Times* announces digital subscription plan. *The New York Times*. Retrieved from http://www.nytimes.com

Peterson, C., & Seligman, M. E. P. (2004). *Character strengths and virtues: A handbook and classification*. New York: Oxford University Press.

Petty, R. E., Briñol, P., & Priester, J. R. (2009). Media attitude change: Implications of the elaboration-likelihood model of persuasion. In J. Bryant and M. B. Oliver (Eds.), *Media effects: Advances in theory and research* (3rd ed., pp. 125–164). New York: Taylor & Francis.

Petty, R. E., Priester, J. R., & Briñol, P. (2002). Mass media attitude change: Implications of the Elaboration Likelihood model of persuasion. In J. Bryant & D. Zillmann (Eds.), *Media effects* (2nd ed., pp. 155–198). Mahwah, NJ: Erlbaum.

Pew Research Center (2011a). Pew Internet and American Life Project. Retrieved from http://pewinternet.org/

Pew Research Center (2011b). Pew Research Center's Project for Excellence in Journalism: The state of the news media 2011, an annual report on American journalism. Retrieved from http://stateofthemedia.org/

Pewewardy, C. D. (1999). The deculturalization of indigenous mascots in U.S. sports culture. *The Educational Forum*, 63, 342–347.

Pezdek, K., & Hartman, E. F. (1983). Children's television viewing: Attention and comprehension of auditory versus visual information. *Child Development*, 54, 1015–1023.

Pezdek, K., Lehrer, A., & Simon, S. (1984). The relationship between reading and cognitive processing of television and radio. *Child Development*, 55, 2072–2082.

Pezdek, K., & Stevens, E. (1984). Children's memory for auditory and visual information on television. *Developmental Psychology*, 20, 212–218.

Pfau, M., Mullen, L. J., Deidrich, T., & Garrow, K. (1995). Television viewing and the public perception of attorneys. *Human Communication Research*, 21, 307–330.

Phillips, D. P. (1977). Motor vehicle fatalities increase just after publicized suicide stories. *Science*, 196, 1464–1465.

Phillips, D. P. (1984). Teenage and adult temporal fluctuations in suicide and auto fatalities. In H. S. Sudak, A. B. Ford, & N. B. Rushforth (Eds.), *Suicide in the young* (pp. 69–80). Boston: John Wright.

Phillips, D. P., & Carstensen, L. L. (1986). Clustering of teenage suicides after TV news stories about suicides. *New England Journal of Medicine*, 315, 685–689.

Phillips, J. M., Urbany, J. E., & Reynolds, T. J. (2008). Confirmation and the effects of valenced political advertising: A field experiment. *Journal of Consumer Research*, 34, 794–806.

Phillips, K. (1993, January–February). How *Seventeen* undermines young women. *Extra!* 6(1), 14.

Phillips, K. (2007, September 27). Rwandan radio soap opera might help end violence. *Kansas State Collegian*, 4.

Picard, R. G. (1993). *Media portrayals of terrorism: Functions and meaning of news coverage*. Ames, IA: Iowa State University Press.

Pierce, M. C., & Harris, R. J. (1993). The effect of provocation, race, and injury description on men's and women's perception of a wife-battering incident. *Journal of Applied Social Psychology*, 23, 767–790.

Pinedo, I. C. (1997). *Recreational terror: Women and the pleasures of horror film viewing*. Albany NY: State University of New York Press.

Pingree, R. J., Scholl, R. M., & Quenette, A. M. (2012). Effects of postdebate coverage on spontaneous policy reasoning. *Journal of Communication*, 62, 643–658.

Pingree, S., & Thompson, M. E. (1990). The family in daytime serials. In J. Bryant (Ed.), *Television and the American family* (pp. 113–127). Hillsdale, NJ: Erlbaum.

Pinkleton, B. E. (1998). Effects of print comparative political advertising on political decision-making and participation. *Journal of Communication*, 48(4), 24–36.

Pinsky, M. I. (2007). *The gospel according to The Simpsons. Bigger and possibly even better edition*. Louisville, KY: Westminster John Knox Press.

Pitkanen-Pulkkinen, L. (1981). Concurrent and predictive validity of self-reported aggressiveness. *Aggressive Behavior*, 7, 97–110.

Pitta, P. (1999). Family myths and the TV media: History, impact, and new directions. In L. L. Schwartz (Ed.), *Psychology and the media: A second look* (pp. 125–145). Washington, DC: American Psychological Association.

Pollard, P. (1995). Pornography and sexual aggression. *Current Psychology: Developmental, Learning, Personality, Social*, 14(3), 200–221.

Poniewozik, J. (2006, February 6). How reality TV fakes it. *Time*, pp. 60–62.

Pope, H. G., Jr., Olivardia, R., Gruber, A., & Borowiecki, J. (1999). Evolving ideals of male body image as seen through action toys. *International Journal of Eating Disorders*, 26, 65–72.

Pope, H. G., Jr., Phillips, K. A., & Olivardia, R. (2000). *The Adonis complex: The secret crisis of male body obsession*. New York: Free Press.

Postman, N. (1982). *The disappearance of childhood*. New York: Delacorte.

Postman, N. (1985). *Amusing ourselves to death*. New York: Viking Penguin.

Potter, W. J. (1986). Perceived reality and the cultivation hypothesis. *Journal of Broadcasting & Electronic Media*, 30, 159–174.

Potter, W. J. (1988). Perceived reality in television effects research. *Journal of Broadcasting & Electronic Media*, 32, 23–41.

Potter, W. J. (1989). Three strategies for elaborating the cultivation hypothesis. *Journalism Quarterly*, 65, 930–939.

Potter, W. J. (1991a). Examining cultivation from a psychological perspective: Component subprocesses. *Communication Research*, 18, 77–102.

Potter, W. J. (1991b). The relationships between first-and second-order measures of cultivation. *Human Communication Research*, 18, 92–113.

Potter, W. J. (1993). Cultivation theory and research: A conceptual critique. *Human Communication Research*, 19, 564–601.

Potter, W. J. (1999). *On media violence*. Thousand Oaks, CA: Sage.

Potter, W. J. (2001). *Media literacy* (2nd ed.). Thousand Oaks, CA: Sage.

Potter, W. J. (2004). *Theory of media literacy: A cognitive approach*. Thousand Oaks, CA: Sage.

Potter, W. J. (2011). Conceptualizing mass media effect. *Journal of Communication*, 61, 896–915.

Potter, W. J., & Tomasello, T. K. (2003). Building upon the experimental design in media violence research: The importance of including receiver interpretations. *Journal of Communication*, 53, 315–329.

Potts, R., Doppler, M., & Hernandez, M. (1994). Effects of television content on physical risk-taking in children. *Journal of Experimental Child Psychology*, 58, 321–331.

Potts, R., & Martinez, I. (1994). Television viewing and children's beliefs about scientists. *Journal of Applied Developmental Psychology*, 15, 287–300.

Potts, R., & Sanchez, D. (1994). Television viewing and depression: No news is good news. *Journal of Broadcasting & Electronic Media*, 38, 79–90.

Potts, R., & Swisher, L. (1998). Effects of televised safety models on children's risk taking and hazard identification. *Journal of Pediatric Psychology*, 23, 157–163.

Pouliot, L., & Cowen, P. S. (2007). Does perceived reality really matter in media effects? *Media Psychology*, 9, 241–259.

Pratap, A. (1990, August 13). Romance and a little rape. *Time*, p. 69.

Pratkanis, A. R. (1992). The cargo-cult science of subliminal persuasion. *Skeptical Inquirer*, 16, 260–272.

Pratkanis, A. R., & Greenwald, A. G. (1988). Recent perspectives on unconscious processing: Still no marketing applications. *Psychology & Marketing*, 5, 339–355.

Preston, E. H. (1990). Pornography and the construction of gender. In N. Signorielli & M. Morgan (Eds.), *Cultivation analysis* (pp. 107–122). Newbury Park, CA: Sage.

Preston, I. L. (1975). *The great American blow-up: Puffery in advertising and selling.* Madison, WI: University of Wisconsin Press.

Preston, I. L. (1994). *The tangled web they weave: Truth, falsity, and advertisers.* Madison, WI: University of Wisconsin Press.

Preston, I. L., & Richards, J. I. (1986). Consumer miscomprehension as a challenge to FTC prosecutions of deceptive advertising. *The John Marshall Law Review*, 19, 605–635.

Preston, J. (2011, February 5). Movement began with outrage and a Facebook page that gave it an outlet. *The New York Times.* Retrieved from http://www.nytimes.com

Price, M. E. (Ed.). (1998). *The V-chip debate: Content filtering from television to the Internet.* Mahwah, NJ: Erlbaum.

Primetime shows with the most product placement 2011 (2012). Retrieved from http://www.cnbc.com/id/45884892/Primetime_Shows_With_the_Most_Product_Placement

Pritchard, D., & Hughes, K. D. (1997). Patterns of deviance in crime news. *Journal of Communication*, 47(3), 49–67.

Propper, R. E., Stickgold, R., Keeley, R., & Christman, S. D. (2007). Is television traumatic? Dreams, stress, and media exposure in the aftermath of September 11, 2001. *Psychological Science*, 18, 334–340.

Quackenbush, D. M., Strassberg, D. S., & Turner, C. W. (1995). Gender effects of romantic themes in erotica. *Archives of Sexual Behavior*, 24, 21–35.

Quan-Haase, A., & Young, A. L. (2010). Uses and gratifications of social media: A comparison of Facebook and instant messaging. *Bulletin of Science, Technology & Society*, 30, 350–361.

Quinn, G. P., Ellery, J., Thomas, K. B., & Marshall, R. (2010). Developing a common language for using social marketing: An analysis of public health literature. *Health Marketing Quarterly*, 27(4), 334–353.

Quinsey, V. L., Chapman, T. C., & Upfold, D. (1984). Sexual arousal to nonsexual violence and sadomasochistic themes among rapists and non-sex offenders. *Journal of Consulting and Clinical Psychology*, 52, 651–657.

Raacke, J. D., & Bonds-Raacke, J. M. (2008). MySpace and Facebook: Applying the uses and gratifications theory to exploring friend-networking sites. *CyberPsychology & Behavior*, 11, 168–174.

Rabinovitch, M. S., McLean, M. S., Markham, J. W., & Talbott, A. D. (1972). Children's violence perception as a function of television violence. In G. A. Comstock, E. A. Rubinstein, & J. P. Murray (Eds.), *Television and social behavior: Vol. 5. Television's effects: Further explorations*. Washington, DC: U.S. Government Printing Office.

Rader, B. G. (1984). *In its own image: How television has transformed sports.* New York: The Free Press.

Rains, S. A. (2008). Health at high speed: Broadband Internet access, health communication, and the digital divide. *Communication Research*, 35, 283–297.

Raju, P. S., & Lonial, S. C. (1990). Advertising to children: Findings and implications. *Current Issues and Research in Advertising*, 12, 231–274.

Ramasubramanian, S., & Oliver, M. B. (2007). Activating and suppressing hostile and benevolent racism: Evidence for comparative media stereotyping. *Media Psychology, 9,* 623–646.

Ramirez Berg, C. (1990). Stereotyping in films in general and of the Hispanic in particular. *Howard Journal of Communication, 2,* 286–300.

Ramirez Berg, C. (2002). *Latino images in film: Stereotypes, subversions, and resistance.* Austin, TX: University of Texas Press.

Ramirez, A., Jr., Dimmick, J., Feaster, J., & Lin, S.-F. (2008). Revisiting interpersonal media competition: The gratification niches of instant messaging, e-mail, and the telephone. *Communication Research, 35,* 529–547.

Raney, A. A. (2002). Moral judgment as a predictor of enjoyment of crime drama. *Media Psychology, 4,* 305–322.

Raney, A. A. (2006). Why we watch and enjoy mediated sports. In A. A. Raney & J. Bryant (Eds.), *Handbook of sports and media* (pp. 313–329). Mahwah, NJ: Erlbaum.

Raney, A. A., & Bryant, J. (2002). Moral judgment and crime drama: An integrated theory of enjoyment. *Journal of Communication, 52*(2), 402–415.

Ratzan, S. C., Payne, J. G., & Massett, H. A. (1994). Effective health message design: The America Responds to AIDS campaign. *American Behavioral Scientist, 38,* 294–309.

Ravaja, N. (2004). Contributions of psychophysiology to media research: Review and recommendations. *Media Psychology, 6,* 193–235.

Rawson, H. (2003, June/July). The road to freedom fries. *American Heritage, 12.*

Rayner, K., Miller, B., & Rotello, C. M. (2008). Eye movements when looking at print advertisements: The goal of the viewer matters. *Applied Cognitive Psychology, 22,* 697–707.

Reeve, D. K., & Aggleton, J. P. (1998). On the specificity of expert knowledge about a soap opera: An everyday story of farming folk. *Applied Cognitive Psychology, 12,* 35–42.

Reeves, B., & Nass, C. (1996). *The media equation: How people treat computer, television, and the new media like real people and places.* New York: Cambridge University Press.

Reeves, B., Thorson, E., Rothschild, M., McDonald, D., Hirsch, J., & Goldstein, R. (1985). Attention to television: Intrastimulus effects of movement and scene changes on alpha variation over time. *International Journal of Neuroscience, 25,* 241–255.

Reid, S. A. (2012). A self-categorization explanation for the hostile media effect. *Journal of Communication, 62,* 381–399.

Reid, S. A., & Hogg, M. A. (2005). A self-categorization explanation for the third-person effect. *Human Communication Research, 31,* 129–161.

Reinecke, L., Tamborini, R., Grizzard, M., Lewis, R., Eden, A., & Bowman, N. D. (2012). Characterizing mood management as need satisfaction: The effects of intrinsic needs on selective exposure and mood repair. *Journal of Communication, 62,* 437–453.

Reinemann, C., & Maurer, M. (2005). Unifying or polarizing? Short-term, effects of postdebate consequences of different rhetorical strategies in televised debates. *Journal of Communication, 55,* 775–794.

Rice, M. L., Huston, A. C., Truglio, R., & Wright, J. C. (1990). Words from *Sesame Street:* Learning vocabulary skills while viewing. *Developmental Psychology, 26,* 421–428.

Rice, M. L., Huston, A. C., & Wright, J. C. (1986). Replays as repetitions: Young children's interpretation of television forms. *Journal of Applied Developmental Psychology, 7,* 61–76.

Rich, F. (1997, December 26). Mental illness still needs a spokesman. *Manhattan Mercury,* A7.

Richards, J. I. (1990). *Deceptive advertising.* Hillsdale, NJ: Erlbaum.

Richardson, G. W., Jr. (2001). Looking for meaning in all the wrong places: Why negative advertising is a suspect category. *Journal of Communication, 51*(4), 775–800.

Richardson, S. M., Paxton, S. J., & Thomson, J. S. (2009). Is BodyThink an efficacious body image and self-esteem program? A controlled revaluation with adolescents. *Body Image*, 6, 75–82.

Riddle, K., Potter, W. J., Metzger, M. J., Nabi, R. L., & Linz, D. G. (2011). Beyond cultivation: Exploring the effects of frequency, recency, and vivid autobiographical memories for violent media. *Media Psychology*, 14, 168–191.

Rideout, V., Robert, D. F., & Foehr, U. G. (2005). *Generation M: Media in the lives of 8–18-year-olds*. Menlo Park, CA: Kaiser Family Foundation.

Riffe, D., & Freitag, A. A. (1997). A content analysis of content analyses: Twenty-five years of *Journalism Quarterly*. *Journalism and Mass Communication Quarterly*, 74, 873–882.

Riffe, D., Lacy, S., & Fico, F. G. (1998). *Analyzing media messages: Using quantitative content analysis in research*. Mahwah, NJ: Erlbaum.

Riggle, E. D. B., Ellis, A. L., & Crawford, A. M. (1996). The impact of "media contact" on attitudes toward gay men. *Journal of Homosexuality*, 31(3), 55–69.

Riggs, M. (1992, June 15). *Color adjustment*. [Documentary.] New York: PBS.

Rimmer, L. (2002, October). Brand-new day. *World Press Review*, pp. 36–37.

Ritchie, D., Price, V., & Roberts, D. F. (1987). Reading and television: A longitudinal investigation of the displacement hypothesis. *Communication Research*, 14, 292–315.

Rivadeneyra, R., Ward, L. M., & Gordon, M. (2007). Distorted reflections: Media exposure and Latino adolescents' conceptions of self. *Media Psychology*, 9, 261–290.

Roberts, D. F. (2000). Media and youth: Access, exposure, and privatization. *Journal of Adolescent Health*, 27(2), 8–14.

Roberts, D. F., & Christenson, P. G. (2001). Popular music in childhood and adolescence. In D. G. Singer & J. L. Singer (Eds.), *Handbook of children and the media* (pp. 395–413). Thousand Oaks, CA: Sage.

Roberts, D. F., Henriksen, L., & Christenson, P. G. (1999). *Substance use in popular movies and music*. Washington, DC: Office of National Drug Control Policy.

Robinson, A. R., Hohmann, K. B., Rifkin, J. I., Topp, D., Gilroy, C. M., & Pickard, J. A. (2004). Direct-to-consumer pharmaceutical advertising: Physician and public opinion and potential effects on the physician-patient relationship. *Archives of Internal Medicine*, 164, 427–432.

Robinson, J. D. (1989). Mass media and the elderly: A uses and dependency interpretation. In J. F. Nussbaum (Ed.), *Life-span communication* (pp. 319–337). Hillsdale, NJ: Erlbaum.

Robinson, J. D., & Skill, T. (2001). Five decades of families on television: From the 1950s through the 1990s. In J. Bryant & J. A. Bryant (Eds.), *Television and the American family* (2nd ed., pp. 139–162). Mahwah, NJ: Erlbaum.

Robinson, M. J., & Sheehan, M. A. (1983). *Over the wire and on TV: CBS and UPI in Campaign 80*. New York: Sage.

Robinson, P., Goddard, P., Parry, K., & Murray, C. (2009). Testing models of media performance in wartime: U.K. TV news and the 2003 invasion of Iraq. *Journal of Communication*, 59, 534–563.

Robinson, T. N., Saphir, M. N., Kraemer, H. C., Varady, A., & Haydel, K. F. (2001). Effects of reducing television viewing on children's request for toys: A randomized control trial. *Journal of Developmental and Behavioral Pediatrics*, 22, 179–184.

Robinson, T. N., Wilde, M. L., Navracruz, L. C., Haydel, F., & Varady, A. (2001). Effects of reducing children's television and video game use on aggressive behavior. *Archives of Pediatric and Adolescent Medicine*, 155, 17–23.

Rogers, E. M., & Singhal, A. (1990). The academic perspective. In C. Atkin & L. Wallack (Eds.), *Mass communication and public health* (pp. 176–181). Newbury Park, CA: Sage.

Rogers, E. M., Vaughan, P. W., Swalehe, R. M. A., Rao, N., Svenkerud, P., & Sood, S. (1999). Effects of an entertainment-education radio soap opera on family planning behavior in Tanzania. *Studies in Family Planning*, 30(3), 193–211.

Rojahn, K., & Pettigrew, T. F. (1992). Memory for schema-relevant information: A meta-analytic resolution. *British Journal of Social Psychology*, 31, 81–109.

Rolandelli, D. R., Wright, J. C., Huston, A. C., & Eakins, D. (1991). Children's auditory and visual processing of narrated and nonnarrated television programming. *Journal of Experimental Child Psychology*, 51, 90–122.

Romer, D., Jamieson, K. H., & Aday, S. (2003). Television news and the cultivation of fear of crime. *Journal of Communication*, 53, 88–104.

Romer, D., Jamieson, K. H., & DeCoteau, N. (1998). The treatment of persons of color in local television news: Ethnic blame discourse or realistic group conflict. *Communication Research*, 48, 286–305.

Romer, D., Jamieson, P. E., & Jamieson, K. H. (2006). Are news reports of suicide contagious? *Journal of Communication*, 56, 253–270.

Romero, S. (2000, December 19). A cell phone surge among world's poor in Haiti. *The New York Times*. Retrieved December 19, 2000, from http://www.nytimes.com/2000/12/19/technology/19CELL.html

Rosenbaum, J., & Prinsky, L. (1987). Sex, violence, and rock'n'roll: Youth's perception of popular music. *Popular Music and Society*, 11, 79–90.

Rosenberg, T. (2003, July 3). In Colombia, muckrakers have become scarce. Retrieved July 3, 2003, from http://www.nytimes.com

Rosencrans, M. A., & Hartup, W. W. (1967). Imitative influences of consistent and inconsistent response consequences to a model on aggressive behavior in children. *Journal of Personality and Social Psychology*, 7, 429–434.

Rosengren, K. E. (1992). The structural invariance of change: Comparative studies of media use (some results from a Swedish research program). In J. G. Blumler, J. M. McLeod, & K. E. Rosengren (Eds.), *Comparatively speaking: Communication and culture across space and time* (pp. 140–178). Newbury Park, CA: Sage.

Rosengren, K. E., Wenner, L. A., & Palmgreen, P. (Eds.). (1985). *Media gratifications research: Current perspectives*. Newbury Park, CA: Sage.

Rosenkoetter, L. I. (1999). The television situation comedy and children's prosocial behavior. *Journal of Applied Social Psychology*, 29, 979–993.

Rosenzweig, J. (1999). Can TV improve us? *The American Prospect*, 45, 58–63.

Rossler, P., & Brosius, H.-B. (2001). Do talk shows cultivate adolescents' view of the world? A prolonged-exposure experiment. *Journal of Communication*, 51(1), 143–163.

Rotfeld, H. J. (1988). Fear appeals and persuasion: Assumptions and errors in advertising research. *Current Issues and Research in Advertising*, 11, 21–40.

Rothenberg, D. (1998, June 5). The sounds of global change: Different beats, new ideas. *The Chronicle of Higher Education*, p. B8.

Rowling, C. M., Jones, T. M., & Sheets, P. (2011). Some dared call it torture: Cultural resonance, Abu Ghraib, and a selectively echoing press. *Journal of Communication*, 61, 1043–1061.

Roy, A., & Harwood, J. (1997). Underrepresented, positively portrayed: Older adults in television commercials. *Journal of Applied Communication Research*, 25, 39–56.

Rozendaal, E., Buijzen, M., & Valkenburg, P. M. (2012). Think-aloud process superior to thought-listing in increasing children's critical processing of advertising. *Human Communication Research*, 38, 199–221.

Rozendaal, E., Lapierre, M. A., Reijmersdal, E. A., & Buijzen, M. (2011). Reconsidering advertising literacy as a defense against advertising effects. *Media Psychology*, 14, 333–354.

Rubin, A. M. (2002). The uses-and-gratifications perspective of media effects. In J. Bryant & D. Zillmann (Eds.), *Media effects: Advances in theory and research* (2nd ed., pp. 525–548). Mahwah, NJ: Erlbaum.

Rubin, A. M. (2009). Uses-and-gratifications perspective on media effects. In J. Bryant and M. B. Oliver (Eds.), *Media effects: Advances in theory and research* (3rd ed., pp. 165–184). New York: Taylor & Francis.

Rubin, A. M., & Perse, E. M. (1988). Audience activity and soap opera involvement. *Human Communication Research*, 14, 246–268.

Rubin, A. M., Perse, E. M., & Powell, R. A. (1985). Loneliness, parasocial interaction, and local television news viewing. *Human Communication Research*, 12, 155–180.

Rubin, A. M., Perse, E. M., & Taylor, D. S. (1988). A methodological examination of cultivation. *Communication Research*, 15, 107–134.

Rubin, D. C. (1995). *Memory in oral traditions: The cognitive psychology of epic, ballads, and counting-out rhymes*. New York: Oxford University Press.

Rubin, D. M., & Cummings, C. (1989). Nuclear war and its consequences on television. *Journal of Communication*, 39(1), 39–58.

Rubin, G. C., Brewin, C. R., Greenberg, N., Simpson, J., & Wessely, S. (2005). Psychological and behavioural reactions to the bombings in London on 7 July 2005: Cross sectional survey of a representative sample of Londoners. *British Medical Journal*, 331, 606.

Rubin, R. B., & McHugh, M. P. (1987). Development of parasocial interaction relationships. *Journal of Broadcasting & Electronic Media*, 31, 279–292.

Rumelhart, D. E. (1980). Schemata: Building blocks of cognition. In R. J. Spiro, B. C. Bruce, & W. F. Brewer (Eds.), *Theoretical issues in reading comprehension* (pp. 33–58). Hillsdale, NJ: Erlbaum.

Ruoff, J. (2002). *An American family: A televised life*. Minneapolis: University of Minnesota Press.

Russell, D. E. H. (1998). *Dangerous relationships: Pornography, misogyny, and rape*. Thousand Oaks, CA: Sage.

Russo, J. E., Metcalf, B. L., & Stevens, D. (1981). Identifying misleading advertising. *Journal of Consumer Research*, 8, 119–131.

Russo, V. (1981). *The celluloid closet: Homosexuality in the movies*. New York: Harper & Row.

Sacchi, D. L. M., Agnoli, F., & Loftus, E. F. (2007). Changing history: Doctored photographs affect memory for past public events. *Applied Cognitive Psychology*, 21, 1005–1022.

Sachs, A. (2002, April 15). Oprah turns the page. *Time*, p. 63.

Saegert, J. (1987). Why marketing should quit giving subliminal advertising the benefit of the doubt. *Psychology & Marketing*, 4, 107–120.

Sagarin, B., Britt, M. A., Heider, J. D., Wood, S. E., & Lynch, J. E. (2005). Intrusive technology: Bartering and stealing consumer attention. In W. R. Walker & D. J. Herrmann (Eds.), *Cognitive technology: Essays on the transformation of thought and society* (pp. 69–88). Jefferson, NC: McFarland.

Saito, S. (2007). Television and the cultivation of gender-role attitudes in Japan: Does television contribute to the maintenance of the status quo? *Journal of Communication*, 57, 511–531.

Salomon, G. (1984). Television is "easy" and print is "tough": The differential investment of mental effort in learning as a function of perceptions and attributions. *Journal of Educational Psychology*, 76, 647–658.

Salomon, G. (1987). Television and reading: The roles of orientations and reciprocal relations. In M. E. Manley-Casimir & C. Luke (Eds.), *Children and television* (pp. 15–33). New York: Praeger.

Sanborn, F. W. (2004). Cross-sex friendships: A cross-sectional exploration (unpublished doctoral dissertation). Kansas State University, Manhattan, KS.

Sapolsky, B. S. (1984). Arousal, affect, and the aggression-moderating effect of erotica. In N. M. Malamuth & E. Donnerstein (Eds.), *Pornography and sexual aggression* (pp. 85–113). Orlando, FL: Academic Press.

Sapolsky, B. S., & Molitor, F. (1996). Content trends in contemporary horror films. In J. B. Weaver & R. Tamborini (Eds.), *Horror films: Current research on audience preferences and reactions* (pp. 33–48). Mahwah, NJ: Erlbaum.

Sargent, J. D., Beach, M. L., Dalton, M. A., Mott, L. A., Tickle, J. J., Ahrens, M. B., et al. (2001). Effect of seeing tobacco use in films on trying smoking among adolescents: Cross sectional study. *British Medical Journal, 323*, 1394–1397.

Schachter, S., & Singer, J. E. (1962). Cognitive, social, and physiological determinants of emotional state. *Psychological Review, 69*, 379–399.

Schacter, D. L. (1996). *Searching for memory.* New York: Basic Books.

Scharrer, E. (2005). Hypermasculinity, aggression, and television violence: An experiment. *Media Psychology, 7*, 353–376.

Scharrer, E. (2006). "I noticed more violence": The effects of a media literacy program on critical attitudes toward media violence. *Journal of Mass Media Ethics, 21*(1), 69–86.

Scheele, B., & DuBois, F. (2006). Catharsis as a moral form of entertainment. In J. Bryant & P. Vorderer (Eds.), *Psychology of entertainment* (pp. 405–422). Mahwah, NJ: Erlbaum.

Schenk-Hamlin, W. J., Procter, D. E., & Rumsey, D. J. (2000). The influence of negative advertising frames on political cynicism and politician accountability. *Human Communication Research, 26*, 53–74.

Scheufele, D. A., & Tewksbury, D. (2007). Framing, agenda-setting, and priming. *Journal of Communication, 57*, 9–20.

Schiappa, E., Allen, M., & Gregg, P. B. (2007). Parasocial relationships and television: A meta-analysis of the effects. In R. W. Preiss, B. M. Gayle, N. Burrell, M. Allen, & J. Bryant (Eds.), *Mass media effects research: Advances through meta-analysis* (pp. 301–314). Mahwah, NJ: Erlbaum.

Schlenger, W. E., Caddell, J. M., Ebert, L., Jordan, B. K., Rourke, K. M., & Wilson, D. (2002). Psychological reactions to terrorist attacks: Findings from the national study of Americans' reactions to September 11. *Journal of the American Medical Association, 288*, 581–588.

Schleuder, J., McCombs, M. E., & Wanta, W. (1991). Inside the agenda-setting process: How political advertising and TV news prime viewers to think about issues and candidates. In F. Biocca (Ed.), *Television and political advertising: Psychological processes* (Vol. 1, pp. 265–309). Hillsdale, NJ: Erlbaum.

Schmitt, K. L., Anderson, D. R., & Collins, P. A. (1999). Form and content: Looking at visual features of television. *Developmental Psychology, 35*, 1156–1167.

Schmitt, K. L., Woolf, K. D., & Anderson, D. R. (2003). Viewing the viewers: Viewing behaviors by children and adults during television programs and commercials. *Journal of Communication, 53*, 265–281.

Schmitt, K. M., Gunther, A. C., & Liebhart, J. L. (2004). Why partisans see mass media as biased. *Communication Research, 31*, 623–641.

Schneider, A. (1998, January 9). Advising Spielberg: A career studying the Amistad rebellion. *The Chronicle of Higher Education, 44*, p. A12.

Schneider, J. A. (1987). Networks hold the line. In A. A. Berger (Ed.), *Television in society* (pp. 163–172). New Brunswick, NJ: Transaction Books.

Schneider, J. P. (2001). Effects of cybersex addiction on the family: Results of a survey. *Sexual Addiction and Compulsivity, 7*, 31–58.

Schneider, J. P. (2003). The impact of compulsive cybersex behaviours on the family. *Sexual and Relationship Therapy*, 18, 329–354.

Schneider, S. L., & Laurion, S. K. (1993). Do we know what we've learned from listening to the news? *Memory & Cognition*, 21, 198–209.

Scholfield, J., & Pavelchak, M. (1985). The Day After: The impact of a media event. *American Psychologist*, 40, 542–548.

School of hard knocks (1992, October 12). *Time*, pp. 31–32.

Schooler, C., Chaffee, S. H., Flora, J. A., & Roser, C. (1998). Health campaign channels: Tradeoffs among reach, specificity, and impact. *Human Communication Research*, 24, 410–432.

Schooler, C., Flora, J. A., & Farquhar, J. W. (1993). Moving toward synergy: Media supplementation in the Stanford Five-City Project. *Communication Research*, 20, 587–610.

Schooler, C., Sundar, S. S., & Flora, J. (1996). Effects of the Stanford Five-City Project Media Advocacy Program. *Health Education Quarterly*, 23(3), 346–364.

Schouten, A. P., Valkenburg, P. M., & Peter, J. (2007). Precursors and underlying processes of adolescents' online self-disclosure: Developing and testing an "internet-attribute-perception" model. *Media Psychology*, 10, 292–315.

Schulkind, M. D., Hennis, L. K., & Rubin, D. C. (1999). Music, emotion, and autobiographical memory: They're playing your song. *Memory & Cognition*, 27, 948–955.

Schumann, D. W., & Thorson, E. (Eds.) (1999). *Advertising and the World Wide Web*. Mahwah, NJ: Erlbaum.

Schwan, S., & Ildirar, S. (2010). Watching film for the first time: How adult viewers interpret perceptual discontinuities in film. *Psychological Science*, 21, 970–976.

Schwarz, N., & Brand, J. F. (1983). Effects of salience of rape on sex role attitudes, trust, and self-esteem in non-raped women. *European Journal of Social Psychology*, 13, 71–76.

Seefeldt, C. (1977). Young and old together. *Children Today*, 6(1), 22.

Seggar, J. F., Hafen, J., & Hannonen-Gladden, H. (1981). Television's portrayal of minorities and women in drama and comedy drama, 1971–1980. *Journal of Broadcasting*, 25(3), 277–288.

Seiter, J. S., & Gass, R. H. (2005). The effect of patriotic messages on restaurant tipping. *Journal of Applied Social Psychology*, 35, 1197–1205.

Selnow, G. W. (1997). *Electronic whistle-stops: The impact of the Internet on American politics*. New York: Praeger.

Senn, C. Y., & Desmarais, S. (2004). Impact of interaction with a partner or friend on the exposure effects of pornography and erotica. *Violence and Victims*, 19, 645–658.

Shaheen, J. G. (1984). *The TV Arab*. Bowling Green, OH: Bowling Green State University Popular Press.

Shaheen, J. G. (2001). *Reel bad Arabs: How Hollywood vilifies a people*. New York: Olive Branch Press.

Shaheen, J. G. (2008). *Guilty: Hollywood's verdicts on Arabs after 9/11*. Northampton, MA: Olive Branch Press.

Shain, R., & Phillips, J. (1991). The stigma of mental illness: Labeling and stereotyping in the news. In L. Wilkins & P. Patterson (Eds.), *Risky business: Communicating issues of science, risk, and public policy* (pp. 61–74). Westport, CT: Greenwood Press.

Shanahan, J., & McComas, K. (1999). *Nature stories*. Cresskill, NJ: Hampton Press.

Shanahan, J., Morgan, M., & Stenbjerre, M. (1997). Green or brown? Television's cultivation of environmental concern. *Journal of Broadcasting & Electronic Media*, 41(3), 305–323.

Shankman, A. (1978). Black pride and protest: The Amos 'n' Andy Crusade. *Journal of Popular Culture*, 12, 236–252.

Shanteau, J. (1988). Consumer impression formation: The integration of visual and verbal information. In S. Hecker & D. W. Stewart (Eds.), *Nonverbal communication in advertising* (pp. 43–57). Lexington, MA: Lexington.

Shanteau, J., & Harris, R. J. (Eds.). (1990). *Organ donation and transplantation: Psychological and behavioral factors.* Washington, DC: American Psychological Association.

Shapiro, M. A. (1991). Memory and decision processes in the construction of social reality. *Communication Research*, 18, 3–24.

Shapiro, M. A., & Chock, T. M. (2003). Psychological processes in perceiving reality. *Media Psychology*, 5, 163–198.

Shapiro, M. A., & Kim, H. K. (2012). Realism judgment and mental resources: A cue processing model of media narrative realism. *Media Psychology*, 15, 93–119.

Shapiro, M. A., Barriga, C. A., & Beren, J. (2010). Causal attribution and perceived realism of stories. *Media Psychology*, 13, 273–300.

Sheafer, T., & Weimann, G. (2005). Agenda building, agenda setting, priming, individual voting intentions, and the aggregate results: An analysis of four Israeli elections. *Journal of Communication*, 55, 347–365.

Sheikh, A. A., Prasad, V. K., & Rao, T. R. (1974). Children's TV commercials: A review of research. *Journal of Communication*, 24(4), 126–136.

Sheldon, K. M., Abad, N., & Hinsch, C. (2011). A two-process view of Facebook use and relatedness need-satisfaction: Disconnection drives use, and connection rewards it. *Psychology of Popular Media Culture*, 1, 2–15.

Shen, F., & Eveland, W. P. (2010). Testing the intramedia interaction hypothesis: The contingent effects of news. *Journal of Communication*, 60, 364–387.

Sherry, J. L. (2001). The effects of violent video games on aggression: A meta-analysis. *Human Communication Research*, 27, 409–431.

Sherry, J. L. (2002). Media saturation and entertainment-education. *Communication Theory*, 12, 206–224.

Sherry, J. L. (2007). Violent video games and aggression: What can't we find effects? In R. W. Preiss, B. M. Gayle, N. Burrell, M. Allen, & J. Bryant (Eds.), *Mass media effects research: Advances through meta-analyses* (pp. 245–262). Mahwah, NJ: Erlbaum.

Shimp, T. A., & Gresham, L. G. (1983). An information-processing perspective on recent advertising literature. *Current Issues and Research in Advertising*, 5, 39–75.

Shoemaker, P. J., Chang, T., & Brendlinger, N. (1987). Deviance as a predictor of newsworthiness: Coverage of international events in U.S. media. *Communication Yearbook*, 10, 348–365.

Shoemaker, P. J., Danielian, L. H., & Brendlinger, N. (1987). Deviant acts, risky business, and U.S. interests: The newsworthiness of world events. *Journalism Quarterly*, 68, 781–795.

Shoop, T. J. (2010). From professionals to potential first ladies: How newspapers told the stories of Cindy McCain and Michelle Obama. *Sex Roles*, 63, 807–819.

Shope, J. H. (2004). When words are not enough: The search for the effect of pornography on abused women. *Violence against Women*, 10, 56–72.

Shrum, L. J. (2001). Processing strategy moderates the cultivation effect. *Human Communication Research*, 27, 94–120.

Shrum, L. J. (2002). Media consumption and perceptions of social reality: Effects and underlying processes. In J. Bryant & D. Zillmann (Eds.), *Media effects: Advances in theory and research* (2nd ed., pp. 69–95). Mahwah, NJ: Erlbaum.

Shrum, L. J. (2009). Media consumption an perceptions of social reality: Effects and underlying processes. In J. Bryant and M. B. Oliver (Eds.), *Media effects: Advances in theory and research* (3rd ed., pp. 50–73). New York: Taylor & Francis.

Shrum, L. J., & Bischak, V. D. (2001). Mainstreaming, resonance, and impersonal impact: Testing moderators of the cultivation effect for estimates of crime risk. *Human Communication Research, 27,* 187–215.

Shrum, L. J., Lee, J., Burroughs, J. E., & Rindfleisch, A. (2011). An online processing model of second-order cultivation effects: How television cultivates materialism and its consequences for life satisfaction. *Human Communication Research, 37,* 34–57.

Siegel, A. N. (1956). Film-mediated fantasy aggression and strength of aggressive drive. *Child Development, 27,* 365–378.

Sigesmund, B. J. (2003, July 3). XXX-ceptable. Retrieved July 3, 2003, from http://www.msnbc.com/m/pt/printthis main.asp?storyID-934252

Signorielli, N. (1989). The stigma of mental illness on television. *Journal of Broadcasting and Electronic Media, 33,* 325–331.

Signorielli, N. (1990). Television's mean and dangerous world: A continuation of the Cultural Indicators perspective. In N. Signorielli & M. Morgan (Eds.), *Cultivation analysis: New directions in media effects research* (pp. 85–106). Newbury Park, CA: Sage.

Signorielli, N. (1993). Television, the portrayal of women, and children's attitudes. In G. L. Berry & J. K. Asamen (Eds.), *Children & television: Images in a changing sociocultural world* (pp. 229–242). Newbury Park, CA: Sage.

Signorielli, N. (2001). Television's gender role images and contribution to stereotyping. In D. G. Singer & J. L. Singer (Eds.), *Handbook of children and the media* (pp. 341–358). Thousand Oaks, CA: Sage.

Silver, R. C., Holman, E. A., McIntosh, D. M., Poulin, M., & Gil-Rivas, V. (2002). Nationwide longitudinal study of psychological responses to September 11. *Journal of the American Medical Association, 288,* 1235–1244.

Simmons, R. (2002). *Odd girl out: The hidden culture of aggression in girls.* New York: Harcourt.

Simons, D. J., & Ambinder. M. S. (2005). Change blindness: Theory and consequences. *Current Directions in Psychological Science, 14,* 44–48.

Simons, D. J., & Chabris C. F. (1999). Gorillas in our midst: Sustained inattentional blindness for dynamic events. *Perception, 28,* 1059–1074.

Simons, R. F., Detenber, B. H., Cuthbert, B. N., Schwartz, D. D., & Reiss, J. E. (2003). Attention to television: Alpha power and its relationship to image motion and emotional content. *Media Psychology, 5,* 283–301.

Simons, D. J., & Levin, D. T. (1997). Change blindness. *Trends in Cognitive Science, 8,* 261–267.

Simons, D. J., & Levin, D. T. (1998). Failure to detect changes to people in a real-world interaction. *Psychonomic Bulletin & Review, 5,* 644–649.

Singer, D. G., & Singer, J. L. (1983). Learning how to be intelligent consumers of television. In M. J. A. Howe (Ed.), *Learning from television: Psychological and educational research* (pp. 203–222). London: Academic Press.

Singer, D. G., & Singer, J. L. (1998). Developing critical viewing skills and media literacy in children. *The Annals of the American Academy of Political and Social Science, 557,* 164–179.

Singer, D. G., Singer, J. L., & Zuckerman, D. M. (1981). *Getting the most out of TV.* Santa Monica, CA: Goodyear.

Singer, D. G., Zuckerman, D. M., & Singer, J. L. (1980). Helping elementary school children learn about TV. *Journal of Communication, 30*(3), 84–93.

Singer, J. L., & Singer, D. G. (1976). Can TV stimulate imaginative play? *Journal of Communication, 26,* 74–80.

Singer, J. L., & Singer, D. G. (1981). *Television, imagination, and aggression: A study of preschoolers.* Hillsdale, NJ: Erlbaum.

Singer, J. L., & Singer, D. G. (1998). *Barney & Friends* as entertainment and education. In J. K. Asamen & G. Berry (Eds.), *Research paradigms, television, and social behavior* (pp. 305–367). Thousand Oaks, CA: Sage.

Singer, M. I., Slovak, K., Frierson, T., & York, P. (1998). Viewing preferences, symptoms of psychological trauma, and violent behaviors among children who watch television. *Journal of the American Academy of Child and Adolescent Psychiatry, 37*(10), 1041–1048.

Singhal, A., & Rogers, E. M. (1989a). Prosocial television for development in India. In R. E. Rice & C. Atkin (Eds.), *Public communication campaigns* (2nd ed., pp. 331– 350). Newbury Park, CA: Sage.

Singhal, A., & Rogers, E. M. (1989b). Entertainment-education strategies for family planning. *Populi, 16*(2), 38–47.

Singhal, A., Cody, M., Rogers, E., & Sabido, M. (Eds.). (2004). *Entertainment-education and social change: History, research, and practice.* Mahwah, NJ: Erlbaum.

Singhal, A., & Rogers, E. M. (1989c). *India's information revolution.* New Delhi: Sage.

Singhal, A., & Rogers, E. M. (1999). *Entertainment-education: A communication strategy for social change.* Mahwah, NJ: Erlbaum.

Sintchak, G., & Geer, J. (1975). A vaginal plethysymograph system. *Psychophysiology, 12,* 113–115.

Sivulka, J. (1998). *Soap, sex, and cigarettes: A cultural history of American advertising.* New York: Wadsworth.

Sivulka, J. (2001). *Stronger than dirt: A cultural history of advertising personal hygiene in America, 1875 to 1940.* New York: Humanity Books.

Singhal, A., & Rogers, E. M. (2002). A theoretical agenda for entertainment-education. *Communication Theory, 12,* 117–135.

Skal, D. (1993). *The monster show: A cultural history of horror.* New York: Faber & Faber.

Skeggs, B., & Wood, H. (2012). *Reacting to reality television: Performance, audience, and value.* New York: Routledge.

Skill, T., Wallace, S., & Cassata, M. (1990). Families on prime-time television: Patterns of conflict escalation and resolution across intact, nonintact, and mixed-family settings. In J. Bryant (Ed.), *Television and the American family* (pp. 129–163). Hillsdale, NJ: Erlbaum.

Skill, T., Lyons, J. S., & Larson, D. (1991, November). Television and religion: Content analysis of the portrayal of spirituality in network primetime fictional programs. Summary report to the American Family Association, Tupelo, MS.

Skill, T., Robinson, J., & Wallace, S. (1987). Family life on primetime television: Structure, type, and frequency. *Journalism Quarterly, 64*(2/3), 360–367, 398.

Slater, D., & Elliott, W. R. (1982). Television's influence on social reality. *Quarterly Journal of Speech, 68,* 69–79.

Slater, M. D. (1990). Processing social information in messages: Social group familiarity, fiction versus nonfiction, and subsequent beliefs. *Communication Research, 17,* 327–343.

Slater, M. D. (2003). Alienation, aggression, and sensation seeking as predictor of adolescent use of violent film, computer, and website content. *Journal of Communication, 53*(1), 105–121.

Slater, M. D., Hayes, A. F., & Ford, V. L. (2007). Examining the moderating and mediating roles of news exposure and attention on adolescent judgments of alcohol-related risks. *Communication Research, 34,* 355–381.

Slater, M. D., Henry, K. L., Swaim, R. C., & Cardador, J. M. (2004). Vulnerable teens, vulnerable times: How sensation seeking, alienation, and victimization moderate the violent media content-aggressiveness relation. *Communication Research, 31,* 642–668.

Slater, M. D., & Rasinski, K. A. (2005). Media exposure and attention as mediating variables influencing social risk judgments. *Journal of Communication, 55,* 810–827.

Slater, M. D., & Rouner, D. (2002). Entertainment-education and elaboration likelihood: Understanding the process of narrative persuasion. *Communication Theory*, 12, 173–191.

Slovic, P., Finucane, M. L., Peters, E., & MacGregor, D. G. (2004). Risks as analysis and risk as feelings: Some thoughts about affect, reason, risk, and rationality. *Risk Analysis*, 24, 311–321.

Smith, M. E., & Gevins, A. (2004). Attention and brain activity while watching television: Components of viewer engagement. *Media Psychology*, 6, 285–305.

Smith, S. L., & Atkin, C. (2003). Television advertising and children: Examining the intended and unintended effects. In E. L. Palmer & B. M. Young (Eds.), *The faces of televisual media: Teaching, violence, and selling to children* (pp. 327–346). Mahwah, NJ: Erlbaum.

Smith, S. L., & Boyson, A. R. (2002). Violence in music videos: Examining the prevalence and context of physical aggression. *Journal of Communication*, 52, 61–83.

Smith, S. L., & Choueiti, M. (2010). Gender disparity on screen and behind the camera in family films: The executive report. Retrieved from http://www.thegeenadavisinstitute.org/research.php

Smith, S. L., & Cook, C. A. (2008). Gender stereotypes: An analysis of popular films and TV. Retrieved from http://www.thegeenadavisinstitute.org/research.php

Smith, S. L., & Donnerstein, E. (1998). Harmful effects of exposure to media violence: Learning of aggression, emotional desensitization, and fear. In R. G. Geen & E. Donnerstein (Eds.), *Human aggression: Theories, research, and implications for social policy* (pp. 167–202). San Diego, CA: Academic Press.

Smith, S. L., Lachlan, K., & Tamborini, R. (2003). Popular video games: Quantifying the presentation of violence and its context. *Journal of Broadcasting & Electronic Media*, 47, 58–76.

Smith, S. L., Nathanson, A. I., & Wilson, B. J. (2002). Prime-time television: Assessing violence during the most popular viewing hours. *Journal of Communication*, 52, 84–111.

Smith, S. W., Smith, S. L., Pieper, K. M., Yoo, J. H., Ferris, A. L., Downs, E., et al. (2006). Altruism on American television: Examining the amount of, and context surrounding, acts of helping and sharing. *Journal of Communication*, 56, 707–727.

Smith, T. J., Levin, D., & Cutting, J. E. (2012). A window on reality: Perceiving edited moving images. *Current Directions in Psychological Science*, 21, 104–113.

Smith, T. M. (1998). *The myth of green marketing: Tending our goats at the edge of apocalypse.* Toronto, Canada: University of Toronto Press.

Snyder, L. B. (2007). Meta-analyses of mediated health campaigns. In R. W. Preiss, B. M. Gayle, N. Burrell, M. Allen, & J. Bryant (Eds.), *Mass media effects research: Advances through meta-analysis* (pp. 327–344). Mahwah, NJ: Erlbaum.

Soley, L. (1983). The effect of black models on magazine ad readership. *Journalism Quarterly*, 60(4), 686–690.

Solomon, D. S., & Cardillo, B. A. (1985). The elements and process of communication campaigns. In T. A. van Dijk (Ed.), *Discourse and communication* (pp. 60–68). Berlin, Germany: de Gruyter.

Sommerfeld, J. (2002, September 17). Most weight-loss ads too good to be true, report shows. *MSNBC online news.*

Sommers-Flanagan, R., Sommers-Flanagan, J., & Davis, B. (1993). What's happening on music television? *Sex Roles*, 28, 745–753.

Sood, S. (2002). Audience involvement and entertainment-education. *Communication Theory*, 12, 153–172.

Southwell, B. G. (2005). Between messages and people: A multilevel model of memory for television content. *Communication Research, 32*, 112–140.

Southwell, B. G., & Torres, A. (2006). Connecting interpersonal and mass communication: Science news exposure, perceived ability to understand science, and conversation. *Communication Monographs, 73*, 334–350.

Spangler, L. C. (1989). A historical overview of female friendships in prime-time television. *Journal of Popular Culture, 22*(4), 13–23.

Spangler, L. C. (1992). Buddies and pals: A history of male friendships on prime-time television. In S. Craig (Ed.), *Men, masculinity, and the media* (pp. 93–110). Newbury Park, CA: Sage.

Sparks, G. G., Pellechia, M., & Irvine, C. (1999). The repressive coping style and fright reactions to mass media. *Communication Research, 26*, 176–192.

Sparks, G. G., & Sparks, C. W. (2000). Violence, mayhem, and horror. In D. Zillmann & P. Vorderer (Eds.), *Media entertainment: The psychology of its appeal* (pp. 73–91). Mahwah, NJ: Erlbaum.

Sparks, G. G., & Sparks, C. W. (2002). Effects of media violence. In J. Bryant & D. Zillmann (Eds.), *Media effects* (pp. 269–285). Mahwah, NJ: Erlbaum.

Sparks, G. G., Sparks, C. W., & Sparks, E. A. (2009). Media violence. In J. Bryant and M. B. Oliver (Eds.), *Media effects: Advances in theory and research* (3rd ed., pp. 269–286). New York: Taylor & Francis.

Special Committee on Pornography and Prostitution (1985). *Report* (Vol. 1). Ottawa: Minister of Supply and Services.

Spencer, J. W., Seydlitz, R., Laska, S., & Triche, E. (1992). The different influences of newspaper and television news reports of a natural hazard on response behavior. *Communication Research, 19*, 299–325.

Sperber, M. (2001). *Beer and circus: How big-time college sports is crippling undergraduate education.* New York: Henry Holt.

Sprafkin, J. N., Gadow, K. D., & Abelman, R. (1992). *Television and the exceptional child: A forgotten audience.* Hillsdale, NJ: Erlbaum.

Springwood, C. F., & King, C. R. (Eds.). (2001a). *Team spirits: The Native American mascots controversy.* Lincoln, NE: University of Nebraska Press.

Springwood, C. F., & King, C. R. (2001b, November 1). "Playing Indian": Why Native American mascots must end. *The Chronicle of Higher Education*, pp. B13–14.

Stall, R. D., Coates, T. J., & Hoff, C. (1988). Behavioral risk reduction for HIV infection among gay and bisexual men. *American Psychologist, 43*, 878–885.

Stanley, A. (2000, September 14). Rome journal. *The New York Times.*

Stayman, D. M., & Kardes, F. R. (1992). Spontaneous inference processes in advertising: Effects of need for cognition and self-monitoring on inference generation and utilization. *Journal of Consumer Psychology, 1*, 125–142.

Steinem, G. (1990, July/August). Sex, lies, and advertising. *Ms.*, 18–28.

Stephens, N., & Stutts, M. A. (1982). Preschoolers' ability to distinguish between television programming and commercials. *Journal of Advertising, 11*, 16–26.

Stephenson, M. T. (2003). Examining adolescents' responses to antimarijuana PSAs. *Human Communication Research, 29*, 343–369.

Stern, S. R., & Mastro, D. E. (2004). Gender portrayals across the lifespan: A content analytic look at broadcast commercials. *Mass Communication and Society, 7*, 215–236.

Stewart, D. (1999). *The PBS companion: A history of public television.* New York: TV Books.

Stewart, D. W., Pavlou, P., & Ward, S. (2002). Media influences on marketing communications. In J. Bryant & D. Zillmann (Eds.), *Media effects* (2nd ed., pp. 353–396). Mahwah, NJ: Erlbaum.

Steyer, J. P. (2002). *The other parent: The inside story of media's effect on our children.* New York: Atria Books.

Stitt, C., & Kunkel, D. (2008). Food advertising during children's television programming on broadcast and cable channels. *Health Communication, 23,* 573–584.

Stodghill, R. (1998, June 15). Where'd you learn that? *Time,* pp. 52–59.

Stolberg, S. G. (2001). C.D.C. injects dramas with health messages. Retrieved July 11, 2001, from http://www.nytimes.com/2001/06/26/health/26CDC.html

Stonehill, B. (1995, Spring). Hearts, smarts, and sparkle. *Los Angeles Times.*

Stout, D. A. (2011). *Media and religion: Foundations of an emerging field.* New York: Routledge.

Stransky, D. (2011, July 22). New product placement hits old sitcom reruns. *Entertainment Weekly,* p. 20.

Strasburger, V. C. (1995). *Adolescents and the media: Medical and psychological impact.* Thousand Oaks, CA: Sage.

Strasburger, V. C., & Donnerstein, E. (1999). Children, adolescents, and the media: Issues and solutions. *Pediatrics, 103,* 129–139.

Strasburger, V. C., & Wilson, B. J. (2002). *Children, adolescents, and the media.* Thousand Oaks, CA: Sage.

Strate, L. (1992). Beer commercials: A manual on masculinity. In S. Craig (Ed.), *Men, masculinity, and the media* (pp. 78–92). Newbury Park, CA: Sage.

Straubhaar, J. D., Heeter, C., Greenberg, B. S., Ferreira, L., Wicks, R. H., & Lau, T. Y. (1992). What makes news: Western, socialist, and Third-world newscasts compared in eight countries. In F. Korzenny & S. Ting-Toomey (Eds.), *Mass media effects across cultures* (pp. 89–109). Newbury Park, CA: Sage.

Straubhaar, J. D. (2007). *World television: From global to local.* Thousand Oaks, CA: Sage.

Strayer, D., Drews. F. A., Crouch, D. J., & Johnston. W. A. (2005). Why do cell phone conversations interfere with driving? In W. R. Walker & D. J. Herrmann (Eds.), *Cognitive technology: Essays on the transformation of thought and society* (pp. 51–68). Jefferson, NC: McFarland.

Strobel, W. P. (1997). *Late-breaking foreign policy: The news media's influence on peace operations.* Washington, DC: Institute of Peace Press.

Strouse, J. A., & Fabes, R. A. (1985). Formal vs. informal sources of sex education: Competing forces in the sexual socialization process. *Adolescence, 78,* 251–263.

Stutts, M. A., & Hunnicutt, G. G. (1987). Can young children understand disclaimers in television commercials? *Journal of Advertising, 16*(1), 41–46.

Stutts, M. A., Vance, D., & Hudelson, S. (1981). Program-commercial separators in children's television: Do they help a child tell the difference between Bugs Bunny and The Quik Rabbit? *Journal of Advertising, 10*(2), 16–48.

Subervi-Velez, F. A., & Colsant, S. (1993). The television worlds of Latino children. In G. L. Berry & J. K. Asamen (Eds.), *Children & television* (pp. 215–228). Newbury Park, CA: Sage.

Suleiman, M. W. (1988). *The Arabs in the mind of America.* Brattleboro, VT: Amana Books.

Sullivan, B. (2003, August 6). Has the spam dam really burst? Retrieved August 6, 2003, from http://www. MSNBC.com

Sullivan, D. B. (2006). Broadcast television and the game of packaging sports. In A. A. Raney & J. Bryant (Eds.), *Handbook of sports and media* (pp. 131–145). Mahwah, NJ: Erlbaum.

Sun, Y., Pan, Z., & Shen, L. (2008). Understanding the third-person perception: Evidence from a meta-analysis. *Journal of Communication, 58,* 280–300.

Sundar, S. S., & Wagner, C. B. (2002). The world wide wait: Exploring physiological and behavioral effects of download speed. *Media Psychology, 4,* 173–206.

Sutton, M. J., Brown, J. D., Wilson, K. M., & Klein, J. D. (2002). Shaking the tree of knowledge for forbidden fruit: Where adolescents learn about sexuality and contraception. In J. D. Brown, J. R. Steele, & K. Walsh-Childers (Eds.), *Sexual teens, sexual media* (pp. 25–55). Mahwah, NJ: Erlbaum.

Sypher, B. D., McKinley, M., Ventsam, S., & Valdeavellano, E. E. (2002). Fostering reproductive health through entertainment-education in the Peruvian Amazon: The social construction of Bienvenida Salud! *Communication Theory, 12*, 192–205.

Tai, Z. (2009). The structure of knowledge and dynamic of scholarly communication in agenda setting research, 1996–2005. *Journal of Communication, 59*, 481–513.

Tal-Or, N., & Tsfati, Y. (2007). On the substitutability of the third-person perception. *Media Psychology, 10*, 231–249.

Tal-Or, N., Cohen, J., Tsfati, Y., & Gunther, A. C. (2010). Testing causal direction in the influence of presumed media influence. *Communication Research, 37*, 801–824.

Tamborini, R. (1996). A model of empathy and emotional reactions to horror. In J. B. Weaver, III & R. Tamborini (Eds.), *Horror films: Current research on audience preferences and reactions* (pp. 103–123). Mahwah, NJ: Erlbaum.

Tamborini, R., & Choi, J. (1990). The role of cultural diversity in cultivation research. In N. Signorielli & M. Morgan (Eds.), *Cultivation analysis: New directions in media effects research* (pp. 157–180). Newbury Park, CA: Sage.

Tamborini, R., Grizzard, M., Bowman, N. D., Reinecke, L., Lewis, R. J., & Eden, A. (2011). Media enjoyment as need satisfaction: The contribution of hedonic and nonhedonic needs. *Journal of Communication, 61*, 1025–1042.

Tamborini, R., & Stiff, J. (1987). Predictors of horror film attendance and appeal: An analysis of the audience for frightening films. *Communication Research, 14*, 415–436.

Tamborini, R., Stiff, J., & Heidel, C. (1990). Reacting to graphic horror: A model of empathy and emotional behavior. *Communication Research, 17*, 616–640.

Tamborini, R., Stiff, J., & Zillmann, D. (1987). Preference for graphic horror featuring male versus female victimization: Individual differences associated with personality characteristics and past film viewing experiences. *Human Communication Research, 13*, 529–552.

Tan, A. S., Fujioka, Y., & Tan. G. (2000). Television use, stereotypes of African Americans and opinions on affirmative action: An affective model of policy reasoning. *Communication Monographs, 67*, 362–371.

Tannen, D. (1990). *You just don't understand: Women and men in conversation.* New York: Ballantine Books.

Tannen, D. (1994). *Talking 9 to 5: Women and men in the workplace: Language, sex and power.* New York: Avon Books.

Tannen, D. (1998). *The argument culture: Stopping America's war of words.* New York: Ballantine Books.

Tannen, D. (2001). *I only say this because I love you.* New York: Ballantine Books.

Tannenbaum, P. H. (1971). *Emotional arousal as a mediator of communication effects* (Technical reports of the Commission on Obscenity and Pornography, Vol. 8). Washington, DC: U.S. Government Printing Office.

Tannenbaum, P. H. (1980). Entertainment as vicarious emotional experience. In P. H. Tannenbaum (Ed.), *The entertainment functions of television* (pp. 107–131). Hillsdale, NJ: Erlbaum.

Tapper, J. (1995). The ecology of cultivation: A conceptual model for cultivation research. *Communication Theory, 5*, 36–57.

Taruskin, R. (2001, Dec. 10). Music's dangers and the case for control. *The New York Times.* Retrieved December 10, 2001, from http://www.nytimes.com/2001/12/09/arts/music.09TARU.html

Tate, E., & Surlin, S. (1976). Agreement with opinionated TV characters across culture. *Journalism Quarterly*, 53(2), 199–203.

Tavris, C. (1986). How to publicize science: A case study. In J. H. Goldstein (Ed.), *Reporting science: The case of aggression* (pp. 23–32). Hillsdale, NJ: Erlbaum.

Taylor, C. (2003, June 16). Spam's big bang! *Time*, pp. 50–53.

Taylor, C. R., & Stern, B. B. (1997). Asian-Americans: Television advertising and the "model minority" stereotype. *The Journal of Advertising*, 26(2), 47–60.

Taylor, C. R., Lee, J. Y., & Stern, B. B. (1995). Portrayals of African, Hispanic, and Asian Americans in magazine advertising. *American Behavioral Scientist*, 38, 608–621.

Taylor, P. (2000, November–December). The new political theater. *Mother Jones*, 30–33.

Taylor, S. (1982). The availability bias in social perception and interaction. In D. Kahneman, P. Slovic, & A. Tversky (Eds.), *Judgment under uncertainty: Heuristics and biases* (pp. 190–200). Cambridge, UK: Cambridge University Press.

Taylor, T. (2005, May 13). Advertisers growing fond of dead celebrities. *Manhattan Mercury*, p. A6.

Teplin, L. A. (1985). The criminality of the mentally ill: A dangerous misconception. *American Journal of Psychiatry*, 142, 593–599.

Tewksbury, D. (1999). Differences in how we watch the news. *Communication Research*, 26, 4–29.

Tewksbury, D. (2003). What do Americans really want to know? Tracking the behavior of news readers on the Internet. *Journal of Communication*, 53(4), 694–710.

Tewksbury, D., & Scheufele, D. A. (2009). News framing theory and research. In J. Bryant and M.B. Oliver (Eds.), *Media effects: Advances in theory and research* (3rd ed., pp. 17–33). New York: Taylor & Francis.

Tewksbury, D., Jensen, J., & Coe, K. (2011). Video news releases and the public: The impact of source labeling on the perceived credibility of television news. *Journal of Communication*, 61, 328–348.

Tewksbury, D., Moy, P., & Weis, D. S. (2004). Preparations for Y2K: Revisiting the behavioral component of the third-person effect. *Journal of Communication*, 54, 138–155.

Thaler, P. (1994). *The watchful eye: American justice in the age of the television trial*. New York: Praeger.

The Faustian bargain (1997, September 6). *The Economist*.

The size of the World Wide Web (2011, June 15). Retrieved from http://www.worldwidewebsize.com/

Thomas, B. (2003, March). What the world's poor watch on TV. *World Press Review*, pp. 30–33.

Thomas, C. B. (2005, January). Wal-Martainment. *Time Inside Business*, p. A4.

Thomas, S. (1986). Gender and social-class coding in popular photographic erotica. *Communication Quarterly*, 34(2), 103–114.

Thompson, R. A., & Nelson, C. A. (2001). Developmental science and the media: Early brain development. *American Psychologist*, 56, 5–15.

Thompson, T. L., & Zerbinos, E. (1995). Gender roles in animated cartoons: Has the picture changed in 20 years? *Sex Roles*, 32, 651–673.

Thomsen, S. R., McCoy, J. K., Gustafson, R. L., & Williams, M. (2002). Motivations for reading beauty and fashion magazines and anorexic risk in college-age women. *Media Psychology*, 4, 113–135.

Thorson, E. (1990). Consumer processing of advertising. *Current Issues and Research in Advertising*, 12, 197–230.

Thorson, E., Christ, W. G., & Caywood, C. (1991). Selling candidates like tubes of toothpaste: Is the comparison apt? In F. Biocca (Ed.), *Television and political advertising: Psychological processes* (Vol. 1, pp. 145–172). Hillsdale, NJ: Erlbaum.

Tickle, J. J., Sargent, J. D., Dalton, M. A., Beach, M. L., & Heatherton, T. F. (2001). Favourite movie stars, their tobacco use in contemporary movies, and its association with adolescent smoking. *Tobacco Control*, 10, 16–22.

Tinic, S. (1997). United Colors and untied meanings: Benetton and the commodification of social issues. *Journal of Communication*, 47(3), 3–25.

Tinsley, H. E. A., & Weiss, D. J. (2000). Interrater reliability and agreement. In H. E. A. Tinsley & S. D. Brown (Eds.), *Handbook of applied multivariate statistics and mathematical modeling* (pp. 95–124). San Diego, CA: Academic Press.

Toney, G. T., & Weaver, J. B. (1994). Effects of gender and gender role self-perceptions on affective reactions to rock music videos. *Sex Roles*, 30, 567–583.

Took, K. J., & Weiss, D. S. (1994). The relationship between heavy metal and rap music and adolescent turmoil: Real or artifact? *Adolescence*, 29, 613–621.

Toplin, R. B. (1995). *History by Hollywood: The use and abuse of the American past*. Urbana: University of Illinois Press.

Topline Report NBC/People (2005). National survey of young teens' sexual attitudes and behaviors. Retrieved from http://msnbcmedia.msn.com/i/msnbc/Sections/TVNews/Dateline%20NBC/NBCTeenTopline.pdf

Torabi, M. R., & Seo, D. C. (2004). National study of behavior and life changes since September 11. *Health Education Behavior*, 31, 179–192.

Tower, R. B., Singer, D. G., & Singer, J. L. (1979). Differential effects of television programming on preschoolers' cognition, imagination, and social play. *American Journal of Orthopsychiatry*, 49, 265–281.

Toyama, M. (2008, July 7). Where older dogs are learning new tricks. *Time*, p. 4.

Trier, J. (2008a). The Daily Show with Jon Stewart: Part 1. *Journal of Adolescent and Adult Literacy*, 51(5), 424–428.

Trier, J. (2008b). The Daily Show with Jon Stewart: Part 2. *Journal of Adolescent and Adult Literacy*, 51(7), 600–606.

Tsay, M., & Bodine, B. M. (2012). Exploring parasocial interaction in college students as a multidimensional construct: Do personality, interpersonal need, and television motive predict their relationships with media characters? *Psychology of Popular Media Culture*, 1, 185–200.

Tsfati, T., (2007). Hostile media perceptions, presumed media influence, and minority alienation. *Journal of Communication*, 57, 632–651.

Tsfati, Y., & Cappella, J. N. (2005). Why do people watch news they do not trust? The need for cognition as a mediator in the association between news media skepticism and exposure. *Media Psychology*, 7, 251–271.

Tsiantar, D. (2006, April 10). Getting on board. *Time*, 167(15), pp. A1–A4.

Tuchman, S., & Coffin, T. E. (1971). The influence of election nights television broadcasts in a close election. *Public Opinion Quarterly*, 35, 315–326.

Tulloch, J., Kippax, S., & Crawford, J. (1993). *Television, sexuality, and AIDS*. Sydney, Australia: Allen & Unwin.

Tunstall, J. (2007). *The media were American: U.S. mass media in decline*. New York: Oxford University Press.

Turkle, S. (2011). *Alone together: Why we expect more from technology and less from each other*. New York: Basic Books.

Tversky, A., & Kahneman, D. (1973). Availability: A heuristic for judging frequency and probability. *Cognitive Psychology*, 5, 207–232.

Tversky, A., & Kahneman, D. (1974). Judgment under uncertainty: Heuristics and biases. *Science*, 185, 1124–1131.

Tye, J. B., Warner, K. E., & Glantz, S. A. (1987, Winter). Tobacco advertising and consumption: Evidence of a causal relationship. *Journal of Public Health Policy*, 8, 492–508.

Tyler, T. R. (2006). Viewing CSI and the threshold of guilt: Managing truth and justice in reality and fiction. *Yale Law Journal*, 115, 1050–1085.

Ume-Nwagbo, E. N. E. (1986). "Cock Crow at Dawn": A Nigerian experiment with television drama in development communication. *Gazette*, 37(4), 155–167.

Vaid, J. (1999). The evolution of humor: Do those who laugh last? In D. H. Rosen & M. C. Luebbert (Eds.), *Evolution of the psyche: Human evolution, behavior, and intelligence* (pp. 123–138). Westport, CT: Praeger.

Valentino, N. A. (1999). Crime news and the priming of racial attitudes during evaluations of the president. *Public Opinion Quarterly*, 63, 293–320.

Valentino, N. A., Hutchings, V. L., & Williams, D. (2004). The impact of political advertising on knowledge, Internet information seeking, and candidate preference. *Journal of Communication*, 54, 337–354.

Valkenburg, P. M. (2001). Television and the child's developing imagination. In D. G. & J. L. Singer (Eds.), *Handbook of children and the media* (pp. 121–134). Thousand Oaks, CA: Sage.

Valkenburg, P. M. (2004). *Children's responses to the screen: A media psychological approach.* Mahwah, NJ: Erlbaum.

Valkenburg, P. M., & Beentjes, J. W. J. (1997). Children's creative imagination in response to radio and television stories. *Journal of Communication*, 47(2), 21–38.

Valkenburg, P. M., & Buijzen, M. (2005). Identifying determinants of young children's brand awareness: Television, parents, and peers. *Journal of Applied Developmental Psychology*, 26, 454–468.

Valkenburg, P. M., & Cantor, J. (2001). The development of a child into a consumer. *Journal of Applied Developmental Psychology*, 22, 61–72.

Valkenburg, P. M., & Peter, J. (2006). Fantasy and imagination. In J. Bryant & P. Vorderer (Eds.), *Psychology of entertainment* (pp. 105–117). Mahwah, NJ: Erlbaum.

Valkenburg, P. M., Peter, J., & Schouten, A. (2006). Friend networking sites and their relationship to adolescents' well-being and social self-esteem. *CyberPsychology & Behavior*, 9, 584–590.

Valkenburg, P. M., & van der Voort, T. H. A. (1994). Influence of TV on daydreaming and creative imagination: A review of research. *Psychological Bulletin*, 116, 316–339.

Van Biema, D. (2008, March 17). The evangelical Onion. *Time*, p. 55.

Van den Bergh, B., Dewitte, S., & Warlop, L. (2008). Bikinis instigate generalized impatience in intertemporal choice. *Journal of Consumer Research*, 35, 85–97.

van der Meij, L., Almela, M., Hidalgo,V., Villada, C., Ijzerman, H., van Lange, P.A.M., & Salvador, A. (2012). Testosterone and cortisol release among Spanish soccer fans watching the 2010 World Cup final. *PloS ONE*, 7(4), 1–7.

van der Voort, T. H. A. (1986). *Television violence: A child's eye view.* Amsterdam: North-Holland Publishing.

van der Voort, T. H. A., & Valkenburg, P. M. (1994). Television's impact on fantasy play: A review of research. *Developmental Review*, 14, 27–51.

Veale, J. (2008, May 26). Dreamer. *Time*, p. 59.

Vega, V., & Malamuth, N. M. (2007). Predicting sexual aggression: The role of pornography in the context of general and specific risk factors. *Aggressive Behavior*, 33, 104–117.

Verser, R., & Wicks, R. H. (2006). Managing voter impressions: The use of images on Presidential candidate web sites during the 2000 campaign. *Journal of Communication*, 56, 178–197.

Vettehen, P. H., Nuijten, K., & Peeters, A. (2008). Explaining effects of sensationalism on liking of television news stories: The role of emotional arousal. *Communication Research*, 35, 319–338.

Vidmar, N., & Rokeach, M. (1974). Archie Bunker's bigotry: A study in selective perception and exposure. *Journal of Communication*, 24(1), 35–47.

Vincent, R. C., Davis, D. K., & Boruszkowski, L. A. (1987). Sexism on MTV: The portrayal of women in rock videos. *Journalism Quarterly*, 64(4), 750–755.

Vokey, J. R., & Read, J. D. (1985). Subliminal messages: Between the devil and the media. *American Psychologist*, 40, 1231–1239.

Volgy, T. J., & Schwarz, J. E. (1980). TV entertainment programming and sociopolitical attitudes. *Journalism Quarterly*, 57, 150–155.

Vorderer, P., & Knobloch, S. (2000). Conflict and suspense in drama. In D. Zillmann & P. Vorderer (Eds.), *Media entertainment: The psychology of its appeal* (pp. 59–72). Mahwah, NJ: Erlbaum.

Vorderer, P., Wulff, H. J., & Friedrichsen, M. (Eds.). (1996). *Suspense: Conceptualizations, theoretical analyses, and empirical explorations*. Mahwah, NJ: Erlbaum.

Vraga, E. K., Edgerly, S., Bode, L., Carr, D. J., Bard, M., Johnson, C. N., Kim, Y. M., & Shah, D. V. (2012). The correspondent, the comic, and the combatant: The consequences of host style in political talk shows. *Journalism and Mass Communication Quarterly*, 89, 5–22.

Vraga, E. K., Edgerly, S., Wang, B. M., & Shah, D. V. (2011). Who taught me that? Repurposed news, blog structure, and source identification. *Journal of Communication*, 61, 795–815.

Wahl, O. F. (1995). *Media madness: Public images of mental illness*. New Brunswick, NJ: Rutgers University Press.

Walgrave, S., & Van Aelst, P. (2006). The contingency of the mass media's political agenda setting power: Toward a preliminary theory. *Journal of Communication*, 56, 88–109.

Walker, J. R., & Bellamy, R. V., Jr. (2001). Remote control devices and family viewing. In J. Bryant & J. A. Bryant (Eds.), *Television and the American family* (2nd ed., pp. 75–89). Mahwah, NJ: Erlbaum.

Walker, M., Langemeyer, L., & Langemeyer, D. (1992). Celebrity endorsers: Do you get what you pay for? *Journal of Consumer Marketing*, 9, 69–76.

Wallace, A. (1998, August 6). "Ryan" Ends Vets' Years of Silence. *Los Angeles Times*. Available at http://articles.latimes.com

Wallack, L., Dorfman, L., Jernigan, D., & Themba, M. (1993). *Media advocacy and public health*. Newbury Park, CA: Sage.

Wallis, J. (2005). *God's politics: Why the right gets it wrong and the left doesn't get it*. San Francisco: Harper San Francisco.

Walma van der Molen, J. H., & van der Voort, T. H. A. (2000). The impact of television, print, and audio on children's recall of the news. *Human Communication Research*, 26, 3–26.

Walters, R. H., & Willows, D. C. (1968). Imitative behavior of disturbed and nondisturbed children following exposure to aggressive and nonaggressive models. *Child Development*, 39, 79–89.

Walther, J. B., & Bunz, U. (2005). The rules of virtual groups: Trust, liking, and performance in computer-mediated communication. *Journal of Communication*, 55, 828–846.

Walther, J. B., Gay, G., & Hancock, J. T. (2005). How do communication and technology researchers study the Internet? *Journal of Communication*, 55, 632–657.

Walther, J. B., Van de Heide, B., Kim, S.-Y., Westerman, D., & Tong, S. T. (2008). The role of friends' appearance and behavior on evaluations of individuals on Facebook: Are we known by the company we keep? *Human Communication Research*, 34, 28–49.

Wang, Y., Mathews, V. P., Kalnin, A. J., Mosier, K. M., Dunn, D. W., Saykin, A. J., & Kronenberger, W. G. (2009). Short term exposure to a violent video game induces changes in frontolimbic circuitry in adolescents. *Brain Imaging and Behavior*, 3, 38–50.

Wang, Z., & Lang, A., (2012). Reconceptualizing excitation transfer as motivational activation changes and a test of the television program context effects. *Media Psychology*, 15, 68–92.

Wang, Z., & Tchernev, J. M. (2012). The "myth" of media multitasking: Reciprocal dynamics of media multitasking, personal needs, and gratifications. *Journal of Communication*, 62, 493–513.

Wann, D. L., Melnick, M. J., Russell, G. W., & Pease, D. G. (2001). *Sports fans: The psychology and social impact of spectators*. New York: Routledge.

Wanta, W. (1997). *The public and the national agenda: How people learn about important issues*. Mahwah, NJ: Erlbaum.

Wanta, W., & Ghanem, S. (2007). Effects of agenda-setting. In R. W. Preiss, B. M. Gayle, N. Burrell, M. Allen, & J. Bryant (Eds.), *Mass media effects research: Advances through meta-analysis* (pp. 37–51). Mahwah, NJ: Erlbaum.

Ward, S., Wackman, D., & Wartella, E. (1977). *How children learn to buy: The development of consumer information-processing skills*. Beverly Hills, CA: Sage.

Warren, R. (2005). Parental mediation of children's television viewing in low-income families. *Journal of Communication*, 55, 847–863.

Wartella, E., & Jennings, N. (2001). Hazards and possibilities of commercial TV in the schools. In D. G. Singer & J. L. Singer (Eds.), *Handbook of children and the media* (pp. 557–570). Thousand Oaks, CA: Sage.

Watkins, B. (1988). Children's representations of television and real-life stories. *Communication Research*, 15, 159–184.

Watson, J. M., & Strayer, D. L. (2010). Supertaskers: Profiles in extraordinary multitasking ability. *Psychonomic Bulletin and Review*, 17, 479–485.

Weaver, J. (2003a, May 14). A hot "Hispanicized" consumer market. Retrieved May 14, 2003, from http://www.msnbc.com/news/912895.asp?0cv=CB20

Weaver, J. (2003b, July 7). College students are avid gamers. Retrieved July 18, 2003, from http://www.msnbc.com

Weaver, J. (2003c, July 24). Teens tune out TV, log on instead. Retrieved July 25, 2003, from http://www.msnbc.com

Weaver, J. B., III. (1991). Responding to erotica: Perceptual processes and dispositional implications. In J. Bryant & D. Zillmann (Eds.), *Responding to the screen* (pp. 329–354). Hillsdale, NJ: Erlbaum.

Weaver, J. B., III, Masland, J. L., & Zillmann, D. (1984). Effects of erotica on young men's aesthetic perception of their female sexual partners. *Perceptual and Motor Skills*, 58, 929–930.

Weaver, J. B., III, & Tamborini, R. (Eds.). (1996). *Horror films: Current research on audience preferences and reactions*. Mahwah, NJ: Erlbaum.

Weaver, J. B., III, & Wakshlag, J. (1986). Perceived vulnerability to crime, criminal victimization experience, and television viewing. *Journal of Broadcasting & Electronic Media*, 30, 141–158.

Webb, T., Martin, K., Afifi, A. A., & Kraus, J. (2010). Media literacy as a violence-prevention strategy: A pilot evaluation. *Health Promotion Practice*, 11(5), 714–722.

Webel, A. R., Okonsky, J., Trompeta, J., & Holzemer, W. L. (2010). A systematic review of the effectiveness of peer-based interventions on health-related behavior in adults. *American Journal of Public Health*, 100, 247–253.

Weber, R., Ritterfeld, U., & Kostygina, A. (2006). Aggression and violence as effects of playing violent video games? In P. Vorderer & J. Bryant (Eds.), *Playing video games: Motives, responses, and consequences* (pp. 347–361). Mahwah, NJ: Erlbaum.

Weber, R., Ritterfeld, U., & Mathiak, K. (2006). Does playing violent video games induce aggression? Empirical evidence of a functional magnetic resonance imaging study. *Media Psychology*, 8, 39–60.

Wedding, D., Boyd, M. A., & Niemiec, R. M. (2005). *Movies & mental illness* (2nd ed.). Cambridge MA: Hogrefe.

Wei, R., & Lo, V.-H. (2007). The third-person effects of political attack ads in the 2004 U.S. Presidential elections. *Media Psychology*, 9, 367–388.

Weigel, R. H., Loomis, J., & Soja, M. (1980). Race relations on prime time television. *Journal of Personality and Social Psychology*, 39(5), 884–893.

Weimann, G., & Brosius, H.-B. (1991). The newsworthiness of international terrorism. *Communication Research*, 18, 333–354.

Weiss, A. J., & Wilson, B. J. (1998). Children's cognitive and emotional responses to the portrayal of negative emotions in family-formatted situation comedies. *Human Communication Research*, 24, 584–609.

Weisz, M. G., & Earls, C. M. (1995). The effects of exposure to filmed sexual violence on attitudes toward rape. *Journal of Interpersonal Violence*, 10, 71–84.

Wenner, L. A., & Gantz, W. (1998). Watching sports on television: Audience experience, gender, fanship, and marriage. In L. A. Wenner (Ed.), *MediaSport* (pp. 233– 251). New York: Routledge.

Wernick, R. (1996, August). Let's hear it for the lowly sound bite! *Smithsonian*, 27(5), 62–65.

West, D. M. (2005). *Air wars: Television advertising in election campaigns, 1952–2004* (4th ed.). Washington DC: Congressional Quarterly.

Weston, M. A. (1996). *Native Americans in the news: Images of Indians in the twentieth century press*. Westport, CT: Greenwood.

Weymouth, L. (1981, January–February). Walter Cronkite remembers. *Washington Journalism Review*, p. 23.

What's so funny? (1997, December 20). *The Economist*.

What's up, doc? (1995, February 5). *Manhattan Mercury*, p. A7.

Wheeler, D. L. (2001, January 5). Embracing technology and spirituality, at the top of the world. *The Chronicle of Higher Education*, 47, p. A64.

Wheeler, T. H. (2002). *Phototruth or photofiction? Ethics and media imagery in the digital age*. Mahwah, NJ: Erlbaum.

Whillock, R. K. (1997). Cyber-politics: The on-line strategies of '96. *American Behavioral Scientist*, 40, 1208–1225.

White, L. A. (1979). Erotica and aggression: The influence of sexual arousal, positive affect, and negative affect on aggressive behavior. *Journal of Personality and Social Psychology*, 37, 591–601.

Whiteside, E., & Hardin, M. (2011). Women (not) watching women: Leisure time, television, and implications for televised coverage of women's sports. *Communication, Culture & Cognition*, 4, 122–143.

Wicks, R. H. (2001). *Understanding audiences: Learning to use the media constructively*. Mahwah, NJ: Erlbaum.

Wilcox, B. L. (1987). Pornography, social science, and politics: When research and ideology collide. *American Psychologist*, 42, 941–943.

Wilkes, M. S., Bell, R. A., & Kravitz, R. L. (2000). Direct-to-consumer prescription drug advertising: Trends, impact, and implications. *Health Affairs*, 19(2), 110–128.

Wilksch, S. M., & Wade, T. D. (2009). Reduction of shape and weight concern in young adolescents: A 30-month controlled evaluation of a media literacy program. *Journal of the American Academy of Child & Adolescent Psychiatry*, 48, 652–661.

Will, E. (1987). Women in media. *The Other Side*, 23(4), 44–46.

Williams, B. (1979, November). Report of the Departmental Committee on Obscenity and Film Censorship. London: Her Majesty's Stationery Office. Command 7772.

Williams, B. A., & Delli Carpini, M. X. (2002, April 19). Heeeeeeere's democracy! *The Chronicle of Higher Education*, 48, pp. B14–B15.

Williams, T. M. (Ed.). (1986). The impact of television. Orlando, FL: Academic Press.

Williamson, V. J., Jilka, S. R., Fry, J., Finkel, S., Mullensiefen, D., & Stewart, L. (2011). How do "earworms" start? Classifying the everyday circumstances of involuntary musical imagery. *Psychology of Music*, 39, 1–26.

Willman, C. (2005). *Rednecks and bluenecks: The politics of country music*. New York: New Press.

Wills, E. (2005, June 3). Pride or prejudice? *The Chronicle of Higher Education*, 51(39), pp. A29–A30.

Willwerth, J. (1993, February 15). It hurts like crazy. *Time*, p. 53.

Wilson, B. J. (1987). Reducing children's emotional reactions to mass media through rehearsed explanation and exposure to a replica of a fear object. *Human Communication Research*, 14, 3–26.

Wilson, B. J. (1989). Desensitizing children's emotional reactions to the mass media. *Communication Research*, 16, 723–745.

Wilson, B. J. (1991). Children's reactions to dreams conveyed in mass media programming. *Communication Research*, 18, 283–305.

Wilson, B. J., & Cantor, J. (1987). Reducing fear reactions to mass media: Effects of visual exposure and verbal explanation. In M. McLaughlin (Ed.), *Communication Yearbook 10* (pp. 553–573). Newbury Park, CA: Sage.

Wilson, B. J., Colvin, C. M., & Smith, S. L. (2002). Engaging in violence on American television: A comparison of child, teen, and adult perpetrators. *Journal of Communication*, 52(1), 36–60.

Wilson, B. J., Hoffner, C., & Cantor, J. (1987). Children's perceptions of the effectiveness of techniques to reduce fear from mass media. *Journal of Applied Developmental Psychology*, 8, 39–52.

Wilson, B. J., Linz, D., Donnerstein, E., & Stipp, H. (1992). The impact of social issue television programming on attitudes toward rape. *Human Communication Research*, 19, 179–208.

Wilson, B. J., Smith, S. L., Potter, W. J., Kunkel, D., Linz, D., Colvin, C. M., et al. (2002). Violence in children's television programming: Assessing the risks. *Journal of Communication*, 52(1), 5–35.

Wilson, B. J., & Weiss, A. J. (1992). Developmental differences in children's reactions to a toy advertisement linked to a toy-based cartoon. *Journal of Broadcasting & Electronic Media*, 36, 371–394.

Wilson, B. J., & Weiss, A. J. (1993). The effects of sibling coviewing on preschoolers' reactions to a suspenseful movie sequence. *Communication Research*, 20, 214–248.

Wilson, J. R., & Wilson, S. L. R. (1998). *Mass media/Mass culture* (4th ed.). New York: McGraw-Hill.

Wilson, R. E., Gosling, S. D., & Graham, L. T. (2012). A review of Facebook research in the social sciences. *Perspectives on Psychological Science*, 7, 203–220.

Wilson, S. N. (2000). Raising the voices of teens to change sex education. *SIECUS Report*, 28(6), 20–24.

Wilson, W. (1999). *The psychopath in film*. Washington, DC: University Press of America.

Winn, M. (2002). *The plug-in drug: Television, computers, and family life*. New York: Penguin.

Wirth, W., Hofer, M., & Schramm, H. (2012). The role of emotional involvement and trait absorption in the formation of spatial presence. *Media Psychology*, 15, 19–43.

Witte, K. (1992). Preventing AIDS through persuasive communications. In F. Korzenny & S. Ting-Toomey (Eds.), Mass media effects across cultures (pp. 67–86). Newbury Park, CA: Sage.

Wittebols, J. H. (1991). The politics and coverage of terrorism: From media images to public consciousness. Communication Theory, 1, 253–266.

Wober, J. M. (1986). The lens of television and the prism of personality. In J. Bryant & D. Zillmann (Eds.), Perspectives on media effects (pp. 205–231). Hillsdale, NJ: Erlbaum.

Wojcieszak, M. E., & Mutz, D. C. (2009). Online groups and political discourse: Do online discussion spaces facilitate exposure to political disagreement? Journal of Communication, 59, 40–56.

Wolfson, T. (2012). From the Zapatistas to Indymedia: Dialectics and orthodoxy in contemporary social movements. Communication, Culture, & Critique, 5, 149–170.

Wood, J. M., & Duke, N. K. (1997). Inside Reading Rainbow: A spectrum of strategies for promoting literacy. Language Arts, 74, 95–106.

Worden, N. (2011, April 14). Web advertising eclipsed newspapers in 2010. The Wall Street Journal. Retrieved from http://online.wsj.com

Worthen, B., & Tuna, C. (2011, February 1). Web running out of addresses: Internet sites, carriers are laying the groundwork for a new routing system. The Wall Street Journal. Retrieved from http://online.wsj.com

Wresch, W. (1996). Disconnected: Haves and have-nots in the information age. New Brunswick, NJ: Rutgers University Press.

Wright, C. R. (1986). Mass communication: A sociological perspective (3rd ed.). New York: Random House.

Wright, J. C., Huston, A. C., Reitz, A. L., & Piemyat, S. (1994). Young children's perceptions of television reality: Determinants and developmental differences. Developmental Psychology, 30, 229–239.

Wright, J. C., Kunkel, D., Pinon, M., & Huston, A. C. (1989). How children reacted to televised coverage of the space shuttle disaster. Journal of Communication, 39(2), 27–45.

Wright, J. C., St. Peters, M., & Huston, A. C. (1990). Family television use and its relation to children's cognitive skills and social behavior. In J. Bryant (Ed.), Television and the American family (pp. 227–251). Hillsdale, NJ: Erlbaum.

Wroblewski, R., & Huston, A. C. (1987). Televised occupational stereotypes and their effects on early adolescence: Are they changing? Journal of Early Adolescence, 7, 283–297.

Wu, F. H. (2002). Yellow: Race in America beyond Black and White. New York: Basic Books.

Wulf, S. (1996, July 29). An old sweet song. Time, pp. 67–69.

Wyer, R. S., & Collins, J. E. (1992). A theory of humor elicitation. Psychological Review, 99, 663–688.

Xenos, M., & Moy, P. (2007). Direct and differential effects of the Internet on political and civic engagement. Journal of Communication, 57, 704–718.

Yalch, R. F. (1991). Memory in a jingle jungle: Music as a mnemonic device in communicating advertising slogans. Journal of Applied Psychology, 76, 268–275.

Yamamiya, Y., Cash, T. F., Melnyk, S. E., Posavec, H. D., & Posavec, S. S. (2005). Women's exposure to thin-and-beautiful media images: Body image effects of media-ideal internalization and impact-reduction interventions. Body Image, 2, 74–80.

Yang, M., & Roskos-Ewoldson, D. R. (2007). The effectiveness of brand placements in the movies: Levels of placements, explicit and implicit memory, and brand-choice behavior. Journal of Communication, 57, 469–489.

Yanovitzky, I., & Bennett, C. (1999). Media attention, institutional response, and health behavior change: The case of drunk driving, 1978–1996. Communication Research, 26, 429–453.

Yates, E., Barbaree, H. E., & Marshall, W. L. (1984). Anger and deviant sexual arousal. *Behavior Therapy*, 15, 287–294.

Yegiyan, N. S., & Grabe, M. E. (2007). An experimental investigation of source confusion in televised messages: News versus advertisements. *Human Communication Research*, 33, 379–395.

Young, S. D., Boester, A., Whitt, M. T., & Stevens, M. (2008). Character motivations in the representation of mental health professionals in popular film. *Mass Communication & Society*, 11, 82–99.

Zelizer, B. (1992). CNN, the Gulf War, and journalistic practice. *Journal of Communication*, 42(1), 66–81.

Zhao, X. (2009). Media use and global warming perceptions. *Communication Research*, 36, 698–723.

Zhao, X., & Cai, X. (2008). The role of ambivalence in college nonsmokers' information seeking and information processing. *Communication Research*, 35, 298–318.

Zhao, X., & Gantz, W. (2003). Disruptive and cooperative interruptions in prime-time television fiction: The role of gender, status, and topic. *Journal of Communication*, 53, 347–362.

Zhao, X., Leiserowitz, A. A., Maibach, E. W., & Roser-Renouf, C. (2011). Attention to science/environmental news positively predicts and attention to political news negatively predicts global warming risk perceptions and policy support. *Journal of Communication*, 61, 713–731.

Zielinska, I. E., & Chambers, B. (1995). Using group viewing of television to teach preschool children social skills. *Journal of Educational Television*, 21, 85–99.

Zill, N. (2001). Does Sesame Street enhance school readiness? Evidence from a national survey of children. In S. M. Fisch & R. Truglio (Eds.), *"G" is for "growing": Thirty years of research on children and Sesame Street* (pp. 115–130). Mahwah, NJ: Erlbaum.

Zillmann, D. (1978). Attribution and misattribution of excitatory reactions. In J. H. Harvey, W. J. Ickes, & R. F. Kidd (Eds.), *New directions in attribution research* (Vol. 2). Hillsdale, NJ: Erlbaum.

Zillmann, D. (1996). The psychology of suspense in dramatic exposition. In P. Vorderer, H. J. Wulff, & M. Friedrichsen (Eds.), *Suspense: Conceptualizations, theoretical analyses, and empirical explorations* (pp. 199–231). Mahwah, NJ: Erlbaum.

Zillmann, D. (2000). Humor and comedy. In D. Zillmann & P. Vorderer (Eds.), *Media entertainment* (pp. 37–57). Mahwah, NJ: Erlbaum.

Zillmann, D. (2002). Exemplification theory of media research. In J. Bryant & D. Zillmann (Eds.), *Media effects* (2nd ed., pp. 19–42). Mahwah, NJ: Erlbaum.

Zillmann, D. (2006a). Empathy: Affective reactivity to others' emotional experiences. In J. Bryant & P. Vorderer (Eds.), *Psychology of entertainment* (pp. 151–182). Mahwah, NJ: Erlbaum.

Zillmann, D. (2006b). Dramaturgy for emotions from fictional narration. In J. Bryant & P. Vorderer (Eds.), *Psychology of entertainment* (pp. 215–238). Mahwah, NJ: Erlbaum.

Zillmann, D., & Bryant, J. (1982). Pornography, sexual callousness, and the trivialization of rape. *Journal of Communication*, 32(4), 10–21.

Zillmann, D., & Bryant, J. (1984). Effects of massive exposure to pornography. In N. M. Malamuth & E. Donnerstein (Eds.), *Pornography and sexual aggression* (pp. 115–141). Orlando, FL: Academic Press.

Zillmann, D., & Bryant, J. (1988a). Pornography's impact on sexual satisfaction. *Journal of Applied Social Psychology*, 18, 438–453.

Zillmann, D., & Bryant, J. (1988b). Effects of prolonged consumption of pornography on family values. *Journal of Family Issues*, 9, 518–544.

Zillmann, D., & Bryant, J. (1988c). A response to Linz and Donnerstein. *Journal of Communication*, 38(2), 185–192.

Zillmann, D., & Bryant, J. (1991). Responding to comedy: The sense and nonsense in humor. In J. Bryant & D. Zillmann (Eds.), *Responding to the screen: Reception and reaction processes* (pp. 261–279). Hillsdale, NJ: Lawrence Erlbaum.

Zillmann, D., Callison, C., & Gibson, R. (2009). Quantitative media literacy: Individual differences in dealing with numbers in the news. *Media Psychology*, 12, 394–416.

Zillmann, D., Bryant, J., Comisky, P. W., & Medoff, N. J. (1981). Excitation and hedonic valence in the effect of erotica on motivated intermale aggression. *European Journal of Social Psychology*, 11, 233–252.

Zillmann, D., Bryant, J., & Sapolsky, B. S. (1979). The enjoyment of watching sport contests. In J. H. Goldstein (Ed.), *Sports, games, and play: Social and psychological viewpoints* (pp. 297–355). Hillsdale, NJ: Erlbaum.

Zillmann, D., & Mundorf, N. (1987). Image effects in the appreciation of video rock. *Communication Research*, 14, 316–334.

Zillmann, D., & Weaver, J. B. (1996). Gender-socialization theory of reactions to horror. In J. B. Weaver & R. Tamborini (Eds.), *Horror films: Current research on audience preferences and reactions* (pp. 81–101). Mahwah, NJ: Erlbaum.

Zillmann, D., & Weaver, J. B., III. (1997). Psychoticism in the effect of prolonged exposure to gratuitous media violence on the acceptance of violence as a preferred means of conflict resolution. *Personality and Individual Differences*, 22, 613–627.

Zillmann, D., & Weaver, J. B., III. (1999). Effects of prolonged exposure to gratuitous media violence on provoked and unprovoked hostile behavior. *Journal of Applied Social Psychology*, 29, 145–165.

Zillmann, D., Weaver, J. B., Mundorf, N., & Aust, C. F. (1986). Effects of opposite-gender companion's affect to horror on distress, delight, and attraction. *Journal of Personality and Social Psychology*, 51, 586–594.

Zinkhan, G. M., Qualls, W. J., & Biswas, A. (1990). The use of blacks in magazine and television advertising: 1946 to 1986. *Journalism Quarterly*, 67, 547–553.

Zuckerman, M. (1994). *Behavioral expressions and psychobiological bases of sensation seeking.* New York: Cambridge University Press.

Zuckerman, M. (1996). Sensation seeking and the taste for vicarious horror. In J. B. Weaver & R. Tamborini (Eds.), *Horror films: Current research on audience preferences and reactions* (pp. 147–160). Mahwah, NJ: Erlbaum.

Zuckerman, M. (2006). Sensation seeking in entertainment. In J. Bryant & P. Vorderer (Eds.), *Psychology of entertainment* (pp. 367–387). Mahwah, NJ: Erlbaum.

Author Index

Subject Index